# An Integrated Play-based Curriculum for Young Children

Play provides young children with the opportunity to express their ideas, symbolize, and test their knowledge of the world. Through play, young children become active learners engaged in explorations about themselves, their community, and their personal–social world. *An Integrated Play-based Curriculum for Young Children* explores how play fits into various curriculum areas and helps pre- and in-service teachers create an early childhood curriculum that is both developmentally and culturally appropriate for all children. Offering important theoretical and practical frameworks to pre-service teachers, this book equips them with foundational knowledge about the field, the work that practitioners do with young children, and how to best assume a teacher's role effectively. Through Saracho's integrated approach to early childhood education, this text explains how all young children are able to successfully learn and develop.

Special Features Include:

- Suggestions and guidelines for activities and choosing classroom materials.
- Discussion of a full range of curriculum areas and topics including literacy, language, science, social studies, mathematics, art, music, blocks, and movement.
- Vignettes of children's conversations and examples of how children learn through play.
- End-of-chapter summaries to enhance and extend an understanding of young children.

**Olivia N. Saracho** is Professor of Education in the Department of Teaching, Learning, Policy, and Leadership at the University of Maryland.

# An Integrated Play-based Curriculum for Young Children

OLIVIA N. SARACHO

Routledge
Taylor & Francis Group

NEW YORK AND LONDON

First published 2012
by Routledge
711 Third Avenue, New York, NY 10017

Simultaneously published in the UK
by Routledge
2 Park Square, Milton Park, Abingdon, Oxon OX14 4RN

*Routledge is an imprint of the Taylor & Francis Group, an informa business*

*Library of Congress Cataloging in Publication Data*
Saracho, Olivia N.
   An integrated play-based curriculum for young children/
Olivia N. Saracho.
      p. cm.
   Includes bibliographical references and index.
   1. Play. 2. Early childhood education—Curricula. I. Title.
   LB1139.35.P55S27 2011
   372.21—dc23
                                                                    2011021460

ISBN: 978–0–415–88774–8 (hbk)
ISBN: 978–0–415–88775–5 (pbk)
ISBN: 978–0–203–83327–8 (ebk)

Typeset in Sabon by
RefineCatch Limited, Bungay, Suffolk
Printed and bound in the United States of America on acid-free paper by
Sheridan Books Inc.

To my parents Francisca S. and Pablo J. Villarreal:
With all my gratitude and love for instilling in me a
love of learning and the importance of an education,
for their work ethic, and their love of life.

# Contents

# Preface

The early childhood education curriculum is the most comprehensive but most misinterpreted, although it has been firmly based on philosophy, theory, and research. The philosophers (such as John Amos Comenius, John Locke, Jean Jacques Rousseau), theorists (such as Jean Piaget, Lev Vygotsky, Erik Erikson), and educators (such as Friedrich Froebel, Maria Montessori) contributed to a scientifically based early childhood education curriculum. Although their approaches differed, all of them believed in a child centered curriculum that would focus on the children's individual needs, abilities, and interests. The knowledge we have gained from them on how children learn and develop and the American public's increased acceptance of early childhood education and children's play make this a particularly opportune time for a curriculum book on children's play. In addition, there has been an increase in time, energy, and resources across various fields to better understand and communicate thoughts and research findings that contribute to theory and practice on the relationship between play and curriculum. Researchers' and educators' enthusiastic interest in children's play continues to persist and is expected to expand, which will have an impact on the preparation of future generations of early childhood education professionals and children whose ages range from birth through eight years of age.

Young children's learning differs from older children or adults; how children attempt to understand their world strongly depends on their play, exploration, and imagination. *An Integrated Play-based Curriculum for Young Children* is a curriculum text for students who are preparing to teach children ages three through five. It is intended to provide basic knowledge about play in the field of early childhood education, about the work that practitioners do with young children, and about the ideas that underlie that work. It is an appropriate text for graduate and undergraduate courses in four-year colleges and universities as well as in community colleges. Due to the rich resources included in this book, students will wish to keep it as a reference when they begin their teaching career. This book introduces practical ways to integrate play into the children's learning, especially in the different subject areas such as science, mathematics, music, and art. Throughout this book, each chapter integrates research, theory, and practice in relation to children's play so that the reader can understand what things happen in schools for young children as well why they happen. The book is written in a clear, concise style using understandable language. Concepts are carefully explained, and practical examples and appropriate illustrations are provided to clarify the most complicated ideas.

This book describes the early childhood curriculum, educational play, and historical perceptions of children's play. It also presents the developmental theories of children's play that are essential in teaching young children. A separate chapter is included for each curriculum area (such as social studies, literacy). All of the chapters integrate the children's play into each of the curriculum areas to help the reader focus on the specifics of program planning and implementation.

Within each topic, basic theory and research are related and integrated with practical knowledge gained from classroom teaching. Careful attention is given to provide the most current research and to address emerging issues in the field. Examples, practical applications, and guidelines for practice as well as verbal descriptions are generously supplied to help students explore the implications of the concepts, ideas, and theories presented throughout *An Integrated Play-based Curriculum for Young Children*.

Each chapter in this book presents a specific curriculum area and suggests ways to teach young children the subject area's forms of knowledge through play. Forms of knowledge for each subject area are fully discussed and the chapters then incorporate discussion of children's play into the different content areas including social studies, language, writing, literature, literacy, science, mathematics, music and movement, art, and blocks. Before presenting the different subject areas, the book provides the reader with background information on play including the developmental theories of play, learning through play, historical perceptions of play, and early childhood curriculum and educational play. Specifically, chapters address the following:

- Chapter 2: *Learning Through Play* discusses the importance of play in the children's learning. It reviews the definitions of play and discusses how play is used in the children's social learning and social education.
- Chapter 3: *Developmental Theories of Play* reviews the developmental theories of children's play (such as classical, modern, cognitive), postmodern theories (such as theory of mind, cultural play theory), and sociocultural play theories.
- Chapter 4: *Historical Perceptions of Play* presents historical perceptions of children's play and historical representations of children's play that have been symbolized in the visual arts and literature.
- Chapter 5: *Early Childhood Curriculum and Educational Play* describes historical curriculum interpretations, child development and early childhood influences, how to integrate play into the different subject areas in the early childhood education curriculum, educational play, and the play environment (like centers, prop boxes, materials). Finally guidelines for designing learning centers and facilitating children's play are discussed.
- Chapter 6: *Play Experiences of Children with Diverse Needs* describes the importance of play for various groups of diverse children (like those with disabilities, at risk,

English language learners). Then it proposes a variety of settings to promote their play experiences.

- Chapter 7: *Social Studies-play Learning Experiences* describes early childhood education pioneers, contemporary early childhood influences, the program, curriculum knowledge, play learning centers, prop boxes, field trips, museums, and thematic units in social studies.
- Chapter 8: *Language-play Learning Experiences* describes learning oral language, the relationship between language and play, language experiences, the language environment, learning written language, and writing in children's play.
- Chapter 9: *Literature-play Learning Experiences* describes the relationship between literature and play, literature experiences that support play, guidelines for reading children's books, and visual literacy in children's literature.
- Chapter 10: *Literacy-play Learning Experiences* describes emergent literacy, the children's developmental levels in literacy, experiences that promote their literacy development, the relationship between play and literacy, a literate-themed play environment, literacy-enriched play centers (traditional vs. themed), the organization of literacy-play centers, and guidelines for organizing literacy-play centers.
- Chapter 11: *Science-play Learning Experiences* describes the children's learning, standards and expectations (like the science benchmarks), children's play, learning centers, and learning in a social context in science.
- Chapter 12: *Mathematics-play Learning Experiences* describes daily classroom experiences, standards and expectations, children's play, learning centers, and play themes in mathematics.
- Chapter 13: *Music and Movement-play Learning Experiences* describes the music in children's lives, music curriculum, music appreciation, aesthetic music experiences, music play, developing a play-based music program, and music learning centers (music vs. non music).
- Chapter 14: *Art-play Learning Experiences* describes artistic play, developmental stages in art, art media, play art environment, and children's understanding of classic works of art.
- Chapter 15: *Block-play Learning Experiences* describes the value of blocks in the curriculum, how block building contributes to adulthood, how blocks are used as a building toy, the different block categories, the unit or blocks by Caroline Pratt, the block building stages, the block accessories, the block center, and children as builders.
- *References* contains the compiled references for all of the chapters.

# Acknowledgments

Writing a textbook is usually a very lonesome undertaking, but this type of book is hardly written on your own. I wish to acknowledge my debt to the many individuals who directly and indirectly contributed to this book. I owe a great deal to the many teachers, undergraduate and graduate students, and children with whom I have worked throughout my professional career. The ideas that are communicated in the book have developed from my interactions with them over the years. Bernard Spodek—my teacher, mentor, colleague, and friend—interacted and discussed with me ideas about play. He helped me make sure that my ideas on play would be spontaneous, flexible, and enjoyable to children. Frances Hancock, my colleague and friend, who provided me with her moral support, suggestions, and discussion of ideas; and most importantly, for her belief in the joy of play and its role in the early childhood curriculum. My colleague, Francey Kohl, a faculty member in the Department of Special Education at the University of Maryland, who helped me select the appropriate terminology for the children with disabilities. Vincent J. Novara, Curator for the Special Collections in Performing Arts, and Leahkim Gannett, Assistant Curator for the Special Collections in Performing Arts, for the Michelle Smith Performing Arts Library at the University of Maryland helped me identify resources for the music and movement chapter. Two excellent early childhood education professionals, Elida de La Rosa and Sharon Gilder, who helped me identify some of the resources that I used. Two of my university students, Santiago L. Sere and Shyueh-Rwong C. Cheng, who used their computer expertise to help me convert my diagram sketches to Microsoft Word. Jeanene Varner reviewed an earlier version of the manuscript and provided valuable suggestions. Last, but not least, I would also like to thank Heather Jarrow, my editor at Routledge/ Taylor and Francis Group, for her excellent comments on my manuscript as well as her support, assistance, and encouragement in getting this book published.

# Section I
# Play in the Context of Early Education

# Chapter 1
# Introduction
## Play and Teaching in Early Childhood Education

> Teachers need to engage in "observing children as they play and building curriculum that's appropriate for each child from what we see and hear" . . . teachers need to deeply understand that intellectual development occurs through play. Children integrate everything they know in all domains when they play. Play should have a big place in a curriculum for children from toddlerhood through the primary grades.
>
> (Millie Almy, 2000, p. 6)

Early childhood teachers are now responsible for the education of a diverse group of children in their classes. This requires that teachers learn to be sensitive to individual differences among these children and become more competent in providing a developmentally appropriate education. For example, children with special needs were withheld from school or were provided with a segregated education. These children are increasingly being integrated into the regular classrooms to provide them with a degree of educational equity that was not previously available to them. Peterson (1987) compares the previous and present concepts about the education of children with disabilities (see Table 1.1). In addition, educating children from diverse backgrounds and with diverse abilities is considered to be more effective for all children (Spodek & Saracho, 1994a).

One of the first things early childhood teachers do at the beginning of the school year is to decide how to fill the days with worthwhile activities. The teachers need to plan for the school year, decide what the children will do during each school day, what materials will be provided and how they will be organized within the classroom, and how to schedule each day. In other words, teachers are planning the early childhood curriculum. Much of the planning begins before teachers ever meet their classes of young children. Once the

**TABLE 1.1. Previous and Present Concepts about the Education of Children with Disabilities**

| Previous Concepts | Present and Emerging Concepts |
| --- | --- |
| Education is a privilege for those who are able to benefit from it | Education is a right for *all* children and is a means to help them to (a) confront the challenges in their environment, (b) learn, and (c) live fulfilling and productive lives |
| Education is composed of academic instruction in literacy, writing, mathematics, and other subject areas relating to the arts and sciences | Education includes any skills children need to obtain optimal functioning in society and their environment. For example, some children may need instruction in skills as basic as walking, eating, talking, and attention, or in motor functions encumbered by a disability |
| Only children who are 'ready' to begin formal education can attend public school programs. Otherwise, they must wait until they have mastered their basic social, self-help, cognitive, and language skills | School prepares children to be "ready" through learning, experience, and training. Their lack of prerequisite skills clearly indicates their immediate need for education and training |
| Children who are not able to learn through the school's curriculum need to be removed from the classroom and placed elsewhere (a special classroom or school) | The curriculum and instructional methods are based on the children's individual needs. Within reason, teachers and specialists modify instruction and the environment to promote all of the children's learning in inclusive settings |
| Children with disabilities are assigned to special classrooms where they can be together with other children with disabilities and will not disrupt the learning of typically developing children in a regular classroom | Children with disabilities are in an integrated classroom with their typically developing peers to learn to participate and function as members of society. The only time they are isolated is when they are receiving special services |
| Children with disabilities are expected to fail in school, because their disabilities limit their learning | All children are able to learn at their own pace based on their individual differences. It is the responsibility of the teachers and specialists to select appropriate learning alternatives, to break down instructional tasks into small, sequential steps, and to monitor their progress to facilitate these children's learning |

children arrive and the teachers get to know them well, plans can be modified and adjusted to be responsive to a particular group of children.

In designing the early childhood curriculum, teachers ponder on the following questions:

- What materials and activities should be provided?
- What makes activities educationally worthwhile?
- What activities are developmentally appropriate for young children?

Teachers may feel that whatever keeps the children busy and happy is an appropriate activity. Other teachers may be concerned about maintaining some degree of order in the classroom. However, an early childhood curriculum needs to go beyond keeping children happy, busy, and safe. Activities should provide some form of education to the children and need to be based upon a set of guidelines that underlie educational experiences for young children.

For educational activities to be worthwhile, they must be both developmentally appropriate and content rich. Children's development goes beyond a simple biological process. As Bruner (1990) argues, it is a cultural process as well. "Cultures characteristically devise 'prosthetic devices' that permit us to transcend 'raw' biological limits—for example, the limits on memory capacity or the limits on our auditory range" (Bruner, 1990, p. 34). Similarly, Vygotsky (1967) argues that human beings acquire "cultural tools" that extend their developmental capacity. These cultural tools include language as well as the various ways of knowing that are critical to cultural development. The scholarly disciplines and language are considered to be the tools that children must come to understand in order to achieve optimal development in society. It is only when an early childhood education curriculum helps children access the various ways of knowing—including the disciplines of formal knowledge—that it can truly be considered developmentally appropriate. A way to ensure that educational activities are developmentally appropriate and content rich is by developing a curriculum that builds on children's play.

Unfortunately, play is being eliminated from the early childhood curriculum. The Alliance for Childhood reports radical changes in kindergarten practice in the last 10 to 20 years, stating that,

> Children now spend far more time being instructed and tested in literacy and math than they do learning through play and exploration, exercising their bodies, and using their imaginations. Many kindergartens use highly prescriptive curricula linked to standardized tests. An increasing number of teachers must follow scripts from which they may not deviate. Many children struggle to live up to academic standards that are developmentally inappropriate . . . At the same time that we have increased academic pressure in children's lives through inappropriate standards, we have managed to undermine their primary tool for dealing with stress—freely chosen, child-directed, intrinsically motivated play (Miller & Almon, 2009, p.15).

This same movement is being spread to preschools (Hirsh-Pasek et al., 2009) and most early childhood education programs. The rigid emphasis on teaching academic skills through direct instruction is replacing play. The determined and inflexible substitution of using more didactic academic and content-based methods in the young children's education forces early childhood education programs to reject more child-centered, play oriented, and constructivist methods (Nicolopoulou, 2010). Young children's learning differs from older children or adults and the children's approaches to understanding their world strongly depend on their play, exploration, and imagination (Gopnik, 2010).

Society has specified the schools' learning goals in relation to basic skills, stressing the learning of letters, numbers, words, and colors even at the preschool level. This concentration on academic skills diminishes the importance of the children's play. Play allows young children to select their learning, especially if it facilitates their attainment of a broad range of developmental goals; therefore, it must be a vital component in the early childhood education curriculum (Spodek & Saracho, 1987).

Play is an essential element in early childhood education programs, because it provides young children with the opportunity to (1) express their ideas and their feelings, (2) symbolize and test their knowledge of the world, and (3) acquire effective support for academic and pre-academic learning. Through play, young children engage in active learning when they reconstruct their experiences, generate ideas, and test these ideas. Teachers need to develop play activities that relate to the program's educational goals. Play also allows children to integrate the ideas and experiences so that they construct knowledge and achieve most of their goals (Saracho, 2002a).

Throughout the book, research and theory are used to justify the use of children's play as a curricular tool in the children's education. Then practical applications in relation to children's play are suggested for each subject area. In a play curriculum, different forms of knowledge must be addressed and different forms of intelligence must be nurtured. These and other ideas are presented in the chapters that follow. In addition, the chapters explore how these ideas—some of them rather abstract in nature—can be turned into the concrete elements of children's school experiences. In doing this, each chapter addresses how teachers can choose the resources available to them—the resources of time, space, physical materials, and human resources—in establishing a high quality educational program for young children.

This book takes the position that the value of play does not lie in a specific set of methodological structured "play" practices to teach specific skills. Play is valuable to young children mainly as a medium for learning. In play, Bergen (1988) refers to the word medium based on Webster's (2008) definitions.

- *A condition in which something may function or flourish.*
  Play can be thought of as a condition in which learning may flourish and the cognitive structures of the mind can be noting the interaction of structure and function from which adaptive intelligence is created (p. 3).
- *A means of effecting or conveying something.*
  Play is often the means by which the child's thoughts and feelings are conveyed, facilitating understanding of thoughts and feelings by the child. Since the young child is less able to use "internal" language as a means of conveying and understanding the complexity of his thoughts and feelings, the play medium provides a means of effecting his learning to himself (p. 3).
- *A channel or system of communication.*
  Similarly, since the language that provides adults with their prime channel of communication is less available to the child, play often provides the channel by which thoughts and feelings are communicated to others. Many of the misconceptions of the child's understanding are made clear to adults through observations of play activities and the complexities of the child's learning are communicated through the channel of play (pp. 3–4).
- *A surrounding or enveloping substance.*
  Observers of young children are often aware of how completely enveloped the child becomes in play. Almost every activity in which the young child engages has elements of play behavior. Thus, play is a surrounding environment through which the child's learning is filtered (p. 4).
- *Material or technical means of artistic expression.*
  In the young child active expression is vitally important: indeed, sensorimotor activity is a major mode of behavior. Play seems to be used by children as a technical means of actively expressing learning. Exploring a material from many perspectives, finding out all of the things which can be done with an object, playing out different ways to deal with a social situation all provide means of active expression of learning (p. 4).

Thus, play is a medium for different types of learning (such as achieving social competence, learning about their world, developing knowledge in the different subject areas). Play provides the optimum learning conditions when the environment and approaches focus on the children's interests and developmental levels. In each chapter, the book is primarily concerned with discussing the medium of play in relation to the specific types of children's learning that will help them succeed in life. Each chapter in the book also addresses the adult's role in facilitating the development of play as an increasingly rich medium for learning.

# Chapter 2
# Learning through Play

Imitation is natural to man from childhood, one of his advantages over the lower animals being this, that he is the most imitative creature in the world, and learns at first by imitation. And it is also natural for all to delight in works of imitation. The truth of this second point is shown by experience: though the objects themselves may be painful to see, we delight . . . in the most realistic representations of them in art . . . The explanation is to be found in a further fact: to be learning something is the greatest of pleasures not only to the philosopher but also to the rest of mankind, however small their capacity for it . . . the reason of the delight . . . is . . . gathering the meaning of things . . .

(Aristotle, 1958)

The meaning of play in the early childhood education curriculum has changed throughout the years. Early childhood pioneers (such as Friedrich Froebel, Maria Montessori, and John Dewey, who will be discussed in Chapter 4) believed in the value of young children's play and developed systematic ways to integrate play into child rearing and in education. Although Froebel and Montessori's approaches differed, their play activities were prescriptive and children had to follow precise directions when using the materials, which were far from playful. The lack of spontaneity in their activities would not be considered play today.

In contrast, John Dewey's (1916) concept of children's learning is the basis for the present view on the educational use of children's play. He believed that the young children's education should be based on their experiences and on the world surrounding them. Teachers would establish an environment to cultivate the children's play that would support their mental and moral growth. Presently, play is considered a serious activity that is essential in young children's education (Spodek & Saracho, 1987), although not everybody is convinced of its value. This chapter discusses the importance of play in the children's learning. It reviews the definitions of play and discusses how play is used in the children's social learning and social education.

## Justifying Play

One of the remarkable aspects of early childhood education is the unique need to justify the use of play in the curriculum. This justification becomes difficult in our present world that is obsessed with academics. Professionals, whose major concern is children's play, frequently deny their concern with play by using words that are misrepresentative and communicate a different definition of play. For example, they state that "play is the work of the child," thus relate work with play and convert play into work. Professionals believe that if they define play as work, everybody will consider play a serious activity and they can preserve their professional self-esteem (Spodek & Saracho, 1987).

For a long period of time, the requirement to defend play has created difficulties in early childhood education. For numerous decades, educators, psychologists, philosophers, researchers, and others have investigated the natural phenomenon of play. They attempted to define it, interpret it, understand it, develop criteria for it, and relate it to other human activities. Play occurs in many forms, which makes its concept complex and difficult to understand. Even though young children, adults, and nonhuman animals participate in play, it differs for each player (Saracho, 2008). A look at the definitions of play can help us become knowledgeable about the reason for misunderstanding children's play. Philosophers and researchers have developed a wide range of definitions and set of criteria for play. These will be discussed in the next section.

## Definitions of Play

The word "play" has been used in a variety of ways (Spodek & Saracho, 1987) without a consensus definition. Attempting to define the word "play" has presented a challenge. Some observers (i.e., Lorenz, Thorpe) suggest it is wise to avoid defining the word, because there is a high inter-observer agreement in identifying play (cited in Dobbert, 1985). Inter-observer agreement measures how much two or more observers agree on their observation, and in the case of play it is risky to take for granted that an observer can designate the purpose for an individual's behavior. The observer may suggest that a play behavior takes place without a reason, simply because the observer does not understand the subject's behavior (Ellis, 1973). According to Schlosberg (1947), many times the reasons for play may be vague, and without manipulating the situation, the evidence that the observer uses to make the inferences is weak. This may be why many observers think that if it is not work, it is play.

In contrast, Fagen (1981) attempts to use an extensive review of the literature to define play. This is a challenging task, because the definition of play is different among researchers, educators, and philosophers. For example, Mitchell and Mason (1948) compare these thinkers' definitions:

*Seashore*:    Free self-expression for the pleasure of expression.
*Froebel*:    The natural unfolding of the germinal leaves of childhood.
*Hall*:    The motor habits and spirit of the past persisting in the present.
*Groos*:    Instinctive practice, without serious intent, of activities which will later be essential to life.

*Dewey*:      Activities not consciously performed for the sake of any result beyond themselves.

*Schiller*:   The aimless expenditure of exuberant energy.

*Spenser*:    Superfluous actions taking place instinctively in the absence of real actions. Activity performed for the immediate gratification derived without regard for ulterior benefits.

*Lazarus*:    Activity in itself free, aimless, amusing, or diverting.

*Shand*:      A type of play directed at the maintenance of joy.

*Dulles*:     An instinctive form of self-expression and emotional escape value.

*Curti*:      Highly motivated activity, which is free from conflicts is usually, though not always, pleasurable (pp. 103–104).

Sapora and Mitchell (1961) cited the following definitions of play, because they capture the sense of the layman's definition:

*Gulick*:     What we do because we want to do it.

*Stern*:      Play is a voluntary self-sufficient activity.

*Patrick*:    Those human activities which are free and spontaneous and which are pursued for their own sake. Interest in them is self-sustaining, and they are not continued under any internal or external compulsion.

*Rainwater*:  Play is a mode of behavior . . . involving pleasurable activity of any kind, not undertaken for the sake of reward beyond itself.

*Pangburn*:   Activity carried on for its own sake (p. 114).

Each definition provides a different understanding and interpretation of play, which motivates scholars to continue their attempt in defining play (Schartzman, 1978), identifying "paradigm cases" of the phenomenon, postponing definitional problems until later (Matthews & Matthews, 1982), and disagreeing on a definition of play. All the definitions maintain that play is not motivated by any other motive than for an immediate inherent reward in the activity itself. The activity is a reward of itself.

   The problem of defining play has yet to be settled. Smith and Vollstedt (1985) propose combining the characteristics of a play activity to define play instead of examining the literature in search of the presence or absence of one perfect quality. This requires that a set of criteria be specified to identify play behaviors (Sokal, 1974). Others (including Spodek, Saracho & Davis, 1991) have each specified a set of play criteria. Krasnor and Pepler (1980) suggest that a play activity needs to have flexibility, positive affect, intrinsic motivation, and nonliterality. However, Sutton-Smith and Kelly-Byrne (1984) make the case that several patterns of play behavior are involuntary or inflexible and show a negative affect. Rubin et al. (1983) suggest a broader set of criteria:

1.  Play is personally motivated by the satisfaction embedded in the activity and not governed either by basic needs and drives, or by social demands.
2.  Players are concerned with activities more than with goals. Goals are self-imposed and the behavior of the players is spontaneous.
3.  Play occurs with familiar objects, or following the exploration of unfamiliar objects. Children supply their own meanings to play activities and control the activity themselves.
4.  Play activities can be nonliteral.

5.  Play is free from the rules imposed from the outside and the rules that do exist can be modified by the players.
6.  Play requires the active engagement of the players (cited in Spodek & Saracho, 1994a, 1994b, pp. 3–4).

Using a set of criteria helps identify play behavior, while a set of specific criteria can help understand play; but it fails to describe the reason people (including children) play. Smith and Vollstedt (1985) tested many researchers' sets of criteria to describe a play activity. They reported that a combination of nonliterality (Krasnor & Pepler, 1980), positive affect, and flexibility (Krasnor & Pepler, 1980) were used most frequently to identify a play activity. Smith and Vollstedt's (1985) definition seems to be the most accepted definition of play. Play is joyful, flexible, imaginative, spontaneous, and essential to the children's development and learning. A dependable definition is needed to assist in identifying play behaviors, but in order for this definition to be trustworthy, it needs to be based on the developmental theories of play, which are discussed in Chapter 3.

## Spontaneity in Group Play

Children are born into a social world. From birth, they begin by exploring that world. At each stage of early development (infant, toddler, preschool, primary-age), children look around and try to make sense of their social and physical environments. They gradually learn more about their expanding community and eventually come to see themselves as citizens (Mindes, 2005).

Young children need to understand themselves, the world around them, and their relationship to it. They learn about themselves when they test their knowledge on their physical and social worlds and receive feedback from their outside world. They learn about their environment and try to understand it as they identify the boundaries between themselves and the surrounding world. Young children develop the knowledge and abilities that they need both for their everyday life and to prepare them for future learning. They directly approach the physical world and test what they know about physical things by touching, listening, or viewing. Young children have direct contact with individuals and observe their behavior. However, only the *meaning* of the observed behavior is important, which suggests that the meaning needs to be understandable.

The consequence of social behavior and the context in which the behavior occurs provides meaning to the behavior (Spodek & Saracho, 1994b), such as when children play. For example, dramatic play promotes the children's personal and social learning. It helps them understand their social world. In dramatic play, young children act out roles that relate to their social settings the way they perceive and understand them. This type of play assists children to interpret their social world, family, school, and community and role play their perceptions of those worlds. When children play with others, they communicate their understandings and test them against their peers' point of view.

In preschool, children usually play together. They might be pretending, running, or making "cakes" in the sandbox. Early pretend play with peer play is associated with competent social development. Therefore, it is important that children engage in play. Some children do not play, because their peers tell them "You can't play," or because they have anxious behavior with peers that prevents them from making an effort to play. These children do not learn how to play. Children need many opportunities to play with peers to learn (a) how to engage in prosocial and complex play with peers and (b) how to find solutions to their conflicts (Howes & Lee, 2007). This is of extreme importance for children with disabilities.

For preschool-aged children with disabilities, the educational possibility of peer influence in inclusive settings is determined by their peers' social acceptance and rejection, which affects the developmental benefits of such settings. Odom et al. (2006) found that in inclusive classrooms half of the children with disabilities were well accepted, but the other half of children with disabilities were at risk of social rejection by peers. Diamond et al. (2008) suggest the use of peers to support the development of young children with disabilities. They suggest that children with disabilities be provided with multiple opportunities to participate in school and community programs that include peers without disabilities. They believe that the children's development and acceptance will be enhanced if children with disabilities have multiple opportunities for social interaction with their peers without disabilities. Children without disabilities need to understand "what it means to have a disability and children's decisions to include a child with a disability in activities with peers, along with individual children's peer-related social competence, can be critical for understanding the social environment of children with disabilities" (p. 142).

Young children are energetic, imaginative and curious to behave and interact within their environment. Since they are self-centered, they have a narrow and unilateral view of their environment. Most of their life, they reside with their family, play with their peers, and determine how they should relate to others, how to spend their free time, whom to play with, which books to read, and even how to spend money. Although young children learn about the larger social world through television and other media, travel, family, and friends, they usually need the conceptual base to integrate knowledge from new experiences into their familiar immediate social environment. In addition, they need the social skills to consider their peers' point of view to be able to resolve problems or to anticipate consequences of their behavior (Saracho & Spodek, 2007c).

Young children display various patterns of social organization. In spite of their exclusive behavioral characteristics and their own distinctive personalities, they organize themselves over time into logical groups. Young children's development has an impact on the organization of their social groups (e.g., the development of social, regulatory, communication skills). Researchers have considered the social organization of both the classroom and school and reported on the patterns and the processes that motivate these dynamics (Martin et al., 2005). Young children need to improve their social competence through social education and social learning.

## Social Learning

Social learning refers to the acquisition of essentials in social competence. Initially young children become socialized into the family through their relationships with family members. They learn their roles and expectations within the family as a member of that social group. Through their family interactions they learn to integrate the behavior and thought processes of successful interpersonal relations (Saracho & Spodek, 2007c).

Early pretend play with peer play leads to the children's competency in social learning (Howes & Lee, 2007; Kavanagh, 2006). The beginning of social learning begins in early infancy. During the first half-year of life, infants show their social interest when they smile, make sounds, and reach towards peers. At age one, infants watch, make sounds, reach out, and smile at others. At age two, toddlers start to show more advanced social exchanges in terms of interchange, give-and-take, and co-ordination. By age three, more prosocial behaviors (like helping, sharing) are observed. The children's social play becomes more obvious and it includes more frequent social contacts. For the younger children, the peer group gives them an important and unique context for the acquisition and implementation of social skills (Rubin & Copla, 1998).

Social learning theory suggests how (a) children learn from peers and (b) they are socialized by their interactions and relationships with peers. The following are the social learning premises (Ladd, 2007):

- *Peer interactions and relationships give children social information.*
  When children interact and engage in relationships with their peers, they receive information about: (a) themselves and their behavior; (b) peers, peer behavior, and peer relationships; and (c) the situations and contexts where social interactions and relationships take place.
- *Children process the information they receive from peer interactions and relationships.*
  Children actively process, sort out, interpret, and form conclusions about the information they obtain from peer interactions and relationships, and store it for future use.
- *Children use the information they receive from peer interactions and relationships.*
  Children use the information they have received from peer interactions and relationships to change their future behavior toward peers where they apply the change with their peer interactions and relationships.
  As children use their changed behavior, they receive information about their behavior which they can use to (a) keep or modify their previous behavior or (b) keep or modify their existing behaviors.

Children learn appropriate behaviors from peers in social play contexts. The nature and form of early social learning in peer contexts consist of children learning from

- peers' responses to their behaviors
- watching peers
- processing information received from peer interactions
- creating, practicing, and changing the ways they interact with peers (Ladd, 2007).

Toddler and preschool children are very sophisticated in their peer interactions. They engage in pretend play when they need to take turns, reverse their actions, use scripts, and assume roles. However, the sophistication of the toddlers and preschoolers' peer interaction depends on the size and composition of the peer group. The interaction quickly breaks down if there are too many players or too few players who know the script (Howes & Lee, 2007). The children's development of social play contributes to their interactions with peers.

When children engage in social play, they learn how their peers influence the children's behaviors (like social skills), thoughts (like understanding themselves and others), feelings (like emotional states, reactions), and characteristics of their development. For example, in peer context, children learn (a) about themselves as persons, (b) about peers as persons, (c) how to manage their emotions and overcome distress, (d) that adverse experiences can endanger children's health and development, and (e) that gender segregation can cause children to learn unique ways of relating to each other (Ladd, 2007).

In pretend play, children explore and interpret the world including social situations. Children who engage in pretend play are the ones who are more socially competent with peers and adults (McAloney & Stagnitti, 2009). Howes and Lee (2007) also reported that even children between 10 and 59 months of age who engage in more complex play are found later to be more sociable, less aggressive, and less withdrawn. They concluded that complicated play with peers can be used as an indicator of social competence with peers, which shows their social competence. Preschool children play with a broader range of playmates than do toddlers. Sociodramatic play and games-with-rules show an increase in social activities (Rubin & Copla, 1998).

Sociodramatic play becomes important. As children get older, they integrate pretense themes in their play. Sociodramatic play creates a context to help children communicate with meaning and provides children with opportunities to learn to discuss, control, and negotiate pretend roles and scripts and the rules for the pretend episodes in their play. In social pretense play, children feel safe to explore and discuss issues of intimacy and trust (Howes & Lee, 2007).

Children need to play in a social–emotional climate where children engage in conversations, spontaneous laughter, and enjoyment when they participate in a variety of activities and interactions. Some classrooms have clear, but flexible rules and expectations for classroom routines. Children usually understand these rules in a positive environment. Children will engage in peer play in an environment that values play (Howes & Lee, 2007). Children need to be provided with physical space to play and materials that motivate them to engage in pretend play (Sutterby & Frost, 2006).

Young children need to develop knowledge and skills that help them function in their everyday life. They use their senses, seeing, touching, and listening to physical things to immediately learn about their physical world; while children learn about their social world when they interact with others and become aware that their behavior is important. The nature of young children's learning processes depends on their personal experiences that help them to construct knowledge and create meaning, which makes it important to provide young children with immediate and first hand experiences to facilitate their learning (Saracho & Spodek, 2007b).

## Social Education

Young children need to learn social ways in order to function within a democratic society. Social learning helps them to improve their emotional and practical competence, their perception of themselves, and their acceptance of others, disregard of their competencies and limitations. The episode below provides an example of the children's social learning.

> Cody, Brianna, and Dylan are gathered around the sand table during free play time in their preschool classroom. Cody is carefully playing with one of the sand toys when Brianna reaches over and grabs it out of Cody's hands. Cody immediately reacts by reaching out to hit Brianna and yells out "that's mine!" After she gets hit, the toy falls out of her hand, she starts to cry, and Dylan moves closer to hug and comfort her. A nearby teacher hears the commotion and comes over to the sand table. Dylan tells the teacher that Cody hit Brianna. The teacher asks Cody to apologize. Cody responds by saying "she took the toy from me!" and starts yelling and gesturing as if he plans to hit Brianna or the teacher. It takes Brianna nearly a minute to stop crying, and Cody ends

up sitting in the time out chair for three minutes due to his temper tantrum (Trentacosta & Izard, 2007, p. 59).

The above observation is a comparatively common argument in an early childhood classroom, especially in a classroom that provides education to at-risk or economically challenged children. The behaviors that emerged in the observation are examples that indicate that these young children need support in their social and emotional learning. Although these children have a similar chronological age, they indicate different degrees of emotional and social maturity. Usually preschool-aged children lack basic social skills and the ability to deal with their emotions. Nevertheless, in the described episode the preschool play context provides these children with an exceptional setting for them to learn these skills and abilities that will help them to adjust to any challenges that they encounter throughout their lives (Trentacosta & Izard, 2007). Thus, young children will receive the support they need in a social learning environment.

The National Council for the Social Studies (NCSS, 1984), the largest professional organization in the United States that is dedicated exclusively to social studies education, believes that social learning helps young children understand and function in their personal and social worlds. They are active, curious, and need to develop their competence in socialization, social values, and self awareness.

- *Socialization* is the way young children interact with and respond to the different groups' expectations and responsibilities. Their social group goes beyond the family. Children are introduced to a larger society as they enroll in their early childhood class, which requires them to learn a new role within a new social institution. They have to learn their role in the school or center, the rules of behavior, their expectations, society's way of life, and the social values. They need to learn appropriate school behavior, become competent in meeting their own needs, and to interact with others. Young children also need to learn to share and effectively interact with others, including family members, peers, and teachers. These are behaviors that are compatible with the standards of a specific society. Young children need to become personally competent within a social context, which is a major goal in social learning in early childhood education.
- *Self-awareness* focuses on the young children's affective development. Children become aware of their self-concepts, manage those feelings about themselves and others, and develop effective ways to communicate and interact with others. They need to learn how to come to terms with their emotions and become responsive about themselves. Young children learn self-awareness when they are provided with opportunities to express their feelings or concerns with the teacher, alone, or in a group. Discussions, role playing, storytelling, and several play experiences help children achieve self-awareness.
- *Social Values* that are essential to convey to children include concern for the worth of the individual, concepts of freedom and responsibility, the importance of democratic decision making, and care for the safety of persons and property.

Children develop appropriate social values when they experience a wide array of opportunities for individual selection of goals and activities and consider the alternatives and possible consequences of their actions and of their own feelings. Young children learn social values through role playing, creative dramatics, literature, and art experiences. They also pick up the values of those around them whom they consider important, including parents and teachers. Children's values relate to their concept of morality, like what they consider to be fair and appropriate. Stages of moral development, which relate to moral reasoning and values, are part of the children's developmental processes. It is important for children to understand the moral judgments they can make at their own level. Children develop social values when they are allowed to select goals and activities (Wolfson, 1967).

Many consider that education reflects socially or culturally accepted standards or rules of behavior. Young children learn to identify with and accept the standards or norms of their society, which relate to moral education. Moral education is also essential for social learning. Moral education helps young children differentiate between right and wrong. Although there is a general moral code, the sources of morality differ in our society. Lawrence Kohlberg (2008) identified three levels, with two stages at each level, of moral development in children (see Table 2.1, from Turiel, 1973). Kohlberg's framework shows that the way children judge moral dilemmas indicates their level of development. Very young children usually function below stage two or three. Young children can learn proper behavior, but they will not understand the reason the behavior is considered proper in relation to higher-order ethical principles. The children's moral stage can be identified when they discuss the reasons for moral judgments and when they respond in role playing situations and question the reasons for their actions.

Young children show different patterns of social organization. They have their personal behavioral characteristics and personalities; but over time, they organize themselves into logical groups. The young children's development affects how they organize their social groups (like the development of social, regulatory, communication abilities). They have

**TABLE 2.1.** Stages of Moral Development

| Stage | Description |
| --- | --- |
| Stage 1 | *The punishment and obedience orientation.* The physical consequences of action determine its goodness or badness. Avoidance of punishment and unquestioning deference to power are valued in their own right |
| Stage 2 | *The instrumental-relativist orientation.* Right action consists of that which instrumentally satisfies one's own needs and occasionally the needs of others |
| Stage 3 | *The interpersonal concordance or "good boy–nice girl" orientation.* Good behavior is that which pleases or helps others and is approved by them. Behavior is frequently judged by intention—"he means well" becomes important for the first time. One earns approval by being "nice" |
| Stage 4 | *Authority and social order maintaining orientation.* There is orientation toward authority, fixed rules, and the maintenance of the social order. Right behavior consists of doing one's duty, showing respect for authority, and maintaining the given social order for its own sake |
| Stage 5 | *The social-contract legalistic orientation.* Right action tends to be defined in terms of general individual rights and standards (laws), which have been critically examined and agreed upon by society |
| Stage 6 | *The universal ethical principle orientation.* Right is defined by a decision of conscience in accord with self-chosen ethical principles. These principles are abstract and ethical; they are not concrete moral rules like the Ten Commandments |

very complicated social systems in any context (like playgrounds, classroom) that the dynamics of their social interactions may be difficult to understand. Researchers have developed special procedures to study the children's social behaviors and their peer interactions. They have attempted to identify the children's social organization in the classroom and school as well as the patterns and the processes that underlie these dynamics (Martin et al., 2005).

## Curriculum Components of Play

Society has specified the school's goals in relation to basic skills, stressing that children should learn letters, numbers, words, and colors even at the preschool level. The focus on academic skills diminishes the importance of the children's play. This is unfortunate, as play is an important tool to support young children's learning. Play permits children to select their learning, especially in relation to the attainment of a broad range of goals (Spodek & Saracho, 1987). Play provides young children with the opportunity to (1) express their ideas and their feelings, (2) symbolize and test their knowledge of the world, and (3) acquire effective support for academic and pre-academic learning. Through play, young children engage in active learning when they reconstruct their experiences, generate ideas, and test these ideas. Young children learn through hands-on experiences; when they manipulate symbolic materials, young children understand the concepts that these symbols represent. Therefore, symbolic play is a natural way to teach young children (Saracho & Spodek, 1987), and it is wise for teachers to develop play activities that relate to the program's educational goals. They can design play activities that (a) integrate children's ideas and experiences, (b) construct their knowledge, and (c) help them achieve most of their goals (Saracho, 2002b).

Play promotes children's development of knowledge, meaning of inquiry, creativity, and conceptual understanding (Wassermann, 1992). At all ages children need learning experiences within the integrated curriculum to play with words, paints, cubes, problems, materials, and music in their future roles of writers, poets, artists, architects, scientists, and musicians (Stone, 1995–1996).

Essential components in the play curriculum are symbolic play, social play, and educational play. When children engage in symbolic play, they use symbolic representations to communicate their thoughts. When children engage in social play, they interact with others to develop and improve their social skills. Educational play, which will be discussed in Chapter 5, is composed of different types of play including manipulative, block, physical, dramatic, and games.

## Symbolic Play

Children at a very early age initiate their understanding of imagination, drama, and narrative. Their involvement in a fantasy world at such an early age is extraordinary. First year-old infants usually manipulate and explore objects interminably, although they rarely use objects in a symbolic fashion, that is, to let one object represent another. For example, children between the ages of 12 to 24 months like to explore the physical features of household utensils. They manipulate objects (such as pots, pans, spoons) perhaps to bang them together but not to play as if they were something else. Two-year-olds pretend actions with familiar objects. For example, they may place a pot on their head and pretend that it is a hat or propel a spoon across the floor, moving it like a racing car while shouting, "broom, broom" (Kavanaugh & Engel, 1998).

When young children use these symbols, they are beginning to use symbolic representations that communicate their thoughts. They also learn that one object can represent another. Although symbolic behaviors emerge as temporary and separate actions in young children's play (Kavanaugh & Engel, 1998), they indicate that young children are acquiring an innovative and distinct manner of thinking. These children are able to move beyond the here-and-now to understand incidents that are pictured in their mind. Shortly these "symbolic children" will be able to verbalize the past, refer to the future, participate in pretend play, and introduce the construction of narrative segments that relate short "stories" about life incidents. The appearance of symbolic understanding in young children can influence their understanding of the non-literal, fantasy world that surfaces during early childhood.

When children engage in symbolic or dramatic play, they become better abstract thinkers. Their make-believe play helps them to interpret the meaning of objects. At the beginning, the actual objects are used to convey meaning. As children progress into higher stages of their symbolic development, objects are substituted. For instance, two-year-olds might "feed" themselves and a doll in a make-believe tea party. Slightly older children may build replica objects to convey their own pretend actions (Fenson, 1984; Wolf et al., 1984). This thought is a more advanced application of pretense that integrates actions, feelings, and thoughts to inanimate objects (such as making a doll go to sleep because "she's tired" or making a toy animal say, "Ouch, too hot!" as it steps into a make-believe bathtub) (Wolf et al, 1984).

## Social Play

Social play occurs when children assume a role that represents one seen in their social world. In social play they learn to get along with children who have a different point of view from them. For example, a child may say, "No, I don't want to be the mommy! I want to be the daddy!" This situation requires that children negotiate each other's request. Players regularly negotiate, compromise, and settle conflicts among themselves (Lillard, 1998).

### Stages of Social Play

Social play with peers is important in children's development of pretend play. Contemporary developmental perspectives focus on the influence of the social context on the cognitive processes. This theoretical strategy considers the categories of social interaction that affect the development of cognitive processes. These social interactions are enhanced in the children's pretend play (Vygotsky, 1934). Children's play behavior advances with age as does their social competence. Children who engage in play appropriately, solve problems, and share information normally accumulate friendships. Even children who do not know one another ultimately become friends when they play with each other (Creasey et al., 1998). According to Doyle et al. (1992), children enter social play using three approaches: (1) negotiation of pretend play plans (such as "Hey, the Ninja Turtle just bashed you!"), (2) spontaneous pretend play acts by one member of the dyad, or (3) a merger of children's solitary pretend play activities.

Studies have identified children's stages of social play since 1932. Mildred Parten (1932) first identified a series of stages of social play. Three-year-olds, she noted, engaged in *unoccupied play* (not playing at all), *solitary play* (playing alone), or *onlooker* (observing other children play). Four-year-olds participated in *parallel play* (playing side by side with others). Five-year-olds engaged in *associative play* or *cooperative play* (playing with other children). Parten (1932) believed that cooperative play is more advanced than solitary play and that parallel play was a transition from solitary play to cooperative play.

In the last three decades, several researchers (e.g., Rubin, 1976; Saracho, 1997, 1998a, 1998b, 1999a) have challenged the regularity of these stages. Their observations of children's play show that at any age children's play may reflect many stages. Some children like to play by themselves, being independent thinkers, and prefer to play alongside others; while others prefer to join their peers in associative or cooperative play. Saracho (2002a) suggests that the children's personality may influence their sociability. Social children who are interested in people participate in parallel, cooperative, and associative play; while less social children participate in solitary play (Saracho, 1997, 1998a, 1998b, 1999a). Parallel play (children playing alone next to their peers) indicates that children are developing a more sophisticated form of play that may facilitate more advanced, interactive play. Often children are able to alternate between solitary and cooperative play behaviors (Saracho, 2002a). Play behaviors have several attributes (Saracho, 1984). See Table 2.2.

Social play provides an important context that helps children develop and improve their social skills as they interact with others. They may acquire conflict management skills, intimacy, and role-taking opportunities. Peer-play offers children protection from

**TABLE 2.2.** Attributes of Play Behaviors

| Attribute | Description |
|---|---|
| Frequency of play | The extent to which children engage in the different forms of educational play and exhibit the distinctive play behaviors |
| Communication of ideas | The extent to which children communicate their thoughts and ideas in play through language or symbols (such as words, pictures, gestures, objects, a combination of these) |
| Social participation | Parten's (1932) five stages of social participation: solitary play, onlooker behavior, parallel play, associative play, and cooperative play |
| | (a) *Solitary* play indicates that children play alone. They play in a secluded area or initiate their own play activity without their peers |
| | (b) *Onlooker* indicates that children stand or sit within speaking distance of their peers to observe their play. |
| | (c) *Parallel* play indicates that children play alone beside other children |
| | (d) *Associative* play indicates that children play with other children to engage in an activity that is of interest to them |
| | (e) *Cooperative* play indicates that children engage in group play that is systematized (1) to produce some material product, (2) to accomplish a predetermined purpose, (3) to role play incidents from the adults' and group's life, or (4) to play formal games |
| Leader or follower | Indicates how the children participate in the play activity. Leaders initiate their own play activities, whereas followers depend on others to initiate their own play activities |

adult controls so that children can share information and concerns with their classmates. Children's play is a reflection of their overall social competence.

The quality of the children's peer play displays their typical social competence. Teachers can help young children improve their social competence by using role-playing activities to help children learn how to make critical and valuable decisions. Role playing can be used to solve problems, to help children understand their peers' point of view, and to improve their social competence. A role playing situation consists of an incident or a problem involving two or more children in which a situation needs to be explored and problems solved. Box 2.1 shows how to guide children in solving problems and Box 2.2 provides examples of role playing activities that help young children improve their social competence (Shaftel & Shaftel, 1982).

---

**Box 2.1. Using Role Play to Guide Children in Solving Problems**

1. *Defining the problem*. Teacher reads a story, waits for volunteers to respond, and gives children time to think.
2. *Delineating alternatives*. This is a projection process.
3. *Exploring alternatives*. Teacher allows the children to provide impulsive, negative, or anti-social solutions to solve the story problem as well as socially accepted solutions.
4. *Decision-making*. After the group has arrived at some clear understanding of the alternatives that they can explore and of the consequences they cause, the teacher asks the group which is the best solution, what are the consequences, and why.

---

**Box 2.2. Role Playing Activities that Improve the Children's Social Competence**

1. Read the book *The Little Red Hen* to the children. The teacher and children can identify the problem (others did not want to help). They can discuss the problem and solutions that would encourage cooperation. They can also role play the story by reversing the characters and discussing what the characters thought. The teacher can ask, "What can we change so that everybody gets along and can be happy?" A discussion can occur along these lines. Along the discussion, the teacher can ask, "At what point in the story can a change be made to help everybody be involved in the baking of the bread?" The children can then role play the modified story, discuss their perceptions and evaluation, and compare the original story with the modified story. The teacher can ask, "What do you think will happen now?" or "Is there another way to make everybody feel better?" Then they can role play the stories that the teacher feels would give the children an understanding of the feelings of others. Putting the children in the shoes of the character may help them understand what others feel about the actions of others.
2. Teachers can describe a situation to children where someone has to make a choice, discuss the situation, role play the situation, alternate the characters, and arrive at an appropriate solution on how the roles of the characters could be handled. For example, the following situation can be used:

Sarah has promised Jane that she would go to her birthday party. Then Sarah had a chance to go to see the movie *Harry Potter* with Mary Lou and Becky who are the popular girls in her class. Jane is a lonely and unpopular girl who nobody likes or plays with. Sarah wants very much to be popular and to play with others. She tells Mary Lou and Becky that she will go see *Harry Potter* with them and tells Jane she will not go to her party. Jane asks, "Why?"

The children can role play this situation and then role play it again and reverse the roles. Then teachers and children can provide alternative solutions to the problem.

3.  Teachers can use photographs of problem solving situations. If they are not able to find these photographs, teachers can use the photographs from the book, *Words and action* (Shaftel & Shaftel, 1967b). It illustrates photo-problems developed for preschool, kindergarten, and primary (first- and second-grade) children. Its focus is primarily on language development and the initiation of problem-solving skills. Teachers may elicit responses by asking questions such as, "What is happening here?" Teachers may help set the stage by asking children such questions as, "Who are you in this story? Where is this story? Who are the other children in the story? How does this make _____ feel? What do you think will happen now? Are there any ways that this situation can end?" The story and its solution can be role played.

It is important that teachers wait to role play the solution to the problem until it has been fully discussed and understood by the children. Teachers also have to be careful that these activities are developmentally appropriate (in length and content) for the children. Teachers may need to extend these activities to several days in order that children remain interested and do not become restless and frustrated.

## Social Aspects of Play

Play is critical to children's development. When children play, they understand the meaning of play and its role in life, civilization, and culture. For example, on the wall outside a classroom of four-and-a-half-year-olds was a Statue of Liberty covered with the children's printing of Emma Lazarus' beloved poem, "Give me your tired, your poor, your huddled masses."[1] There was also a large map of the fifty states, covered with postcards from all over the country. The children were engrossed in their work and never looked up from it. The teacher shared with Chenfeld (2004) the following story about the Statue of Liberty and a map of the United States.

Believe it or not, it started with puzzles. We had a pile of puzzles, as part of play time. One of the puzzles was a map of the United States. One of the "puzzle kids" picked up one of the states and asked which one it was. A few kids gathered round, looking at the other state puzzle pieces and began sharing the names of familiar states where they had relatives or friends. We found the puzzle piece for every state they named. They were SO

1 Emma Lazarus (July 22, 1849 B November 19, 1887) was an American poet who was born in New York City. In 1883, she wrote a famous sonnet titled "The New Colossus." In 1912, the last lines of the sonnet were engraved on a bronze plaque in the pedestal of the Statue of Liberty (Cavitch, 2006).

interested in that map puzzle. Well, you know how one thing leads to another . . . they went home very excited and, a few days later, one of the parents brought in a push button talking map that told nicknames, capitols, and sings "God Bless America," and even tells about the Statue of Liberty. The kids were enchanted. Every day they played with the puzzle map and the talking map. Soon, many of the children knew the names of rivers, cities, mountain ranges, state birds, and even insects! We decided to pay attention to one state at a time. We started with New York because most of the children had families that came from or lived in New York. We read books about Ellis Island and the Statue, about grandparents who came across the ocean from Europe and landed in New York. We sang "Give My Regards to Broadway" and "New York, New York." We spent about two weeks talking about and learning about New York. Then we paid atten- tion to our own state, Ohio. We even had cheers and projects to celebrate the legendary Ohio State/Michigan football game! We did so many wonderful things together! For Massachusetts, we made a Tea Party! For Kentucky, we made miners' hats and drew charcoal pictures to help us remember how important coal is to that state. We made stalagmites out of crystals and blue dye honoring Kentucky's blue caves. The kids loved constructing horse farms with horses made of clay to celebrate Kentucky's horses and blue grass country. We sang. We ate. We kept adding more and more ideas. This is just a fraction of what's been going on. Look at the postcards we've been receiving from people ALL over the country! We've been counting them, separating them into the states they represent (at the time of this conversation, twenty states were counted for in the numbers of postcards delivered to the class). We're comparing, counting, graphing. Imagine all this ongoing fascination just from ONE puzzle! (Chenfeld, 2004, p. 141).

Play also gives children a way of dealing with unconscious pressures (McCaslin, 2006). Young children use pretend play to make sense of the world and their experiences and to negotiate these meanings with others. When children engage in social pretend play, they experience an enjoyment that describes the children's creative development throughout life. Social pretend play also creates magic or the investigation of the boundaries of the children's experiences that identifies the life mysteries that are found in intellectual and aesthetic fields (Nourot, 1998).

Children's play is one of the most important ways for them to learn social studies. They look at the world around them and play what they see. They see people go to the office, drive a bus, work at stores, or go to parties. Children try a variety of ways to dramatize different roles and challenge themselves with all kinds of problems. Since they are only playing, children can try out new things without being afraid to fail. Children need to strengthen their understanding of social norms during pretend play by participating in imaginary situations that provide social opportunities and consequences (Peter, 2003). The children make sense of their pretend experience and create mental representations, which influences their attitudes, behavior, and understanding of their peers' behaviors. Their ability to use representations in shared environments that are meaningful to their peers is vital to the children's development of social competence, because they are learning how to understand and take different perspectives (Fein, 1981). Pretend play helps children to explore and experiment with their understanding of familiar social situations in imaginary contexts where they create their own cultural patterns (Vygotsky, 1978). Children's play behavior will show their growing understanding of objects and situations, as well as their feelings about others and their relationships with them in a variety of circumstances as they act out significant emotional stresses and themes (Howe & Lee, 2007).

Through play, children are "learning how to do it while doing it", an approach to partici-pate more meaningfully in a social world and leading towards greater social awareness and understanding. (Peter, 2003, p. 21). They examine objects and events in their immediate envi-ronment. Children find, inspect, and attempt to understand the natural objects and events that surround them. For example, on the way to and from school, children stop to stare at everything that is in their environment. They seem to be capturing the essence of the civiliza-tion that surrounds them. In their classroom, children will role play what they observed. They will spontaneously talk about their concerns with people and materials in their environment. Children are continuously searching for answers to questions like "How?" "How does it work?" "How did it get there?" "How do you know?" Children need to have access to infor-mation that will help them answer their questions. It is the best way for them to be provided with opportunities for first hand investigation and vicarious experiences. Children need to be presented with any source of information that is simple, clear, and accurate. They need to collect information using firsthand experiences, such as trips and personal contacts, or vicar-ious experiences like pictures and books. These experiences need to be carefully selected and developed to make sure that they are altogether comprehensive to help young children iden-tify details, use the knowledge they learned in their play, and develop their understanding through their interactions with others (Rudolph & Cohen, 1984).

In facilitating the children's play, it is important to consider the context for play (Darvill, 1982). The play environment includes both the social and physical elements that interact with each other and the children's individual developmental levels. In the subject areas, it is important that the children be provided with support in symbolic play. Play-drama lays the groundwork for the foundations for social relationships and develops the children's symbolic understanding and use of pretense (Peter, 2003). Basic guidelines to support pretend play are found in Table 2.3 (Rogers & Sawyers, 1988).

**TABLE 2.3.** Basic Guidelines to Support Pretend Play

| Guideline | Description |
| --- | --- |
| Support without force pretend play | Dress up clothes, books (such as *Caps for Sale*), and other props that will encourage children to engage in make-believe events |
| Give children the freedom to engage in their own make-believe play | The children's play rarely needs intrusion. As long as the children are playing safely, they need to be allowed to develop and engage in their own play. Children need to define the events. If they want to act out a story, they determine its course including any variations from the story |
| Let children determine if the play is real or fantasy | Make-believe can be an imitation of reality, but children may decide to change the order or the characters in the story or have animals do tricks |
| Select appealing props | Hats, replicas of food, suitcases, stethoscopes, beach towels, and cash registers can be the basis for children to build themes |
| Provide familiar experiences | Field trips, books, holidays, visitors, and everyday activities with family and friends can be used for pretend play. The children can use these experiences to expand on interesting themes |

Children need to be provided with a safe, interesting environment and the freedom to experiment with roles, resolve conflicts, and solve problems (Way, 1967). Play, acting, and thought are interrelated. They are mechanisms by which children test reality, get rid of their anxieties, and master their environment (Courtney, 1982, p. 177).

Many have used several interchangeable terms (like imaginative play, make-believe play, fantasy play, dramatic play, sociodramatic play) in relation to pretend play. Dramatic play, sociodramatic play, symbolic play, and pretend play represent related phenomena. All terms refer to play in relation to "pretending" or the use of symbols that "stand in" for that which is real. For example, one child becomes a dog and another child is the owner; a puppet speaks for a child; or a pile of blocks symbolizes a cave for bears (Mendoza, & Katz, 2008).

## Play, Dramatic Play, or Creative Dramatics

Regular educators usually use the term dramatic play or some type of drama, although early childhood educators usually use the term dramatic play. Regular educators teach their content through role playing to an audience; whereas early childhood educators motivate young children to engage in spontaneous play to act out situations in their world. Box 2.3 describes these differences. Young children participate in drama without having to memorize, to structure behavior patterns, to imitate, or to perform for an audience. Examples of drama that have been used in the early childhood classroom are found in Box 2.3.

---

**Box 2.3.  Examples of Drama**

- *Dramatic play* consists of role playing, puppetry, make-believe, and fantasy play. It may be individual or group play. In dramatic play, children assume different roles according to a specific value and to solve social and emotional problems. Dramatic play permits children to fit the reality of the world into their own interests and knowledge. It is one of the purest forms of symbolic thought available to young children, because dramatic play contributes strongly to the children's intellectual development (Piaget, 1951). Symbolic play is a necessary part of the children's language development (Saracho & Spodek, 2003a; Spodek & Saracho, 2003a). Dramatic play in childhood is a rehearsal for life. It is the children's way of (a) studying life itself; (b) studying the adults' world; and (c) learning more about the reality (Koste, 1995).

- *Sociodramatic play* is dramatic play that requires social interaction with others (such as a peer, adult). Sociodramatic play gives children the opportunities (1) to understand their peers' point of view and (2) to compromise and to stand firm in their beliefs and purposes. It is rich, complex, and uses the children's abilities to construct meaning, frame stories, and make sense of their world (Nourot, 1998).

- *Creative dramatics* is spontaneous and offers creative ways in which children reenact a scene or a story.

- *Role playing* is what young children do in dramatic play (McCaslin, 2006). They create magical worlds in their pretenses. Children's dramatic play is spontaneous, child-initiated, open-ended, and encourages individual expression. Shaftel and Shaftel (1982) advocate that role playing helps young children become decision-makers; because when children engage in role playing, they learn in a real life related way to solve problems between people.

■ *Story drama* is when children spontaneously role play a story that may be similar or different from the actual story. It gives the children the opportunity to "become the co-constructor of the story, the story itself, and the characters living the story" (Booth, 2005, p. 8). This is similar to creative dramatics.

Young children profit when they engage in creative dramatics. They enjoy the freedom of large movement and physical activity, but they get to develop a number of areas such as those in Box 2.4 (McCaslin, 2006).

---

### Box 2.4. Benefits of Creative Dramatics

■ *Develop their imagination* when children project themselves into another situation or into another person's life.

■ *Develop independent thinking and planning* when the children plan together in a group and communicate their own ideas and contribute to the situation.

■ *Develop their own ideas* when the group works together. Children share ideas and solve problems together.

■ *Develop their ability to cooperate* when the group builds something together. They learn ways to cooperate when they share ideas and improvise scenes.

■ *Build social awareness and human understanding* when children project themselves into another person's life. When children act out roles they have decided who is the character, the reason for the character's behavior, the character's relationship to others, and how the character manages problems.

■ *Feel and release emotion* when children actively engage in play. They use appropriate and acceptable channels to release emotions such as anger, fear, anxiety, jealousy, resentment, and negativism.

■ *Develop oral vocabulary and oral expression* when children use and practice words in their creative drama, which promotes their conceptual thinking and their characteristics of cognitive language.

---

Creative drama is a way of learning, a means of self-expression, a social activity, or a form of art. It also helps young children to assume responsibility, accept their peers' decisions, cooperate with their peers, acquire new interests, and search for new information. Creative drama needs to be based on situations and interests that make it very personal and highly socialized (McCaslin, 2006). Children can learn from drama when there is a relationship between their life and the content, issues, and themes. Their make-believe play theme should be connected with their real life to help children get immediate feedback about their specific actions and learn the consequences of their actions (Peter, 2003).

Although there are differences between dramatic play and drama, they have many characteristics in common. Both require children to interact, use their imagination, make symbolic transformations, make use of movement exploration, and conserve/replenish their energy. They also meet the children's creative, emotional, intellectual, and physical needs. Both should be labeled dramatic play (Mellou, 1996). According to Sutton-Smith and Magee (1989)

> Play . . . is a kind of drama more than it is a kind of speech, particularly when you consider that the players adopt role-type voices (mothers, gangsters, etc.), adopt voice tones with expressive phonology (conversational, authoritative, interested, questioning, laughing, announcing, insistent, excited, directive, surprised, defiant, sing song, telephoning, sighing), make dramatizations, sounds (screeching cars and exploding guns), and include expressive gestures (coquettish moves, skipping, prancing, flaring arms, leaping, jumping, exaggerated fearful faces) (p. 56).

The mutual component in all characteristics of dramatic play is that children imitate the behavior they observed in adults and themselves. For example, children may play dramatically when they pretend to be a spaceperson or a doctor (Mellou, 1996). The characteristics of dramatic play are characterized by the children's abilities to perceive, imagine, impersonate, and imitate actions when they identify with a specific person, thing, or event that is meaningful to the children. Children step into the shoes of another person to experiment with this person's situation from this person's point of view. Such approach broadens the children's expressive procedure of dramatic play to the creative process of making drama. According to Siks (1983),

> It happens when four-year-old Margo, who has a new baby brother, plays alone with her doll, imitating her mother caring for the baby. It happens when a group of boys on playground act out an encounter of their perception of Space Wars (p. 6).

This kind of play has in common a make-believe or pretend quality, that is *the child uses his imagination to amplify and modify the concrete and immediately present stimulus* (Saltz & Johnson, 1974, p. 623). The evolution from children's natural dramatic play to the art of drama forms a bridge between the children's expressive abilities in dramatic play to their creative abilities to develop and perform the dramas they create. The children's learning experiences reinforce their expressive abilities and cultivate their communication and aesthetic perception abilities. Children experience and learn fundamental concepts when they are actively involved with the concepts in the process of learning to create and communicate drama (Siks, 1983).

## Summary

In the American culture, where the ethical values persist, play is considered a frivolous activity, without any important consequences. Although researchers fail to support this belief, it still has an impact on the early childhood education curriculum. Several early childhood programs maintain the cultural belief that learning only occurs from work, which suggests that teachers need to set up a work curriculum. They justify play by referring to it as "child's work." In fact, play can be fun and fanciful and still have critical educational consequences for young children (Saracho, 1999b).

Through play young children learn about their world. The teachers have a major role in the play curriculum. They need to use appropriate arrangement, interpretation, and intervention strategies to motivate and encourage the children's participation in play, which ultimately develops their learning (Saracho, 1999b). When young children play, teachers need to observe their play to obtain insight about the children's view of their world, and create strategies that facilitate the children's learning. Teachers become facilitators rather than directors of the children's learning through play. Then children are able to learn complex concepts that will help them live successfully in modern society. Young children need the type of play experiences that can assist them to assimilate and accommodate knowledge. An effective early childhood education curriculum needs to use play as a learning medium (Spodek & Saracho, 1987). In this play curriculum teachers (1) set up a supportive environment with sufficient play areas, materials, and equipment; (2) nurture positive social interactions; and (3) integrate children's play to make it more beneficial. Teachers need to know the effects of the various types of play that are appropriate for young children (Saracho, 1999b).

# Section II
# Theoretical Perspectives

# Chapter 3
# **Developmental Theories of Play**

Play is the principal instrument of growth. Without play there can be no normal adult cognitive life; without play, no healthy development of affective life; without play, no full development of will.

(Courtney, 1977, p. 95)

Most theorists affirm that play develops the children's cognitive and social competence (Erikson, 1950; Piaget, 1951). Young children (including toddlers) who participate in sophisticated pretend play (like using a crayon to represent a phone) are often considered to be more intelligent than children who participate in simple forms of play. Also preschool children who use highly developed sociodramatic themes (like Star Wars) in their play are more socially competent and are more popular than their peers who engage in a simpler form of play (Creasey & Jarvis, 2003). Since play is a predominant premise to the children's performance across many societies, it is essential to better understand its development. Multiple theories frame the children's developmental progress in their play. This chapter reviews the developmental theories of children's play (such as classical, modern, cognitive), postmodern theories (such as theory of mind, cultural play theory), and socio-cultural play theories.

## Theories of Play

Over the years, philosophers have introduced related theories of play to help understand the nature of children's play behavior. They have been characterized as classical and modern theories of play. Classical theories emerged in the 19th century and continued throughout the 20th century, whereas modern theories appeared after 1920. Classical theories describe the reason and purpose of play, whereas modern theories describe the practices of play and their relationship to children's development. The modern theories of play use theoretical concepts and empirical research to understand play activities, especially for the psychoanalytic and cognitive theories of play. Among the modern theories, Spodek and Saracho (1994b) integrated dynamic theories of play, which are discussed in the following sections.

## Classical Theories

*Classical theories* justify the reason and explain the meaning of play. They consist of the (1) Surplus Energy, (2) Recreational or Relaxation, (3) Practice or Pre-exercise, and (4) Recapitulation theories.

The Surplus Energy Theory was created by Friedrich Schiller (1759–1805), the 18th century German poet, historian, and philosopher. His theory indicates that after meeting basic survival needs, play gets rid of "excess energy." Schiller's theory of play suggests that animals develop more energy than they need to survive, and all human and nonhuman animals must dispose of any surplus energy.

The British philosopher Herbert Spenser (1820–1903) related his surplus energy theory of play to evolution. For example, higher species animals play more than lower species animals. Since these species use less energy for survival (such as meeting the organism's fundamental needs), they have more time to play.

Schiller considered play to be related to "surplus energy," while Spenser considered it to be a "superfluous activity." Neither of these philosophers believed that play was essential for human development. Rather they believed that it was a mechanism that helped the organism balance its energy.

Recreational or Relaxation Theory sees play activity as a way to restore energy. Moritz Lazarus (1883), the German poet, saw play as the reverse of work, renewing the energy that was depleted during work. Play is a recreational activity (Lazarus, 1883) or a behavior pattern that emerges as a need to relax (Patrick, 1916). Recreational or Relaxation theory is considered the opposite of surplus energy theory (Lazarus, 1883).

Practice or Pre-exercise Theory was created by Karl Groos (1898, 1901), and recognized countless traditions and functions of children's play in adult games, rituals, and competitions. Play prompts children to reproduce and carry out adult roles that get children ready for adulthood and their future. For example, children act out their parents' roles in dramatic play and are rehearsing roles that they will take up as adults in the future. Numerous modern developmental theorists (e.g., Bruner, 1976; Sylva et al., 1974) reflect Groos' Practice or Pre-exercise Theory. Many constructivist theories presently support this theory, because they believe it develops the children's intellectual functioning (Piaget, 1951, 1976).

Recapitulation Theory was created by G. Stanley Hall (1844–1924), an American psychologist. It assumes that the individual's development reestablishes the species' development. Hall (1906) used Charles Darwin's theory of evolution as a source for his recapitulation theory. Hall theorized that each human being begins at the embryo stage and continues through evolutionary stages that are paralleled to those of the human species. In this progression children dramatize the human being's developmental stages (like animal, savage, tribal member) in their play, which gives children a catharsis freeing them from any primitive impulses that are inappropriate for our present society.

## Summary of Classical Play Theories

The classical theories of play can be grouped into pairs: (1) Surplus Energy Theory with Recreational/Relaxation Theory and (2) Practice/Pre-exercise Theory with Recapitulation Theory. See Table 3.1 for a summary of these theories.

Each set of theories opposes the other on the way play uses energy or controls instincts. The Surplus Energy and Recreational/Relaxation theories explain the way play manages energy. One theory disperses excess energy, while the other restores the lack of energy. Both the Practice/Pre-exercise and Recapitulation theories describe play and their relationship to instincts. The Practice/Pre-exercise theory familiarizes children with adult life as they practice the roles in adulthood, while the Recapitulation theory helps children to free themselves of maladaptive instincts of previous stages.

The classical theories are based on philosophical principles instead of empirical research. Ellis (1973) considers these theories to be extremely deficient. In addition, they are missing the up-to-date theoretical knowledge of energy, instinct, evolution, and development (Johnson et al., 2005). Nonetheless, they provide a foundation for the modern theories of play (Rubin, 1982) that are presented in the following sections.

## Modern Theories of Play

Modern theories of play provide an understanding of its essential role in children's development. Typically, the modern theories of play yield an understanding of play by justifying the strength of the theoretical concepts and by supporting it with empirical research. Modern theories view play as a system that fosters cognition or symbolization. Such theories consist of Psychoanalytic, Arousal Modulation, Metacommunicative, and Cognitive theories (Mellou, 1994). These theories are summarized in Table 3.2.

**TABLE 3.1.  Classical Theories of Play**

| Theories | Theorists | Purpose for Play | Areas of Concentration |
|---|---|---|---|
| Surplus Energy | Friedrich Schiller (1759–1805) Herbert Spenser (1820–1903) | Eliminates excess energy left over beyond what individuals need | Physical |
| Recreational or Relaxation | Moritz Lazarus (1883) G. T. W. Patrick (1916) | Restores sufficient energy to continue again | Physical |
| Recapitulation | G. Stanley Hall (1844–1924) | An inherent manner of discontinuing primitive skills and drives that individuals have inherited from former epochs of civilization and becoming prepared for the endeavors of modern life | Physical |
| Practice or Pre-exercise | Karl Groos (1896, 1901) | An instinctive manner of preparing children for the endeavors of adult life | Physical, intellectual |

**TABLE 3.2. Modern Theories of Play**

| Theories | Philosopher | Purpose of Play | Area of Concentration |
|---|---|---|---|
| Psychoanalytic | Sigmund Freud<br>E. H. Erikson<br>L. E. Peller<br>L. Murphy<br>V. M. Axline<br>Margaret Lowenfeld<br>Susan Isaacs | Children are helped to cope with repressed problems that took place at their previous stages of development and were buried in their subconscious. Children use play as a device to conquer their own hidden feelings related to their apparent actions | Emotional, social |
| Arousal Modulation | M. J. Ellis<br>D. E. Berlyne | Play enables the organism to look for sources of arousal to acquire specific information. It is a stimulus-seeking activity that offers children with opportunities to manipulate objects and actions in new and rare ways. It expands both the stimulation and arousal levels | Physical, emotional |
| Meta-communicative | G. Bateson | Claims that play is based on the children's interactions when they participate in pretend play. In play, children learn to function at the same time on two levels: (1) pretend meaning of objects and actions and (2) reality of life (e.g., real identities of players and real purpose of objects and actions). Play scripts and experiences are constantly shifting based on their situations and the environment | Social, intellectual |
| Cognitive | Jean Piaget<br>Lev S. Vygotsky<br>Jerome Bruner<br>Brian Sutton-Smith | Play fosters the children's cognitive development and abstract thinking. In play children get information and meaning from their experiences. Their make-believe play helps them in their interpretations of the objects. Play is the children's creation of make-believe incidents of real life problems | Intellectual, social |

*Psychoanalytic Theory* was created by Sigmund Freud and his followers. It was derived from their clinical practice. Freud believed that play carried out a unique purpose in the children's emotional development. Since it helped children to deal with negative emotions and replace them with more positive ones, play performs a cathartic effect, which helps children manage situations that result from negative feelings and traumas. Play helps them to develop a better emotional equilibrium.

Freud (1938) noticed that children use play as a device to conquer their own hidden feelings. The children's active participation or inactive observation controls their internalized thought system and their intentional physical movements. Distress affects the individuals' social dealings or interpersonal discourses. Play activities and explorations assist children to better understand stressful situations and look for a different meaning that incorporates enjoyable feelings and avoids bad ones. Play helps children to interpret situations and connect symbolic properties of people and objects in both the present and past. As such, play assists children to express their feelings (Wehman & Abramson, 1976).

Other theorists made independent analyses that modified Freud's psychoanalytic theory. Each theorist analyzed a separate purpose of play in human development. Psychoanalysts associate play with wish fulfillment, anxiety, and ego development (Takhvar, 1988). Erikson (1950), one of Freud's followers, modified Freud's stages of psychosexual development to begin at birth and continue throughout the individual's life (Erikson, 1950). Erikson believed that children play to act out the past, present, and future. Their play dramatizations help children to resolve problems they find at each particular developmental stage. Peller (1952), another of Freud's disciples, thought that children's basic emotional feelings (love, admiration, fear, aggression) motivated them to engage in rehearsals of life during play. Both Erikson and Peller assumed that the structure of play affects the individual's psychosocial or psychosexual development (see Table 3.3).

Psychoanalysts speculated that children use fantasy play situations to act out adult roles, which provides them with a feeling of achievement that makes it possible for them to manage actual problems. Children act out personal upsetting experiences to overpower the hurt, because they can understand them during their play experience. Being able to cope with the incident can help them to deal with the affective elements of positive life situations (Murphy, 1956). For example, a child becomes sick and is taken quickly to a hospital. This situation can be traumatic and leave various negative emotional feelings. This separation from family, in addition to the child's pain and suffering from the illness, can create an emotional trauma. Once the child has recuperated, the experiences at the hospital can be acted out by the child. By dramatizing scary situations, play gives the child a means to cope with the world, understand it, and handle its problems.

Play therapy has been used as a clinical treatment, which is used with children who have emotional problems. It helps children to naturally express themselves and act out emotions of tension, fear, and insecurity. Therapists give children toys to observe their

**TABLE 3.3.** Freud's Stages of Psychosexual Development

| Stage | Age | Description |
|---|---|---|
| Oral Stage | Zero to one year | The focal point of sensual stimulation and pleasure |
| Anal Stage | One to three years | The focal point of pleasure is in withholding or eliminating feces |
| Phallic Stage | Three to six years | The parents are identified |
| Latency Stage | Six to 12 years | The focus is on industriousness and suppression of sexual interest |
| Genital Stage | 12 years and up | Mature sexual interests develop |

behavior and discover the children's emotions through play therapy. They observe children during play therapy to get an understanding about the child's problems and be able to help them cope with their problems. Through play therapy children learn to deal with their emotions and become secure (Axline, 2002).

In 1928 Margaret Lowenfeld (1979), a British pediatrician and child psychiatrist, opened her Clinic for Nervous and Difficult Children in London. She discovered how children think, how they play, and how they deal with pain and grief. Lowenfeld used these insights to create her own original theories and techniques. She developed a projective play therapy technique for unhappy or disturbed children. Since Lowenfeld's play therapy technique did not require the children to use words or language, it was successfully used in cross-cultural research. Lowenfeld considered the World Technique to be a way for children to communicate and express their thoughts and emotions as well as to release any conflicts and tensions resulting from inconsistencies between their inner and outer realities. Lowenfeld believed that children's and adults' thinking processes were very different. Her technique would permit children to directly communicate their mental and emotional experiences, which she could keep a record of and study. Lowenfeld did not superimpose any theories onto the children's constructions. She let the theory develop from the children's work itself (Turner, 2009).

Lowenfeld became well known for her therapeutic use of miniature figures in a tray of sand. She based her work on Herbert George Wells' (1866–1946) *Floor Games* (1911) that describes the sensation of the miniature worlds.[1] Wells developed many different small toys and blocks to be used on the floor (Turner, 2004). Lowenfeld called the small toys and materials the "wonder box." In 1929, she referred to the wonder box as the World Technique. The field immediately started to shape miniature worlds and scenes in the sand boxes in the playroom at their clinics (Lowenfeld, 1979).

Lowenfeld's play therapy and the Dramatic Productions Test (DPT) by Erik Homberger Erikson (1937) were simultaneously developed. Erikson did not know about the World Technique. Coincidentally, he used miniature figures in a defined space to try to better understand human behavior. In his DPT, Erikson asked the subjects to create a dramatic scene and concluded in his studies that what seemed to be their miniature arrangements on top of the table were scenes that represented the subjects' childhood trauma. The DPT arrangements were the subjects' extensions of where they had left off in their childhood efforts to triumph over their trauma in their active repetition of play (Turner, 2009).

In 1937, Lowenfeld introduced the World Technique at a clinical conference in Paris. She documented the therapeutic value of the World Technique in her children's clinic (Turner, 2009). Other specialists (e.g., Isaacs, Erikson) became attracted to the study of the World Technique and adapted or modified it to meet their own specific therapeutic or diagnostic purposes because of its similar characteristics to dramatic play.

Susan Isaacs (1885–1948) made important contributions to both the young children's education and to the children's psychoanalysis. She was also known for her belief that the environment was a natural starting point for children's education. She attributed this idea to John Dewey. Isaacs emphasized the children's introduction to the natural world. While she was head of the Malting House School (1924–1927), Isaacs (1930) collected and analyzed observations and developed the following principles of children's inquiry into the natural world:

---

1 *Floor Games* has a cheerful and entertaining discussion about the theory, purpose, and methodology using models, miniatures, and other props to play a variety of children's games.

- Children learn from physical contact with the world. Their testing and measuring of reality weans them from personal schemas (p. 80).

- Children's knowledge increases through experiences of experimenting, observation and discovery. For example, after burning bits of wool and cotton, a Malting House School child observed that wool does not burn so easily as cotton (p. 51).

- Children have strong, spontaneous interests in and raised questions about the things and events of the natural world. (pp. 80–81).

- Children can reason, when their interests are engaged. Although young children cannot sustain verbal thinking, it does spring up and die down, like wave crests (pp. 84–85).

- Given the right environment and degree of response from influential adults, children will pursue interests. Sustained conversations between one child and one adult . . . occur . . . in the course of free practical activity in a varied setting, and in play with other children and with adults who share in the practical pursuits (pp. 82–83).

- . . . children's thinking in everyday life . . . And on any day, [the children] would pass easily between the realms of pure fantasy and occasionally of magic, and those of practical insight and resource, and of verbal argument and reasoning (p. 92).

- Children can hypothesize and make inferences. Cognitive behavior was not to be thought of as a set of single-unit acts of relation-finding, but as a complex dynamic series of adaptive reactions and reflections. These crystallize out here and there into clear judgments or definite hypotheses or inferences, which, however, gain all their meaning from their place in the whole movement of the child's mind in its attempt to grasp and organize its experience (p. 52).

In the 1930s, Isaacs presented her principles at the London Institute of Education. In the 1960s, publications of Susan Isaacs' started to flourish. Friedrich Froebel and John Dewey influenced Isaacs' educational approach, and she in turn influenced others with her activity methods (Hall, 2000). These three thinkers believed in an individualized approach to learning where children are encouraged to discover the nature of the world for themselves (Graham, 2008). Isaacs used her approach at the Malting House School. Isaacs (1930) describes how the school building was modified to be used as a school. The following is Graham's (2008) interpretation of Isaacs' description.

> The striking feature of her description of the school is the lack of any mention of class-rooms, and in fact there were none. However, there was plenty of space in the garden and an abundance of stimulating equipment whose use the children could explore for themselves. In the garden there was a sandpit with a water tap, a tool-shed, a summer house with roof and open sides, a see-saw (which had detachable weights hung at inter-vals underneath), sliding boards, movable ladders, and a 'Jungle-gym' climbing cage.

> Among the equipment indoors were paints, both artist's colours and 'real' (house-painter's) paints with suitable brushes, rolls of thin coloured muslin; plasterer's laths for woodwork and, later on, pieces of small timber; hammers, pincers, nails, and other tools of the proper size and weight for carpentry (including a double-handled saw for cutting up logs), bricks for building (both a variety of wooden ones, and old 'real' bricks of small size for building in the garden); small movable pulleys that could be screwed in where desired; maps of Cambridge town and county; an HMV portable gramo-phone and selection of records; a pendulum, with movable weight, fixed on the wall.

The carpenter's room in the second and third years included a lathe with a variety of tools, a drilling machine, and such oddments as a spirit level and callipers.

After the first year, Bunsen burners were fitted to the benches both in the large hall, and in the laboratory for the older children, and there were tripods, flasks, glass rods and tubing to use with them. (The supply of gas was controlled by a detachable key for each burner, so that the burner could not be used by the children unless one of the staff was there to supervise.) In the laboratory there were dissecting instruments and dishes, jars for specimens, a human skeleton and anatomical diagrams.

The living animals (kept mostly in the garden) included several families of mice and rabbits, guinea pigs, two cats and a dog, a hen and chickens, snakes and salamanders, silkworms, a fresh-water aquarium and a wormery.

There was also some formal educative material, including some Montessori equipment. The reading material included a wide variety of the 'look and say' type—pictures of things with names attached, pictures with short stories, commands, labels and so on. Much of this was made by the staff and the children as required. The older children had a typewriter and a library of suitable books.

The richness of the material available to the children is surely remarkable. Perhaps even more remarkable to the contemporary reader is the ready accessibility of such potentially dangerous equipment. One is relieved to hear that the supply of gas to the Bunsen burners was individually controlled and their use supervised. All the same, one has the strong impression that a visit from one of today's health and safety inspectors would have rapidly resulted in at least a temporary closure of the school. (pp. 8–9)

Isaacs believed in observing the children to see their development and what they did under free conditions. The children needed to be provided with the freedom to explore and experiment with (a) the physical world; (b) the way things are made; (c) how they break and burn; and (d) the properties of water, gas, and electric light, the rain, sunshine, the mud and the frost. Children needed to have the freedom to engage in either fantasy or imaginative play (Graham, 2008). Isaacs (1930) notes that dramatic play assists children to understand the behavior of objects and people.

## Commonalities

Developmentalists like Susan Isaacs, Erik Erikson, and Margaret Lowenfeld found a way that helps children work out their problems and be able to meet any challenges in their world with self-assurance. The descriptions of their observations are remarkably comparable in meaning. For instance, Erikson (1940) states, ". . . to play it out is the most natural auto-therapeutic measure childhood affords. What ever other role play may have in the child's development the child also uses it to make up for defeats, sufferings, and frustrations" (p. 561). In her written observations, Susan Isaacs (1930) says, ". . . Play is not only the means by which the child comes to discover the world, it is supremely the activity which brings him psychic equilibrium in the early years. In his play activities the child externalizes and works out to some measure of harmony the different trends of his internal psychic life. In turn he gives external form and expression, now to the parent, now to the child within himself . . . And gradually he learns to relate his deepest and most primitive fantasies to the ordered world of real relations" (p. 425). In discussing repeated temporary neurotic episodes of childhood, Margaret Lowenfeld (1931) believes that symbolic play is very important, because it helps children draw off "some of the excess emotional energy which has become dammed up behind the neurosis" (p. 226). If children are allowed to play freely in a setting of security and acceptance, they will be able to satisfactorily and healthily cope with their most urgent problems (Hartley & Goldenson, 1963).

One of psychoanalytic theory's major influences on early childhood education has been that it made the use of expressive activities with young children more educationally legitimate. The resolution of conflicts in the early years was seen as important to children's mental health. Children are able to deal with and resolve conflicts on their own level through play (Murphy, 1962). The expression of feelings as well as ideas is also important for their mental health. The expressive arts are important tools that allow young children to express their ideas and feelings. Young children may not have the competence to use language to express all their thoughts and feelings, and various forms of expression—art, music, and movement—allow children to express those ideas they cannot express in words (Alschuler & Hattwick, 1947). They also use play to act out disturbing situations, providing a way to cope with negative feelings and to resolve emotional conflicts they may not be able to do in real life. While play could provide a form of therapy for children (Axline, 2002), play is also central to the activities of schools for children below the primary grades.

Because children use the arts and play to express personal feelings, many early childhood educators believe that teachers should not interfere with children's creative activities. Adult interference, they feared, would hinder children's personal expressions. With adult intervention, the play and art activities would become expressions of the supervising adult rather than of the children, and the emotional needs of the children would not be met. Teachers were told instead to closely observe children's play and to record these observations to gain insights into children's minds and hearts (Hartley & Goldenson, 1963). Information from direct observation of the preschool children's physical activity can identify the children's activity behaviors and the related social and environmental events of those behaviors (Brown et al., 2009).

Arousal Seeking/Modulation Theory was created by Berlyne (1969). It explains how play is the organism to search for sources of arousal to acquire specific information. Berlyne believed that a need or drive in the children's central nervous system maintains arousal at the best possible level. Being overstimulated (like seeing a strange object) increases arousal to alarmingly high levels and guides children to engage in activities that will diminish stimulation (like looking at an object to become familiar with it). A deficiency of stimulation decreases arousal to lesser levels and develops monotony. Then the organism struggles to look for more stimulation, which Berlyne identifies as "diverse exploration." Looking for activity reduces the motivation for arousal.

Ellis (1973) proposed a second arousal-seeking theory of play. It is a stimulus-seeking activity that provides children with opportunities to manipulate objects and actions in new and rare ways. Ellis assumed that play would expand both the stimulation and arousal levels. He suggests that individuals constantly concentrate on sensory adjustment. Sensory input continues to set when individuals only focus for a short period of time. They search for a collection of complimentary sources of information to increase stimulation. On the other hand, too much information encourages them to avoid stimulation by ignoring several information sources. Individuals are better thinkers when conditions give them a wealth of novelty, uncertainty, and complexity. Play helps children to achieve their fullest potential if reinforced with the appropriate amount of stimulation.

Metacommunicative Theory, developed by Bateson (1955), claims that play is based on the children's interactions when they participate in pretend play. Children inform their peers that the play episodes are fictitious and are only life imitations. When children play, they learn to function at the same time on two levels: (1) pretend meaning of objects and actions and (2) reality of life (like real identities of players and real purpose of objects and actions).

Bateson's Metacommunicative theory also states that play scripts and experiences are constantly shifting based on their situations and the environment. Play motivates children to develop meaningful scripts within the context based on their cultural experiences. During play, they are also able to distinguish the difference between fantasy and reality which is essential to the children's cognitive development. Bateson's theory stimulated researchers to examine the relationship between play and cognition. Wolf and Grollman (1982) show a developmental age trend in the narrative qualities that occur while children are shifting in their play. Schartzman (1978) reports that the children's social status changes during their play. The perceived relationship between text and context is similar to the relationship between communication and metacommunication (Takhvar, 1988).

## Cognitive Theories of Play

Child development theorists have shown the relationship between play and cognitive development. Jean Piaget, Lev S. Vygotsky, and Jerome Bruner are the theorists who have contributed the most knowledge about this relationship. Their theories are discussed below.

### Piagetian Theory

Jean Piaget (1896–1980) established that children gain knowledge through the dual processes of assimilation and accommodation. Through *assimilation*, children acquire information from their experiences in the external reality. Then they assimilate or merge this information into existing mental structures. Through *accommodation*, children compare new information that differs from the information that they already know and modify their mental structures. Typically this difference leads the child to reach a state of balance or *equilibrium*. For spontaneous play, assimilation considers primacy over accommodation. In other words, children accommodate their world into their mental structures. Children use their current mental schemes and movement patterns to solve their present problems when they consider that their world is different (Fein & Schwartz, 1982).

Piagetian theory states that dramatic play occurs at the children's developmental level. In dramatic play, children acquire information and meaning from their experiences (Saracho & Spodek, 1995). Piaget (1951) shows that the children have three consecutive stages of play: (1) sensory-motor play, (2) symbolic play, and (3) games with rules. Children progress through these stages while their mental structures slowly integrate into their later stages.

In the first of Piaget's stages of play, children have repetitive actions that focus on physical activity; therefore, accommodation is essential. In other words, during all development stages, children experience their environment using the mental representations they have developed. A repeated experience will fit without difficulty (or is assimilated) into the child's cognitive structure, which helps them keep mental "equilibrium." If the experience is unfamiliar (either different or new), the children will fail to keep their equilibrium and will instead modify their cognitive structure to accommodate the new experiences, adding to their cognitive structures.

In the second stage (from about age 18 months to age seven years) pretend or symbolic play emerges. Since this stage of play has a symbolic nature, it strongly contributes to the children's literacy development. In symbolic play, any object is represented and assigned original characteristics. For example, a wooden box can represent a car or truck. Piaget's final stage of play is games with rules. It emerges during Piaget's concrete operational stage between the ages of six to seven years. Games with rules (like checkers, chess, card games) need to have at least two children in order to play. Once children start playing these games, both sensorimotor and symbolic play decrease throughout the children's lives. Piaget maintains that modifications in his stages of cognitive development create the foundation for modifications in his stages of play. Piaget's theory that play advances the individual's cognitive development is opposed by Vygotsky.

### Vygotskian Theory

In 1924 the Russian psychologist Lev S. Vygotsky (1896–1934) stated that play contributed to more than the children's cognitive development. He proposed the general theory that children's symbolic play can be understood as a very complex system of speech with the help of gestures that indicate the meaning of different playthings. Thus, an object provides support for the matching gesture. Later, children begin to use verbal symbols; together children may decide on the representation of the objects ("this will be a house for us," or "this is a plate") and begin to use rich verbal associations to indicate, explain, and communicate the meaning of each movement, object, and action. Children gesture and verbalize their explanation of their own play, and ultimately link their gestures with their speech (Vygotsky, 1935, cited in Smolucha & Smolucha, 1998). Vygotsky first described his research on play in a publication titled, *The Prehistory of Written Language* (Vygotsky 1935, 1978, 1987) where he discusses the gestural-symbolic nature of the object substitutions that children make during pretend play:

> . . . The child's own movements, his own gestures are what assign a symbolic function to the corresponding object that communicate meaning to it. All symbolic representational activity is full of such indicatory gestures; thus, a stick becomes a riding-horse for the child, because it can be placed between the legs and it is possible to apply a gesture to it, which will indicate to the child, that a stick in this case designates a horse.

> From this point of view children's symbolic play can be understood as a very complex system of speech with the help of gestures, communicating and indicating the meaning of different playthings. It is only on the basis of these indicatory gestures that playthings gradually acquire their own meaning, just as drawing, at first supported by gesture becomes an independent sign. Only from this point of view is it possible for science to explain two facts, which up to this time still have not had a proper theoretical explanation.

> The first fact consists in this, that for the child anything can be anything in play. This can be explained thus, the object itself acquires an unction and a symbolic meaning only thanks to the gesture, which endows it with this. From here follows the idea that meaning consists in the gesture and not in the object. That is why it is unimportant

what an object is in any given case. The object is only a point of support for the corresponding gesture.

The second fact consists in this, that it is only early in the play of 4- to 5-year old children that the verbal conventional symbol appears. Children agree among themselves "this will be a house for us, this is a plate" and so on; and at about this age extraordinarily rich verbal connections arise, indicating, explaining, and communicating the meaning of each movement, object, and action. The child not only gesticulates, but also converses, explaining his own play. Gesture and speech mutually intertwine and are united. (Vygotsky, 1935, pp.77–78, cited in Smolucha & Smolucha, 1998, pp. 49–50)

In his research, Vygotsky discusses the type of object substitutions children imitate during their play such as:

The object itself performs a substitution function: a pencil substitutes for a nursemaid or a watch for a drugstore, but only the relevant gesture endows them with meaning. However, under the influence of this gesture, older children begin to make one exceptionally important discovery—that objects can indicate the things they denote as well as substitute for them. For example, when we put down a book with a dark cover and say this will be a forest, a child will spontaneously add, "yes, it's a forest because it's black and dark." She thus isolates one of the features of the object, which, for her, is an indication of the fact that the book is supposed to be a forest . . . Thus, the object acquires a sign function with a developmental history of its own that is now independent of the child's gesture. This is second-order symbolism, and because it develops in play, we see make-believe play as a major contributor to the development of written language—a system of second-order symbolism. (Vygotsky, 1935, pp. 79–80, cited in Smolucha & Smolucha, 1998, p. 50)

In 1933 Vygotsky's publication entitled *Play and its Role in the Mental Development of the Child*, he discusses that play develops a "zone of proximal development" (ZPD) for preschool children (Vygotsky, 1967). He describes the zone of proximal development as *"the distance between the actual developmental level as determined by independent problem solving and the level of potential development as determined through problem solving under adult guidance or in collaboration with more capable peers"* (italics in the original text, translated from *Mind In Society*, Vygotsky, 1978, p. 86).

According to Vygotsky (1934), symbolic or dramatic play fosters the children's abstract thinking. Their make-believe play helps them in their interpretations of the objects. While initially, the representation needs to be similar to the objects, in later stages of development this becomes less relevant. Vygotsky characterizes play as the children's creation of make-believe incidents of real life problems.

Vygotsky's theory added to Piaget's theory manifesting that the children's play experiences stimulate their cognitive development in the social context of culture where the cultural aspects of cognitive development occur. Playing with peers promotes the children's cognitive development.

Lev Vygotsky's work of the 1920s and 1930s was continued by Bruner in his earlier work. Bruner believed that knowledge and learning were gained most effectively when children learned through personal discovery instead of just being "taught."

*Bruner's Theory*

Jerome Bruner (1915–) initially theorized that children's play promoted problem-solving abilities that were to become important in their later life, which suggests that his early work is an extension of the classical theory of play. Bruner (1972) believed that through play children obtain information about and experience the environment, which can maximize their flexibility. He thought that play provides children with the opportunities to test a mixture of behaviors and use these experiences to learn. Bruner thinks that especially social play offers a way to minimize the consequences of the children's actions and reduce the risks in a situation. Thus, social play is a type of communication system where the children's behaviors are transmitting messages. Play is a way of learning appropriate social communication.

According to Bruner, in play the means are more important than the ends. When children are playing, they do not have to be concerned about achieving goals. They have the freedom to explore with innovative mixtures of behavior without any pressure to reach a goal. After they have tested the new behavioral combinations that they used in play, the children can then use them to solve real life problems. As a result, play supports flexibility in problem solving and extends its usefulness in human development and evolution. Burner makes a case that if the immaturity period is extended, young children will be able to develop flexible problem solving skills through play (Johnson et al., 2005).

Bruner views play as beneficial to the children's cognitive development and their preparation for their practical social life that is found in human culture. He contends that play helps children practice to become proficient in their social abilities and to test out combinations of behaviors without any risks. In play children explore and test out materials and in social play children learn their society's rules and rituals. Bruner feels that all of children's play has rules from the beginning. In his well known Peek-a-Boo experiment, Bruner shows that all children understand the rules of turn taking that are the source of this game (Curtis & O'Hagan, 2008). On the other hand, Bruner believes that not all types of play are equal. For example, rough and tumble play is less intellectually challenging than other play activities like construction or drawing activities that are more goal oriented (Sylva et al., 1974).

In Bruner's (1990, 1996) later work, he stressed the importance of play in the children's development of narrative modes of thinking. Bruner advocated the use of scaffolding to foster the children's learning. He believed that children's interests and scaffolding learning support their learning. According to Spodek and Saracho (1994b), Bruner identified three styles of representation that children can use to process information.

- *Enactive mode* is when children represent things through doing, which usually concentrates on the process instead of the product.
- *Iconic mode* is when children document experiences using photographs, pictures, videotapes, DVDs, and any kind of media.
- *Symbolic mode* is what children use to represent something. Young children often use a code to communicate what they mean. Older children may write a word or a number, while younger children may use marks (scribbles, reverse letters) to communicate their meaning. Children use many different kinds of symbolic codes to express themselves such as drawing, painting, making crafts, dancing, pretend play, language, and numbers.

Bruner sustains that young children organize their knowledge in a sequential, narrative like manner. According to Kavanaugh and Engel (1998), long before children independently create their own real or imagined stories, they compose make-believe scenarios that an adult play partner can mold into a brief narrative. For instance,

> consider the remarks of a father while playing with his 2 1/2-year-old. During the course of their play, the child picked up a wooden spoon and stirred the contents of an empty bowl. As he did this, the father said, Oh, you're baking a cake, are you? Are you going to have a party? With cake? And balloons? That'll be a great cake (p. 92).

This scenario illustrates how young children's pretend play has an implicit narrative structure which an adult can make obvious to the child. When adults narrate the children's pretend gestures, as in the example above, they give structure and meaning to the children's non-literal actions, which emphasizes the narrative characteristics that are implicit in the children's actions. Also by acting out make-believe sequences, young children can become proficient with elements of narrative structure, similar to their initial experience with grammatical structure through their nonverbal play routines (Bruner, 1975). This process offers a direct connection between play and the verbal and logical cognitive elements. In sociodramatic play, children will enact child-constructed narrative stories, which provides them with opportunities to learn and perfect their narrative abilities (Johnson et al., 2005).

## Commonalities

Psychologists have noted that children's cognitive abilities are developed through play that uses practice, imagination, and re-creation of situations. Bruner thinks that play is critical for the children's intellectual development (Sylva et al., 1974). Bruner and Vygotsky endorse the socio-constructivist theory of play. In this type of theory, children advance to higher levels of cognitive development by scaffolding through sensitive and intelligent adult interactions and social interactions with peers. In contrast, Piaget's theory states that in play children progress through each specific developmental stage with or without adult intervention. His belief contradicts the socio-constructivist theory of play (Maynard & Thomas, 2009).

### Sutton-Smith's Theory

Brian Sutton-Smith (1924–) is a play theorist who has been seeking the cultural significance of play in human life. He concluded that play is important for both children and adults, although it is a natural and an intentional ambiguous concept. Brian Sutton-Smith's theories of play changed over the past decades, making a connection between modern and postmodern theories of play (Johnson et al., 2005). Sutton-Smith's (1967) initial theory of play represents the modern theories, with an emphasis on play's role in cognitive development. He stressed the inconsistency of play behavior and its positive influence on creativity and problem solving. Sutton-Smith's initial theory and Bruner's (1972) theory about play are alike in that both propose that play prepares children for adult life by developing flexibility (Johnson et al., 2005).

Later Sutton-Smith's (2001) theory of play becomes more complex and he considers play to be *adaptive variability*. In his present theory, the variability of play is the basis of its meaning in human development. Gould (1997) compares this to the importance of physiological and behavioral variability to evolution. Since it is difficult to predict the future with its drastic shifting environments, it is difficult to predict the skills and knowledge that are needed for future environments. Therefore, the adaptive capabilities of developing children (or evolving species) do not need precise adaptations that can prompt rigid behavior. Instead, adaptability should have great flexibility in behavior like "quirkiness, sloppiness, unpredictability, and massive redundancy" (Gould, 1997, p. 44), which Sutton-Smith considers to be the trademarks of play behavior. Therefore, play is important in human development, because it guarantees a wide range of adaptive capacity, even if the connection between play and adaptation is spontaneous in nature and more indirect than in his earlier theory (Johnson et al., 2005).

When Sutton-Smith (2001) proposed his theory of adaptive variability, he published his book on *The Ambiguity of Play*, where he suggested that play theories can be analyzed and better understood in relation to rhetorical thoughts and values that motivate them. He claims that there are rhetorics of play, where each rhetoric has its own series of values, play styles, and play theories. Sutton-Smith (2001) identified seven rhetorics of play (See Table 3.4).

His rhetorics of fate, power, identity, and frivolity are ancient rhetorics that have a more influential position in classical literature. The modern rhetorics emerged with the shifts in philosophical and psychological movements over the past 200 years. Sutton-Smith (1995) maintains that these rhetorics form the science that researchers use to investigate play and have a tremendous impact on the way they interpret and understand play. This means that the researchers' interpretations of play relate to the rhetoric

**TABLE 3.4.** Brian Sutton-Smith's Rhetorics of Play

| Rhetorics of Play | Description | Major Disciplines |
|---|---|---|
| Progress | Emphasizes that children learn something useful from play | Biology, psychology, education |
| Fate | Refers to gambling and other games of chance | Economics, statistics, mathematics |
| Power | Is usually applied to sports and festivals, in which power is wielded or inverted and mocked | History, sociology, anthropology, cultural, psychology, multicultural education |
| Identity | Is often applied to festivals and celebrations which are viewed as creating group identity | History, anthropology, folklore |
| Imaginary | Refers to the improvisation, creativity, and imagination found in the artistic endeavors | Arts (music, dance, visual arts, drama) and literature |
| Self | Emphasizes the role of play in shaping personality and in providing peak subjective experiences | Leisure studies, psychiatry, therapy |
| Frivolity | Refers to the activities of tricksters, clowns, and comedians. | History, folklore, popular culture |

that they believe. Apparently, no absolute truths about play behavior exist except for the relative ones. This is a major characteristic of postmodernism, which is discussed in the next section.

## Post-Modern Theories

Several modern scholars proposed a foundation to consider play theories and the children's individual differences in today's society. As usual, while each scholar's proposal differs, modern scholars are beginning to agree on several characteristics about play, although some challenging debates have appeared in relation to its effect in present society.

The individual differences heritage has been monitored in developmental psychology. It is considered important, but its competitive domain-general theories related to age or phase have been criticized and avoided. Regardless, the issue of the importance of considering individual differences is very persuasive. The following sections discuss theories of mind, play culture, and socioculture as examples of an individual differences process.

### Theory of Mind

Theory of mind is the capacity to assign mental states (like beliefs, intents, desires, pretending, knowledge) to oneself and others as well as to understand that others have different beliefs, desires, and intentions. Recently the children's understanding of the mind has become the focus of research within cognitive development, which has extended into social development. Understanding the mind is essential to human interaction. In most social experiences, individuals, at least implicitly, extract from their knowledge of minds to understand if someone hears something, the reason someone is surprised, or the way to motivate someone to work harder. Such a body of social knowledge is usually considered theory of mind, including the social context in children's play.

A theory of mind is part of social knowledge, because (1) mental states are theoretical constructs and (2) knowledge about minds becomes a type of theory when it affects certain ontological differences, has a causal-explanatory framework, and explains its constructs with other constructs in the theory (like surprise is described in relation to belief). Knowledge is persuasive to human support in social circles. Developmental psychology has helped to understand young children's responses to a false belief task. According to Lillard (1998):

> In the original false belief task (Wimmer & Perner, 1983), children are shown a doll [Maxi], who hides a piece of chocolate in a blue cupboard. Then Maxi leaves the scene. During his absence, his mother arrives, moves the chocolate from the blue cupboard to a white one, and then also leaves. Maxi returns. The chocolate is not visible as both cupboards are closed, and Maxi has clearly not seen his mother move the chocolate. Children are asked, "Where will Maxi look for his chocolate?" One should say, "The blue cupboard" since that is where Maxi left the chocolate, and he has no way of knowing that it has been moved. But what Wimmer and Perner found is that children under four years of age tend to fail the test by claiming that Maxi will go to the white cupboard, where his mother put it. Possible problems with the paradigm (the story is hard for young children to follow, children do not understand the question, and so on) have been examined, and while the issue is not entirely resolved, most would agree that young children do have a genuine problem understanding that people

can have false beliefs. Like many of Piaget's classic tasks, the false belief task brings into sharp relief how truly different the world is in some ways for young children as compared with adults. Also like many of Piaget's classic tasks, one can push down the ages at which children "pass" by altering the test situation, but the result with the original version is easily replicable and remains compelling in its own right (p. 11–12).

Wimmer and Perner's (1983) study stimulated researchers to examine the way children understand the mind. They have examined many topics, including pretend play. Theoretical and practical foundations that interface pretend play and theory of mind are based on understanding mental representation. Lillard (1998) describes mental representation as a mental model of a person or concept, that is, its "re-presentation" inside the mind. Mental representations can be misleading, because one person's mental representation of something can be different from another's, which is an important characteristic of theory of mind. A person's interactions with the world are influenced by their interpretations of the mental models of the way the world is rather than the explicit knowledge of reality.

It is important to understand the unrealistic assurance and the basic understanding that everybody has their own truths. Social cognitive theorists generally characterize these double meanings to pretending and theory of mind, because both capabilities rely on understanding mental representational differences. Pretense certainly uses mental representations. When young children engage in pretend play, they assume their internal, mental representation of some real instance or object (Lillard, 1998). Several studies show a relationship between pretending and social understanding. A basic principle is that this relationship progresses when children use social reasoning in their pretend play. It is assumed that the relationship of pretend play contributes to social understanding.

Pretense play obviously requires the use of mental representations. When children pretend, they communicate their internal, mental representation of something to a real event or object (Lillard, 1998). If children pretend that a pencil is an airplane, they mentally represent it as both objects (pencil and airplane). They think of it as an airplane and make it fly; but when children consider it is actually a pencil, they do not try to fly it to Hawaii. And if all of a sudden they need a real pencil, they probably would use it even if they thought it was an airplane. The claim is that when this object has two cognitive representations, it becomes a complicated process. In distinguishing between pencils and airplanes, children need to keep the pretense representation cordoned off or "decoupled" [Leslie's (1987) term] from the airplane's typical representation, which is a real airplane. If not, children imagine that real airplanes are made out of wood and filled with lead. Distinguishing between the mental representation used in pretense and the real object, children need to understand that their pretense mental representations are merely representations that they can assign to a variety of objects and that we are able to assign multiple representations to the self-same object (Lillard, 1998).

Pretense and understanding false beliefs are in a way conceptually parallel and a benchmark to understanding the mind (Leslie, 1987). When children pretend, they perceive in their mind a situation that differs from reality. For instance, if children pretend that their back yard is a beach, then they can create a pretend representation on a beach, although the reality is their back yard. The children's pretense representation is a false one, but they consider it in reference to a real situation, which is their back yard. Similarly, if the children were confused about their location and they actually believed that a beach was just out of their back door, then they would plan a false representation of a beach onto the reality of their back yard. Theory of mind researchers have become fascinated with this similar resemblance, because children seem to naturally understand pretense way before they seem to understand false belief (Lillard, 1998).

In summary, pretending depends on understanding mental representation. It is perplexing that two-year-olds engage in pretend play while four-year-olds understand mental representation, usually in the belief realm. There is sufficient support to show that children are not able to understand mental representation in belief domains before four years of age.

Theory of mind suggests a number of basic problems in understanding the mental elements of pretense. Very young children consider pretending to be a mental state. Their pretend play is barely the remotest presentation (such as actions) that is connected to a theory of mind. Pretenders negotiate their pretend roles by challenging and agreeing on various propositions and wishes. During pretend play, children practice perceiving one object or situation in two opposing ways at once, and imagining one object to represent another. In addition, they consider their peers' point of view during pretend role-play. Since the real meaning of pretense is usually emotional and challenging, pretending provides children with the opportunity to experience dealing with these circumstances. The children's pretense play helps understand the children's theory of mind. Pretend play is how children imitate their world and think about internal states and the social order. It also provides information about the children's major problems, responses to certain incidents, and present functioning. It suggests the children's behaviors and guidelines that help children to improve their understanding. Obviously, pretending provides information to use in modifying any predictions and in teaching children about minds and subjectivity (Lillard, 1998), which can be influenced by their culture.

## Cultural Play Theory

Multicultural scholars differ in the way they define culture. Carter and Quareshi (1995) classify theorists into five major groups: (1) the Universal or Etic group who believe that all human beings are similar because intra-group differences are larger than inter-group differences; (2) the Ubiquitous group who have a "liberal" position; they believe that individuals have multiple cultures based on their cultural attributes (like ethnicity, gender, mental and physical abilities, race, religion, sexual orientation, socioeconomic class). The outstanding and relevant cultural characteristics depend on the individuals' setting; (3) the Traditional or Anthropological group who believe that individuals' country of birth and geographical area where they were raised shape their culture; (4) the Race-Based group who believe that race is the leading locus of culture (like being a member of a racial entity exceeds all other experiences relating to culture); and (5) the Pan-National group who think that global racial oppression is the major structure in cultural difference (López & Mulnix, 2004). Culture is "an ongoing pattern of life, characterizing a society at a particular stage in its development or at a given point in history" (Coon & Mitterer, 2008, p. 5). This stage is integrated in Piaget's cognitive developmental phase (preoperational).

In Piaget's (1976) stages, children between two and seven years of age use symbolism through language and mental imagery even if thinking continues to be instinctive (have limited reasoning and logic) and egocentric (unable to take the other's point of view). Young children need (a) developmentally appropriate ways of communication, (b) a careful analysis of their level of cognitive refinement, and (c) a use of their independent or interdependent relationship style. For example, they learn when toys, concrete words, role place events related to their exclusive circumstance, stories, and metaphors are used.

Keeping this in mind, López and Mulnix (2004) maintain that young children's learning requires a diverse classroom culture. The content needs to be introduced in an atmosphere that will provide young children with an effective culture-centered educational experience. They also need to become culturally aware and sensitive to other cultures.

Multicultural societies must provide young children with multicultural education where they learn multiple values and appreciate the value of being different. Young children need to learn different systems of value to expand their cultural perspectives. In a pluralistic society, young children need to expand their knowledge, to become more culturally aware, and to be sensitive to cultural differences as well as become informed about different cultural values (López & Mulnix, 2004).

As young children are growing up, they encounter the same challenges and worldwide principles (Coon & Mitterer, 2008). When children attend school, between the ages of two to seven, they are progressing through Erikson's (1950) theory of psychosocial dilemmas stages 2 (autonomy vs. shame and doubt), 3 (initiative vs. guilt), and 4 (industry vs. inferiority). At this time, the adults in the children's lives need to help them become autonomous, take initiative, and become industrious. Adults in young children's lives are very important. Therefore, it is important that during the second stage (three years), children are not ridiculed or overprotected. These actions may cause children to distrust their abilities and feel ashamed about their actions. When children are in the third stage (between three and five years) and are severely criticized, restricted from playing, or forbidden to ask questions, children will feel guilty about instigating activities. When children are in stage 4 (between five and seven years) and their attempts are considered to be messy, childish, or unsatisfactory, children will feel inferior. Stages 2 through 4 are the foundation of stage 5 (adolescence) when children struggle with their identity, wondering who they will become. The children's socialization experiences need to integrate an appreciation for cultural differences and experience an environment where they are encouraged to express, explore, and develop diverse perspectives (López & Mulnix, 2004).

*Culture and Play*

In 1938, Johan Huizinga (1872–1945), the Dutch historian, cultural theorist, and professor wrote the book *Homo Ludens*, or "Man the Player." In the book, Huizinga (1950) discusses the importance of the play element of culture and society. He uses the term "Play Theory" to define the conceptual space where play takes place. Huizinga believes that play is fundamental and essential in the generation of culture. He emphasizes the play element *of* culture rather than the play element *in* culture. He clarifies that his book was based on a lecture titled, "The Play Element of Culture," which was continuously corrected to "in" Culture, a revision Huizinga strongly objected. He explains:

> it was not my object to define the place of play among all other manifestations of culture, but rather to ascertain how far culture itself bears the character of play (Huizinga, 1950, Foreword, unnumbered page).

In the 19th century anthropologists were interested in the "science of man" and began the concepts of biological (Darwin) and social (Spencer) evolution. According to Schartzman (1978), the theory of social evolution used the metaphor as a source for cultures to be biological organisms that showed similar systems of growth and development. Potts (1996) stated, "Culture makes man makes culture" (p. 182). Culture depends on modifications in noncultural phenomena (like biological, social, ecological) that the structure of the organism has an impact on modern human beings and the nature of human information systems, particularly the emergence of symbolic behavior. Bodily ornaments, statues, musical instruments, regional stylism, and painting characterize symbolic culture (Roberts, 2001).

Considering children as delegates in a transactional state with their environments, childhood can provide a feasible procreative origin for evolution that can be reached and developed. Repeatedly, in learning about the origins and predecessors of the present human species, children are viewed as having to make an obligatory effort to care for them or as passive storage knowledge segments. According to Opie and Opie (1959), children are the keepers of rich cultural heritage. "Any consideration of the role of children in human evolution would be incomplete without emphasis on one of the most important aspects of childhood, indeed human behavior, at which children are the experts: play" (Roberts, 2001, p. 106).

Views of play are subjective to one's culture. In the West, play is understood through shared attitudes about what play is not. Western theories of play request a search for principles. They challenge the value of play in learning and cognition. Most theorists and researchers ignore an across-the-board theory of play that critically combines the infinite real meaning of culture. Acknowledging the diversity in culturally continuous and discontinuous play contexts is essential. The different societies throughout the world (like industrialized pluralistic, industrialized homogeneous, post-colonial, hunting–gathering) make it difficult to include culture (Roberts, 2001). Schartzman (1978) believes that present research on play suffers from too much definitional familiarity, even when studies use several theories and results.

The works of Bruner (1976), Rogoff (1990), Vygotsky (1978), and others provide an understanding of the children's development through their sociocultural interactions. More studies need to be conducted to develop a theory on culture and play. Since it is premature to develop a theory of culture and play, Roopnarine et al. (1998) provide several guidelines to use in studying children's play across cultures:

- Biosocial factors, both somatic and reproductive, influence parent-child participation.
- Differences also exist in the psychology of the importance of play whether it is in the peer group or parent–child system.
- Finally, in preindustrial societies education occurs in formal and informal settings . . . Theories of play must account for the myriad of ways in which play is used for learning social and adaptive skills that are essential for successfully negotiating the demands of the individual's socio-cultural world. The socio-ecological contexts that represent the work-play mixture are antithetical to most Western frameworks regarding children's play (pp. 197–198).

As the world unites through travel, trade, and internet, agricultural lands and rain forests diminish, industrial and residential buildings decrease space that at one time was used for play; technological devices take the place of traditional toys; and developing countries establish better educational goals, which has stimulated obvious improvements for both the context and nature of young children's play across cultures. For instance, educational goals in Africa have become more formal where work and play are more precise. Therefore, children lack time to informally observe, learn, and accommodate their knowledge of their environment and roles using work and play. Preschool concepts in Western countries concentrate on constructive and symbolic play in educational settings (Roopnarine et al.,

1998). In Taiwanese children's play activities, the preschool children prefer slides and swings and transportation toys over more traditional objects (such as kites, paper folding) (Pan, 1994). For more than a decade, in Japan the use of video games has intensely increased. Japanese children would rather watch television, read comic books, and play with video games than play traditional Japanese games (Saracho & Shirakawa, 2004).

In many cultures play spaces have disappeared. The elimination of the rain forests in Africa and South America has led to families and children becoming detached from the environments of the Aka, Efe, and other hunting–gathering societies that have become hazardous. Play materials from the surrounding areas highly limit the play activities, which also includes survival societies. In the industrialized world, play spaces have been reduced in large cities (Pan, 1994) while fashionable technological devices have been substituted for conventional games. Fashionable play materials have primarily hidden away the children's imaginative and aggressive nature (Roopnarine et al., 1998).

The "Western" cultural attitudes influence worldwide the distribution of well-defined manufactured toys. Billboards advertise Barbie Dolls and other play materials that are culturally related to the United States in South Asia, South America, and the West Indies. Nevertheless, toys are selected in these countries based on the cultural values of the post industrialized societies, because these societies challenge and often at times ignore native toys and play practices in their countries. They think that play objects from the industrialized world are better. Current educators from abroad and the United States are concentrating on the restoration of ethnic dignity (Roopnarine et al., 1998).

## Sociocultural Play Theories

For a number of years, sociocultural perspectives have been present in the literature without any attention. Recently, scholars have developed systematic and coherent improvements to understanding children's play and culture in relation to development. Cultural characteristics need to be considered when constructing learning and socialization theories to meet the needs of all children including diverse groups of children (Roopnarine et al., 2007).

The Russian psychologist Lev Vygotsky (1967, 1978) believed that play was an essential source for young children's learning and development, which takes place when they observe and interact with members of their culture. Children learn when they engage in social interactions with more knowledgeable members of the culture, who guide them and support them in the different culture related activities. In many cultures, families support the children's play when they guide them to learn about the play elements (like taking turns) or their world (like buying materials with money) (Vandermass-Peler, 2002).

### Ecological Theory

Urie Bronfenbrenner's (1917–2005) environment contributed to his interest in the children's social and physical surroundings. He spent time in the rich biological and social terrain where his father worked. He learned how the social and physical environment can influence individuals, which he tested in his cross-cultural research. Bronfenbrenner (1979) defines ecology of human development as:

> . . . the scientific study of the progressive, mutual accommodation between an active, growing human being and the changing properties of the immediate settings in which

the developing person lives, as this process is affected by relations between those settings, and by the larger contexts in which the settings are embedded (p. 21).

The idea that environment influences development relates to Bronfenbrenner's theoretical model. Bronfenbrenner's bioecological model indicates the importance of environmental factors that range from the broader cultural context to their environment in their daily lives. When children interact with individuals at all the various levels of context, they become aware and learn to accept each individual's different cultural characteristics. Looking at the similarities and differences across diverse societies is a cultural extension of Bronfenbrenner's bioecological model (Johnson et al., 2005). Thus, Bronfenbrenner's ecological model focuses on the importance of children's environments and their interactions with different members of the culture. Bronfenbrenner noted that children develop in the context of numerous social systems (like family, caregivers, teachers, peers) that interact in critical ways with the children's cultural context. The degree that their play is supported and encouraged as well as the play opportunities that are provided to children directly affects the children's development (Vandermass-Peler, 2002).

An extensive degree of impact on children comes from cultural values and societal beliefs. The physical environment is a cultural element that forms children's play. In some societies children are given several toys, while other societies leave children to play on their own with anything that that they can find (Berger, 2008). For example, in agrarian societies children have responsibilities for the family's land and crops as well as going to school. Children lack the time and adults lack the interest to support play and games. On the other hand, in cultures where the families work outside the home and do not involve the children in their economic life, families may directly or indirectly support the children's play (Rogoff et al., 1993). Accordingly Bronfenbrenner's ecological model offers a valuable framework to use the children's play in their development at the center of the different social systems (Vandermass-Peler, 2002).

All children play regardless of their environment. They play on Arctic ice or desert sand. Since culture, gender, and sex influences the children's play, it provides a perfect opportunity for children to learn the social skills they need in the social context (Sutton-Smith, 2001).

Play scholars have attempted to describe a sociocultural perspective on play. Göncü and his associates (Göncü et al., 1999) view play as a cultural activity and explanation with interdisciplinary ideas. Economic, social, and political elements that function within the higher culture are needed to understand the meaning of children's play in cultural contexts. In any culture or cultural community the meaning of the children's play depends on the adults inside the culture. They convey to children their beliefs and values about play in the way adults encourage play, participate in play with children, or support play. These attitudes and values become apparent in the various ways that adults set up accessible materials, time, and space for children's play or, if not, they will use their own influence to promote the children's play in a cultural community (Göncü et al., 1999). Cultural customs and opportunities influence the types of play that are motivated by the physical and social environments such as the following:

- Do adults encourage work or play?
- Are children free to explore and motivated to practice adult roles through play?
- Does the environment provide children with easy access to models and materials to engage in creative and constructive play?

To address these questions, Edwards (2000) reanalyzed the data that were collected in the 1950s in the Whiting and Whiting (1975) study on children's play in six cultures focusing on specific cultural practices, instruction, history, climate, and geography and their relationship to specific play behaviors. Beatrice and John Whiting concluded that children in more complicated cultures play with more and more sophistication. In addition, within the most complex groups, children played more when they had the freedom to select their playmates and wander about the community (Sutton-Smith & Roberts, 1981). Sutton-Smith and Roberts (1981) called this observable fact *cultural leeway*, which suggested the importance of allowing children to have the freedom to explore the environment to understand the purpose in supporting culture in the children's play.

The children's culture and traditions are essential in selecting the amount and the ways to motivate the children's imaginative and cognitive play. Sutton-Smith (2001) believes that play with toys is "mediated through social interactions and social traditions" (p. 8) in many ways.

1. Cultural traditions determine the value of play: whether it should be supported or neglected.
2. Cultural traditions determine their child rearing practices such as whether to initiate and promote independence and autonomy in both girls and boys.
3. Economic and historical conditions are essential resources to motivate both physical and intellectual play. Children engage more in play when they are exposed to models that they can imitate. Communities need to provide them with raw materials, as natural materials (such as wastepaper, wire, bottle caps, buttons, scrap lumber, cloth, tires, glass, cans) for children to use to create toys to play with. An overflowing of materials will motivate children's imaginations and creativity. Making toys is integrated in the dynamic process of culture change (Rossie, 1998) in both industrial and nonindustrial societies. Information about new playthings will immediately spread among the children throughout the community without any adult involvement and the conception of fashions, fads, and crazes in the local, regional, and global cultures of childhood will emerge (Edwards, 2000).

The sociocultural perspective analyzes settings (a) to shed light on the meaning of play and nonplay behaviors in a cultural community and (b) to use culture to integrate the person and the environment. Traditional developmental psychologists perceive nature and nurture or the person and the environment to be disconnected, although they interact with each other. The sociocultural perspective rejects the suggested view of this interactionism, where culture is usually considered to be independent of the individual; rather an individual's mind or awareness about the events in the environment are considered to be both sides of the same coin. Put differently, based on the sociocultural perspective, culture takes place "between the ears" (in the individual's mind) just like everything that takes place in the external environment. Experiences are symbols of integrating the individuals and the environment (Johnson et al., 2005).

Sociocultural scholars attempt to find out the way that children interpret their experiences of the world in their play. For instance, how do children select the adults' roles and activities to act them out in their dramatic play? A sociocultural perspective needs to be integrated in studies of play to determine which ideas can be transferred from one cultural community context to another. In addition, knowledge about the children's cultural environment, social ecology, and extensive cultural foundations and values can be used to provide positive interethnic communications between teacher and child and home and community.

## Summary

Originally, theories of play were used to study the play of humans or animals. Currently play is considered appropriate for young children, adults, and nonhuman animals. Children, adults, and nonhuman animals participate in play and it must be perceived in the context of the individual's development and education (Spodek & Saracho, 1987).

For centuries, play was originally viewed as essential in children's lives. Presently it has become important as an educative force in early childhood education. The increased concern about educational play and its effects on young children's development and education stimulated the materialization of numerous theories of play (such as modern theories, post modern theories, sociocultural theories) that have similarities and differences.

Modern theories were developed to understand play from a human development perspective that speculates on the way play promotes young children's development. Postmodern theories perceive play to communicate the way children make sense of the world and the way they understand the nature of understanding, by this means establishing a theory of mind. Postmodern scholars also integrated a sociocultural perspective that includes the children's environment and culture in relation to play. Initially, they identified the differences in the way children from various cultures would play. Recently the increased international commerce and communication has made the children's play more global where modern societies influenced more traditional societies both on the way children play and in what they play with.

# Chapter 4
# Historical Perceptions of Play

In play a child is always above his average age, above his daily behaviour; in play, it is though he was a head taller than himself. As in the focus of a magnifying glass, play contains all developmental tendencies in a condensed form; in play, it is as though the child were trying to jump above the level of his normal behaviour.

(Vygotsky, 1967, p.16)

Traditions in early childhood education have changed over time. Many traditions emerge and then completely disappear. Others reemerge over and over again in related forms, now and then with new embellishments that make it seem that they are actually new. Many times traditions swing back and forth like a pendulum (Spodek & Saracho, 2003b). These traditions have influenced the history of play and had an impact in the way play has been perceived over time. This chapter presents historical perceptions of children's play and historical representations of children's play in the visual arts and literature.

## Historical Perceptions

Since the times of Classical Greece, theorizing about play has had an irregular development. With the increased interest in play, theories were analyzed based on thoughts of the current era. In the early 1970s, new theoretical movements emerged with an increased concern for play (Ellis, 1973). An awareness of historical perspectives on children's play provides a better understanding of children's play and how it has been perceived through the centuries.

## Play in Renaissance Europe

The eastern Mediterranean world believed that children were naturally innocent and pure. Ancient Egypt had wall paintings of children playing with balls and dolls and jumping rope. They understood and accepted play to be part of the children's lives (French, 1977). In Plato's *Republic* the ancient Greek philosophers believed that children's play experiences promoted their learning. Plato (1941) wrote, "enforced learning will not stay in your mind . . . let your children's lesson take the form of play" (p. 536). The Greeks used the term child to refer to the word *play*. Both words *play* and *education*; adults played to make a living, whereas play helped children learn through experiences. For example, adults' play consisted of participating in competitions such as Olympic games, mating games, work, and occupations (Terr, 1999).

Children and adults' play activities are portrayed in paintings that depict scenes from everyday life in Renaissance Europe. Both children and adults played the same games and chanted the same nursery rhymes. The nursery rhymes that were specifically composed for the nursery and lullabies were the only chants that were focused on the world of childhood (Tucker, 1974). Adults composed riddles for adults. Most of the popular chants that are used today from that period were originally sung by adults and usually had interesting political or social messages. For example, the children's rhyme "Sing-a-Song-of-Sixpence" was an adult song about King Henry VIII's love for Anne Boleyn and other dealings at the beginning of the Protestant Reformation period (Borstelmann, 1983; Opie & Opie, 1969).

Throughout the centuries the concepts of childhood, play, and education continued to be related. At times, many (like Plato) considered play to be compatible with education, but to others (like the Christian Puritans) it was also viewed as being at odds. At all times, both play and education were associated with childhood. All individuals, regardless of age, were always old enough to play (Terr, 1999), in spite of any views on play during that era. The Western world continued to recognize the unique nature of childhood until the Middle Ages, where special childhood activities, including play, were considered both acceptable and appropriate (Borstelmann, 1983).

During the Renaissance, the toy manufacturing industry was established in southern Germany. They produced the homemade toys (like kites, tops) of the Middle Ages and also developed new toys (like lead soldiers, elaborate wooden dolls, glass animals). The Renaissance toys were for both children and adults. Most of the toys from this period as well as from the 17th and 18th centuries were so complicated and fragile (like teasers, dolls, dollhouses) that children were not permitted to even touch them (Sommerville, 1982).

In the 17th century, almost at the end of the Renaissance era, the European attitudes about play started to change and a new consciousness of childhood appeared (Pinchbeck & Hewitt, 1969). Children were considered to be valuable with different developmental needs and with problems different from those of adults. During the 17th century, there was an interest in the colonization of the New World. Its colonization patterns had the most important European influences on American attitudes toward work and play, which originated in the countries of France and England (Hughes, 2010).

### French Perceptions

Europe surfaced from the Renaissance at the beginning of the 17th century. During this time, the French accepted and presently continue to accept play. Although the Catholic clergy repressed the value of play without the social value of work, they were not able to stop its attractiveness (Ariès, 1962). A comprehensive record of children's play in 17th century France may be a diary by Jean Heroard, young King Louis XIII's physician. This diary gives an account of the French view of play in the 17th century. Young Louis played with windmills, hobby horses, and whipping toys that looked like the modern tops. When Louis was 17 months old, he could play the violin and sing at the same time. When he was a toddler, he played ball just like the adults. At age two, he banged on a little drum and could dance well. At age four, he played cards and could shoot with a bow and arrow. At age six, he started to play chess and take pleasure in parlor games (Ariès, 1962). Although these descriptions are based on Louis' physician's diary, which may be subjective or wishful thinking, these do give an idea of the thinking at the time.

Since most of Louis' playmates were his adult servants and courtiers, Louis' play was similar to the adults' of his time. Children, noblemen, and noblewomen of all ages engaged in play that consisted of music, athletic skills, board games, and parlor games. Since in the early 17th century there was no difference between the children's and the adults' world, beyond the age of infancy the children's and adults' games were the same. There was no awareness of childhood innocence or the difference between work and play (Hughes, 2010).

During the progression of the century, a difference surfaced between the children's and adults' worlds and their games. The children's games were physical in nature, while adults from the nobility only played intellectual games. Work and play were considered different activities. The adults' life had a focus on work. France appreciated the period of childhood play and the children's natural activities, which were later represented in the writings of France's most influential philosopher of the 18th century, Jean-Jacques Rousseau (1712–1784). Rousseau (1762) emphasized a naturalist philosophy. In the opening of his book, *Émile*, Rousseau states, "God makes all things good; man meddles with them and they become evil" (p. 3). Children are born and develop based on their experiences. He wrote that "Childhood has its own way of seeing, thinking, and feeling. Nothing is more foolish than to try to substitute our own methods for these" (p. 52).

Rousseau proposed to let children develop with little adult supervision; they needed to enjoy their first years of life with free time. The role of adults should be to avoid teaching virtues to children but to protect them from becoming sinful. He wrote, "Give him no orders at all, absolutely none" (p. 45) and "Do not even let him think that you claim authority over him" (p. 45). The prevalent acceptance of Rousseau's ideas describes this era and the French people. Although some French people neither agreed with Rousseau's vision of child development nor read his books, it conveys the French people's view of life. Rousseau's ideas may have been popular in France, but they were rejected in England (Hughes, 2010).

*British Perceptions*

In 17th century England, as in other European countries, children were considered to be unique individuals separate from adults. This did not include the acceptance of children's play. While the French approved children's play, the English emphasized the value of work for both children and adults in the 17th and 18th centuries. Both religious and philosophical influences were the reasons for England's lack of interest in play. The Protestant and Catholic religions were mostly responsible for England's depreciation of play. Catholics believed that faith was essential to achieve salvation. The Protestants believed that faith, hard work, and self-discipline were necessary for good moral character. Since play contradicted work, it was viewed as both sinful and irresponsible. For example, the theologian John Wesley would say, "He who plays as a boy will also play as a man" (Hughes, 2010).

Rousseau became a distinguished philosopher in France; while in England, John Locke (1632–1704) became the most widely accepted philosopher. He represented the 17th century's thinking that all children were unique and valuable human beings and believed that adults needed to recognize children's developmental needs. Locke was the son of Puritan parents; therefore, he represented this religious tradition and his ideas on child rearing were in harmony with Puritan and other Protestants' views. Locke did not criticize play; but he was firm in his belief that work, rationality, and discipline were the major elements in the children's optimum development. The Protestant reformers' beliefs influenced the British views on child rearing, work, and play. Work and self-discipline were perceived as leading to eternal salvation, material success, and mature rationality. Play was considered a distraction and a sign against God. Several English towns passed laws forbidding specific types of play, like playing with tops or running races in the public streets (Hughes, 2010).

## United States' Perceptions in the 19th Century

The beliefs in the American colonies differed from those of the British and French. The Puritans did not condemn play, but they discouraged it in Puritan children's lives. Play was considered a distraction from study and vocational training that were needed for self-discipline. Since children went to school from seven until four or five in the afternoon and went home where they had to do household chores, Puritan children did not have enough time to play (Illick, 1974).

The 19th century showed an uncertainty about children and play. However, American children were motivated to play, develop mobility, and manage their environment. Toys became complicated and realistic such as miniature vehicles like trains and cars. In 1859 the first cap pistol was created to encourage children to communicate aggression and control their environment (Davis, 1976). During the progressive era, adults started to develop an interest in children's play and created playthings and play areas for indoor and outdoor play. Outdoor play had pets and natural objects such as wild flowers, butterflies, or frogs. Children built things out of stones, snow, or wood. Children were also provided with home made toys (simple puppets, dolls, kites, balls, spinning tops). Frequently, traditional play consisted of sports, games, music, folktales, songs, and dances that were seen in communities as part of festivals and special events. Inactive or unruly solitary or social play promoted the children's social and physical development (Johnson et al., 2005).

In the United States, Puritans' beliefs about play persisted through the 19th and into the 20th century (Hughes, 2010). Although they continued with their strict discipline, they became more child-centered. They also began to use play to assist children in becoming complete participants in social life (Johnson et al., 2005). Conventional play helped with group functions and ethnic identity (Lee et al., 2001).

## United States' Perceptions in the 20th Century

The first decade in the 20th century showed an increase in letting children express their feelings openly (Davis, 1976). During the era, the child study movement began to prosper.

This movement described the beginning of a science of child development and the writings of the well-known American psychologist G. Stanley Hall (1844–1924). Although the movement was starting to appreciate the children's developmental characteristics, a new influence was on the rise in American psychology. Between 1910 and 1920, John B. Watson (1878–1958), an American psychologist, proposed the behaviorism theory. He believed that children would become what the environment made them. He wrote, "Give me a dozen healthy infants and my own specified world to bring them up in and I'll guarantee to take any one at random and train him to become any kind of specialist I might select—doctor, lawyer, artist, merchant, chief, and yes, even beggar man and thief, regardless of talents, penchants, tendencies, abilities, vocations, and race of his ancestors" (Watson, 1925, p. 82). In the behaviorist theory, play was only used as a means to lead to social reform. It was a learning experience that helped children nurture socially acceptable behaviors (Davis, 1976). In the middle and later 20th century, many thought John Watson's theory was considered both strange and cruel toward children.

For more than five decades, the children had been allowed to have autonomy and freedom of expression that was representative of ancient or modern history (Davis, 1976). Play had been important in the children's development. Children were permitted to play, because it gave them the opportunity for intellectual and social development as well as for emotional release, which are part of both psychoanalytic and cognitive development theories (Hughes, 2010).

It is important to know how play has been perceived in history to better understand the nature of play, and therefore it's useful to understand about the early pioneers of play.

## Pioneers of Play in Early Childhood Education Programs

Early pioneers and theorists such as the German educator, Friedrich Froebel (1782–1852) and the Swiss educator, Johann Heinrich Pestalozzi (1746–1827), supported the importance of young children's play in their education. Friedrich Froebel, Maria Montessori, and John Dewey created methodical approaches to integrate play in child rearing and in education.

Friedrich Froebel was the founder of the original kindergarten. He believed he used play as an educational method. The Froebelian curriculum required the manipulation of objects like wooden blocks as well as wooden cubes and woolen balls that he called *Gifts*. Children also engaged in craft activities that he called *Occupations* including paper weaving and paper folding. The Froebelian curriculum also had children sing songs and play games that he called *Mother's Plays and Songs*. The activities and materials represented the spiritual meanings that Froebel intended for children to learn. The children did not participate in free, expressive forms of play; the activities were manipulative. The basis of a kindergarten activity was the German peasant children's natural play. Froebel summarized and organized the necessary features of their play in his method (Lilley, 1967).

Maria Montessori (1870–1952) also took the important components in children's natural play activities, restructured them, and organized them. She designed materials, took them to her classroom, and observed children play with them freely. From her observations, she took what she thought were the critical factors of play and organized their use in her method (Montessori, 1914). Both the Froebelian kindergarten and the Montessori approach were based on their observations of children's play activities; but the educational methods they developed from their play observations were different, reflecting their differing opinions on the nature of knowledge. Froebel used his kindergarten materials and activities to assist young children to understand the abstract ideas and spiritual meanings they represented. Montessori thought that her method would assist children to understand the properties of the materials they were manipulating. Montessori wanted children to collect and arrange their sensory impressions to develop knowledge. Both Froebel's and Montessori's approaches were based on children's play. Unfortunately, each removed most of the characteristics (such as allowing children to be spontaneous, free, expressive) of play.

John Dewey (1859–1952) disapproved of Froebel's concepts of play. Dewey founded the laboratory school at the University of Chicago, which included a "sub-primary" class instead of a kindergarten. Dewey's notion of children's learning provided a basis for the contemporary point of view on the educational use of children's play. Dewey moved away from earlier beliefs of children's play activities that originated in colonial times, when adults urged children "to avoid the frivolity of play" (Hartley & Goldenson, 1963, p. 1). Dewey proposed that young children be educated using their experiences in the real world. In play, children were able to recreate these experiences to acquire meaning from them and to be able to function at higher levels of consciousness and action (Dewey, 1900). However, he believed that play was not a completely free activity; teachers needed to provide an environment that would cultivate the children's play and support their needed mental and moral growth (Dewey, 1916).

According to Froebel, play consisted of manipulating the *gifts* and using the *occupations* in specific patterned ways. Montessori's activities required the manipulation of materials to acquire and arrange sensory experiences or the exercise of practical life skills such as pouring water or sweeping floors. The progressive kindergarten and the modern nursery school believed that the play where children were in control was educational. In dramatic play, children personified their understanding of the adults' lives around them. They communicated these concepts in their play activities. Dramatic play is a mutual activity where children play together and test their understanding of their world to compare it against the other children's understanding.

In the emergence of both the Progressive kindergarten and the modern nursery-school movements in the first quarter of the 20th century, children's play became broadly recognized as a means for learning. The children's natural play experiences were encouraged and cultivated as being educationally important.

The modern concept of play as a way to learn and develop in the early years and the value of dramatic play (like imitating the adults' roles and tasks) has its roots in the Progressive Era. Progressive early childhood educators distinguished between play and other children's activities. Play (a) requires the children to use their free and natural impulses, (b) is an activity ready for external reward, and (c) is an activity finished for its own sake, although it is not a frivolous activity. Play is different from work, but it can be serious and is an essential component of early childhood education (Spodek & Saracho, 1987).

The Progressive concept of play continues to spread throughout early childhood education programs that have equipment and materials to promote children's play in classrooms. For instance, usually preschool and kindergarten classrooms have a dramatic play area that has miniature representations of kitchen equipment (like toy pots, pans, dishes), household furniture, dolls, cleaning equipment, plastic food, and other similar objects. Children use them to act out their depictions of home life. The dramatic play area may also represent a different theme that reflects the children's world, like a supermarket, a doctor's office, or a garage for repairing automobiles. In the block area, children can construct buses, airplanes, or trains and pretend that they are drivers, pilots, or engineers. They may act out several scenarios such as transporting toy vehicles (cars, buses, vans, trucks) through streets, superhighways or rivers that they built in the block area.

The Progressive concept considers play in context of the children's development, learning (Spodek & Saracho, 1987), experience, and knowledge when they engage in both indoor and outdoor play. For example, Saracho and Spodek (1998a) observed the following situations in a nursery school:

Situation 1:

The children run into the playground area. Two children, Nikki and Elizabeth, head immediately for the sandbox. They each grab a bucket and a shovel, and sit down next to each other.

"Let's make mud cakes," says Elizabeth.

"OK," replies Nikki.

The girls work quietly, digging in the sand, filling their buckets. Elizabeth gets up and walks over to the teacher. "Would you like a mud cake?" she asks. The teacher answers, "Oh, how wonderful," and pretends to taste the mud cakes. When Elizabeth returns, Nikki is no longer in the sandbox. Instead, Nikki is sitting in the middle of the sandbox. Elizabeth says, "Nikki, move! You're in the way" (p. 1).

This situation can be compared with another one that occurred with two different children.

Situation 2:

Two children, Matthew and Bobby, are pretending to be Robin Hood. They both are crawling on the floor, pretending to hide from the enemy. Every once in a while, they reach for an imaginary bow from their backs, and shoot an arrow at the oncoming enemy.

Matthew screams, "I got you, Prince!"

Bobby hollers, "Watch out, Robin, they're coming behind you!" Matthew rolls around the ground, pretending to fight with the enemy. Bobby comes to the rescue and pretends to scare away the enemy (p. 2).

The children's play experiences have characteristics that add to or modify their knowledge when their new and familiar experiences are integrated. The children's make-believe play creates their different patterns of thought (Freud, 1937; Lewin, 1935; Luria, 1932; Piaget, 1951). Their make-believe play generally has a social element that represents their world. Its interpersonal interactions, incidents, and adventures call for numerous characters and places in space and time. Usually make-believe play takes place with pairs or groups of children, but supplementary invisible characters and/or inanimate objects may be used to portray absent people or animals. When children play, they imitate the roles of adults, adventures that they have been introduced to in children's stories or that others have read to them, or they have seen on television.

Presently, attitudes towards play continue to be ambivalent. Pioneer researchers in play worried that many misunderstand play. People may think of play as a natural part of childhood but with little developmental value. Elkind (1987) has continuously stated that today children are being required to grow up very fast while childhood activities, like play, are substituted with a "meaningful" life search of educational and occupational success (Hughes, 2010).

## Play Represented in the Visual Arts

Throughout history, society has been interested in young children's play experiences. Early artistic contributions portray such play experiences. The quality of children's play is represented in the visual arts. For example, children's play has been represented in several classical paintings. Blizzard's (1993) book, *Come Look with Me* has paintings, print, and sculpture of people playing. The painting *Children's Games* (1560) by the Flemish painter Peter Bruegel (1525–1569) shows more than 80 different childhood games, many of which are still known today. Throughout the ages, children have played most of these games. For example, during Nero's era, children played the children's game titled "Buck Buck," illustrated in Bruegel's painting. Petronious refers to it in the well-known Satyricon (Opie & Opie, 1969). This game continues to be played in American city streets and is called "Johnny-on-the-Pony."

Several artists in China portrayed *One Hundred Children at Play* during the Sung Dynasty (960–1279). The artists did a series of paintings, which are exhibited in the Palace Museum in Taipei, Taiwan, as well as in collected works of Chinese art in museums throughout the United States and other parts of the world. Such Chinese paintings portray children participating in sociodramatic play. Upper-class or aristocratic children imitating adult roles in their play were the ones who were represented in the Chinese paintings. In contrast, Bruegel painted children in the village who are more active, more vigorous, more concerned with direct motor experiences, and more distinctive of a lower socioeconomic group. The children in Bruegel's and the Sung Dynasty's paintings characterize two cultures and are different in time and space. The inconsistencies between the Bruegel and Sung Dynasty paintings reflect the different cultures (Flemish vs. Asian). Both represent the style of the art world of their time. Bruegel's painting has multiplicity with numerous fine points while Sung Dynasty's paintings have simplicity with few fine points.

At the beginning of the 20th century, the American artist Maurice Prendergast (1859–1924) painted a playground in lower Manhattan called, *The East River* (1901). The painting shows both children and adults enjoying a leisure day in New York City. In this urban location, both children and adults are playing with equipment (like swings, a sandbox) that is still found in present-day playgrounds.

In the early 1870s and throughout, Winslow Homer, one of America's leading artists, painted the outdoor games he played as a child in 19th century rural America. Homer's fresh and realistic background in his paintings made him a well-known painter. In many of his art works, he painted a one-room schoolhouse as a backdrop. He also had children gathered in a one-room schoolhouse, playing in the countryside, or sitting on the beach on a summer day. In 1872, he painted his most popular painting, *Snap-the-Whip*, which shows barefoot boys holding hands in a line and running across a field that is in front of a red schoolhouse. The leader suddenly stops, which makes the children at the very end of the line lose their hold and fall down. This painting shows the way Homer makes use of numerous fine points to illustrate the healthy, energetic children, their environment, and the consequences of weather and light (Blizzard, 1993). *Snap-the-Whip* provides contrasting descriptions like the play of stillness and motion, running and falling, stones and flowers, interior and exterior, wilderness and construction, physical and mental. This final comparison is especially important, because the shadow of a high sun from behind the schoolhouse conveys that the game took place at a noon break.

Diego Rivera, a Mexican painter and muralist, had a natural ability to paint historical murals and respect down-to-earth folk traditions, which made him one of America's most eminent artists and one of Mexico's favorite painters. In 1953 Diego Rivera painted *La Piñata*, a star shaped clay piñata that is filled with treats and hangs from a rope just out of reach of a group of excited children. A blindfolded boy is striking the piñata with a stick while other children excitedly rush to collect the treats, which consist of fruits and peanuts but do not include candy. On the right, a boy with a blue and white poncho is crying. At the same time, his mother is consoling him, touching him on the head, and handing him a piece of Mexican bread, which is called tortilla (Blizzard, 1993).

Paintings of children's play that were described represent children from various cultures, placed apart by time and space. The paintings suggest society's attitudes toward play in a variety of contexts. However, the paintings convey the same view: that play is a natural activity of children.

## Play Represented in Literature

Many of the children's literature stories (such as *Three Little Pigs*, *Little Red Hen*, *Goldilocks and the Three Bears*) feature pretend play. The characters in the stories take on a make-believe role that usually imitates the activities and troubles of humans. For instance, in the *Three Little Pigs*, the pigs pretend to be people who build houses to live in. Children listen to the story and dramatize the roles of the different characters (pigs, mother, wolf). Some classic literature also represents play.

A number of English writers wrote about children's play in their work (Singer, 1973). For example, Samuel Taylor Coleridge (1772–1834), an English romantic, wrote at length about the nature of children's fantasy. William Wordsworth (1770–1850), another English romantic, romanticized the child's mind in its innocence. These English authors are examples of how classic literature calls attention to the children's fantasy and their world of make believe, which are essential elements in the children's pretend play.

The English writers actually began writing about children's play in about the middle of the 19th century. In the 20th century, many English writers and psychologists had difficulty accepting children's make-believe play. Auden's (1965) memoirs describe incredible incidents about how his mother's closeness could have provided the basis for one of the 20th century's greatest poet's imaginative power. Auden (1965) writes:

> When I was eight years old, she taught me the words and music of the love potion scene in "Tristan and Isolde" and we used to sing it together (p. 166).

Auden also commented how the novelist Evelyn Waugh's father daily played charades all through his life (Singer, 1973). Count Leo Tolstoy (1828–1910), the Russian novelist, social reformer, and moral philosopher, shared his childhood experiences and their impact upon his own development. His brother would set up games where all the players pretended to be "ant people" (Tolstoy, 1852).

In his plays, Denis Daudet (1713–1784), the French Encyclopedist, philosopher, and man of letters, wrote naturalistic portraits of middle class family life. Anatole France (1844–1924), a French poet, journalist, and writer, was a successful novelist, with several best sellers. In his period, he was viewed as the ideal man of letters. He also won the Nobel Prize for Literature. In his memoirs, he wrote *Le Livre de Mon Ami* (My Friend's Book), where he successfully illustrates the imagination and comprehensive pictures of children who were secluded in their room at night. Gustave Flaubert (1821–1880), another French author, describes Madame Bovary's dreams when she was a young girl in a convent trying to imagine the saints' lives and her personal future. This is an impressive instance of the consciousness of the children's solitary behavior.

The Scottish novelist, poet, and essayist Robert Louis Stevenson (1850–1894) more than any author has been known to have romanticized children's fantasy and pretend play in countless of his small poems and in numerous of his semi-autobiographical writings. On September 1878, he wrote in *Cornhill Magazine* a composition on childhood titled "Child's Play" (Stevenson, 1930), where he creates a concept of imaginative play. He proposes that play is a means of changing reality and writes:

> In the child's world of dim sensation, play is all in all. "Making believe" is the gist of his whole life, and he cannot so much as take a walk except in character. . . . When my cousin and I took our porridge of a morning, we had a device to enliven the course of the meal. He ate his with sugar, and explained it to be a country continually buried under snow. I took mine with milk, and explained it to be a country suffering gradual inundation. You can imagine us exchanging bulletins; how here was an island still un-submerged, here a valley not yet covered with snow; what inventions were made; how his population lived in cabins on perches and traveled on stilts, and how mine was always in boats; how the interest grew furious, as the last corner of safe ground was cut off on all sides and grew smaller every moment; and how in fine, the food was of altogether secondary importance, and might even have been nauseous, so long as we seasoned it with these dreams (pp. 161–162).

Since children are like this, Stevenson adds,

> One thing, at least, comes very clearly out of these considerations; that whatever we are to expect at the hands of children, it should not be any peddling exactitude about matters of fact. . . . I think it less than decent. You do not consider how little the child sees, or how swift he is to weave what he has seen into bewildering fiction; and that he cares no more for what you call truth, than you for a gingerbread dragoon (Stevenson, 1930, p. 163).

In Stevenson's (1998) book titled, *Where Go the Boats?: Play-Poems of Robert Louis Stevenson* he explains the joy of play. The joy of both past and present childhood team up in his timeless verse when he discusses young children (1) constructing a ship using chairs and pillows, (2) building a city using blocks, (3) playing with toys on a bedspread, or (4) sailing a toy boat down the river to an indefinite location. His poem "Where Go the Boats?" is about a voyage of two toy boats that discharge from the country down a river that tours through a patchwork landscape and moves easily past a large city where urban children find them. To motivate enjoyment in the children's imagination, Grover (the illustrator) offers a sparkling interpretation of Stevenson's words and presents the poetry that children have enjoyed for generations (Bromer, 1999). Children as young as five years of age enjoy the poems enthusiastically.

Robert Louis Stevenson wrote about his own childhood and the nature of childhood before he started writing *A Child's Garden of Verses* (Stevenson, 1885). Four poems from Stevenson's book are rhymes that are about playing. For example, In "A Good Play," two boys construct a sailboat on a set of stairs with sofa pillows and chairs and "go a-sailing on the billows." In "Block City," a young girl imagines that the pattern of green trees on a purple overstuffed chair is a mountain in her make-believe town by the sea; whereas in "The Land of Counterpane," a green bedspread is thought to be green hills (Bromer, 1999).

Stevenson's poems focus on make-believe play in a new and perceptive way. The poems rejoice in the joy obtained from the changing power of creativity. Stevenson thought that young children needed to be allowed to play, use their imagination, be innocent, and be afraid. They may not be rational. Make-believe play is interesting and a wonderful break from the boredom in their lives. Such innovative ideas were inappropriate in 1879 (Rosen, 1995). Although this type of play was present at that time, the adult world lacked a genuine interest in childhood experiences. For instance, Mark Twain's compositions imply that sociodramatic play appeared before the 19th century (Singer, 1973). He clearly was aware about the importance of the adults' responsibility in becoming good role models, selecting appropriate stories, and supporting the children's make-believe play.

Many of Mark Twain's books and stories offer the earliest, most realistic narration of make-believe play in fiction. His stories show how Tom Sawyer (Twain, 1876), Huckleberry Finn, and their friends' role-play being pirates, river boat captains, and numerous different characters. At the end of *Huckleberry Finn* (Twain, 1884) in the complicated farce into which Huck and Jim become involved, Twain explains Tom's own fantasies and play when he is developing a wish to become a pirate. In *The Prince and the Pauper*, Twain (2000) gives details about Tom's growth when he and his companions are participating in make-believe play and he becomes the leader. Many times, Twain explains how the adults' enthusiasm in storytelling influences the children's play (Singer, 1973).

Each of the authors discussed here suggests a cultural attitude about children's play. Although none of the authors were ingrained in a "science of play," each one was a sensitive observer who communicated a view of humanity that "rang true." Examining the work of these writers who were from various eras provides the best descriptions of the children's play during different times. Such features of the popular culture suggest that play emerged centuries ago and that it continues to be valid in childhood.

## Summary

Play is a natural part of all children's behavior. It has been documented in numerous cultures and in many periods of history that play is universal. The history of play is complicated. Many of the historical sources differ in information and interpretations provided. Different perspectives on both descriptions of childhood and perceptions about children's play are presented. For example, didactic and prescriptive texts from Puritan and Victorian eras describe children to be cold and serious, approaches to education and child rearing to be adult-centered and authoritarian.

Children's play is considered trivial or counterproductive to learning and the development of character. Records from medical documents, doctor's reports, and recommendations for individual children contradict these interpretations of children's play in the historical period (Johnson et al., 2005). For example, artistic contributions characterize the quality of children's play experiences. The famous 16th century painting by the Flemish artist Peter Bruegel (1525–1569), *Children's Games*, and the 18th century Chinese artist Chin T'ing-Piao's *Children at Play in the Hall (Ch'ing Dynasty)* also document the children's play. The painting *Playing Children* show a child centered and humanistic view of children and their play (Hsiung, 2005). Micklethwait (1996) illustrates several art pictures that also depict the children's play. In a section that she titles, "Let's Play," she has Bruegel's *Children's Games* (1560), which shows children at play. On the opposite page she has a Japanese version of Bruegel's painting titled *Children's Games* (1868–1912) that is displayed in the Van Gogh Museum in Amsterdam. The paintings were completed three centuries apart. The settings are different in culture, but the paintings are children at play and both include a concession stand. For example, in Bruegel's painting, the children are playing tug-of-war, leapfrog, headstand, rolling hoops, and riding a hobby horse. Similarly, in the Japanese painting *Children's Games* (1868–1912), the children are riding piggyback, jumping rope, spinning tops, rolling a hoop, stilt walking, bouncing a ball, and flying a kite. More of these examples are found in the visual arts and literature section.

In addition, distinguished authors such as William Shakespeare, Leo Tolstoy, Mark Twain, and William Wordsworth have portrayed play in their classic literature. Several well-known artists such as Bruegel in Europe and the Sung Dynasty painters in China have also illustrated play in their paintings. Numerous games that children played centuries ago are presently played by children, even though some have been modified. It is apparent that for long periods of time, many have recognized and included children's play in their work. This trend remains present today (Saracho, 2010b).

# Section III
## Educational Perspectives

# Chapter 5
# Early Childhood Curriculum and Educational Play

> . . . the great instinctive forces of civilized life . . . law and order, commerce and profit, craft and art, poetry, wisdom, and science. All are rooted in the primeval solid of play . . . genuine, pure play is one of the main bases of civilization.
>
> (Huizinga, 1950, p. 5)

An early childhood education curriculum is any program or planned experiences for young children. It is a comprehensive instructional guide for day-to-day interactions with young children. Curriculum is the "what" of early childhood education and the content that the young children need to learn (Lieber et al., 2008). It is designed to make sure *all* children (including diverse children) have the opportunity to actively engage in the context in which the curriculum is presented. One of the early childhood teachers' major responsibilities is to make sure that young children with disabilities also have access to the general curriculum including the most critical knowledge across developmental and content areas that all children are expected to learn (Division for Early Childhood, 2007). Such "knowledge" then becomes the most important concern in considering all of the children's individual differences to make sure that all children progress within the general curriculum (Lieber et al., 2008).

In curriculum-related play, children are able to use and combine new concepts and skills that they are learning. Play also develops a context where children select the kind of play activities based on their current interests and needs. The early childhood curriculum has an impact on the children's play because the curriculum is the schools' educational program that includes academic subject areas, objectives, goals, instructional strategies, learning activities, and assessment methods (Johnson et al., 2005). This chapter describes historical curriculum interpretations, child development and early childhood influences, how to integrate subject areas into the play curriculum, educational play, and the play environment (like centers, prop boxes, materials). Finally, guidelines for designing learning centers and facilitating children's play are discussed.

## Historical Curriculum Interpretations

A curriculum is a collection of learning experiences, planned and organized based on the program's educational goals. Each curriculum specifies what children "ought to be and become" (Biber, 1984, p. 303), conforming to perceptions of social values that are integrated into the learners' experiences (Saracho & Spodek, 2002). The first curriculum book was published in 1918 (Bobbit, 1918). In the United States, the contemporary curriculum was introduced in the early 1890s as a result of major committees that debated the form and structure of public education at all levels (Saracho & Spodek, 2002).

For decades, various curriculum interpretations emerged. Caswell and Campbell (1935) believed that curriculum is "composed of all of the experiences children have under the guidance of the teacher" (p. 66). Tyler (1957) thought that the curriculum was composed of all the students' learning that the school plans and directs to achieve its educational goals. Smith, Stanley, and Shores (1957) described the term curriculum to be a sequence of possible experiences that are established in a subject area to help students develop their ways of thinking and caring. The curriculum for young children differs from that for older students. Usually *all* subjects are integrated within the early childhood curriculum, which is based on social values that children learn to become successful members of the community. Young children learn to value themselves as individuals and become self-assured to independently make their own decisions. Thus, it is important that young children become autonomous and independent thinkers.

The curriculum needs to be carefully planned in order that children of all ages learn concepts. It is essential that the curriculum has a balance among the cognitive, physical, and affective areas, which can only be achieved through play. Teachers have the responsibility to make sure that the children engage in educational play, but it is equally important to preserve the spontaneity and creativity of children's play. The early childhood curriculum's structure, process, and content (Saracho & Spodek, 2002) involves arranging, organizing, and interpreting the educational programs' plans into a natural environment. An experience-centered curriculum focuses on the developmental effects that result from specific experiences. A high quality curriculum that incorporates both an experience-centered curriculum and natural experience is one with strong play implementation (Hurwitz, 2002–2003).

## Integrating Play into the Early Childhood Education Curriculum

The Association for Childhood Education International (ACEI)—a respected organization that is dedicated to promoting the optimal education and development of children in a changing world—acknowledges children's need to play and the importance of play in children's lives (Isenberg & Quisenberry, 2002), suggesting that play should be integrated into the early childhood education curriculum. According to Bergen (1988), "play has been undervalued as a curricular tool by educators and parents because society has defined the goals of learning, especially school learning, very narrowly . . ." (p. 1). Play helps achieve learning goals and provides a highly successful way for making it possible for "students to learn more about what is important in the 'hard line' curriculum areas of math, science, social studies, and language arts . . . virtually every important concept to be taught—whether it be at the primary, intermediate or graduate level or whether it be in science, math, economics or business management—can be taught through the medium of serious play" (Wassermann, 1992, p. 136–137). It is important to know that play

- is valuable,
- helps children learn,
- is a beneficial curriculum element for all age levels, and
- must be integrated into the curriculum.

An integrated curriculum takes into account the importance of play in relation to the curricular components. When play is integrated into the curriculum, children have the opportunity to explore, discover, solve problems, invent, experiment, imitate, dramatize, and benefit from both the content and learning experiences. According to Wassermann (1992), ". . . play allows children to make discoveries that go far beyond the realm of what we adults think is important to know" (p. 133). Play promotes children's development of knowledge, meaning of inquiry, creativity, and conceptual understanding (Wassermann, 1992). At all ages children need learning experiences within the integrated curriculum to play with words, paints, cubes, problems, materials, and music in their future roles of writers, poets, artists, architects, scientists, and musicians (Stone, 1995–1996).

Play should have a genuine integration into the school curriculum where teachers make a concentrated effort to exploit the learning potential of the connections between play and curriculum (Johnson et al., 2005). The curriculum can create or contribute to the children's play activities, while the children's play behavior assists in establishing the curriculum content. This process is described as Curriculum-generated play and Play-generated curriculum (Van Hoorn et al., 2011).

- *Curriculum-generated play.* The children's play experiences assist them in learning academic concepts and skills. The play centers are academically enriched, because they are prepared with theme-related literacy and mathematics materials where children engage in reading, writing, and mathematics play experiences. In curriculum-generated play, young children learn, combine, and practice concepts and skills from the academic curriculum. The children's behavior indicates what they learned during this kind of play.
- *Play-generated curriculum.* The children's play experiences indicate their interests, which guides the development of the curriculum activities. For example, if during play children are interested in gardening (like pretending to plant and grow flowers or vegetables), a project or unit that focuses on the way plants grow can be developed. Experiences can consist of field trips to a nearby garden, science experiments (like growing lima bean seeds in a Zip lock bag), reading books about plants and gardening to create a class garden on the playground. Projects and integrated units should focus on the children's interests. When children play, their behavior will signal their areas of interest.

Children are excellent learners when concepts are introduced in a play environment. The foundation for providing academic learning to children is through the use of familiar themes as tools to learn analytic knowledge. Children explore to develop their own knowledge, which they relate to important concepts in a variety of situations. According to John Dewey (1902):

> It is just to get rid of the prejudicial notion that there is some gap in kind (as distinct from degree) between the child's experience and the various forms of subject-matter that make up the course of study. From the side of the child, it is a question of seeking how his experience already contains within itself elements—facts and truths—of the same sort as those entering into the formulated study; and, what is of more importance, of how it contains within itself the attitudes, the motives and the interests which have operated in developing and organizing the subject matter to the plane which it now occupies. From the side of the studies it is a question of interpreting them as outgrowths of forces operating in the child's life and discovering the steps that intervene between the child's present experience and their richer maturity (pp. 15–16).

For John Dewey (1902) in his book, *The Child and the Curriculum*, for William Kilpatrick (1918) in his book, *The Project Method*, and throughout the period of Progressive Education, the integration of young children's learning was considered reasonable. The British infant schools supported this integration in their *Integrated Day*. It continues to be a respected practice in early childhood programs (Saracho & Spodek, 2003b).

## Child Development and Early Education Influences

By the 1960s many theories of child development were available to educators. Early childhood education came to be seen at that time as a way of helping children deal with environmental limits. A number of different early childhood curricula were developed, each inspired by a different developmental theory or a particular view of that theory. Within the Head Start and Follow Through programs, a set of planned variations was developed to test these different curricula. However, the test that was conducted was far from conclusive (Vinovskis, 2008). Most of the programs have faded in the ensuing years. The one exception might be the High/Scope curriculum, which was inspired by Piagetian theory (Hohmann et al., 2008).

Since there has been a lack of funding to develop new curriculum models, early childhood educators were concerned about the improvement of developmentally appropriate practices. Early childhood programs have adopted practices from the follow through models (e.g., Bank Street approach, the High/Scope Curriculum). In their practices, the models recognized that children learn best through active participation with materials, ideas and people. Teachers encourage children to be curious, test their ideas, enjoy learning, be respectful and accepting of individual differences, become involved with the world around them, and become independent learners. Sometimes the justification for these practices is related to their learning outcomes. Often these new practices are justified, because they are seen as the most appropriate practices for young children.

Sometimes the goals of early childhood education are articulated in terms of the various developmental domains. Thus, teachers may suggest that the goal of early childhood education is to foster the social, emotional, intellectual, and physical development of children. Stating the goals this way reflects the close relationship between early childhood education and child development that has unfolded over the past 100 years. But the two fields are quite different from each other. Some suggest that development influences education by establishing principles of readiness that suggest when children are capable of learning specific skills or concepts. But in fact, levels of development are determined by the individual's genetic makeup rather than the experiences one has. Others suggest that what is learned by children influences their development.

Rather than basing curriculum on the principles of child development, we can explore these principles as coming from the nature of the society in which the child is growing up, the resources available within that society, and the demands placed upon the child and the developing adult by that society. For example, early childhood teachers are being asked to educate in their classroom an increasingly diverse group of children. Such a request requires teachers to become more (a) sensitive to individual differences among diverse children and (b) competent in offering an appropriate education to each child including children who were not able to navigate the school's stairways and corridors because of an orthopedic problem. These children were educated in a separate school or at home and prevented from having contact with any non-handicapped children. Children who were denied attending school before or who were educated in a segregated setting have increasingly been integrated in the regular classroom with a wide variety of children. Integration is considered to offer a degree of educational equity and to be more effective for children from diverse backgrounds and with diverse abilities. Presently, young children are being educated in inclusive settings, that is, in classes with regular children. Studies indicate that their education is more effective, because they learn to perform more like their peers. Simultaneously, regular children benefit when they learn to live with other children who are different from themselves in a variety of ways (Saracho & Spodek, 2003a).

Children are born with capacities to function, but how they will function—physically, intellectually, socially, and morally—is determined to a great extent by each society. Societies provide their members with a set of tools that extend their abilities to function. Language is one of these fundamental tools. Thus, though each normally developing child has the capacity to learn a language, which language will be learned and how that language will be mastered and adapted to various uses is determined by the context in which the child grows up. A child may learn a particular variation on a specific language or a particular dialect. For some children, the language or dialect learned first at home may be different from that studied in the school. This means that teachers of young children may have to modify their language learning activities as they would modify their other learning activities to respond to the needs and abilities of the children in their particular class (Saracho & Spodek, 2003a).

The values that we, as a society, hold also provide us with principles upon which to base our curriculum. We believe that children need to be physically capable, should have good social relations with others, have the right to live in a safe and healthy environment, should be honest and trustworthy, and should respect the individual characteristics of others. These values suggest the things we need to teach young children. We teach about health and nutrition; we help children develop physical skills; we want children to learn how to get along with others, to develop and maintain friendships, to manifest prosocial rather than antisocial behavior, and to resolve conflicts peacefully. We want children to respect their environment and do things to sustain a safe and healthy environment. We want children to be aware of the diversity of cultures both in our own country and throughout the world. We want children to resist cultural and racial stereotypes and to avoid acting in a biased manner against individuals who are different from themselves. Each of these values suggests an area of content (subject area) that should be addressed in the early childhood curriculum. An essential goal is to help children learn such subjects like social studies, art, mathematics, language arts, and social science through natural experiences.

## The Play Curriculum

Educational play is a fundamental component of the early childhood education curriculum. Teachers can use the different forms of educational play, flexibly yet intentionally guiding children's learning and carefully guiding their play. However, if teachers are too heavy-handed, then play becomes distorted and the activity is no longer play.

Young children become content literate in the different subject areas (such as arts, science, mathematics, social studies, language, literacy) through their play. According to Judith Van Hoorn and her associates (2011), play is the core of the early childhood curriculum. Early childhood programs use play as a medium for learning, because it provides children with the opportunities to generate and test their ideas about knowledge (Spodek & Saracho, 1987). Play develops the children's language, mathematics, science, and creative arts learning, which are briefly described in the following section.

## Integrating Subject Areas into the Play Curriculum

All subject areas should be integrated into a play curriculum that is used to achieve educational goals in the early childhood education program. Play can be integrated into social and personal learning, science, mathematics, language, and creative arts areas of the curriculum (Spodek et al., 1991). A brief description of these curriculum areas is provided below and expanded upon in future chapters.

- *Social Learning.* Play helps children understand their social world. They act out roles that assist young children to interpret their social world, family, school, and community and role play their perceptions of those worlds.
- *Language and Literacy.* Play becomes an essential source where children explore and develop the purposes and characteristics of the written language. During play, they use language in literate ways; whereas they use literacy the way they see others practice it (Saracho & Spodek, 2006).
- *Science.* Through play children learn science concepts in different ways. Play promotes science learning for individuals of all ages. After children engage in science play, or "mess about" with a scientific phenomenon, they can effectively understand science (Hawkins, 1965),
- *Mathematics.* Play provides young children with opportunities to understand mathematical concepts. When young children play grocery store, they weigh merchandise. They can also count play money when they collect money and give change to the customers. When young children use money in several play situations, they learn to differentiate denominations and count the money that must change hands.
- *Creative Arts.* Both play and the arts help young children communicate their ideas and feelings and provide a means for the children's creativity. For example, children play with different media as a form of communicating creatively.

## Educational Play

Play can be educational when it is natural, is spontaneous, and occurs in a variety of settings without adult interference. The difference between educational and noneducational play reflects the purposes and proposed outcomes expected from a play activity. Children reach a goal in educational play when they (1) explore and acquire information from their world; (2) expand that information to create meaning; (3) develop physical, social, and intellectual goals; and (4) understand and manage their feelings. Educational play requires teachers to plan in order that the children's play is spontaneous but that it includes educational value. Children carry the activity forward and determine its content (Spodek & Saracho, 1987). Manipulative play, block play, physical play, dramatic play, and games are essential in the early childhood curriculum (Spodek & Saracho, 1994b, see Box 5.1). The different forms of educational play in relation to children with disabilities are discussed in Chapter 6.

---

**Box 5.1. Types of Educational Play**

1. *Manipulative Play* identifies how children maneuver little bits of equipment such as puzzles, cuisenaire rods, and pegs. Most of the movements are self-contained and a dramatic quality hardly exists in the play activity. The Montessori materials are a good example of manipulative play materials. Children can manipulate a set of wooden cylinders, compare their lengths or diameters, and insert them into a specifically designed case to seriate them.
2. *Physical Play* occurs when children use large actions (e.g., running, jumping, riding a tricycle). This develops the children's physical skills.
3. *Dramatic Play* provides children with the opportunity to assume and act out a role with their classmates who usually play other roles. These dramatic events usually depict the children's life experiences. In dramatic play children reconstruct their world using various themes (e.g., a beauty salon, post office, restaurant, grocery store) that are familiar to them.
4. *Block Play* includes the children's use of small unit blocks or the large floor blocks.
5. *Games* are structured activities with rules and directions that must be followed. Four- and five-year-old children are usually at the level where independent game playing is possible. Easy games or musical exercises that have components of games are indeed acceptable for this age group. Children need to learn techniques to play games, but they need guidance with the games to know rule-appropriate behavior.

---

The differences among the kinds of play are important, although they may have overlapping characteristics. For example, several manipulative aspects can be found in the other forms of play, and dramatic dispositions can also be found in all forms of play. However, the nature of each kind of play is important in developing play-learning activities and approaches that support play in school (Saracho, 2002a).

## Manipulative Play

The manipulative play area includes manipulative materials that may be arranged based on themes or subjects. Materials are placed on open shelves that can be reached by the children. Materials are saved in their own case or in plastic see-through boxes, bins, baskets, or trays. Children can sit on chairs to work at tables or on a carpet. The children can remove the materials from the shelf and carry them to the table or carpet to work with them and return them when they are finished. Manipulative materials (see Box 5.2) can develop the children's perceptual motor and conceptual skills (Spodek & Saracho, 1994b).

---

**Box 5.2. Manipulative Materials**

1. *Stacking and nesting toys* are those toys that can be arranged by size. Young preschoolers are able to stack one upon the other, weave them on a dowel, or nest them into each other. They are also able to classify each part by size and arrange them appropriately from the largest to the smallest. Since young children are able to see if they can correctly arrange the parts, these materials are self-correcting. These toys may include cups, dolls, or rings.

2. *Puzzles* are different levels of jigsaw puzzles varying from simple to complex. They range from three- to four-piece puzzles to complicated puzzles that have two or three dozen pieces. The simplest puzzles are from boards where simple shapes (squares, circles, triangles, trapezoids) are to be inserted into matching cut-out spaces. More complex picture puzzles are composed of many pieces where the shape of the pieces may have nothing to do with the picture itself. Several indestructible puzzles made out of wood or Masonite that vary in difficulty need to be included. Children must be taught ways to care for their puzzles such as how to carefully remove and restore puzzles so that all the pieces are recovered. Each piece can be labeled with a common design that will help children detect the missing pieces. If pieces are lost, teachers can construct substitute shapes out of wood putty and paint them to match the lost piece. Puzzles can be stored and organized based on their level of difficulty to help teachers monitor the children's progress. Many children may have been introduced to working with puzzles at home, but they may not have acquired the proper skills. At the beginning of the school year, children need to have precise instructions on how to complete a puzzle.

3. *Parquetry blocks and pegboards* teach children form and color discrimination and retention. Parquetry blocks consist of wooden pieces of different shapes and colors, whereas pegboard sets consist of different colored pegs. Elastic bands can accompany the pegboard sets to help children design several shapes. To help children to independently manipulate these materials, they need model cards with different manipulative figures that children can use to replicate them. The model cards are displayed according to difficulty levels.

4. *Construction sets* are small sets of materials that children use to build small structures, as they engage in miniature dramatic play on a table surface. They include table blocks, which are small forms of unit blocks, and plastic interlocking blocks (such as *Lego, Tinker Toys, Lincoln Logs*), which are commercially designed by various brands. Many manufacturers sell this type of construction material. Children can construct small buildings and structures. Children can add miniature figures (people, animals, doll furniture, toy vehicles) to their constructions as they act out their miniature dramatizations.

5. *Locking devices* are commercial locking boards that have several locking devices. They may look like small doors or windows that open and close. Teachers can use materials from a hardware store to create comparable devices. Moving parts can be fastened with hinges. Hooks and eyes, barrel bolts, sliding door bolts,

hasps, cupboard catches, window locks, and locks with keys can be mounted on a board for children to use. Locking devices promote hand–eye coordination and teach practical skills.

6. *Fastening frames* are stretched pieces of cloth that are attached to a wooden frame. Many fastening gadgets (zippers, buttons and button holes, hooks and eyes, snaps, eyelets and shoe laces) are used to help children learn to dress and undress themselves. These gadgets are attached to wooden frames. Fastening frames promote the children's hand–eye coordination.

7. *Games* that help children become more autonomous, understand their peers' points of view, formulate interesting ideas, solve problems, raise questions, and make associations should be included in the manipulative area. These games include dominoes, card games (*Old Maid, Animal Rummy*) and board games (*Candyland, Chutes and Ladders, Lotto*). Bankauskas (2000) suggests games such as chess, checkers, and tic-tac toe. Teachers who prefer to use these games should consider that children make up their own rules, which they may change each time they play. Teachers must be careful that in presenting these games, play keeps its spontaneity, and children are encouraged to play with the game. Although teachers need to encourage cooperation among children, they must adapt the games to the children's thinking and avoid the teachers' authority as much as possible.

8. *Commercial manipulative materials* are materials from an educational supply catalogue that require children to manipulate objects. Hardware stores also have such materials that children can use in this way. Teachers can use their creativity in searching through hardware stores and their own homes to find stimulating and exciting materials for educational purposes.

9. *Natural manipulative play materials* are natural materials (such as sand and water with relevant objects) that children can use for manipulative and educational purposes. For example, sand and/or water can be placed in an appropriate container such as a galvanized or a plastic bucket. Accessories (different size containers, spoons, shovels) are added to the sand and water. Although children use these materials freely, they must be taught how to care for them and the limitations for their use. Children can take wet sand to create many shapes or they can filter dry sand and run it through funnels. Materials (e.g., sponges, floor brush, dustpan) must be included for children to use for cleaning up when they are finished playing with these materials.

## Dramatic Play

Dramatic play creates a micro world of social roles and relationships that children use to express their feelings. Through dramatic play, young children test out their ideas, learn to work with others by negotiating conflicting social situations, make sense of the world around them, and learn to cope with their environment. Children act out roles spontaneously. The children's dramatic play may have elements of fantasy. Children create their own scenarios, plan activities, set the stage, develop plots through conversations, and use objects to represent something that differs from what they really are. Teachers can help children modify their dramatic play scenarios. They can rearrange or add materials and props to the learning center to create new interests among the children. Judith Bender (1971) and Susan Myhre (1993) recommend the use of "prop boxes" in the classroom to enhance the dramatic play area. A prop box requires a collection of materials to motivate children to engage in play themes. An empty box (like a xeroxing paper or computer box) can be filled with materials that stimulate children to construct a specific scenario and dramatic play theme. The theme, materials, and supplies can be written on the outside of each box so as to keep things organized. For example, a prop box for automobile repair play has discarded, cleaned auto parts, tools, and other related materials. Prop boxes can include a camping box, a beautician's box, or various other boxes. Prop boxes will be further discussed in relation to themes in the different subject chapters.

The dramatic play area should include materials that reflect the children's home life and community life. Play situations can be created that reflect the children's world. Teachers can help children construct knowledge by guiding the play situation. They need to be aware of and sensitive to the children's play activities; have a sense of the goals of play; and be able to join the play, give suggestions, and become a player when necessary. Teachers can help children acquire and practice knowledge in their play by providing them with information. They can read books; show pictures, videotapes or DVDs; guide discussions; invite resource persons; and take the children on trips.

## Block Play

Block play overlaps with the other forms of physical, manipulative, block, and dramatic play. In early childhood education, blocks are one of the most effective tools that young children use to play, work, and become self-educated. Blocks provide young children with the opportunity to model their experiences and then act them out using their block structures.

When young children engage in block play, they develop their small and large muscle coordination and hand–eye coordination. Blocks motivate children to construct and engage in dramatic play as they create imitations of buildings around them. Children are also engaging in physical play. The large and heavy blocks induce children to get extensive physical exercise and practice in coordination as they lift, carry, put down, and return blocks to their proper storage place.

Block building, as a learning tool for young children to create and represent ideas, continues to challenge teachers (Hewitt, 2001). Teachers come to understand this activity when they observe what children do in their block building experiences. Teachers should offer daily opportunities for block building, provide encouragement, guidance, suggestions, and ask open-ended questions that stimulate thinking. Teachers must stimulate the children's thinking and focus on the process that children are involved in rather than the outcome or product. They need to provide a classroom environment that has open-ended materials and teachers need to understand, encourage, build on, and even join this fundamental complicated way of learning. In a separate chapter, block play will be fully discussed with practical applications.

## Physical Play

Children engage in physical play both outdoors and indoors. In physical play children use large muscle actions (like running, jumping, riding a tricycle), which usually take place during the children's outdoor play in the yard or playground. The classroom environment can be extended to include the outdoor play area when it is adjacent to the classroom.

Indoor and outdoor environments can be stimulating, safe, and accessible to children with disabilities (Sutterby & Frost, 2006). A well-designed outdoor environment encourages children to test and challenge their abilities at a range of developmental levels. For example, an obstacle course can serve this purpose when children engage in outdoor play.

An obstacle course has a series of activities that require children to crawl under, jump over, climb through, or walk around them. The activities are adequately spaced so that a number of children can independently but consecutively work on them. Figure 5.1 shows

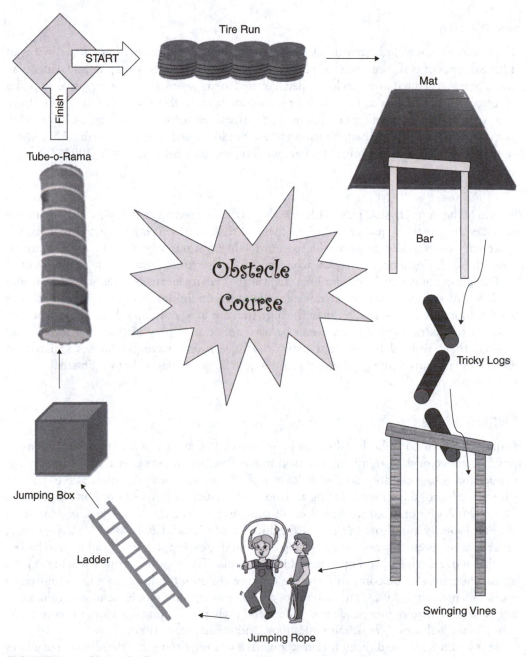

**FIGURE 5.1.   Obstacle Course.**

an obstacle course where a child may move in different ways between the tractor tires on the ground (like jumping on one foot, jumping on two feet, turning in the air while jumping). Another child may crawl or run through a ladder, while a third child may do a forward roll. In the obstacle course, various children are able to use the separate pieces of equipment simultaneously, without having to wait or interfering with each other (Spodek et al., 1991).

The physical surroundings prompt the children's sense of inquiry, stimulate their imaginations, invite them to explore, communicate a sense of belonging and cultural identity, and support their sense of development and competence over time.

### Outdoor Play

The outdoors can include structured, semi-structured, and unstructured areas in support of different types of play. Unstructured play areas include open spaces, sand pits, and water play areas. Semi-structured areas include open, covered areas (overhangs, porches, free-standing covered areas). Children can use these areas outdoors when there is a need for shelter from rain, sun, and other weather conditions. Semi-structured areas can also be used for other purposes (observation, making transition to the outdoors, outdoor science lab). They allow children to observe nature, other children, wildlife, and weather (McGinnis, 2002).

### Indoor Play

Several of the same physical play outdoor activities can be used for indoor play, although these activities are generally quieter and more confined than outdoor play. Activities that require space have to be scaled down to the space available. Various schools have a multipurpose room to use during more active play, while most schools are confined to a children's room.

The classrooms can have climbing apparatus and integrate boards, sawhorses, and ladders into extravagant enjoyable frames that need minimum storage space. Wheel toys used indoors need to be smaller than the ones that are used outdoors. For example, sturdy wooden trucks or variplay boxes can be used for indoor play instead of tricycles and wagons that are used for outdoor play. Some classrooms have playhouses situated on elevated platforms, ladders, staircases, slides, and other artifacts that are in small spaces in a classroom.

## Games

Games can be used in both indoor and outdoor play. Games range from using extensive physical movement to minimum physical movement, but most require problem solving. Games for young children need to be easy with simple and obvious rules. These types of games can be combined with singing and movement (such as *Looby Loo*, *London Bridge*). There should be only a few directions in these games, such as those in *Old Maid* and *Animal Rummy* and those in the board games *Candy Land*, *Chutes and Ladders*, *Lotto*, and checkers. Board games require young children to develop strategies and to plan before making moves, which promotes their thinking skills. These games require teachers (1) to adjust the games to be compatible to the way the children think, (2) to allow children to work independently, and (3) to foster cooperation among children. Educational games can help children acquire independence, understand their peers' points of view, develop interesting ideas, solve problems, raise questions, and make associations.

Many games are too difficult for preschoolers, so it's important that the selection of games should be developmentally appropriate. Teachers need to guide preschool children when they play games. As young children acquire experience with games, they become interested and very competent at playing games if teachers introduce games that are at the children's developmental levels. There are simple games that preschoolers can play with help from a teacher, such as simple sing-along games like Ring Around the Rosie. Box 5.3 presents games that help children develop skills in game playing and understanding of how games work.

---

**Box 5.3. Games that Help Children Understand and Develop Skills in Game Playing**

- Roll the Ball
- Hokey Pokey
- Nursery Rhymes
- Mulberry Bush
- Hide and Seek
- Follow the Leader
- Horseshoes
- Simon Says

---

## The Play Environment

A high quality play environment is essential in promoting the children's learning. The environment should include learning centers stocked with play materials in both indoor and outdoor areas. Each play center should contain appropriate space, materials, and equipment for learning and educational play. Play centers are captivating and support the curriculum goals. Frost and Dongju (1998) suggest integrating indoor and outdoor play centers. Teachers must consider not only the learning potential but also the safety of play areas both indoors and out of doors.

Teachers need to be aware of the different elements in each type of play and should be flexible in using them with children. Play must be spontaneous and children must have control of the play situation; too much interference by the teacher terminates the play activity. The teachers need to understand how the elements of play can be applied to individual children's characteristics to provide them with careful guidance in their play. Teachers can set these different types of play into learning centers, which are areas with a variety of materials to support children's learning activities. Each center is designed to provide activities that are based on the children's interests and support valuable learning.

## Learning Centers

The terms *learning centers*, *interest centers*, and *activity centers* are often used interchangeably. Learning centers are identifiable areas that have many different materials that help children learn. Teachers need to provide some degree of balance in the learning centers. An abundance of dependence on self-contained centers can lead to a shattered program. Early childhood classrooms should be organized into learning centers that support educational learning, and the environment should be child-centered rather than teacher-centered. To individualize learning, each center provides learning alternatives that focus on the children's interests to motivate them for valuable learning. The learning alternatives reflect each child's developmental levels and experiential backgrounds. Therefore, children select the learning alternatives that are of interest to them and learn at their own pace about the world around them. The learning alternatives allow children to manipulate objects, build, immerse themselves in dialogue, assume a variety of roles, and participate in the classroom actively and independently.

A theme center can be introduced and should be displayed for a number of weeks before another theme center should be introduced. Theme centers should be near the permanent housekeeping corner in order that children are able to integrate the theme center activities with the housekeeping play center activities. For example, children who are pretending to be parents in the housekeeping center area might take a "sick" baby to be examined at the doctor theme center (Woodard, 1984).

Learning centers for three- to five-year-old children may include centers for dramatic play, science, mathematics, technology (like cameras, computers), manipulative, library, block play, woodworking, music, and art. Learning centers will be discussed and described for each subject area throughout the book. Spodek and Saracho (1994b) provide the following examples of learning centers.

- *Block Center* provides opportunities to construct houses, stores, schools, and transportation systems. Play can be extended with the addition of block accessories (such as a traffic light to control the movement of cars, toy farm animals and people to help simulate a farm, or toy airplanes to allow for the construction of an airport).
- *Puzzle and Game Center* includes puzzles and games of different difficulty levels to help children select an activity that they are able to complete successfully. Puzzles and games can be coded by color or shape of some form based on the level or area of skill. These materials can be both commercially-made and teacher-made, but they must be appropriate for the children's interest and level of skill.
- *Library Center* is situated in a quiet area of the room away from traffic. Books are displayed in a way that children can select those books that are of interest to them. The books displayed consist of favorite books and those that relate to the topic the children are studying. Carpets or rugs and soft chairs or pillows along with paintings and flowers make the library area comfortable and attractive.
- *Mathematics Center* helps children solve mathematical problems with materials such as counting rods, geoboards, containers for measurement, felt figures for comparing, and task cards that present children with problems to solve.
- *Science Center* engages children in simple experiments, observing natural phenomena, or caring for a pet. It has games for children to engage in classifying or categorizing objects from the natural environment (like seeds, sea shells, leaves, insects, or tastes).
- *Sand and Water Centers* can be used both outside and inside. Inside centers are set up on a table that is situated in an area where the floor has the appropriate material for sand and water.
- *Sound and Music Center* has simple musical instruments and other materials that produce sounds. Children develop an appreciation for sounds and rhythm with materials such as sand blocks, drums, or bells.
- *Art Center* has at least basic materials such as easels, large table, paints, paper, paste, clay, and similar materials. It includes an appropriate and ample storage space. Children need to have easy access to materials and put them away during their independent clean up.
- *Physical Education Center* has equipment such as balance beams, hopscotch, hula-hoops, jump ropes, romper stompers, beanbag games, and balls. For classrooms that

lack adequate space, equipment can be set up in another inside space (such as a multi-purpose room) or outside such as a patio or playground area.

- *Dramatic Play Center* has materials linked to several play themes that relate to different facets of adult and community life such as housekeeping, a store, a restaurant or any theme that reflects the children's social life. "Prop boxes" support any themes.

Two learning centers that are often overlooked will be discussed in detail to emphasize their importance. These are the technology center and the woodworking center.

### The Technology Center

Technology is important in every aspect of life today and its importance will continue to increase in the future. Electronic information technology and electronic digital interactive devices provide young children with additional tools to play with. Young children transfer their mark-making media patterns across media areas. Young children can shift the representations and expressions that they make with pencil and paper to electronic and digital media. Young children use technology with ease and teachers need to use technology to benefit children. Computers can supplement highly valued early childhood activities and materials (art, blocks, sand, water, books, dramatic play). They can be used in developmentally appropriate ways that benefit young children. Developmentally appropriate software offers young children opportunities to engage in collaborative play, learning, and creation (National Association for the Education of Young Children NAEYC, 1996).

Computers can be used actively or passively in their learning. As passive users, children use tools without understanding the concepts they see on the screen. The computer becomes an electronic worksheet as children memorize but do not understand concepts. To avoid this, teachers need to monitor the quality of the software children use, the amount of time children work with it, and the way in which they use it. Box 5.4 provides suggestions on how to check software (Robinson, no date).

---

#### Box 5.4. Judging the Quality of Software for Children

1. Good software uses pictures and spoken instructions rather than written ones so that children will not need to ask for help.
2. In good software, children control the level of difficulty, the pace and direction of the program.
3. Good software offers variety: children can explore a number of topics on different levels.
4. Children receive quick feedback in good software, so they stay interested.
5. High quality program utilizes the capacities of today's computers by appealing to children through interesting sights and sounds.
6. To determine a product's appropriateness for a child's current level of development, parents have evaluated the skill list and activities as described on the package, and previewed the product through store demonstration or a friend's computer.
7. Good software engages children's interest by encouraging children to laugh and use their imagination in exploring.
8. A good program allows children to experience success and feel empowered through learning.

The technology center can provide children with opportunities for digital imagery (both still and video), which is an exciting technological application. Children can use photography and video to document their learning and to remember and reflect on their experiences. Video imagery can help young children relive and process their experiences. Digital cameras provide excellent photos with a "point and shoot" technology that young children can learn to use. The technology center should have

- Word processing and writing tools such as WriteOn (published by Software Production Associates).
- Computer art programs like Kid Pix (published by Broderbund) that introduce children to open-ended exploration on the computer. The children's art programs offer them a wide range of choices to communicate ideas, from freehand drawing to the use of stamps, text, or other special effects that children can combine to create a complex visual display. Several of these programs also offer multimedia options (like sounds, animation, and voice recording for children to allow children to create multimodal work). Children as young as three-year-olds can use these programs.
- Software like HyperStudio (published by Robert Wagner Publishing), with art programs where children create multimedia presentations to communicate to others their ideas, experiences, and understanding.
- Research tools that include both age-appropriate websites and software programs helping young children to obtain information. They can use them formally and informally to research topics that are of interest to them. Such applications can supplement the classroom library and offer multimedia databases on a broad range of topics.
- Concept mapping software like Kidspiration (published by Inspiration Software) that provides children the opportunity to portray many of their ideas and concepts and relate them to one another pictorially. Young children can use these tools to create webs and other schematics that visually represent their understanding of a topic. Children can use these schematics to play with ideas and communicate to their teachers their understanding and thought processes (Murphy et al., 2003).

Teachers need to select products that promote the children's learning. They need to use technology resources that complement their teaching practice, build on children's different learning styles, offer depth to content mastery, and help children construct knowledge (Bergen, 2000).

## The Woodworking Center

The woodworking center should include a heavy wooden table or workbench, some good 8- to 10-oz. hammers, a hand drill, miter box, backsaw or short crosscut saw, "C" clamps, soft wood, and common nails. The use of wood and tools helps children develop their large and small muscles and hand–eye coordination. Woodworking offers young children opportunities to experiment with different kinds of materials and equipment, exercise muscles, develop skills, and express themselves creatively. They can also improve their social relationships when they share, take turns, and develop appreciation for the work of their peers. They can learn to solve problems. This center should be located where it can be supervised at all times. Woodworking gives children opportunities like those in Box 5.5.

**Box 5.5.  Opportunities for Woodworking**

1.  Learning to care for tools
2.  Converting ideas into completed products
3.  Working with others on group projects
4.  Respecting rules of safety
5.  Performing control
6.  Asking for and giving assistance
7.  Planning, designing, measuring, constructing, completing

The woodworking center can include materials and equipment like the ones in Box 5.6.

**Box 5.6.  Items for the Woodworking Center**

- Workbench or workhorse equipped with wood vise
- Cross-cut saw (short but not toy)
- Hammer
- Iron clamps
- Screwdriver
- Sandpaper
- Nails
- Tacks
- Containers for nails of various sizes
- Pliers
- Ruler and yardstick
- Wood (soft pine scraps)
- Vises (G or C clamps)
- Screws
- T-square
- Tool board for keeping tools ready to use

## Woodworking

Children can experience different ways of working with wood. Hammering and sawing is a simple activity that gives pleasure and satisfaction to very young children. Unfortunately, many teachers prefer to avoid woodworking in their classroom. These teachers usually lack experience with carpentry and tools. They need to learn the proper way of teaching young children how to use hammers, saws, and other tools safely. Young children can learn how to use the tools and skills to use them safely. However, at all times adult supervision is required in this area.

A school that is not equipped for any type of real carpentry can use wood-with-glue-and-beautiful-junk activity, which is an activity without using tools. Teachers can use wood with children without the use of tools. Wood materials can be combined with glue. There are many constructions children can make with just wood and glue such as a small table and bench or chair for a doll or a small box for treasures and innumerable other things. For example, young children can easily create a boat using a large block of wood with a smaller one on top for a cabin or construct an airplane using two narrow strips glued at the right angles and paste small pieces in place for a tail, motor, etc.

Once children understand that things can go together to create objects and have experienced selecting shapes and sizes of wood, they can develop simple skills with tools, such as driving one nail into crossed pieces of wood to make an airplane, drilling one hole to insert a piece of doweling for a smokestack or a mast on a boat making two cuts with a saw to produce a point for the bow of a boat.

Scrap wood can often be obtained in any lumber yard, building supply store, or at a carpenter's or cabinetmaker's shop. They usually have problems disposing of the scraps. Thus, they are willing to save the scraps for teachers to select any usable pieces. Teachers need to find out when these sites dispose of their rubbish and visit these sites when they have the largest selection. Teachers need to select wood of different sizes and shapes. They need to check to make sure that it is safe for children to use these scraps of wood. The wood scraps should not have any knots or blemishes and should be finished so that it does not have any splinters. Finished one-inch boards are actually only about three fourths of an inch thick, even if they are referred to as one-inch lumber.

The best wood to hammer and saw is usually one-inch clear, finished pine. These vary in length. The most useful dimensions are the one inch by two inches, one by four, one by six, two by four, and two by two. Teachers need to collect as many scraps as they can of this type of wood in all shapes and sizes. They need to check that the pieces of wood they select do not have any splinters, jagged edges, or knots. Thickness, width, and length should be considered in selecting the wood.

An appropriate woodworking area has positive activities, has safety precautions, is supervised, and is isolated from other activities. Tools and supplies must be (1) stored where they are readily accessible, (2) in good order, (3) in proper repair, (4) include appropriate materials (sharp saws; handles firmly embedded in the heads; hammers with a good supply of soft wood such as common pine). Several woodworking accessories can be added as the children get experience and become proficient in using the wood and tools. See Box 5.7.

---

**Box 5.7. Woodworking Accessories**

- Short crosscut saws and hammers that are lightweight and of good quality.
- Sandpaper, block planes, rasps, and wood files.
- A brace, drill bits, and hand drill.
- Screwdrivers can be added as children learn to use screws.
- Nails for fastening boards together.
- A woodworking vise, workbench or saw horses, and "C" clamps.

---

Children start building simple constructions, which are put together with nails and glue. The projects can be expanded by adding dowels, empty paper rolls, spools, and anything the teachers and children find useful. Children can paint their woodworking projects with tempera and cover them with shellac or lacquer to keep the color from running. It is harder to work and clean up enamel paint.

## Wood Sculptures

Children can create wood sculptures. Box 5.8 shows children's books related to wood sculpture. The teacher and the children can read them before deciding on their wood sculpture project. Teachers can follow the following procedures for the wood sculpture process, which takes several days or weeks (Bisgaier et al., 2004; Samaras, & Freer, 2003). See Table 5.1.

---

### Box 5.8. Children's Books on Wood Sculpture

- Barton, B. (1990). *Building a house*. New York: Harper Trophy.
- Browne, A. (2003). *The shape game*. New York: Farrar Straus Giroux.
- Fleming, D. (2000). *Where once there was a wood*. New York: Henry Holt.
- Hunter, R. A. (1998). *Cross a bridge*. New York: Holiday House.
- Johnson, A. (2001). *Those building men*. New York: Blue Sky Press.
- Laden, N. (2000). *Roberto the insect architect*. San Francisco: Chronicle Books.
- Lipman, J. (1999). *Calder's universe*. Philadelphia, PA: Running Press Publishers.
- Pinkwater, D. M. (1993). *The big orange splot*. New York: Scholastic.

---

**TABLE 5.1.** Guidelines to Help Children Create Wood Sculptures

| Guideline | Description |
|---|---|
| ▪ Get wood scraps from suppliers | Local lumberyards, local builders, and martial arts competitions have disposable scraps of wood as noted earlier. Ask children to bring twigs, small branches, nuts, acorns, leaves, and other natural resources. Although bases for the sculptures can be purchased, they can be made from cut up corrugated cardboard boxes or large scraps of wood. Bases need to be strong enough to hold a heavy block structure that is around 12 inches by 12 inches in size. |
| ▪ Discuss pictures from books on building, sculpture, architecture, or wood to encourage the children | Introduce and display these books in the wood working center to help children focus on specific elements of design. Read aloud and discuss children's literature books on wood sculpture (see Table 5.6 on children's books related to wood sculpture). |
| ▪ Set up a wood center and provide scraps of wood in a bin for children to create wood sculptures | Children can look at the children's books to get ideas for the sculpture. This may take several days or weeks. |
| ▪ Leave sculpture bases in the wood center with the loose scrap wood pieces for children to explore their ideas | Children may arrange the wood into a variety of configurations and discuss balance, shapes, sizes, and textures of the wood pieces. |
| ▪ Provide wood glue in deli containers to apply using popsicle sticks or tongue depressors | Children need to know how to use the glue to attach wood pieces permanently to each other and to the base. Children may glue larger wood pieces to the base first. Allow only small groups in the wood center so that you can assist them with their work. |
| ▪ Allow children to work on their project over time so that children can add pieces to their sculptures | Encourage children to use a variety of shapes, sizes, and colors and consider painting and adding collage materials (such as fabric, paper, ribbon, string, pom-poms, feathers, beads) to their sculptures. |

*(Continued)*

**TABLE 5.1.** (*continued*) Guidelines to Help Children Create Wood Sculptures

| Guideline | Description |
| --- | --- |
| ▪ Display the children's finished sculptures | Allow children to share their work with their classmates. |
| ▪ Host a sculpture exhibition in the classroom | Other classrooms, teachers, and families can come to view them. Children can assume the role of museum tour guides for the visitors. |

*Setting up Learning Centers*

A classroom that is planned for learning invites children to engage in activities that are interesting and educationally worthwhile. Learning centers that are carefully planned provide interesting and appropriate learning alternatives, overcome many discipline problems, and give teachers the opportunity to recognize individual children. Children need to be able to choose from several learning alternatives and be able to change to a different activity. They need to learn in as natural a context as possible and have many first hand experiences. Teachers need to provide children a large daily block of time (30 to 60 minutes) for center activities. Children should be able to independently access and return equipment and supplies to their appropriate place without the assistance of an adult.

Teachers can make sure that the learning centers are in functioning areas in the classroom. For example, noisy and quiet learning centers need to be separated. The art center should be near a source of water. Classrooms without water must have the art center near the door to be close to the water (such as the children's restrooms). A suggested floor plan for learning centers is found in Figure 5.2.

Box 5.9 provides some suggestions to assist teachers plan and organize learning centers (Spodek & Saracho, 1994b).

---

**Box 5.9. Suggestions for Planning and Organizing Learning Centers**

1. Although the activity period is one in which children engage in self-selected activities, the teacher needs to design centers to engage children into learning activities and provide ideas to them.
2. Consider the children's muscle development and coordination, social maturity, language skills, interests, and needs in planning and arranging the classroom.
3. Plenty of space, time, and equipment should be provided for uninterrupted play. Through involvement in play activities, children experiment with social relationships with others their age. There should be opportunities for physical and intellectual development, language practice, and critical thinking. Well-planned activities provide varied learning experiences of a concrete and sensory nature.
4. Many experiences should be available each day during center time. Children should be able to move freely from one activity to another, depending upon their interests and their attention span.
5. During the activity period, provide a balance between quiet and vigorous activities, and between individual and group activities. Plan for dramatic play, block play, science and math learning with manipulative materials, and work in the creative arts. Frequently, include experiences with music and books. Children

should not be limited to the experiences set out for that day. They only serve as beginnings, as invitations to involvement. Teachers should respond to learning opportunities that occur spontaneously.

6. Make yourself available to the children during the activity period. Observe frequently. Children's play reveals interests, abilities, and needs. At times it is advisable for teachers to step in, to increase the potential or encourage fullest play.

7. This is the time that teachers guide children toward self-discipline, by saying things such as, "Look at the progress you've made, Frankie! You were just learning to do that last week!" Or perhaps you will notice that a new play material will help a group to add to their sand city.

8. Adults need to supervise children who are engaging in activities (such as carpentry) to ensure their safety.

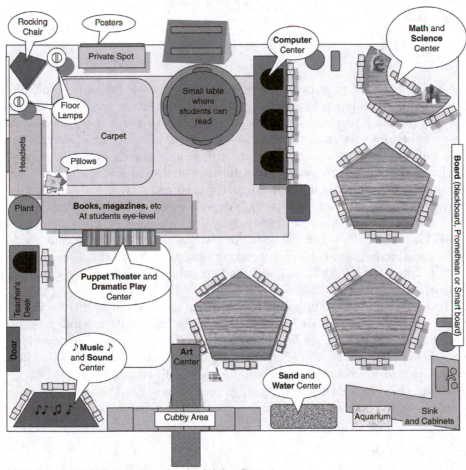

Library includes the following to create a soft and secluded reading area:

- **2 throw rugs** (green and orange): soft to lie on
- **various pillows**: nice to cuddle with
- **small table with chairs**: good for all types of activities
- **rocking chair**: for author's chair and read alouds
- **headsets**: to listen to recorded stories
- **bookshelves** filled with books
- **freestanding bulletin board** to display new books

**FIGURE 5.2. Floor plan-diagram.**

*Joint Children–Teacher Planning for Learning Centers*

Teachers need to have a well-organized classroom plan to help children function in the learning centers in an orderly manner. Teachers should plan together with children to select the learning centers and activities that are of interest to them. They can introduce to the children the activities that are available in the learning centers and determine the number of children who can be at each center at one time. A planning board positioned in a central place in the classroom can be used to show children which learning centers are available. Teachers can also use the board to record in which learning center each child is working. The planning board may include a picture of each learning center. Under each picture, a number is recorded to identify how many children can work in that center. A hook is also installed under the picture so that children can insert a tag with their name in the hook to let other children know that another player has joined the learning center and to let the teacher know where each child is working. If the block center only has room for five children, for example, there should only be five hooks representing that area on the planning board.

## Materials

Toys in early childhood education are texts, the equivalent of books for older children (Cuffaro, 1999). The children's developmental level should be considered in selecting toys, because play materials vary with age. For example, three- to five-year-old children usually play with miniature toys that represent objects and symbolize the children's life (for example, dolls, doll furniture, wagons, engines). Toys motivate children to assume several adult roles in their play, introduce meaningful information to young children, and help them to understand the social life of their home and community.

The quality and quantity of play materials depend on the children's interest and way of using the materials in the different forms of play. Children may play alone when playing with play-dough, clay, and sand and water. In contrast, art materials prompt children to engage in constructive, nonsocial play. Teachers need to make a careful selection of play materials to promote the children's play and to help children achieve the program's educational goals.

Play materials vary according to the topic or play theme of study. Play activities that contribute to the children's knowledge (such as going for a walk around the neighborhood, visiting the post office, reading a book on a specific play topic, seeing a video) can motivate them to become interested in a play topic or theme (Saracho, 1999b). Table 5.2 provides criteria in selecting play materials (Neuman & Roskos, 1990).

These criteria can be used in selecting play materials. Providing the appropriate environment and materials encourages young children to engage in complex play experiences.

*Multicultural Materials*

Teachers are responsible for providing activities and materials that are multicultural. It is important that materials that portray people (like dolls, books, puzzles) reflect the children's culture. Dramatic play materials (like dress-up clothes, props, toys) need to reflect the classroom children's diversity (race, ethnicity, gender, culture, family structures, profession, disabilities). Johnson and Colleagues (2005) provide Wardle's (2003) guidelines in using toys and materials that are multicultural:

- Materials should increase each child's self-acceptance, knowledge, and understanding of his or her heritage and identity by showing the child's culture in a positive light.
- Materials should increase each child's acceptance, knowledge, and understanding of people who are different from him or her by showing those people and their cultures in a positive light.
- Materials should expand children's view of the world and people in the world.
- Materials should address a variety of areas of diversity at the same time, such as gender, disability, and family structures.
- Materials that expose children to diversity should be integrated within the whole program and its curricula, not isolated in a token manner.
- Diversity represented in materials should be realistic and authentic, such as Native Americans in real jobs with contemporary clothes rather than dancing in headdresses.
- Materials should continually challenge every kind of stereotype, whether it be that women can only be nurses and men cannot be nurses, that Asian boys are always good at math and black boys are always good at athletics, or the like.
- Materials need to emphasize diversity within large groups and not convey the idea that all African-Americans, all Latinos, all women, and so on look the same and think the same.
- Materials should emphasize the choices, freedoms, and uniqueness of each individual, who have attributes from a variety of diverse groups (gender, race, etc.)
- Materials should never convey that one group is somehow better than another group. Unfortunately, if people are not represented in play materials, this invisibility is a powerful indicator of lack of importance.
- Materials must not exclude any person or any part of a person; thus multiracial and multiethnic children and their families must be represented as unique individuals, not just part of the minority parents' cultures (pp. 234–235).

**TABLE 5.2.** Criteria to Select Play Materials

| Criteria | Description |
|---|---|
| Appropriateness | The materials need to be used in a natural way and be safe for young children to use. Some safety precautions may be needed for some materials. For example, materials in the woodworking center need adult supervision |
| Authenticity | Materials (like props) need to be authentic. They should be real objects from the environment. Telephones, recipe books, and play money are considered authentic because children are familiar with these objects |
| Utility | Materials need to serve a specific purpose that children know from their daily life. For example, materials relating to the post office (such as pencils, envelopes, stamps, stationery) have a purpose |

Selection of materials for young children with disabilities needs to be modified, because they have a combination of immature and mature play patterns. They need play models and materials that encourage more mature play stages. Materials and social grouping need to be carefully selected to help exceptional children develop higher play stages. They seem to prefer blocks, vehicles, books, dolls, rolling objects and puzzles. If children are not able to use a specific material, teachers can develop a task analysis for the material. First they introduce materials that require similar skills and then present the children with materials that require different skills. For instance, a truck, a set of blocks, and a ball require similar skills. Children with disabilities can then (1) establish eye contact with each material; (2) hold or pick it up; (3) place it for appropriate play (e.g., turn the truck around before rolling it to a play partner, put the block above a tower or building, or put the ball in so that a push would send it off to a playmate); and (4) let go it (e.g., push the truck toward a playmate, put a block on top of a building, or roll the ball toward a playmate).

## Guidelines for Designing Learning Centers

When children play in well-designed play learning centers, they engage in a purposeful academic conceptual framework. It is important that children are involved in designing their learning in play. For example, the following are guidelines to organize meaningful play learning centers that integrate social studies concepts (Labbo, 1998).

### I. Designing the center

Step 1. *Select and share thematic books*. At the beginning, a thematic set of children's fiction and non fiction books related to important concepts is introduced to the children and displayed at the appropriate play center. For example,

> Ms. Martin began by selecting books on travel and vacations that could provide information about geography and transportation, map skills, and economic principles. She introduced the theme and helped children build their vocabulary by reading and discussing books such as *Arthur's Family Vacation* (Brown, 1993) and *On the Go* (Morris, 1990). Because the books were displayed with covers showing on a open shelved book case, the children were free to revisit key concepts and retell stories to each other (Labbo, 1998, p. 19).

Step 2. *Raise questions, find fact, and keep records*. Children help in designing the play center to be able to ask questions, look for facts, and keep records. Both children and teachers work together in developmentally appropriate research-oriented inquiry. For example,

> After Ms. Martin invited students to help her design and set up a travel agency center, they brain stormed a list of questions about how travel agencies work. They used information from a variety of sources including a fact-finding trip to a travel agency, interviews with experts who visited the class, supplementary books suggested by the school media specialist, and electronic or digital sources (e.g., the internet, e-mail, CD-ROMS, and video). These activities gave Ms. Martin the opportunity to model research methods (such as generating questions, making up categories of information, and taking notes from interviews) and to make use of conventional forms of literacy as the data took form on large chart paper that was displayed on a bulletin board (Labbo, 1998, p. 19).

## II.  Implementing the center

Step 3.  *Plan and equip the center*. When children plan and equip the play center, they combine the gathered information. For example,

> Ms. M used a diagram of the play center and cutouts of various pieces of furniture to help children create a map to guide the center design. In addition, she helped the children apply what they had learned about the purpose and forms of office work as they made literacy props (e.g., tickets, time schedules, note pads and pens for phone messages, travel maps, a cardboard model of a computer). Children also received guidance in translating the lists, sketches, diagrams, and maps from two dimensional paper into three dimensional reality in the play center (Labbo, 1998, p. 19).

Step 4.  *Introduce play at the learning center*. Some children may not know about role-playing to create an appropriate scenario with dialogue and activities for the characters that they have been studying. For these children, it may be necessary to have a discussion about the roles, activities, and use of props. For example, children may need more information on assuming the role of a customer or travel agent when they play.

## III.  Responding to the center

Step 5.  *Enjoy, elaborate, and contemplate their experiences*. Children need to enjoy, elaborate, and contemplate their playful experiences to be able to refine or expand the new social studies information. To reinforce their social studies learning, children may be provided with materials for them to draw, write about, or dictate their playful experiences. These are important opportunities for children to communicate their ideas.

The five steps presented above provide young children with opportunities to obtain meaningful learning by using many excellent sources. Children will engage in several methods of inquiry and be able to organize, interpret, and use the knowledge they acquired (Labbo, 1998). Usually the learning centers are set up to represent thematic themes (e.g., community helpers, our ancestors). One way of supporting these themes is to create play within the themes, such as using prop boxes. Materials are needed to facilitate play that can be organized into prop boxes or learning centers.

## Facilitating Children's Play

Teachers need to make sure the children's group play is educational. They can provide materials that (a) nurture the children's group play, (b) assist with the children's thinking and planning, and (c) provide sufficient information for the children to have the knowledge of what and how to engage in pretend play. The children can engage in meaningful play if teachers offer them information through field trips, reading a book, or other instructional ways.

Teachers can promote the children's play by becoming a facilitator and, sometimes, a participant. As facilitators, they select; coordinate and present objects, materials, and props; and develop experiences in relation to concepts or themes. When there is a purpose in mind, they can also intervene to expand and enrich the children's play. This intervention stimulates, clarifies, and accounts for the play event; although the intervention must encourage rather than control the play activities. Teachers must observe the children's play to identify the critical play elements to appropriately intervene, employ props, and use language. Teachers initiate and motivate children when they introduce the children's play.

Teachers can use many means to introduce play. They can design environments that encourage children to absorb themselves in educational play. Their introduction must provide children with attractive play materials, play possibilities, and some type of innovation to the play context. A brief child–teacher planning period where children are presented with various choices can be held to assist children in choosing play activities and centers. In this planning discussion children learn about the new equipment or toys and their functions, uses, and limitations (Saracho, 1999b).

Teachers can motivate children by providing them with diverse and new play activities. Thus, they need to include familiar and unfamiliar play activities that are displayed in different formats. In addition, play centers are organized or changed, new labels are displayed in the play centers, and/or numerous new materials added to re-create an old play activity into a fantastic new one. Fresh play activities must prompt the children's attention and creativity as well as extend their play.

Teachers can extend the children's play in a variety of ways. They can cautiously join the children's play by minimizing their intervention and not violating the children's autonomy. Teachers need to refrain from becoming the center of attention or the dominant source of play ideas, because it diminishes the children's incentive to play. Teachers should assess how their actions can affect the play situation to become responsive to the children's play and their development of their play behaviors (Saracho, 1999b).

Teachers need to be aware of the children's play behaviors and their play developmental level to introduce play interventions, adjust the play environment, choose new play materials, or lightly engage in the children's play to clear up ideas. Teachers' interventions must refrain from causing children to focus on reality or to relinquish control of the play situation. They can encourage young children's play by accepting a variety of their play patterns and their choice not to play. Teachers can offer children a variety of activities that can motivate them to play (Saracho, 1999b) and interact during their play.

Teachers need to encourage play interactions between children. They may have to join and participate in the children's play to promote the quality of the interactions. Box 5.10 offers suggestions that teachers can use to encourage play interactions between children (Christie, 1982).

Play is an important component of the early childhood curriculum. Early childhood teachers integrate self-selected and self-directed play activities into the early childhood education curriculum. They must have the responsibility to make sure that the children's play provides an educational function. Teachers at all times must make sure that play is spontaneous, flexible, and creative so that it continues to be play.

**Box 5.10. Suggestions to Encourage Play Interactions Between Children**

1.  Model the role by demonstrating it and saying, "A lifeguard would put on a pair of sunglasses and visor and go save somebody."

2. Demonstrate how objects can represent something else (for instance, a box can be a fishing boat or a broomstick can be a horse).
3. Show how to expand a play episode by adding to the story. If the children are bored of playing auto repairperson, teachers can say, "Now that the car is fixed, you may want to drive it."

Teachers plan and implement the learning experiences and, when necessary, guide the children. However, teachers first need to let the children solve any problems on their own before interfering in their group play. Teachers need to let children have the freedom to correct and learn from their mistakes. They should only interfere in the children's play to help them clarify concepts. For example, children may be building a farm and using block accessories with farm animals. If the teacher sees that children have included an elephant, the teacher may join the group to discuss the reason for including the elephant in the barn. Teachers need to help children to advance in their play. However, teachers must understand that some children may not be ready to advance in their play. Teachers must know their classroom children to assess when children need guidance to advance in their play or when the children can only develop if they are left to play independently.

The teachers' interference needs to be carefully considered. The decision as to when to join the play group and when to leave children alone in their play is a difficult one. A decision to interfere must only be made when children need help in conveying their ideas and progressing in their play. Teachers who decide to leave the children alone must give attention and support to the players. They need to be sensitive about the play situation before deciding when to interfere.

Many of the elements of children's play are beyond the teachers' capacities, but there are many situations that the teachers can control. Teachers can assure the quality of the children's classroom play by being well prepared in educational play, carefully planning, and providing careful guidance. Worthwhile educational results can occur when teachers appropriately guide the children's educational play in the way they play and initiate it.

## Summary

Play can be recreational and educational. It can introduce young children to their world. Using the play curriculum, teachers can design an effective environment, choose appropriate materials, and implement appropriate intervention strategies that motivate and develop the children's learning.

Teachers must be sensitive about what the children perceive as play. Children perceive that play is work in self-selected and self-directed activities. Some teachers may use games to teach concepts in their play. However, the children identify these games as work, when the teachers select and guide the games instead of the children. Box 5.11 provides reasons why teachers need to understand the children's perceptions of play activities in early childhood settings (Ceglowski, 1997).

**Box 5.11.  Reasons Teachers Need to Understand the Children's Perceptions of Play Activities**

- Teachers need to be aware that play to children is like work to adults;
- Children consider play seriously;
- Adults need to work with play;
- Enrich play;
- Facilitate the children's play.

# Chapter 6
# Play Experiences of Children with Diverse Needs

If you approach each new person you meet in a spirit of adventure, you will find yourself endlessly fascinated by the new channels of thought and experience and personality that you encounter.

Eleanor Roosevelt, Wife of President F. D. Roosevelt, activist, UN diplomat

Play has usually been provided in programs for typically developing children and frequently restricted to children with diverse needs, that is, children (a) with disabilities, (b) who are at risk, and (c) with linguistic and cultural differences. Many programs for these children concentrate exclusively and consistently on confined teaching methods to assist children to cope with difficulties caused by their specific disability, including cultural diversity, which many educators consider a disability. These educators focus on ways to remedy the children's disability and view play as irrelevant to the education of children with diverse needs. These educators often believe that the children with diverse needs are incapable of playing.

Both of these suppositions are incorrect. Preventing children with diverse needs from playing prohibits their potential for developing in as normal a way as possible. Play contributes to the development of *all* children. Play allows children to communicate their ideas and feelings as well as to represent and test their knowledge of the world. This is as much needed for children with diverse needs as for typically developing children. Although most of the education for children with diverse needs focuses on providing direct support for academic and pre-academic learning, play should not be denied its rightful place in the education of children with diverse needs. Actually, an integrated classroom offers the best support for play experiences that promote their learning. Educators need to acquire the necessary knowledge to work effectively with the multiple cultures, languages, and abilities of the children they serve (Ryan & Hyland, 2010), particularly in using play to promote the learning of children with diverse needs.

This chapter describes the importance of play for various groups of children with diverse needs (such as those with disabilities, at risk, with linguistic and cultural differences). It discusses the play experiences for children with disabilities, symbolic and social play, educational play, and the physical environment. Then it proposes a variety of educational settings to promote the play experiences of children with diverse needs. This chapter will serve as an introduction to children with diverse needs. Throughout the following chapters, examples are offered on ways to modify the curriculum for children who have diverse needs and are placed in inclusive settings.

## Play Experiences for Children with Disabilities

Play helps children with disabilities to master motor skills, to follow directions, to laugh, and to interact with other children. They also learn to communicate their satisfaction and enjoyment through smiles, laughter, and several expressive movements of the head, arms, and body. Through play children with disabilities (a) develop gross and fine motor skills, a higher level of social skills, and language skills; (b) achieve their program's educational goals; (c) decrease their socially unacceptable behavior; and (d) experience enjoyment. Thus, young children with disabilities need to be provided with opportunities to play. In inclusive classes where these children are integrated into a regular classroom, teachers need to be just as caring about their play as about that of the other typically developing children in the class. Children with disabilities may have specific difficulties that prevent them from playing in the same way as their typically developing peers. For these children, teachers need to consider their particular disability and cautiously select activities and materials for their learning. For example, children with visual impairments and autism need more assistance in their play than do other children. Young children with disabilities need imitation games where they can imitate adults' and peers' behavior.

In helping children with disabilities play in the preschool classroom, teachers need to consider the nature of the children's disability and the type of play to be supported in the class. Each kind of disability will require different kinds of program modifications in various types of play such as symbolic play, social play, and educational play. Both symbolic play and social play are discussed in Chapter 2, while educational play is described in Chapter 5.

## Symbolic and Social Play

Children who participate in symbolic play use symbolic representations to convey their thoughts. Children who engage in social play interact with others to develop and improve their social skills. Spodek and Saracho (1994a) report a series of studies with children with Down Syndrome and autism. Children with Down Syndrome have a systematic progression in different hierarchal stages of symbolic play. On the other hand, children with autism exhibit serious deficits in symbolic play. Their initial levels for symbolic play skills and multischeme sequences relate to their skills in receptive language and nonverbal communication skills. Children with autism participate in less doll-directed play and in immature forms of play than other children including children with an intellectual disability. Their play skills depend on the seriousness of their disability. Teachers need to focus on improving the play skills of children with autism.

Since most children with disabilities have trouble communicating their ideas, they need to engage in symbolic play activities. The symbolic play of children with communication disorders can be improved when they use objects in their play. Abnormalities in the development of symbolic play relate to the severity of the children's language and vision disabilities. Children with visual impairments and autism have play skills that develop abnormally in both their sensorimotor and symbolic play.

Young children with disabilities develop a combination of immature and mature play patterns. These children can use play models and materials that promote more mature play levels. Careful selection of materials and social groups can help children with disabilities develop higher levels of play. Materials such as blocks, vehicles, books, dolls, rolling objects, and puzzles can be used. For those children with disabilities who have difficulty using a particular toy, teachers can introduce toys that require them to use skills that they have developed and then provide the child with toys where they have to learn to use different skills. For example, children with disabilities can play with a truck, a set of blocks, and a ball, because these toys require that the children use similar skills. Children with disabilities will then (1) establish eye contact with each toy; (2) grasp or pick it up; (3) position it for appropriate play (turn the truck around before rolling it to a partner, position the block above a tower or building, or place the ball in a way that a push would send it off to a playmate); and (4) let it go (push the truck toward a playmate, roll the ball toward a playmate).

Adapting toys can make up for various deficiencies in hand functioning. Toys can be attached to a surface with masking tape to make them stable. Toys that have a base can be fastened to a table. A restricted area can be established by putting toys on top of a cardboard box or tray with boundaries. Pull toys can be positioned on a track while objects that require a banging motion (such as tambourines) are placed in a wood frame with springs. Grasping aids (such as a universal cuff, quip cuff) assist children to grasp sticklike objects (for example, crayons). Cylindrical foam or tape and foam can be wrapped around the objects to add to the width of an object, which help children with cerebral palsy to hold the object.

## Children with an Intellectual Disability

Children with an intellectual disability lack spontaneity in play. They need to play with toys and materials that encourage and motivate their play behavior. Appropriate toys and materials need to

1. *Be durable enough to last for a long period of time.* Some children with an intellectual disability tend to bang toys or materials, especially if they become aggressive. They also put them in their mouth or push, pull, and throw them.
2. *Encourage concrete experiences.* Young children with an intellectual disability have not reached the symbolic or abstract stage. They overlook houses, dolls, or transportation vehicles that support symbolic and imaginative play, because they have not learned how to use them.
3. *Offer a positive psychological effect.* Some children with an intellectual disability may have a young mental age. Toys and materials need to be appropriate for their mental age.

Children with an intellectual disability have the same play needs and interests as their typically developing peers. Although they usually play in isolation and have difficulties in groups, they need to engage with a social group. Children with an intellectual disability need continuous social approval. Their social success motivates them to socially engage with their peers. They have difficulty coping with competition and may become aggressive when they lose. For these children, the cooperative qualities of play should be the focus.

## Children with Emotional Disabilities

Play can assist children with emotional disabilities to control their behaviors. When they learn to control materials, they will be able to control themselves and their interactions with peers. Children with emotional disabilities who have a limited range of experiences may lack social skills and are inadequate in their socialization experiences. They will be able to participate in group play experiences and acquire familiar friendships that prolong their interactions with their peers throughout the day. Group play fosters the relationships for the children with emotional disabilities and their peers. In addition, group play develops their social acceptance.

Play can reveal or control the feelings of the children with emotional disabilities. It can also decrease their confined hostility and anger. Through play, children with emotional disabilities are able to express themselves by their actions and obtain emotional satisfaction.

## Children Who Are Deaf and Hard-of-hearing

Children who are deaf and hard-of-hearing engage in more simple and unsocial play than typically developing children, although their social play improves in integrated settings. Play interactions are indispensable for all of the children's development. Children who are deaf and hard-of-hearing have the same sequence of normal patterns in developing their play skills. However, the developmental progress of children who are deaf and hard-of-hearing is influenced by their socioeconomic status, acquisition of hearing aids at an early age, and training or therapy they obtain in the early years. For example, some children who are deaf and hard-of-hearing may have difficulty with both object substitution and dramatic play. Their socioeconomic status and language experiences are crucial influences that affect their development of symbolic play.

The children who are deaf and hard-of-hearing have a communication deficiency that may delay their play development. Since verbal conversation is critical in the children's play, their limited verbal language capacity restricts the development of their cooperative make-believe play including the symbolic use of objects and sophisticated peer interactions.

Various children only have an expressive communication disorder, while others have a mixed receptive–expressive language disorder, which means that they have difficulty understanding and communicating meaning. These children struggle in symbolic play. Children with language disorders are unable to function in both unstructured and structured play situations like their typically developing peers. Conversely, they have more advanced symbolic play skills in different play situations than younger typically developing children with the same developmental level in their language. Some children who are deaf and hard-of-hearing and have communication disorders are able to interact through actions and objects without using speech.

Spontaneous play experiences can help children who are deaf and hard-of-hearing. They develop their natural movement capability. Complications that limit their freedom of movement become social disabilities instead of physical limitations. Social play offers them many opportunities for their social development.

Play can also help children who are deaf and hard-of-hearing to improve their speech. They need to communicate their interests and use play words as action words. Even though speech is usually less important to actions during the young children's play, through play children who are deaf and hard-of-hearing can expand their vocabulary.

Children who are deaf and hard-of-hearing may have play interests that resemble those of younger children. Their immature interests generally suggest a deficit in psychosocial maturation. Children who are deaf and hard-of-hearing typically need a range of experiences that can develop their social skills.

## Children with Visual Impairments

Children who are blind or who have other visual impairments develop their symbolic play slowly. When the eyes, hands and mouths of four-month-old or older infants who are blind become coordinated, they are able to explore objects, although their sensorimotor play is considerably delayed, but initially these infants constantly play with their own body, which defers their play with objects (like playing with dolls). However, they possess the same play needs and interests as their typically developing sighted peers. Vision is important for the play of infants with other visual impairments, These Children have the required movement skills, but they are usually scared to move freely. Once they become confident and lose their fear, they will become physically secure. Children with visual impairments need to use their other senses to do well in play. They like tactile games with blocks, toys, and materials that have a variety of textures and forms. Most of these children like to play with objects that have a specific form and they use touch to easily recognize objects. Complex shapes and soft, rather undefined objects, such as those made from fur or cotton, are confusing for children with visual impairments. They have difficulty recognizing these objects and may avoid using them. They can be provided with games where they change directions, stop, and begin to develop their kinesthetic sense and have opportunities to move flexibly. Children with visual impairments can develop movement skills better with games and other physical activities than through gymnastics and apparatus work. Many of them have difficulty with balance activities; but they generally can climb ropes or play with push toys, swings, seesaws, parallel bars, rings, and other equipment that mainly requires the sense of touch. They can communicate and be creative when they use their body and facial expressions in dramatics, mimetics, art, and dance.

Children with visual impairments like socializing with their peers and frequently develop close relationships with small groups within larger groups, which restricts their social development. They need to be presented with opportunities for social contact with large groups of children in order to learn to play effectively with their peers. They need to become secure, know that they are socially accepted, and understand that their impairment does not limit their participation and enjoyment of play. They need to be provided with personally satisfying play experiences that they enjoy both independently and with their peers.

## Children with Orthopedic or Physical Disabilities

The play experiences of children with orthopedic or physical disabilities need to be well-planned, modified, and organized in a way that they will be able to fully participate in their play. Their play experiences need to provide them with the opportunities to make choices. Pictures of different activities can be displayed a few inches apart on heavy laminated cardboard for children with orthopedic or physical disabilities to select an activity that is on the picture. They may use their fist to point to the appropriate picture to show their selection. Young children with cerebral palsy need materials and toys that they can see rather than touch. They have a limited range and less frequent play behaviors, but they have more frequent social behaviors among other groups of children with disabilities.

Many children with orthopedic or physical disabilities may find play challenging and complicated when they spend many hours in treatment or in the resource room. Those with the more serious disabilities are restricted in their participation in active games because they are not able to stand without support, walk or run with ease, or coordinate their hands and arms without difficulty. Since most children with orthopedic or physical disabilities are unable to move with ease, they may become more frustrated. Those of them who are able to move and enjoy active play can usually decrease their frustration. Many refuse to play with groups of children because they feel inferior, are self-conscious, and fear competition or self-testing.

## Children Who Are At-Risk

Although children who are at-risk do not have specific disabilities where their play environment needs to be modified, their needs must be taken into account in relation to their play. Children who are at-risk are described in relation to family poverty, alcohol and/or drug consumption, child abuse, school attendance, educational failure, and race and ethnicity. Studies indicate that many children who live in conditions of poverty display a developmental and intellectual disability. An impoverished environment and the parents' social environment affect the play of children who are at-risk.

## Children with Linguistic and Cultural Differences

Children with linguistic and cultural differences are born and socialized in a family environment to become productive citizens in their society. Family members belong to various cultures and have different languages. The children's hereditary environment makes them unique individuals within their family of origin and cultural heritage. The schools communicate society's values to children of different cultures and languages.

Language and culture are the predominant elements in children's lives. Culture defines their distinctive experiences whereas language assists them to communicate their culture in society. The children's curriculum needs to be "thoughtfully planned, challenging, engaging, developmentally appropriate, culturally and linguistically responsive, comprehensive, and likely to promote positive outcomes for all young children"(NAEYC, 2003, p. 2). The indicators of an effective curriculum are that: "children are active and engaged; the goals are clear and shared by all; the curriculum is evidence-based; the valued content is learned through investigation, play, and focused, intentional teaching; the curriculum builds on prior learning and experiences; and the curriculum is comprehensive" (NAEYC, 2003, p. 2).

Children with linguistic and cultural differences speak a language that differs from English. They become English language learners (ELLs) and need their curriculum to be modified. Multiple factors influence the effectiveness of a particular curriculum or instructional approach. Factors such as the children's exposure to their primary language and to

English, opportunities to experience learning in multiple languages, and varied of family involvement affect their early education experiences and learning.

Teachers need to help ELLs develop English vocabulary through incidentally multiple exposures to words in a variety of meaningful social contexts. An important adaptation for ELLs in preschool settings is to address the meaning of everyday words, phrases, and expressions in the context of play. In addition, teachers can help children learn vocabulary by using the children's first language strategically, such as using storybook reading activities and role playing the stories.

When children who are linguistically and culturally different learn how to use language, they understand social situations, develop their thinking skills, and are able to control their own actions and thoughts. Their culturally driven and socially mediated progression of language development helps them construct mental frameworks (or schemas) to understand their world. Language is a tool of thought that helps ELLs develop a repertoire of complex-thinking skills, which are the mental representations through which language and culture represent their world as play. This point of view is particularly important for young children dealing with two or more languages (García & Jensen, 2010) and cultures.

## Children Who Are Gifted

Children who are gifted have play abilities that are similar to those of older typically developing children, but they also have equivalent characteristics of typically developing children of their own age. Their peers enjoy playing with them. They are more imaginative and engage in more physical, social, and cognitive play; but their humor and usual impact in a play situation is the same as that of their typically developing peers.

Some teachers expect the children who are gifted to have the social maturity that corresponds with their cognitive ability. This expectation can only pressure children who are gifted to assume responsibilities they are not ready for. In the integrated classroom, children who are gifted are able to interact with their same-age typically developing peers in mutual areas of interest and also have the opportunity to do extremely well. Children who are gifted need to engage in areas that challenge and extend their intellectual ability. Play activities can (a) consist of special projects that are appropriate for them, (b) have mutual special interest areas, (c) be community-based learning activities, or (d) promote advanced academic work.

Children who are gifted need enrichment activities that are appropriate and reasonable for them. They need activities that promote their creativity and higher cognitive processes (like predicting, planning, decision-making). Activities need to develop their inquiry, problem solving, and affective abilities. The children who are gifted need to be provided with the most appropriate instructional processes ranging from scaffolding to acceleration and from direct instruction to inquiry. They need opportunities to develop and explore their interests and to select appropriate content, processes, and products (Henshon, 2010). It is important that teachers use play to promote their creativity, higher cognitive processes, executive operations, inquiry and problem solving abilities, and affective development.

Advanced materials need to be modified to keep the interest of the younger children who are gifted. They need opportunities to engage in independent and solitary work, explore self-selected activities, coordinate self-selected activities, and manage their own time. They need to learn how to socially and constructively interact with peers, share responsibilities, and comply with classroom rules. In play children who are gifted can learn to make group decisions and develop social skills.

## Educational Play

Preschool classes typically have four types of educational play, which are appropriate for *all* children and need to be part of play in an integrated class. A broad range of educational play experiences need to be provided for children with disabilities in an inclusive setting. Modifications for children who are at risk or children with linguistic and cultural differences would be to include stories and materials in their own language and from their own culture and home. This is particularly important in dramatic play. Educational play, which was discussed in Chapter 5, is composed of different types of play: Physical play, dramatic play, manipulative play, and games (see Table 5.1). The following are Saracho's (1984) brief descriptions of these types of play.

- In *manipulative play*, children manipulate miniature pieces of apparatus, such as puzzles, pegsets, or table-top construction sets. It also includes materials that teach self-help skills.
- *Physical play* requires large physical motions, either with or without equipment.
- In *dramatic play*, children imitate roles and relationships when they play with their peers.
- Simple *games* can be played by preschool children who are beginning to restrict their spontaneity, to become aware, and to follow rules in these games.

### Manipulative Play

In manipulative play children with disabilities play with small pieces of equipment like puzzles, cuisenaire rods, or pegs and pegboards. The manipulative materials help them learn self-care skills, which are essential for those young children with disabilities who have difficulty dressing themselves. They can use large dolls and dressing frames to practice dressing skills, to learn how to dress themselves. When children with disabilities dress a two foot tall, stuffed doll, they engage in snapping, buttoning, zippering, buckling, hooking, and lacing. The clothes have large heavy-duty fasteners, large hooks and snaps (like the ones on pants), large and flat buttons about one inch in diameter, and heavy zippers with a zipper-pull ring. They can also use dressing frames to learn self-care skills. Dressing frames have several fasteners (like the ones on their clothes) that are sewn to pieces of material.

Children with an intellectual disability usually use the manipulative materials in repetitive ways. When they explore the manipulative materials, they generally push, pull, and throw them. They typically put a puzzle together but may place pieces of the puzzles in their mouth. This behavior generally indicates a lower level of intellectual development. They are still exploring in their play and use the materials for self-stimulation. As they gain experiences using the materials, their play behavior becomes more organized. The children with an intellectual disability gradually gain manipulative skills with materials and learn to use the materials appropriately, for example spinning the wheels of a truck, turning a nut on a bolt, or placing pegs into a pegboard. Once the children with disabilities know how to use the materials, they can learn to classify different materials, eventually combining their various uses. For instance, children with an intellectual disability will be able to disconnect cars from a train, undress a doll, or untie a knot.

In using manipulative materials to teach skills to children with an intellectual disability, teachers may have to use task analysis, which refers to breaking down complex skills into sets of simpler skills that are easier for these children to learn. The children with an intellectual disability may need a considerable amount of guidance to help them learn how to use the materials.

Children with visual impairments have a malfunction in the eye or optic nerve due to their development or caused by an injury. The most apparent forms of visual impairment are blindness or limited visual acuity, such as myopia (nearsightedness), hyperopia (far sightedness), and astigmatism (an irregularity in the cornea or lens of the eyes). In reality, a small number of children with visual impairments are completely deficient in vision. Numerous kinds of visual impairments can be resolved with eye glasses or contact lenses, and then these children are able to function without a disability.

Manipulative materials offer children with visual impairments concrete experiences that help them to understand their environment and to learn cognitive concepts similarly to the other children in the classroom. When they use many different materials in manipulative play, they learn to identify and discriminate the physical attributes of objects.

Manipulative play activities need to allow children with visual impairments to use whatever residual visual skills they might have. Manipulative play can provide a range of tasks that require them to use many of their senses. They can learn to become aware of the sensory qualities of manipulative materials, either visually or by holding, tasting, smelling, shaking, and maybe dropping or throwing them. The materials should stimulate sensory awareness as well as help them to develop concepts and skills. Children with visual impairments manipulate objects, which stimulate their sensory awareness to the fullest. Manipulative materials serve more than one single purpose. For example, a set of pliable, rubber squeaky toy creatures can be squeaked with a light touch to encourage repetitive hand activities (tapping, squeezing, touching). Toys with several textures and bright colors motivate the children to explore the surface and help them to develop their pincer-grasp reflex. Also different figural characteristics of a toy can help the children with visual impairments to identify the various parts of the toy that represent the different parts of an animal such as the animal's face. The level of difficulty planned for these activities depends on the ability of the children with visual impairments.

Matching objects by shape or texture is one way that manipulative play can help the children with visual impairments improve their sensory experiences. Everyday objects that children with visual impairments know can be placed in a box; then they can put their hands in the box and identify the objects by touch. In another activity, children with visual impairments can match pieces of material by texture. They can select from two separate sets of cardboards that are covered with several materials of different textures (e.g., rough, smooth). A texture book can be made by gluing different textured materials to sheets of paper or cardboard for children to feel and compare. Manipulative materials can be comparable materials but of various sizes (such as various sized balls or boxes). They can be provided with a broad range of materials with different characteristics that the children with visual impairments can feel and compare in ways that do not require vision.

Children with orthopedic or physical disabilities need several modifications in their environment to engage in manipulative play. If they are not able to sit in a wheel chair, even when the furniture has been modified, they can lie down on the carpet to be able to use their hand–eye positioning. Children who have weak muscular control throughout their bodies can use a foam rubber roll under their chests when they sit at a table or lie on the floor. The foam roll raises their body weight from the floor, allows them to use their hands out in front of them, and places their head in a way that they are able to see their hands and the objects in front of them. In this position, they can control their head and shoulders. To make the roll more secure, foam rubber can be rolled with corrugated cardboard. If additional layers of cardboard are taped or tied together or if a hollow plastic pipe is used, rolls should be thicker. It is essential that the rolls are firmed and strong enough to stand the weight of the children with orthopedic or physical disabilities. The rolls can be wrapped with canvas bags that can be removed to be washed.

Tables for manipulative play need to be high enough for a wheelchair to be rolled under. Wooden or rubber stops are used to stabilize those wheelchairs that do not have locks, then children with orthopedic or physical disabilities can use their arms in manipulative play. Children who are not able to stand (such as those with crutches) or sit without support need to have tables that are built with recesses and strap harnesses. Wooden or metal poles are strapped to the child's body to free their hands and allow them to participate in manipulative play.

Several commercially made toys are available to help children with cerebral palsy manipulate materials independently. Such toys allow these children to use skilled fine movements and manipulate small parts. Effective modifications to develop active and independent play consist of stabilizing the toys, limiting the movement of movable toys, and offering grasping aids, manipulation aids, and switches.

## Physical Play

Children with an intellectual disability have limited physical skills, although they may seem to have a more normal physical than intellectual ability. They can perform primary reflex motor activities (jumping, running, throwing, climbing); but they learn how to hop, skip, and gallop later than their typically developing peers. Children with an intellectual disability may try to catch a ball with their wrists and arms rather than using their hands. Play materials need to be adapted for them to use. If they have trouble catching and throwing a ball, they may need larger, softer balls as well as additional opportunities to practice catching. They prefer concrete materials that they can control. Children with an intellectual disability are able to use toys without engaging in make-believe. They need to play with toys of interest to them. For instance, they will explore the characteristics of a new ball rather than how to use it. If children with an intellectual disability are not able to play with the ball immediately, they usually become frustrated. They may have to be directly taught how to use playground equipment that other children are able to use with ease. It is important that when children with an intellectual disability are not able to use the equipment appropriately, they don't become overly frustrated and instead continue to have a desire to play.

Children with an intellectual disability tend to have less physical energy and will tire easily. During physical play, teachers need to be aware of and assist those children who show signs of fatigue. They need to be encouraged to rest during their play or shift from more active play to play that does not require such high energy levels.

Children with emotional disabilities find physical play relaxing and emotionally satisfying, although hyperactive children need to have their play controlled to help them avoid becoming overly tired. Children who are hyperactive can engage positively in large motor activities. Some children with emotional disabilities have a fear of failure and will avoid playing. Teachers need to modify these children's physical play to make sure that they will succeed and not become frustrated. Teachers need to use strategies that will encourage children with emotional disabilities to participate and succeed in their physical play.

Children with emotional disabilities need to have a feeling of emotional satisfaction and relaxation from successful physical play.

Children with visual impairments are scared of falling and sometimes refuse to engage in physical play. Physical play activities that require them to use a great deal of skill may be worthless to them and must be adapted for them to enjoy these activities. These children, however, can participate in several physical play activities. Children with visual impairments have limited vision and need to adapt to movement to an environment they are not able to see completely. With appropriate adaptations, they can engage in a broad range of physical play activities, such as water play. In water play, they learn to pour; they listen to the sounds they hear when pouring to determine the degree to which a container is filling up. Learning to pour is related to practical life skills, like serving juice or milk. They need to be provided with auditory discrimination exercises, such as listening to the sound of liquid pouring into a container and learn the concepts of full and half-full. They need to learn to use sound to estimate the depth of the liquid and avoid spilling. Children with visual impairments can engage in variations of this activity. They can pour sand rather than water and discover that all of the sand in a small jar can be poured into a large jar whereas if the sand from a large jar is poured into a smaller one, some of the sand will spill.

While visual imperfections of the children with visual impairments do not interfere with their ability to function physically, sometimes they refuse to engage in physical activities. They are scared of falling or hurting themselves. Frequently their fear keeps them from developing and performing physical skills. In addition, children with visual impairments need to develop a feeling of balance in moving about and to learn to use auditory clues to acquire better skills in their movements. They need to have balance to be able to use specific play equipment (e.g., seesaws, swings, push toys, climbing ropes, rings). Fortunately, children with visual impairments are able to learn to move about skillfully and to bounce a ball, skip, hop, and even roller skate.

Children with visual impairments can enjoy outdoor play. They are able to use swings, slides, ropes, rings, and seesaws. They find the trees, wind, rain, and other natural elements to be exciting. They can learn about seasonal changes in nature and enjoy seasonal activities (like kite flying, snow games).

Additional physical activities for children with visual impairments consist of bouncing a ball, skipping, and hopping. They can be provided with ropes, ground rails, and special markers to help them move around the playground without difficulty. Balls can have bells inside them to help children with visual impairments locate them as they listen to the sound the ball makes and catch or hit it after detecting its sound. In learning a game, children with visual impairments may be unable to imitate their peers' actions; therefore, they need to be verbally guided on how to use equipment or how to join in play. Teachers may have to physically guide the children's movement when introducing a physical activity. They can learn to roller skate with one skate first and then two.

Children who are deaf and hard-of-hearing can participate in physical play without any modifications. Their physical skills are typically the same as the other classroom children. They enjoy participating in physical activities and find physical play rewarding.

Children with orthopedic or physical disabilities need special attention during physical play. Impaired body mechanics is a characteristic of children with orthopedic or physical disabilities. They require special attention during their physical play. The physical therapist can offer special recommendations or the equipment may be especially adapted based on their disability. Precautions need to be taken for their safety. For example, a grass or pebble surface may create difficulties in the navigation of children who are in a wheel chair or on crutches. In planning physical play, it is important to consider the extent of the child's disability, particularly the physical features of the classroom, the outdoor play area, and the school. Regardless of their limitations, the physical play of children with orthopedic or physical disabilities can help them develop their basic motor and social skills.

The physical play of children who are in wheel chairs may depend on the help of others (such as teacher aides, volunteer adults, high school students). These children need wheelchair leaders to help them participate in some physical activities. Both the leader and the children with orthopedic or physical disabilities benefit when they participate in a favorite game.

Some children with orthopedic or physical disabilities are unable to run fast. Since running is part of their program, they can run slowly and wear small football helmets or felt headbands to protect them from falls. They can also be paired with a peer to complete a task. If each child finishes part of a task, then both can complete the task together.

## Dramatic Play

Children with an intellectual disability have limited imaginations, which affects their dramatic play. Their dramatic play is usually simple (such as playing cops and robbers, playing house and dolls). Children with an intellectual disability pursue and capture; shoot and escape; and play with dolls, toy dishes, and furniture. They play in the housekeeping center and engage in feeding, dressing, and group living. They imitate roles that are simple, nonverbal, and from their daily lives. Teachers can read stories to children with an intellectual disability for them to act out the roles in the stories. When they act out stories with their peers, peer play tutoring can occur.

Children with emotional disabilities use dramatic play as catharsis. In acting out conflicting situations, they free themselves of feelings with which they cannot cope in the real world. However, children with emotional disabilities should be allowed to disclose only those feelings that they can deal with. Since dramatic play is symbolic, teachers may have difficulty interpreting the meanings of these children's dramatic play. Dramatic play for children with emotional disabilities is important, because it helps them to cope with difficult feelings, to participate in play that they enjoy and to communicate their thoughts. Puppets, pantomimes, charades, and field trips (for example exhibits, museums, libraries) can enrich the dramatic play of children with emotional disabilities.

Children with visual impairments usually spend most of their dramatic play time in a world of fantasy. Acting out the different roles in dramatic play increases their imagination, gives them enjoyment, and reduces their self-consciousness. These children need to be encouraged to assume different roles in addition to pretending to be other people. Children with visual impairments can pretend to be the wind, a kitten, or a flower. They also can act out events from their daily lives such as setting the table or baking a cake. Dramatic play helps such children to become more aware of both the physical and social world that surrounds them. Play activities need to be carefully planned for children with visual impairments to be able to engage in dramatic play with all of the classroom children.

Children who are deaf and hard-of-hearing need to engage in dramatic play, because play of a social nature is of great importance to them and helps them to develop their social skills. Experiences in dramatic play help them to engage in various social situations. Also, since dramatic play is socially interactive, its play activities enhance their speech and language development.

Children who are at-risk may not have definite disabilities that require that their play be modified. Nevertheless, their needs must be considered in relation to their play. Parents' social environment affects their children's social development. For example, parental rejection influences the social isolation of the parent–child relationship, whereas parental acceptance increases the children's involvement with other adults. Parents (mothers and/or fathers) can be invited to participate with the children in the classroom during their play. Children who are at-risk can act out roles with other children's parents or with their own parents in the dramatic play area. They will be able to identify with and assume different roles. Children who are at-risk can use play as a catharsis for feelings they need to cope with. In dramatic play, they can express their feelings about their situations. Children who are at-risk enjoy the experiences, express their feelings, and obtain meanings from the activities. Puppets, pantomimes, and an assortment of props can motivate them to act out the different roles of other persons.

The play environment needs to stimulate the imagination of children who are at-risk to act out family roles. Stories, pictures, and interesting field trips can motivate them to assume different roles. Children from various socioeconomic statuses can act out their family situations, or circumstances they may wish to take place at their home. Most children who are at risk have a network made up of relatives and friends. When these children face a situation that needs a social readjustment and assistance to relieve their stress, they rely on this network. Teachers can assist families to build networks that can increase the children's play.

## Games

Children with an intellectual disability enjoy playing games with simple rules and much repetition. Games need to be carefully selected. Through games they gain and retain knowledge as well as learn concepts and skills. Children with an intellectual disability need games that (a) have few simple directions, (b) place no strain on their memory, (c) have appealing names, and (d) use simple equipment. At first, some children with an intellectual disability may have trouble understanding a game. They can perform sections of the game (such as ball throwing, running, tagging) and finally merge all the different parts. Teachers need to patiently explain the games and provide children with an intellectual disability with opportunities to practice parts of the game until they become sufficiently competent to fully participate in a game without causing frustration to the rest of the class. For example, if they practice throwing a ball or running along a line, they can recall the appropriate progression. Movements (running, climbing, turning, jumping) that they enjoy make it possible for them to learn games and stunts. Games that involve singing, dancing, and storytelling help children with an intellectual disability develop their reasoning and memory. These games should be introduced at the beginning of the school day to avoid any distractions.

Children with emotional disabilities may have difficulty participating in games, even if these games promote their cooperative or competitive skills. Cooperation may not always be possible; games that are intellectual, competitive, or require separate score-keeping may be too stressful for some children. Children with emotional disabilities need to participate in simple games, because they have a short interest span. Games that require physical contact between players may cause problems and need to be avoided. However, if children with emotional disabilities experience success, they will experience an extreme fulfillment from playing out a game, which is a similar feeling to the one they get after they finish a product or a work of art.

Children who are deaf and hard-of-hearing are able to play active games with other children, but they have problems with imaginative language games. Since they have difficulties learning new games, they cling to the old games. They do not want to modify games, make up new ones, or learn new games. Children who are deaf and hard-of-hearing do not have any problems with the structure of games, but they have difficulties with the language elements. They may have problems hearing the directions and are not able to follow the rules. Games such as tug-of-war, relay races, and any team games do not require verbal communications and promote both competition and cooperation. The children who are deaf and hard-of-hearing need to understand the directions in a game. Teachers need to provide instructions at the beginning of the game and should not expect for these children to learn them from other children. If the teaching method used is comprehensive, the children will learn what to do. They will not forget a game, skill, or dance.

Teachers can introduce verbal games to children who are deaf and hard-of-hearing as group games where responses are provided in unison. They need to know the details of a new game. If they are not able to understand all of the auditory cues, such cues need to be modified.

Children with visual impairments need games that are neither so difficult as to cause frustration nor so simple as to cause resentment. Simple games suggest to them that they are incompetent whereas difficult games frustrate them. Through games children with visual impairments learn size, shape, and physical arrangement. When they play the game repeatedly in the same location, children with visual impairments feel safe. Since these children memorize everything in a play space (like equipment, movable facilities), they need to be informed if anything changes. Teachers can assist these children when they play in a small group. Children with visual impairments cannot read nonverbal messages (such as glances, facial expressions); therefore, during the game, everybody needs to talk about the game for these children to hear so they do not feel left out of anything. They also need to know exactly where everybody (teacher, other players) is located. Everybody needs to talk to one another and to the children with visual impairments, identify themselves and their locations, and let the children with visual impairments know where they are and what they are doing. Teachers need to (a) provide them with encouragement, (b) offer them a permissive approach, and (c) motivate their imagination. Children with visual impairments do not need to be spoiled. They need to enjoy a game that is fun and challenging.

Children with orthopedic or physical disabilities can play basic childhood games using vigorous, skillful movements of their arms and move objects through space. They can also play with equipment they can handle. Large, light balls, beanbags, or balloons can be used for throwing. Children with orthopedic or physical disabilities can also use projectiles that return automatically, because there is a string attached or because the surface is tiled. They also need additional teacher guidance, limited play space for games, and light equipment to limit the movement area. Children with orthopedic or physical disabilities usually prefer games that they already know, particularly noncompetitive ones, over new and unfamiliar ones. Games need to be modified to accommodate children who use crutches or a wheelchair. For example, they can play circle toss or volleyball games with a rubber balloon, because the balloon moves and falls slowly. They can just tap it lightly enough to keep the balloon in the air, while a strong hit will not knock it out of bounds.

Children who are at risk enjoy attractive games and prefer games that are of interest to them. They like games that have bright colors, texture, and shape. They prefer games that involve singing, pantomiming, and stories that are appealing to them.

## Children with Linguistic and Cultural Differences

Children need to be exposed to games from multiple cultures to promote understanding, tolerance, and interest in other languages, cultures, and societies. Multicultural games can help young children understand and appreciate different languages and cultures. Young children need to play fun and stimulating multicultural games such as the ones discussed below.

1, 2, 3 Dragon is a Chinese game that can be discussed and played during the Chinese New Year. The children stand in a line where the first child in line is the head and the last child is the tail. Children hold on to the shoulders of the child in front of them. All scream, "1, 2, 3 Dragon!" At this point, the "head" runs around to catch the "tail." When any of the children lose hold of the child in front, the round is over, the "head" becomes the tail, and the next child in line becomes the "head."

Stick game from Chile is a popular game and is usually played outside. For indoor play, use a Christmas-tree stand.

1. One end of the stick is buried to make it stand up straight.
2. Draw a circle around the stick that is approximately three feet or one meter in diameter leaving the stick in the middle of the circle.
3. Place a penny on top of the stick.
4. Children will stand around five feet away from the stick.
5. Each child will use a different penny and take turns trying to knock the penny off the stick.
6. Each child will get a point every time the penny is knocked off the stick and out of the circle. The child with the most points wins.

## Physical Environment

The physical environment needs to be meticulously assessed to assist the children with diverse needs to function more effectively. Each child's abilities must be taken into account in creating a play environment and modifying the play experiences in an integrated setting. It is essential that the classroom is safe for all children, particularly for the children with disabilities. An environment may be safe for typically developing children but not for children with disabilities. For instance, the arrangement of the furniture in a class might seem to be safe; however, children with visual impairments use their memory and kinesthetic senses to move around in the classroom's physical space. These children need to be notified before any change in the classroom's physical arrangement is made. Also the classroom furniture needs to be modified for children with orthopedic or physical disabilities. The indispensable modification is to place rubber tips on the table legs to keep the table from sliding.

In addition to making sure that the environment is safe for the children with disabilities, teachers need to find ways to increase the opportunities for these children to play in satisfying and educational ways. Play materials must be carefully selected to motivate these children to use them with ease. Teachers have to be aware of the modifications required in arranging the play environment and making materials available for children with diverse needs. Two elements of play for *all* young children are novelty in play and flexibility in exercises of several schemas on specific play objects.

The social environment is also important. Teachers may invite typically developing children to play with children with diverse needs. Teachers need to determine how many of these children at a time might be invited to play, and what type of guidance these children need. The social environment is very important to children who have linguistic and cultural differences. Young children and their families characterize an increasing diversity of language and culture. Teachers need to provide children with an environment that values diversity and supports their relationship with their families and community as well as maintaining the children's home language and cultural uniqueness. Such support requires that teachers recognize, understand, respect, and accept their cultural and language differences (Saracho, 2010c).

## Summary

Play is an important part of young children's life both at home and in school. It is essential that the play environment includes young children both with and without disabilities, as well as that teachers recognize the specific needs and limitations resulting from each child's specific disability. Such knowledge is used in designing an environment as productive as possible and in providing valuable play opportunities that are fun, educational, and practical for all children. Children with diverse needs are challenged by a condition that interferes with the normal progress of their development. As is true of every child, all have a need and right to play and it is the teachers' responsibility to provide the appropriate environment and opportunities for this to occur.

A play environment for children who have diverse needs must include a variety of play centers that support *all* children in their play. Learning centers (such as housekeeping, block building, manipulative materials, library, music) are a practical way to arrange play materials. Each learning center should include materials for all children to use. Learning centers are discussed in detail in Chapter 5.

The play environment must be safe for all children. Some situations may be safe for typically developing children but may be dangerous for children with disabilities. The safety of play materials and settings is as important as their developmental appropriateness. Boundaries and rules must be established and clearly communicated, such as acceptable behaviors within the play centers. Dramatic play centers need to include props for play, such as dress-up clothing and different artifacts that describe the play themes of interest to all of the children.

Manipulative play centers should include tables and chairs that are appropriate for all children. Manipulative materials need to be displayed in ways that convey easy access for *all* children and easy return of materials for storage and cleanup. Either indoor or outdoor physical play must offer sufficient space and appropriate equipment. Attention should be given to the children's safety. Children can play games in different settings based on the type of game.

While it is important to consider the situations and requirements of children with diverse needs, it is important to keep in mind the fact that they are first and foremost children, whose basic needs are similar to those of *all* children. These basic needs must be the teachers' major focus to be able to guide children with diverse needs toward productive educational experiences and to help them become an important member of the class.

This chapter introduced children with diverse needs in relation to their characteristics when they play. It also discussed the importance of play and how play can be adapted based on the characteristics of children with diverse needs including those children with disabilities, those at-risk, and those who have linguistic and cultural differences. In this chapter, it is assumed that children with diverse needs are challenged by a condition that interferes with the normal progress of their development. It described play experiences for children who have diverse needs and their symbolic and social play, educational play, and physical environment. In addition, throughout the following curriculum chapters, more examples are provided on using play with children who have diverse needs and are placed in inclusive settings.

# Chapter 7
# Social Studies-play Learning Experiences

Education in its broadest sense, is the means of this social continuity in life.

(Dewey, 1916, p. 3)

A major educational goal is to transmit culture or a way of life to young children. Social studies helps them to gain the knowledge, skill, attitudes, and values that are required to persevere in society. It focuses on people and their interactions with others and the whole environment to impart a way of life, while at the same time it builds the skills, knowledge, attitudes, and values children need to change and improve their way of life. Social studies embraces all disciplines from the social science field. Everything concerning the nature of people and the world, the heritage of the past, and all of contemporary living is considered to be social studies (Seefeldt et al., 2009). The National Council for the Social Studies (NCSS, 2008a), the most prevalent professional organization for social studies educators in the world, describes social studies as:

> the integrated study of the social sciences and humanities to promote civic competence. Within the school program, social studies provides coordinated, systematic study drawing upon such disciplines as anthropology, archaeology, economics, geography, history, law, philosophy, political science, psychology, religion, and sociology, as well as appropriate content from the humanities, mathematics, and natural sciences. The primary purpose of social studies is to help young people make informed and reasoned decisions for the public good as citizens of a culturally diverse, democratic society in an interdependent world (p. 6).

Social studies promotes the children's civic competence including the knowledge, intellectual processes, and dispositions that they need to be active and engage in groups and public life. Civic competence helps children learn the ideas and values of democracy. It also helps them develop the ability to use knowledge about their community, nation, and world. Young children need to become knowledgeable, skillful, and committed to democracy so as adults they can help sustain and improve their democratic way of life as members of a global community (NCSS, 2008a).

Young children need to be provided with purposeful and meaningful learning experiences that are challenging, of high quality, and developmentally appropriate. Social studies education needs to be integrated into the children's curriculum for them to become effective participants in a democratic society. They need to become independent and cooperative to solve problems that focus on complex social, economic, ethical, and personal concerns. Young children need the knowledge, skills, and attitudes to become informed and thoughtful members of society. The social studies curriculum needs to focus on concepts from the four core social studies disciplines: civics, economics, geography and history.

Young children who are in a strong social studies program learn to develop a crucial foundation to participate as citizens throughout their lives. Both America and the world are quickly changing and are living in a far more multiethnic, multiracial, multi-lingual, multi-religious and multicultural context. Early childhood teachers need to be prepared to value and to teach a far more diverse group of young children and their families than they did in the past. Social studies is essential in the early childhood curriculum, because it prepares young children to understand and participate effectively in an increasingly complex world.

Young children need to be provided with opportunities to explore the variety and complexity of human experience through a dynamic and meaningful education. They need to be grounded in democratic principles and immersed in developmentally appropriate democratic strategies to obtain the basic skills that prepare them to respectfully and intelligently work together in a country and world marked by globalization, interdependence, human diversity, and societal change. The purpose of this chapter is to describe early childhood education pioneers in Social Studies, contemporary early childhood influences, the program, curriculum knowledge, play learning centers, prop boxes, field trips, museums, and thematic units in social studies.

## Social Studies Early Childhood Education Pioneers

Several early childhood education pioneers proposed innovative and meaningful social studies approaches for young children. Patty Smith Hill, who was influenced by John Dewey, believed that the children's social experiences are the basis for knowledge. Dramatic play themes can help children learn about the world. Children role play their experiences with their family, friends, and community. Such experiences can be repeated, interpreted, and expanded (Hill, 1913).

Another early childhood pioneer, Lucy Sprague Mitchell (1934), developed a program where the young children's experiences in their personal environment helped them to learn basic concepts about geography. She included concrete materials that would help young children understand abstract ideas that provided them with sophisticated knowledge. Maria Montessori (1912) also created concrete materials to help young children understand abstract ideas. She used time lines to help young children place historical events within a temporal framework. For example, children could understand the relationship between events within the framework of historical time when they measured distance with a rope to represent time. Children were able to get a sense of geography when they worked with map puzzles.

In the 1930s, progressive educators like John Dewey suggested that social studies be the basis for activity-based learning using the children's interests. Dewey advocated that learning required firsthand experiences and various instructional resources. He believed that developmentally appropriate learning and teaching activities were needed to help children go from familiar to unknown daily life experiences (Dewey 1916). For farming communities, children can plant wheat in the classroom, observe the process of the plants' growth, and document their progress, whereas city children can learn about the work of the milk wagon driver and the chimney sweep (Mindes, 2005).

## Contemporary Early Childhood Influences

In the 1960s, Jerome Bruner's (1960) work supported the child-centered curricular and instructional approach for social studies. Bruner suggested a spiraling curriculum to teach children social studies topics, such as democracy, in a developmentally appropriate way. For example, young children could establish classroom rules to keep order and be fair to everybody (Mindes, 2005). Bruner's approach contributed to inquiry-based teaching that became the major way to teach social studies. He also emphasized learning by doing in the social studies learning process.

## Social Studies Program

In social studies, young children study the political, economic, cultural, and environmental components of societies in the past, present, and future. The social studies content includes the areas of history, economics, geography, political science, sociology, anthropology, archaeology, and psychology. These rich, interrelated disciplines are essential to the background of thoughtful citizens. Pace (2007), a university professor who has a point of view that is widely held by social studies educators, believes that

> depth of historical, political, and cultural understanding is essential if this democracy is to survive and thrive. Powerful social studies teaching helps students develop enduring understandings in the core content areas of civics, economics, geography, and history, and assures their readiness and willingness to assume citizenship responsibilities. Powerful social studies learning leads to a well-informed and civic-minded citizenry that can sustain and build on democratic traditions.

For young children and all age groups, social studies serve several purposes. The social studies curriculum provides them with the knowledge and understanding of the past that is important for them (1) to manage the present and plan for the future; (2) to help them to understand and participate effectively in their world; and (3) to communicate their relationship to other people and to social, economic, and political institutions. According to NCSS (2008b), the purpose of social studies for young children is

> to establish a learning environment and instruction to enable each student to understand, participate, and make informed decisions about their world. Social studies explain students' relationships to other people, to institutions, and to the environment.

It equips them with the knowledge and understanding of the past necessary for coping with the present and planning for the future. It provides them with the skills for productive problem solving and decision making, as well as for assessing issues and making thoughtful value judgments. Above all, it integrates these skills and understandings into a framework for responsible citizen participation, whether in the school, the community, or the world (pp. 1–2).

Social studies content offers young children the ability to be able to effectively solve problems, make decisions, assess issues, and make thoughtful value judgments. Most importantly, social studies assist young children to integrate these abilities and understandings into a framework for responsible citizen participation in their play group, the school, the community, or the world (NCSS, 1988).

A social studies curriculum uses strategies and activities for children to participate in important ideas and helps them (a) to relate what they are learning to what they already know and to current issues, (b) to be critical and creative thinkers about what they are learning, and (c) to apply that learning to their life situations. Active learning goes beyond hands-on. According to the NCSS (2008b)

- Children can understand concepts, make decisions, discuss issues, and solve problems when they work independently and collaboratively with a rich variety of sources.
- Children need to have opportunities to construct meaning. Children need to be provided with clear explanations, allowed to ask and answer questions, discuss or debate implications, and work with projects where they use their critical thinking.
- Children need to be provided with experiences where they analyze the social studies content using several different learning modes.

The social studies curriculum integrates the complete human experience over time and space, connecting the past with the present and the future. It focuses on the core social science disciplines and includes knowledge from the arts, sciences, and humanities, from current events, from local examples, and from the children's personal lives (NCSS, 2008b).

Usually in an early childhood social studies program, the young children's experiences consist of things and events that are close to them in time and space. Themes relate to home and family, school (e.g., the classroom), neighborhood (e.g., stores, supermarkets, gas stations), local community (e.g., community services, agencies, workers), transportation, and communication. Children can compare similarities and differences among communities (e.g., urban community versus rural or suburban community). As young children accumulate experiences, their learning expands to things that are more remote in time and space. For example, their learning about family life can extend to other countries, a broader comparative community study, and concepts from the social sciences. Young children can also learn the relationship between consumers and producers in the area of economics. They can also become aware of the actions and interactions among people from the field of sociology. According to Saracho and Spodek (2007a), developmentally appropriate social studies concepts for young children are obtained from the following areas:

- *Teaching History* is important for the young children's intellectual development, because they learn important concepts about time and history. Four-year-olds can distinguish between past and present and five- and six-year olds understand the cyclical and sequential nature of events. When young children learn about historical events and ideas, they can learn about important time concepts in relation to history. (See Box 7.1.)

### Box 7.1. Teaching about Personal History Using a Time Line

Cut a length of rope allowing about one foot for every year of each child's age. Mark it by one foot (one year) segments, marking one end birth and the other end with the age of the child. Send home notes asking the children's parents to send pictures or souvenirs depicting their child at different ages, noting those ages (for example, photos, first shoes, baby toy, and the like). Have the children attach the article at the proper interval on the rope. Have the children talk about themselves when they were different ages. Discuss how each child has changed (Spodek & Saracho, 1994b, p. 422).

- *Teaching Geography.* The world is a laboratory that helps young children understand space in relation to geographic concepts (Mitchell, 1934) such as topological space (proximity, enclosure, continuity, separation, order). Young children need to know how things relate to each other in space to understand geographic (Sunal, 1993) concepts. Then they can interpret simple maps from their environment. (See Box 7.2.)

### Box 7.2. Creating Maps

Encourage children to draw and make their own maps. They can draw make believe maps of places they have visited or just imagined. They can use felt markers, but let them use blocks and milk cartons as well, for a three-dimensional approach. Children may build, draw, or paint maps well before they are able to read them (Fromboluti & Seefeldt, 1999, p. 10).

- *Political Socialization.* Young children are natural political thinkers (Sunal & Haas, 2007). They can learn about the electoral process, the voting process, and the qualifications for local and national candidates. Taking advantage of these events can help young children become politically socialized. For example, during elections, children can talk about the offices and candidates. Then they can role play the electoral process to understand it. Young children can pretend to have elections for the candidates or elect class officers. (See Box 7.3.)

### Box 7.3. Holding a Class Election

Have the children vote on some element in the curriculum (for example, their favorite story of the ones read that week, their favorite song of those sung that week, their favorite activity center). Talk with the children about the process: that each person makes only one choice and that each person's choice is noted as a "vote," that each vote is tallied, and that the one with the largest number of votes is the winner. Primary grade children can mark secret ballots that they insert into a ballot box. These ballots are then counted by a committee of children and the results are announced to the class. Younger children might be asked to place blocks one atop the other in the pile labeled for their particular candidate. Young children will thus be able to see the results of their vote. Discuss the fact that while not everyone voted for the winner, the final result reflects the views of the entire class.

If there is an election, the children could similarly hold mock elections in their class (Spodek & Saracho, 1994b, p. 424).

- *Economics.* Even five-year-olds can learn and use economic concepts to make decisions. Very young children have economic knowledge such as economic attitudes, their first direct experiences, and cognitive abilities. Young children have daily economic experiences such as when they go with their parents to stores and buy products. They watch the transactions and learn that each item has a price that can be bought using money. Young children can role play these roles. (See Box 7.4.)

### Box 7.4.  A Classroom Bake Sale

The teacher can organize a bake sale with the children. The children can make cookies, brownies, or other treats that they can sell to the children in the school. Let them keep track of what they pay for the ingredients. The children should determine the price of each item sold. They can discuss whether they want to lose money, earn money, or make no profit from their sale. The sale could be advertised in the school, with notices on bulletin boards, announcements over the school public address system (if there is one), or in other ways the children think up. Set a time for the sale and arrange the various roles: who will be salesperson, who will collect money, who will make change. If young children will need help with the sale, parents or older children might be enlisted. After the sale, figure out, with the children, whether they made or lost money. If money was made, the children could decide how to spend it: for example, buy something for the class, have a party, or make a contribution to a charitable cause (Spodek & Saracho, 1994b, p. 426).

Social studies continue to focus on teaching young children through an integrated, project-oriented approach. Preschool children might study why, in December, people in Florida wear different clothes than the people in New York. Children may be provided with opportunities to explore how climate helps people determine which clothes people need to wear during the year. Children might look at weather maps; develop weather charts; read stories about weather and clothes; listen to the weather channel on television; explore the weather on the internet; and draw, cut, and paste pictures from magazines or the Internet to compare climatic differences (Mindes, 2005). *The House of Four Seasons* (Duvoisin, 1956) and *A Tree Is Nice* (Udry, 1987) are good books to help children compare the seasons and discuss the different climates.

Concepts in social studies have been organized around the young children's basic human needs in their home, community, the wider society, and communities more remote in time and space. Children best learn these concepts through themes like the school, family, neighborhood, and municipality. For example, for a theme about a bakery, the children can take a field trip to the bakery. They see that customers select and pay for bread. Children might be given some money so they, too, can buy bread. When they return to their classroom, they can go to the bakery that has been set up in the dramatic play area. Children can role play their interpretations of the field trip to obtain meaning from this experience. All of the children's experiences need to be developmentally appropriate based on the children's learning abilities (Saracho & Spodek, 2007a).

In social studies, young children learn to live and work together with others within small and large communities, beginning with the family, classroom, and community. They also need to learn developmentally appropriate concepts from the social sciences, which are the basis for social education (Saracho & Spodek, 2007b). NCSS (2009) advocate the importance of a high quality social studies curriculum for young children. That is, even the youngest children in schools need powerful, insightful, and active teaching, because they will become the leaders of tomorrow. Therefore, it is important to reinforce children, their community, family, school, and the larger societies in which adults and children, in all their diversity, interact and learn.

Young children need to learn how to become effective members of a democratic society. The world requires them to become independent and cooperative problem solvers of social, economic, ethical, and personal concerns; therefore social studies becomes as important as subject areas like reading, writing, and computing. Young children need to have the knowledge, skills, and attitudes to become informed and thoughtful members of society. However, an effective social studies program builds on the children's prior learning and experiences. A social studies program also values learning that fosters respect for others; equality, fairness, and justice. It also nurtures the children's abilities to become critical and creative thinkers and to become involved in the community. Young children need to gain knowledge and understanding of their world to be able to become successful members of a society that is diverse and global. Social studies in early childhood education can be used to support multicultural education in different ways. It facilitates the presentation of individual cultures of the children in the classroom. In social studies, teachers can plan and integrate a variety of cultural activities in their classrooms. An effective social studies program offers the children the appropriate environment for them to become productive members of a democratic society (NCSS, 2008b).

## Curriculum Knowledge in Social Studies

Social studies helps young children to become responsible within the larger community and to understand the organization of their society. They become aware of our society's values, rituals, symbols, and myths. In social studies young children can learn (1) the different celebrations of holidays, (2) stories about historic figures and heroes, and (3) traditional songs that will help them understand the organization of society and their expected roles and behaviors (Saracho & Spodek, 2007b).

Social studies can be integrated with other areas of knowledge in the curriculum. A social studies unit can facilitate preschool children's learning of math and science concepts (Charlesworth, 1988). They build with blocks, models, or dioramas as part of a unit. Then children act out, learn social roles, and learn ways to express themselves. They use pictures, paintings, drawings, and constructions to informally communicate what they have learned.

Music and literature assist young children to become aware of the symbol system and values of a culture. High quality children's literature helps them to learn about people, institutions, and social relationships that may be difficult for children to understand. When characters in good literature share their feelings, young children are able to sympathize with the characters even before they can intellectually understand them. Ethnic music, songs, stories, and poetry contribute to the young children's social learning. Major topological concepts in geometry assist young children to understand geography and maps. In map reading, young children locate places and estimate proximity and separation.

Young children use puppets to dramatize social events. Books inform children about such social events. They use this information to create and write a story that expresses their understanding of these social events. Language helps young children to understand the information and share it with their peers. They role play to explore the different roles and their relationships in their dramatic play. Teachers can also present dramatic play activities that reflect various cultures in their classrooms.

## Curriculum Standards

The NCSS (2008a) has developed curriculum standards for social studies to provide a principled framework that will guide teachers in selecting and organizing knowledge and modes of inquiry for purposes of instruction. The curriculum standards provide themes to use in organizing the social studies curriculum for all ages. Some themes may be more dominant for a particular age group, although all themes (see Table 7.1) are highly interrelated.

The thematic strands draw from several related disciplines to provide a framework for a social studies curriculum design. They are appropriate for all age levels from several disciplines including history, geography, civics, economics, psychology, and other fields. The Consortium for Interdisciplinary Teaching and Learning (1994), which included the major national subject-matter organizations (e.g., National Council of Teachers of Mathematics, the National Council of Teachers of English, the International Reading Association, the National Science Teachers' Association, the National Council for the Social Studies, the Speech Communication Association, and the Council for Elementary Science International) developed a joint position paper to address the need for curricula that would focus on conceptual learning that is integrated across traditional subject areas from preschool to the fourth grade. These organizations claim that young children's educational experiences must stimulate their natural curiosity and their drive to create meaning. They emphasize the importance of a relationship across disciplines that can nurture the children's creative problem solving and decision making. Such a relationship provides young children with the opportunity to consider the perspectives, knowledge, and data-gathering skills of all the disciplines. It would also motivate young children to interact with others in a learning community where diversity in cultures is valued.

## Designing Social Studies Integrated Play Learning Centers

The classroom environment can be set up to recreate the real world where children play, explore, and learn. Thus, "the entire spirit of school is renewed. It has a chance to affiliate itself with life, to become the child's habitat, where he learns through directed living instead of only a place to learn lessons, having an abstract and remote reference to some possible

**TABLE 7.1.** Curriculum Standard Themes in Social Studies

| Curriculum Standard Theme | Description |
| --- | --- |
| Culture | Social studies curriculum should include experiences that provide for the study of culture and cultural diversity |
| Time, Continuity, and Change | Social studies programs should include experiences that provide for the study of the ways human beings view themselves in and over time |
| People, Places, and Environments | Social studies curriculum should include experiences that provide for the study of people, places, and environments |
| Individual Development and Identity | Social studies curriculum should include experiences that provide for the study of individual development and identity |
| Individuals, Groups, and Institutions | Social studies programs should include experiences that provide for the study of interactions among individuals, groups, and institutions |
| Power, Authority, and Governance | Social studies programs should include experiences that provide for the study of how people create, interact with, and change structures of power, authority, and governance |
| Production, Distribution, and Consumption | Social studies programs should include experiences that provide for the study of how people organize for the production, distribution, and consumption of goods and services |
| Science, Technology, and Society | Social studies programs should include experiences that provide for the study of relationships among science, technology, and society |
| Global Connections | Social studies curriculum should include experiences that provide for the study of global connections and interdependence |
| Civic Ideals and Practices | Social studies curriculum should include experiences that provide for the study of the ideals, principles, and practices of citizenship in a democratic republic |

living done in the future. It gets a chance to be a miniature community, an embryonic society" (Dewey, 1943, pp. 31–32). The real world can be recreated through learning centers that offer children many opportunities to learn social studies and real world concepts.

Young children play in a well-designed learning center that offers them rich opportunities to acquire knowledge related to social studies. Labbo (1998) offers the following example.

> Five-year-old Francis sits in the kindergarten travel agency play center cradling a toy telephone receiver on her shoulders as she adds two wavy squiggles beneath a line of numbers she has already written on a pad of paper. As she speaks into the pretend phone, she places a check by each scribbled line. "Okay. You can leave on your trip today. You [can] go on a train or on a plane or on a bus. (She pauses and pretends to listen.) [You want to go on a] train? You [can] come see me to get your ticket, okay? Have a nice day."
>
> After she hangs up the phone, Marquise and Atresia, who each carry a small suitcase and a fistful of play money, immediately enter the play center. "We want the tickets . . .

the tickets for the train, please," Atresia explains. Francis reaches across the table to several piles of brightly-colored rectangles and picks up two child-designed train tickets and a child-designed map. After a brief exchange of the play money for the pretend tickets and map, Francis says, "The map shows you where to go. Have a nice trip." When Marquise and Atresia exit, Francis crumbles the "phone message" and tosses it into a trash can (p. 18).

After the three children finish playing, they discuss and then dictate a story to an adult about their experiences. Francis adds an illustration to her story and shares it with the class during circle time. Then her story is displayed on the bulletin board for others to see and read. In this learning center, children are learning about the service industry, different kinds of transportation and travel, major principles of economics, the purposes of maps, the brief use of notes, and the communication systems that are used in business.

Learning centers provide young children with the freedom to develop social studies concepts. They are easy-to-find spaces within the room. Each learning center has equipment, materials, and furniture arranged to meet specific purposes, goals (Seefeldt et al., 2009), social studies concepts, and subject areas or themes. The environment for children's play is very important (Bagley & Klass, 1997). Thematic play complements the different equipment, props, materials, and classroom arrangements. The props need to match the theme and the setting. It is important that children be provided with a friendly, familiar, and warm environment to promote their social abilities.

Learning centers should invite individual and small groups of children to explore and learn social studies concepts. For example, in the restaurant center, a delivery truck only requires one driver, which means that children will engage in solitary play. On the other hand, in a bakery learning center that has baking equipment and playdough, a group of children will participate in this center (Petrakos & Howe, 1996). Learning centers are specific areas in the classroom that have a variety of materials related to thematic concepts (Johnson et al., 2005). The learning centers should be well defined, distinct, and easy to see. The similarity in the materials prompt the children to engage in certain activities or experiences (Norris et al., 2004). When children interact with these materials and with other children in the learning center, they will discover and learn essential concepts (Johnson et al., 2005). Learning centers help young children learn appropriately from (Copple & Bredekamp, 2009) experiences when they engage in activities that are

- hands-on, social, and active experiences with play,
- meaningful experiences with materials given to them,
- working at their own individual pace.

The arrangement and use of the learning centers should be similar to a workshop rather than a traditional classroom. Children should have the freedom to select the learning centers, the activities in each learning center, and their own learning, which individualizes their instruction (Seefeldt et al., 2009).

A learning center can focus on social studies content such as an event of historical importance. Children will become interested in history when they become emotionally involved with the historical people they are learning about. Children can see historical individuals as real when they act out their life. Children will become aware that people in the past, like people today, had problems without quick or easy solutions (Witte Museum, no date). Children can learn by engaging in learning activities within learning centers that focus on a single topic or theme. For social studies, the dramatic play center is the one that is used the most.

## Dramatic Play Center

Dramatic play centers offer children opportunities to acquire knowledge when they act out their personal experiences. The typical dramatic play center is designed as a housekeeping area and includes props for engaging in work and family roles. Based on the social studies theme, additional dramatic play centers beyond the traditional housekeeping center may be set up in the classroom. These could include a grocery store, restaurant, rocket ship, pharmacy, or pirate ship. Research show that these type of learning centers motivate young children to engage in play as well as facilitate their social and cognitive play interactions (Petrakos & Howe, 1996). Learning centers can be set up to reinforce social studies concepts. Other shops in the community may be set up as learning centers based on the children's interests and experiences. A large packing crate, with a variety of signs, curtains, and pertinent props, can be displayed for a post office, card shop, beauty shop, barber shop, hardware store, gasoline station, drugstore, toy shop, Laundromat, or bank. Children have experiences in these kinds of shops. If they are interested in them, children will be able to recreate their experiences with these shops (Seefeldt et al., 2009).

The children's social studies experiences can be reinforced through props that will motivate young children to assume various roles. A trip to the dentist's office suggests the addition of a mirror, chair, and white shirt; a trip to the airport suggests the addition of suitcases, and a ticket desk; if a mail carrier talks to the class, a shoulder bag and hat may be added to the dramatic play center. Centers of interest may include those in Box 7.5.

---

**Box 7.5. Social Studies Centers**

- Post Office
- Newspaper
- Police Station
- Fire Station
- Library
- Beauty Salon
- Barber Shop
- Construction Work

- Restaurant
- Supermarket
- Doctor's Office
- Veterinarian's Office
- Hospital
- Airport
- Gasoline Station

---

## Housekeeping Center

The housekeeping learning center encourages children to act out future adult roles. They re-create the adult world to be able to understand it and interact with others and objects. Children enjoy playing in the housekeeping center, especially with adult-like equipment and familiar materials. "From this familiar baseline, the child can make forays into the unknown under the drive for stimulus variation, and can return to this baseline when he finds too much incongruity between what he already knows and the novelty he encounters" (Curry, 1974, p. 66).

The housekeeping learning center needs to include an assortment of dress up items; pieces of clothing that encourage children to take on different roles. They may use a discarded lace curtain panel as a wedding gown, a grandmother's shawl, or skirt. A variety of hats can motivate young children to assume many different roles. Other items that can be included in the housekeeping center are dolls, stove, kitchen utensils, pans, chairs, and other items that are found in the home. All areas that have been suggested by the NCSS can be reinforced with props in the housekeeping center such as the following props (Seefeldt et al., 2009):

- *Economics*: play money for purses and wallets, scales for weighing groceries, cash registers, blank receipt books.
- *History*: sunbonnets, long skirts, ranch-hand hats.
- *Geography*: road maps, dress up clothes for traveling, wheel toys, steering wheel.
- *International education*: clothing, games, or other objects used in other countries.

Since dramatic play contributes to the young children's social and emotional growth, Bagley and Klass (1997) recommend making the housekeeping center a permanent center in the classroom. They believe that other thematic centers should be an addition to the housekeeping center, which supports and promotes the children's overall development.

A more elaborate dramatic play center is the one McKinney and Golden (1973) used as part of their social studies program. This dramatic play center is described in Box 7.6 with the integrated activities that they used.

---

### Box 7.6.  A Model Community Dramatic Center

Dramatic play helps children learn social studies concepts, productive thinking, and classroom behavior. McKinney and Golden (1973) developed a social studies program where children engaged in dramatic play to build and construct a model community. Children were provided with information about what they were learning before they played in their learning center. The dramatic play social studies program allowed the children to engage in realistic play. The objectives of the social studies program were:

1. To develop an understanding of the concept of community and the structure of social organization within the community.
2. To provide the child with basic information regarding the various workers, types of services, and social institutions in the local community.
3. To develop an awareness of the interdependence of various occupations in a community.
4. To develop an understanding of the position and size of a local community in relation to neighboring communities and the state.
5. To supplement other aspects of the total curriculum by providing math, reading, and language arts lessons related to the dramatic play.
6. To promote the development of productive thinking and positive attitudes towards members of the community (p. 173).

The children built a child size community out of modular blocks in an open classroom space in the Frank Porter Graham Research Building. At first the community consisted of only houses, a store, and a post office. As the children played in the community they found out that they needed more buildings and workers. For example, when they played in the post office and used air mail, they realized that they needed airports that included air traffic control officers and pilots. Airplane and car crashes led the children to include a hospital with doctors, nurses, and ambulance drivers in their community. They also found out that they needed police officers to control traffic and a gas station attendant and mechanic to service cars. At the end of the project, the community contained a bank, fire station, school, restaurant, craft shop, traffic court, U.S. Mint, U.S. Government Printing Office, and a major's office with a city council.

The social studies program had three sessions for dramatic play:

1. *Pre-play discussion*: Children would select a job before each dramatic play period and briefly discuss the activities to be held in the community that day. Children were free to change jobs and explored different activities in the community as often as they wanted.
2. *Dramatic play*: Spontaneous dramatic play took place for 15 to 25 minutes.
3. *Post-play discussion*: After each play period, children discussed the play experiences in the community for that day and any problems that might have emerged. At this point, the children would find out if they needed more information and props, which might require them to (1) read teacher prepared charts; (2) read books; (3) see movies, filmstrips, pictures, slides; (4) listen to records; and (5) take field trips.

The children took 10 field trips to local agencies and centers. The social studies program integrated several subject areas such as writing, arithmetic, and geography. For example, children learned how to count and multiply when shopping at the store and post office. They also wrote stories about their field trips and wrote letters to mail in the post office. The children developed a map of their own community that people in the police station and construction company would use. They looked at a map of the Untied States and the world to decide how to plan the destinations for the airplanes and give the information to the pilots to share with their passengers. This experience required children to learn information, mathematics, letter writing, and map reading. During their art experiences, they developed menus and other props that they needed for their play.

McKinney and Golden (1973) related the children's outcomes to a social studies program that was influenced by the dramatic play in a model community that the children designed and built. They defined dramatic play as a classroom activity where children engaged in social studies through dramatic play. Shaftel and Shaftel (1967a) support the motion that dramatic play offers an environment that encourages exploration and motivates and interests children in playing and learning.

These centers can be set up based on the social studies concepts that the children are learning. In addition, it is important to provide the children with learning centers that reflect themes and activities that are of interest to them. In addition to these centers, the classroom can include activities that reinforce the social studies concepts in the different areas such as sand and water, blocks, library, writing, and art.

## Sand and Water Center

The sand and water center can be a resource for social studies learning. When children play with natural materials, they become aware of the nature of the world. If a sand table is not available, plastic bathtubs, or wading pools can be used.

Young children can build roads, tunnels, bridges, cities, farms, airports, and anything they know. They can keep the sand moist to make it easier to build by filling a clear squirt detergent bottle with water. The sand and water center needs to include buckets, plastic containers, sieves, bottles, sponges, funnels, and sticks to explore the properties of sand. After children have experienced manipulating and exploring the sand, props including animals, people, cars, shops, airplanes, shells and sticks can be added.

## Block Center

Dramatic play with blocks is a self directed activity for children. Children build structures based on their experiences, fantasies, and information. Pratt and Stanton (1926) illustrated how the children's experience with railroad tracks contributed to the block building structures.

Young children may make spur of the moment changes. They may build a house with only four walls, and then realize they need a roof. Then they need to determine which size block will extend on the building to make sure that the roof will not collapse. During the early stages of block building, the simplest roofs are flat; at a later stage in block building, children usually construct peaked roofs on their structure (Brody, 1996).

The context for dramatic play requires appropriate space, numbers, different types of blocks, and a variety of block accessories such as rubber and wooden people and animals, cars, planes, boats, cloth, paper, string, colored cubes, containers, and sticks. The block center differs from the other learning areas. For example, the housekeeping center has a refrigerator, stove, sink, bed, tables, chairs, and other related replicas. In contrast, the block area has blocks and accessories for children to build. They need to create the context for their play to evolve. Children need to construct their own stove (Cuffaro, 1996) and create their make-believe environment. Children use blocks to construct structures in their world like the zoo, airport, apartment house, mobile house park, and the neighborhood. To make their structure more realistic, they can add props such as toy animals, people, street signs, cars, boats, planes, trains, and ladders. They can also use natural materials, pieces of shrubs, plants, shells, cables, wires, ropes, lumber, and stones to make their block construction seem real. They may also wish to add signs to their structures to label their store, street, or airport and provide signs with directions.

When children build, they usually know what they mean. They are able to discuss and describe their construction. Their reality is based on their wishes, their feelings, and their thoughts. The sequence of their thinking is observed (Brody, 1996).

When young children talk about the height of a building, they generally mean something that is taller than they are. Their concept of proportion and relationships is based on their size. The child who built the stable that was too small for the horse was unable to compare the size of the horse in relation to the stable until she had tried to put the horse inside (Brody, 1996).

Children consider their block structures to be serious work. Pratt (1948) describes how children see their work in block building:

They were indeed developing work habits. Their play with blocks made this very clear. Building a railroad with blocks may look like play to an adult, but to the children it is work. There comes the moment when it is even drudgery, like building a structure over and over until it stands. The discipline of work is surely present as it is in any adult creative venture. As a matter of fact, it was at about this time that we dropped the name Play School because the children resented it! (p. 17).

When children build in the block center, they discover that their environment makes many demands on them. During their construction, they must communicate, exchange ideas, plan, and finish their structure. After they are finished, they must continue to communicate, exchange ideas, and probably modify their building plans. In block building, children learn to preplan, to cooperate, to give, and to take, which goes beyond the block center. Such abilities become part of them. They learn to become disciplined to be able to concentrate and become a contributing member of their peer group. Thus, they learn how groups function, which helps them be on their way to becoming adults. The relationships with others is the basis for social studies. "In social studies, children learn to cope with people and their relationships to each other through time and space. Children need the time and the space to experience, to learn, and to grow" (Brody, 1996, p. 118).

## Library Center

A library center includes books (literature books and books authored by the children). The area should be filled with color and beauty including growing plants, dried flower arrangement, prints, children's art, and children's books. A rocking chair, overstuffed chair, carpet, pillows, and anything that makes children comfortable may be added. Dioramas can be displayed for children to tell and retell stories. It should include bulletin boards that the children create and book jackets. The library center should be designed for children to read by themselves or with a friend.

Simple reference books, picture dictionaries and encyclopedias as well as books on many topics that children have studied can be valuable resources for children's social studies learning. Such books can provide an excellent way for children to explore many social studies themes. Books help children learn about their own culture and family, cultures around the world, geography, history, community, and more. Young children's books provide them with a good opportunity to explore the many social studies themes (such as their own culture and family, cultures around the world, geography, history, community). Box 7.7 has examples of books that represent these themes (NAEYC, 2005).

---

**Box 7.7. Exploring Social Studies through Children's Books**

- *Adelita: A Mexican Cinderella Story* by Tomie dePaola. 2002. New York: Grosset & Dunlap. Ages 5–8.
- *Building a House* by Byron Barton. 1990 (Reissue ed.). New York: Harper Trophy. Ages 3–6.
- *Castles, Caves, and Honeycombs* by Linda Ashman, illus. by Lauren Stringer. 2001. New York: Harcourt. Ages 3–8.

- *Daddy Makes the Best Spaghetti* by Anna Grossnickle Hines. 1999. New York: Clarion. Ages 2–6.
- *Everybody Works* by Shelly Rotner & Ken Kreisler. 2003. Brookfield, CT: Millbrook. Ages 2–5.
- *Lots of Grandparents* by Shelley Rotner & Sheila Kelly. 2003. Brookfield, CT: Millbrook. Ages 3–7.
- *Machines at Work* by Byron Barton. 1997 (Board ed.). New York: Harper Festival. Ages 3–6.
- *Our World: A Child's First Picture Atlas.* 2003. Washington, DC: National Geographic Society. Ages 4–7.
- *Recycle! A Handbook for Kids* by Gail Gibbons. 1992. Boston: Little, Brown. Ages 4–8.
- *Stars and Stripes: The Story of the American Flag* by Sarah L. Thomson, illus. by Bob Dacey & Debra Bandelin. 2003. New York: HarperCollins. Ages 4–8.

## Writing Center

A writing center allows children to communicate social studies concepts. Writing materials can include sharpened pencils, soft tipped pens in several colors, blank booklets (several sheets of paper stapled together), and an assortment of different sizes, shapes, and colors of paper for children to write. They may have a story to dictate, write, or draw. Usually social studies content offers children a springboard that helps children to draw their experiences and ideas. They may dictate, draw, or write the story about how it feels to go to the moon, everything they saw on a field trip, how it feels not to have a friend, about their friend, or any other topic.

## Art Center

When children create in the art center, they prepare and share needed materials, work individually or in a group, and clean up, which helps them to practice and learn social skills. Being artistic with their work becomes emotionally satisfying. Children become aware that they have power and are able to control the materials and things, which provides them with a safe, appropriate way of releasing feelings and communicating ideas.

Art helps children learn about other cultures. The art center should have a variety of materials that encourage children to draw, paint, model, construct, cut and paste, sew, weave, or build. These materials need to provide children with the opportunities to communicate through art in their social studies experiences. Social studies (like field trips, observations, interactions with others) give children ideas for their art work.

## Developing Prop Boxes

Prop boxes are based on themes or topics that the children are learning or they may contain objects related to a shared experience or a field trip. For example, after going on a field trip to an animal hospital or pet store, a veterinarian prop box can be used. Prop boxes can be developed to respond to the children's emerging interests.

Several "prop boxes" should be provided in the classroom based on a theme (Bender, 1971). Each box has materials that assist the children to create a specific dramatic play theme like a restaurant, store, or office. The box has real things from the real world. It includes specialized items that are appropriate for a specific theme. For example, a sport shop prop box can include backpacks, climbing books, heavy socks, motorcycle helmet, baseball caps, baseball gloves, baseball shoes, baseball cards, football helmet, football, jersey's shoulder pads, hockey mask, basketball, basketball hoop, stop watch, hand-held weights, headbands, sweat bands, tennis shoes, tennis rackets, sports banner, sports poster or pictures, ski goggles, stocking caps, ski gloves, child-size skis, ski boots, scuba-diving fins, scuba-diving goggles, diving gloves, and snorkel.

When learning about a specific theme, the appropriate prop box can be taken out for children to engage in dramatic play. After the prop box is used, its contents need to be cleaned, and any consumable materials that were used must be replaced before it is stored. This way the prop box is ready to be used as soon as it is needed. Sample prop boxes based on themes are found in Box 7.8.

---

**Box 7.8. Sample Prop Boxes Based on Themes**

- *Forest Ranger:* canteen, flashlight, rope, mosquito netting, canvas for tent, knapsack, food supplies, nature books, small logs, grill, binoculars, and other appropriate items (Bender, 1971).
- *Plumber:* piping (all lengths, widths, shapes for fitting together), spigots, plungers, tools, hose and nozzles, spade, old shirt, cap, hardware supply catalogues, measuring devices, and other appropriate items (Bender, 1971).
- *Office:* pads of paper, desk accessories (pen holder, plastic paper files, etc.) stamps, stapler, rolls of scotch tape, tape dispenser, memo holder, magnets for memos, small tables and chairs, posters or pictures of office workers, file folders, envelopes, telephone, adding machine, computer, pens and pencils. Since it's an office, more than one item may be needed, for example two telephones, several hole punchers (Myhre, 1993).
- *Flower shop:* flower and garden magazines, small garden tools, aprons, garden hats, garden gloves, posters or pictures of flowers, plastic flowers, Styrofoam squares, vases, baskets, cash register, play money, empty watering pitcher, empty seed packets (Myhre, 1993).

---

Teachers and children can create prop boxes that reflect different cultures in the classroom. A culture prop box would include artifacts related to a particular cultural theme. Both children and teachers can add to the cultural prop box resources from a specific culture including music and art. For example, cultural prop boxes reflecting the Mexican-American culture can include boxes of Tejano musicians and Quinceañeara celebrations. A Tejano musician's prop box can have a guayavera, a cowboy straw hat, a shawl, a short skirt, flowers for hair, a guitar, an accordion, and the like. These props can motivate young children to role play a Tejano musician's group. The Quinceañeara prop box may contain a formal gown, a tiara, a veil, gloves, musical instruments, and similar items. Children can dramatize a Quinceañeara celebration, which is a 15th birthday festivity.

Prop boxes are easy to make. Local stores can be contacted and asked to save empty paper boxes with lids (like computer paper boxes). Families or businesses may donate some of the items or items may be bought at yard sales, thrift shops, and dollar stores (NAEYC, 2008). Children and parents may also donate odds and ends to include in the prop box. These objects can be placed in easy to carry boxes. Each box is labeled and decorated according to its theme. Outside the box should be a list of materials and supplies that are inside the box. These boxes are based on a theme for different types of role playing. Children should be able to identify them. The boxes should have pictures cut from magazines or children's drawings that identify the theme of the prop box. Once the prop boxes are ready, use the guidelines in Box 7.9 to use the prop boxes (Myhre, 1993).

---

### Box 7.9. Guidelines for Using Prop Boxes

- Introduce the props to small groups of children to facilitate their discussion and participation. They might identify the items and discuss how to use them safely and carefully. They might brainstorm on creative ways to use them.
- It is important that children are safe. Objects need to be developmentally appropriate for children. If the objects are too small, too sharp, or conceptually inappropriate, they need to be replaced with objects that are more developmentally appropriate objects for the children's age.

   All children who want to play need to have the opportunity to use the prop boxes. For popular prop boxes, a waiting list needs to be posted for children to see and know whose turn is next.
- Children need to know how many children can play with the prop box at a time. They need to know how many are able to use the space and props based on the number of props available.
- Consistency is important. If children know that everyone must wear safety goggles when they are using the repair shop prop box, this rule must be carried out each time this prop box is used. When the same rules are applied each time, children quickly learn what is expected of them.
- Prop boxes can be used in any play area in the classroom, such as traffic cop directing traffic in the large block area.

---

Thematic prop boxes are invaluable in developing rich play environments. They offer an excellent way to create an authentic setting where children have the freedom to use materials in their play.

Prop boxes provide the means to guarantee an extensive amount of ideas and materials that are promptly available to the children. Children are then motivated to create stories, pictures, and drama. During their pretend play, children sort out their relationship to others (Soundy & Gallagher, 1992).

## Taking Field Trips

Field trips provide children with opportunities to see in real life what they have seen in pictures or books or have heard in conversations. Field trips offer the children the opportunity to develop lasting memories and develop concepts (Saul, 1993). The benefits of social studies field trips to the children's learning are found in Box 7.10 (Seefeldt et al., 2009).

**Box 7.10. Benefits of Social Studies Field Trips to the Children's Learning**

1. Increase the children's knowledge of their environment, give them firsthand experiences that are not available in the classroom.
2. Introduce children to their environment and help them to orient themselves in the environment.
3. Help children develop concepts of directions, maps, and space.
4. Assist children in learning about their social world and develop the children's knowledge about occupations in the world.
5. Give children the opportunity to use the methods of the scientist as they acquire information, observe the environment, and make conclusions.
6. Provide a standard core of experiences where children play, work together in solving a problem, share, and discuss.
7. Cultivate the parents' relationship when children visit the places their parents work or visit the same places they have visited with their parents. Parents can also serve as volunteers to help take care of the children on field trips.
8. Provide children with new ideas and information where they develop new interests, questions, and responses.

Field trips are an essential component of the social studies program (Mitchell, 1934). They help young children observe social systems, such as fire and police protection, traffic control, and banking. Field trips give children first-hand experiences where they observe, collect information, and draw conclusions. They are meaningful experiences where children learn about social studies concepts (Taylor et al., 1997).

Field trips require proper planning. In addition to the technical planning, the children need to know the purpose and focus of the field trip. While spur of the moment incidents can improve a field trip, it is better to have everything well planned. Simple field trips can be very meaningful. For example, taking a walk to the corner to watch the traffic control operations or visiting a local supermarket can be a productive experience (Spodek & Saracho, 1994b).

Other field trips may be more complex. For example, Rudolph and Cohen (1984) describe a children's field trip on a train journey. The four-year-olds went to a railroad station, bought tickets, and traveled approximately 15 minutes to a nearby familiar town. This field trip was selected because in dramatic play children played with the interlocking wooden trains and asked questions about the caboose, which the children thought was an intriguing word. The children saw pictures of trains and a caboose. They shared experiences, developed thoughts, and sang songs about trains and the caboose. Although there was a thoughtful discussion about different transportation vehicles, the children selected the train for their field trip. When they arrived at the train station, the teacher bought the tickets while the children watched what she did, then they enjoyed their field trip. After the field trip and children are in their classrooms, they can be provided with photographs from their trip and play props to motivate them to engage in dramatic play about their experience on the train. Children can adopt roles and use make-believe transformations to act out their experience.

Young children use dramatic play to communicate their thoughts and feelings. During their play, they identify with persons or objects and imitate the persons' actions or objects. Children get their sources of information for dramatic play from personal contacts and vicarious experiences like children's books, pictures, and field trips. For example, children will engage in dramatic play when on a field trip with classmates, they see and sit in a helicopter and spontaneously envision that they are pilots in action (Siks, 1983). Successful field trips need to provide meaning to the children. They also give children information about their community. Other possible places for field trips are repair shops, garden shops, pet stores, farms, farmers' markets, department stores, hospitals, airports, fire stations, city hall, bus terminals, church buildings, children's theaters, and museums.

On a field trip for one school, children were taken to an art museum. The themes of "fantasy and reality" followed by "animals in the world" were bridged by embarking on an "art safari." Beforehand, the mixed age class of 3- to 5-year-olds was asked which animals they would look for in the paintings at the art museum. "Dogs, cats, horses, lions, and dinosaurs" were popular responses. One 4-year-old, however, was determined to find a camel. The teacher, on her pre-trip, did not recall a camel and feared the child would be disappointed. However, in the quiet of the museum, a delighted squeal was heard followed by, "Oh, my camel and its humps are just for me!" On a subsequent trip to the zoo, this child remarked, "These camels look like the one at that picture place" (Taylor et al., 1997, p. 141).

## Visiting Museums

One of the children's field trips may be to a museum. Museums provide children with an area for them to play. Just like traditional museums, children's museums contain collections of objects and specimens for children to study. In addition, the children's museums have rich physical environments that motivate young children to learn and play. Children's museums are user friendly, interactive, hands-on, attractive, non-threatening, and motivating environments that have been specifically designed and developed for children. Some children's museums provide space for children to make things and display their work. For example, the Copenhagen Children's Museum in Denmark invites children to set up displays with artifacts from the museum or those made by children. Children will put them in museum cases for public display (Mayfield, 2005). Some museums lend displays of social studies materials (such as dioramas or artifacts) to schools.

Children's museums have become child-friendly and provide a range of exhibits and learning experiences in communities all over the United States. Victor Danilov (1986) discusses several museums in large cities, like at the Field Museum of Natural History and the Museum of Science and Industry in Chicago, the Museum of Natural History in New York, and the National Museum of Natural History in Washington, DC. He also identifies several children's museums in many communities like the Exploratorium in San Francisco, the Boston Children's Museum, and the Children's Museum in Indianapolis. Many smaller cities also have children's museums. Such museums display exhibits that are geared for children of all ages. They also give young children opportunities to explore scientific phenomena. These museums are entertaining and educational (Ault, 1987). Successful exhibits in a children's museum need to include at least one of the following (Regnier, 1987):

- Gross motor activities (e.g., crystal climbing boxes and bridges).
- Sand and water (e.g., large seascape settings with boats and ships)
- Collections that show categories (e.g., dinosaurs arranged in order of size; floral exhibits displayed by climate).
- Role play settings (e.g., school, commercial, neighborhood, various historical settings).
- Dressing up in costumes and uniforms (e.g., explorers, archeologists, astronaut outfits).
- Places to hide (e.g., animal homes, life in the forest, storybook gardens).

- Objects to assemble/disassemble (e.g., large scale dinosaur or animal puzzles, matching jobs and tools).
- Age appropriate activities (e.g., explorations children can reach, solve, or complete without adult intervention).
- Activities that provide opportunities for selection and diversity (e.g., child sized tools or equipment and opportunities to apply them to "real" tasks).
- Multi sensory displays (e.g., moving exhibits characterized by bright lights and sounds).

Children can learn about their social studies topics when they visit the exhibits at the museum and about the work of people in the museum. Museums give children the opportunity to see the "real thing" and to relate what they see to their social studies learning. They motivate children to use their thinking skills, especially when they ask questions about what they see (NAEYC, 1999).

A museum helps children learn more about how the larger community works. For example, at the University of Maryland's preschool, a group of young children built rockets and airplanes. They created paper rockets at the art table and later raced them outdoors. One of the children shared a book on how to make paper airplanes. The children's interests led to an airplane study. Since an airplane museum was near the preschool, the children visited and discussed their airplane experiences like their destination and how they felt about the experience. A child was taking a long airplane trip to New Zealand and Australia. When she arrived in Australia, the children contacted her online and asked many questions about the airplane and her flight (Friedman, 2005). Electronic mail and telecommunications provide children with opportunities to use the internet to facilitate direct communication and to foster social interactions with children who are in a different physical location (NAEYC, 1996).

In dramatic play, the children engaged in block building. They used hollow blocks to build airplanes and a control tower. They dressed up and pretended to be on business trips and vacations. Then the children took a field trip to the airport to look at the control tower, although security officers only allowed them to see the control tower from a distance. They also visited the observation deck and the baggage claim area. When they returned to their classroom, they read a book to learn more about control towers and to find out what they look like and how they work (Friedman, 2005).

Later a commercial pilot visited the class, talked to the children, shared a model of a cockpit, and answered their questions. For example, the children wanted to know the difference between a pilot and a copilot. As a culminating experience, the children used blocks and accessories to build an airport. They made a baggage conveyer belt out of fabric. They also built an airplane and several vehicles they saw at the airport. The airport was left on display for about a week (Friedman, 2005).

The trip to the museum is also very important, because they learn social studies concepts along the way. For example, D'Addesio, Grob, Furman, Hayes, and David (2005) describe the concepts that a class of four-year-olds learned on their way to the museum.

> The regularity of the trips to the Newark Museum allowed the children to discover the patterns of life and work on the streets. As we walked from the subway to stop to the museum, we passed a church undergoing renovation. On our first trip we saw a worker sanding the front door. The next week we were surprised to discover that he was still there. This time he was applying stain. Each week we watched the progress of the renovation.

After our first museum visit, as we headed back to the subway, we saw a postal worker emptying a mail storage box into his mailbag. The next week, we saw him again! We said, We saw you here last week! and he said that he remembered us. The children asked him what he was doing and he told them. The trips were valuable firsthand experiences that taught the children about the ongoing life of their community (p. 54).

The children's multiple experiences at the museum helped them to improve their observation abilities. After making many trips to the Newark Museum, the children developed a sense of pride and community ownership. They walked through the galleries with confidence and referred to the Newark Museum as "our museum" (D'Addesio et al., 2005). This kind of excitement can be used to encourage the children to build their own museum in the classroom (see Box 7.11 below).

---

### Box 7.11. Making a Local History Museum

Have the children ask their parents if they have mementos of their earlier years, and of the years of their grandparents. These could be an article of clothing, early radios or home appliances, pictures of people and places. Organize these objects by eras or by people. Have the children or their parents tell stories about these things which can be written up and displayed with the objects themselves.

   Visit the local public library. See if they have collections of photos or objects related to the community from different eras. Display these, if possible along with similar, more modern objects or photos of contemporary scenes. See if there is a local historian that can come to the class. Ask the librarian; they often know of such persons in the community. Have the children discuss things as they are now and as they were long ago. Invite parents and other groups of children to your display (Spodek & Saracho, 1994b, p. 422).

---

Technology extends benefits that help children to collaborate beyond their classroom environment. The internet and the online "user friendly" networks can help young children to collaborate with children in other classrooms, cities, counties, states, and even countries. Electronic museums can be found in real time or via diskette and children can learn about different cultural and environmental experiences (NAEYC, 1996). For example, children can explore the history museums at the Smithsonian in Washington DC or travel through Europe visiting museums using the Internet. They can take a virtual trip to these museums (see Box 7.12).

---

### Box 7.12. Sample Websites Children Can Visit for Virtual Field Trips

- American History from Smithsonian
  http://americanhistory.si.edu/notkid/index.htm
  Explore topics such as The American Presidency.
- Smithsonian National Air and Space Museum
  http://www.nasm.si.edu/

- American Museum of Natural History Kids
  http://www.amnh.org/kids/
  This museum has many online stories and reading opportunities such as How
  Lou Got the Flu, Endangered! and Ology.
- America's Story
  http://www.americaslibrary.gov/cgi-bin/page.cgi
  Lots of readings and activities on American History.

Children can find resources to locate online museums. With the help of a person who can read and write, children can do a search in Google for topics such as "French art museum" or "horse museum." It is important to identify and encourage shared learning opportunities in the communities for the children. Young children need to visit children's museums with some frequency. In addition, museum educators need to be invited to work with children in the classroom (D'Addesio et al., 2005).

## Developing Thematic Units

Occasionally a lesson will take many days to finish. This leads to the development of a series of lessons, taught over a long period of time, and focused on a specific theme, which is called a thematic unit. The unit consists of a set of related lesson plans that are used to introduce, develop, and expand understanding of a topic. The lessons in the thematic unit may integrate art, music, movement education, language arts, literacy, and other subject areas. A thematic unit is developed around key concepts, reasons, values, and inquiry abilities (Sunal & Haas, 2007). It plans instruction using activities, books, and a variety of learning experiences. The thematic unit is designed to help the students meet content-related objectives that give children a feeling of continuity and will avoid providing unrelated experiences (Vacca et al., 2011).

Children interact with books, materials, their peers, and collaborate with their peers to share knowledge, to compare understandings, and to discuss and negotiate meanings. The thematic unit is a planning device that includes the following:

1. A title that reflects the thematic or topical nature of the unit. Ideas for a unit emerge from the world around us. Current events of a national nature (presidential election) or a regional or local incident (a hurricane or state fair) may be an incentive in developing a unit (Sunal, 1990)
2. The main concepts to be learned
3. The materials, books, and information sources that will be needed
4. The thematic unit's instructional experiences
5. Assessment to determine the children's learning after participating in the unit (Vacca et al., 2011).

The thematic unit can reinforce the social studies concepts through the use of a wide range of literature. Children's books can be used to provide an information base, but the basis for individual and group learning of a theme or topic will be the use of both fiction and nonfiction books based on the children's interests and question needs. A variety of children's literature, both imaginative and informational, can help children become intensely involved in the topic they are learning. Trade books, pamphlets, periodicals, reference books, newspapers, magazines, and audiovisual materials can be used as supplements to acquire information (Vacca et al., 2011).

Children can explore social studies areas through dramatizations of the topic they are learning. Dramatic play can be used to motivate the children to explore, learn, and become interested in the subject of study (Shaftel & Shaftel, 1967a). Young children learn better with appropriate experiences that use direct experiences (McKinney & Golden, 1973). Box 7.13 provides an example of a thematic unit that emphasizes play experiences.

---

### Box 7.13. Neighborhood Thematic Unit

#### The Neighborhood

Krown (1975) describes a thematic unit where children ages three and four learned about their neighborhood through dramatic play, looking at books, talking to people, and taking field trips. The purpose of the thematic unit in the neighborhood was to study the children's lives and environment. The children (ages three and four) collected information, summarized it, and combined the knowledge they learned. The neighborhood thematic unit lasted two months. The major goals were

1. To examine the buildings in the neighborhood and think about their purposes;
2. To understand why buildings are where they are and how they meet the needs of the people in the area;
3. To understand the concept of neighborhood as a unit made up of homes, and services for the people living in the homes;
4. To learn what goes on in a neighborhood and how it is all related (p. 139).

The children would (1) learn words (such as near, far, small, large, high, low, wide, narrow, crowded, in front of, behind) to describe objects and the objects' relationship to the neighborhood; (2) become aware of the interrelations of people, businesses, and services in the neighborhood and know that there are more houses and a few stores to serve many people; and (3) find out the components (such as the children's houses, the stores, market, area, baby, health station, nursery school, schools, youth center, synagogues, roads, buses, police, hairdresser, carpenter, workshops) that represent a neighborhood.

*Introduction*

The children had been building houses, cars, stores, bus stops, and roads in the nursery school. They were asked to think about the following questions:

- What do we call a place where there are many houses together?
- What kinds of buildings are there in your neighborhood?
- Why did the city build roads?

The children were not expected to provide an immediate and complete answer to these questions, but it was expected for them to begin thinking about the neighborhood and its different buildings. The questions motivated the children to go out and look at the neighborhood and learn the names of things. Then the children took a field trip around the neighborhood.

*Taking a Trip*

The children took a field trip to see where their classmates lived. They discovered that the streets had names and the houses had numbers. They learned that this was a neighborhood and what made a neighborhood. They visited the shopping center and looked at the different kinds of shops. They discussed how all the shops were together in one area and the purpose of each shop. After the neighborhood trip, the children discussed the field trip in their classroom. They made a list about what they saw and decided to build a neighborhood in their block play.

*Pretend Play*

The next morning, the children reviewed the field trip, planned their neighborhood, and decided to build their own house or a building from the neighborhood. The children made a list of houses, roads, and the nursery school. Several children decided to build cars, a grocery store, a garage, and a hairdressing shop. Then the children planned their neighborhood by making sketches. They made chalk markings of streets and the location for each building.

The children began building and ran out of building blocks. They started to use large boxes, pieces of wood, cardboard boxes, and anything they found in the nursery school. For the next two weeks, the children discussed their buildings to make sure that buildings were not interfering with each other. They also made several trips to the neighborhood to look at specific buildings and their special characteristics to be able to make an accurate reproduction.

Group discussions continued about the building and the plan. The following is a discussion between the teacher and two girls.

| | |
|---|---|
| Dafna: | *We built a house. I'm the mother and Aliza is the baby.* |
| Teacher: | *Have you arranged to finish your house yet?* |
| Dafna: | *Yes, we have a bed, a table, chairs, and curtains.* |
| Teacher: | *What are you doing now?* |
| Dafna: | *I want to feed the baby cereal.* |
| Teacher: | *Where will you get the cereal?* |
| Dafna and others: | *The grocery.* (Dafna takes a basket and goes to the grocery.) |
| Teacher (to Naomi): | *What did you build?* |
| Naomi: | *I built a hairdressing shop.* |
| Teacher: | *What do you do there?* |
| Naomi: | *I cut hair.* |
| Teacher: | *How do you know what kind of haircut to give?* |
| Naomi: | *I ask how they want it.* |
| Teacher: | *Children, be careful; remember to tell Naomi how to cut your hair or she might cut it too short if you want it long.* (In this way, the children were encouraged to talk, and often they themselves took over the teacher's role in making conversation.) (p. 141) |

The children engaged in pretend play. They imagined that they were taking trips on the bus to the health clinic, grocery store, and hairdresser. The nursery school had miniature equipment, pictures on the wall, tiny pieces of plasticine on the table, a place to hang clothes, a toilet, kitchen, and outdoor equipment. Then the neighborhood grew with the additions of a supermarket, several food shops, and a very active restaurant where actual cooking took place. The family houses and shops had signs for their name. The children made a rule about those who would ride on the bus: "You can't ride on the bus unless you pay." However, some children sneaked to the back of the bus.

The children continued to play and discuss several issues such as the specifics about buying and selling, ways to earn and spend money, and problems that emerged during their play. They also discussed the need of supplies for the shops and the geographical orientation of the neighborhood. That is, the exact position of the roads and the buildings in the neighborhood, which led to making various additional trips. Then the children dealt with important details of the neighborhood including the water tanks and the electric lines and poles. They looked at the way the electric wires ran into the houses and built a miniature neighborhood to their block buildings.

*The Model Neighborhood*

In addition to the block building, the children built a miniature model of their neighborhood. Krown (1975) provides photographs of model neighborhoods that children built.

They set up the model in a large sand table. The children made the buildings out of cardboard, cigarette boxes, match boxes, plasticine, and small interlocking plastic blocks. The first building they built was the nursery school, which was located in the middle of the box. A group of children looked at the details of the buildings (such as the synagogue, the youth center) near the nursery school. They examined the buildings' geographical location in relation to the nursery school. Then they organized on the table (using wet sand) the shapes of the neighborhood with its hills and roads. The children calculated the relative positions (close to, far from, behind, higher, and lower than the nursery school) of the miniature buildings they had built. They built the houses with more detail, such as miniature "people" on the balconies. They started adding the shops, health clinic, fire station, bus line, electric wires, and other details. One of the groups added automobiles in front of their houses, while another group added their "Uncle's" truck or the bus that the teacher rode.

The model neighborhood was placed in the middle of the room. The children played, discussed the model, and added details to it. For example, they added people made of plasticine, wood and pipe cleaners, small automobiles, street signs, and trees. A rule was developed stating: if you play with the model you must say what you are doing. For example,

Danny, holding a doll in his hand: *I am leaving the house. I am passing the store. Now I am going near the fence of the park. The road is going up hill.*

Teacher:   *How do you feel, going uphill?*
Danny:      *Hot, my legs hurt.*

> Teacher:   *Yes, going uphill makes a person feel hotter and sometimes our legs hurt if we are going fast. What else is happening on your walk?*
> Danny:     *Here is the synagogue. Now I am going into the gate of the nursery.*
>
> Yaakov takes a police car from the police station and announces that he is driving around the neighborhood: *Now I am on the main road and going to Hadassah Hospital* (pp. 144–145).

The children featured in Box 7.13 played with the model. They acted out the cause of fires and fire engines, accidents and ambulances, and visits to each other's houses. During their play, they became aware of the need to keep the "neighborhood" neat and clean. The children made paintings and collages that reflected the theme of the neighborhood.

At the end of the thematic unit, the children had shown a high interest in the project, which enhanced their questioning and thinking abilities. The children were able to use words to communicate their thoughts, actions, and intentions. Even the most timid children engaged in this interesting project. They had a positive experience in cooperation and maintained their interest throughout the project. They learned (1) the purpose of each building, (2) to ask questions, and (3) to search for answers. The children started to become aware that they are a part of their environment, which affects them (Krown, 1975).

## Summary

In a social studies program for young children, students can learn to understand social processes and develop abilities in social inquiry. They can also learn to understand themselves better in relation to their social world. In addition, in a social studies program, children learn to understand and appreciate people from other backgrounds and cultures. They need to understand their physical world to be able to make logical decisions about situations in their life (Saracho & Spodek, 2007b).

The success of social studies programs needs to focus on the children's imaginations, relate it to the children's lives outside of the school, and focus on their prior knowledge. Children also need experiences that (a) foster the children's empathy, (b) encourage them to consider their own and others' emotional responses, and (c) encourage them to be concerned about others. They need to learn to become responsive to the others' feelings, issues, and historical events. Children also need to develop social understanding and intellectual reasoning (Fertig, 2007). Children can easily learn the above when their social studies program focuses on dramatic play, where children use role playing or sociodrama techniques to learn about historical events and to understand their peers' interpretation of their behaviors (McKinney & Golden, 1973).

# Chapter 8
# **Language-play Learning Experiences**

The development of power and efficiency with any form of language derives from using language for genuine purposes, not from studying about it.

(Walter Logan, 1978, p. 100)

Teachers need to be aware of the beauty of language that can be found in the ways children express themselves. Often the idiosyncratic phrases of children in the nursery years are subdued, because they do not seem proper. Subcultural groups have expressions that enrich children's language, yet teachers frequently exclude these from their classroom. Teachers need to support and cherish these rather than try to eliminate them. The beauty of language is enhanced when communication is a personal statement rather than a predetermined series of phrases. The purpose of this chapter is to describe the learning of oral language, the relationship between language and play, language experiences, the language environment, learning written language, and writing in children's play.

## Learning Oral Language

Oral language requires an analytic process that children use in order to construct meaning and monitor their thoughts and activities (Antonacci & O'Callaghan 2004). Children's oral language development is critical to their learning. Language assumes a distinct and important function in developing the young children's mental processes (Vygotsky, 1934).

Young children differ in the way they develop their language. They range from early talkers to late talkers or from being talkative children to being quiet ones. Several of these differences may be developmental, while others may be caused by the children's environment and culture. The culture in which children develop influences the patterns of their language. When children enter school, they have different levels of language acquisition, although most young children know how to effectively use the basic sentence forms of the language of their culture. Young children typically develop language at a rapid pace; they learn between six to ten new words per day, beginning at about age three (Saracho & Spodek, 1993). Children at age three and one-half have completely acquired a basic grammatical speech and six-year-olds are competent performers in language. They usually have a listening and speaking vocabulary of about 2500 words and know the basic rules for combining these words into complex sentences and phrases. They have also acquired an intuitive sense of the structure of the language.

Young children listen to the language and build their representations of the speech sounds. Infants listen to many sounds, view sights, and feel from the emotions of their care providers. Initially young children view these to be "a buzzing, blooming confusion," but they slowly develop form and definition (Handel, 2005). Children learn language and relate sounds to words, words to utterances, and utterances to larger logical thoughts (Baquedano-López, 2003). Young children give meaning to the sounds that they hear, which become part of their own language repertoire.

When children interact with others, they learn language rules. For example, they learn that adding "-ed" to a verb places it in the past tense. Many times children make mistakes, because they apply rules to words that are exceptions to their language rules, although young children usually apply the correct form of the rules. For example, children may say, "He dided it," but they will rarely add the "ed" to the end of a noun.

Both nature and nurture informs the learning of language. Children learn to talk in a predictable sequence (nature), but they also need a linguistically invigorating environment (nurture) for proper learning development. Usually, young children utter their first meaningful words between the age of 11 and 12 months. Without having any language instruction, the children's first words frequently are, "mama" or "dada." Obviously, children learn their family members' language, although the family members do not "teach" the children how to talk. They also tend not to correct mispronounced words or grammatically inaccurate sentences. Some parents and their infants mutually interact when they engage in their daily habits, behaviors, and conversations (Caulfield, 2002), which become important in the child's language development.

Children use their experiences to develop a language structure. They simultaneously learn language, learn about language, and learn through language, which are interactive processes (Halliday, 1969). The children's oral language indicates their perceptions about the world, knowledge, interpretations, and thought processes. Nevertheless, language is "a tool not just for communicating existing meanings but for generating new meanings" (Pinnell & Jaggar, 2003, p. 895). Children use language to clear up confusion and to construct and share interests and ideas, which develops their vocabulary, knowledge base, and understanding (Kalmar, 2008). They use oral language for inquiry, for "making connections with others in an attempt to build understanding, or to learn" (Pinnell & Jaggar, 2003, p. 901).

Preschool children who are at-risk learn language when they are frequently exposed to vocabulary across multiple contexts and when definitions are integrated in context, even when they are introduced to words from content materials (like science, social studies). Children who are at-risk learn vocabulary knowledge by associating concepts and word relationships. They understand relationships between words and concepts by using their background knowledge. Children who are at-risk need to learn language through themes (such as broad, universal ideas about life, nature, society). They learn new information when they relate it to what they already know (Pollard-Durodola et al., 2011).

## Language Interactions

In developing new concepts, children test their ideas by interacting with others who provide them with feedback (McGee & Richgels, 2004). Children also need to talk about a new problem or new concept in order to understand it and use it in their language. Children learn language by using it in a natural setting as they attempt to meet their communication needs. Young children need to be provided with natural language experiences that focus on helping them to develop the necessary language skills to engage in purposeful communication. They need a repertoire of oral language experiences that assist them to construct new understandings about receptive and expressive language (Kirkland & Patterson, 2005). Children all over the world use language for different reasons: informational purposes (such as asking why questions), entertainment, recreation (songs and stories), socialization purposes, and several others (Soderman & Farrell, 2008). The children's language can be developed in a variety of settings (see Box 8.1, Hall, 1987).

---

### Box 8.1.  Children's Language Development in Different Settings

- children are the primary builders of language;
- parents, teachers, and caregivers facilitate, rather than transmit, language development;
- language is integrated into the children's context of their daily lives;
- children construct language in their search for meaning and comprehension related to their world;
- the situations for developing language are similar to those for learning about the world;
- social interaction is the basis for language development;
- children understand the purpose of language when they use it to clarify information about themselves and others; and
- language is learned in a child-initiated, holistic way.

---

It is important to provide oral language development opportunities in the early childhood classroom, and developing the children's vocabulary is a major goal of early childhood programs. A language program should focus on the language that is generated by the children themselves (Pigdon & Woolley, 1993).

## Language in a Social Context

Social behavior relates to the development of interpersonal understanding of "meaningful behavior." Thus, a primary purpose for the use of early language is the ability to establish and maintain interpersonal social interaction. As a result, the children's talk can be used to help them learn those concepts that form the foundation for social communication (Garvey & Hogan, 1973). Dewey (1916) proposes that a language program needs to include the children's social interactions and interests (such individual, small group, classroom inquiry). He believes that children actively engage in genuine investigations. Vygotsky's (1934) observations show that preschoolers are able to verbally plan, explain outcomes, and describe the results of their inquiry. He reports how preschoolers use private speech to plan, guide, and monitor their behaviors in a self-regulatory way.

Language learning first occurs in a social context (Vygotsky, 1978). When two or more children converse as they go about their everyday informal lives, these children are together constructing their social interactions and their worlds (Turnbull & Carpendale, 2001). Dewey (1916) also believes that social interactions (such as small group discussions and peer dialogue) promote learning. According to Hymes (1972), "The key to understanding language in context is to start, not with language, but with context" (p. 57). The context refers to the environment and the persons in the environment as well as what they are doing and saying, and where and when they are doing it. The social contexts help children create meaning when they interact, experiment with, make use of, and play with both oral and written language.

Children create social contexts where they become speakers who act and behave using the constructive natural language (Vygotsky, 1978). Vygotsky's theory on social constructivism provides an understanding of how children develop specific ways of knowing, thinking, and communicating about the world. He explains that young children create meaning when new information interacts with their existing knowledge in a social context. This knowledge is influenced by the "children's cultural experiences and interactions with others in that culture (McRobbie & Tobin, 1997, p. 194). The children's cognitive and language skills are best developed in a more natural setting and experiences such as play. Children dominate language faster through playful activities (Bruner, 1983).

## Language and Play

Opportunities for language learning should be provided in a natural context, where the functional purpose of language is emphasized rather than skill acquisition (Saracho, 2004). This approach within a natural context can be facilitated through play. During play, young children use social conventions and skills that are essential in their language development and they inquire into the meaning of the written language (Roskos & Neuman, 1998). For example, Neuman and Roskos (1993) provide a play excerpt to illustrate how language and literacy are integrated in communication.

> *Jackie and Ericka (two 5-year-olds) are playing pharmacy in the Play Office. They are filling prescriptions for pretend customers.*
> **Jackie (taking a phone-in prescription):** *Write this down, Ericka. 55 purple. No, no, 55 pink and 2 purple.*
> **Ericka (scribbling this down on paper):** *There ya go. (She hands it to Jackie.)*
>    *(Ericka writes down a name copying from a child's name tag, then hands it and a small medicine bottle to Jackie).*
> **Jackie (reading the paper):** *You forgot the name (she points and hands it and a small medicine bottle to Jackie).*
> *(Ericka writes down a name copying from a child's name tag, then hands it down and a small medicine bottle to Jackie).*
> **Jackie:** *Ok, a lady's comin' over now. Ding, ding, ding. Come in . . . (She talks to the pretend customer.) Hello! Here you are ma'am. She got it all ready. Your name is back and your medicine too . . . 55 pink and 2 purple (p. 15).*

In this play excerpt children are developing both their oral and written language.

Children's interactions with peers in play support both oral and written language. When children play, they talk about what is, what was, and what can be. They suspend reality and play with concepts, thoughts, and language. The talk that occurs in play, their language play such as rhyming (Soderman & Farrell, 2008), and play episodes contribute to both their language and literacy development. Young children imagine, expect, see, feel, want, and respond to objects and situations with different emotions. They learn how words can be used to describe their emotions and experiences (Turnbull & Carpendale, 2001). They usually play with language and thinking or test the literacy functions and its applications (Saracho, 2004).

The social nature of play also nurtures the children's intellectual development. Children use meanings and objects to represent the real world. They use signs and tools to create mental patterns. Pretend play helps children to acquire higher-order thinking processes. It also frees them from the boundaries of the real world that confine them. When children interact with their peers in play, they process information that varies from their existing knowledge. This process frequently occurs when two or more children act out roles to recreate a real-life situation (Saracho, 1999b), such as pretending to be having dinner with their family members or being fire fighters who are putting out a make-believe fire (Christie, 1982). In play children gain the ability to talk about their mental world and to reflect on their own experiences, providing them with insight and self-understanding. When children acquire the vocabulary to mentally describe their experiences through a social process, they will experience that the concept of reflection makes sense (Vygotsky, 1978, 1986). This reflective resource makes it possible for the children to recall memories or to envision likely situations related to their mental situation (Turnbull & Carpendale, 2001).

Stories can help English language learners (ELLs) develop their vocabulary. ELLs use stories to share their lives and memories, which becomes a foundation for new learning. Sharing stories helps ELLs with their language acquisition, because they focus on oral language skills. The term "acquisition" relates to learning language that is "picked up" rather than being directly taught. It is an informal, "natural" way of learning a second language through meaningful learning experiences.

Language is one of the symbolic components of pretend play. Young children use symbolic objects (like a doll for a baby or a piece of paper for a blanket) and words to express themselves. Both language and objects represent reality and communicate meaning in pretend play (Saracho, 1986). At the beginning, young children manipulate objects to communicate thoughts. Later they assume several roles to separate meaning from actual objects (Vygotsky, (1934). In play, children learn to separate meanings and objects, and flexibly connect signs with their referents. For example, in play children learn that they can indiscriminately determine that a piece of wood (like a building block) will represent a car, a person, or any other object. The meaning of the block is not specified or built into the object, but rather it is based on the meaning assigned by the children. This knowledge permits the children to make use of socially defined signs (such as written words) to represent meanings. In these sign components, children verbally explain such transformations.

During play, young children usually participate in speech play to explore and manipulate the many principles in their language that guide their actions with verbal descriptions. Speech play promotes the foundation of metalinguistic awareness, which makes young children aware of the rules in their language. In pretend play, young children verbally assign the functions of both role and objects. For example, when children play, they use language to negotiate roles and to identify objects (e.g., saying, "No! You're the Mom, and I'm the baby!" Rowe, 1998, p. 13) that will connect objects and meanings. Young children organize representations of habitual situations from their daily lives, which provide knowledge about their behaviors and actions. Young children organize their knowledge of events into words that communicate their experience, which enhances some elements of carrying on a conversation. The children's knowledge (like situations, social rules on turn taking, topics) determines the quality of their conversation including interactions during play. When the children engage in a conversation, they generate a context for making inferences where they make meaningful connections between speaking and planning responses.

Young children learn more words when they engage in pretend self-play, pretend other play, and symbolic play. The children begin to use and remember the words that they use in the play situation. Garvey and Kramer (1989) show that children who engage in social pretend play develop more language, linguistic forms, and expressions than those children who did not engage in pretend play. Children assume roles and verbally communicate when they engage in pretend play. They also use language to plan, develop, and maintain play. The verbal communication in play helps young children to learn new words and concepts from experience. When children play, they use longer words and more adjectives and adverbs (Kostelnik et al. 1989), and the "language used in play is far more complex than that used in regular conversations" (Kostelnik et al., 1989, p. 169).

Preschoolers who engage in play have the required knowledge to participate in longer conversations that are more structurally complex. For example, preschoolers may make pretend birthday cakes in a sandbox instead of just pouring sand from one bucket to another. Short-Meyerson and Abbeduto (1997) believe that a conversation is better when both children know what they are talking about. They feel that children are able to adapt to their peer's level of expertise by explicitly showing mutual knowledge about it. Providing children with the same knowledge promotes the quantity, quality, and nature of the children's conversation.

To help children extend their conversation abilities, they can play together with a set of toys that are appropriate to one of the topics of study. Toys should be child-sized, and can be commercially available, everyday objects, or objects that are constructed from cardboard. For example, an airplane should be large enough for the children to enter, sit inside, and engage in conversation. Pairs of children can engage in conversations when they play together for ten minutes with child size toys related to topics like those in Table 8.1.

**TABLE 8.1.** Children's Topics of Conversation

| Coversation Subject | Objects to Aid in Conversation |
| --- | --- |
| Baking cookies | Oven, playdoh, cookie sheet, mixing bowl, mixer, spoon, measuring cup, ingredients (e.g., sugar, milk, eggs), rolling pin, cookie cutters, spatula |
| Airplane trip | Airplane, ticket counter, tickets, boarding passes, travel brochures, luggage, clothes, baggage checking counter, waiting area |
| Dentist office | Large chair, clip-on bib, toothbrushes, paper cups, X-rays, clipboard with forms, receptionist desk and chair, phone, calendar, paper, pens, waiting area with magazines |
| Doing laundry | Washer and dryer, ironing board, iron, hangers, clothes, laundry basket, laundry detergent, fabric softener |
| Metrorail trip | Interactive map, rail schedules, fare vending machines, visitors' kit guide to use the metrorail, brochures, publications with information, metro pocket guide, system map, points of interest near stations and information on system hours, fares, passes |
| Carpentry/painting/ construction work | Hard hats, plastic tools, toolbox and tools, measuring tape, lunch boxes, blue prints, empty paint cans, pipe fittings, golf tees for nails, Styrofoam to hammer golf tees into and pictures of people building, paint caps, paint sticks, rollers, rolling pans, paint samples, aprons, brushes, step stool |

At birth, children lack the social and language skills they need to communicate with others. Communication among children centered initially on play is concerned with manipulating the physical environment. Language develops with this context of action and rule-governed play. As children mature and become more able to sustain an interaction, play activity becomes less important and children gradually develop the ability to interact solely by verbal means. Garvey and Hogan (1973) proposed that these early activities, which promote the acquisition and use of verbal forms of interpersonal contact, are biologically useful and that they precede what later becomes thought, writing, and adult dialogue.

## Language Experiences

Many programs provide children with the opportunity to engage in spontaneous sociodramatic play. However, a language program needs to go beyond this kind of activity. Young children need to be provided with language learning opportunities that promote their normal language development. These opportunities need to be rich enough to motivate the children's interest and to help them increase their vocabulary and concept development. For example, if sociodramatic play opportunities are provided, they need to be carefully designed to include a variety of play topics, themes, and experiences (such as field trips, stories, films) to build shared background knowledge. In addition, a wealth of interesting props as well as sufficient time and space need to be provided (Levy et al. 1986).

In the early childhood classroom, children receive verbal messages from a variety of sources. They get specific directions for actions; information about the world; and opportunities for enjoyment, aesthetic appreciation, and comfort. The children respond based on the messages they receive and understand. They also communicate messages to others. MacCleod (2004) emphasizes the importance of language learning through activities that children find familiar and meaningful. Children's language can be developed in a play setting when teachers provide the appropriate opportunities such as those in Box 8.2.

---

**Box 8.2. Teachers' Roles in Developing Children's Language**

- Allow enough time and space for play in the classroom
- Provide the needed material resources
- Develop children's background knowledge for the play setting
- Scaffold the rehearsals of dramatic retellings; and
- Become involved in play settings as to guide the children's attention and learning through modeling and interaction (National Research Council, 1998, p. 184).

---

Young children enjoy and use oral language in the classroom as they assume social responsibility. Teachers can provide young children with many opportunities for oral language learning. Some of these opportunities are large group activities such as group discussion, story reading, story sharing, and "show and tell." However, in large group activities children can spend most of the time waiting for a turn. In promoting natural language learning, small group activities and interactions are usually more effective for oral language learning than are total class instructional settings. Additional opportunities to develop oral language learning can be provided through individual conversations with the children.

## Conversations

Oral language can be developed in an environment that provides children with thoughtful, genuine opportunities to participate in conversations. These opportunities should be within a non-threatening and predictable environment where children feel safe to express themselves in any way they choose. Conversation requires children to cooperate in a social activity and to develop a considerable trust in others. All of the children's ideas must be valued, honored, and reinforced; children should not be afraid of making mistakes. Teachers stimulate conversations between themselves and young children when they have a warm attitude, openly accept their ideas, and offer sensitive responses to their ideas. Clay (1991) states,

> If children have been slow to acquire speech or have been offered few opportunities to hold conversations (for many reasons) there can be limitations in the grammar they control, which might mean that they have difficulties with comprehending oral and written language. Such children may not have control of some of the most common sentence structures used in storybook English, and therefore are unable to anticipate what may happen next in the sentences of their reading texts (p. 38).

Children who are shy and untalkative in groups can be provided with opportunities to interact individually with the teacher and/or their classmates. They can engage in conversations about the activities, materials they are using, or about anything that focuses on something outside of themselves. Conversations increase the children's vocabulary and teach them about using language in a variety of contexts including their abstract thinking. Conversations can be initiated through open-ended questions that can elicit language expressions such as, "Tell me what you have there," or "Are there other ways you could make something like it?" Such questions can lead to a continuous conversation.

English language learners can engage in conversations in their first language. Teachers need to support the children's acquisition of their first language. They can (a) encourage parents to engage in meaningful conversations with their children using their home language, (b) encourage space within the school building for first-language instruction, and (c) use first-language resources that are within the community to motivate the children's conversations.

## Sharing Time

Sharing time can contribute to children's language development. Sharing time, also referred to as "show and tell," are discussion sessions with the whole class, which have many advantages. It is a sharing period where each child takes a turn to speak to the entire class. Often children bring an object from home and share it with the class. These objects should be displayed to the group instead of passing them around. They may prefer to share and discuss an event. The teacher and other children may make observations, ask questions, and make comments. All objects or events need to be accepted. Box 8.3 provides teachers with guidelines to use with children for sharing time (Brewer, 2007).

---

**Box 8.3. Children's Guidelines for Sharing Time**

- Describe in detail how the class created objects such as a clay object. Cooking and block building experiences can also be interesting topics for discussion.

- Bring objects from home that relate to a theme or topic of study such as something square when the class is learning shape concepts.
- Share important personal experiences such as a special trip or an interesting home event.
- Brainstorm to solve class problems or plan class activities.

## Discussions

Teachers need to provide many other opportunities in the classroom to initiate discussion. Informal discussions between the teacher and a child or group can take place on any occasion and should be encouraged by the teacher. The greater the amount of the child's verbal expression and the greater the number of adult–child interactions that take place, the greater the opportunities for language learning in the classroom.

Pictures provide a good basis for discussions. Photographs or magazine pictures can stimulate oral language as children discuss the contents of the picture. Many magazines, like *National Geographic*, publish excellent pictures that can be used in the classroom for language learning. *National Geographic* also publishes a children's version of the magazine.

## Photographs

From a very early age, young children are fascinated by photographs of themselves, families, and friends. A photograph provides an immediate feeling of being there. Photographs provide incentives for language with their constant conversations. Children look at photographs and talk about what they see. Photographs, memory representations, or family objects can be used during sharing time or while discussing a thematic concept. Photographs provide a visual image of everyday life, representing both the ordinary and the dramatic. They record a special memory that can be used to motivate the creation of stories. Children can use these items to create family stories that can be told and retold in the classroom (MacCleod, 2004). Photography can be used to find out about the children's out of school lives like in the following anecdote.

> Miguel took a picture of an old car seat covered with pine straw in the middle of the woods. Through his photographs and narrations, Miguel was able to continue his special relationship with his grandparents, who had moved back to El Salvador. He wrote, "This is my abuelito [grandfather]. He lived with us a while ago. He found a secret place in the woods. It had seats. He read books there. We found him in his secret place. He said to come." Miguel's photograph of his grandfather's secret place is one of many examples of how we learned what was important to children in their out of school lives (Allen et al., 2002, p. 313).

Photographs contribute to the children's language development, because they draw language out of children. The expression "A picture is worth a thousand words" acquires a literal meaning when children are doing the looking and talking.

Teachers can keep several cameras in the classroom and check them out to children to take home on a rotating basis (Allen et al., 2002). Or they can provide children with disposable cameras for them to photograph anything that is of interest to them in their families and communities. In either case, it's important to teach children how to use the cameras and how to take care of them.

The children's photographs represent their world, because they describe detailed culturally meaningful things and events of the children's experiences. They also indicate the children's interpretation of the image in the photograph, which motivates and guides the children's discussion. Teachers can also use photographs from home collections and historical archives within communities.

Photographs of the children can be available in the classroom for perusal, sharing, or play. They can also be used as language related materials. Children can match or sequence photographs, which are more meaningful for children than commercial cards. Teachers can make transparencies of each child's photograph (Woods, 2000), which can be taken at school or brought from home. They can set up an overhead projector for children to view their photographs. Children can collect, sort, and interpret a variety of photographs from various places. Small groups or pairs of children can discuss the photographs, interpret each photograph, and have someone write their interpretations. Then vocabulary lists can be generated to describe and interpret photographs using descriptive words (Schiller & Tillett, 2004). When using photographs to stimulate the children's conversation, teachers need to display them appropriately. See the guidelines in Box 8.4 (Woods, 2000).

**Box 8.4. Guidelines for Displaying Photographs to Stimulate Children's Conversations**

- Display a group photograph in an attention-grabbing and convenient location in the classroom.
- Create a photograph gallery of their class group photograph from past years. Children like seeing their siblings in this gallery.
- Place a photograph of each child in a container and listen to children's monologues and dialogues.
- Make charts using the children's photographs and next to their photograph write a sentence about each child (e.g., hair or eye color or favorite color, food, or animal).
- Take photographs of classroom events (e.g., field trips, celebrations, visitors) and put them in an album. These photographs can also be displayed around the classroom. For example, children can become fascinated by the spooky effect of a photograph of a dusk jack-o-lantern that has a candle burning inside. The face of the pumpkin will glow, while it has a bluish tint on the top from the reflection of the deep blue sky.
- Create an album that has all of the children's and teachers' baby and current photographs.
- Ask parents for a set of photographs of all the family members participating in activities they enjoy. Each week, display photographs of a different family.

Photographs can be used as part of the classroom activities. Woods (2000) suggests the following classroom activities:

- Photographs can be used as sequence cards to teach events in sequence for a regular activity such as baking cookies, getting a haircut, washing the dog, carving a pumpkin, or stories of real life experiences. These types of activities will stimulate conversation and storytelling among the children. Photographs can be used as story starters for dictated work.

- Mount pairs of photographs on cards for the children to match. Since this is a matching activity, teachers need to develop two prints of each photograph. For example, take pictures of different snowmen after a snowfall and develop prints of each. Or take two similar photographs of the children, mount them, and write their names below their photograph.

- Photographs of experiences for different seasons can reinforce concepts in a science unit on weather. Children can classify these photographs. Classification of photographs is both important and challenging to young children. Other photographs that can have a similar use include photographs of foods from different food groups, methods of transportation, or objects of assorted colors.

Children can have discussions and fun with a camera. Photography develops the children's language, visual literacy skills, and literacy skills.

Children can use photography to record all types of school activities that are taking place around the school. Schiller and Tillett (2004) report how children use digital cameras to record the progress in constructing a playground outside their school. The children looked at the playground models, listened to playground experts, and designed their ideal playground. Children provided input into the new playground that they wanted constructed.

## Digital Images

Information and communications technologies (ICT) extend the children's ability to explore information that will respond to their inquiries. Children can better understand what they are learning (like author stories or news events) using powerful digital media and technologies that are available. The interactivity of new digital technologies and use of the internet has facilitated communication beyond the classroom. Children can see that the author can publish and exchange views through graphics, animation, sound, and video.

Young children interact with visual images when they watch television, browse through magazines, read books, listen to stories, notice advertising images, and observe several images available through information and communication technologies. These images include some type of clip art, images created by the child through a software paint application, scanned images, or an image made using a digital camera (Schiller & Tillett, 2004).

## Narrative Stories

Everyone likes to hear a good story. When we were children, our parents or grandparents would tell us a story. Telling a story or writing a narrative is an important part of learning. A narrative story can be true or imaginary, but it is often easier to tell a story about an experience. A personal experience helps the narrator remember specific situations. Personal narratives can transfer the storyteller's experience to the listeners (audience), because the narrators retell the personal events that they experienced. "In a narrative, then, referents and events become serially active in the mind of the speaker, who, by using language, activates something resembling them in the mind of the hearer" (Chafe, 1986, p. 144). In addition, the structure of an original story emerges from the storytellers' unconscious knowledge so that the listener can "create the imaginary experience as the narrators are themselves creating it, with its sights, sounds, emotions, and actions" (Clark, 1994, p. 1019). Thus, narrative stories mark the retelling of specific personal events. The narrators unconsciously tell spontaneous narratives and shift during their story into "story-now" grammar and intuitively change tense, aspect, and pronoun in relation to present and past events. The grammatical shifts in their narration show that they as narrators are cognitively immersed in their past scenario. The sequences in their story are derived from a spontaneous oral narration and time sequences.

Children are natural storytellers. Storytelling has existed for centuries; it has been used to share with future generations the family's culture, beliefs, and traditions. A narrative can inform and preserve cultural identity as well as establish reality and the meaning of experience. The children's worlds are full of diverse narratives that they both hear and tell. Children's narratives are based on their real experience and on their fantasies. They use narratives to communicate their understanding of the world, to make factual and emotional sense of it, and to discover their place in it (Nicolopoulou, 2009).

Narratives can be part of a storytelling and story-acting practice that is part of the regular schedule in the preschool classrooms. Young children can be provided with opportunities to share stories with their peers. These stories may also be dictated and recorded by their teachers (like the language experience approach that is described in a later section). Later they can act them out during a group-time activity that includes the whole classroom. According to Ahn and Filipenko (2007), five-year-old

> Kathy experiences many different roles through her imaginary play. These diverse roles allow her to build a concept of herself, i.e., she tries on the mantles of a variety of characters and experiences what it is to be a doctor, a cashier, a mother or a daughter. These different roles provide different perspectives on her social world. Thus, through her narratives and imaginary play, Kathy constructs her understanding of her social world and the ways in which she can position herself within it (p. 282).

Kathy and her friends continued to play for several days where Kathy explored several social roles. She has an extraordinary understanding of the responsibilities and expectations that each role demands. For example,

> In the first scene, Kathy assumed the role of a doctor. During this scene she participated in the enactment of the birth of a baby and revealed her knowledge of the ways in which a doctor would participate in the birthing process. In the next scene Kathy adopted the role of sales person, and positioned herself in the world of commerce. Her role was carefully and precisely executed. In the role of sales person, she followed strict rules for determining what would be sold and the price of each item to be sold. In these examples and well as in her other imaginary play narratives, Kathy disclosed her understanding of authority, gender, dynamic family relationships, and economics. Through the appropriation of a variety of social roles she explores the social world from different perspectives as well as exploring her identity in terms of where she may fit into her social world (p. 283).

When children play, they explore emerging ideas and create "possible roles in possible worlds" (Dyson, 1997, p. 14). Fantasy and collaborative story-telling spontaneously occur in play. Children use language during play to describe other worlds, events, and characters. They also are starting to experiment with "decontextualized" language, how to acquire multiple perspectives, and how to settle the conflict between what was meant, what was said, and what was understood (Vygotsky, 1934).

An important major form of children's play focuses specifically on the portrayal of narrative scenarios. The children's pretend play and storytelling complement the narrative activity on a continuum that ranges from the discursive interpretation of narratives in storytelling to their act in pretend play. Box 8.5 provides guidelines to motivate young children to create narratives that are richer, more ambitious, and more meaningful (Nicolopoulou, 2009).

## Box 8.5. Guidelines to Motivate Children to Create Rich and Meaningful Narratives

- Storytelling is voluntary, self-initiated, and essentially spontaneous.
- Stories are not requested by adults nor prompted by props, story stems, or implied topics.
- Children have the freedom to select their own characters, subjects, and plots.
- Children act out the story to the class and to each other in a shared public setting.
- Children's storytelling and story-acting are part of the ongoing context of the classroom miniculture and the children's everyday group life.
- Children's narratives can be borrowed and cross-fertilized between the group. They can use these stories as vehicles for seeking or expressing friendship, group affiliation, and prestige.

Nicolopoulou (2009) observed a classroom of three- and four-year-old children who dictated stories. On the same day, children acted out their story in the order that each story was dictated. Then the teacher read the story aloud, after which the child/author selected which character he or she wanted to play and assigned children other roles that they would act out. After all the characters were assigned, the teacher read the story aloud again and the child-actors acted out the story as they listened to it. The rest of the children listened attentively. This procedure continued until all the stories dictated that day were acted out. A single storybook was used to write all of the stories.

Although it is important to have all children participate in this activity, teachers might find that this experience can be more productive if they consider the children's attention span. Perhaps only a small number of children will tell their stories each day. The number of children should be based on the children's attention. Children can be scheduled alphabetically and a chart should be displayed so that they know when it is their turn.

Stories and narratives give insight into the children's construction of their social world. Narrative stories are the children's autobiography; they describe their past, present, and their relationship to each. They become social actors who organize their lives and experiences through stories, which help them make sense of their world. As social actors, they retell their experiences and lives. Young children are able to create stories from their experiences. When children tell stories, they express the meaning and understanding of their experiences. Children mentally organize situations and solve a problem. The children's stories are based on characters and situations that focus on their experiences. They organize the events and experiences and obtain an understanding of them. Children tell stories to understand their world as well as their emotions, and stories help children heal from a bad emotional experience; they use storytelling to gain control over their feelings and understand their bad emotional experiences. When children tell or role play a story, they offer a self-portrait that can help teachers understand them. Their stories are often about events real or imagined, experiences, ideas, and dimensions of themselves. These stories show how children experience the world (Brewer, 2007).

## Creative Dramatics

Creative dramatics (briefly described in Chapter 2) is a form of improvised drama that is created by the children themselves and played with spontaneous dialogue and action. Children start with imaginative play that reflects their perceptions of life through simple dramatizations. Then they improvise their dialogue rather than memorize written scripts. Their purpose is to promote the children's growth and development rather than to entertain an audience. If children decide to share their ideas with the group, their dialogue is always spontaneous. Creative dramatics develops the children's language skills, socialization skills, creative imagination, understanding of human behavior, and abilities in working with their peers and in solving problems. Creative dramatics includes pantomimes, improvised stories and skits, movement and body awareness activities, and dramatic songs and games. Creative drama consists of three basic building blocks: *imagination*, *movement*, and *improvisation* (Bontempo & Iannone, 1988).

- *Imagination* is the basis of creative work. Children need to be presented with experiences that require them to use their imagination. These activities assist children to become aware of their senses, feelings, and perception. Imagination gives children the ability to observe accepted facts and see them in new and different ways.

    Activity: *The teacher dims the lights and children close their eyes. The teacher asks the children to imagine themselves (1) on top of the tallest house in their neighborhood, (2) looking at the other houses, people, and cars below, (3) floating in the air to get a better view of (name of town), and (4) flying next to an airplane. Based on the children's attention span, the teacher can provide directions where children rise high enough to see the rivers, mountains, other land, water forms, the world, and a space shuttle.*

- *Movement* requires children to use their bodies. Movement activities help children use their bodies through dance or pantomime. Children communicate their feelings, moods, and thoughts with their bodies as they gain confidence in their ability.

    Activity: *Children use a sheet to become a caterpillar egg inside the sheet. Then they grow out of the egg, become a tiny caterpillar by covering themselves in the sheet, grow out of their skin a number of times, becoming the caterpillar in the chrysalis stage (cocoon), breaking out as a butterfly, and flying like a butterfly using the sheet as wings.*

■ *Improvisation* requires immediate expression through speech and movement. The teacher or the children create a situation. When children have not had experience with improvisation, it is introduced with simple situations in which dialogue is used. For example, children express their thoughts and feelings about situations such as when their mothers find that their room is a mess or their feelings and thoughts on their first day at school.

Activity: *The children return from outdoor play and find that their room is in a mess. Have children talk about how they feel when they cannot work with materials. Have them pantomime what they would do to clean up the room* (Spodek & Saracho, 1994b, pp. 307–308).

## Language Environment

In general, children will benefit from a rich language learning environment that immerses them in language. Table 8.2 provides guidelines for creating a favorable language environment (Dudley-Marling & Searle, 1988).

**TABLE 8.2.** Guidelines to Create a Favorable Language Environment

| Guideline | Description |
|---|---|
| Physical setting that promotes interaction | Opportunities need to be provided for discussion such as learning centers or pets (e.g., gerbils or fish). Concrete manipulative materials (e.g., toys, magnets, lenses) need to be accessible to help children use language as they plan, observe, and report cause-and-effect relationships |
| Language opportunities that promote interaction and learning | Children need learning experiences where they are able to discuss and share what they know. For example, they can discuss and share their own personal experiences with bears with a story such as *The Three Bears* by Paul Galdone (1985). Several children may share their bear experiences with cartoons, trips to the circus or zoo, or camping where food was locked in cars, or supplies were hung from trees to keep unwanted intrusions from bears |
| Language experiences that are used for different purposes and audiences | All learning experiences need to have a purpose (e.g., decision-making, problem-solving, predicting). Children can share their experiences and feelings in small groups without the teacher. Computer programs can provide several rich language experiences |
| Teachers' responses that stimulate the children's discussion | Language is best learned when children engage in a conversation that is personal and meets their own needs. Teachers need to listen to the children attentively to encourage their initiated discussion. If a child says, "Boy you should *have* seen the neat stuff at the circus." The teacher's response needs to encourage the child to want to talk more about the circus. The teacher may say, "You had a good time at the circus." A show and tell language activity also invites children to engage in conversation |

Language experiences need to take into consideration the audience, the setting, and the purpose for communication. Children need many opportunities to use a wide range of language forms to develop their language and learning. Spontaneous and practical expressions about relevant objects and the use of appropriate syntactical structures increases the children's vocabulary. Box 8.6 provides guidelines for developing children's vocabulary (Kirkland & Patterson, 2005).

## Box 8.6. Guidelines for Developing the Children's Vocabulary

- Classrooms need to display print that reflects the children's language and work. Their displayed work should include a self-selected title and any other related information.
- Print that is displayed needs to have a purpose and represent the concepts that they are learning. Easy duties (e.g., signing in, marking lunch choices each day) and daily activities schedules need to be displayed with picture clues and words to help children follow them on their own. Meaningful charts, graphs, signs, symbols, logos, and language experience activities can also be displayed in the classrooms. These experiences help children to increase their vocabulary. When children see and hear themselves and others engaging in language experiences, they understand the purpose and use of language, which builds on their knowledge and use of language as they attempt to make sense of their classroom and their world.
- Libraries in the classroom need to be displayed in a way that children select, take care of, and use the books.
- Times need to be scheduled for children to socially interact with each other, which will extend their knowledge about language use. For example, children can have a class meeting each morning and afternoon. In the morning, they can share the home events; while in the afternoon (15 to 20 minutes), they can discuss their day's experiences in the classroom including their challenges and successes during the school day. The afternoon meeting can also have a ritual song, poem, or book that will send children home with language echoing in their minds.
- Language areas should be provided in the classroom. In these areas, there should be opportunities for children to retell favorite stories. Opportunities can consist of having flannel board stories, dress-up areas, puppets, stories on overhead transparencies, and listening centers that will encourage children to experiment and explore stories repeatedly. Children's books that promote their language can be made available. Box 8.7 provides examples of information books about the children's social world.

## Box 8.7. Children's Books for Language Development

- Brett, Jan. *Daisy Comes Home.* New York: G. P. Putnam's Sons, 2002. 32 pp., $16.99. Ages 4 to 8 years.
- Doyle, Malachy. *Sleepy Pendoodle.* Julie Vivas, Illustrator. Cambridge, MA: Candlewick Press, 2002. 32 pp., $12.99. Ages 3 to 6 years.

- Lee, Tae-Joon. *Waiting for Mama*. Doug-Sung Kim, Illustrator. New York: North-South Books, 2007. 32 pp., $16.95. Ages 3 to 8 years.
- McBratney, Sam. *Colors Everywhere*. Anita Jeram, Illustrator. Cambridge, MA: Candlewick Press, 2007. 24 pp., $7.99. Ages 2 to 5 years.
- McBratney, Sam. *When I'm Big.* Anita Jeram, Illustrator. Cambridge, MA: Candlewick Press, 2007. 24 pp., $7.99. Ages 2 to 5 years.
- Putock, Simon. *A Story for Hippo: A Book About Loss*. Alison Bartlett, Illustrator. New York: Scholastic Press, 2001. 22 pp., $15.95. Ages 3 to 6 years.
- Stevens, April. *Waking Up Wendell*. Tad Hills, Illustrator. New York: Random House Children's Books, 2007. 40 pp., $15.99. Ages 4 to 8 years.
- Vail, Rachel. *Sometimes I'm Bombaloo.* Yumi Heo, Illustrator. New York: Scholastic, 2002. 24 pp., $15.95. Ages 3 to 5 years.

A language and literacy environment should be provided where children are surrounded with books, printed materials, and writing materials to motivate them to enjoy books by looking at pictures, pretending to read the stories, and sharing them with others (Saracho, 2004), which serves as a dependable basis in learning. Rich language environments facilitate the children's transition to the formal school context. Meaningful language experiences are best for the children's learning.

## Learning Written Language

Play promotes the children's oral and written language, especially when they engage in symbolic thought. Symbolic thinking is similar to the kind of thinking that children use in reading and writing, where children understand what the symbols (letters) represent such as the letters in "cat" (Soderman & Farrell, 2008).

Children begin the writing process from the time they can hold a writing tool. Initially, children's drawing and writing may look like the same thing. Over time, as the children are surrounded by print, they come to see drawing and writing as two different symbols and will differentiate between the two. Through writing, children learn that the purpose of text is to be understood. They learn that written language is not exactly the same as spoken language and that it can be used for a variety of purposes. Children communicate this understanding through the differentiation they make between various types of writing they use in lists, letters, and stories (McGee & Richgels, 2004). For example, the extract below describes the writing experience of a Spanish-speaking child who is deaf and hard-of-hearing. Elena had contracted meningitis when she was 13 months old and was left with a profound hearing loss in both ears. Before her illness, her parents spoke Spanish at home and then switched the language of their home to English and a signed version of English.

> At age 3½, Elena picked up a telephone at her grandmother's house, cradled the receiver to her ear, and began making scribbles on a pad of paper, vocalizing unintelligibly as she wrote. She hung up the telephone after filling one page of the small pad and filled five more pages with varying sorts of script. Some pages had sticks, while others seemed to have attempts at making the first letter of her name. On the next to the last page she drew a picture of her abuela (Spanish for grandmother) that overlaid (or underlaid) some scribbling and told me that was Abuela (p. 209).

Young children have a variety of writing concepts. See Box 8.8 (National Council of Teachers of English, 2006).

---

**Box 8.8.  Young Children's Writing Concepts**

1. Young children know about written language and different kinds of writing such as stories, lists, and signs. Writing instruction needs to reflect the children's experience and knowledge.
2. All families participate in writing-related experiences. Family and school writing experiences should be related to guarantee greater participation and success with school tasks.
3. Writing goes through multiple forms before it becomes standard writing.
4. The "language arts" are in agreement as drawing supports writing and writing supports reading. Opportunities to use multiple expressions of language develop the children's language learning and ability.
5. Writing instruction needs to be a social activity that is integrated into the social contexts.
6. Extensive language, reading, and writing experiences within a specific category increases successful performance.
7. Writing effectively develops the children's thinking and learning throughout the curriculum.
8. The children's writing and language relate to their communities and social world.

---

The natural event of letter writing begins in infancy (Vygotsky, 1978) with the infant's actions, gestures, speech, play, and drawing, which are all forms of representation. Young children create several symbol systems to create meaning. They use writing to draw, tell, and act stories. Drawing is critical in the children's writing process. They draw to organize and plan their written text (Dyson, 2006).

Young children usually draw pictures first, write words or mark symbols, and read their recorded story. Young children's readings of their stories will be longer than their written version. When children read the stories, they communicate their messages (McGee & Richgels, 2004).

Children often begin writing at home. Children enjoy writing their names. Children's signatures are their first understanding of written language. At first young children assume that pictures, numbers, and letters relate to print. They are not able to distinguish among them. As children progress in their understanding of literacy, they begin to tell the difference between pictures and letters. For example, in a study (Saracho, 1990) of children's writing, children were asked to write their name on an eight and one-half inches by 11 inches piece of white xeroxing paper. A three-year-old kept drawing pictures and was therefore given a blank piece of paper over and over again. Finally, frustrated, the child rolled his eyes and said, "I guess I have to write my house." He drew what he called a house around a stick figure of himself. The children's experience with print leads them to make a scribble to represent their name; later they add a shape or two, then they include the first letter in their name, and finally they write their full name. For example, Table 8.13 and Figure 8.1 show the levels of progression in three-year-old children's writing (Saracho, 1990).

**TABLE 8.3.** Levels of Progression in Three-Year-Old Children's Writing

| Progress Level | Description |
| --- | --- |
| Level 1 Scribbling | Children attempt to write their name by moving the writing tool on the paper. Using their arms and hands, they make longitudinal and circular motions. Many times they draw a picture instead of writing their name |
| Level 2 Horizontal Movement | The children's marks on paper have a considerable tendency toward the horizontal and some systematic "up and down" squiggling. They make hasty scribbling in an up and down motion progressing across the page. Children attempt to imitate the adult's manner in rapid cursive writing |
| Level 3 Separate Symbol Units | Though horizontal movement (with greater regularity in the vertical strokes) still exists, children have a tendency to make discrete symbol units, some of which are scarcely recognizable as letters |
| Level 4 Incorrect Written Letters | Letters are written incorrectly. The waviness in imitation of adult cursive writing is almost absent. Most letter units are recognizable. There is more construction in space. Subjects have discovered separate letter units and have developed an interest in writing those letter symbols |
| Level 5 Correct Spelling of First Name | A mixture of correct and incorrect letters appears in this level. Correct spelling of the first name is seen. |

*Level 1*   **Scribbling**

Mathew
3–1

Michael
3–2

Montine
3–5

*Level 2*   **Horizontal Scribbling**

Nancy
3–1

Mathew
3–1

Justine
3–5

Romualdo
3–6

*(Continued)*

*Level 3*   **Discrete Units**          *Level 4*   **Letters**

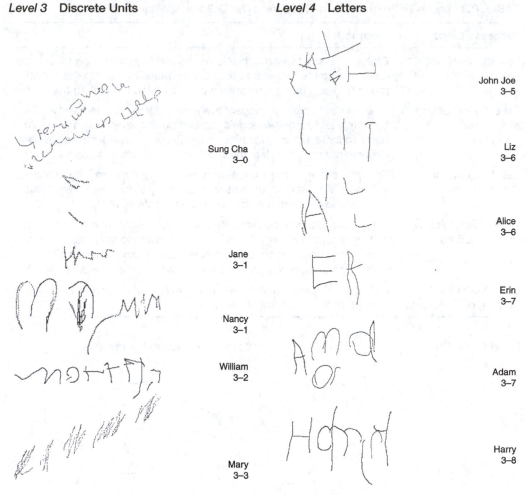

Sung Cha
3–0

Jane
3–1

Nancy
3–1

William
3–2

Mary
3–3

John Joe
3–5

Liz
3–6

Alice
3–6

Erin
3–7

Adam
3–7

Harry
3–8

*Level 5*   **Correct Spelling**

**FIGURE 8.1.   Levels of progression in Three-Year-Old Children's Writing.**

Saracho's levels reflect the results of one study of young children's early writing attempts. They are examples of the children's understanding of the written symbols rather than a proposal of developmental stages. Young children develop their own ideas about writing such as the following (Saracho & Spodek, 1996):

> **Maria** *likes to write because she likes to make words, but she knows that some children would rather play than write. She likes to use markers and some of the things she likes to do to write when not told to, are to draw pictures, make a plane, and write numbers and letters.*

> **Steve** *likes to write in order to learn how to write his name and those of other members of his family. He also thinks that some children would rather play than write. He prefers pens to pencils because they "write pretty." He likes to draw a house with boys playing with a small dog and its mother. He does not like to be told what to write.*

> **Flora** *likes to write because if she does not learn her mother will get mad. She thinks all children like to write because they like to work in school. She likes to use markers because they come in all colors. She likes to draw a picture of a clown and prefers to be able to write what she wants to, not what a teacher tells her to write. But teachers can help because "they know what to do."*

Young children can appropriately learn to hold and use crayons and paint brushes to help them make the transition from drawing to writing with ease. Children need to be provided with a variety of writing experiences such as computer-based writing, writing letters, and writing stories about themselves or storybook characters.

Writing is a visual and motor activity, which has an impact on children with visual impairments. Children who are blind can use braille, but they must also learn to use other kinds of communication (such as special devices that assist them to write letters, spell words, sign their names). Children with visual impairments need dark lined paper and large pencils. Sand and clay writing experiences help them develop their motor skills. Learning to type is also a useful skill. Children with physical disabilities (such as severe motor difficulties) can use an electric typewriter or a computer with a word processing program. They can also use computers with joysticks. Writing experiences for children with disabilities must transpire from meaningful experiences and be integrated with other activities that have definite writing purposes.

## Writing Experiences

During writing experiences, children need to interact with others, explore print on their own, try out a variety of written forms, and make up their own literacies. These meaningful experiences provide young children with the knowledge about the forms and functions of written language in situations that describe their surrounding environment. As a matter of fact, environments (both physical surroundings and human relationships) that integrate rich written language experiences allow the children to naturally participate in literacy-related situations (Neuman & Roskos, 1997) such as writing invitations to a birthday party. Children have the opportunity to brainstorm who to invite to the party, write lists of friends that they want to invite to their birthday party, write the invitations at the writing center, sign their names to the cards, and put in the envelope a map to their house with the landmarks labeled, and drop the invitations in the classroom mailbox (Soderman & Farrell, 2008). Writing experiences need to be part of the children's knowledge about language. They need to explore, initiate, and practice writing. Writing experiences need to be spontaneous such as those on Table 8.4.

**TABLE 8.4. Spontaneous Writing Activities**

| Activity | Description |
| --- | --- |
| Catalog Shopping | Children can go through catalogs or store brochures. Each child writes his/her name or initials next to the items they would order |
| Graffiti Bulletin Board | Poster boards or bulletin boards can be used for children's messages. Children can post comments, illustrations, or/and cartoons with dialogues. Children might also record a story or message using a cassette or CD recorder |
| Stationery Design | Children can design their own stationery, using potato prints, for example, at the top or along the borders. The children can write their messages on this stationery |

Table 8.5 provides suggestions to promote writing in young children (Spodek & Saracho, 1994b).

## Language Experience Stories

When young children actively participate in their social and cultural world, they learn and understand written language. Many teachers use the language experience approach. With this approach, the children go on a field trip or participate in another exciting activity. After

**TABLE 8.5. Experiences to Promote Children's Writing**

| Experience | Description |
| --- | --- |
| Interrupted Episode | At a climactic point in a story or film, stop reading or viewing. Ask the children what happens next. Write down and discuss their responses. There is no one right response, but discuss which of the responses are plausible |
| Story Illustration | When introducing a story, the teacher identifies a character that children need to pay particular attention to. Children will not see the illustrations so that at the end of the story, they will depict the character through drawings. Later children compare their illustrations with those of the book. A bulletin board is made with the children's drawings and the original illustration in the middle |
| Inkblot Writing | A large sheet of newsprint is placed on the floor. The teacher adds cornstarch or flour to ink to make it thick. Let the children throw the ink mixture onto the paper, Then fold the paper in half, and reopen it. Ask the children to identify and describe the hidden pictures within the blob they have created |
| Mystery Box | Make a fist-size hole in the top of a shoe box and attach a toeless sock to the edge of the hole. (A long sock over a coffee can also be used.) Place different things in the box. The children will place their hand through the sock into the box and describe what they feel. The teacher records their descriptions on a chart. Children should be encouraged to review mystery box charts from previous sessions (p. 325) |

the experience, the children and teacher discuss the experience and the teacher makes sure children understand the concepts. In this type of group story, each child dictates a sentence. The teacher writes the child's precise words and reads it back immediately, focusing on left to right sequence. Then the children read the sentence, while at the same time the teacher moves his or her arm from left to right as the children are reading. The children discuss and give a title to the story. The children will read the story many times and the teacher will use this story to help the children to acquire developmentally appropriate reading skills such as rhyming words and identifying words with the same meaning, words with opposite meaning, words that sound the same but have different meaning, and vocabulary words. The chart with the story is put on display for children to read at their convenience. The story can be xeroxed for children to take home and read to their parents. The individual experience story follows the same steps as the group experience story. A child may prefer an individual story because of a personal experience such as a birthday party or a new baby at home. All language experience stories need to be personally meaningful to children, because they see themselves as the authors of the stories. Children use their own personal experiences and their own language to express their thoughts in written language.

## Writing in Children's Play

Play helps young children develop their communication abilities, make representations of real and imaginary characters and events in fantasy play, and prepare a variety of narratives based on their daily experience (Cook, 2000). The children's writing experiences need to reconstruct and represent their daily experiences. Vygotsky (1983) points out that the connection between writing and other forms of symbolic representation (like make-believe play and drawing) are "different moments in an essentially unified process of development of written language" (p. 116). Children's writing develops from the children's pre-speech gestures, from the language they hear and later use, and when they become aware that the written word, like the spoken word, represents reality. Children can understand what writing is for and what it is like through social interaction and many storybook experiences (Wells, 1986). Young children convert the speech of others and storybook language into their own written texts. They use drawing and invented spelling to negotiate meaning and understand the complex world around them.

## Writing and Dramatic Play

The play environment can stimulate the children to write. According to Dyson (1989), "children's dramatic play and their imaginative drawings are their own replayings and graphic organizations of their experienced worlds" (p. 25). A supportive environment that has writing and art areas for children to engage in dialogue extends their writing knowledge when they learn the roles of authors and audience as they encounter new ideas and conflicts about print construction and meaning (Rowe, 1998). Children learn about writing when they use it as part of their personal and social lives.

Children find dramatic play to be a very exciting experience; because it has a feeling of authenticity and seriousness that differs from most other experiences. When children play, they engage themselves with elements of life that frequently require them to think and behave like individuals (adults, parents, children, babies) in the real world. The reality in play is a very complex place, although reality in play has an adaptable connection with the unreal (Hall, 1998). Heath (1983) stresses that:

> The constraints of reality enter into the play which accompanies these socio-dramas in yet other ways. Once the children have announced a suspension of reality by declaring a sandbox a city, a rock a little girl, or a playroom corner a kitchen, they paradoxically more often than not insist on a strict adherence to certain details of real-life behaviour. In playing with doll babies, girls insist they are not dressed unless a diaper is pinned about them. Children in a play kitchen will break their routine of washing dishes by reaching over to stir the contents of a pot on the stove. When asked why they do this, they reply "It'll burn" (pp. 164–165).

Children need play experiences that help them to distinguish between reality and fantasy in their world. Even the housekeeping area can provide opportunities to support the development of writing skills. Children can write shopping lists, and can also write recipes, using pictures to represent some things they cannot spell or write. Children learn the functions of writing when it is integrated in their play, such as in centers that focus on the office, grocery store, and publishing setting. See Table 8.6.

**TABLE 8.6.** Writing Play Centers

| Play Center | Description |
| --- | --- |
| Office | An office center can be created in the early childhood classroom. It can include an old typewriter, telephone, chairs, and tables. Other office equipment and materials may be added as needed. The children can assume the role of office workers, having conversations on the telephone, writing notes, and filling out forms (Korat, Bahar, & Snapir, 2002/2003) |
| Grocery Store | A grocery store can be created in one corner of the classroom. The children can be asked to bring things from home to stock the store, including empty boxes and packages of food, paper and plastic bags, printed advertisements to promote business, a cash register or calculator, as well as pencils and paper to make notes (Korat et al., 2002/2003) |
| Publishing Center | Four- and five-year-old children should be encouraged to be independent writers, to think of themselves as authors, and to have confidence in their writing ability. Children can take on different roles as authors, illustrators, printers, binders, and customers |
| Garage | The children can build a garage to be located in a corner of the classroom. They would decide how to play in this area, which might include different tools and car parts that are safe for children to play with. They could build a ramp out of large hollow blocks and use the school's tricycles as vehicles to repair. The children might visit a local garage that repairs cars to be able to replicate a garage in their classroom. The children can draw what they see or make notes to refer to when they return to school |

The garage can also be used as a thematic unit. Box 8.9 provides an extensive example of a garage thematic unit to help children understand that writing-play experiences are part of the children's real world (Hall, 1998; Hall & Robinson, 2003).

## Box 8.9.  Garage Thematic Unit

Four- and five-year-old children planned to build a garage to be located in a corner of the classroom. They decided how to play in this area, although outside that space they experienced several "special events" related to the whole process in constructing the garage. One of these events, the complaint, occurred at the beginning stage of building the garage. A complete description of this experience can be found in Hall and Robinson (2003).

The children visited a local garage that repaired cars so they would be able to replicate a garage in their classroom. The children noticed environmental print both inside and outside the garage. They were particularly interested in the ramp (car lift). The children drew what they saw, recorded notes on clipboards, discussed the visit, and wrote individual thank you letters to the garage owner. To get permission to build the garage, the children wrote to the Town Hall and requested planning application forms. Some children completed these applications, drew plans, and mailed them. Although they received permission to begin building, the children received a letter of complaint from a school neighbor, Mrs. Robinson. She wrote the following letter:

*Dear Mrs. Booth's Class,*

*I have heard that you are going to build a garage. I wish to complain about it. Garages are very noisy, very dirty, and very dangerous. Someone may get hurt with all the cars. I do not think you should be allowed to build a garage.*

*Yours faithfully,*
*Mrs. Robinson* (Hall & Robinson, 2003, p. 78).

The class opened and discussed the letter. The children were shocked with the letter and thought they needed to challenge Mrs. Robinson's position to continue building their garage. They had extensive discussions with many disagreements. One solution was to keep on building the garage and should Mrs. Robinson ever visit their classroom, they would take the signs down to trick her into believing that they had stopped building. They wrote to Mrs. Robinson letting her know that there was no garage, but she found out the garage was still being built. Again she wrote to the children. The children had to cope with being discovered; they had more extensive discussions, and finally wrote persuasive letters to convince her to let them build their garage. The children's convincing letters were successful.

In building the garage, the children experienced a series of special events and participated in a variety of writing activities that were meaningful to them, because they focused on the life of their community. For example, they,

- wrote thank you letters;
- made notes during their visit;
- wrote letters requesting application forms to get permission to build;
- completed the planning application form;
- read the letter that complained about their garage;
- responded with persuasive letters to the letter of complaint;

- read the reaction to their letters; and wrote a reassuring letter;
- wrote lists of things that they needed in the garage;
- read the guide on accidents at school, developed their own accident guide, instructions, and rules;
- composed advertisements for jobs in the garage;
- completed application forms to work in the garage;
- wrote lists for the stock; and made labels and posters;
- wrote to a newspaper;
- wrote grand opening invitations;
- developed a program with a schedule of events;
- created name tags;
- wrote a description of the garage for the blind lady;
- developed a "feely" book for the blind lady;
- created an audiotape for the blind lady;
- read letters that the nursery school children wrote;
- read the nursery school children's response;
- wrote estimates for the repairs of the nursery school children's bike;
- wrote letters to explain their repair prices;
- read the letter from the airport; and
- responded to the airport to share their position.

This noteworthy list only represents some of the many writing experiences that had a high and rich range of forms of text. The young children engaged in meaningful experiences for a 12 week period. This kind of writing seemed difficult for young children, but the children seemed to enjoy these challenges; because they wanted to build their garage and they cared about keeping it in the classroom. The children's writing experiences were based on the special events, which were socially constructed activities that had meaning to them.

The garage consisted of a shared nature of events, where children engaged in writing experiences through play. The writing activities would have no meaning without the play. The play experiences placed their learning into context and provided a purpose. The experiences with the garage related to the community's daily life with real situations.

## Summary

Language development occurs in the context of play. When children play, they interact with others, label, organize a sequence of situation events, negotiate, and engage in "pretend talk," which motivates them to communicate with peers and adults. Children plan their play event, negotiate their roles, what the available materials represent, and how they will play. Their play is a shared meaning-making activity. They cooperate in dramatizing a meaningful story and at the same time depend on their play experience to understand their world. Children develop plans of action, which are their blueprints of ways to relate and sequence actions and events.

Within the play context children interact with others, create in sequence a series of play situations, and negotiate procedures through conversation. They discuss the play procedures and negotiate rules, relationships, and roles such as saying, "You be the baby and I'll be the mother." At the beginning of a play episode, young children engage in ongoing explicit and implicit negotiations for joint meaningful play (DeZutter, 2007). Children use both their eyes and speech to learn about their social world (Vygotsky, 1978). When young children play, they become aware of their physical world and act out several roles from their social world, which develops their language. For instance, children may pretend to be at a restaurant, order from a menu, and use "pretend talk." Pretend play is an important experience, because children have the opportunity to act out their plans and several roles to convey their thoughts and feelings about their social world (Garvey, 1990).

Play researchers believe that more social interaction and types of language are drawn out among children in the housekeeping area (Pellegrini, 1984) through sociodramatic play. Sociodramatic play promotes the children's language development (McGee, 2003), since children obtain some level of meaning of a new word when they are introduced to it. They frequently use "rare words" during toy play, mealtime, and storybook reading. Young children learn and generate meaning from new words based on the (a) action or object, (b) their interpretation of new vocabulary, (c) social norms, and (d) explanation of their meaning.

The children's writing needs to reflect the nature of their daily life within their environment. Teachers need to be sensitive to and support the young children's social and educational needs. They need to help children relate their writing to life, its school culture, and peer culture activities. Young children find writing to be a difficult process. They can understand its shape, pattern, and texture if it relates to their individual needs and it evolves around the specific purposes and themes of a school experience related to their social situations. Writing is something to learn about where the learners are able to "empower action, feeling, and thinking in the context of purposeful social activity" (Wells, 1986, p. 14) that can help them advance toward becoming literate (Kantor et al., 1992) in their preschool years.

# Chapter 9
# Literature-play Learning Experiences

Children's books are "printed words produced ostensibly to give children spontaneous pleasure."

(Darton, 1932)

Children's literature links children's emotional and intellectual experiences to their wider world. It provides children with aesthetic experiences that are beneficial in all aspects of their lives including their language and linguistic development. Reading aloud to children supports their understanding of narrative structures, including features such as story beginnings and endings, and character behavior (Kiefer, 2004).

Children's literature provides words and illustrations that help them to become aware of the order of events, unity of action, balance of occurrences, or new frame of reference of events. They learn to understand character, setting, issues, and problems. They enjoy the beauty, wonder, and humor of the story or experience the anguish in the sorrow, injustice, and ugliness of it. The story can help children identify with story characters to provide them with vicarious experiences in other places, times, and lifestyles. They can experience a variety of perspectives, risks, mystery, and suffering. Children also find pleasure in a feeling of accomplishment and belonging. Literature gives children the opportunity to dream, to think, and to ask questions about themselves (Galda et al., 2009). The purpose of this chapter is to describe the relationship between literature and play, literature experiences that support play, guidelines for reading children's books, and visual literacy in children's literature.

## Literature and Play

Literature should be an integrated component in children's play. Literature can offer a context where children have meaningful interactions with different genres and it can promote children's social development and help them develop alternative perspectives. Children will read or listen to the story and build relationships with information that they hear or listen to. In these situations, children interact with each other to integrate, construct, and relate knowledge to the printed text (Vygotsky, 1978). These literature experiences need to be well planned to help young children understand and appreciate literature, but the experiences should be spontaneous, pleasurable, and enthusiastic to enrich the children's lives and promote their appreciation of language and literature.

## Literature Experiences to Support Play

Literature experiences provide children with the opportunity to explore and experiment with interesting materials such as books and puppets. Literature offers many opportunities for children to interpret, improvise, and pretend by creating their own scripts, engaging in storytelling, and assuming a variety of roles. It motivates children to engage in drama that may or may not follow the content of the story, but may instead build on themes, characters, or ideas within it. Children may assume the role of one of the characters and behave the way they perceive the character in the story. Children may use literature as a source and improvise when they develop a new story with the same characters or identify with characters who are like them. It is important that children be provided with a variety of literature experiences such as reading books, storytelling, poetry, puppetry, and creative dramatics.

### Books

Studies of children's literature in school-based settings showed an improvement in reading achievement when children are read to and allowed to respond to books through talk, creative drama, art, and writing (Kiefer, 2004), which contribute to the children's language learning. Children's literature integrates many genres including ABC and counting books, nursery rhymes and poetry collections, picture storybooks, novels, and nonfiction. The accepted criteria for these books are that they provide literary and artistic experiences for children, that is, they provide children with meaningful information and contain a variety of media that makes the book attractive to the child. Such criteria are exemplified in such prestigious awards as the Newbery and Caldecott Medals (Association of Library Service to Children (ALSC), 2007).

The language used in children's books is very important. Children store up all the words, phrases, and story elements they hear and after a time this language becomes their own. Books can fill out their storehouses of beautiful words. Even simple stories can do this. Children enjoy Wanda Gág's book *Millions of Cats* and repeat the words, "Millions of cats, millions of cats, billions and trillions of cats" Brewer (2007). Books need to be carefully selected to provide a balanced literature program (Galda et al., 2009) such as a collection of books from several categories (see Table 9.1). A small collection of books from the following categories can provide a balanced literature program (Spodek & Saracho, 1994b).

**TABLE 9.1.** Children's Books from Several Categories

| Type of Book | Useful Examples |
|---|---|
| Mother Goose | *Book of Nursery and Mother Goose Rhymes* compiled and illustrated by Marguerite de Angeli, Garden City, N.Y.: Little, Brown & Co., 1970<br>*The Real Mother Goose* illustrated by Blance Fisher Wright. New York: Dover Publications, 2008 |
| Alphabet Books | *Peter Piper's Alphabet* illustrated by Marcia Brown. New York: Charles Scribner's & Sons, 1959<br>*The ABC Bunny* by Wanda Gág. Minneapolis, MN: Univ Of Minnesota Press, 2004 |
| Counting Books | *My First Counting Book* written by Lilian Moore and illustrated by Garth Williams. New York: Simon & Schuster, 2001<br>*The Very Hungry Caterpillar* (pop up edition) written by Eric Carle. New York: Philomel |
| Concept Books | *Cubes, Cones, Cylinders, & Spheres* by Tana Hoban. N.Y. Greenwillow Books, 2001<br>*Symbols and their Meaning* written and illustrated by Rolf Myller. New York: Atheneum, 1978 |
| Machines Personified | *Mike Mulligan and His Steam Shovel* written and illustrated by Virginia Lee Burton. New York: Houghton Mifflin, 2006<br>*The Little Engine that Could: Deluxe Edition* by Watty Piper & George and Doris Hauman. New York: Grosset & Dunlap, 2009 |
| Animal Stories | *Millions of Cats* by Wanda Gág. NY: Puffin, 2006<br>*The Complete Adventures of Curious George: 70th Anniversary Edition* by Hans A. Rey. New York: Houghton Mifflin Co., 2010 |
| Humorous and Nonsense Books | *Horton Hatches the Egg* by Dr. Seuss (Theodor Seuss Geisel). New York: Random House, 2004<br>*Sylvester and the Magic Pebble* by William Steig. New York: Simon & Schuster, 2005 |
| Picture Books | *Cinderella* by Charles Perrault and illustrated by Marcia Brown. Publisher: Anonymous, 2007<br>*Crow Boy* written and illustrated by Taro Yashima. New York: Penguin, 1976 |
| Easy-to-Read Books | *Grasshopper on the Road* written and illustrated by Arnold Lobel. New York: Harper Collins, 1986<br>*Little Bear's Visit* written by Else Holmelund Miniarik and illustrated by Maurice Sendak. New York: Harper Collins, 1992 |
| Participation Books | *Brian Wildsmith's Puzzles* written and illustrated by Brian Wildsmith. Minneapolis, MN: Millbrook Press, 1996<br>*Zoo City* written and photographed by Stephen Lewis. New York: William Morrow & Co. Inc., 1976 |
| Information Books | *Kites* written and illustrated by Larry Kettlekamp. New York: William Morrow & Co., 1959<br>*Your Friend, the Tree* written by Florence M. White and illustrated by Alan E. Cober. New York: Alfred A. Knopf, Inc., 1969 |
| Poetry | *Hailstones and Halibut Bones* written by Mary O'Neill and illustrated by John Wallner. Garden City, New York: Doubleday & Co., 1990<br>*Hey Bug! and Other Poems About Little Things* selected by Elizabeth M. Itse and illustrated by Susan Carlton Smith. New York: American Heritage, 1972<br>*Oxford Book of Poetry for Children* compiled by Edward Blishen and illustrated by Brian Wildsmith. New York: Oxford University Press, 1996<br>*The Complete Collection of Nonsense Books* by Edward Lear. New York: Benediction Books, 2009 |

Early childhood classrooms should have a balance of well-written and well-illustrated books for children, including collections of stories or anthologies, even without illustrations. Other teachers, supervisors, librarians, local colleges, and universities can provide guidelines for teachers in selecting books if they require guidance. Every year a committee of the ALSC (2007) identifies children's books that are worth noticing, important, distinguished, and outstanding. The committee's selection includes books that have a specific commendable quality, display venturesome creativity, and are of different genres (e. g., fiction, information, poetry, picture books) that would be of interest to children in several age levels (birth through age 14). The ALSC also identifies children's books that were identified in the past, children's recordings, videos, and computer software for children's books (see web link in the reference section).

Teachers need to select a variety of books that are of interest to children. Humorous books can motivate children, encourage discussion, and provide an active environment. The interpretation of humor requires children to use their insight, thinking skills, and critical skills. Books provide children with information about things outside their immediate world, broadening their perspective. Teachers need to select informative books that are accurate and authoritative. Children's books need to integrate the children's literary experience with the world of whimsy and fantasy.

Preschool children who are at risk need to be presented with books from a variety of genres (like traditional storybooks, informational texts). They will learn text conventions and to read this type of genre to obtain information. Informational texts use a topical theme that makes this text genre highly appropriate to communicate factual information about the social or natural world of the children who are at risk (Pollard-Durodola et al., 2011).

Books for children who are gifted need to attract their interest and motivate them to independently search for additional information after they have finished reading a book. They can search for information in handbooks, biographies, fictional stories, and picture books. Then children who are gifted need to engage in enrichment activities that will further their knowledge about the topic they are reading.

Engagement with books provides the foundation for the different subject areas (such as language, social studies). Books and their pictures communicate the mores, attitudes, and values of the culture. For example, teachers can use children's storybooks that reflect Mexican American families and themes. They can learn about Pat Mora, who is a children's author and poet. Children enjoy storybooks about the family like *Family Pictures/ Cuadros de Familia* (1990), written by Carmen Lomas Garza. This picture book is an album of paintings of the artist's memories when she was growing up in a small Texas town. Her Mexican American community is portrayed in these paintings, doing things such as celebrating a birthday, picking cactus, making tamales, and going to church. Another book that can be used is *Too Many Tamales* (1996), written by Gary Soto and illustrated by Ed Martínez. It is a story about a girl named Maria. She helps her family make tamales at Christmas. She also tries on her mother's wedding ring, which is lost. While trying to find the ring, the children eat all the tamales.

Factual, realistic, and imaginative literature stimulates the children's curiosity and nurtures their interests. Books help children learn the language, explore the meaning of language, and stimulate their higher order mental processes: thinking about meanings, seeing relationships, remembering similar feelings and events, developing concepts, generalizing, and abstracting. The language in books helps to increase children's vocabulary in supportive and creative ways. Books should be selected for their use of beautiful language

(Brewer, 2007). However, books should focus on the children's interests and should be fun. A classroom's collection of books should reflect a balance between contemporary works and classics, between realistic and fanciful literature, between fictional and informational material, between popular and precious reading matter, between expensive and inexpensive books, between periodicals and books, and between prose and poetry. Humorous books encourage discussion and children need to use their insight and thinking skills to interpret their humor.

## Predictable Books

Books that are written in a predictable format have a rhythmical and repetitive pattern that helps young children to guess what is on the following page. A good example is Bill Martin's (1986) *Brown Bear, Brown Bear, What Do You See?* After reading a few pages of words, phrases, and themes that repeat throughout the book, children can easily figure out the pattern. The following phrases from *Brown Bear* are an example of this repetitive pattern.

> Brown bear, brown bear, what do you see?
> I see a red bird looking at me.
> Red bird, red bird, what do you see?
> I see a yellow duck looking at me.

Other predictable books use a cumulative pattern where previous ideas are incorporated into subsequent ones, such as *I Know a Lady Who Swallowed a Fly* (Hoberman, 2004) or *The Gingerbread Man* (Kimmel, 1993). Some predictable books have familiar sequences such as *The Very Hungry Caterpillar* (Carle, 2008). Predictable books provide young children with a rewarding experience and offer a practicable and excellent way to supplement reading instruction.

## Big Books

Big books are large versions of children's books. Big books allow young children to see the text, which contributes to their visual discrimination, letter and word recognition, and critical thinking skills. Big books may be expensive or may not be available for all of the children's books. Teachers and children can turn their own version of a popular story into a big book. The production process can stimulate the young children's interest in reading and develop a sense of ownership and pride in their big book. Box 9.1 provides directions for making big books (Meinbach, 1991).

### Box 9.1. Making Big Books

1. Select a favorite story.
2. Copy each page of text onto a blank piece of paper approximately 25" X 15".
3. Write the text in print large enough for a group of children to see. Once the text is written, reread the story and discuss possible illustrations.
4. Illustrate the text. If groups of students are making the illustrations, the teacher needs to assist them.

5. Determine the correct sequence of illustrated text by displaying them along the chalkboard, bulletin board, or clothesline.
6. A title page listing the names of the illustrators, a photograph of the class, the date of publication, and the name of the class as publishing company are a nice addition to the book.
7. The pages can be joined to make a Big Book, adding a cover and a title page. A heavy-duty stapler, metal rings, or heavy stitching (dental floss works well) are good for binding. The spine of the book can be strengthened with heavy book-binding tape.
8. Laminate the covers for durability and place a loan pocket on the inside of the back cover to encourage children to check out the books.
9. Provide children with opportunities to read and reread the story.

Stories created by individual or groups of children can be made into big books. Stories can be from their experiences or an extension of a children's book. Young children can collaborate as authors of a shared big book. Stories can be read many times, dramatized, and discussed to foster the children's comprehension and encourage them to read the book. The children's reading of the story can be tape recorded.

*Reading Stories*

When children are read to, they take a literary journey where they expand their experience, language, feelings, and knowledge of their world. Teachers need to know the story in advance. It is helpful if teachers take the books home and practice reading them aloud. The environment needs to be set up to provide young children with a pleasurable reading experience. Teachers can informally seat children on a rug in a way that they will be able to see both the teacher and the book. Chairs can also be informally arranged during this period.

A discussion can follow after reading stories. Such discussion develops the children's language and thinking skills. Usually teachers read the stories to children themselves, although at times an aide or a parent volunteer may read the story. When more adults are available, story reading may occur in small groups. When the story-reading period is more intimate, it promotes language learning. Children in the primary or upper grades may also be invited to read the stories.

Children with visual impairments depend on listening more than other children. Listening to stories are rewarding experiences for them. When they share a good book with the teacher and classmates their literary world expands and they live vicariously through the literary characters in the story. Children with visual impairments may respond to the story or may write about it using Braille. They can frequently listen to a recording of their favorite story. Commercial recordings are available of favorite stories like (a) Beatrix Potter's and A. A. Milne's stories; (b) the *Mother Goose Stories*; (c) other nursery rhymes; (d) the *Babar, Paddington, Curious George,* and *Madeleine* stories; and (e) *Charlotte's Web, The Biggest Bear, and Winnie-the-Pooh.*

Any nursery or kindergarten class should have a good stock of well-written and well-illustrated books for children. Collections of stories, or anthologies, even when not illustrated, are also useful. Teachers can get help in selecting books from other teachers and

**TABLE 9.2.** Guidelines for Reading Children's Books

| Guideline | Description |
|---|---|
| Set the Environment | Children sit on the floor close to the teacher to be able to see the illustrations and print. The Big Book can be positioned on an easel to make it easier to turn the pages and point to the words as the book is being read. At times, a child may turn the pages |
| Introduce the Story | Provide a brief introduction. Discuss the front cover illustration, title, related past experiences, and other relevant information. For example, for Ezra Jack Keats' *The Snowy Day*, appropriate questions for the introduction may be: What is snow like? How does it feel? Have you ever played in the snow? If not, what do you think it should be like to play in the snow? The purpose of the introduction is to motivate children to listen to the story |
| Read the Story | First read the story for enjoyment and pleasure; successive readings can offer a way for learning to read. Teachers who have difficulty pointing to the words while reading with expression, can postpone pointing to upcoming readings. Some teachers prefer a pointer to assist children in seeing exactly what is being read. When rereading the Big Book, point to the words and encourage children to participate. They enjoy repeating a familiar refrain or chant or making simple hand actions or appropriate sound effects. When teachers point to the words, children can see that print follows certain conventions, and they begin to recognize sound-symbol relationships and words |
| Discussion | After the initial reading, discuss the illustrations, characters, or favorite part of the book. The discussion should have a natural flow. Discuss the author's proposed meaning and monitor the children's comprehension. Since the story will be read and discussed many times, the initial discussion should be brief and end before the children lose interest |
| Follow-up Activities | After the initial or subsequent rereading of the Big Book, implement appropriate follow-up activities, such as independent reading of the story, dramatization, art, music, and writing. Independent reading is one of the most important activities because children become part of a reading community. Small versions of the Big Books can be made accessible for independent reading to encourage children to reread their favorite books as often as possible. Children learn to read by engaging in the reading act |
| Evaluation | During and after the reading experience, evaluate each student's progress. |

supervisors, librarians, and local colleges and universities. The following suggestions have been adapted from Meinbach's (1991) guidelines on reading books (see Table 9.2).

## Storytelling

Storytelling may be the oldest art form in the world. It is the first conscious form of literary communication and appeals directly to the children's imagination. It can be better than reading a story from a book, because in the case of a book the illustrations force all the children to see the same picture rather than allowing children to create their own mental picture. Marie L. Shedlock (2004), a 1890 London professional storyteller, believes that storytelling gives children

- dramatic joy, for which they have a natural craving;
- help to develop a sense of humor, which is actually a sense of proportion;
- the consequences of the characters' actions;
- the interpretation of ideals, and
- the development of their imagination.

Teachers can take a small group of children, ask them to close their eyes, and tell them a story using intonation and inflection in their voice for emphasis. This is meant to keep the children's attention so they can concentrate on the storyteller's voice to seize the dramatic interest of the story.

Storytelling (Box 9.2) is a direct communication between the listener and the teller. When children listen to a story, they become active listeners. They participate in the story, repeat phrases or words, and create voices and gestures for the characters. The repetitious language patterns and story events from predictable books and stories assist children to predicate the meaning and to anticipate language patterns, plot, and sequence. Storytelling assists young children to acquire sophisticated language patterns and prompts them to experiment with their own written and oral language. Teachers need to be sensitive to the children and respond accordingly. If the children become restless, they can make the story more dramatic using gestures and voices, reduce the length of the story, or finish the story immediately. During storytelling, teachers need to use language that children understand. Stories should relate to topics and situations that are of interest to them. Teachers usually use stories from the children's books and retell them in their own words. Spodek and Saracho (1994b) describe the following storytelling experience in a preschool.

---

**Box 9.2.**

The teacher sits with four children in the corner of the room. From a bag she brings out a grey puppet. "Do you know what this is?"

The children knew immediately that it was an elephant. "But," the teacher asked, "what is different about this elephant than those that you have seen in books or at the zoo?"

Karissa jumped up and said, "Its trunk is funny."

"That's right, Karissa," the teacher said. "Look. Its trunk is short. Don't elephants usually have long trunks? I have another animal that I would like to show you." The teacher brings a green animal out of her bag. "What do you think this little creature is?" she asked.

"It's a crocodile, like in Peter Pan," said Marsha.

"Wow, that's great," said the teacher. "Now, these two animals are puppets. I am going to need two of you to be my puppet holders during the story." She gives the elephant to Peter and the crocodile to Jill.

"I will tell you a story about how the elephant got its trunk. We said this elephant doesn't have a trunk. But the story I am about to tell you will explain how all the elephants got their trunks," the teacher says. The teacher begins the story about the elephant that asked too many questions, but the one question that he asked more than any other was, "What does the crocodile eat for breakfast?"

"Peter," the teacher asked, "can you hold up your elephant and ask the question."

Peter raised the elephant in the air and said in a loud voice, "What does the crocodile eat for breakfast?"

The teacher continues, "one day a bird told him to go to the river and ask the crocodile what he eats for breakfast. So off the elephant went. And what do you think he said when he found the crocodile?" the teacher asked. "This crocodile said, 'Come closer and I'll tell you.' Can you say that to the elephant, Jill?"

So Jill said, "Come closer and I'll tell you."

Peter moved the elephant close to the crocodile.

The teacher continues. "Well, the crocodile kept telling the elephant to come closer and closer until, guess what, he grabbed hold of the elephant's face and would not let go. Can you do that Jill?"

Jill grabbed the elephant. The children laughed and squirmed. Peter pulled his elephant away.

The teacher said, "That's exactly what the elephant did. He pulled and pulled and pulled until finally the crocodile lost his grip. But guess what. When he got up on his feet and looked down, he had this long, long, long nose. Guess what we call that long, long, long nose?"

"A trunk!!" all the children shouted.

"Do you think the elephant liked his trunk?" the teacher asked. "He did," she continued. "He liked it very much. He could spray water all over himself with it and catch bugs. He liked it so much that he went home to all of the other elephants and told them to go down to the river and ask the crocodile what he eats for breakfast so they too could get a trunk" (pp. 310–311).

Storytelling might consist of a fanciful, contemporary tale, or a traditional story picked from folk literature. Stories may also branch out from the children's experiences. Retelling the events of a trip or another event from the children's experiences are excellent resources for stories as well (see Table 9.3).

**TABLE 9.3.** Resources for Storytelling

| Type of Book | Publishing Details |
|---|---|
| Anthologies | *Caroline Feller Bauer's New Handbook for Storytellers: With Stories, Poems, Magic, and More* by Caroline Feller Bauer. Chicago: American Library Association, 1993<br>*Storytelling: Art and Technique* by Ellin Greene and Janice M. Del Negro. Santa Barbara, CA: Libraries Unlimited, 2010<br>*Tell Me a Story* by Eileen Colwell. New York: Penguin, 1983 |
| Storybooks | *Ask Mr. Bear* by Flack, M. New York: Simon & Schuster, 1971<br>*Caps for sale: A Tale of a Peddler, Some Monkeys and Their Monkey Business* by Slobodkina, E. New York: HarperCollins, 2008<br>*Goldilocks and the three bears* by Marshall, J. New York: Penguin, 1998<br>*Harold and the purple crayon* by Johnson, C. New York: HarperCollins, 1998<br>*Mr. Brown can moo! Can you?* by Dr. Seuss. New York: Random House, 1996<br>*The Gingerbread boy* by P. Galdone. New York: Houghton Mifflin, 2008 |

| | |
|---|---|
| | *The little engine that could: Deluxe edition* by Piper, W. New York: Grosset & Dunlap, 2009 |
| | *The little red hen* by Galdone, P. New York: Houghton Mifflin, 2011 |
| | *The noisy book* by Brown, M. & and Leonard Weisgard. New York: Scholastic, 1995 |
| | *Too much noise Mr. Brown* by McGovern, A. New York: Houghton Mifflin, 1992 |
| Books for Storytelling | *Merry Tales for Children* by Carolyn Sherwin Bailey. Memphis, TN: General Books LLC., 2010 |
| | *Stories for Little Children* by Pearl S. Buck. New York: The John Day Co., Inc., 1940 |
| | *Tales from Grimm* by Wanda Gág. Minneapolis, MN: University of Minnesota Press, 2006 |

Teachers need to engage children to participate in the story. Playing with stories that they enjoy encourages children to select their own books and motivates them to become authors (Williams & Hask, 2003). The following activities can be used with stories (Brewer, 2007):

- Children can dramatize a story during storytelling.
- Children can use materials to retell stories during learning centers. Materials may include flannel board pieces, wooden characters, or puppets.
- Children can tell their own stories in several forms such as a skit, scroll story, or a flannel board story.
- Children can join in telling the story by repeating certain phrases or sounds.

Props or pictures can assist in story telling. Also simple figures can be used on a flannel board. Characters can easily be made out of flannel and used to tell stories on a flannel board.

Children can use the computer and work as a team to develop computer interface technologies that help them search, browse, read, and share books in electronic form. The International Children's Digital Library (ICDL) has a collection of more than 10,000 books in at least 100 languages that children and teachers can use via the internet. Children are able to elaborate on the stories to develop games using the collection. The variety of books with a multicultural nature helps to teach languages. In addition, children can engage in the following activities.

- Scavenger Hunt: Children can learn how to navigate the ICDL and search for specific books such as their favorite books. The teacher can also provide parts of familiar stories and children can look for these books.
- Complete the Story: Children can complete a story or suggest a different ending to a story by drawing pictures.
- Creative Writing: Children can look at a picture book in a language they do not know and write or draw a story to go along with the pictures (International Children's Digital Library, n.d.).

## Folktales

For centuries people have shared stories with their children. These narratives have often taken the form of folktales, a form of traditional literature that has been in existence since before recorded history. People began telling folktales in an attempt to explain and understand the natural and spiritual world. Folktales also help children to understand social issues, history, and natural phenomena (Lynch-Brown & Tomlinson, 2004). The source of the folktale depends on the oral traditions of each culture. Folktales provide a feeling of security, usually while making fun of things people want to change. Such culturally treasured tales have mutual plots in which good overcomes evil, justice is served, and a happy ending occurs.

Folktales offer children rich and interesting literary experiences. They also help young children expand their understandings of the world. Folktales have many of the same qualities that children enjoy in a story (Carney, 2004). Quick beginnings, spiced action, and humor attract the young children's interest. In addition, young children are drawn to the folktales' concept of justice where good is rewarded and evil is punished. Many folktales have appealing rhyme and repetition and short, specific endings. Children can identify with the characters in the story, because folktales respond to the children's basic questions such as "Who am I?", "How can I solve my problems?", and "Is it too scary to think about these things?"(Howarth, 1989). Several major types of folktales are appropriate for young children. See Box 9.3 (Carney, 2004; Russell, 2007).

### Box 9.3. Folktale Categories

- *Cumulative Tales* are stories that have repetition of what has come before with some addition. Examples: *The House That Jack Built*, *The Gingerbread Man*, *There Was an Old Woman Who Swallowed a Fly.*
- *Pourquoi Tales* (Pourquoi is French for "Why?") are stories that explain why or how something occurred or came to be. Examples: *How the Birds Got Their Colors*, *Why the Elephant has a Long Trunk.*
- *Beast Tales* are anthropomorphic stories where animals are like people; they wear clothes and talk. Examples: *The Three Billy Goats Gruff*, *The Three Little Pigs*, *Goldilocks and the Three Bears*.
- *Noodlehead Tales* are stories where the main character is a silly person, makes foolish decisions, and gets into trouble. These characters are good and get involved in humorous situations that end well. Example: *The Three Sillies*.
- *Trickster Tales* focus on a small creature who uses intelligence instead of strength or size to outsmart a stronger and bigger opponent. Examples: *Anansi the Spider*, *Brer Rabbit*.
- *Realistic tales* are stories where the characters are people from real life without magic.
- *Fairytales* are stories that have magic and fantasy. Examples: *Cinderella*, *Snow White.*

Folktales can help children to understand customs and culture, fears and frailties, and morals and messages. If they are presented to children in a sensible way, folktales can be of benefit to young children. They are full of moral meanings, and children learn that they can find rewards in growing up, overcoming hardship, and acting righteously. The themes in folktales have an ageless attraction and the stories are authentic and exciting. They are also part of the children's heritage, which helps them make a connection between their past, present, and future generations (Rupiper & Zeece, 2005).

## Puppetry

Puppetry is an old art form. A puppet is a visual metaphor; it can symbolize a person, an object, or a shape. Puppets can represent real life and help children explore the world of fantasy. They can become characters in a story that is read or told by one child while the other children manipulate the puppets based on the plot. Children may create their own story to manipulate and talk for their own puppets. Puppets make it easy for children to enter a magic world of fantasy where they can solve their problems. When children engage in puppetry, they give evidence of their inner world. Puppetry helps young children confront their self-consciousness and permits them to convey their feelings more freely. For example, shy children can communicate through a puppet to avoid becoming the center of attention. See Box 9.4 for reasons puppets are useful with young children.

---

### Box 9.4.  Importance of Using Puppets with Young Children

- Develops the children's creative thinking and imagination.
- Gives children the opportunity to test life situations.
- Helps children become aware of their own behavior.
- Allows children to expose their anxieties and release their tensions.
- Develops communication skills.
- Promotes critical listening skills and critical thinking.
- Expands children's attention span.
- Assists children in acquiring knowledge.
- Offers children opportunities to work cooperatively and share ideas.
- Develops problem-solving skills.

---

When introducing puppets to young children, teachers can use soft toys that children know, improvise the movement of the toy, and encourage the children to explore the puppets' movement. While a variety of commercial hand puppets can be purchased in supply houses, children like to create their own simple puppets to share a story. Teachers can provide children with the materials such as ribbons, bows, twine, scraps of fabric, different lengths of old yarn, paper bags, worn-out but clean socks, gloves, paper plates, a variety of buttons, and other odds and ends. They can make stick puppets, hand puppets, and papier-maché puppets. Stick puppets can be made by pasting a child's picture, a magazine face, or a picture the children have drawn on paper onto a flat stick. Children can hold and manipulate the puppet stick in a play situation.

Hand puppets can be made out of paper bags or socks. Children can draw a face on a paper sack. They need to draw the mouth on both sides of the point at where the square bottom of the bag is folded, which children can open and close by holding it between finger and thumb. The inside of the flap can be colored so that it looks like the inside of a mouth. Eyes, ears, hair, and other features can be added to the puppet. A clean sock puppet or glove puppet is made in a similar way with buttons for eyes and a piece of felt for the mouth.

Puppet shows are best developed in small groups. Teachers can have children in small groups where each child creates a puppet, then create a story as a group, and present it to the class. Although children do not need a stage for their puppet shows, teachers can easily construct a puppet stage from a cardboard box. They can also take a table and turn it on its side to become a puppet stage.

Shadow puppets can be used without a stage. They have a magic like no other puppets. Children hold the puppets behind a thin curtain while a strong beam of light shines from behind the puppets through the curtain. The puppets look like silhouettes in a dark room. Teachers may hang the thin curtain and dim the light in the classroom to create a dark room. Or they may prefer to use a shadow screen. Shadow puppets are transformed so that the children's art becomes exaggerated, which is the purpose of the puppet form.

Children can use puppets to learn about the different disabilities. Puppets that represent both children with disabilities and typically developing children can interact and ask questions of each other in a presentation. Children can create scripts to obtain information on the different disabilities. Puppet presentations assist typically developing children to dismiss myths and fears and at the same time understand and accept the children with disabilities. Scripts need to be realistic with an active conversation. They need to include any similarities that exist in the lives of children with disabilities and typically developing children (such as family situations). Puppets depicting typically developing children might show that the children with disabilities have fulfilling lives. Puppeteers may be used with younger children. Puppeteers need to be knowledgeable about the disabilities in the classroom, script, and how to present the script so that it is developmentally appropriate for young children. They can also use puppets to retell a story about someone with disabilities. For ideas, the following stories can be read to children.

- Brightman, A. (2006). *Connections in the Land of Disability*. Palo Alto: Palo Alto Press.
- Brightman, A. (2008). *DisabilityLand*. Blaine, Washington: SelectBooks Publications.
- Choldenko, G. (2004). *Al Capone Does My Shirts*. New York: G.P. Putnam's Sons.
- Peterson, J.W. (1984). *I have a sister, my sister is deaf*. New York: HarperCollins.
- Schaefer, L.M. (2001). *Some Kids Use Wheelchairs*. Manakato, MN: Capstone Press.
- Seeger, P. & Jacobs, P.D. (2006). *The Deaf Musicians*. New York: G.P. Putnam's Sons.
- Wilkie, K. (2002). *Helen Keller: From Tragedy to Triumph*. New York: Aladdin Paperbacks.

## Creative Dramatics

Children can experience creative drama using a specific plot from a familiar story book that has a relatively simple plot line. When children act out a story, they play with the language of books and stories at a very personal level. Since they meet the characters of books "face to face," they gain a better comprehension of the text. Children who act out the stories develop vocabularies, use complex language, and have better comprehension of the story (McGee & Richgels, 2004). When children act out a story, they play with the language of books and stories at a very personal level.

The story can be a retelling in the children's own words, especially the story dialogue. Children select their characters and the way they will be portrayed, including the story's words, which they may continually change to develop their own script. They may decide if some dialogue is repeated at different times in the story or by different characters. When the script is finished, children can have a copy to read with their families. Scripts can be typed with a large font and the characters' speaking parts set in boldface. The children's names should be listed as the authors of the script (Morado & Koenig, 1999).

Children are able to interpret the stories, poems, and songs they hear in many ways, selecting characters and making up their own dialogue. The creative element of the dramatic presentation depends on the children's interpretations, the dialogue they develop, and the actions they assign to specific characters. The children's dramatic presentation can also be based on their own original stories, which allows them to control the plot and character. For example, three-year-old Joey and his classmates love pigs and selected *The Three Little Pigs* folktale to be the height of suspense, action, and drama. The children built houses where giggling "pigs" hide from a big bad wolf that has trouble blowing the house down. In their play, the children suspended their disbelief and pretended that they were in a place and time outside of reality. Children used their imagination and fantasies to act out the story. In the children's sociodramatic play with *The Three Little Pigs*, they had to use their problem solving, motor skills to build block houses, and understand the story structure to act out the parts of the story. The sociodramatic play gave the children several opportunities to enter, retell, and recreate the tale's drama (Moran, 2006).

The children's creative dramatic presentations only need a few props and no audience. They can use (a) a couple of chairs to represent a car; (b) a table to represent a bridge; (c) a piece of carpet to represent an ocean; or (d) leftover pieces of drapery material; skirts, and floppy hats can also be used for costumes.

The play script and content needs to be the child's product. The teachers (a) introduce a story that children can become familiar with after they have listened to the story several times, (b) propose actions and sequences, and (c) refer to the original story as a source of dialogue and action. Usually a suggestion like, "What happens next?" or "What did he say in response?" is the only direction that children need. Children may act the part of a character from a story. These types of story re-enactments are informal, child initiated, and child directed. Since action and dialogue follow a selected story, re-enactment is different from dramatic play. In story re-enactment, children are able to explore stories in a familiar environment and can either have or lack an audience. Morado and Koenig (1999) provide an example of a story re-enactment of a kindergarten class (See Box 9.5).

---

### Box 9.5. Story Re-enactment of an Early Childhood Class

"Once upon a time there were five little kittens who wanted to go out to play . . ." As the narrator begins this new version of the "Three Little Kittens," five kindergartners stand in a row, their excitement barely contained as they face an audience of class-mates and family members. The five wear pairs of mittens cut from felt; their kitten identities are suggested by the whiskers drawn on their faces and the cat ears attached to their headbands.

"Let's go out to play!" suggests Sara. One by one the other performers chime in with the line each has thought up and rehearsed.

"I'm going on the sliding board," says Nikisha.

"I'm going in my treehouse," says Kevin.

"I like to roll in the leaves," says Chrissy.

"I'm going to play ball," says Dion.

"I'm going on the swings," says Arnetta.

The kittens skip out to play to the accompaniment of piano music. Each pretends to play at his or her chosen activity and each, of course, loses his or her mittens. As the music stops, the kittens sing to Mom and Dad who have been standing quietly in full view of the audience since the beginning of the story: "The five little kittens, they lost their mittens and they began to cry. Oh, Mom and Dad, we sadly fear, our mittens we have lost!"

Thoroughly enjoying their roles of disapproving parents, Mom and Dad almost shout, "What! Lost your mittens, you naughty kittens! Then you shall have no pie."

It's the kittens' turn again, and they sadly sing the traditional words and tune: "Meow, meow, meow, meow. We shall have no pie!"

"Let's go find our mittens," shouts Arnetta, and the piano music begins again as the five kittens skip around, finding and putting on their mittens (Morado & Koenig, 1999, p. 116).

The following are sample stories that children can use in a mini performance (Box 9.6) (Morado & Koenig, 1999).

---

**Box 9.6. Stories for Mini Performances**

- Aardema, Verna, Gail E. Hailey, Ann Grifalconi and Gerald McDermott. (2008). *Who's in rabbit's house? and other Stories from the African Tradition*. Chagrin.
- Falls, Ohio: Findaway World LlcBrett, Jan. (1998). *The mitten: A Ukrainian folktale*. New York: Scholastic.
- Gannon, Janell. (2006). *Stellaluna*. Hamburg, Germany: Carlsen Verlag GmbH.
- Galdone, Paul. (2011). *Three little kittens*. New York: Houghton Mifflin.
- Kimmel, Eric. (1994). *The gingerbread man*. New York: Holiday House.
- London, Jonathan. (2007). *Froggy gets dressed*. New York: Puffin.
- McCloskey, Robert. (2010). *Blueberries for Sal*. New York: Puffin.
- McGovern, Ann. (1992). *Too much noise*. New York: Houghton Mifflin.
- Michels, Tilde. (1993). *Who's that knocking at my door?* Hauppauge, NY: Barron's.
- Morgan, Pierr. (1996). *The turnip: An old Russian folktale*. New York: Puffin.
- Slobodkina, E. (2008). *Caps for sale: A Tale of a Peddler, Some Monkeys and Their Monkey Business*. New York: HarperCollins.
- Wells, Rosemary. (2000). *Noisy Nora*. New York: Puffin.

---

The children's maturity and experience with stories help them develop more elaborate dramatic presentations. They begin to use more extensive stories and characterizations and more elaborate props and settings. The children will usually dramatize the story in different ways. Children can interpret a story in creative dramatics, with puppets, or with flannel board pieces. They can also act out the story through pantomime where they only use actions to communicate their interpretation of the story.

## Language Play in Literature

At school young children enjoy the language they hear and spontaneously repeat expressions that are most appealing to them. They also enjoy innovative and general ways to use language, such as in poetry and action plays. Children benefit from language play, because it establishes their pleasure with poetry with its reliance on rhythm, rhyme, and patterns in language. Children discover that the tone and feeling of a word affects its meaning, and that words have and imply a meaning. Language play occurs in several forms. It may focus on the sound of language, patterns within the language, visual aspect of the written language, or on the meanings of words or phrases. Books can motivate children to engage in word play. For example, children aged three and four made their own poem from the book *Good Night Moon* (Brown, 2005). They can say, "Good Night" to anything that is meaningful to them such as

Goodnight Mommy,
Goodnight, Daddy,
Goodnight dolls,
Goodnight blanket,
And goodnight Grandma.

In language-play children experience the phonological, syntactic, and/or semantic rules of language like those found in poetry, action plays, and nursery rhymes. These experiences will promote the children's linguistic abilities, insights about constructing meaning (Labbo, 1996), and language-play responses to literature, which will organize their thinking. Through language play discourse like in telling stories, children will integrate their mental imagery with their literature experiences. Children use language play to invent language by disregarding the standard rules of speech and using reversals, substitutions, ambiguities, sound similarities, or rhymes. Children base their inventive language on traditional language usage, although they also use existing, conventional, and folkloric language play (folk speech, metaphorical proverbs) to arrange their thinking. In conveying meaning, they may combine their inventive language play with the traditional language.

Children learn early forms of language play (rhyming and word play) as part of their daily lives. Language play experiences (such as repeating nursery rhymes, action plays, poetry, story book sharing) can help children develop their forms of language play and begin their stages of phonemic awareness, which is of critical importance in learning to read and write. Phonemic awareness procedures differ in their level of difficulty. The following sections will focus on language play experiences that can promote the children's phonemic awareness.

### Children's Books

Children enjoy word play. They need to be provided with experiences with words in a rich context. The more they emerge themselves in word play to communicate with others, the better they will become. Books that can be used for word play are found in Box 9.7.

**Box 9.7. Books for Word Play**

- Brothers Grimm (2011). *Little Red Riding Hood*. New York: HarperCollins.
- Brothers Grimm (2008). *Hansel and Gretel*. New York: Penguin.
- Gág, Wanda (2006). *Millions of Cats*. New York: Puffin.
- Loebel, Arnold (1988). *The Book of Pigericks*. New York: HarperCollins.
- Polacco, Patricia (1999). *Babushka Baba Yaga*. New York: Puffin.
- Wells, Rosemary (1998). *Max's First Word*. New York: Dial.
- Wells, Rosemary (2003). *Max's Ride*. New York: Dial.

*Poetry*

Teachers can introduce poetry to young children. Like poets, young children explore and arrange their experiences through facts and emotional symbols. They are fascinated with the sound of words and with poetry's rhythmic attributes. They organize and move their body in a rhythmic manner and become fascinated with the expressive qualities of the time, sight, and sound of poetic language. Poetry for young children must be meaningful, use poetic language, and have appropriate and fascinating content. Criteria for selecting poetry for young children are displayed in Box 9.8 (Coody, 1996).

---

**Box 9.8.  Criteria for Selecting Children's Poetry**

- *Rhythmic language* where words and phrases continuously sound melodious and harmonious. Rhythmical language distinguishes poetry from other literature. An appropriate poem for young children must have rhythm and melody in its language.
- *Emotional appeal* where the children are motivated to respond emotionally including sadness, delight, reflection, empathy, or anger. Poetry motivates the children's emotions.
- *Familiar themes* that relate to the children's life experiences. Young children prefer poems that tell a story; that are about animals, people, or places; or that are fun, humorous, and silly.
- *Sensory appeal* that prompts young children's senses of touch, taste, smell, sight, and sound.

---

Teachers need to share good poetry with young children to help them develop a lifelong fondness for different kinds of poetry. Children need a variety of experiences with poetry (see Box 9.9).

---

**Box 9.9.  Activities for Engaging Children with Poetry**

- Listen to poetry on a regular basis, including poems that children have written themselves.
- Listen to poetry that relates to familiar situations such as the season, weather, holiday, or experiences in science, social studies, mathematics, or reading.
- Pantomime and dramatize poetry.
- Illustrate their poetry using a variety of media such as crayons, paint, clay, wood, or wire to illustrate poems. Children can create murals of their favorite poems.
- Sample different types of favorite poems from newspapers, magazines, books, and those composed by the children.
- Listen to poetry recordings with or without music.
- Provide their own interpretations of poetry.
- Write poetry.
- Listen to poems with action or humor.

---

Children may be more interested in contemporary poets than traditional poets, because young children may be able to understand them better. Local poets can be invited to work with the children. These poets are able to help children create astonishing poetry.

Poetry is unique in its aesthetic qualities and association with the arts. The relationship between language and art is captured in the poetry books and helps them see illustrations through the rich poetry. Words lightly spoken, deeply pondered or skillfully written entwine with all aspects of the children's lives and become the cornerstone for the music of their hearts. The way children interact with language, what they do with actual words, help each of them define life as they see it. Language play is evident in the *Eensy Weensy Spider* (Hoberman, 2000) and *Henny Penny* (Wattenberg, 2000), a classic theme retold and famous story retold. Wattenberg's (2000) interpretation, riddled with incredible humor and photographs of the actual animals, makes this book a fascinating version. Just seeing ducks swimming in a chlorinated pool with the Great Pyramids of Giza in the background is enough to get a laugh out of anyone.

## Nursery Rhymes

A nursery rhyme is a traditional song or poem that young children learn, enjoy, and participate in rhythmically. The verses in the nursery rhyme help with children's language and mathematics (such as basic counting skills) and motivates them to enjoy music. The rhymes are usually silly and appealing to children. For example, "Hickory Dickory Dock" is a classic nursery rhyme that fascinates the children's view of silliness. An extensive range of rhymes has been used in the preschool classroom (Opie & Opie, 1959) with groups of children or the whole class, because they have a real social benefit as children chant and sing in unison (Holdaway, 1979). Children spontaneously respond to the nursery rhymes; because they are short, full of fun, dramatic, pleasing to the ear, and easy to remember (Hopkins, 1998).

Many nursery rhymes have been orally passed down from one generation to the next. The best collection of nursery rhymes is that of Mother Goose, which was an anthology of fairy tales referred to as *Tales of Mother Goose*. Nursery rhymes encourage language play, because the verses are catchy, usually humorous, and exhibit a range of types of play with language. The teachers can select nursery rhymes and poems that are rich in rhyme and alliteration, such as "Hey Diddle, Diddle," which has several rhyme pairs: *diddle/fiddle; moon/spoon*; and alliteration in the repetition of the initial consonant *d* in the opening phrase: "Hey Diddle, Diddle." The teachers can read and recite while the children can recite to enjoy the language delight in the alliterative and rhythmic language of "Hey Diddle, Diddle," "This Little Pig," and "Shoe a Little Horse."

In addition to reciting and singing the nursery rhymes, children can interpret and dramatize them. For example, on the first day the children can read or listen to and recite "Mary Had a Little Lamb." The next day, they can recite it again. Then the children can close their eyes and pretend that an animal followed them to school. The children can discuss the kind of animal that they would like to follow them, the size of the animal (big or little), the color of the animal, and what the animal would do at school (Scholastic, 2004). Children's interest in nursery rhymes can be stimulated. After listening to several nursery rhymes from a storybook, young children can determine the adventures of the main nursery rhyme characters and then they can create a different nursery rhyme book. Specifically, the children can select their favorite nursery rhyme and create a sequel, such as future adventures of "Jack and Jill" or "Mary Had a Little Lamb." Children can describe the nursery rhyme characters' personality when they are not in the story and design these characters' future adventures. They can consider, "What could the shattered Humpty Dumpty do?" (Evans, 2000, p. 17) and what would his future adventures be? Sean thought,

> *Perhaps every broken bit of Humpty's shell will grow other body bits and become complete eggs like worms when they get chopped up* (Evans, 2000, p. 18). When Humpty Dumpty broke into many pieces, Sean's different nursery rhyme was
>
> *Sellotape Dumpy*
>
> *Humpty Dumpty sat on a wall and then he cracked.*
>
> *The King's men couldn't put him together so they sellotaped him together then he watched Man. United, every time they scored. Once they scored he crashed and all the yolk came out then he died* (Evans, 2000, p. 21).

Evans (2000) used this experience with a small group of young children. In using this experience, it is important that the experience maintains its playful qualities. A major recommendation is to make these types of activities playful and fun for the children. It is important that drill and rote memorization be avoided. Instead these activities need to be presented in a way where children interact with each other, are motivated to become curious about language, and are free to experiment with language (Yopp, 1992).

## Action Stories

Several stories, poems, and rhymes have actions that children can perform. In a story someone can both present the story and carry out the actions. The "Bear Hunt" is an example of an action story. The children use actions to show how the hunter is going through grass, mud, hills, and so on. Children can create their own original stories including the actions, story characters, and words that are frequently used. Individual children can act out each word or groups of children can act out specific words. Children usually create their own action stories based on their experiences. They can also select a popular story such as *The Hare and the Tortoise* (Galdone, 1962) and decide on a dialogue to act out the story with actions such as the following:

| | |
|---|---|
| Characters: | Hare, Tortoise, Fox |
| Setting: | woods |
| Hare: | Good morning, Mr. Tortoise. Ha! Ha! Ha! Ha! |
| Tortoise: | What's so funny? |
| Hare: | Ha! Ha! Ha! Ha! |
| Tortoise: | What's so funny!!! |
| Hare: | Your little legs. Ha! Ha! How can you walk? |
| Tortoise: | I can walk and even run faster than you. |
| Hare: | What? |

The dialogue continues until the end of the story. Three children or three groups of children can act out this story. They can do choral speaking, which consists of developing a dialogue for a character and the group of children will speak in unison on the agreed dialogue. For example, if the Hare speaks the group of children who selected that character will speak and act out that role together.

Action stories also include action/finger plays, which are rhymes that sustain the children's interest. Popular action plays include "I Am a Little Teapot," "Hickory Dickory Dock," and the "Eensy Weensy Spider." Action plays and rhymes usually take place during circle and large group times where children communicate word meaning through simple actions and body movements. They improve the children's memory and recall skills when children continuously sing and recite the songs and poems. Action plays are recited using matching words and body movements. Action plays can be used to introduce poetry and new concepts, which can also be taught through themes. For example, to learn about the work of the people in the children's communities, children can do action stories such as the following:

### The Mail Carrier
I see the mail carrier in his 2-ton truck
He looks in his pocket and finds a buck
He gets out with this satchel
He has letters and postcards for you
He puts them in the mailbox, too.

## Visual Literacy in Children's Literature

We use several means of communication that are embedded in a variety of media. Literacy is generally considered as focusing on written language, but it can refer to other systems of representation and communication as well. Visual literacy is the process of gaining meaning through visual images. Children find visual images everywhere, which they consistently use and interpret. Young children communicate in every way. They may merge several symbolic forms to express themselves. For example, they merge drawing with writing or making gestures when speaking. They are involved in meaning-making by combining different forms of communication, such as oral language, written and printed symbols, drawings, and other visual elements. It is natural for young children to attempt to control a variety of alternative "literacies," or ways of symbolic representation like drawing, painting, gesture, construction, dramatic play, and words. Most children communicate through a variety of forms (e.g., songs, chants, marches, rituals, dramas, games). Visual images (like photographs, drawings, diagrams, paintings) overwhelm children's experiences; their world is full of complex multimedia.

Young children select a variety of media to convey their message. They use their experience with each: (1) they think about the media as they change media and (2) they are sensitive to the qualities of each medium. Edwards and Willis (2000) report the following event:

. . . a child has been playing house with her friends and decides she wants to paint a picture of this house. As she uses her brush, the paint flows onto the paper in bold colorful lines and the child relives the inner experience of having "my house"—something big and beautiful that gives her a strong sense of belonging. As she stops to admire her painting, she looks at the closed door and begins to think about the act of going inside her house. Now she experiences a problem—wanting to open the door. She does not know how to paint a door that can open, so she decides to use clay to make a new house. She spends a great deal of time learning how to create a little slab of clay for a door and a "frame" of clay around it. She enjoys manipulating this door even though the clay tends to squash into the clay of the door frame every time she closes it. She realizes that she now wants to make a house with a door that opens and closes easily and that swings open as one goes through. Talking over this problem with her teacher and friends, she obtains a shoe box. She cuts out a door and windows, decorates the house, and fills it with furniture and people. By this point the child has gained a great deal of experience through her explorations of the three different materials for representing her house (p. 262).

This child seems to be aware that materials have different qualities that can be used to communicate a certain message. Children learn how to use the materials and also learn to interpret the authors' message that is conveyed through their illustrations. They also analyze and think critically about the meaning of these images. The beautiful and creative illustrations provide children with the opportunity to prompt their aesthetic thinking in readers (Giorgis et al., 1999).

Picture books for children need to have both an engaging story and appealing art. The elements should complement each other to help young children gain meaning. Children learn to appreciate the way illustrations complement the text. When children look at picture books, they consider the artists' use of line, color, space, shapes, and properties of light and dark within the illustrations that are on each page or throughout the book. Children look at each to understand the way each artistic element communicates meaning (Giorgis et al., 1999).

## Illustrations in Children's Books

The illustrations in children's books, especially in picture books, have been changing to reflect new forms and creativity levels. The illustrators of children's books provide exciting and appealing art, which has contributed to the emersion of visual literacy. Illustrators use various techniques to illustrate children's books. Artists may use illustrations to (a) create visual images that supplement or strengthen the storyline, (b) improve or elaborate on the text to communicate their own interpretation of the story, (c) emphasize a strong connection to the text, and (d) use characters to help children interpret the story in the book. Children love "reading" the illustrations as well as the text (Giorgis et al., 1999).

Children can learn that illustrators use their techniques to personally express themselves. Young children can understand that the illustrators' art is a personal expression when teachers share children's books that show this concept. For example, Cynthia Rylant's (1988) *All I See* is about a young boy named Charlie who watches Gregory, an artist who paints beside a lake. Then Gregory stops painting and rides his canoe. Charlie looks at Gregory's picture and is surprised. Charlie sees that Gregory keeps painting the same thing—a blue whale. After Charlie and Gregory become friends, Charlie asks Gregory why he always paints whales. Gregory answers that it is all he sees (Giorgis & Glazer, 2008).

Young children can see that in both books the artists create what they "see." The teachers can ask children to look back at their drawings to see if what they drew was important to them. Then they can look at one or two paintings of well-known artists. They can use the artists' drawings to determine what was important to that artist (Giorgis & Glazer, 2008).

Some books express how children can be artists, too. In a story from Haiti, Ti Marie in *Painted Dreams* (Williams, 1998) takes paints and other art materials from the trash to draw on the wall behind the stall where her mother sells vegetables. She draws the tomatoes and onions that they sell. Her drawings catch the attention of people who become customers. To give her neighbors relief from the heat, Ali in *Cool Ali* (Poydar, 1996) draws chalk pictures of a lake, shade, and snow storm on the sidewalk (Giorgis & Glazer, 2008).

Another way teachers can show that art is a personal expression is to compare the work of two or more artists who use the same or similar subject matter. Songs and folktales can be used because they usually have several illustrated versions. *Over in the Meadow* by Olive A. Wadsworth (2003) has several illustrated versions. It has been illustrated by Ezra Jack Keats (1999), Paul Galdone (1989), Feodor Rojankovsky (1999), Louise Voce (2000), Anna Vojtech (2002, 2003), Michael Evans (2007), and many others. Children can tell or sing the rhyme or song, look at the pictures in the books, and compare them by holding the books side by side to match the text. Children can compare the way each illustrator portrays the characters and the actions. They can compare the way Keats' collage portrays the subject of each verse with Vojtech's (2002) soft watercolor illustrations of owl mother and babies. Children can choose their favorite illustration to learn that artists portray subjects differently and that others respond to these illustrations differently (Giorgis & Glazer, 2008).

An example game for children is to have them choose an animal and compare the way it is illustrated in several books of fiction. Then teachers can select and provide children with books that are developmentally appropriate to their age level. For example, if children choose a pig, they can see that artists use different media and different styles to show different pig characters. Teachers can provide children with appropriate books on pigs to compare—for example, the illustrations of the pig in William Steig's (1997) *Zeke Pippin* with the drawings of Arthur Geisert (1991) in *Oink*, the pencil sketches with vivid watercolors of Colin McNaughton (2000) in *Oops!*, the pencil and ink outlines with watercolor washes of Felicia Bond in *If you Give a Pig a Pancake* (Numeroff, 1998), and the charcoal and gouache illustrations of Falconer's (2003) *Olivia and the Missing Toy*. At the beginning young children usually can compare only two books at a time. Later, teachers can add a third, fourth, and fifth book; but they should only add one at a time (Giorgis & Glazer, 2008). Teachers can follow this activity by asking children to draw their own pig illustrations. Children can be encouraged to use a variety of media to illustrate their own pigs and create a class mural. Children need to learn a broad range of art that is found in the children's books. Before examining the art in children's books, it is important that teachers read to children books on visual literacy such as those in Box 9.10 (Giorgis et al., 1999).

---

### Box 9.10. Books on Visual Literacy

- Archbold, R. (2010). *An Artist in Nature*. Toronto, Ontario: Black Walnut/Madison Press.
- Bateman, R. (1998). *Safari*. Boston: Little, Brown.
- Carle, E. (2003). *Hello, red fox*. New York: Simon & Schuster.
- Christelow, E. (1997). *What do authors do?* New York: Houghton Mifflin.
- Christelow, E. (2007). *What do illustrators do?* New York: Houghton Mifflin.
- Cummings, P. (1999). *Talking with artists volume 3*. New York: Clarion.
- Johnson, S.T. (1995). *Alphabet city*. New York: Viking.
- Johnson, S.T. (2003). *City by Numbers*. New York: Puffin.

- Lasky, K. (2002). *The emperor's old clothes*. Ill. D. Catrow. San Diego, CA: Harcourt Brace.
- Wilbur, R. (2001). *The disappearing alphabet*. Ill. D. Diaz. San Diego, CA: Harcourt Brace.
- Winter, J. (2003). *My name is Georgia: A portrait*. San Diego, CA: Harcourt Brace.
- Zimmerman, A.G., & Clemesha, D. (1999). *Trashy town*. Ill. D. Yaccarino. New York: HarperCollins.
- Zimmerman, A., Clemesha, D., & Rosenthal, M. (2004). *Dig*. San Diego, CA: Harcourt Brace.

Young children need to learn to see the diversity in the art found in picture books and other two-dimensional forms of art. They can start by using several different media and different styles in their own art. It is important to share and record the illustration approaches that children are observing. Children can explore and compare the illustrations in relation to the story of several books with different media (Giorgis & Glazer, 2008).

A focus study can help children learn everything about being an illustrator. They can select an illustrator who has illustrated many books and examine the illustrations more closely. It can help children learn and understand the artistic techniques and styles from several books. It is better to use hardcover editions of the books, because the soft cover books usually lack a high level of color intensity (Giorgis et al., 1999).

Children can be encouraged to react to and discuss the art in picture books. They can express their opinions about what they think about the paintings. It is important to begin with illustrations that children will like right away. Children can discuss their opinion whether the illustrations make the story better for them as compared to just listening to the story. They can discuss specific pictures telling what they liked about the illustrations or telling why the illustrations were not helpful to them. Children can be helped to look at the illustrations carefully, but they should not be guided into what to say (Giorgis & Glazer, 2008).

Children need to engage in art in a personal way. When children look at the illustrations in a book, they can imagine themselves somewhere in the picture. They can discuss what would happen if they actually were in the painting or if the painting was in their world. Children need many experiences where they see and become involved with a variety of artistic styles and media. They can paint using the illustrators' media or observe and discuss the illustrators' work. Children need to learn that diversity in art needs to be both valued and enjoyed (Giorgis & Glazer, 2008).

## Book-related Play

Young children use book-related play to deal with social situations and to explore the problems presented in books and the real world. In book-related play, children use language, gestures, pantomime, costumes, and props to test their ideas and interpretations. In a play environment, they feel safe in testing their ideas and temporary conclusions.

Play is a medium for literacy learning. In a study of two and three year olds, Rowe (1998) observed several characteristics in book related play in their literacy interactions including (a) connection, (b) ownership, (c) flexibility, (d) openness, (e) multiple sign systems, (f) transmediation, and (g) community. Table 9.4 shows the characteristics in book related play.

**TABLE 9.4.** Characteristics in Book-related Play

| Characteristic | Description |
| --- | --- |
| Connection | Through dramatic play children relate the books to both their present and past experiences. They take imaginary characters into reading events and integrate the themes and information in the books into their play, which help them to connect their world with that of pretense |
| Ownership | Since children initiate and develop the play events and scripts, they hold ownership of play events. When children direct the play events, they explore literacy and manipulate the setting. In this type of situation, children relate the experiences in the books and their life experiences and understand the relevance of books to their life |
| Flexibility | Play provides the children with the flexibility to learn about and from books. The children's play ranges from responding to books to solving personal problems. The children's follow up play events need to be based on their interests and knowledge of a specific book along with its available resources |
| Openness | According to Spodek and Saracho (1987), play needs to be free from rules that have not been developed by the children. The openness of play allows the children to create links between books and their life experiences and between knowledge domains. Play permits children to create their own interpretations of books instead of being rigidly restricted to those interpretations by others. In play children consider the elements of books that are of personal interest to them |
| Multiple Sign Systems | In play children communicate and interpret meanings through oral language, gestures, movement, props, wardrobe, and set designs, which give them a lived-through experience of books that is multisensory, concrete, and more real than the books themselves. When children touch objects and move through space to act out play episodes, they are using their regular ways of experiencing the world, which helps them to understand and explore the world of books |
| Transmediation | During play, children create ways to convey book-related meanings in a new sign system. Drama requires the use of dialogues, actions, props, and elements that are partially reported in the text and illustrations of picture books. When children experience books (e.g., manipulating props or modifying their physical expectation in relation to another character), they realize that there are several ways to interpret meaning rather than those they read or talked about in the books, which teaches them new communication systems |
| Community | Play is integrated into the social community of the home and school. Young children may assign their peers the role of audience and coplayers. If children play by themselves, their dramatic portrayals reflect their interactions with others. Community also limits the children's imagination and inventions. Since children usually include others in their play, they create their play events based on their playmates' understanding and experience; thus, community restricts them to the traditional uses of signs and the shaping of shared understandings |

Evidently, young children are able to connect books and play, which indicate that they may also use dramatic play as a means of exploring the content of books.

Young children who have experiences listening to stories can make the connections between dramatic play and the meanings they find in books. Thus, play in relation to children's literature refers to those meanings conveyed in the books' text or illustrations. Children are read stories and then role play these stories (Morrow, 2009). When children have access to props such as a stuffed animal or a puppet to hold while they are listening to the story, they can reconstruct the story. Storybook props can be provided at the library area to encourage children to dramatize the story.

## Library Center

There are several things that need to be considered in creating a library center. These include the physical environment, books, and materials.

### Physical Environment

The physical environment needs to be inviting and accessible to the children. It can have a throw rug, various pillows, and an oversize cardboard box that is painted or covered with contact paper in the area to give a sense of a cozy, soft, and secluded reading area. The library center can include a small table with chairs for children to look or create their own books, a rocking chair for them to read comfortably, and headsets to listen to recorded stories. Listening to stories on a headset can help children to privately enjoy stories. The center can also be secluded using bookshelves, a piano, file cabinets, or freestanding bulletin boards that enclose the area. Children and teacher can plan and design the library center together. Books need to be changed frequently based on the children's interests and topics of study. They can also continuously evaluate the center, develop rules for its use, care for books, be responsible for keeping it neat and orderly and naming it (like Book Nook, Look at a book).

Books are displayed on a shelf or rack where children are able to see and select the books that are of interest to them. An area is provided where children can comfortably browse through the books, look at the pictures, read them, and discuss them with their peers. A rocking chair, a table and chairs, a group of pillows on the floor, or even a small rug offer an inviting setting to browse through books. Appropriate lighting and privacy should be provided at the library center. Books from the children's culture should also be displayed. For instance, young children can learn about American Indians through appropriate books. They need to be introduced to modern day stories with Native children involved in everyday activities (like bike riding and eating at restaurants with parents who are lawyers and engineers). They can use books to learn about tribes that have historical and/or contemporary roles in society. Roberts, Dean, and Holland (2005) provide the following examples.

- *A Rainbow at Night: The World in Words and Pictures by Navajo Children,* by Bruce Hucko. 1996. San Francisco: Chronicle. This book presents artwork by Navajo children. Each painting or drawing has an explanation and the artist's photograph. The explanations help children learn about the Navajo culture.
- *Firedancers,* by Jan Bourdeau Waboose. Illus. by C.J. Taylor. 2000. New York: Stoddart Kids. This is an Anishinawbe (Ojibway) picture book. Noko (Grandmother)

shouts, "Slow down, Fast One," to her young grandchild. Both leave their home late at night and travel by motorboat to Smooth Rock Island, where their ancestors once danced. In the firelight, the grandmother gains her youth while the child gains the knowledge of understanding heritage.

- *Red Is Beautiful (Chiih Nizhoni),* by Roberta John. Illus. by Jason David. Trans. into Navajo by Peter A. Thomas. 2003. Flagstaff, AZ: Salina Bookshelf. Since Nashasha has rough skin, she fears her classmates' teasing. Her grandmother teaches her about *chiih*, a healing cream of red earth mixed with mutton fat. When Nashasha grows up, she teaches others about traditional medicine and using natural resources.
- *SkySisters,* by Jan Bourdeau Waboose. Illus. by Brian Deines. 2000. Toronto, Ontario, CAN: Kids Can Press. When two sisters climb Coyote Hill under Grandmother Moon, they enjoy the wildlife, cold air, and snow. Then they wait for the appearance of the Sky Spirits (Northern Lights).

Materials encourage young children to create their own books, and felt stories should be available at the library center. Children's magazines (new or old) and newspapers are inexpensive and accessible to teachers. These magazines can be displayed with the books and other materials at the library center. In addition, the library center and the literature experiences need to include a variety of materials.

The library center can also include figures of story characters from favorite books to manipulate on a flannel board. Different types of puppets can encourage children to act out their favorite stories. To make the library center more inviting, mobiles from book jackets and attractive posters are very motivating and should be displayed in the area.

Dolls and/or stuffed animals can be used for cuddling while listening to a story or just holding them while they look at books. Children like to pretend to read to dolls and stuffed animals. Dolls and stuffed animals that relate to a story can be displayed at the library center with the corresponding book. For example, a stuffed bear and/or doll with blond hair can be displayed along with the book *Goldilocks and the Three Bears* (Galdone, 1985), a stuffed pig can be displayed along with the book *The Three Little Pigs*, and a stuffed rabbit can be displayed next to the book *Peter Rabbit*.

## Summary

In the classic *A Critical History of Children's Literature*, children's literature is defined as: "those books which are to establish standards and crystallize taste, and which will present much vicarious experience and will be long remembered" (Meigs et al., 1969, p. XXI). Literature for young children consists of several categories of books (picture books, concept books, information books, poetry). Regardless of the category, the visual element in the illustrations is as important as the text. Both the text and illustrations in children's books need to be presented together, because the literary and aesthetic quality of children's books are equally important in the children's acquisition of knowledge. Schickedanz and McGee (2010) add that literature activities (like storytelling, art, cooking) promote the children's learning. If children are provided with opportunities to talk in the literature experience, they achieve gains in vocabulary, language development, and listening comprehension. Justice, Kaderavek, Fan, Sofka, and Hunt (2009) also report that literature experiences contribute to the children's print knowledge and vocabulary, particularly with low-income and language-delayed learners. They recommend that the literature experiences are beneficial to children at-risk and who have language, developmental, and intellectual impairments. Sipe (2008) proposes that children's literary understanding of books be expanded to include the children's "literary-meaning making" which he compares to low-level labeling, simple retelling of plots, and answering questions. He believes that it is important to consider the literary qualities of books and the children's responses during story reading.

During story reading, the children make sense of the text and interpret it based on their own experiences, background, and beliefs. Children with different experiences, attitudes, beliefs, and family differences, develop different interpretations. In pretend play, children can explore a social problem when they dramatize a story in the book. In dramatic activities children discuss, explore, and act the roles of the characters in the story. While role playing situations, children are encouraged to think critically, analyzing the lives of the characters in the story.

The major characteristic of pretend play is the "assimilative manipulation of symbols." Children create stories and scripts. Then they use make-believe transformations of objects and act them out. In pretend play, children assume that real-world objects and people have other identities. Acting out a story influences the children's comprehension, because it helps them to develop mental recollections of story situations and to develop story schemas, both of which are used to foster the children's comprehension. In acting out a story, children also may engage in fantasy play. Rudolph and Cohen (1984) justify the importance of fantasizing when children are allowed to imitate or act out what they would like to be.

> The world of make-believe has an almost real quality for children and they can pretend within a wide range of possible behavior. They can wish themselves anything they like, and play that it becomes a reality. They can pretend to be glib and powerful and authoritative, even if they really are only little children with very little power indeed. They can pretend that they are angry tigers, growling dogs, and fierce lions, even if in reality they are gentle and well-mannered boys and girls. They can try on for size the feeling of being a mother, father, a street cleaner, or a truck driver. They can go back to babyhood or forward to adulthood, they can frighten others or be the thing they are themselves afraid of. This inner life of children we call their fantasy life and it represents an integral part of children's efforts to comprehend themselves and the world around them (p. 100).

Pretend play in stories may be personal; children adjust their points of view even when they focus on the story's events, plot, and characters.

Listening to the stories several times helps young children to act out the stories on their own. At first, the children may pretend to read the story by following the book's illustrations. At the beginning, the children's stories may not be well formed, but with practice the children's role playing of the story will be similar to the original story. Reading the story several times is important in the children's storytelling. They become familiar with the story and acquire a structure to be able to use different levels of texts. Children will gradually take over and pretend to read the story. When children learn the story very well, they are able to act out the stories or pretend to read them on their own.

Children may find it necessary to use new sign systems to create dialogue and actions for the characters in the books using their personal experiences or experiences from other texts. For example, when playing "The Three Little Pigs," a child who was role playing the brick seller to the three little pigs extended his role beyond the text and illustrations of the story. To bring his role to life, he related the actions, dialogue, and intonation used by the peddler in *Caps for Sale* (Slobodkina, 1989), a book that that had already been read in class. Goodman (1990) observed that young children engage in book-related play at the dramatic play center. She saw that children use familiar stories (like fairy tales) to create play scripts.

Children engage in pretend play in responding to book-reading events. They pretend to read and act out roles of characters in the text, creating play scripts in their play. They may develop their play scripts as their focus for their interactions ("I'm the Mom") instead of using the words and pictures in a book (Rowe, 1988). They also pretend to read and act out the roles of characters in the text. Children interpret stories and respond playfully to the stories in the books, which are beyond literal re-enactments or recall of stories.

# Chapter 10
# **Literacy-play Learning Experiences**

I struggled through the alphabet as if it had been a bramble-bush; getting considerably worried and scratched by every letter.

Charles Dickens (1861, p. 79)

Literacy refers to those behaviors that are related to receptive (listening, reading) and expressive language (speaking, writing) (Saracho, 2004). Most young children begin to read at a very early age (Saracho, 2002c). According to Ferreiro and Teberosky (1983):

it is absurd to imagine that four- or five-year-old children growing up in an urban environment that displays print everywhere . . . do not develop any ideas about this cultural object until they find themselves in front of a teacher (p. 12).

Children develop literacy concepts at an early age when they become aware and interact with readers and writers as well as when they attempt to read and write. Children scribble and write, pretend to read, react to books that have been read to them, and read environmental print (Saracho, 2003), all of which are considered emergent literacy behaviors. An emergent literacy perspective broadens the literacy development concept to integrate literacy-like behaviors (such as making believe they are reading) as genuine and contributory, where social contexts become a necessary means for introducing children to literacy knowledge and practices. Such systems consider that the children's language and literacy develops through their daily social activities. In play experiences, young children have the opportunities to use language in literate ways and to use literacy as they see it practiced. In emergent literacy, the relationship between play and literacy is evident as play assists young children to explore and understand the interactions between these two specialties (Saracho & Spodek, 2006). The purpose of this chapter is to describe emergent literacy, the children's literacy developmental levels, experiences that promote their literacy development, the relationship between play and literacy, a literate themed-play environment, literacy-enriched play centers (traditional vs. themed), the organization of literacy-play centers, and guidelines for organizing literacy play centers.

## Emergent Literacy

Emergent literacy usually refers to children from birth through five years of age and characterizes young children's development towards reading and writing. Although researchers have not agreed on a single definition of emergent literacy, they consider the richness behind young children's unconventional scribbles and their early attempts at reading (e.g., pretend reading, picture reading, reading text based on their interpretation). It suggests that children's abilities to read and write emerge simultaneously and that written literacy skills emerge gradually in the context of oral language development.

Emergent literacy places children in the position of active learners, problem-solvers, and meaning makers. It acknowledges that early literacy behaviors and knowledge are not pre-anything, as the term pre-reading suggests. Emergent literacy relates to young children's reading and writing behaviors that provide the way to formal reading instruction (Sulzby, 1991); thus, reading, language, and writing are considered an integrated event.

Emergent literacy refers to the concept that literacy is best learned as a developmental continuum, beginning early in the children's lives. It includes the skills, knowledge, and attitudes that are considered a developmental foundation to standard ways of reading and writing (such as shared book reading). Emergent literacy also takes into account the importance of social interactions in literacy-rich environments for pre-readers. Children's emergent literacy depends on the (a) pre-readers' characteristics that provide the basis for later reading and writing, (b) experiences that contribute to emergent literacy development, and (c) practices that promote the pre-readers' social interactions in a literate environment. The emergent literacy perspective suggests that children learn about reading and writing before formal reading instruction.

Children develop knowledge of vocabulary, syntax, narrative structure, metalinguistic aspects of language, letters, and text that immediately helps them learn how to read and write. The emergent literacy elements introduce children to the skills that they need to become literate. Young children gain knowledge of the functions, uses, conventions, and importance of text. Such knowledge is apparent in the literacy activities that involve emergent reading, emergent writing, reading environmental print, and conventional print motivation. These activities disregard skills that are directly related to decoding, encoding, or comprehension, which are usually taught through meaningless drill and practice. Instead this knowledge relates to the children's reading and writing awareness. It also interacts with both formal and informal learning opportunities that promote the children's literacy learning (Whitehurst & Lonigan, 1998).

In the process of reading, young children identify words, interpret their meanings, and understand the context of the words' grammatical structure, speech phrasing and intonation, literary forms and devices, and print conventions (National Reading Panel, 2000). Good readers are usually successful in society, are highly respected, and contribute to social and economic prosperity (Saracho, 2002c).

## Children's Literacy Developmental Levels

Literacy development begins early in the children's lives and continues until they become competent readers and writers. Literacy usually emerges in infancy and continues through age seven, although some children start reading and writing at ages four and five (Sulzby & Teale, 2003). Children develop literacy concepts at an early age. They develop an awareness of their existing models of written language when they observe and interact with readers and writers. Then they try to read and write in order to explore language, text, and meaning. Their engagement with text helps them with their literacy development (Saracho, 2002c).

When children interact with readers and writers, they develop an understanding of how literacy develops, especially when they observe existing examples of written language. Knowledge of these models changes as children explore language, text, and meaning. The way children become interested in text determines how they learn literacy. Young children learn how to read when they learn a number of concepts, know letter names and shapes, have a phonological awareness, become interested in literacy, cooperate with peers (National Research Council (NRC), 1998), and understand that each letter in the alphabet represents a unique sound.

The NRC (1998) developed a set of specific literacy behaviors of successful learners. Table 10.1 identifies the successful behaviors for preschool and kindergarten children. Although this index of behaviors is seen as only a partial list and is somewhat controversial, it focuses on the way children learn how to read (listening to stories, pretending to read books, labeling objects in books). However, it's important to remember that these behaviors depend on the child's maturation and experience.

**TABLE 10.1.** Developmental Accomplishments of Literacy Acquisition

| Age of Child | Literacy Acquisition Stage |
|---|---|
| Birth to Three-Year-Old Accomplishments | • Recognize specific books by cover<br>• Pretends to read books<br>• Understands that books are handled in particular ways<br>• Enters into a book-sharing routine with primary caregivers<br>• Vocalization play in crib gives way to enjoyment of rhyming language, nonsense word play, etc.<br>• Labels objects in books<br>• Comments on characters in books<br>• Looks at a picture in a book and realizes it is a symbol for a real object<br>• Listens to stories<br>• Requests/commands adult to read or write<br>• May begin attending to specific print such as letters in names<br>• Uses increasingly purposive scribbling<br>• Occasionally seems to distinguish between drawing and writing<br>• Produces some letter-like forms and scribbles with some features of English writing |
| Three- and Four-Year-Old Accomplishments | • Knows that alphabet letters are a special category of visual graphics that can be individually named<br>• Recognizes local environmental print<br>• Knows that it is the print that is read in stories<br>• Understands that different text forms are used for different functions of print (e.g., list for groceries) |

- Pays attention to separable and repeating sounds in language (e.g., Peter, Peter, Pumpkin Eater, Peter Eater)
- Uses new vocabulary and grammatical constructions in own speech
- Understands and follows oral directions
- Is sensitive to some sequences of events in stories
- Shows interest in books and reading
- When being read a story, connects information and events to life experiences
- Questions and comments demonstrate understanding of literal meaning of story being told
- Displays reading and writing attempts, calling attention to self: "Look at my story"
- Can identify 10 alphabet letters, especially those from own name
- "Writes" (scribbles) message as part of playful activity
- May begin to attend to beginning or rhyming sound in salient words

Kindergarten Accomplishments

- Knows the parts of a book and their functions
- Begins to track print when listening to a familiar text being read or when rereading own writing
- "Reads" familiar texts emergently, i.e., not necessarily verbatim from the print alone
- Recognizes and can name all uppercase and lowercase letters
- Understands that the sequence of letters in a written word represents the sequence of sounds (phonemes) in a spoken word (alphabetic principle)
- Learns many, though not all, one-to-one letter sound correspondences
- Recognizes some words by sight, including a few very common ones (a, the, I, my, you, is are)
- Uses new vocabulary and grammatical constructions in own speech
- Makes appropriate switches from oral to written language situations
- Notices when simple sentences fail to make sense
- Connects information and events in texts to life and life to text experiences
- Retells, reenacts, or dramatizes stories or parts of stories
- Listens attentively to books teacher reads to class
- Can name some book titles and authors
- Demonstrates familiarity with a number of types or genres of text (e.g., storybooks, expository texts, poems, newspapers, and everyday print such as signs, notices, labels)
- Correctly answers questions about stories read aloud
- Makes predictions based on illustrations or portions of stories
- Demonstrates understanding that spoken words consist of a sequence of phonemes
- Given spoken sets such as "dan, dan, den" can identify the first two as being the same and the third as different
- Given spoken sets such as "dak, pat, zen" can identify the first two as sharing a same sound
- Given spoken segments can merge them into a meaningful target word
- Given a spoken word can produce another word that rhymes with it
- Independently writes many uppercase and lower case letters

*(Continued Overleaf)*

**TABLE 10.1** *(Continued)* Developmental Accomplishments of Literacy Acquisition

| Age of Child | Literacy Acquisition Stage |
| --- | --- |
|  | • Uses phonemic awareness and letter knowledge to spell independently (invented or creative spelling)<br>• Writes (unconventionally) to express own meaning<br>• Builds a repertoire of some conventionally spelled words<br>• Shows awareness of distinction between "kid writing" and conventional orthography<br>• Writes own name (first and last) and the first names of some friends or classmates<br>• Can write most letters and some words when they are dictated |

## Literacy Stages: Birth through Preschool

During their first years of life, young children can use symbols effectively. Two- and three-year-olds progress from looking at print in books to making marks as they try to write. At the end of age two or at the beginning of age three, most children make (1) reading-like and drawing-like scribbles and (2) recognizable letters or letter-like forms. Two and three-year-olds may learn some letters and sounds when they see television programs like *Sesame Street*. Three-year-old children often know that the golden arches "stand for" McDonald's. They can use symbols in a few situations, but they need a lot of practice to be able to use this knowledge in all situations. Young children begin to understand how symbols such as these are used: (1) both hash marks and number concepts, (2) the difference between numbers and letters, (3) the use of letters in their name and their friends' written names, and (4) knowing how letters and their sounds are connected within words (Saracho, 2002c).

## Literacy Stages: Preschool Years

Several three- and four-year-old children begin to identify obvious sounds within words, while many four-year-olds use initial consonants to write words using invented spelling. Their writing consists of scribbles, random strings of letters, and letter-like forms. Three-year-olds often think that reading is a mysterious activity, four-year-olds begin to understand that the reading process is like what is read to them, five-year-olds begin to connect reading with print, six-year-olds begin to notice patterns in print, seven-year-olds see reading as learning, and eight-year-olds think reading is reading books and learning to read (Saracho, 1983). Four-year-olds can print and recognize letters and words (Mason, 1980). With assistance, young children can identify patterns in letters, understand that letters are reading clues, and sound out letters in words. These children have experience using toys and manipulatives that have letters, numbers, and playful letter sounds and other symbol systems. Shows on television, CD-ROMS, DVDs and computers also help young children learn letters, sounds, words, and text levels (Saracho, 2001).

When children are read to frequently, they can "read" their favorite books by remembering the written language in the books and imitating the reader. Three- and four-year-old children show emergent reading behaviors like reading pictures, illustrations, or labels. Some young children notice the print in books, but others read from their favorite books. Afterward most children discuss pictures, combine actions with pictures, participate in occasional question-and-answer conversations, and/or generate voices for characters in pictures (Kaderavek & Sulzby, 1998). Children usually begin "real" reading between the ages of five to seven, after they have entered kindergarten. According to Lenters (2004/2005), reading instruction for young second-language learners should integrate the following:

### Comprehension
- Use a language experience approach to provide meaningful materials the child is able to read.
- Pay attention to cultural biases in text and illustrations presented to young second-language learners.
- Fill in the missing cultural information when materials must be used that are culturally unfamiliar to the learner.
- When possible, use translations alongside English texts to enhance comprehension and support first-language reading skills.
- Allow students to respond to text in their first language.

### First-language reading support
- Form strong home–school connections with the families of second-language learners.
- Value the child's first language.
- Find any means possible to ensure that the child receives reading instruction in his or her first language (p. 332).

## Literacy Stages: Beginning Reading

Young children become readers before formal reading instruction. Children bring to school their own unique background, set of experiences, and set of abilities. While most kindergarten children have been in a school setting for several years, some are attending school for the first time; thus, they range in reading ability levels. Some children are independent readers, while others are beginning to learn some fundamental literacy knowledge and skills. What this means is that some kindergartners may have the skills characteristic of the typical three-year-old, while others might be functioning at the level of the typical eight-year-old (Riley, 1996). Therefore, even teachers of young children need to use a developmentally appropriate approach in teaching young children literacy strategies.

## Literacy Development

Teachers develop the young children's literacy development by reading books to them that encourage verbal interaction, develop the children's language (especially vocabulary) development, and help them understand the concepts of print; and provide them with activities that focus on the children's attention to the sound patterns within spoken words, such as songs and poems that have rhymes, jokes, and games that switch sounds within words (NRC, 1998). Children can learn how to read through activities that help them to connect oral and written language. They need to learn the skills that contribute directly to successful reading such as knowledge of word meanings, print that communicates meaning, phonological awareness, printed letters and their sounds, and identifying letters, numbers, shapes, and colors.

Most children can learn these skills, but their individual differences in learning and interests must be considered with all of their literacy experiences. It is important that the children's literacy experiences be at their emergent literacy developmental level where children explore and experiment with print (Vacca et al., 2011).

A reading program that facilitates initial reading instruction must reflect the children's interests, characteristics, developmental level, and knowledge or understanding of concepts. It should implement active experiences and explorations (Saracho, 1987), because (1) reading is acquired through socially interactive and emulative behavior, (2) children acquire the ability to read as a result of life experiences, (3) children acquire reading skills when they see a purpose and a need for the process, and (4) being read to plays a role in the acquisition of reading (Morrow, 2009).

Labeling objects can also help children develop literacy concepts. They learn the purpose of letter symbols, letter sounds, and printed words, which is the basis for learning to read successfully. Learning to read requires that children learn the meaning of letter shapes, drawing those shapes, pronouncing sounds, and their relation to letters. Learning meaningful words and following print with their eyes also help to provide skills that are essential to learning to read. Children need to understand the nature and purpose of reading. Learning to read has a foundation in a deep layer of meanings and is cultivated by intellectual development. In 1958, James Lee Hymes suggested that reading sells itself to young children, because print messages are in the limelight continually (Vacca et al., 2011).

## Literacy Experiences

Children need a variety of literacy experiences that help them learn the difference between print and non-print and to understand the purpose of letters and sounds of the alphabet. These experiences should encourage young children to invent symbols and messages that lead to their literacy development such as left to right and top to bottom progression, and to apply capitalization and punctuation. Literacy experiences and materials must be consistent with the children's developmental level, interests, and ability to concentrate. Such activities include books on tape, puppet theater; computer-based reading, writing, and storybook activities; playing board games; looking through children's magazines; and all kinds of individual and group projects. Having a collection of well-chosen materials within a reading community can have an impact on children's engagement and achievement.

Literacy experiences should include reading situations that integrate scripts where children dictate, write, and read stories; talk about the alphabet and its sounds; read familiar signs and stories; and print labels on pictures, projects, and personal belongings. Young children should be encouraged to create these scripts to help them understand the purposes of reading. Young children can develop these scripts relating to the functions of reading. Children need to be provided with experiences such as discriminating and labeling letters, calling out (reading) signs and labels, and printing and spelling short words (Mason, 1980). Children develop concepts about letter characteristics through such activities as identifying similarities in letters and words, listening to stories, looking at books, writing names, labeling pictures, looking at books while listening to a CD/tape recording or cooking from a recipe. These activities require children to examine the relationship between print and objects and between print and speech, and to learn the ways that sounds and letters of words can be analyzed. When children compare likenesses and differences in letters and words, listen to stories, look at books, write names, label pictures, and look at books as they listen to a CD/tape recording of the book or cook from a recipe, they develop concepts about letter characteristics. These literacy experiences assist children to see the connection between (a) print and objects, (b) print and speech, and (c) letters and their sounds. Appropriate literacy experiences for these children are found in Box 10.1 (NRC, 1998).

---

**Box 10.1. Developmentally Appropriate Literacy Experiences**

- Oral language activities for fostering growth in receptive and expressive language and verbal reasoning;
- reading aloud with children to foster their appreciation and comprehension of text and literacy language;
- reading and book exploration by children for developing print and concepts and basic reading knowledge and processes;
- writing activities for developing children's personal appreciation of the communicative dimensions of print and for exercising printing and spelling abilities;
- thematic activities (e.g., sociodramatic play) for giving children opportunity to integrate and extend their understanding of stories and new knowledge of spaces;
- print-directed activities for establishing children's ability to recognize and print the letters of the alphabet;
- phonemic analysis activities for developing children's phonological and phonemic awareness; and
- word-directed activities for helping children to acquire a basic sight vocabulary and to understand and appreciate the alphabetic principle (p. 189).

---

Children's literacy development should focus on the communication of oral and written language in a meaningful context (Saracho, 1993). Their learning of oral and written language may appear as playing and exploring. Reading stories and poems, telling stories, listening to children's stories, engaging children in predicting and sequencing stories, expanding the children's vocabulary based on the stories, using puppets to retell stories, reading poetry, dramatizing stories, discussing stories, writing stories, and interacting about stories promotes the children's literacy development. These literature experiences are discussed in Chapter 8. See Box 10.2 (Spodek & Saracho, 1994b).

---

**Box 10.2. Experiences to Promote Young Children's Literacy Development**

- *Reading stories and poems*. Stories and poems can be read to young children to share the joy and wonder of broadening their knowledge about the world of books. Children will enjoy the stories and poems read.
- *Telling stories*. Children need to listen to stories rather than having them read to them. At times the content of the story can be modified to make it more meaningful and to maintain the children's interest. For example, stories can be personalized by substituting the characters' names with those of the children.
- *Listening to children's stories*. Children can share stories of an important event, such as a visit to a relative. Teachers can listen to the children's stories

and engage them in conversation or record the story for the children to later illustrate. These can be read many times and taken home to share with family members.

- *Engaging children in predicting and sequencing in stories*. Predictable books, such as *The Gingerbread Man* (Kimmel, 1993), can engage children in the prediction process. They can predict what is going to happen next and check their predictions as the teachers read the story. For example, *Sylvester and the Magic Pebble* (Steig, 1969) is a good book that can be used to help children predict the next event. Sylvester Duncan is a young donkey who discovers a magic pebble and experiences a series of humorous and suspenseful situations. Another book that is good for prediction is Benjamin's (1992) *What's Up the Coconut Tree?* Children can predict every time a coconut bumps on one of the animals' heads. When the animals ask the Lion (King of the Jungle) for assistance, they can predict what the lion would find up the coconut tree. The children can illustrate the story with a palm tree with coconuts and different animals (such as a puzzled lion, zebra).

- *Expanding the children's vocabulary based on the stories*. Some books can be used to expand the children's vocabulary with repetitious phrases, such as *The Gingerbread Man* (Kimmel, 1993) and *Millions of Cats* (Gág, 1928). Children enjoy repeating the phrase, "I run as fast as I can. You can't catch me. I'm the Gingerbread Man." They also find delight in Wanda Gág's phrases in *Millions of Cats*. They love repeating, "Millions of cats, billions and trillions and zillions of cats." The repetition helps the children learn new vocabulary or reinforce well-known words.

- *Using puppets to retell stories*. Puppets can be used to expand the meaning of the story and extend the children's interest. Teachers and children can use the puppets together to dramatize the stories. Teachers can provide children with commercially made puppets (such as a Lady Bug, spider, or crab). They also can make puppets with their classroom children, including stick puppets, paper bag puppets, sock puppets, and puppets made out of a garden glove. The children can then use the puppets to retell a story in a playful way.

- *Reading poetry*. Poetry can be read to children to encourage them to engage in language play. Children can play with the words in the poem or make up words. Children may have a different interpretation and play with a different set of words each time they hear the same poem. Their stories and illustrations may vary each time they listen to the poem. For example, Stevenson's (1987) "From a Railway Carriage" suggests the speed and rattle of a train as it journeys through the country. The lines below may prompt the children's stories and illustrations.

*From a Railway Carriage*

> *Faster than fairies, faster than witches,*
> *Bridges and houses, hedges and ditches;*
> *And charging along like troops in a battle,*
> *All through the meadows the horses and cattle.*

The children's stories and illustrations may express the way they imagine themselves looking out the windows. A group of children drew a picture of themselves in a train looking out the window at bridges, houses, ditches, trees, and fairies and witches flying in the sky. Children prefer poetry that has concrete poems, because these concrete poems can be seen or touched. Some poets stress the meaning of a concrete poem by shaping it into the form of a picture. For example, the poem "Dead Tree" (Froman, 1974) from *Seeing Things: A Book of Poems* has the words written in the shape of a dead tree trunk. Saracho and Spodek (1998b) observed that after the teacher provided the children with experiences using concrete objects and listening to a picture poem about them, they composed some concrete poems themselves.

- *Dramatizing stories.* Teachers can give children the opportunity to act out a story that is their favorite or has been frequently read. They like to tell favorite stories that are easy to remember and often learn or memorize some of their cherished lines. For example, for the story *Goldilocks and the Three Bears* (Cauley, 1981), children will narrate the dialogue word for word such as "'Someone has been sitting on my chair!' said Papa Bear." They also will act out the stories and use improvised actions and dialogues rather than committing the written scripts to memory. Saracho and Spodek (1998) observed that children acted out stories through pantomime and spontaneous stories and skits. In addition, they also used movement and body awareness activities as well as dramatic songs and games. These activities help young children to carry the written language into their own world as they depict the roles of the characters in the story or poem. Children can understand the dramatic quality of the stories as seen when they act out these roles. They interpret stories and poems in several ways. Teachers can provide children with assorted pieces of props, drapery material, clothes, and hats to dress up when dramatizing the story.
- *Discussing stories*. Teachers and children can discuss stories (1) that are familiar, (2) they have illustrated, (3) found in favorite books, or (4) that are retold. Teachers can ask questions about a story they have shared. In the discussion, teachers can suggest actions, sequences, and use the original story as a source of dialogue and action. In discussing the story, teachers can enquire, "What happens next?" or "What did [the character] (such as the King of the Jungle) say in response?" They can also encourage children to raise questions, provide comments, and make observations.
- *Writing stories*. Teachers and children can write stories. Usually children will dictate the story, but teachers can still encourage children to make some marks on their drawings about the story and to try writing using inventing symbols and messages.
- *Interacting about stories.* Teachers can engage children in many interactions about the stories read. In addition, teachers can also interact to support and extend the children's literacy development.

Other literacy experiences can include providing children with time to share alphabet letters, to read to children, and explore the written language.

*Sharing Letters Time*

Teachers can provide a sharing time where children share their favorite letters. Teachers can put plastic commercial letters or cardboard letters in a zip lock bag, and pass out these bags during sharing letters time. Children can use these letters to write words, sentences, and stories. They can also discuss their favorite letter and words that begin with the same letter. Younger children can show letters that they have seen somewhere such as in a McDonald's bag, book, cereal box, or any other label.

*Reading Time*

Teachers can provide a time to read to children. Reading to children helps them to understand that reading is for enjoyment and information and helps them to see reading models. Children try to read books that have been read to them. After a four-year-old girl had listened to *The Little Engine that Could* (Piper, 1954), she said, "Show me where it says 'I think I can, I think I can.' I want to see it in the book." She continued to look through the rest of the book and read with great enthusiasm every time she saw the line "I think I can, I think I can." Reading to children helps them to acquire meaning from the printed written word.

  Literacy requires that children acquire representation skills that help them learn to read and write. Words that are written on a page require children to interpret the meanings of these symbols. The printed visual characteristics help young readers to interpret meaning. Children need to learn the essential skills to identify written codes to acquire meaning; therefore, teachers need to provide young children with learning experiences that will develop their representation skills (Saracho, 2002c). Children need to learn oral meanings and written language in a way that is meaningful to them. Five-year-old children are knowledgeable about print when they ask, "What's that say?" Children who are watching a television advertisement or are listening to a story from a picture storybook may say, "I can't read all the words but I know what they say." (Clay, 1972, p. 28). These children may not be reading the text, but they can be considered to be reading a book when they use a book-like pattern such as "Once upon a time . . ." or "Mother said, 'Do you want a piece of cake?' " Rather than the general "Reading is talk written down." An extensive and meaningful vocabulary helps children learn the other important components in the written language.

*Writing Language Time*

Children develop their written language the same way they develop their oral language. Read (1975) and Chomsky (1972) were among the first to discover that young children's writings were untaught spellings that focused on phonetic and phonological analysis of speech. These children already know the conceptual classifications for consonant and vowel sounds in spoken English. Such classifications are linguistically sound and underlie the invented spellings that children use in their writing. Their experiences with written language in a setting that is meaningful to them make them learn the important characteristics of the written language. Scribbling, printing, spelling, and copying are clear emergent literacy abilities. Very young children use scribbles to copy the adults' writing. Scribbling and writing are an integrated literacy element. Young children learn the characteristics of the written language when they experiment with print in a meaningful way;

they can do this when they use written language within a familiar context. They construct a variety of texts and kinds of writing systems. When children use early nonconventional writings (such as scribbles and nonphonetic letter strings), they are exploring features that they see in print. Teachers can use developmentally appropriate strategies to promote the children's literacy development. Chapter 7 provides a detailed description of children's writing development.

When young children interact in an environment that is full of print, they learn to identify printed word symbols. They detach the printed word symbols from the contextualized setting, categorize and organize them, and integrate or systematize them in their own language system. The children's learning to write is based on their experience, exploration, and conceptual insights.

## Environmental Print

Children find print everywhere in their environment. They see print in toys, clothes, books, television, signs, captions, printed containers, logos, and billboards. They also see print in their environment such as on stop signs and on cereal boxes; in scribbled letters, and in their written names; and in the reading of familiar stories. In all situations, young children become aware of print in their environment and observe adults using print for different reasons. Sometimes adults and older children involve young children in a print experience. They read stories to them or read them a menu at a restaurant. Such experiences give young children information about print and the reason and purposes of print. The great amount of print that young children deal with on a daily basis motivates them to learn to read for personal and social purposes.

The environment influences the way children interact, explore, and express their literacy behaviors. Teachers need to provide young children with a variety of print-related experiences. Purposeful interactions with print and story-related activities are considered important steps in developing emerging writing and oral language skills, more so than working on concepts such as shapes and color recognition (International Reading Association, 1986). Children become literate by being immersed in a literacy-rich environment and engaging in literacy activities with adults and older children who can read. They come to understand the reading process by being read to and by seeing others reading. Before young children can actually read, they learn the parts, products, and purposes of the writing system and how reading and oral language activities relate to and differ from each other (NRC, 1998).

Children are curious and like to imitate adults; they want to read and write when they see adults reading and writing. Teachers need to display an appropriate set of literature books that are of interest to young children. They can read them to the children and display them throughout the school year in the library area. This display should be attractive enough to stimulate young children to browse or read what is within their power to read. Teachers can carefully select books that fit the children's mental age and interests, which helps children to develop a positive attitude toward reading and books. Teachers can sit with a small group of children on a carpet or in the library area and read simple stories to them. The children should find that stories and books are a treasured possession. Children are interested in stories that relate to situations that occur in their own lives, families, community, and world. They also like listening to stories about new experiences.

Teachers can provide children with reading materials as soon as possible. For example, on the first day of school, teachers can create a bulletin board or a door display with a title such as "The Stars from Room 25." The bulletin board or display can have a star for each child with his/her name and/or picture inside a star. Teachers can initiate the year with a unit on the home. They can read stories to children about families such as *Diversity in Families* by Scholastic or Eric Carle's (1986) *Papa, Please Get the Moon for Me*. The children can be encouraged to act out the different roles that their family members assume. They can write and illustrate their own stories about these roles. For example, Amanda, a five-year-old, illustrated and dictated the following story:

> When it's my birthday or anyone's birthday, we usually have a cake and ice cream. I get a piñata like Pocahontas and my brother gets other things.

> When we go to the park my father, mom, brother, my aunt and me play on the monkey bars. My brother Hector and me play always. My father, mom and my aunt Theresa eat a snow cone while we play.

> We also go to the movies with my dad, aunt Theresa, mom, Hector, my brother, me. After the movies we go home and order pizza to eat at home.

> We go visit my grandparents at Dallas and my uncle Bet usually takes us to the park and barbecues fish. He likes cooking.

These stories can be displayed on the wall. If teachers print cards or sentence strips for children, they can match these sentence strips to the text of the original story.

Teachers can promote the children's literacy in a play environment where children are encouraged to use objects (such as paper, pencil, books) and events (such as a story) to understand the meaning of the written word. In a play environment, teachers focus on the purpose and use of literacy instead of the acquisition of skills. The children's literacy-oriented behaviors can be developed in a literacy-related play environment. The natural contexts or enhanced literacy environments emphasize reading, writing, speaking, listening, and knowing in a play environment. Recently, a "social turn" in literacy (Gee, 2000) has emerged, where literacy is considered a social activity and focuses on how literacy develops during the children's interactions with others (DeZutter, 2007).

## Play and Literacy

Play offers young children many opportunities to participate in social experiences that use their reading and writing abilities (Neuman & Roskos, 1990a). Play serves as a medium for developing emergent literacy. Young children explore and test their ideas through play. In play, particularly pretend play, children practice and experiment with written language in many ways (for example, reading stories to their pretend babies, playing school with make believe or real students, writing prescriptions and writing what looks like a never ending stream of scribbled notes). For example, five-year-old Claudia is playing travel agency and states, "You don't scribble on tickets! You spell your name!" (Roskos, 1988a, p. 26). Young children engage in beginning literacy with these play activities. In a play-based literacy education program, young children concentrate on real life situations and act them out in dramatic play. Dramatic play provides a rich contextual setting where literacy behaviors can emerge such as in the following example.

Erika pulls an envelope out of the mailbox and says, "look it's for me!" Then she opens it and scans the scribble on the paper inside. "Mom (a playmate), look it, we're supposed to be at the meeting at eight o'clock" (Roskos, 1991).

In this episode, Erika pretends to read scribbles and print. Erika gives meaning to the scribbles on paper, pretends to read actual text, and scans the paper, which is a reading example of pretending to read (Roskos, 1991). When children play, they engage in literacy conversations using language and bodily movements embedded in the social-physical play context. Young children use the literacy context and "tools" in the enriched play environment to communicate their interpretations of the purposes and characteristics of written language. Their peers also help them to increase their knowledge (Neuman & Roskos, 1991), such as in the following interaction between two four-year-olds:

> Jeremy has a case with plastic dinosaurs inside. As he plays with them, Ashley joins him.
> Jeremy:   I'm playin' with these. Don't close the case up. It has the words.
> Ashley:   Can I play, too?
> Jeremy:   Only take one, OK? Look right here [pointing at the words on the case]. This says "stego" with this one (Neuman & Roskos, 1990a, p.214).

These types of literacy interactions are promoted in a play environment that facilitates the young children's literacy acquisition (Neuman & Roskos, 1990a). Children participate in dramatizations in "literate" play settings when they have an abundant supply of reading and writing materials so that they can willingly integrate literacy into their play episodes (Christie, 1990). The integration of print into the children's dramatic play supports the children's acquisition of literacy in several ways, like those in Box 10.3.

---

### Box 10.3.  Ways Dramatic Play Supports Literacy

- Children are able to sit together and show what they have learned about the daily uses of print.
- Children can explore scribble writing, invented spelling, and developing reading in rich, contextualized circumstances.
- Children develop knowledge of story structure as they create and role play their own narrative scripts.
- Children use literacy vocabulary (such as read, write, pencil, paper, book) in meaningful contexts (Christie, 1990).

---

The children need sufficient time in their play to plan and initiate their play scenarios. Before children begin to play, they need to enlist other players, allocate roles, assign make-believe representation of objects, and negotiate scripts to be dramatized. If children are given short periods of time to engage in play, they will shift to less advanced types of play. Young children need at least 30 minutes to be able to participate in rich, continuous play. But children need more than time to engage in their play—in order that literacy behaviors emerge during play, the classroom needs to be appropriately furnished to become a literate environment that is meaningful to the children.

## Literate-themed Play Environment

At an early age, children become aware of the meaning in print. As a result, when children are continuously exposed to print in familiar contexts, they use their inferring abilities to give meaning to common labels, signs, and objects. Children "read" environmental print to obtain meaning. According to ecologists Kounin and Sherman (1979), "what people do is markedly influenced by where they are" (p. 145). Therefore, when a section of the classroom environment is set up to represent a real-life literacy context (for example, an office), children interact with environmental and meaningful print to associate print with meaning (Neuman & Roskos, 1993a).

Even if children are exposed to just a few materials, they will spontaneously integrate literacy into their play. Children need to be provided with a literate-rich play environment with literacy materials (like books, posters, signs, pamphlets) and a variety of paper and writing tools to promote their literacy development (Roskos & Vukelich, 1991). Thematic play provides a perfect environment for young children to practice, elaborate, and develop their emergent literacy abilities (Woodard, 1984). They discover the functional uses of literacy skills that young children integrate into their play themes. During their play, they engage in paper handling, storytelling, and trying to read and write (Roskos, 1991). When creating literacy play environments to promote the children's acquisition of literacy, teahers need to also take into account the children's point of view and their interests such as in the following play situation.

> In one kindergarten classroom, the children decided the next week's play setting would be a library and accepted responsibility for creating the setting. They sorted and labeled the books. They put cards and envelopes in each book. They created a check out center with a date stamp and pad and a sign saying, "Check books out here." They added Librarian to the classroom jobs chart. They hung Sh-h and Quiet Areas signs. They put the stuffed animals in the center to be read to. Perhaps the message is: Let the children help with the development of the settings. They will then become more alert to print-related activities when visiting real life settings (Vukelich, 1990, p. 208).

Vukelich (1990) also reports how children became interested in learning and arranging UPS dramatic play settings.

> one day as the children were playing outside, a UPS truck pulled into the school drive. Jessica yelled, "Uncle Mike!" and the class was off for a "teachable moment" tour of a UPS truck and its packages, packages and more packages. The children saw labels on the packages, an insignia on Uncle Mike's shirt and hat, a clipboard with package recipients' signatures, and samples of forms to complete when mailing a package via UPS (p. 206).

This incident led to establishing a UPS dramatic play setting. Information on the inner workings of the local collection and distribution office can be obtained from a UPS location. Literacy materials (for example, express mailers, weight scales, charts to calculate the costs for packages of several weights, stamps and pads, signs such as "Line forms here" and "Fill out the required forms BEFORE getting in line") can be collected and placed in the classroom UPS dramatic play setting. In this situation, the children thought that the classroom's big wooden trucks should have signs and their hats should have insignias. The literacy props were displayed and before playtime there was a discussion on how to use the props. The following play episode took place.

> Michael organizes how packages could be handled. As Jason receives a package from Jonathon (he had prepared the mailing label noting whom the package was to and from), Michael asks, "Are you stamping that package and getting his money? Be sure to write a receipt." Jason stamps and stamps and stamps the package. Michael directs, "That's enough! Look, you are holding up the line! Write the receipt!" Jason doesn't know how to spell Jonathon's name. Allen tells Jonathon to turn around so Jason can copy his name from his name tag. The package is weighed, the weight recorded on the receipt and the money collected. Michael calls, "Hey, driver, get this package delivered. It's going to Canada." Jessica drives off toward "Canada" (p. 207).

In this short episode, the children read, wrote, and talked by using both oral and written language that takes place at a package collection distribution setting. In packaging and sending packages, the children learned about the purposes of writing (e.g., receipts, mailing labels). They applied their knowledge and understanding of print (such as writing progresses from left to right, capital and lower case letters make words, different letters are needed to make a word) to write on the receipts and labels. In the UPS dramatic play setting, the children engaged in a variety of related learning experiences.

In thematic play settings young children have the opportunity to use materials that encourage them to write, to use print, to read, and to engage in literacy behaviors as they play. Sociodramatic play develops oral language when children plan, negotiate, compose, and carry out their play. Children also practice verbal and narrative language. In dramatic play young children create elaborate scripts that promote literacy. They are encouraged to write when teachers provide appropriate materials (such as paper, markers, pencils, stamp pads) for their language scripts. Teachers can guide children to recognize print that is displayed in the play environment.

Teachers' interactions can support and extend the child's literacy development through play by using literacy-play materials to encourage interactions during reading and by playfully using concrete literacy objects. Teachers can use strategies and activities that integrate play and literacy such as those in Box 10.2. Teachers can assist children with their language and literacy development using play-based literacy instruction if they:

- allow enough time and space for play in the classroom,
- provide the needed material resources,
- develop children's background knowledge for the play setting,
- scaffold the rehearsals of dramatic retellings, and
- become involved in play settings so as to guide the children's attention and learning through modeling and interaction (NRC, 1998, p. 184).

The classroom environment or physical arrangement is important in sociodramatic play. In the sociodramatic environment children can use reading and writing to legitimize their pretend play, express themselves, and record information within play events (Roskos, 1988b). Teachers need to provide children with experiences that help them understand the purposes of the written language. Children can create and use shopping lists, buy goods with food stamps, and get prescriptions from a doctor during their play (Jacob, 1984).

Children's literacy behaviors emerge in a play setting where they learn the purposes and characteristics of print that are important in the children's early literacy development. When children play, they generate assumptions about print as a "sense-making" activity. They also turn into "meaning makers" in their literacy-enriched environments (Wells, 1986).

Literacy interactions in a play environment help and encourage the children's literacy development. These play environments must consider the children's interests and developmental levels. When children engage in literacy-related play experiences, they (1) explore their environment, (2) interact with others, (3) express themselves, (4) confirm events, (5) dialogue with text (Neuman & Roskos, 1989), and (6) select and use abilities that are essential for literacy learning in a social context. Play helps young children explore their developing perceptions of the uses and aspects of print (Saracho, 2002c).

## Literacy-enriched Play Centers

Children's early literacy experiences usually take place in a natural context. Play centers with literacy materials provide young children with outstanding opportunities to promote their acquisition of literacy. Dramatic play theme centers provide children with valuable natural literacy opportunities. The classroom environment should include literacy-enriched play centers. Activities that promote reading can be integrated in the play centers in the early childhood curriculum. Language or literacy components can be integrated in the children's play activities to promote the inventing of symbols and messages in the children's writing. The teachers need to create a literate environment that includes spontaneous play to promote the children's literacy development. Teachers need to keep in mind that children's play must be (1) spontaneous and voluntary and (2) willingly selected by the players (Spodek & Saracho, 1987).

Children exhibit literacy behaviors in the different learning centers. Activities that are flexible should be included in the different learning centers to give children the opportunity to engage in spontaneous play and interact with each other. Spontaneous play is found in manipulative, physical, dramatic, and block play. Teachers can set up play centers in the classroom that focus on language and literacy development such as pretend reading, reading pictures, learning the letters of the alphabet, and writing stories. Literacy play centers can also include language, library, and writing areas. Literacy experiences are found in the block, mathematics, dramatic, writing, and library learning centers. Some representative literacy-play experiences that were observed by Saracho (2001) and Saracho and Spodek (1996, 1998b) are discussed below in relation to the literacy enriched-play learning centers. Since the different learning centers have been described in chapter 5, only the observations will be included. Two types of learning centers can be observed in the early childhood classroom: traditional and theme centers. Traditional centers relate to academic areas (like science, mathematics, language), where themes centers focus on themes that are found the children's environment (like post office, grocery store, bank).

## Traditional Centers

Traditional centers consist of block, manipulative, mathematics, writing, library, computer, language, science, and dramatic play centers.

## Block Center

In the block activity center, the children can build anything they want. For example, in a classroom, five boys were observed building with blocks. Three of them constructed a roadway out of blocks and the other two built a double garage structure. In building these constructions, children had concepts of their structure. During block building, children shifted these concepts (the idea of a garage and roadway) to a concrete reality (Saracho & Spodek, 1996).

Spontaneous play in the block area can encourage the children's problem solving and cooperative behaviors related to the children's literacy development. Saracho (2001) describes two different situations of spontaneous play:

Situation 1:

A group of boys constructed a building with a set of scrap lumber building blocks. During their play, the teacher asked them what they were building.

"A house," was one boy's reply.
"A house?" the teacher asked.
"Yes!" came the response.

The remainder of the building period continued with little conversation as the boys worked cooperatively or independently in their construction.

In this situation, children developed vocabulary concepts and the ability to engage in discussion with others.

Situation 2:

A group of boys were using triangular blocks to represent automobiles. In the block center, a child pretended to be parking a car, one child was holding a roof and another child watched. Children checked the interior of the garage. They had a drop cloth stretched out on the floor. The drop cloth had pictures of streets and logos of traffic signals for children to follow directions when playing with transportation toys. The children drove their cars around the streets and "read" the information on the drop cloth and responded to it, such as stopping their cars at the intersections before resuming the driving of their cars.

Children develop literacy behaviors when they follow oral and written directions, like when they read and followed the directions on the signs. These literacy behaviors represent functional reading in our society.

## Manipulative Center

The manipulative center included games, geoboards, and picture dominoes. Table 10.2 indicates the literacy development in these activities.

**TABLE 10.2. Components of Literacy Behaviors in the Children's Play**

| Play Activities | Literacy Behaviors |
| --- | --- |
| Parquetry Blocks | 1. Use of analytic thinking<br>2. Use of memory<br>3. Read the shapes on the pattern card and match them with the ones on the blocks |
| Bingo and Lotto | 1. Match a written word with a picture and letters (if ready)<br>2. Match a spoken word with a picture beginning sound (if ready) |
| Geoboards | 1. Explore the geometric shapes of letters<br>2. Create the shapes of letters in a tactile medium<br>3. Match the shape of the letter with its spoken sound<br>4. Match words with their initial letters and sounds<br>5. Write letters on the geoboard |
| Picture Dominoes | 1. Match the same pictures<br>2. Learn sequential order<br>3. Follow and establish rules<br>4. Accept other's point of view through communication<br>5. Develop generalizations based on specific examples |
| Sequence Games | 1. Match pairs of related objects<br>2. Learn the use of sequence that occurs in a story<br>3. Learn to look for similarities and differences that occur in the recognition of letters<br>4. Verbal picture representations |

## Mathematics Center

In the mathematics center, a teacher can post a chart with numbers from one to 100. A child can be assigned to point to a series of numbers, while children in this center sit on the carpet and read each number that the child points to. Reading the Arabic numbers correctly requires children to use reading behaviors (Saracho & Spodek, 1996).

In an observation, Saracho and Spodek (1998b) reported that the mathematics center, which was next to the reading center, had five children working in different literacy-related activities. A girl used a 36-inch ruler to point at numbers on a Counting Chart that was hanging from a metal frame. Two other children read the name of the number. They read the numbers in sequence from one to a hundred and then they counted backwards (100 to 0). Some children rocked back and forth as they read the numbers. These observations are examples how useful a mathematics center can be for developing literacy skills.

## Writing Center

In the writing center, children were writing in sequence stories and some of their experiences. First they drew, colored, and attempted to write their stories as pictures. Then they dictated their story to the teacher. During this activity children imitated the teachers' behavior when they pretended to write as they made marks on a piece of paper. When they finished, they read what they had written. The marks children made on a paper differed each time they read to others the written message. To them their own writing was the only text they could read accurately; therefore, the writing of these symbols became very important to the children and writing became important in their literacy development (Saracho & Spodek, 1996).

## Library Center

Library centers have a variety of reading materials such as easy storybooks that have been read to children, picture books, and books and stories that children have written themselves. Saracho (2001) describes how three girls shared a comfortable chair. One of the girls read the story of *The Three Bears* with much animation and expression. She turned the pages as she imitated an adult's reading behavior. She seemed to be reading the story, but upon closer observation it was noted that she was reading her own version of the story. Picture reading and imitating reading behaviors are indications of the children's emergent literacy behaviors.

The library center has several print and non-print materials. It includes several of the children's books and a carpet for children to sit on and listen to a story. Teachers can read stories, while children sit comfortably on the carpet and listen. Teachers may read a story and at the same time ask the children questions about it. Another listening activity may be listening to a variety of stories on tapes. Children listen to the story on the tape or CD as they look at the book and turn the page as directed by the recording. In this literacy experience children have an opportunity to follow a story that is read on a recording using the pictures and print in the book as well as listening to the tape recording (Saracho, 2001). A small group of children followed a story that was read on a commercially-prepared recording. The children listened to the recording, looked at the printed books that accompanied it, and turned the pages when they heard a music sound (Saracho & Spodek, 1996).

## Technology Center

With the appearance of computers in the classrooms, early childhood teachers find themselves with a new technology. They can set up a computer center in the classroom to begin to use high quality and appropriate computer programs including CD talking books. Talking books on CDs have the potential to serve as another vehicle for children's engagement with stories in ways that support their literacy development. Teachers should make use of talking books, because they are interactive, digital versions of stories that use multimedia features such as animation, music, sound effects, highlighted text, and models of fluent reading (Labbo, 2000). Talking books provide a new way to capture children's interest with stories. Some of the children's favorite stories that are found in talking books include *Dr. Seuss's ABC* (1995), *Green Eggs and Ham* (Seuss, 1995), and *Stellaluna* (Cannon, 1996). *On the Go* (Williams, 1995) is a big book that can be used in shared reading. This book tells how each child goes to school in the morning. Children can create their own version of the story in the computer. They type their name and as many sounds as they can for the rest of the message. These stories can be printed and displayed for rereading. The text can also be written in SimpleText (1995) so that the computer can read it aloud. Young children enjoy hearing their names and the group story read aloud in a variety of voices. Another useful software is Kid Pix (1997). This program encourages children to write as they experiment with graphics and special effects (Eisenwine & Hunt, 2000). Children can write or attempt to write something that matches their illustrations.

Eisenwine and Hunt (2000) use the computer with small groups of children. They use Hyperstudio (1997) software to create their own talking books for children. This program allows for easy animation of figures that the software has created. The talking books include illustrated actions, sounds, and music. For example, when the text reads, "I can walk," a man is shown walking along a road to music. In another story, a frog is jumping on one page and on another page a bird is flying. The frog jumps across the grass to the sound of frogs croaking. Teachers need to introduce the stories with various patterns of high frequency words. When children go to the computer center, they read these talking books by themselves. They will enjoy the animated stories and reading along with the computer. The Hyperstudio program can also be used to create talking books that can be integrated in their thematic unit. Box 10.4 includes sample software that can be used with young children.

---

**Box 10.4  Computer Software**

*Cat in the Hat* by Dr. Seuss (2005). The Learning Company. Boston: Houghton Mifflin Harcourt.

*Dr. Seuss's ABC.* (2005). The Learning Company. Boston: Houghton Mifflin Harcourt.

*Green Eggs and Ham* by Dr. Seuss. (2005). The Learning Company. Boston: Houghton Mifflin Harcourt.

*Hyperstudio 5* by Roger Wagner. (2011). Boston: The Software MacKiev Company.

*Kid Pix.* (2011). Boston: The Software MacKiev Company.

*Mr. And Mrs. Potato Head Go On Vacation.* (2001). New York: Infogrames Interactive.

*Stellaluna* by Cannon. (2006), (2005). The Learning Company. Boston: Houghton Mifflin Harcourt.

---

## Science Center

In the science center children follow directions in carrying out an experiment and write its findings. For children who cannot read, teachers can provide them with pictures to help them follow the directions. Books related to the topic of study are displayed in the science center.

Children can plant seeds or bring a plant from home to watch and record its growth. They can water it, observe it, and record its growth on a chart. Children can write a report about the plant's evolution by using drawings and symbols or invented spelling. They may also wish to dictate this report to the teacher so that the teacher writes their report on their illustrations or a chart (Saracho & Spodek, 1996).

## Dramatic Play Center

The dramatic play center can include housekeeping or other role playing activities that encourage the children to role play past experiences and different roles. Teachers provide children with appropriate props to develop stories and activities that enhance the children's vocabularies in their literacy learning. Children use appropriate props to reproduce the social interactions and previous experiences or schemata they have observed in their environment (Saracho, 2001). The dramatic play center can be changed periodically to a theme which is based on the children's interests and lives. The thematic center can also be set up next to the housekeeping center.

## Themed Literacy-play Centers

Theme centers extend the range of children's literacy-related play experiences. Themed centers need to include props and furniture based on surroundings from the children's lives, such as a doctor's office, restaurant, bank, post office, ice cream parlor, or grocery store. For example, a center on the doctor's office can be separated into two areas:

- the waiting room that is furnished with a table for a receptionist and chairs for patients, and
- the examination room that has another table, chairs, and several medical props (e.g., doctor kit, scales).

The inclusion of theme-appropriate literacy and writing materials encourages literacy-related play. For example, the doctor's office could have a supply of pencils, a notebook for the receptionist to write down appointments, magazines for the patients to read at the waiting room, prescription forms, and reference books for the doctor to consult.

## Housekeeping Center

The housekeeping center offers young children opportunities to act out the role of being the mom, the dad, or the baby. Children can engage in family play themes (for example, parents taking care of a baby or a family eating a meal) that are part of the children's daily lives, such as in the following episode.

> Collin and Patrick are playing house in the dramatic play center in their kindergarten classroom. Collin opens the refrigerator and says, "Patrick, there's no food in this refrigerator; no food in this house!" Patrick responds, "I didn't have time to go to the grocery store today. Where's a piece of paper and I'll make a list of the things you want?" (Vukelich, 1990, p. 205).

A home usually has reading materials (books, telephone directory, magazines). The house-keeping play center can be furnished with props that remind children of their own homes. Children will engage in literacy activities they have experienced in their homes. A house-keeping play center that is well furnished has various household props, such as miniature replicas of kitchen furniture, appliances, dishes, kitchen utensils, dolls, doll accessories, telephones, ironing boards, brooms, baby carriages, and cradles (Johnson et al., 2005). The housekeeping center should encourage literacy activities by supplying many reading materials (pens, pencils, note pads, diaries, cookbooks, telephone books, picture books, magazines, catalogs, newspapers). When these kinds of materials are available in the housekeeping center, young children will be motivated to integrate reading and writing into their play episodes (Christie, 1990). The housekeeping play center can be replaced at regular intervals or be combined with another dramatic play center such as a grocery store setting, a hospital setting, and any setting that matches the children's interests.

When children act out household themes in the housekeeping center, they participate in several home literacy practices consisting of writing notes and letters to family members and relatives, constructing shopping lists, taking telephone messages, searching for programs in the *TV Guide,* looking at recipe books to prepare pretend meals, browsing through newspapers and magazines, and reading stories to make-believe babies (Christie, 1990).

## The Shoe Store Play Center

The shoe store play center provides young children with many opportunities to participate in literacy activities. It can include chairs for customers, shelves for displaying shoes, and a checkout counter to buy the shoes. Young children can assume the roles of a salesperson, cashier, and customers. In this play center, young children are able to recreate personal experiences where they use functional literacy. In the shoe store center, children encounter literacy when they read the posters that are displayed advertising a variety of shoes that children can purchase. Shoes are categorized, labeled, and displayed on shelves where shoes are sorted based on products and sizes for women, men, and children. Young children are able to read the labels to select and buy their shoes or as a sales associate locate and stock the shelves. They can measure and read the customers' sizes with rulers or other measuring tools. The sales associates write sales slips, while customers read the sales slip and write a check or use play money for their purchase (Campbell & Foster, 1993).

## The Florist Shop Play Center

The florist shop play center can provide young children with an exciting and creative learning experience. It can include all kinds and colors of plastic or silk "cut" flowers, which are arranged and placed in vases that are labeled with the color and kind of flower (e.g., red roses, pink and white carnations). For this purpose, empty coffee cans, milk cartons, or real flowers storage containers borrowed or donated from a florist can be used. Synthetic plants and floral arrangements can be displayed in pots. The florist shop play center can also have displays of live plants and terrariums for children to compare with the artificial ones. Styrofoam scraps can be glued or taped into plastic vases, bowls, and plates. Arrangements can have marbles at the bottom of the container. Young children can wear gloves and aprons with the florist shop's name that has been written on paper and taped to the aprons. Freshly cut flowers and floral arrangements can be wrapped with tissue, wrapping, and/or cellophane paper with ribbons. Posters and pictures could have short written descriptions for the different floral arrangements and be hung on the walls in the "receptionist" area. A small table could have magazines, books, pamphlets, and newspaper clippings about flowers and plants. The receptionist's desk or table could include a telephone, city telephone book, a class directory, pencils, pads, and a calendar to write the orders; order forms may have blank spaces to write the name, address, kind of arrangement ordered, and delivering date and time. Orders are kept on a clipboard for the receptionist to monitor their deliveries. A sign advertising the name, address, and telephone number of the florist shop could be displayed above the receptionist's desk. Containers that hold the flowers ought to be labeled with both names and/or color words of the flowers. Rebus flower pictures can be used to separate the flowers and place them into the correct storage containers (Campbell & Foster, 1993).

## Camping in a National Park Play Center

The camping play center can include a park station, an area for the camp site, and small paper lake. Props can consist of camping supplies and equipment, a badge for the park attendant, several types of paper fish with attached paper clips in the lake, fishing poles with magnet "hooks," and stones to mark the campfire's borders. Young children can read the park rules that are posted at the station, read the restrictions on how many different kinds of fish can be caught in the lake, fill out an application to get a fishing license, and register to camp in the national park. Magazines and books can be placed inside shoulder bags for children to read while fishing, resting from hiking, or relaxing alongside the campfire (Campbell & Foster, 1993).

## Travel Agency Play Center

The travel agency play center supports a number of study units (such as people of other lands and cultures, ways of transportation, geography) for children of all age levels. It can include small suitcases or travel bags to be used for travel to several destinations such as warm places (e.g., Florida, Hawaii) or cold places (e.g., Alaska, Norway). Belongings packed in a suitcase intended for warm climates can consist of thongs, straw hats, towels, beach toys, suntan lotion, and sunglasses. In contrast, belongings packed in a suitcase intended for cold climates include snow boots, gloves, mittens, a hat, a muffler, and a heavy coat. Belongings for all climates can contain travel "necessities" (e.g., toothpaste, toothbrush, oversized T-shirts for sleep wear, shampoo, slippers). Posters, photographs, and magazine pictures about travel destinations and different types of transportation can be displayed on the walls for children to read. A globe and maps of both the United States and world could be displayed in a location where children are able to see them and find their travel destinations. A table with travel magazines, books, and pamphlets could be displayed for travelers to check out. At the entrance, a sign with the name of the travel agency and signs for the children to know when the travel agency is "Opened," remains "Closed," and has "Office Hours" could be displayed. A clock, computers, telephone, pencils, pads, and calendar to book reservations may be included on the travel agent's desk. Unfilled airline and train tickets could be printed to include the passenger's name, going from _____ to _____, date, time of departure, time of arrival, and flight or train number. Copies of tickets are on a clipboard. The travel agent hands the tickets to the travelling customers when they complete and pay for the travel reservations (Campbell & Foster, 1993).

## Repair Shop Play Center

The repair shop play center should be full of broken objects (e.g., dishes, toys, appliances, clocks). Since it is important to take into account the children's safety, it is important that the electrical cords be removed from the appliances and old televisions or objects with sharp edges be left off and/or removed from the repair play center. Broken objects (without sharp edges), tools, and adhesives are sorted on the shelves that are labeled for children to find and replace objects. The props could consist of a workbench with seating for the workers, a counter for customers, and notebooks with directions that workers can follow to repair broken objects. When the customers take to the shop objects to be repaired, young children can write receipts for the broken objects, read directions to mend the broken objects, and determine how much to charge for services provided. Important signs should be displayed in the shop, such as signs to advertise the prices of particular repair jobs and safety procedures (e.g., Goggles required) (Campbell & Foster, 1993).

Dramatic play can also include themes that draw out real-life uses of literacy. Real life props need to be added to these themes to make them realistic. The themes need to represent the children's real-life and literacy-related experiences to encourage their own creative purposes for reading and writing. Regardless of the theme, it is important that the center be enriched with the addition of many literacy materials, such as those in Box 10.5 (Neuman & Roskos, 1990b).

---

**Box 10.5. Literacy Materials to Use in Different Themed Dramatic Play Centers**

- *Fast food restaurant, ice cream store, or bakery* include menus, order pads, cash registers, list of specials for the day, recipes, and lists of flavors or products.
- *Restaurant* includes child-authored menus, posters that display the various meals, and pencils and note pads for the waiters and waitresses to write down the customers' orders.
- *Newspaper office* includes writing paper, telephones, directories, maps, type-writers, computers, and areas that concentrate on sports, travel, general news, and weather.
- *Supermarket or local grocery store* includes labeled shelves and divisions, food containers, cash registers, telephones, shopping receipts, checkbooks, coupons, and advertising flyers.
- *Post office* includes paper, envelopes, address books, pens, pencils, stamps, cash registers, and mailboxes. A mail carrier needs a hat and bag to deliver the children's mail through reading their names and addresses.
- *Airport* includes signs announcing arrivals and departures, tickets, boarding passes, luggage tags, magazines and books for the waiting area, safety messages on the plane, and name tags for the flight attendants.
- *Gas station and car repair shop* can be added to the block center. Cars and trucks can be used for props. In addition, this center needs to include receipts for sales, road maps to assist with directions for a variety of destinations, auto repair manuals to fix cars and trucks, posters to advertise automobile equipment, and empty cans of various products that are sold in stations.
- *Kitchen* can have telephone books, a telephone emergency number decals, cookbooks, food coupons, and grocery store advertisements.
- *Office* can have calendars, appointment book, signs, magazines for waiting room, and assorted forms.
- *Post office* can have stationery and envelopes, mail boxes, computers, address labels, posters, signs about zip codes, and tote bag for mail.
- *Library* can have library book return cards, children's books, stamps for borrowing books, and sign in/sign out sheet.

---

The selection of themed play centers should be based on situations that all children know and those that can expand their experiences. In promoting optimal literacy-related play experiences, children should contribute to the planning and creation of the center. In addition, both the children and the teacher can discuss the materials and their use.

# Organization of Literacy-play Centers

Literacy-enriched play centers are important in the classrooms, but the organization of the classroom environment influences the effectiveness of the centers. The following describes the daily routines that are observed in classrooms:

> The classroom is spacious and neat. The walls, boards, and bulletin boards are covered with interesting and neatly displayed learning materials and children's work. The classroom environment and interactions between the teacher and children seem to motivate the children to engage in literacy learning. The classroom environment also includes learning play centers that are enriched with literacy activities. Clearly labeled, the play centers are placed around the room and are ready for children to use them (Saracho & Spodek, 1996).

Literacy-play experiences are considered when they contribute to the development of any type of communication. The play activities can be adapted to the children's listening, language, writing, and literacy developmental levels. The literacy experiences need to provide children with opportunities to develop and use literacy behaviors. Before the children engage in the literacy-enriched play centers, teachers need to provide a planning period. Chapter 5 suggests planning procedures that teachers can use. The children are dismissed to go to the play center of their choice. As children finish their work in the learning center, they go to another one. Teachers interact spontaneously with the children in the play centers.

The literacy-enriched play centers influence the children's literacy behaviors based on the way they are physically displayed. It is important to consider their spatial organizations, the general functions of reading and writing among preschoolers, and the children's point of view. Guidelines for organizing literacy play centers can be found in Box 10.6 (Neuman & Roskos, 1990b).

---

### Box 10.6. Guidelines for Organizing Literacy-play Centers

- All play centers should be noticeably separated from each other and be obviously labeled with semi-fixed elements (such as cupboards, screens, tables and hanging mobiles).
- Labeling objects in the physical environment is helpful. For instance, storage bins will help children put blocks and accessories away. Illustrated and printed signs can make it easy to identify art materials.
- Play centers (e.g., Post Office, Library, Office, Kitchen) that are familiar to the children need to have activities that children know to promote their literacy development.
- The physical space needs to be spacious enough for children to move between the literacy-enriched centers. However, close proximity of related theme play centers encourages children to extend the play themes.
- Literacy props that are placed in each play center need to be appropriate (young children are able to use them), authentic (a real object from the environment), and functional (young children are able to use them in their imitative literacy attempts).

Literacy-related play themes in the enriched play centers need to influence the play experience for the children to engage in literacy-related play for a longer period of time. In a play situation, the print activities connect the literacy-related play to a logical theme. For example:

> Michael and Scott are in the Office play center. They are playing "sign-up." They want people "to sign up" for the homeless. Scott has a small clipboard and pencil. He circulates throughout the classroom, asking different teachers and children to sign their names on his clipboard. Michael remains in the office "writing" at the desk. Periodically he looks up and directs Scott to ask someone else. Finally Scott returns with a list of signatures. Both boys pretend to "enter" the list into the computer. Scott points to names on the list and Michael types. When done, Scott removes the paper from the clipboard and is sent out again to gather more names (Neuman & Roskos, 1990b).

In the enriched play centers, children use literacy in a more useful, purposeful, and organized way. They use literacy to gain and communicate information that is important in their play schemes (e.g., to sign up for activities, to "read" recipes to prepare meals). The children's play becomes more firm. Precise play situations (such as the Office, Post Office) suggest a definite structure while the literacy props give children specific ways to use literacy. The situation and literacy props assist in identifying the play themes that encourage and lead the play structure. In addition to increasing interactions, young children assume roles (like postal workers, office managers, advocates of social issues, librarians), establish role definitions, and gain knowledge (like library duties). The children's participation in the literacy-enriched play environment becomes useful and deep-rooted in their play activity. Thus, play gives more understanding and meaning to literacy, where the children's exploration has many purposes in nature. The relationship between play and literacy becomes more obvious in the enriched centers (Neuman & Roskos, 1990b).

Young children learn how to write and read through literacy-related play activities in their social world (Spodek & Saracho, 1987), which can be provided in literacy-enriched play centers. Table 10.3 provides sample literacy behaviors that are developed in these play centers. These play centers can include activities and be organized to promote literacy. Centers need to be enriched to be used for learning and communicating, such as a writing center, role-playing center, and library center. Each learning center should develop essential communication functions in the children's emerging literacy behaviors. Reading should develop naturally in the same way that oral language is learned.

**TABLE 10.3. Sample Literacy Behaviors Developed in the Play Centers**

| Play Centers | Literacy Behaviors |
| --- | --- |
| Library Center | 1. Learn book etiquette<br>2. Learn to use a reading voice<br>3. Learn the conventions of printed text<br>4. Enjoy literacy experiences<br>5. Learn the difference between text and pictures |
| Listening Center | 1. Follow directions<br>2. Match the spoken word with the printed text<br>3. Learn story grammar |

| Science Center | 1. Follow directions |
| | 2. Test ideas |
| | 3. Follow instructions |
| | 4. Read pictures |
| | 5. Discuss ideas |
| Dramatic Play | 1. Engage in symbolic play when they substitute objects for real ones |
| | 2. Interact among the children to develop vocabulary |
| | 3. Use prior knowledge to create their experiences |
| | 4. Sequence events |
| | 5. Write ingredients in a cooking experience |
| | 6. Use of currency in shopping |
| Block Play | 1. Use prior knowledge from previous experiences |
| | 2. Use of language |
| | 3. Use of stories to write at a later time |
| | 4. Label structures |

## Summary

Interactions exist between literacy and play that promote the children's literacy learning. During play young children engage in reading and writing experiences that develop their literacy abilities that are required for formal reading instruction. Children need play experiences that integrate both oral and written language to understand the purposes of print (Saracho & Spodek, 2006). Language and literacy can be developed through play-based literacy instruction (NRC, 1998), when children are provided with developmentally appropriate literacy play experiences. Children can become "meaning makers" in literacy-play enriched environments (Wells, 1986). In a sociodramatic play environment, children use reading and writing to legitimatize their pretend play, to express themselves, and to record information within play incidents (Roskos, 1988b). Children's literacy behaviors emerge in a play environment when they obtain knowledge of the purposes and features of print in early literacy development (Saracho & Spodek, 2006). The children's literacy can be developed through play and its different play-related literacy methods (such as learning centers, setting up a play environment, various literacy-play experiences).

# Chapter 11
# **Science-play Learning Experiences**

Like play, science is a search for order in an imperfect world. It offers a temporary, limited perfection in the face of the blooming, buzzing confusion of everyday reality. It casts a spell and lifts us out of apparent chaos into an idealized world of make-believe.

Chet Raymo (2007)

In the past, early childhood programs have had a minimum interest in the teaching of science because there has been little educational research suggesting that young children are able to understand scientific concepts. However, over the last decade, some researchers such as French (2004) and Gelman and Brenneman (2004) have challenged this view. They have shown from the moment of birth young children use their senses and reach out to their environment to gain information about their world. As children develop, they gain experiences and create both physical and social concepts about their world. They also accumulate knowledge from their experience and develop new powers of understanding (Spodek & Saracho, 1994b). As a result, early childhood educators have become aware that young children can engage in science experiences and learn science concepts. This has motivated more researchers to explore if children are able to learn scientific concepts. The purpose of this chapter is to describe children's learning, standards and expectations (such as the science benchmarks), children's play, learning centers, and learning in a social context in science.

## Learning Science

For many years, early childhood and science educators have tried to understand how young children acquire science knowledge. Science education helps children learn about their world and discover answers through their own mental and physical activity. Young children have a unique way of learning and discovering concepts (Zimmerman, 2005). Young children (including infants) are biologically ready and motivated to acquire knowledge about the world around them. Infants use their personal experiences and any related roles and props to develop an understanding of and become involved in their everyday world. They can (a) identify regularities, (b) understand their everyday experiences, (c) anticipate the behavior of others in different circumstances, and (d) develop appropriate behaviors (French, 2004). Three-year-old children learn concepts and at ages four or five they learn mental representations through listening. They develop a hypothesis in the form of a question to explain the way that they make sense of the world as seen in Malcom's (1999) description of her four-year-old daughter.

> My own children taught me early on that they sought—and would create if necessary—explanations of their world and its workings. They took no part of the material world for granted. What makes it snow? What are clouds made of? My daughter Kelly's fear of thunder led her to a moment of scientific theorizing when she was four years old. As we were racing home during a storm, she announced from the back seat that she knew why the "clouds bumped into each other and make that thunder." "Why is that?" I asked. "Because they don't have any eyes," Kelly replied.

Young children need developmentally appropriate science experiences that can help them create and refine their theories. They need to be provided with developmentally appropriate learning to help them modify their concepts and perceptions of the different natural phenomena. The children's perspectives in science learning are very important. Young children learn science when they have a feeling of wonder, relatedness, and fascination about the world. They need to experience a novelty effect to become creative in science (Osborne & Brady, 2002). Children need to experience science activities that are new or unique to them. The key is to provide them with "developmentally appropriate" science experiences where young children develop their cognitive understanding in science (Hadjigeorgiou, 2001). According to Rachel Carson (1956).

> A child's world is fresh and new and beautiful, full of wonder and excitement. It is our misfortune that for most of us that clear-eyed vision, that true instinct for what is beautiful and awe-inspiring, is dimmed and even lost before we reach adulthood. If I had influence with the good fairy who is supposed to preside over the christening of all children, I should ask that her gift to each child in the world be a sense of wonder so indestructible that it would last throughout life, as an unfailing antidote against the boredom and disenchantments of later years, the sterile preoccupation with things that are so artificial, the alienation from sources of our strength (pp. 42–43).

Young children are naturally curious with a need to inquire about their surroundings. They are anxious to learn about themselves and their world. Their enthusiasm motivates them to spend long periods of time concentrating on their individual interests. Such motivation is important to any educational undertaking, because young children need to be motivated to enthusiastically persevere into unfamiliar areas and learn from the rich science experiences (Henniger, 1987). According to Sher (2003), science teaching needs to "incorporate opportunities to explore findings of science research and to conduct experiments, supporting a view of inextricable integration of science content and science process"

(p. 191) that emphasizes a connection to real world problems. She continues, "The nature of science itself involves inquiry and exploration. Thus, science education should encourage habits of curiosity, observation, and logic, along with the communication skills to share ideas" (Sher, 2003, p. 205). School environments that promote these qualities are usually the ones where young children are more highly motivated to engage in problem solving and see learning as fun and interesting, which can help them develop scientific habits of mind (Bergen, 2009).

Science learning needs to integrate the children's linguistic and cultural experiences, which make science learning meaningful and relevant to them. Linguistic and cultural experiences also promote their learning of the English language. The children's learning in science needs to connect the different relationships between scientific phenomena and the children's experiences in their home and community environment (for example, cooking, weather conditions, plants in their garden). Some English language learners (ELLs) usually have to learn science through an unknown language. ELLs can learn the science concepts through (a) hands-on activities based on natural phenomena that require limited science experiences and limited knowledge of English that can decrease their linguistic frustration and (b) through independent, collaborative, and small-group activities that offer the ELLs opportunities to develop their English proficiency in the context of actually discussing and learning science knowledge. They can also engage in brainstorming activities, narrative vignettes, and science books for children that motivate their prior knowledge about science.

Children with disabilities can also acquire scientific knowledge when instruction is adapted to their disability. They may need more instructional and practice time and more varied experiences to learn science concepts. For example, children who are deaf and hard-of-hearing may require more time to learn the technical vocabulary of science. They may also need to be taught that vocabulary in a different way (perhaps with pictures, or an interpreter). In conducting science experiments, children who are deaf and hard-of-hearing need to be provided with a few written labels or language cards that identify the materials in each experiment. Vocabulary cards need to be displayed during discussion or demonstration periods and referred to when appropriate.

Children with visual impairments may lack visual sensations, but they are able to use their other senses to experience their world. To participate in science experiences, the physical environment may need to be adapted for children with orthopedic or physical disabilities. Children with learning disabilities need to have experiences simplified and be provided with cues to know in which activities they will participate. Children who are gifted are generally curious about everything. They are persistent in problem solving and want to experiment all of the time. Children who are gifted concentrate on tasks without difficulty and stay on a specific task until they have become proficient at it. With such adjustments, all children can acquire scientific knowledge. Science opportunities for children with disabilities should not be limited. Hands-on and problem-solving experiences seem to be more appropriate for them and should be designed in integrating science in an inclusive environment.

## Science Standards and Expectations

Science is a process of inquiry (National Research Council, 1996), "where knowledge can be uncovered, where questions can be asked and answered" (Malcom, 1999); therefore, young children need to engage in learning experiences that assist them to learn the nature of scientific inquiries. In 1990 the American Association for the Advancement of Science (AAAS) set up the goal of "science for all," including for young children. "The AAAS stresses the child's practice with the processes and uses the phenomena only as vehicles and the concepts as tools. An added difference is that the AAAS program attempts to appraise the children's progress more systematically and in greater detail than do the others" (Karplus & Thier, 1967, p. 8).

The *Benchmarks for Science Literacy* indicate that young children have to learn about the Scientific World View, Scientific Inquiry, and Scientific Enterprise. The *Benchmarks for Science Literacy* (AAAS, 1993) recommends that young children learn through an inquiry approach where they become active investigators. For the inquiry approach in science, Jones, Lake, and Lin (2008) propose that young children engage in experiences where they observe, classify, measure, communicate, estimate, predict, and infer. Developmentally appropriate science learning progresses in a pattern that is based on simple principles.

## Observation

Children use all their five senses to make observations from their own point of view; they know how to observe. Even infants can observe and adapt to their environment. One-month-old infants can imitate gestures even when they no longer see the individuals (Meltzoff & Moore, 1989). Twelve-month-old infants watch others and learn new behaviors. Two-year-olds observe situations internally, create mental images, and remember the mental images of objects. When young children play, they are able to test their observations; but they need an opportunity to play with props and toys to test their ideas (Jones et al., 2008).

## Classifying

Classification relies on observation. Children categorize objects into groups according to certain characteristics. Young children create classifications to make sense of their world, which requires them to think logically. They are able to group objects, although they may be unable to explain the reason for the way they organized them. Preschool children organize objects based on single characteristics. Their ability to classify objects develops with age; for instance, children ages two and three can sort and organize into groups their toys such as building blocks, toy cars, or soft toys. Preschool children can group objects such as rocks, shells, seeds, leaves, colored shapes, or stickers. Classifying these objects encourages young children to search for similarities and differences. In the classroom, children of any age can group themselves, such as those with a packed lunch and those who will eat the school lunch (Jones et al., 2008).

## Measuring

When young children observe and classify, they usually describe or compare in relation to quantity. For instance, children may organize objects into groups, count, and compare their groups. Measuring allows children to learn numbers, distances, time, length, area, weight, volume, and temperature. Generally, young children measure length, volume, weight, time, and temperature. Young children can learn measuring concepts when they quantify their observations, such as when they use the terms big, small, tall, short, long, wide, heavy, and light. They can develop their own measurement systems, for example, using body parts such as fingers, hands, feet, or body lengths to measure distances. They can also weigh objects such as marbles, paper clips, peas, plastic bears, or nails. Young children need daily measuring classroom experiences.

## Communicating

Young children need to communicate their science experiences, sharing their ideas or discussing their findings. Communication provides young children with the opportunity to reflect on what they did. This requires them to express their ideas and thoughts. They can communicate through oral language, pictures, models, music, movement, and play acting. The classroom environment can facilitate the children's communication through a display of pictures, graphs, and charts. Children with more experience can use graphs, charts, and tables to communicate their results. They need opportunities to explain, discuss, share, describe, and question. Children can draw pictures, create artifacts, or build models to communicate their thoughts. Their descriptions encourage them to use the terms for the science concepts. Regardless of the mode of communication, young children need to experience it in a natural and meaningful context (Jones et al., 2008).

## Estimating and Predicting

Both estimating and predicting requires young children to draw from their experiences to imagine a future event or an amount. Young children have daily experiences predicting daily events, such as meals, bath time, bedtime. They are also aware of predictable occurrences during play. They know that the toy car will move if they push it. Or if they drop a ball on a hard surface, it will bounce back up. Young children also predict occurrences in their natural world, such as the sunrise and sunset, the ocean's tides, or the four seasons. Although the weather is difficult to predict, young children can look outside and tell if it is going to rain. For example, a young girl who observes that the clouds are dark and black will predict that it might rain and she will need to wear a raincoat before going outside to play (Jones et al., 2008).

Prediction assists young children in their daily lives and in science. Children need many science experiences that support the development of their estimating and predicting abilities. These experiences can be easily integrated during their daily play periods. For instance, if children are building a tower in the block center, they can predict the number of blocks they will use before their tower collapses. Young children can be provided with play experiences where they have valuable opportunities to predict events (Jones et al., 2008).

## Inferring

When young children infer, they draw from their experiences and use logic to speculate and draw conclusions according to their observations.

> If a child smells the aroma of baking bread from the kitchen and says *I can smell something baking*, he or she has made an observation. However, if the child says, *Mommy must be making bread in the bread machine*, he or she has made an inference. Clearly, the first comment is more likely to be accurate than the second. The observation is more likely to be accurate because it is based on information obtained through one of the senses. The inference, on the other hand is an explanation for the observation, and is more susceptible to error (Jones et al., 2008, p. 28).

At a very young age, children need daily experiences where they have the opportunity to make inferences. Children can observe a plant, become aware that it has wilted, and infer that it needs water. When children go to the playground and notice that the grass is wet, they can infer that it was raining.

## Integrating the Science Strategies

Young children learn the science strategies of observing, classifying, measuring, communicating, inferring, estimating, and predicting when they engage in simple science investigations where they have the opportunity to explore and test their ideas. In these simple investigations, young children will develop a plan of study. They will think about their investigations, ask appropriate questions, and complete their investigations. Then they will interpret and explain their findings. This procedure needs to occur in the context of concrete experiences (Jones et al., 2008) in a social context. These science strategies develop when children engage in a dynamic social interaction while they engage in problem solving and scientific inquiry. Learning these strategies is facilitated through the children's play.

## Science-related Play

Scientists study the world. They generate hypotheses and collect data to test them in the field or in the laboratory. They gather and document information on critical evidence and develop explanations and theories. They use specific practices and tools to answer specific questions and problems of the everyday natural world (Eberbach & Crowley, 2009). Scientists examine materials and processes, play with ideas about materials and processes, generate hypotheses, and test these hypotheses.

Children learn science in a way that encourages them to create tentative theories about scientific phenomena, test them, and adapt their theories based on their observations. Thus, children modify their theories when they see that new evidence contradicts or shows a new view of their existing theories (Harlen, 2006). According to Riley and Savage (1994), young children experience this scientific uncertainty through play, because it provides a non-threatening context where they play with their ideas around science. They explore as they play, which helps them to learn science. The play experience simulates their interest and builds a concrete real world of experiences where children learn complex and abstract science (Henniger, 1987). For example,

> Two children are building a sandcastle and are experiencing difficulties with collapsing walls. Several procedures are tried until a combination of sand and water proves the necessary consistency for durable walls. These children are practicing important problem solving skills crucial to science learning (Henniger, 1987, p. 168)

The areas of play and scientific inquiry may seem to be worlds apart. On the one hand, play is fanciful, divergent, and subjective. In contrast, scientific inquiry is logical, linear, systematic, and objective; but researchers show that play and science complement each other in problem solving. Scientists usually solve problems effectively and progressively when they seek solutions in an essence of play. Science influences systematic behavior whereas play promotes creative behavior; therefore, both components are necessary to effectively solve problems (Severide & Pizzini, 1984). Einstein (1954) related science and play when he explained the way to solve problems. He pointed out that children can be productive thinkers when they are allowed to be curious about their world and the way it works, but teaching methods that are dull or not motivating fail to stimulate curiosity. Specifically, he stated

> It is in fact nothing short of a miracle that the modern methods of instruction have not yet entirely strangled the holy curiosity of inquiry . . . It is a very grave mistake to think that the enjoyment of seeing and searching can be promoted by means of coercion and a sense of duty (Einstein, 1949, p. 17).

> . . . The desire to arrive finally at logically connected concepts is the emotional basis of this rather vague play . . . This combinatory play seems to be the essential feature in productive thought (Einstein, 1954, pp. 25–26).

Play and science have both creative and deliberate elements; both need to be balanced. Severide and Pizzini (1984) have compared children's play to science (see Table 11.1).

Most of science learning can be play. Hawkins (1965) calls this "Messing about" (p. 8). The "messing about" of the science program is a form of play, where children experience unguided exploratory work. They are provided with materials and equipment to construct, test, probe, and experiment without superimposed questions or instruction. First children explore the properties of things. Then they ask reasonable questions of the materials and the phenomena they experience. Later they look for ways to answer these questions. According to Ganschow and Ganschow (2006), "Science is about asking questions, and

TABLE 11.1. Play and Science in the Classroom

| Play | Science |
|------|---------|
| Develops skills and attitudes that are important for effective thinking | Provide a wide variety of play materials on a topic and allow the children time to experiment with them |
| Make believe play increases the number of solutions children generate | Use imaginary stories and settings, imaginary, role playing and "what if" games in science lessons |
| Helps children develop flexible problem solving strategies as well as a wide range of solutions | Let the children become acquainted with materials before providing structure for the activity. Let them imagine what they will do before you begin the activity |
| Lessens the risk of failure and reduces frustration | Begin guided play in preschools and maintain throughout |
| Promotes positive learning attitudes at all ages, but especially in young children | Watch for repetition of play activities and then redirect play to extensions or elaborations of the play theme |
| Is most effective and innovative when adults observe before offering guidance | Be a playful model, ask open ended and/or higher level questions, be receptive to spontaneous ideas, and suspend judgment until after the play period |
| Open teaching strategies can facilitate productive play | Include play lessons that are new and/or difficult |

playfulness facilitates the process at the proper place and time. Best of all, engaging in scientific discovery is something that scientists enjoy doing. What could be more playful than having fun?" (p. 459).

A playful attitude towards science learning helps children learn more about science than if they learn specific science facts by rote learning. According to Elkind (1999),

> early childhood is a most important period for math, science and technology, but only if we adapt such instruction to the unique needs, interests, and abilities of young children (p.70).

Young children's natural activities of manipulation, exploration, and lively finding out is the basis for science learning. Rudolph and Cohen (1984) provide a vivid demonstration of a young child's self-initiated activity:

> After watching a gardener digging out shrubbery roots, four-and-a half-year-old Darius found a sharp stone and proceeded to dig for roots. "Look here is a root," he said excitedly, holding a stringy grass root in one hand and his stone-shovel in another. He became so preoccupied doing it that he was reluctant to leave for lunch and talked about different kinds of roots.
>
> Later, after coming home from the beach, Darius immediately went into the backyard to resume digging, but this time he preferred to use a shovel. He kept digging laboriously, until he succeeded in making a sizeable hole and another discovery. He rushed into the house with an announcement: "I found a lot of ants in my hole!" He continued watching the ants with absorption and amusement for the rest of the afternoon.
>
> In the house, the subject of roots was still on his mind.
>
> "What are roots for?"
>
> "To hold the plant in the ground. Roots are strong."
>
> "Yes! Roots are strong. I had to pull and dig hard to get them out."
>
> After supper Darius went to dig again, and again the first thing the next morning. Impressed and satisfied with the depth and dimension of a hole, Darius this time asked for water to make mud. How good the mud seemed to him! With it his fervor cooled; he relaxed; his intellectual–physical passion seemed spent (p. 174).

Although Darius' play may not be considered a formalized scientific investigation, his focus in digging for roots, for exposed space, and for crawling ants is a path toward science. He, like other children, was able to calm down from his intense attempts. When young children manipulate, explore, and find out, they are viewed as natural scientists. They learn with their senses; are driven by their curiosity, and tempted to test; they can observe, classify, identify, and describe. They want to solve problems and arrive at conclusions. They will continue to practice these and other skills, which are characteristics that are similar to those of scientists, especially their curiosity (Rudolph & Cohen, 1984).

In play children experience a sphere of imaginary activity that is more delicately structured, more meaningful than ordinary life. The world of play is the children's world of common reality (Raymo, 1973). Like play, science seeks order in an imperfect world. It offers a temporary, confined perfection in the prospect of the flourishing, buzzing confusion of everyday reality. It casts a spell, dismisses any confusion, and transfers children into an idealized world of make-believe (Raymo, 2007). For example,

> Fifteen preschool children and two teachers are outdoors in the play yard. Four children are in the large sandbox playing with buckets, bottles, spoons, shovels, and an assortment of wheeled toys. One of the teachers and three children are digging in the garden plot in preparation for the spring planting of seeds. Two children have discovered an ant hill and are intently watching the activity there. Near the large storage shed two more children are using colorful plastic building blocks to construct their version of a fort. Wheeled vehicles, always popular on preschool grounds, are being ridden by two other children in a game of "follow the leader." Finally two children are lying on the grass staring at the sky and talking about the funny shapes they see (Henniger, 1987, p. 168).

Play situations like these offer young children excellent opportunities to learn about their world. Through play experiences, young children can discover the fundamental science relationships for later learning (Henniger, 1987). Children solve problems and develop and refine their skills when play is integrated in their science experiences (Severide & Pizzini, 1984). These are the processes that scientists use, and these processes can be used by young children as well.

Young children can assume the role of scientist during play. They carry on playful experiments when they bake mud pies or build worm playgrounds. They may giggle and discuss their observations or well thought-out theories with their playmates. The children's early experiences with nature and real objects help them to generate ideas about their world. Since they enjoy exploring with nature, they need to be provided with time, space, and equipment that will help them explore their world (Ross, 2000). Henniger (1987) describes the children's science play experience.

> The children in the garden plot are having similar learning opportunities. When a shovel of dirt uncovers two fat earthworms, the teacher and children take time to observe and discuss the life cycle and importance of worms. Some plants from last year's garden remain and children remove the seeds and sort them by size and shape. As the dead plants are removed to make room for the new garden, the teacher points out the root systems and discusses with the children how plants get nutrients needed for healthy growth (p. 168).

Children are able to grow things from seeds, tubers, and cuttings. For those classrooms that do not have access to a garden, children can plant in window boxes or flower pots. The children can describe the way things are growing and what they think helped them grow. When the plants sprout, the children can record on a chart the plants' growth (Spodek & Saracho, 1994b). For example, one Saturday I went to clean my preschool classroom and noticed that one of the potatoes that the children placed in a jar for them to study was dying. I did not want the children to be disappointed so I went to a Mart store and bought a potato. Unfortunately, the store only had red potatoes so I bought one.

I thought that it would have enough sprouts and the children might not notice the difference (originally the children had placed white potatoes in the jar). On Monday morning when I was collecting the lunch money, I noticed there was a commotion at the science center. Children were looking at their charts and running to the library area. The children were having very intense discussions. After I finished with the lunch money, I went to the science center to check on the situation. The children were trying to figure out how the potato had turned red. When I confessed what I had done, the children were upset; because I had disrupted their investigation.

The children's interest in nature can be fostered throughout the day. Rainy days provide children the opportunity to investigate earthworms and puddles. During a snowstorm, children can bundle up and examine the crystals in the snowflakes. Beaches, woods, parks, backyards, and vacant lots are a promised land for the young scientists. If they take a walk in the park, they may find hidden caterpillars or sparkling rocks. Children need to be encouraged and provided with many materials and tools. If they grow gardens or collect small critters as visitors, they are experiencing adventures (Ross, 2000).

Children can observe and pretend to be scientists in their daily lives. They can observe practical and natural experiences such as knowing that "sweaters keep us warm though a sweater sitting on a table is not warmer than the surrounding room" (Chinn & Malhotra, 2002, p. 339) or being aware that some objects sink and others float. Children can learn to observe and think logically like scientists, but they need supportive learning environments and tools. Children can be provided with lab coats and other lab materials to assume the role of a scientist. A stethoscope can help children to hear sounds they cannot hear with the ear alone. A magnifying glass can help children see things in a larger size or be able to see things that they are not able to see with the naked eye (Eberbach & Crowley, 2009).

Children will explore as they select the right tool that will help them focus on their studies. For example, children will select a mirror to experiment with light or use a magnifying lens to look closely at things (Ross, 2000). According to Herman (1987), a magnifying glass helps children to explore the properties of light. They are able to see the way light bends through the double convex lens of a magnifying glass, or how objects may be seen upside down, and how a specific distance from an object can be identified for the proper focus of the magnifying glass. They are able to compare how things look through (a) the naked eye, (b) a magnifying glass, and (c) a clear container of water (e.g., a glass or an aquarium). Fish and small animals can be placed in appropriate containers for children to study.

Play helps young children to discriminate and classify information that they observe such as a collection of autumn leaves, acorns and nuts, rocks, seeds, or sea shells. Children need to inspect and manipulate the materials and hypothesize about any possibilities. Rudolph and Cohen (1984) describe how a teacher took a box that had a variety of shells to the classroom to promote the children's interest. Children added to the collection, played with them, arranged them according to size and shape, discriminated among them, discussed them, and raised questions such as the following:

"What is this kind of purplish shell?"

"A mussel," the teacher answered.

"This one looks like a saucer; I want to drink out of it," said Joyce.

"Oh, I saw millions of those," said Harley. "What do you call them? I forgot."

"Clam shells," the teacher said helpfully and allowed Dina to use them for 'tea' in the housekeeping section.

"What's the name of this one? That's a beauty!" Harley asked the teacher, showing her an intricate snail shell.

"Let me look in the book to make sure," the teacher answered.

"Let me look, too. I want to see the picture." The teacher opened a picture book, *Beachcomber Bobbie*, and Harley promptly identified the picture of his shell, observing both the shape and the special 'eye' design in the middle; he laid the shell directly on the picture. Three more children followed suit and picked up moon shells and scallops and clams and cockles. They were particularly impressed with the similarity between the actual starfish shell and the picture of it. For a few minutes the children used the book with studious concentration, the way one uses a laboratory manual. A majority of the twenty-two children that year showed curiosity about the shells, sometimes pocketing a few, breaking some, or using them for dishes or as block building decoration. A few children referred to the pictures of shells constantly, asked their names and inquired about the whereabouts of the former inhabitants of the shells (pp. 181–182).[1]

A collection of rocks can provide a similar experience. Children can observe, touch, feel and intellectually inquire about them. According to Rudolph and Cohen (1984),

Using a heavy stone and finding out how its crushing weight cracks an especially hard black walnut, a child wants to know; "Can one stone break another stone?" and he spends considerable time testing the stone for size and weight, hardness and durability. Another child becomes fascinated with the doughnut shape of a stone in the collection and stimulates several other children to speculate on the causes of its odd shape. The teacher accepts the children's own imaginative and spontaneous names for the stones, such as "potato stone" because of its shape and color, or "hand stone" because it fits especially nicely in a child's hand. This kind of spontaneous personal naming of stones sharpens the children's observation and perception. There are, however, occasions when the teacher can appropriately introduce correct names, which not only builds a scientific vocabulary but arouses further interest. The teacher must judge at which point to say: "this rock you hold (or this tree you see) has a real name," thus introducing the children to the rock or the tree.

"I saw this shiny kind of stone before," said Delma, inspecting a fine one on a brief excursion.

"It has a name," said the teacher.

"What?" Delma asked as another child joined them.

"It's called mica."

"Mica," Delma repeated.

1 Florence Bourgeois (1935) *Beachcomber Bobbie*. New York: Doubleday, Doran, and Company.

"And what about this one?" Another child took a crumbly stone out of his pocket.

"Hm . . . this must be shale." Now other children wanted to know the names of their stones, and unable to identify them herself, the teacher promised to look them up (p. 183)

The children's curiosity and inquiring minds are stimulated when they physically engage with natural phenomena. Books and magazines that are appropriate for young children can help them understand and guide their quest for knowledge. Children can browse through these books, listen to a read-aloud story, and look at the illustrations (Rudolph & Cohen, 1984). Young children need to be provided with play activities where they have the opportunity to discover properties and relationships and what to do with them. They can learn about force and how it can be increased or changed in direction when they use a pulley system in the block area to help them build a structure. This experience can help children learn that a pulley makes it easier to lift things.

A doorbell and buzzer operated on batteries can be placed in the housekeeping area for children to use each time they enter the area. They can learn the effects of electricity and the need for a circuit in operating electrical devices. Battery-powered electric lights complete with switches can be wired into a playhouse. A bulb, battery, and a couple of wire extensions can be placed in a box for the children to use for manipulations and discovery. The children's play activities can also include magnets, magnifying glasses, and other items for them to be "messing about".

In all science inquiry children need to be allowed (a) to ask questions about what they see and (b) to find the answers. Some questions may not have answers such as "What is electricity?" In these cases, teachers need to be honest to the children. Teachers can answer, "I don't know, but we can see some of the things that electricity can do." Such responses can help children feel comfortable with the unknown.

## Science Learning Centers

Play offers many excellent opportunities for children to learn fundamental science concepts. Children need to be optimally involved in their science experiences to interpret within a fresh experience a wonderful variety of understandings based on their past experiences and present observations (Hawkins, 1983). This means that their environment needs to encourage their interpretations and understandings. Science is playful, multifaceted, multidisciplinary, conditional, and emerging. To promote the children's understanding of science concepts, children should be given space to play in an environment that reflects the nature of science in a variety of contexts. This play environment should suggest to children that science is creative and can be stimulated in many ways. When children play, they have the freedom to interact with ideas, actions, and things. The classroom needs to be organized in a way that the environment will encourage the children's learning, which can occur in separate areas that children can identify. These areas offer children activities and materials that prompt them to test their ideas. Activity areas or learning centers can be set up around the classroom with science experiences.

Learning centers need to be located near a closed storage space (such as a cabinet) where science equipment and materials that are not currently in use are stored. In addition, some open shelf space needs to be available for children to have access to a range of science equipment and materials. Children also need space to solve problems. For centers that are relatively isolated, a problem can be established and children can attempt to solve it individually or in small groups. Scientific inquiry is an important goal and requires that individuals or small groups do most of the science work.

The science area needs to be arranged in a way that it encourages young children to study, compare, and contrast these riches of nature. Through play young children learn about nature when they collect and analyze science materials. Their playful exploration of meaningful materials from their local environment provides young children with important conceptual understanding (Henniger, 1987).

Several learning centers can be set up to promote science concepts. In each center, the children will experiment and test their ideas as they manipulate objects, build, and engage in conversation as they learn at their own pace. Science, library, sand and water, woodworking, and cooking are also learning centers that offer children opportunities for learning scientific concepts. Children can describe the observations they make in a science project. They can write narratives (some may be scribbles or marks) or draw pictures for their descriptions. A display or bulletin board that is created by the children can be set in the appropriate science area. This display contains the children's thoughts and actions on the topic they are studying. It makes it easier to keep the children's focus and expand their interest. See Box 11.1 for suggestions for developing a panel (Lewin-Benham, 2006).

### Box 11.1. Suggestions for Developing a Panel

1. At the beginning of an experience, set up a background using a large panel made out of sturdy cardstock or illustration board.
2. For the headline on the panel, write a question, a child's comment, or use an appropriate title. Add photographs, drawings, or objects that motivated the science project.
3. As the experience continues, add information to the panel. The information can be recorded using the children's language, drawings, or photographs or a series of photographs or objects. It needs to show a pivotal moment that led to the next steps. Lewin-Benham (2006) observed a class that was studying a goldfish. The panel had a photograph of the class at the beginning of the project and a fish bowl in the middle of a child's comment, and two questions posed by two other children. Throughout the project children drew their thoughts on ways to clean the fish bowl.
4. Anytime a panel is hung or words or photos are added, the children who are involved retell, or read about it to the class including what has happened thus far. The children may revisit the panel at least once a day.
5. The science project concludes with photographs, comments, or questions that are added to the panel. Lewin-Benham (2006) observed that the classroom had procedures for cleaning the fish bowl, finding out that the goldfish named Big Eyes was dead, how everybody cried, and making the fish's grave. At the end, two of the children's questions that stimulated new projects were added to the panel. They were "What are we going to do with the dirty water?" and "What will happen to the dead fish?"

The completed documentation panel communicates what motivated the experience, how and why it was developed, what they discovered, and the open-ended questions it aroused. When children revisit the panels, they retell the experience to themselves, their peers, their parents, or the classroom visitors. Revisiting the panel helps (a) move the experience forward, (b) keep the children focused, and (c) intensify their understanding of their experiences (Lewin-Benham, 2006).

Science learning can take place in a variety of centers. For example, the science center places a large emphasis on science concepts while other centers integrate science concepts into a variety of learning areas. These include the library, carpentry/woodworking, cooking, and sand/water play centers. Both the science and other centers are described in the following sections.

## Science Center

Play offers many opportunities for learning basic science concepts. A science center can facilitate this learning. A science center needs to be organized in such a way that children can study, compare, and contrast the treasures of nature. When the children play in collecting and analyzing materials, they have an ideal opportunity to learn about nature and other science concepts (Henniger, 1987). The science center needs to allow children to have sensible access to water. It might also have a display area for plants and animals and shelves that hold magnifying glasses and magnets. Containers of different sizes and a range of measuring devices can be organized and placed in shallow trays for children to arrange in an orderly fashion. Plastic boxes with sets of science materials can also be included. For example, a set can consist of a battery, bulb, and several lengths of bell wire. Another set can consist of a magnet with some small bits of material, including some that are magnetic and some that are not.

A range of materials needs to be displayed to encourage children to explore. The materials and tools in the science center should be together and children need to have access to these materials. There should be open shelves for storage and a display area for ongoing projects. Additional materials can include a plastic jar covered with a rubber membrane, half-filled with water, and containing a medicine dropper; a small basin of water and some materials that float and some that sink; and a box of different textured materials. The materials in the center should be changed based on the science concepts that the children are learning. For example, a science learning center can be based on the following:

In the learning center,

1. Children will use all of their senses to observe in a variety of ways.
2. Children will be encouraged to ask questions, look for answers, test their ideas, and become aware of their world.
3. Children will observe and care for pets and growing plants.
4. The materials can include items such as those in Box 11.2.

---

**Box 11.2. Items for the Science Center**

| | |
|---|---|
| Science pictures | Dry cell batteries |
| Flashlight bulbs | Bulbs and wire |
| Magnifying glass | Bar and horseshoe |
| Magnets | Prisms (glass) |
| Pulleys and gears | Hand mirrors |

| | |
|---|---|
| Computer | Microscopes |
| Tweezers | Measuring cups and spoons |
| Rulers | Yardsticks |
| Scales | Thermometers |
| Hot plate | Electric frying pan |
| Tape measure | Pan balances |
| Timers | Basins |
| Funnels | Animal cage |
| Aquarium and terrarium | Sea shells |
| Rocks | Leaves |
| Bird's nest | Plants, pots, soil, and watering cans |
| Clear plastic containers with covers | |

## Library/Writing Center

An adjacent library/writing center needs to allow children to record and search for information about science concepts. Several children's books relating to science concepts that the children are learning can be available, as could audiovisual aids to help children understand the meaning of the science concepts they are learning. For example, if children are learning about how a caterpillar turns into a cocoon and then into a butterfly, this center can have a variety of science books for children, such as *The Very Hungry Caterpillar* by Eric Carle (2008). Puppets that denote caterpillars, butterflies, and other props can be made available for children to retell the story. The children might have created a chart during sharing time that can be displayed. The chart can be a story that was retold by the children and/or it can be one that shows the caterpillar's life cycle for the week and a written story at their developmental level.

### Story Writing

Children can engage in story writing about their learning. Paper, crayons, markers, pencils, and other writing materials should be available in this area. For example, children can pretend to be the caterpillar and write a diary of the caterpillar. Individual or groups of children can write reports about their scientific explorations of something of real importance to them. Very young children may just write marks and pictures in their report. They can use graphs and charts, create books, and dramatize ideas. They can record their observations in science journals. Children can become a research team and create written reports about their scientific explorations. For example, Conezio and French (2002) describe how in their classrooms three- and four-year-old children "used drawings and words to document the growth and changes that occurred as their caterpillars transformed into colorful lady butterflies." The science is an activity that has a process of inquiry consisting of theorizing, hands-on investigation, and discussion.

### Science Books and Materials

Science books (see Box 11.3) and materials to be used with books can be displayed in this area. Materials (such as puppets, stuffed caterpillars, cocoons, leaves, animals) need to complement the books and the science concepts that children are learning in the classroom.

---

**Box 11.3. Science Books**

- Barner, B. (2001). *Dinosaur Bones*. San Francisco, CA: Chronicle Books
- Conway, D. (2007). *Lila and the Secret of Rain*. London: Frances Lincoln; 2008 ed. Distributed by Publishers Group West, Berkeley, CA
- Sill, C. (2003). *About Insects: A Guide for Children*. Atlanta, GA: Peachtree Publishers
- Steckel, R & M. (2007). *My Teeth*. Berkeley, CA: Tricycle Press
- Weinstein, E. S. (2008). *Everywhere the Cow Says "Moo!"*. Honesdale, PA: Boyds Mill Press

---

## Carpentry/Woodworking Center

Woodworking is another area that offers children a source of scientific knowledge. When children play in the woodworking center, they are able to develop many scientific skills like observation; inference; and development about sizes, shapes, and balance. They become aware of the physical world. Anderson and Hoot (1986) provide the following example.

> One four-year-old boy was observed in the "Carpentry Shop" boring a hole into a piece of wood with a brace and bit. He exclaimed, "Look at all the saw dust I'm making!" When finished drilling he removed the brace and bit, and put his finger down in the hole to brush away the wood shavings. He jerked his finger out and exclaimed, "Wow! It's hot down here!" (p. 13).

Woodworking contributes to the children's learning in issues like parts to whole (e.g., a whole piece of wood versus its parts), understanding cause and effect, and solving problems (Fuller, 1974). Children get sensory feelings when they handle the wood and learn the basic procedures of fitting, fastening, connecting, and cutting. They find out about the grain of wood and the cause of sawdust. They also learn the physical properties of a variety of materials such as roughness, softness, and sharpness (Rudolph & Cohen, 1984). Children learn about textures, for example, rough versus smooth and hard versus soft. They use their senses of smell, touch, hearing, and sight when they work with wood. Most important, children make decisions and solve problems. These processes are an integral part of learning about science. The following example shows how opening acorns can arouse the children's curiosity.

> A boy of four-and-a-half, playing with a can full of acorns that he has collected on the way to school, decides to poke one acorn open to see the nut inside. The teacher encourages him by advising the use of a hammer at the workbench. Instead of finding a nut inside the shell the boy finds the acorn of soft, dry brown matter and some small, pale, grubby worms.
>
> Look! This is news indeed. Not only the boy who discovered the acorn worms but also everyone in the classroom becomes fascinated with the looks, movements, diet, and

family life of the worm. Every child grabs an acorn and eagerly hammers or cracks it open, looking for worms. For days the children collect acorns, excavating the worms and giving them acorn meat to eat. How disappointed Donna is when her three acorns prove empty, and she begs for a worm from lucky J. W., who has a whole bunch (Rudolph & Cohen, 1984, pp. 183–184).

### Safety Rules

The children need to be given an important and interesting introduction to woodworking. In addition, the children need to know the rules for using the learning center and how to handle the tools. Young children have strong impulses, curiosities, and energies, which require them to be supervised and guided in relation to their safety in this area. Good supervision in woodworking protects the children's safety and provides them with interesting individual experiences, discoveries of their own powers, strengthening of techniques, and a great deal of exciting learning (Rudolph & Cohen, 1984).

In woodworking safety is extremely important. Young children need to see and feel the jagged edge of the saw blade and the point of a nail (Rudolph & Cohen, 1984) to understand that they need to be careful with these tools. They need to know the proper use and care of each tool. For instance, they need to know that the hammer is used to drive tools like nails and children need to avoid using it to hit each other. They also need to know that when they saw or pound nails, they must always wear safety glasses. Additional safety guidelines such as stabbing the point of the nail in a bar of soap before pounding will greatly decrease possible risks (Anderson & Hoot, 1986). Children need to know the safety rules. These rules should be posted in the woodworking area. The posted rules can be in simple words and pictures for children to read and understand.

## Cooking Center

Cooking experiences can be used to support science learning in young children. Children of all ages learn science concepts when they observe the way foods change at different temperatures or when they are mixed. Cooking stimulates children to use all of their senses and arouses their curiosity, which makes them question what is going on. The children's observations and descriptions lead them to develop speculations, which need to be accepted but the child should also be encouraged to test them further.

The classroom can have a cooking center that includes a table, chairs, work space, and storage space. It also needs to have tasting and smelling ingredients. Foods are affected when they are heated, cooled, frozen, beaten, and mixed. When rising agents (yeast or baking powder) are added, a dramatic effect will occur on a combination of flour, water, and other ingredients. Cooking experiences also offer excellent opportunities for talking about nutrition and what is needed for healthy growth.

Ingredients and instructions that have simple words and pictures can be placed in the cooking center for children to follow. Recipes can include a fruit salad, vegetable soup, a nutritious drink, or any other simple recipes that young children can follow with ease.

### Making Vegetable Soup

The children can be asked to each bring a fresh vegetable from home to make vegetable soup (e.g., a carrot, a stalk of celery, a potato, a tomato). The teacher can provide a beef bone or some bouillon, beef, chicken, or more vegetables. Start in the morning boiling water in a large pot on a hot plate. The different vegetables are washed, scrubbed with a brush, and cut into pieces with plastic knives. If there are enough vegetables, the children can taste them before they are put in the pot. After putting the vegetables in the pot, seasonings can be added with spoons. By lunchtime the vegetable soup will be ready for the children to eat. Children can check on the pot throughout the morning to observe the rising and spreading of the steam as the lid comes off. They can talk about how hot the soup is, the nature of the heat, the cause of the heat, and the danger of the heat. At lunchtime, the soup can be ladled out, cooled, and eaten. After the soup is eaten, the children can discuss the process and the changes that took place in the vegetables. The recipe for the soup can be written up and made into a wall chart. The children's observations can also be written up on a chart that will be mounted on the wall.

Making the vegetable soup is a whole day project for the children. This activity will dominate the classroom, because it takes hours to prepare and discuss later. While the cooking project is in progress, other learning centers can be available. All of the children will participate in the big cooking event and share their enthusiasm, wonder, and intense curiosity.

Teachers can provide cooking experiences from the different cultures. For example, Mexican American foods can include cooking pinto beans, Mexican soup, and guacamole. Pinto beans, water, salt, and pepper are placed in a pot that will sit on a hot plate for several hours. Cold dishes (such as guacamole or Mexican salsa) can be part of the children's cooking experiences. For guacamole, avocados are smashed and other ingredients (such as onions, salt, parsley) are mixed in (Saracho & Martínez-Hancock, 2004).

## Sand and Water Play Center

Young children enjoy water play. It is soothing and children are motivated to "make something." It is both an outdoor and indoor activity. While generally not included in the manipulative materials center, natural materials (such as sand and water) are important adjuncts to play. Spodek and Saracho (1994b) describe the following event.

> The children run into the playground area. Emily and Elizabeth head immediately for the sandbox. They each grab a pail and shovel and sit down next to each other.
>
> "Let's make mud cakes," says Elizabeth.
>
> "OK," says Emily.
>
> The girls work quietly, digging sand and filling their buckets. Soon Elizabeth gets up, walks over to the teacher and asks, "Would you like a mud cake?"
>
> "Oh, how wonderful!" the teacher answers, and pretends to taste the mud cake.
>
> When Elizabeth returns to the sand, Emily is no longer there. In her place, Kristen is sitting in the middle of the sandbox.
>
> "Kristen, move! You're in the way," says Elizabeth.

Kristen ignores Elizabeth and rubs her hands in the sand.

Elizabeth looks over to the climbing apparatus, sees Emily, and runs towards her (p. 275).

While specially designed sand and water tables are available commercially, a galvanized tub or a plastic wash basin can also be used. Children need freedom to use these materials, but they need to learn how to care for them and know the limitations on their use. Sand can be loaded, dumped, dug, and tunneled. Children can sit on it, pat it, make pies out of it, and run it through their fingers. Dry sand can also be sifted while wet sand can be compared to dry sand. A thermometer can be used to compare the temperature of surface sand with the one that is deep in the sand pile. Children can paint the sand and make drawings with it.

Children at the water table can wash the dolls' clothes, paint with water, and experiment with objects that sink or float. They can pour water from one container into another, use tubes to make siphons, and use egg beaters to make the water churn. When children become bored with water play, the teacher can add food coloring or dish detergent to the water table to stimulate interest. A number of accessories including containers, spoons, and shovels should go with the water and sand area. Wet sand can be molded in many shapes; dry sand can be sieved and run through funnels. Equipment for cleanup such as sponges, a floor brush, and dustpan should be readily available for children to use. A place needs to be available for some of the toys to dry before storing them. Box 11.4 offers some suggestions for this area.

---

**Box 11.4. Suggestions for the Water Table**

- Cover a table with large towels or place old rugs under the water play area.
- Have sponges ready for children to wipe up any spills.
- Have the water play area outdoors where spills will not make a difference.
- Place a rotary beater next to a dish with soapy water in it. Include cups and extra pans for scooping off soap suds as they take shape.
- Have floating materials such as corks, balls, boats, cotton balls, rocks, and nails.
- Have painting materials (paints and brushes) to paint with plain water outdoors.
- Have pouring materials available (cups, sieves, plastic bottles, funnels, dish pan, tub of water).
- Other materials like those in Box 11.5 may be displayed in this area.

---

**Box 11.5. Materials for the Water Table**

| | |
|---|---|
| Plastic pool | Straws |
| Metal tub or commercial sand and water table | Soap |
| Spoons and shovels | Sifters |
| Trucks | Raincoats or plastic smocks |
| Cars | Objects to sink and float |
| Boats | Soap suds |

| | |
|---|---|
| Plastic containers | Food coloring |
| Pitchers | Hoses |
| Watering cans | Funnels |
| Bowls of different sizes | Measuring cups |
| Plastic bottles | Strainers |
| | Egg beaters |

*Telling Stories at the Water Table*

Conversations at the water table are beneficial. The water table may be filled with cornmeal, although it might have rice, macaroni, mixed beans, or snow. Cornmeal has a beautiful color and smell with a smooth texture that children enjoy touching. It is compressed which makes it easy to mold and build structures. It accumulates a static electrical charge which forces individual grains to leap and jump or create interesting swirling patterns at the bottom of the table. Young children become fascinated with it. They examine its properties and engage in imaginative fantasy play. They can use it to cook and build houses and landscapes. During play, children will discuss their activities and discoveries through spontaneous conversations. Osborne (Osborne & Brady, 2001) participates in one of the children's conversations.

I am playing myself; after setting up for the morning I sat down and began by trying to use a bulb baster to suck up cornmeal and blow it back out again. If done carefully this creates a "puff" of particles. I didn't discover this, Darius did. K'nisha and Tiffany are pouring cornmeal from one container to another using a funnel. I send them back to get smocks on and when they return, they settle into this activity—pouring cornmeal from small jars and bowls into large, filling up the large and then pouring those into the basin of the table with much satisfaction. Tiffany grabs a tube and begins stirring the cornmeal as she adds it to a jar. She is talking about making soup and K'nisha chimes in. I ask them, "What kind of soup do you like?" and this begins a lengthy conversation about the likes and dislikes of everyone and anyone. Conversations with four year olds are a patchwork of things they do and know, things they have seen and basic fantasy. I wonder about Tiffany—does she make supper for her baby sister (which is what she is telling me)? I know she did take care of the baby until her mother, an alcoholic, abandoned them. Then her aunt had custody until she too abandoned the children. K'nisha, on the other hand, is a mystery to me. She comes to school with her hair freshly put into twisty ponytails, carefully finished with Goody barrettes. Her clothes are clean and she is too. The criteria for qualification for "at-risk" services are many-fold.

While this conversation is going on, Andrew and Jake arrive. K'nisha and Tiffany continue their fantasy cooking projects but Andrew and Jake have begun molding a building with the cornmeal. This causes a certain amount of competition between the two groups, for space and for cornmeal and actually the boys start stealing cornmeal from the girls causing a great deal of outrage and some whining. Not too much though—both girls are pretty assertive. Finally the girls start building castles too. Theirs involve piling the jars and bowls on top of each other and then sifting the cornmeal down the sides. Occasionally they will mound some cornmeal on the tops and mold this, then brush it off again.

The conversation turns to home renovation. Jake, like Tiffany, is also four years old and called by Mary Jo the primary caregiver for his baby sister. His mother is what I'd term an opportunistic sex worker at a local bar managed by her mother. The children have different fathers and the family lives in the local trailer park. Jake is into construction. The talk at the table is a complex discussion of construction principles and electrical wiring. How do you wire a castle made of cornmeal? Interesting question I'd say and finally do. I ask, "What kind of lights are you planning on installing?" Jake: "Christmas tree with colors." I ask, "Where'd you learn how to do that wiring?" Andrew: "Second shift with the good old boys" (pp. 7–8).

The children's activities at the water table are a blend of fact and fiction that is an interpretation of "truth" which is part of their lives. The social context of play helps them to work out with their peers important relationships and understandings, such as caring and friendship. In their fantasy play the children participate in the realities that are part of their lives. They are reconstructing reality in this context and in every setting (Osborne & Brady, 2001).

## Science Learning in a Social Context

Science experiences for young children are enriched in a social context where they engage in social interactions, reflect on the meaning of their experiences, and refine their science strategies. It is through social exchanges that children develop and refine their science process skills. In short, it is through oral language that children come to understand science concepts. Children develop and refine their science strategies in social contexts. When they directly observe science phenomena, children interact with materials and peers. In the social context, children develop conflict-resolution skills, reflect on the meaning of their interaction, and understand the science concepts. Therefore, children should be provided with sufficient opportunities to interact in groups where they use their science process strategies together with their peers. In addition, the nature of the children's peer relationships may affect how they come to understand the meaning of their science observations, classifications, measurements, and understanding of science phenomena (Jones et al., 2008). There is an extraordinary connection between the children's science and social life experiences where children accumulate the learning that is spontaneous.

## Science Prop Boxes

The materials that are displayed in the learning center can be put in a themed activity prop box such as an empty box of computer or Xerox paper. Prop boxes are similar to learning centers and offer children opportunities to engage in dramatic play. When children use the prop boxes to engage in dramatic play, they are able to learn and remember difficult science concepts. For example, an "All About Weather" prop box can include multiple items of clothing for the weather such as those in Box 11.6 (Hommerding, 2007).

**Box 11.6. Items for a Prop Box for Different Types of Weather**

| | | |
|---|---|---|
| Shorts | Beach towels | Baseball bats |
| Tank tops | Scarves | Winter caps |
| Sunglasses | Mittens | Winter jackets |

During group time, children can discuss several scenarios on dressing appropriately for the weather. For example,

- It is very cloudy outside and the weather forecaster said it might rain. How do you dress?
- There is not a cloud in the sky and the sun is shining. How might you dress?
- Dress for your favorite type of weather (Hommerding, 2007, p. 44).

Also items for a forecaster prop box can include multiple items such as those found in Box 11.7.

**Box 11.7. Items for a Prop Box for a Forecaster**

- Cookie sheets.
- Laminated maps of the United States.
- Laminated weather shapes (sun, cloud, raindrop, etc.) with magnets on the back.
- Laminated weather maps cut from the newspaper.

The children can look at the weather maps and create a forecast. They can also use real weather maps and reproduce the forecast by using the weather shapes on the blank map. Children can place suns on the sunny location and raindrops on the rainy location. Cookie sheets can be used as a backdrop to secure the maps and magnetic weather shapes. Newspaper weather maps can be used to reproduce the forecast on the cookie sheet weather maps that children can share with their classmates. When children use the newspaper weather map, they become aware that understanding a weather map is important to the world outside of their school (Hommerding, 2007). Children's books can be included in the weather prop box (See Box 11.8).

**Box 11.8. Fiction and Nonfiction Books for "All About Weather" Prop Box**

- Bauer, M.D. (2003a). *Snow*. New York: Simon & Schuster
- Bauer, M.D. (2003b). *Wind*. New York: Simon & Schuster
- Bauer, M.D. (2004a). *Clouds*. New York: Simon & Schuster
- Bauer, M.D. 2004b. *Rain*. New York: Simon & Schuster
- Berger, G., & Berger, M. (2000). *Do tornadoes really twist? Questions and answers about tornadoes and hurricanes*. New York; Scholastic
- Cole, J. (1996). *The magic school bus inside a hurricane*. New York: Scholastic
- Cole, J. (2000). *The magic school bus kicks up a storm*. New York: Scholastic
- Cole, J. (2001). *The magic school bus explores the senses*. New York: Scholastic

- Cole, J. (2010). *Lost In The Solar System* – Audio Library Edition (The Magic School Bus). New York: Scholastic
- DeWitt, L. (1993). *What will the weather be?* New York: HarperCollins
- Mayer, M. (2003). *Just a thunderstorm*. New York: Random House
- Nankin, F. (1998). *Wonders of weather*. Newburyport, MA: Kidsbooks
- Staub, F. (2005). *The kids' book of clouds and sky*. New York: Sterling

Young children learn when they play with the themed materials that they find in the prop boxes. Prop boxes encourage young children to act out what they know, to reinforce and practice difficult concepts in a meaningful context, and to learn with their peers during their dramatic play and interactions with the materials.

## Field Trips

Children can take science field trips outside the school. They can be short or long field trips. Children can learn about and come to appreciate nature when they take short field trips through the school yard and along the streets near the school. They will find a variety of rocks and plants that grow unattended in areas such as around fences and in cracks in the sidewalks. They can gather and study them by taking the plants, rocks, and other elements of nature into the classroom to observe them closely. These might be left on tables at the science center for continued observation. Young children can make a terrarium from a jar or large glass container with the material they gathered in their field trip. They can observe the effects of different environmental conditions on plants when different materials are used (e.g., sand rather than soil) and when they are taken care of differently (e.g., some will have more light than others or have more or less moisture). Field trips to parks, wooded areas, and nature preserves offer children opportunities to both learn and practice observation skills and to appreciate and develop a sense of wonder about nature.

Children can take schoolyard hikes to learn about science. They can record the information that they observe. The recorder can be a child in the class, an older child, the teacher, or a parent. One hike can be used to look for shapes in the environment. They can identify objects that are oval, spherical, square, crescent shaped, and the like. Another hike can focus on touch. Children examine objects that feel soft, hard, rough, smooth, bumpy, oily, or gritty. Other hikes can focus on different themes such as number, color, or sound. When they return to their classroom, the children can discuss and record what they observed. A record of their observations can be posted on a bulletin board (Jenness, 1987).

Field trips can also be extended for a longer period of time. Children can observe how the seasons change when they take a trip to a farm or a park. They can visit farms, zoos, or animal shelters to look at animals. Field trips are determined by the resources available near the school. Box 11.9 shows an activity to use on a field trip to a playground or a park.

**Box 11.9. A Field Trip to a Neighborhood Playground or Park**

Take the children to a neighborhood playground or park where they can observe and collect materials. Give each child a paper bag to store and carry things that are collected. Select a focus for each trip, for example one trip might be taken to observe and collect rocks while another trip might focus on leaves. Before leaving, discuss the purpose of the trip and how the children should behave as they go about their collecting. Also set conditions and limits of collecting. Only rocks smaller than a child's fist might be collected or only one sample of each type of object. Thus, children might look for leaves that are shaped differently or that have different colors. They might select rocks of different sizes, shapes, textures, or colors.

Upon return to the classroom, have each child sort and arrange his samples by categories that are established by the class, for example, rocks that were collected could be organized by size, shape, texture, or color. They could also be ordered from the biggest to the smallest or from the smoothest to the roughest. If a child wishes to create a different category, that would be all right, but the child should have to explain it to the class. The class should discuss what they have collected. They might select from each child's material for a class display. The children could also engage in art projects with the materials they collect. They can trace leaves, or make spatter prints with them. They could use small rocks in a collage, or make a miniature rock garden with them. Teachers might want to use a reference book to come up with the proper names of plants or rocks observed (Spodek & Saracho, 1994b, p. 378).

## Children's Museums

Children need to play in a variety of contexts that are safe, accessible, stimulating, and approved play spaces. A context with a play space that has emerged in the children's science play is the children's museums or children's exhibits in larger museums. When children visit a museum, they usually remember specific social contexts and specific content (Anderson et al., 2006). Museums help children to identify with scientists through a variety of materials and science programs. In the museum, children play with the real things. Many museums provide children with an educational environment. The museum's philosophy is for children to experience "Play with Real Stuff." Therefore, they provide children with opportunities to explore the museum's hands-on activities and exhibits throughout the day. Their philosophy focuses on hands-on learning, interaction with real materials, and intergenerational participation in a community context. The children's museums focus on the following goals related to science (Mayfield, 2005); see Box 11.10.

---

**Box 11.10. Science Learning in the Children's Museums**

- *Learning* that would enrich the children's lives, expand their cultural experience, and offer them a creative space to learn about their world.
- *Interactive/hands-on* that would help children learn more about themselves and their world within an interactive learning environment.
- *Fun/enjoyment/joy* that would motivate children to learn.
- *Play* that would motivate children to learn with their families.
- *Creativity/imagination* that would promote the children's creative behavior.
- *Discovery* that would motivate children to discover the mystery of the way things work.

- *Children/families/intergenerational* that would encourage children and families to learn through interactive exhibits and educational programs.
- *Multicultural/intercultural* that would allow children to play and enjoy diverse cultural beliefs and celebrations of life.

The children's museums have increased the diversity of their exhibits and programming. Some museums have a large studio for children to paint, draw, and create many projects. In the museum's theater, children use props to create stories and act them out. In the museum's water play area, the children explore science concepts as they play. The museums offer exhibits and activities to reinforce the children's learning in their classroom (Mayfield, 2005). When children see the "real thing" in a museum, they are able to relate the things they see and already know to their every day learning. Box 11.11 provides information and suggestions that will help young children enjoy and learn at the museum (NAEYC, 1999).

### Box 11.11. Information and Suggestions to Help Children Enjoy and Learn at the Museum

- Children's museums cultivate hands-on learning and interaction experiences. They touch, feel, and manipulate materials. Some children's museums provide them the opportunity to build miniature model cities, conduct scientific experiments, play musical instruments, or slide down a firefighter's pole. Young children enjoy listening to expert storytellers.
- Children's museums have special collections and their treasures. Zoos and aquariums foster the children's interest in the natural world. Children get a first-hand look at animals and aquatic species, their habitats, and their ways of living. Botanical gardens and arboretums, with their glass houses and surrounding grounds, introduce the children to familiar and exotic plants and flowers.
- Children's museums develop their interest in history when they visit restored areas or historic homes. Some areas have been restored to recreate complete villages similar to the way they were centuries ago. Historic homes give children a flash back of the way different groups of people lived in the past. Cultural heritage museums contain collections from certain specialized cultural groups of people and provide an understanding about their cultural and historical traditions. For example, children can visit a museum that has a dinosaur bone exhibit.
- Children's museum visits need to be planned in advance. It is important to know ahead of time the admission fees, hours of operation, and travel directions. It is best to go during the days and hours when the museum is the least crowded, admissions are free, or have admission discounts. The visit needs to be developmentally appropriate. For example, a Van Gogh exhibit that is crowded may not be an appropriate visit for two-year-olds.
- Children's museums have an Information Desk that provides visitors with floor plans to find the locations of exhibits, museum gift shops, restrooms, wheelchair ramps, and rest areas. The Information Desk also identifies the times and locations for hands-on rooms, children's performances, special presentations, musical events, and storytelling sessions.

- Large children's museums can be overwhelming if children are expected to see everything at one time. Children should not be expected to see everything in one visit. Young children can learn best in 10- to 15-minute periods.
- Children's museums stimulate the children's thinking skills. Children need to be provided with opportunities to discuss and ask questions about what they see. A docent or tour guide can respond to the children's questions.
- Resources for children's museums can be found under Museums + Learning: A Guide for Family Visits, U.S. Department of Education. http://www.ed.gov/pubs/Museum

## Science Museums

There are several museums that relate to science, such as those in Table 11.2 (Greene, 2001).

Museums in large cities differ from other museums, such as those in Box 11.12 (Danilov, 1986).

**TABLE 11.2. Science Museums**

| Type of Museum | Description and Use |
| --- | --- |
| Natural History Museums | Have specimens of animals, fish, birds, plants, reptiles, and other natural forms (such as rocks and minerals). They also help children understand how the Earth has changed over time and how it has stayed the same. Children are provided with firsthand experiences on how big dinosaurs were, how to tell a turtle's age, or how giant squids change their color and texture. They may see mummies of people who lived centuries ago |
| Science and Technology Museums | Describe the past history, present, and future of technology as well as how things work. They have exhibits of working models of inventions and some museums encourage the children to test out scientific laws by posting signs with directions (e.g., push a button here, pull a lever there, and see the way gravity works). Children may turn a crank and make their own electricity, see how an engine works, or walk inside a spaceship. When they see the astronauts' spacesuits, they may imagine what it is like to walk on the moon or float in space |
| Zoos | Stimulate the children's interest in the natural world and introduce them to animals, their habitats, and their ways of living |
| Aquariums | Allow young children to see the life in the oceans and lakes. As they observe, children learn about the miniature universe that shows nature's balance such as coral reefs, starfish, electric eels, giant octopuses, and aquatic plants |
| Botanical Gardens | Introduce children to both familiar and exotic plants and flowers that are displayed in glass houses and surrounding grounds |
| Nature Centers | Help children learn about natural beings such as butterflies, beavers, bull frogs, and creeping, crawling bugs. Children learn about local plants and wildlife |
| Planetariums | Show children the complete night sky in all of its glory. Children can see the mysteries of the skies come to life when they view the rings of Saturn through telescopes or when they weigh themselves on scales to find out their weight on the moon or on Mars |

**Box 11.12.  Science Museums in Large Cities**

- Field Museum of Natural History and the Museum of Science and Industry in Chicago
- Museum of Natural History in New York
- National Museum of Natural History in Washington, DC
- Exploratorium in San Francisco
- Boston Children's Museum
- The Children's Museum in Indianapolis.

These museums display exhibits that are designed for children of all ages and allow them to explore scientific phenomena. Many smaller communities also have museums that display exhibits appropriate for young children, and provide them with activities. Museum curators display exhibits that are both entertaining and educational (Ault, 1987).

## Exhibits

Today, a wide range of exhibits are found in children's museums, which may have both permanent and temporary displays. Some museums provide space for the children's work and usually display it. The range of exhibits varies with each museum. A sample list of exhibits in some children's museums are found in Box 11.13 (Mayfield, 2005).

**Box 11.13.  Exhibits in the Children's Museums**

- *Children's Games* (The Children's Museum, Helsinki)
- *Monkey King: A Journey to China* (Children's Museum of Manhattan)
- *Colours* (Explora il Museo dei Bambini di Roma)
- *Let's Grow*! [gardening] (Whatcom County Children's Museum)
- *AFLOAT C The Art (and Science) of Water Play* (Tucson Children's Museum)
- *Food in Art* (Youth Wing of the Israel Museum)
- *R & D Dream Lab* (Port Discovery)
- *Pack Your Bags! A Kid's Ticket to Travel* (Canadian Children's Museum)
- *Paradijs & Co. Iran* (Kindermuseum/Tropenmuseum)
- *Jump to Japan: Discovering Culture through Popular Art* (The Children's Museum, Seattle, WA, USA)
- *Illusions* (Science World, Vancouver, Canada)
- *International Village* (Canadian Children's Museum)
- *How a Rocket Works* (Children's Museum of Caracas)
- *Imagination Station* (The Children's Museum, Seattle)
- *Artville* (Arizona Museum for Youth)
- *The Lab* (The Louisiana Children's Museum)
- *Viking Ship and Castle* (Copenhagen Children's Museum, Denmark)
- *Kid City Market* (Children's Museum, Portland)
- *Grandparent's Attic* (Children's Museum, Boston)
- *The Tree and Me* (Manitoba Children's Museum)

## Class Visits

Class visits can be arranged to these museums, but they must be planned and scheduled in advance. Greene (2001) believes that schools and families assume an important role in introducing children to museums and using them as learning resources. Both schools and families need to work together to assist children in getting the most out of visits to museums. Each group needs to assume a set of responsibilities (see Box 11.14).

---

**Box 11.14. Families & Schools' Responsibilities for Museum Class Visits**

*Schools and Parent-Teacher Organizations*

- Have a parent committee that plans field trips to museums.
- Find out which exhibits in the museums relate to the curriculum and the exhibition schedules (both permanent and temporary).
- Develop partnerships with local museums so that they can work with children both during and after school. Museum staff can visit classes, provide workshops for teachers, answer any of the children's questions, help children set up an in-school exhibition, and share their expertise in many ways.

*Teachers*

- Prepare family members to act as chaperones by telling them the purpose of the visit and how it relates to what their children are learning.
- Invite families to cooperate in planning field trips. Parents can scout their local community for developmentally appropriate learning opportunities. They can identify local collections, collectors, and researchers.
- Become involved in local museum-sponsored workshops and programs. Look for appropriate museum-prepared lessons and curricula that can be used in the classroom.
- Join the museums' mailing list to find out about the museums' activities. Many museums with education departments or teacher services offices sponsor workshops, and give out free or low-cost materials such as posters, curriculum coordination information, brochures for chaperones, and audiovisual materials.

*Families*

- Reinforce classroom lessons when they attend family visits to the museum after school, on weekends, and during the summer.
- Volunteer in planning and helping chaperone field trips to museums.
- Search in newspapers, radio stations, or television channels for special announcements and programs about exhibits and opportunities that reinforce the children's classroom learning or topics of interest. Focus on television programs that target collectors and hobbyists.
- Join the museums' mailing lists and become a member of their favorite museum.

Children's museums vary. However, there is a consensus that the museums are hands-on and provide rich physical environments that encourage children to learn and play together. The children's museums respect, nurture, and celebrate childhood. They are institutions that have made a commitment to provide exhibits and programs that would meet all of the children's (babies, toddlers, preschoolers, elementary school children) needs and interests, as well as to stimulate their curiosity and motivate their learning. This learning is empowered by providing them with contact and direct experience with objects that are as important as an exhibit's subject or content focus. Since its origin, the Association of Children's Museums (ACM) has established relationships with several early childhood organizations to continue to promote the importance of young children's learning and play (ACM, 2007). Children's museums are user friendly, interactive, hands-on, attractive, non-threatening, and stimulating places designed and developed for children.

## Summary

Science education is an integrated part of the curriculum that requires children to learn through inquiry. Children use the science strategies of observing, classifying, measuring, communicating, inferring, estimating, and predicting in simple science investigations where they explore and test their ideas. Science introduces children to a way of understanding their world—a way of thinking about things. This viewpoint requires that children learn to actively think about the experiences provided for them and that their thought processes about physical and natural phenomena match their acquisition of scientific information. In addition, the classroom environment needs to have activities where children *act upon* materials and experiences to infer and make their own conclusions. This means that teachers need to continuously provide children with opportunities to explore, test their hypotheses, and discover concepts on their own. In science learning, children engage in scientific inquiry to classify concepts and make conclusions. The important aspect in this process is the way such conclusions are generated and the reasons and methods of developing a set of classifications. Therefore, an early childhood science program needs to have an environment of inquiry pervading the class (Spodek & Saracho, 1994b).

At different ages, children play with science learning in a variety of forms. Very young children explore the magic of unpredicted science transformations. As children grow older, their learning of science progresses from hands-on manipulations of household materials to more abstract symbolic manipulations. New developments (such as thematic, activity based learning) offer promise for more playful learning processes at different age levels (Kean, 2006). Young children are able (a) to develop a rich understanding of the nature of the scientific processes and (b) to recognize through playful experiences that there are many ways of knowing science concepts (Osborne & Brady, 2001).

When teachers provide a science experience in the children's play, they create situations that will motivate children to engage in scientific inquiry to obtain scientific understandings. Children engage in what Hawkins (1965) refers to as "messing about in science." Children use materials to investigate their hypotheses; conduct tests, observe, gather, classify and record data; examine assumptions, evaluate findings, and reflect on their investigations. During play, children acquire information and develop concepts through direct, hands-on experience (Wassermann, 1988).

Science should relate to the children's everyday lives. Children need to learn science concepts through playful learning. For example, cooking experiences help children to learn about nutrition. Field trips around the neighborhood can be used to learn about ecology. Children may not be able to understand all the principles behind eating a balanced diet or taking care of their environment, but they are able to learn which foods are the most nutritious ones as well as learn to appreciate and protect the physical environment and keep it clean.

Science needs to become concrete for the children. The classroom can be organized with learning centers to help children learn science concepts in an area that they can identify and have a degree of isolation. The centers need to have within them or nearby some closed storage space, such as a cabinet to store science materials that are not currently being used. Also materials may be set up in the learning centers to motivate the children's learning in certain scientific concepts.

Science learning increases through play, because the children act out concepts and ideas that they fall short in understanding. Playful interactions with science help young children to better understand and remember difficult concepts. In play children engage in self-selection activities that promote their critical thinking and learning (Hommerding, 2007).

# Chapter 12
# Mathematics-play Learning Experiences

Children's learning begins long before they attend school . . . Consequently, children have their own preschool arithmetic, which only myopic psychologists could ignore.

(Vygotsky, 1978, p. 84)

Children are born mathematicians. Their relationships and interactions with people and the environment set the stage to develop mathematical concepts (Geist, 2001). For example, in their first days of life, infants can differentiate between a set of two objects and a set of three objects (Antell & Keating, 1983). At six months, they relate a set of three sounds to a set of three objects (Starkey et al., 1990); at five months, infants are able to foresee the changes in small sets. For example, they are surprised if they see two puppets that are behind a screen and they only see one puppet when the screen is raised. As infants become toddlers, their natural quantitative competencies develop. Four-year-olds are able to compare quantities and count (Griffin & Case, 1997). Five- and six-year-olds are able to match numbers to quantity. They can make several quantity judgments without using physical objects. For example, they can determine the number of objects they would have in all if they had four objects and received three (Griffin, 2004). According to Ginsburg, Lee, and Boyd (2008),

- At an early age (infancy to age 5) young children develop informal mathematical concepts (more and less, take away, shape, size, location, pattern, position). Their mathematical concepts are both concrete and abstract and can be extended spontaneously.
- Young children can learn more and deeper mathematics than teachers usually expect.
- Young children solve informal addition and subtraction problems during their play.

Young children enter school with a broad background of experiences in mathematical learning similar to their knowledge of spoken language and their physical world. Their experiences have occurred in a world of quantity where they constantly need to determine if something is "too small," "too large," or "all gone." Young children might have learned how to count at home; they may possess an intuitive understanding of mathematical processes and ways to solve simple mathematical problems (Spodek & Saracho, 1994b).

Before children enter school, they have developed a large amount of informal knowledge of mathematics. By the time they enter kindergarten, they have a large amount of procedural and conceptual knowledge about mathematics, including knowledge of geometry, numbers, money, and measurement. They can identify the numerals with names, provide the next number in the sequence, form groups of three and seven, count up to five items on a card, identify the number of items in a group up to eight, point to the first and last item in a sequence, and compare the number of items in two groups that have four items each. They can also distinguish between coins such as penny, nickel, and dime, and between one, five, and ten dollar bills (Rea & Reys, 1971). They can count and solve simple addition problems.

Once children are in school, they use their personal intuitive strategies to understand standard algorithms (Ginsberg, 1980). The informal sense of number and mathematical processes children have before they enter school can be used as the basis for a sound mathematics program. This program can be based on the children's use of their intuitive and informal strategies to solve mathematical problems (Carpenter, 1986). Their relationships and interactions with adults set the stage for the development of more formal mathematical concepts. There are many opportunities for children to count, which helps them understand one-to-one correspondence and quantity. When children compare groups of objects or quantities, they come to understand concepts of more, less, and the same (Geist, 2001). The purpose of this chapter is to describe daily classroom experiences, standards and expectations, children's play, learning centers, and play themes in mathematics.

## Mathematics Daily Classroom Experiences

Children can learn about mathematics through everyday classroom experiences. However, it is important that teachers systematically plan these experiences in order to integrate mathematical concepts. Young children learn about quantities by comparing things, and finding out whether one object is "bigger than," "smaller than," "longer than," and "shorter than" another object. During group time, they can add or take away one, two, and three objects to understand the process of addition and subtraction. Young children can understand division when they share goodies, for example, when they distribute equal quantities to a group of children by giving each child one piece of candy in turn until there is no more. They also learn that a whole becomes smaller when the object is cut into its parts. Many of these mathematical experiences can be integrated into the classroom routines. See Table 12.1 (Spodek & Saracho, 1994b).

When young children have daily mathematics experiences, they are able to learn more mathematics than adults expect. They can learn a wide range of content (such as number and operations, shape, space, measurement, and pattern) where they are thinking about those processes. Elements of early childhood mathematics education can range from play to organized curriculum (Ginsburg et al., 2008). The National Association for the Education of Young Children (NAEYC) and National Council of Teachers of Mathematics (NCTM,

**TABLE 12.1.** Classroom Experiences Where Children Deal with Quantity

| Type of Experience | Description |
|---|---|
| Snack-time | The tables can be arranged at snack-time by putting out napkins, cups, and other things that are needed for the snack. They can (1) place one napkin, one cup, and one of whatever else is needed for each child; (2) count the number of children sitting at each table; and (3) check that each child has an equal share. After a while, the number of children can change at each table so that the children match the number of objects with the number of places where the children are sitting at each table. The same procedures can be used for setting tables for lunch, if that is part of the program |
| Attendance | An attendance board with hooks can be displayed for each child's tag, which has been previously made. The hooks can be placed in two rows with hooks equally distant from one another. At the beginning of the year the tag might only have the child's picture or it might have any other picture or symbol that the child might recognize. After a while, the children's names are written on the tags. As the children come into the class, they can take their own tags and place them on a hook. The girls can place the tags on one row while the boys will place theirs on another. Ask "How many children are in school today?" "How many children are absent?" "Are there more girls or more boys present?" "How can you tell?" "Are there more children present or absent from school?" They can list these numbers on a chart each day. In time some of the children can engage in these counting and comparing activities alone and report to the class. They can also record the attendance on their own |
| Preparing for Activities | Many activity centers need to have quantities of supplies given out each day. The children can help with these tasks by counting out the number of paint cans or boxes of crayons that should be taken from the shelves and put on the table. Children can check each other to be sure that they have selected the proper amount |
| Planned Experiences | Cooking is a wonderful activity in which informal mathematics can be practiced. The children can follow a recipe when cooking in class. They need to be aware of the different measuring tools that they will use, such as cups, spoons, and the like. They need to learn to carefully fill these and to count out the proper number of measurements they will need according to the recipe they are using. The children can cook food to be eaten or make play dough, finger paints, and other materials |

2010) state that mathematics education should use teachable moments that emerge from the children's everyday play (e.g., building towers of different heights) and everyday experiences (e.g., lining up or distributing snacks). When young children see that adults use mathematics concepts, they also begin to understand number concepts (Geist, 2001).

Effective mathematics education for young children, especially for children aged three to five, is essential. However, many early childhood teachers have difficulty understanding the effective components of preschool and kindergarten mathematics (Ginsburg et al., 2008).

Children with disabilities have difficulty learning mathematics and need several modifications based on their disability. Children with an intellectual disability need to learn simpler mathematical concepts and skills than their typically developing classmates. They learn best when mathematics concepts relate to their daily living situations. Children with learning disabilities have difficulty with concepts that require them to use their intellectual, spatial, and verbal reasoning abilities. They may have difficulty (a) reading mathematical symbols (digits, numbers, operational signs), (b) labeling mathematical terms verbally (number of items, numerals, operational symbols), or (c) understanding mathematical concepts and relationships that require them to use mental calculation. They are not able to add and clearly read or write numbers. Children with learning disabilities, emotional disabilities, orthopedic or physical disabilities, and visual impairments can use manipulative materials, because these materials provide them with immediate feedback and working individually limits their competition with other children. Children with visual impairments can use a braille abacus to solve mathematical problems. If a braille abacus is not available, a memory-assistance device can be made by stringing beads with holes through their centers onto thin wire. Three or more columns of ten beads can be strung onto the thin wire, which can then be placed in a wooden frame or attached to the edges of a cardboard box. Children with visual impairments can use the beads to remember in-between steps in their mathematical functions. The beads are organized to correspond to specific numbers and can be divided into groups by attaching small alligator clips to the wire.

Since children with disabilities have difficulty with mathematics, teachers can apply the general principles of good teaching with *all* children (including children with disabilities and typically developing children). Spodek and Saracho (1994a) reported the following teaching principles for children with disabilities:

- All children are able to learn if they are taught at their level.
- Learning should be planned to ensure some success. Immediate feedback is effective.
- A positive self-concept affects success. Young children must perceive themselves as being important to themselves and to others.
- Practice is important to develop concrete concepts. Practice provided in practical situations allows for transfer of learning to new situations.
- A variety of alternative teaching strategies should be planned. If one approach fails, others can be attempted. Sensory approaches can meet each child's individual learning style.
- Children who have a mathematics disability tend to work slowly and at a concrete level. They may be incapable of performing abstract work; therefore, they may need to fully develop their concrete levels.
- Children's errors should be carefully analyzed to understand their thinking processes and to provide clues about ways to clarify their concepts.
- All children learn differently. An instructional mathematics program should be planned based on careful diagnosis and evaluation (p. 365).

Within the United States, children who are at-risk or with linguistic and cultural differences need to learn mathematics concepts at an early age. Several cross-cultural and within-cultural differences in mathematics achievement derive from the groundwork of informal mathematical knowledge children develop during early childhood. Starkey and Klein (2008) have used informal mathematical knowledge with children in early childhood programs (e.g., Head Start) and different low income and cultural families (like African-American, Latino families). They used this information to develop a Pre-K Mathematics Curriculum (Klein et al., 2004) that they have found to be quite effective at enhancing low-income children's mathematical knowledge. The following are examples of these informal mathematical activities.

- *One-to-one correspondence:* Children distribute a set of objects equally between two puppets
- *Addition and subtraction:* Children share a set of bananas equally between two monkeys
- *Measurement of length:* Two children take two sticks from a box and line up the ends of the sticks to see which stick is longer

Starkey and Klein (2008) believe that their mathematics curriculum will enhance young children's mathematical knowledge. It helps teachers to offer early enrichment in mathematics, which is an important step to guarantee an equal educational opportunity for all children, regardless of their socioeconomic or cultural situation.

## Mathematical Standards and Expectations

Young children have the interest and ability to participate in important mathematical thinking and learning. A mathematics program for young children should be based on a set of standards for early childhood stemming from knowledge of young children's individual needs and mathematical knowledge, which includes acting, thinking, and learning (Clements, 2004). NCTM (2000–2004) recommends that young children be provided with a solid mathematical foundation from prekindergarten through second grade. It states, "In these grades, students are building beliefs about what mathematics is, about what it means to know and do mathematics, and about themselves as mathematics learners. These beliefs influence their thinking about, performance in, and attitudes toward, mathematics and decisions related to studying mathematics in later years."

Young children, as learners, generate beliefs about the meaning, functions, and benefits of mathematics. Their beliefs affect their (1) thinking about, (2) performance in, (3) attitudes toward, and (4) outcomes in mathematics achievement in their later years. The mathematics concepts that young children learn will prepare them for their lifelong work as adults in becoming mathematicians, statisticians, engineers, and scientists. They need to learn to understand the power and beauty of mathematics and have a repertoire of the mathematics basic skills to be able to compute fluently and to solve problems creatively and resourcefully. "Knowledge of what young children can do and learn as well as specific learning goals, are necessary for teachers to realize any vision of high-quality early childhood education" (Clements, 2004, p. 9). It is important that teachers use the natural classroom events in planning play experiences that assist young children to learn and understand mathematics such as the mathematical experiences in Box 12.1 (Spodek & Saracho, 1994b).

---

### Box 12.1. Natural Classroom Mathematical Experiences

- *Grouping.* Children develop concepts of quantity when they group (1) all the pencils in a box, (2) all the red beads in a bead set, (3) the pieces of a puzzle, (4) containers of milk, (5) the children in a class, or (6) matching objects (e.g., pictures, charts, things) to learn one-to-one correspondence. Even before they count, they can line up two sets of objects to match them with each other.
- *Counting.* When young children repeat the names of numbers in sequence without being able to match them to the number, that is not counting. Children

need to learn to associate names, symbols, and quantities with the numbers they represent.

- *Number System*. Once children begin to count and write numbers beyond nine, they need to learn that the numeration system has a base of ten where the place of each digit in a numeral represents its value.
- *Number Operations*. Young children need to learn the basic operations on numbers such as addition, subtraction, multiplication, and division. They need to experience a variety of situations where they put together sets of objects to acquire an intuitive understanding about the facts and the appropriate language. An inappropriate introduction to formal mathematics instruction can prevent the children's intuitive acquisition of concepts and operations.
- *Geometry*. Infants develop an understanding of spatial relationships and begin to understand the basic concepts of topological geometry in their intuitive under-standing. For example,

> *Two toddlers chase each other through a tunnel their teacher made by taping together two cardboard boxes; the children are exploring spatial relation-ships, a foundation for one day understanding geometry and numbers.* (Koralek, 2009, p. 10).

Some of the basic topological concepts that children are learning are *proximity*, the distance of objects from one another; *separation*, the lack of nearness; *order*, the arrangement of objects in space; *enclosure* or *surrounding*; and *continuity*. They learn these concepts through experiences with blocks, beads, or other manipulative materials that illustrate these concepts.

In addition, mathematical topics (e.g., measurement, fractions, graphs, charts, and money) are important elements in the mathematics program for young children. See Box 12.2 (Spodek & Saracho, 1994b).

### Box 12.2. Mathematical Topics for Young Children

1. *Measurement* helps young children to understand quantitative and spatial concepts. When young children measure, they increase their mathematical knowl-edge in relation to their world. Young children learn measurement intuitively when they compare and quantify things in relation to established standards.
   - Young children learn measurement when they *measure distance*. For example, when children play in the block area, they match the heights of two sides of a block structure in order to set up a roof. They will become moti-vated to measure floors, walls, furniture, materials, and people. In addition, they compare the measurements they use in oral and written phrases. These measuring experiences help children to practice mathematical functions such as addition and subtraction.
   - *Measuring weight* may be confusing to understand. Young children need to learn the complicated relationships between units. Children can weigh the

many objects in their school environment and compare them. When children weigh two objects in the balance pans, they are able to see which object is heavier or which object is lighter.

- Young children learn to *measure volume*, when they fill and transfer the contents from containers of different sizes and shapes. Then they learn to measure volume with containers of standard volumes such as one cup, half-cup, pint, quart, and gallon. Measurement of volume is best learned in the sand table and water play area.

- Young children have difficulty learning the *measurement of time*, because time is indirectly measured. In addition, children have difficulty understanding the concept of time. It is better for children to learn to read the instruments (such as calendars, clocks) that measure time. Young children can use simulated clocks to set the time and see the relationship between the movement of the hour and minute hands to understand the concepts and practice reading the clock.

2. *Fractions*. After young children understand whole numbers, they can learn simple fractions as equal parts of a unit. Their life experiences and intuitive sense can help them understand the meaning of one-half, one-fourth, and one-third. For example, young children experience using fractions when they are given half a sandwich to eat or a quarter of a dollar to spend. Classroom experiences with fractions occur when they share snacks, pass out art materials, or work in the block area.

3. *Graphs and Charts*. Young children can use graphs and charts to communicate their thoughts about quantitative information. Geography uses maps for written communication of topographical information. Many graphic representations can be used with young children. For example, children can be compared in the class with just two columns. Comparisons can include the number of boys versus girls, children who go home for lunch versus those who stay at school, or those who live in houses versus those who live in apartments. Initially graphs can be three-dimensional representations. A line of building blocks or wooden cubes can represent each group where each block or cube represents one person. Afterward children can use two-dimensional representations. Children can learn to use more complicated graphs for the children's birthdays (by months), heights, weights, color of hair, or interests. These experiences help children understand that graphs are a practical way of communicating information.

4. *Money*. Young children can learn that our monetary system is like our numeration system. After they learn the value of coins and paper money, they can develop skills of monetary computation. Play money can help young children learn the numeration system. Very young children need to mainly recognize coins of different values and to exchange coins properly. Manipulations with real coins may be used, although play money serves the same purpose. Children can use play money in their pretend play situations such as the supermarket where they practice purchasing, making, and selling objects.

The challenge in any math program is to introduce children to mathematics in a way that will provide continuity from their own intuitive knowledge (Griffin & Case, 1997) to more formal mathematical knowledge. According to Piaget (1947), the children can actively develop new knowledge. Piaget's work has been used to shed light on the mathematical abilities of young children, because of the close proximity of mathematics operations to the formal mental operations that have been studied by Piaget and his colleagues.

Such operations are structured from each child's own actions and the logical sense of these actions. Thus, the children construct these themselves. The Piagetian approach to children's learning suggests that children learn in their environment through hands-on experiences. They can manipulate concrete materials in ways that are comparable to mental operations to solve mathematical problems. In *Principles and standards for school mathematics*, NCTM (2000) states, for grades Pre-K-2, "All students need adequate time and opportunity to develop, construct, test, and reflect on their increasing understanding of mathematics" (p. 76). The teaching of mathematics needs to be based on the understanding of the nature of mathematics and the understanding of the children's capabilities of learning in a specific educational context. NCTM published the *Curriculum and Evaluation Standards for School Mathematics*, which recommends that all children (including young children) learn to understand the mathematics procedures instead of merely memorizing them. In addition, it recommends that children learn mathematics through a problem solving approach where young children discuss the relationship between everyday occurrences, manipulative materials, pictorial representations, and mathematical ideas and symbols. According to NCTM (2000), "[young children's] strategies for computing play an important role in linking less formal knowledge with more sophisticated mathematical thinking" (p. 85–86). Young children develop many strategies where they combine two sets to sum a total set and where they separate a smaller set from a larger one to find out the difference. They develop such strategies when young children intuitively use item-whole coordination without paying direct attention to each item in the sets. In the count-all strategy, children discover about a total set when they count all the items in two specified sets. When children use this strategy, they focus on all of the items that are being combined in the sets. They combine several smaller sets into a single total (Becker & Miltner, 2002).

Developmentally appropriate experiences with actual objects in the children's environment can help children understand the relationship between mathematics and their lives. Then children will understand mathematics when they go to the store, buy groceries for their families, pay the grocer, count the change, and make sure that their transaction was correct (Spodek & Saracho, 1994b). Even the youngest children can develop their mathematical knowledge in an environment that is rich in quantitative experiences and language. They need high-quality programs where children are motivated to be active learners and their thinking is stimulated, uniqueness is valued, and exploration is encouraged (NCTM, 2000–2004). At all age levels, developmentally appropriate experiences can expand their knowledge (Saracho & Spodek, 2008a).

## Math and Play

Mathematical knowledge requires both *conceptual* knowledge and *procedural* knowledge (Heibert, 1986). *Conceptual knowledge* consists of mathematical concepts and understandings whereas *procedural knowledge* refers to mathematical processes, that is, how to apply *conceptual knowledge*. Young children need to learn both kinds of mathematics knowledge (Spodek & Saracho, 1994b). When young children interact with their physical and social environment, they actively construct mathematical knowledge and learn to use their *procedural knowledge* when they solve problems in their environment.

Young children's mathematical actions on objects develop their schema concerning the mathematical order they discover, which leads young children to construct or "invent" mathematics (Spodek & Saracho, 1994b).

Young children progress from intuitive to explicit knowledge in play. That is, they make a transition from what they believe, to what is formal knowledge. Before children enter school, they have emerging abilities in numbers and geometry that range from counting objects to making shapes. They use mathematical ideas in their daily lives to develop informal mathematical knowledge. Teachers can provide developmentally appropriate experiences to help preschool children develop their intuitive mathematical ideas to an explicit level of awareness where they acquire an important mathematical understanding and develop their mathematical vocabulary (Clements, 2004).

As young children develop vocabulary, they start making statements that inform us about the knowledge they have acquired concerning mathematical concepts. The children's play and their statements indicate the mathematical concepts that children have learned in a natural way. Learning mathematics is helped through hands-on activities and problem-solving situations that attract the children's curiosity (Guha, 2002). When young children learn number concepts and other mathematical knowledge through hands-on play activities and discussions, they acquire a full understanding of mathematics. Play experiences motivate and nurture the children's inquisitive minds.

Every day, young children become aware of and consider the mathematical dimensions of their world. They compare quantities, encounter patterns, travel in space, and deal with real problems such as balancing a tall block building or sharing a bowl of crackers fairly with a playmate. Young children use mathematics to make sense of their world outside of school and to build a solid foundation for success in school (NAEYC & NCTM, 2010). Mathematics helps children think about things, organize experiences, try to obtain order, and search for patterns. It requires children to reason and solve problems. At a very early age, young children play with concepts of size, number, shape, and quantity. They learn that there are objects that can be moved and connected together—the beginning of mathematical knowledge.

Early childhood educators are well aware of the value of play for children's mathematics learning. Young children need to be provided with materials and prolonged periods of playful activities that promote counting, measuring, constructing with blocks, playing board and card games, and engaging in dramatic play, music, and art. Young children's interest in play can be the basis for a classroom-wide, extended investigation or project that will build rich mathematical learning. Play continually motivates children to explore and learn mathematics (NAEYC & NCTM, 2010).

The children's daily play experiences can stimulate their thinking about and the use of mathematics. Three- and four-year-olds can learn mathematical concepts when they use them in their play experiences. If they are playing with blocks, the teacher can ask, "How many blocks do you have?" or "How many more do you need?" (Guha, 2002, p. 17). Children enjoy counting objects and making mathematical relationships. When they share snacks or help set the table, they create their own mathematical problem-solving ability in performing the tasks (Geist, 2001).

During play young children manipulate objects, interact with their peers, and explore the world around them, which allows them to develop informal mathematical understanding and a basis for formal mathematics learning. Play can be used as a tool to teach young children mathematics (Seo, 2003). Play and daily activities offer young children valuable opportunities to learn about mathematics. They may sort, classify, compare quantities, and become aware of shapes and patterns. They also test mathematical ideas and processes (NAEYC & NCTM, 2010). Young children also learn that mathematics is part of their everyday life (Guha, 2002).

In mathematics, the focus on natural, play-based activities is the core of developmentally appropriate curricula. Organizations such as NAEYC and NCTM emphasize that the children's natural play to learn mathematics needs to be the focus in early childhood education programs (NAEYC & NCTM, 2010). Young children learn best through play when it is used in an educational context. Play does not guarantee mathematical development, but it offers rich opportunities for this development. Significant benefits are more likely when teachers follow up by engaging children in reflecting on and representing the mathematical ideas that have emerged in their play. The play experiences for mathematics need to be planned to achieve the proposed learning (Uttal, 2003). Teachers enhance the children's mathematics learning when they ask questions that provoke clarifications, extensions, and development of new understandings (NAEYC & NCTM, 2010).

## Mathematics Learning Centers

Most areas in the early childhood classroom offer young children opportunities to group things and to count objects. Opportunities to learn mathematics can be integrated in the daily experiences in the classroom using the learning centers. When children play in a learning center (such as the block or woodworking center), they are required to use a mathematical sense. Music, dance, and games encourage children to count and match. Teachers must make sensible selections of experiences, approaches, strategies, and materials to support the children's interest and ability in mathematics in these learning centers.

The materials in the learning centers should attract the children's interest for an extended period of time for children to have the opportunity to learn mathematics through playful experiences. They may engage in counting, measuring, constructing with blocks, playing board and card games, and engaging in dramatic play, music, and art. In the woodworking area, young children can compare lengths of pieces of wood or count nails. In the art area, they compare the volume of clay they use or group the collage materials based on shape and other attributes. In the sand tables and water play areas, young children use the different containers to compare several measures of volume. Even in the library center young children can count books and other kinds of literature (Spodek & Saracho, 1994b). When teachers use an integrated play curriculum, they can provide a variety of experiences where children engage in mathematics learning. A variety of materials and opportunities can be provided in these learning centers to help young children learn about numbers and number relationships. The following sections discuss examples of learning centers such as the mathematics, block, manipulative, cooking, and dramatic play centers.

## Mathematics Center

A mathematics center needs to be available in the classroom where mathematical materials are kept and used. It can be set up in one section of the classroom to be used regularly. The mathematics center should have materials that stimulate young children to solve mathematical problems. For example, counting rods, geoboards, containers for measurement, and felt figures for comparing. Developmentally appropriate directions can be displayed using easy words and/or pictures printed and displayed for children to follow when they are using the materials. The mathematics center can offer endless opportunities for children to engage in counting, comparing, and measuring, providing children with a wealth of opportunities to engage in mathematics. The materials should be easily accessible and well organized so that cleanup is not cumbersome (Spodek & Saracho, 1994b). Table 12.2 offers examples of items that can be found in the mathematics learning center.

**TABLE 12.2.** Items for the Mathematics Learning Center

| Item | Description and Usage |
| --- | --- |
| Toy Cars | Toy cars can be used for children to park. A parking lot can be drawn on a large poster board. Enough parking spaces for the cars are drawn on the poster board. Parking spaces are numbered to equal the number of cars available. Children are asked to find a parking space for each car (York, 1998) |
| Scales | A scale and items to be weighed can be included in the mathematics center. For example, in the fall children can bring pumpkins for them to weigh and compare according to size and weight. They can also take a piece of yarn or string to measure the circumference of the pumpkin. Children can predict the size by cutting off a piece of string that they estimate to be the circumference of the round pumpkin. Then they can measure their predicted string on a yard stick and record it on a chart that is displayed in the learning center. During group time, the teacher can measure the roundness of the pumpkin with the string, measure the string on a yard stick, and give the children the actual measurement. Children can compare their estimates on the chart with the actual measurements |
| Play Money | Other types of manipulatives include objects that are representative of the children's world and encourage mathematics concepts. For example, play money (coins, paper bills), a sorting tray, a bucket of pennies for counting, store and money puzzles, shopping sequence cars, and board games that encourage children to shop and count money motivate them to use mathematical concepts |
| Plastic Animals | A set of plastic animals and an equal number of small baskets can be displayed for children to compare. They can measure and compare the height and length of baby and adult animals. Young children may develop ways to sort the animals. A toy barn or a barn made out of a shoe box can be displayed. Young children can count the animals and predict how many animals can fit into the barn. A chart can be displayed for children to record their estimate,then they can actually put the animals in the barn and record the correct number. During group time, children can compare their estimate with the correct number on the chart as well as which children had the closest estimate (York, 1998) |
| Mathematical Tools | Tools that promote mathematics concepts can be provided for children to experiment how they work. Tools for in this area can include (1) a timer, hour glass, alarm clock, and stop watch for measuring time; (2) rulers, yard sticks, and measuring tapes to measure; (3) balance scale and bathroom scale for weighing; (4) thermometer with a dish of ice and a pot of hot water to check the temperature; and (5) other useful tools such as a calendar with movable numbers (Stone, 1987) |
| Bag of Halves | Place in a bag both parts of items that have been cut in half (such as paper plates) for children to match both halves (Stone, 1987) |

| Plastic Cups and Containers | Several plastic cups and containers can be available for children to empty and fill with objects such as dried beans. For example, children fill one cup with dried beans, leave the second cup empty, and fill part of the third cup for them to compare. Children will learn concepts like empty, more, or half full (Guha, 2002) |
|---|---|
| Books | Children's books are very effective in assisting them to experience numbers in a variety of contexts, formats, and configurations. Table 12.3 shows examples of mathematics children's books (Dickinson, 2003). They are listed in order of numerical complexity |

**TABLE 12.3.** Mathematics Books for Young Children

| Type of Book | Publishing Information |
|---|---|
| Number Concepts | Anno, M. 1977. *Anno's counting book*. New York: Crowell<br>Bang, M. (1983). *Ten, nine, eight*. New York: Mulberry<br>Crews, D. (1992). *Ten black dots*. Toronto: Scholastic<br>Mallat, K. (1998). *Seven stars more!* New York: Walker<br>Wildsmith, B. (1995). *Brian Wildsmith 1 2 3*. Brookfield, CT: Millbrook |
| Story Mathematics Problems | Baker, K. (1999). *Quack and count*. New York: Harcourt Brace<br>Grossman, B. (1996). *My little sister ate one hare*. New York: Crown<br>Hutchins, P. (1986). *The doorbell rang*. New York: Mulberry<br>Inkpen, M. (1998). *The great pet sale*. London: Hodder<br>Maccarone, G. (1998). *Monster math picnic*. Toronto: Scholastic |
| Counting Backwards, Skip-counting, Counting Higher Numbers | Cuyler, M. (2000). *100th day worries*. New York: Simon & Schuster<br>Jocelyn, M. (2000). *Hannah's collections*. Toronto: Tundra<br>Ryan, P.M. (1996). *One hundred is a family*. New York: Hyperion<br>Sloat, T. (1991). *From one to one hundred*. New York: Penguin<br>Wells, R. (2000). *Emily's first 100 days of school*. New York: Hyperion |
| Some Extras | Minters, F. (2001). *Too big, too small, just right*. New York: Harcourt<br>Van Fleet, M. (1998). *Spotted yellow frogs: Fold-out fun with patterns, colors, 3-D shapes, animals*. New York: Dial Books for Young Readers |

Young children can develop their mathematical concepts in the mathematics center. The mathematics center will have items that will prompt young children to have repeated interactions and dialogue that will lead them to learn some of the mathematics vocabulary and concepts such as equations, fractions, and the concept of zero (Guha, 2002).

## Block Center

Blocks will be discussed in more detail in Chapter 15. Block building promotes young children's thinking; the simple activity of manipulating building blocks requires them to develop several complex and academic skills (Adams & Nesmith, 1996). Blocks can help young children to learn mathematics. They can use blocks as manipulative materials to count and group as well as a way to demonstrate space. In block play, young children can explore concepts from topological geometry. When they build with blocks, they discover that both two dimensional and three dimensional space is represented (Spodek & Saracho, 1994b).

Block building promotes children's intellectual learning, especially mathematics. In block building, young children compare objects, which help them to discover similar and different relationships. For example, when young children build a double track or a two-lane road, the concept of two becomes concrete. They also become aware of four sides when they create a rectangular enclosure, even if they do not know the word *rectangular*. The children's learning of mathematics can be observed when they ask for more blocks to finish constructing a big building or might say they are "not having *enough* for me and Jerry and Jane," (Rudolph & Cohen, 1984, p. 147) and feel that their only recourse is to hoard a specific type of block. Most young children have experiences with numbers, especially when they refer to fingers, toes, television channels, address, or telephone numbers; therefore, when they build with blocks, they have the opportunity to test their knowledge with numbers and practice quantitative concepts of numbers (Rudolph & Cohen, 1984).

Young children have an interest in the different shapes of the blocks, which are another mathematical characteristic. For example, Rudolph and Cohen (1984) reported the following situation in block play:

> "Look," says Bernard, rolling a small and large cylinder block simultaneously. "These are the same, only this one is bigger." And Warren, running out of single unit blocks for his barn, picks up a couple of triangles and turns them around in his hands experimentally, trying perhaps to see if they would do in place of the rectangular piece he needs. Then a light of discovery shines on his countenance as he beholds a definitely four sided block of the right size born of two triangles placed next to each other. The magic of two triangle pieces combining to produce a rectangular one is so fascinating that Warren abandons the completion of his barn and keeps working on his discovery for the rest of the session. Nor does he forget about it the next day (p. 147).

Young children compare and show one-to-one correspondence by matching two walls of a block construction then covering them with a roof. These experiences become the basis for a large number of mathematical concepts, which go beyond simply sorting and seriating. In block building, young children create objects and structures from their daily lives and construct abstract designs by manipulating pattern, symmetry, and other elements.

Young children become aware of geometric concepts that are integrated in the blocks (e.g., two square blocks make one rectangular unit block) and those that are integrated in the structures they build (e.g., symmetric buildings with parallel sides). Young children will make the transition from an intuitive to a more explicit conceptual mathematical understanding (NAEYC & NCTM, 2010). Young children acquire math concepts when they measure, count, create patterns, add, subtract, compare, and discuss blocks. If they build towers and bridges, they learn concepts of gravity and balance (Adams & Nesmith, 1996). Blocks are appealing and familiar materials for young children. Young children usually use blocks and their accessories to build at the block center.

## Block Accessories

To motivate young children to engage in block building, they need to have access to a good set of hardwood unit blocks as a play material to facilitate constructive play. They also need a variety of block accessories that complement the children's block experiences (see the chapter on blocks for a list and information on block accessories). Measuring tapes and other measuring tools can help young children to learn about measuring when they use them to measure blocks. Blocks can also be measured with smaller blocks to find out which block is longer or which is thicker (Guha, 2002).

## Manipulative Center

Manipulatives help children to learn through play or at least in a playful manner. These objects assist young children to learn mathematical concepts and do not require children to use or understand written representations of the same concepts. Manipulative materials are concrete objects (rods, blocks) that facilitate young children's mathematical development. Formal manipulative systems (Dienes Blocks, Cuisenaire Rods) are specifically used to teach mathematics (Uttal, 2003).

Manipulatives help young children to learn naturally through play and exploration. Young children need manipulative materials to help them understand concepts and processes through practical applications with concrete examples of the ideas taught. Manipulative materials can prompt young children to individually or in small groups engage in mathematics activities. This learning center needs to include a wide range of manipulative materials to help children learn about numbers, sizes, shapes, and the like. Children can use puzzles that have geometric inserts, peg-sets, and sets of beads and strings for counting, showing numbers, and patterning. They can also use several structured mathematics materials such as the Stern blocks, Cuisenaire rods, or Montessori beads. However, there are several informal kinds of manipulatives that consist of household objects (e.g., paper clips, coins) and pieces of candy or cereal.

### Digital Manipulatives

Children learn mathematics with manipulatives (such as pattern blocks, base blocks, geoboards, Unifix cubes, Cuisenaire rods, coins, clocks), because they provide children with the opportunity to learn concrete, hands-on exploration and representation of mathematical concepts. Recently online resources have made available virtual versions of these universal manipulatives. In this age of technology, digital manipulatives are available for young children.

Virtual manipulatives consist of interactive, Web-based, computer-generated images of objects. Young children manipulate them on the computer screen; just like when they use their hand to slide, flip, rotate, and turn a concrete manipulative, children can use the computer mouse to perform the same actions and create a dynamic visual representation into a three dimensional object. Children can use virtual manipulatives to apply mathematical concepts and explore ways to represent concepts (Rosen & Hoffman, 2009).

There are various digital libraries of manipulatives, such as those from the University of Maryland (http://www.cs.umd.edu/hcil/research/digital-libraries.shtml), the international children's digital library (http://en.childrenslibrary.org), and the Utah State University National Library of Virtual Manipulatives (http://nlvm.usu.edu/en/nav/vlibrary.html), which presents in English and Spanish virtual manipulatives in (1) number and operations, (2) algebra, (3) geometry, (4) measurement, and (5) data analysis and probability for preschool children.

Computer scientists have designed systems that combine the features of traditional hand-held manipulatives with advanced electronic technologies. Such "digital manipulatives" provide children with electronic feedback to let them know if they have combined the manipulatives correctly or in an expected way. For example, when children place the objects in a certain order, those manipulatives that represent the tens units in an addition problem may turn red while those manipulatives that represent the ones units may turn blue. Any type of manipulative material is considered to be developmentally appropriate for young children, if they help children learn through natural exploration and play (Uttal, 2003). Spodek and Saracho (1994b) suggest the following manipulative materials.

- *Stacking and nesting toys.* Manipulatives are also toys that can be stacked and fitted together. Even the youngest children can arrange toys according to size. Manipulative toys are those that can be stacked one upon the other, threaded on a dowel, or fitted together. These manipulative toys help children to learn to discriminate parts by size and to order these parts from the largest to the smallest. Since children are able to figure out when they have put the parts in the right order, the materials are considered self-correcting.
- *Puzzles.* Puzzles are also self-correcting manipulative materials. The manipulative center can include simple puzzles that are easy for children to use. These simple shapes consist of squares, circles, triangles and trapezoids, which are inserted into matching cut-out spaces.
- *Concrete and virtual manipulatives.* Presently children live in a technology-rich world where classrooms are equipped with computers and internet access. Virtual manipulatives combined with concrete manipulatives and real-world inquiries can motivate children to engage in discussion and critical thinking that will promote their mathematics education. For example, Mrs. Smith reads Anne Grifalconi's book *The Village of Round and Square Houses*, which stimulates a discussion of the geometric composition of houses. Then Mrs. Smith's children begin a project about houses and homes. They combine concrete and virtual manipulatives with real-world inquiry to search for ways to represent and measure shapes. In these types of experiences, children associate the shape manipulatives with those shapes found in actual houses. For instance, they count the number of rectangular windows and oval sinks they had in their own homes and created a class graph to present their results. They constructed house structures with three-dimensional shapes such as wooden blocks (Rosen & Hoffman, 2009).

Manipulative materials help children to explore mathematical concepts and switch abstract mathematical plans into concrete models. Most schools have the means to benefit from virtual manipulatives to supplement the children's developmentally appropriate mathematics education.

## Cooking Center

The cooking area can provide opportunities for children to engage in mathematics experiences. Cooking materials such as measuring cups, spoons, and recipes and appropriate ingredients for children to use need to be available in this area. Young children can learn about math when they follow a cooking recipe. Recipe cards can have the directions using both words and pictures to make it easy for children to follow. They measure appropriate ingredients that are in the picture such as the number of spoons and the number of cups that the recipe requires (Guha, 2002).

Children can follow the measurements like the number of spoons and the number of cups of ingredients for the recipe. The instructions can include a few simple words with appropriate pictures for children to be able to read and follow with ease. For example, Mooney (2008) suggests that children can follow the recipe for orange frosts.

## Dramatic Play Center

The dramatic play center provides the children with playful equivalences of realistic experiences, where they use money, count, and measure. These experiences can help them think about and use mathematics. In dramatic play, young children assume a variety of roles from their environment. The dramatic play center provides excellent opportunities for children to learn and use mathematics. Dramatic play experiences can consist of playing store or driving a bus. Mathematics concepts can be developed through a grocery shopping theme (Spodek & Saracho, 1994b). The dramatic play center can be set up as a restaurant. Children develop grocery lists to count the number of items they need to buy for the menu. They also need to follow a recipe and measure the ingredients during this process. In one of their roles in the restaurant theme, young children can pretend to take orders from customers, determine the price of the food, present the bill (may be scribbles on paper) to the customers, receive play money for payment, and give change to the customers. In determining the prices, young children have the opportunity to think about adding and subtracting (Copley, 2000; Guha, 2002). They can also pretend to be customers who look at the prices in the menu (which may consist of pictures and numbers for the prices), figure out their order, and later use play money to pay for their food and figure out their monetary change.

## Mathematics Play Themes

Children learn mathematics concepts when they apply them in the real world. They gain knowledge that makes them independent, lifelong learners. For example, Wolff and Wimer (2009) describe how they set up a play grocery store. The preschool children were participating in an in-school "field trip" to Consumer Town that was set up in a high school front lobby. The grocery store was four feet tall and had cardboard walls. Rather than having the actual grocery items, the grocery store displayed pictures of the different products that were for sale. The preschool children walked to the local grocery store where they found two of their classmates attending the cash registers. First, they walked around the town to window shop before they made their purchases. If the children found a product they wanted to buy, they informed the shopkeeper, paid for the item, and took the picture off the storefront (stuck with Velcro to be used for the next session). The children experienced counting during transactions. When Sean, a young four-year-old, made a purchase, he was helped to slowly count the money and learned what $3 looked like. Then Sean made another $3 purchase and paid the correct amount without help. The following interactions occurred:

- **Josh** (age four years) asked, pointing to a tool in the hardware store, "What does this product do?"
- **Samhith** (age four years) asked in the Cozy Corner Restaurant, "What's the Special of the Day?"
- **Shawna** (age five years) asked, "Can I have my Mother's Day gift wrapped?"

Then the bell rang and the preschoolers returned to their classroom for a snack and a bathroom break.

Mathematics experiences may be based on themes that naturally emerge from the children's interest. Carter (1985) observed children building a garage, a robot, a rocket, and other building projects that were of interest to them. While children were building, they talked to each other about their building projects. Their conversations indicated that the children had a definite scheme and a planned design for each of their structures. Carter (1985) suggests that teachers use the play situation where young children become master builders and architects who will need sufficient materials for them to build. A construction project (such as making a robot or building a clubhouse) will facilitate the children's use of mathematical concepts when they become master builders.

## Becoming Master Builders

When young children build, they develop measurement and geometry concepts as they engage in activities that are hands on and minds on explorations in mathematics. The architect project helps children learn mathematical principles and concepts such as using basic linear measurement, understanding and creating scale representations, and exploring perimeter and areas. When young children design the structure that they are building, they determine, compare, and analyze characteristics of two- and three-dimensional shapes and acquire geometry vocabulary in a real world situation where they become builders. In planning and implementing a building, young children need to play, buy, and use the materials, and to become knowledgeable in budgeting money, measuring geometric forms, and using geometry principles (Suh et al., 2003).

It is important that the creation of the projects is authentic by having children engage in a real life context. Young children need to be allowed to solve problems that emerge rather than being told what to do. They can cooperatively explore several possibilities and collaborate on the solution. The focus of the project needs to be on problem solving and exploration (Suh et al., 2003) as well as on the children's interests. For example, Carter (1985) observed a young boy who was cutting out a brightly colored robot that had been drawn with magic markers. He carefully set the drawing next to a Lego box and began to assemble a robot that resembled the one in the drawing. When Carter (1985) inquired about the project, the boy said, "Oh, I am making this robot out of my Legos" (p. 9). Then Carter asked why he had made the drawing first and the boy responded, "Well, Mrs. Hawes tells us to always make a plan, and so I planned him like this to have a wide head" (p. 9).

Carter (1985) anticipated the structures that could be built in her classroom. She assumed that children would be able to build superstructures, skyscrapers, and cathedrals. To encourage her classroom children to build, she set up a table and placed scissors, paper, and crayons on it. She also included accessories for the structures, such as paper, dolls, dinosaurs, and soldiers. Additional materials can include clay, yarn, Styrofoam, wood chenille sticks, Tinker Toys, cloth, cardboard, or construction paper. This type of project can be adapted to any age level. Children became excited and began to plan projects such as fortresses for armies, caves and schools for teddy bears, and homes and churches for dinosaurs. Children drew models and built together while Carter took photographs of their creations. In the building area, Carter posted reminders of the steps to follow. The reminders consisted of simple words and drawings to make it easy for children to read. (See Box 12.3.)

**Box 12.3. Reminders in Building**

1. Think
2. Draw
3. Cut
4. Build
5. Talk
6. Read

1. Imagine what you build
2. Think of its details (color, shape, size)
3. Draw it
4. Cut it out
5. Tape it up
6. Build it
7. Compare it to your plan
8. Make changes
9. Tell a story about it
10. Read your story (p. 10)

1. You need:
   - blocks
   - tape
   - crayons
   - scissors
   - paper

2. Ask about:
   - details
   - function
   - size, shape, speed
   - decorations
   - inhabitants

3. You can build:
   - churches
   - forts
   - airports
   - houses
   - cathedrals
   - schools

4. You can build:
   - fire stations
   - rockets
   - robots
   - trains
   - airplanes
   - zoos

Children can become master builders, which can develop their thinking, motor, mathematics skills, and literacy. In the building process children become creative and use their problem solving, comparing and contrasting, estimating, evaluating, predicting, and adapting abilities (Carter, 1985) in assuming the role of architects.

## Becoming Young Architects

Children can become junior architects and develop mathematical concepts in a natural way. As architects, young children can design their dream clubhouse and use measurement and geometry mathematical concepts. Box 12.4 suggests the phases in building a project (Suh et al., 2003).

---

**Box 12.4. Phases in Building a Project**

1.  *Planning the project.* On the first day, teachers introduce the project to motivate the children. They read books on building such as *How a house is built* (Gibbons, 1986) and *Building a house* (Barton, 1981) to show the purposes of and the differences in the buildings in the books. Children discuss the structures and identify the various geometric shapes, symmetry, and congruence in the buildings. *Math in the real world of architecture* (Cook, 1996) is a good resource to study such concepts. Local architects are invited to the classroom and talk to the children about their job and the importance of mathematics to their work. Children look at their measuring tools that they use to draw blue prints as well as pictures and models of several kinds of architecture. When the children are ready to create their own clubhouse projects, they should gather in groups to select a theme for their clubhouses and to make a list of items that they need for it. Themes can consist of sports, animal lovers, art, and dance.

2.  *Focusing on geometric solid figures.* The teacher shows the children that geometric solid figures can be found in items from their daily environment such as milk cartons, cereal boxes, and oatmeal containers. Children use milk cartons to stand for townhouses and the cereal boxes to symbolize apartment buildings. They open the milk cartons and cereal boxes, then cut along the sides of the containers, and become aware of two dimensional and three dimensional objects.

3.  *Perimeter and area.* Children begin to understand the sense of size to determine realistic and proportional dimensions for their clubhouses in relation to the real ones. Children acquire spatial concepts when the teacher lays tape on the floor of the classroom on rectangular shapes that differ in dimensions to represent different room sizes. To compare the different sizes of the room, children measure their length and width to determine the total distance around the tape, which introduces the concept of perimeter. Children count the floor tiles to determine the size of each room. Then they make scale drawings of furniture using graph paper.

4.  *Two-dimensional blueprints.* The teacher shows the children several blueprints from different builders for them to see. On inch paper children design a scale drawing of their clubhouses including the doors, windows, and walls. Then they add drawings of furniture to the floor plan.

5. *Constructing the 3-D models.* The teacher assumes the role of building inspector and inspects the design of the children's clubhouses. Once the building inspector approves the designs, the children construct three dimensional scale models on a poster board or cardboard pieces. They measure and cut the walls based on the calculations and drawings on their blueprints. (This task is very challenging to young children and may need to be modified to be developmentally appropriate.)

6. *Decorating the clubhouse.* In determining how to decorate their clubhouse, children consider the area, perimeter, and money. They look at a catalogue or visit a store to compare prices such as the price and number of coats for paint. The teacher gives children a budget of $10 and displays items such as buttons, colorful straws, cellophane paper, wallpaper samples, toothpicks, fabric swatches, and aluminum foil for children to purchase. Children use bright buttons for doorknobs and decorations, cellophane paper to make stained glass windows, fabric swatches to make curtains for the windows, aluminum foil to make solar panels, and satellite devices (to see the sports channels).

7. *Clubhouse showcase.* The children display and present their clubhouses to their classmates. The teacher encourages them to use as many measurements and geometry concepts and terms as possible in their presentations. Then the children tour their classroom to enjoy the other clubhouses that are displayed.

As architects, young children solve problems and acquire knowledge of construction in a real situation. They work with budgets and cost analysis, which helps them to acquire many mathematical concepts. In addition, they learn to use oral language to communicate their ideas and to accept their classmates' points of view and different solutions. Role playing to be junior architects motivates the children, because they are immersed in an authentic experience that includes the mathematical knowledge that is used in real life. In addition, young children learn important mathematics concepts through their own curiosity and problem solving. Although Suh and colleagues (2003) propose several specific phases for this project, it is important that teachers consider their classroom children and adapt this project based on the children's interests and developmental stages.

## Summary

NCTM (2000–2004) advocates that a solid mathematical foundation be developed for preschool children who are developing beliefs about (a) the meaning of mathematics, (b) the purposes of mathematics, and (c) the benefits of mathematics to them as mathematics learners. These beliefs promote their (1) thinking about, (2) performance in, (3) attitudes toward, and (4) effects in mathematics in their later years.

Young children develop numerous mathematical concepts intuitively. Infants automatically understand and differentiate among small numbers of objects, while preschool children know a substantial body of informal mathematical knowledge. Even the youngest children learn mathematical knowledge in an environment that is rich with mathematic experiences. Their thinking needs to be motivated, individuality respected, and exploration encouraged. Young children who attend a formal school setting usually possess a range of mathematical understanding (NCTM, 2000–2004).

All children can profit from high-quality mathematics programs that consider both the nature of mathematics and the nature of young children. These programs need to (a) build on their intuitive and informal mathematical knowledge, (b) be based on principles and practices of child development, and (c) provide an environment where children are motivated to be active learners and to respond to new challenges. These programs also need to have a strong conceptual framework that encourages and develops the children's mathematical skills and their natural disposition to solve problems (NCTM, 2000–2004).

A comprehensive group of experts in various fields developed standards for preschool and kindergarten mathematics education. They also proposed the following recommendations (Clements, 2004):

- The children's individual differences need to be considered in mathematics education. Children differ developmentally and socioculturally, which will affect their later achievement in mathematics. Such sociocultural and developmental differences indicate "what children know" and "what they bring to the educational situation."
- Early childhood teaching and assessment standards need to be flexible with developmentally appropriate guidelines that are based on current research and practice of young children's mathematical learning.
- The young children's mathematics experiences need to be related to their everyday life.
- High-quality mathematics programs for young children need to incorporate mathematical content, general mathematical processes (e.g., problem solving, reasoning, proof, communication, connections, representation), specific mathematical processes (e.g., organizing information, patterning, composing), and habits of mind (e.g., curiosity, imagination, inventiveness, persistence, willingness to experiment, sensitivity to patterns).
- Curriculum development and teaching need to be based on research and practice. Educators and policymakers require teaching, learning, curriculum, and assessment approaches that have been developed and widely tested with young children.
- Young children learn mathematics through play because it relates learning to life in their daily experiences, interests, and questions.
- Teachers need to provide young children with a mathematical environment and with frequent opportunities that allow them to reflect and extend their knowledge of mathematics into their everyday experiences, conversations, and play. Teachers need to use practical experiences to introduce mathematical concepts, methods, and vocabulary.
- Teachers need to use a combination of teaching strategies and planned sequences of experiences that are integrated throughout the day to promote children's learning.
- Teachers need to consider the children's informal knowledge, everyday experiences, cultural background, language, mathematical ideas and strategies.
- Children's learning can be facilitated through appropriate types of technology, particularly computer tools that enrich and extend mathematical experiences.
- Teachers need to understand each child's own mathematical ideas and strategies and use them to adapt their instruction in the curriculum.
- Teachers need to develop the children's conceptual foundation to help understand the relationships between concepts and skills.
- Assessment should be used to understand young children's thinking and to plan instruction for their mathematical learning. Practical and information forms of assessment consist of interview, performance task, and continuous observations.
- Sustained and coherent professional development needs to integrate research and expert practice. It needs to use multiple strategies and a variety of professional

development models that focus on the importance of teacher leaders and collegial support groups.

- To improve teaching, pre-service and professional development programs need to include a profound knowledge of (a) the mathematics to be taught, (b) children's thinking, and (c) methods to develop the young children's mathematical skills and understandings.

- Professional development programs need to address a high quality of mathematics curriculum materials and programs.

- An interpretation of the information from *The Conference on Standards for Prekindergarten and Kindergarten Mathematics Education* needs to be disseminated to different audiences using a variety of forms.

- State agencies across all states need to join forces to develop clear and related state mandates and guidelines to teach mathematics to young children. Governments need to offer appropriate funding and frameworks to provide high quality mathematics education for all children and high quality professional development for their teachers (cited in Saracho & Spodek, 2008b, pp. 315–316).

In the *Principles and Standards for School Mathematics*, NCTM (2000–2004) suggests that all children need to be provided with rigorous, high-quality mathematics instruction that is developmentally appropriate. They need to learn that mathematics relates to their personal life. Children need to learn the power and beauty of mathematics to obtain a new repertoire of the mathematics basic skills that permits them to compute easily and to solve problems creatively and resourcefully. This means that children need to learn important mathematical concepts and procedures that they understand. They need to have access to technologies that widen and intensify their understanding of mathematics.

A major concern has emerged that mathematics needs to be taught in the early years. Young children have an intuitive feeling of number and mathematical operations that they have obtained from their daily experiences in the world. Teachers need to teach mathematics in a natural context such as play. During play young children learn mathematics naturally rather than by rote memorization. The hands-on approach helps them to understand the mathematics concepts and processes. Young children need to manipulate concrete materials and think about what they do. The mathematics program needs to address many topics that provide teachers with the opportunities throughout the curriculum to have children illustrate and practice their mathematics learning (Spodek & Saracho, 1994b). The young children's mathematics education includes more than arithmetic or "numeracy". It covers a broad range of ideas, such as geometry, measurement, and algebra, as well as patterns.

# Chapter 13
# Music and Movement-play Learning Experiences

Music is the Universal language of mankind.

Henry Wadsworth Longfellow

The importance of music for preschool children was observed in October 1987 when little two-year-old Jessica McClure of Midland, Texas, made national headlines. Jessica had fallen down a hole and remained trapped in a dark and abandoned well for two-and-a-half days. Jessica was found tired, bruised, hungry, but singing in her solitary confinement. Instinctively, Jessica was aware of the strength of music. She knew a song, and her singing may have saved her life. Music seemed to console and support Jessica in her anguish, which suggests that music plays an essential role in children's lives. The purpose of this chapter is to describe the music in children's lives, music curriculum, music appreciation, aesthetic music experiences, music play, developing a play-based music program, and music learning centers (music vs. non music).

## Music in Children's Lives

From the time children are born, they experience the pulse and rhythm of their world (Zur & Johnson-Green, 2008), which begins their musicality (Trevarthen & Aitken, 2001). Infants and preschool children discover that music and play are related activities. As children grow, their musical beginnings continue to be the essence of their life (Dissanayake, 2000) while they respond to and learn from the sounds and patterns of their world (Custodero, 2002). Children engage in musical expressions that take place in different locations, are at times unforeseen, and are typically related to other activities. Gluschankof (2004) describes the following spontaneous musical expressions.

N, a five-year-old boy, sings while swinging on the playground swing, a 1950s-era song heard at his grandmother's house. The first sentence is sung louder than the rest; some of the words are not clearly pronounced (p. 328).

Y, a four-year-old boy, claps his hands, then slaps both his thighs, repeating a pattern several times, while the kindergarten teacher is reading a story aloud (p. 328).

S, a four-year-old girl, is playing by herself with dolls. She describes what the doll does as she moves it. S holds the doll up, then down, repeating the movement and the phrase (in Hebrew): "Hop upward, hop downward, and we start from the beginning." This phrase is chanted and recalls a song taught by the kindergarten teacher (p. 328).

Music exploration and expression occur with frequency in the children's daily lives (Moorhead & Pond, 1942) and are essential components in children's play (Bjorkvold, 1992). Music "happens" to children throughout the whole day. They use music to socialize, express emotions, and entertain themselves. Children stretch, bend, step, hop, and skip in rhythmic forms; while their voices get higher and drop melodically, shifting from fast to slow and from loud to soft. Children engage in both the music that they create and the music that they hear in their environment such as in television, radio, and recordings (Campbell, 2000). Children produce unrehearsed, self-generated music expressions that are normal to them (Campbell & Scott-Kassner, 2006). In particular, children's spontaneous vocalizations can consist of standard songs; rhythmic or melodic variations of standard songs; and/or free-flowing, introverted humming, singing, or chanting (Young, 2002).

Music behavior also consists of moving in a rhythmic way (for example, hopping, skipping, jumping) or making use of objects, toys, or instruments to explore or communicate sounds (Littleton, 1998). Children continuously create music that is fortified from daily life (such as speech, movement, singing), which becomes an outward demonstration of personal practices (Moorhead & Pond, 1942). Young children adapt the music they have learned to accommodate standards in their regional or school culture (Marsh, 2005). Children's daily spontaneous music in schools is composed of singing, chanting, humming, and exploring rhythm even when they walk the halls, carry out class projects, or eat their lunch (Campbell, 1998).

Young children prefer movement (dancing) to music (such as singing songs, playing on instruments) (Denac, 2008; Yim & Ebbeck, 2009). Since dancing and movement are the pre-school children's favorite musical activity, it is important to identify and monitor their music preferences to encourage active participation in their music learning (Temmerman, 2000). The children's music experiences provide them with opportunities for musical expression and establish the basis for successful and effective understanding of life transitions, including the critical transition to formal schooling that can lead to their school success. Children need time and space in their social, emotional, and cognitive development, which is influenced by their daily involvement in making music (Zur & Johnson-Green, 2008).

Recently, an interest in music education has emerged from the way individuals engage with music in their daily lives. The focus has shifted from the laboratory to the intricacies of children's living experiences and the importance of music in their lives

(Lamont, 2006). For example, three-year-old preschoolers' real-life experiences are integrated with music. They like to listen to music. Children's creative and responsive natural play with music is observed in four characteristics of childhood:

1. Concept of inquiry as amazement and the imagining of all possibilities.
2. An exploration of the relationship between the nonverbal nature of the children's initial communication and musical understanding, as they experience the intense, direct emotional nature of the aesthetic in music.
3. Representation that children use for an intimate experience (perspective taking).
4. Freedom to respond and improvise based on their perceived possibilities. For example:

> Four-year-old Samuel picks up two small maracas and begins vigorously playing along with the recording of Virginia Rodrigues' samba performance, his motions reflecting the musical rhythms. A nearby mirror catches his attention and he shakes his maracas in time while exploring the myriad possibilities of facial contortions. He then is drawn to the group of eight other children and three teachers who are also moving and playing along with the recording and he negotiates physical space, weaving through his peers, all the while moving to the beat of the music as he continues shaking the maracas. In the little over four-minute duration of the recording, Samuel tries out several moves, interacting with the music and his cohorts: He shakes the maracas close to a teacher's face, quickly realizing that is not the best possible interpretative move; does the same to his friend with a similar outcome; plays both maracas on his stomach; returns to the mirror and places them on his two ears. His final effort is perhaps the most novel—he reaches to the back legs of his pants and places one maraca in each pocket, proceeding to shake his legs and his bum in synchrony with the music (Custodero, 2005, p. 40).

There are clear differences between the process of composition and the spontaneous improvisation of play with instruments to a samba recording. Samuel received numerous possibilities when he rhythmically shifted the weight of the maracas, from his expression in the mirror, and from his feedback from peers and teachers (Custodero, 2005).

The children's music manifests itself both audibly and visibly in the pitches and rhythms of their play; in the songs they sing; and how they step, sway, bounce, and "groove" to it. Children express and amuse themselves as well as communicate and socialize through the musical sounds they make or that surround them in their world. They are attracted to music as they explore, experiment with, and respond to it; music is the safe haven where they find achievement and safe shelter away from the problems in their young lives (Campbell, 2002). At an early age, the children's musical experiences influence their musical, emotional, and creative development as well. Such musical experiences may be indispensable to the children's healthy "total development" (Kenney, 1989), and it is essential that early childhood education programs provide young children with effective and educationally sound music experiences.

## Music Curriculum

In schools for young children, music can be found both in the spontaneous expressions of children and in adult-directed activities. Teacher-directed activities are very customary and easy to recognize. These include singing in circle time, dancing to music, or singing birthday songs while playing small percussion instruments.

Music experiences for young children are used to develop and refine their perceptions of the music they hear. Children need to be provided with opportunities to listen to various types of music in our lives today as well as the types of music that make up our American musical heritage (for example, bluegrass, blues, jazz, gospel, western swing, new age music, classical music). The children's ability and desire to listen to music provides the foundation for their aesthetic music experience. The basis for the content of a developmentally appropriate music curriculum for young children consists of basic music components, human experience, and repertoire and abilities (Woodson & Johnston, 1989):

- *Basic music components* among others consist of the music rhythm, rate, melody, tone quality, and dynamics.
- *Music human experience* is the unique creation and use of music. It plays an important role in the children's lives, especially because it represents patriotic, religious, and cultural values.
- *Music repertoire and abilities* are part of the children's developmentally appropriate music program. Their repertoire is the children's accumulated musical experiences that they have listened to, moved to, created, played, or sung. They have the abilities to listen to music, play musical instruments, or carry a tune when they sing. Developmentally appropriate abilities for young children consist of moving their body to music, singing familiar songs, learning new songs, making up songs, playing rhythm and pitch games, and using several traditional rhythm band, Orff, home made, and experimental instruments.

Developmentally appropriate music education is too often overlooked in many early childhood programs. A major goal for young children's music experiences is to develop and refine their music awareness, especially understanding the music they hear. As young children hear the basic music components, they become knowledgeable of various styles of music and enhance their affective reactions to music. As children listen and distinguish among various components and styles of music, they learn to completely appreciate music, which becomes the basis for the young children's aesthetic music experience (Woodson & Johnston, 1989).

The music field is composed of concepts about music; a repertoire of songs, patterns, and qualities of sound; and musical abilities such as listening, singing, playing, moving, and reading and writing music. A music program for young children needs to offer them many opportunities to listen to music, learn to understand its components, reproduce them when they sing, play instruments, and combine bodily movements and musical expressions including musical compositions (Aronoff, 1979). A music program needs to integrate other curriculum areas such as language arts and social studies. For example, social studies can assist young children to learn how music is used in many cultures. A music program needs to help children to process music critically, recreate it, and use it to communicate (Wolf, 1992). Song lyrics have characteristics that help young children to see the relationship between oral and written language (Barclay & Walwer, 1992).

The Pillsbury Foundation Studies of 1937 to 1938 (Moorhead & Pond, 1942) were conducted to develop young children's musical understanding, motivate them to engage in free musical expression, and to examine the norms that dominate the children's relationship to music. Four characteristics were evident on how young children relate to music:

1.  Music is basically the discovery of sound.
2.  Music must contain purposive action or involvement.
3.  Music demands that social, environmental and procedural conditions be considered.
4.  Music should be spontaneous (cited in Spodek & Saracho, 1994b, p. 473).

Movement is one of the children's first responses to music. Many fail to use movement as an opportunity to engage children in music experiences (Stamp, 1992). Creative music and movement are loud activities. A time can be scheduled for children to experiment with the sounds of a drum, to allow musical noise, and to involve young children in movement experiences. During this time, a section of the room can be set aside for movement. A multipurpose room, the play yard, an auditorium, or a gymnasium can be scheduled for music experiences (Spodek & Saracho, 1994b) that are loud or require a large room space.

Within schools for young children, group musical activities generally consist of singing, listening, playing musical instruments, dancing, and movement (Yim & Ebbeck, 2009). Children engage in large group music and movement activities, but they need to be allowed to participate in music activities by themselves or in small groups. Music assists children to develop their perceptual motor skills. Children develop hand–eye coordination, when they (a) play a tambourine, (b) develop a sense of rhythm, (c) march to a song, and (d) attain balance and grace during dance (Poest et al., 1990). A few children can play musical instruments or musical toys, while other children can use headphones to listen to a CD.

A music program needs to provide numerous opportunities that incorporate music into the children's learning. They need music experiences that include singing, playing simple instruments, listening to music, and creative movement. Usually creative movement consists of children in mime and creative dramatics.

## Singing

Most young children like to sing. They sing loudly, usually with more liveliness than skill. Children choose songs they hear and sing them to the best of their ability; at times they sing a phrase over and over, sometimes mispronouncing or speaking only part of the words. The children's pitch may be off, but this hardly bothers them and they continue to sing.

Singing with children can be an enjoyable and worthwhile experience. When teachers sing with children, they are able to modify the speed and volume to match the children's abilities. Young children enjoy singing and sing along when they see that the teacher is enthusiastic (Ringgenberg, 2003). Teachers need to take advantage of this enthusiasm. Experience and repetition develops better observance to melody and verse. Young children vary in their levels of singing accuracy. Accuracy levels range from being unable to imitate a melody to singing a song without any help and without any melodic mistakes. Young children eventually are able to imitate a melody correctly (Raut, 1985), which usually occurs by the time they are eight years old (McDonald, 1979).

Young children's singing ranges from infant vocalization to relationships of singing, to spoken language to their use of a singing voice (Custodero, 2006). Children's spontaneous singing is (a) solitary in nature and melodically and rhythmically free and (b) communication in social situations that is more metric and repetitive (Moorhead & Pond, 1942). Children's singing using spontaneous vocalizations in school-based and childcare settings usually occurs in relation to their imaginative world that is different from adults'. This type is integrated into their functional, constructive, and dramatic play (Littleton, 1998). Children's singing provides them with several benefits that affect them interpersonally and intrapersonally (Custodero, 2006). Teachers need to select songs that are appealing to young children. Songs need to have a melodic phrase repetition, repeated word phrases, and the appropriate range for the children's specific stage of vocal development (Smith, 1970).

Singing has been considered to be essential in a music curriculum, which raises the issue of vocal development. It is important to establish good vocal habits in early childhood. Typically, singing is taught through imitation, but music educators suggest that it be reinforced through body movement and the playing of resonator bells. Young children need to shape pitch concepts such as register, and melodic direction should be emphasized, the implication being that development of pitch perception is fundamental in developing their vocal accuracy. Pitch and rhythm abilities in singing can be developed using tonal patterns. Young children can learn pitch concepts by using melodic patterns taken directly from songs that they are singing (Reifinger, 2009).

Teachers need to help children to explore vocal sounds, acquire vocal skills, sing alone and in small groups, extend vocal range, and learn songs to develop their voice. Of course, an enthusiastic music teacher who can effectively model singing is essential. Singing can be combined with movement or visual aids that motivate the senses. Then children will be able to hear the music; feel and move to the rhythms; and see, touch, and play the instruments (Ringgenberg, 2003).

Children's singing has an important element of play. When children play, they exhibit a range of musical and language behaviors. Most self-generated songs are created when children are involved in their play. The children's social interaction during play motivates them to sing for their communication (Mang, 2005). Preschool children spontaneously improvise songs and chants, which reflect the way they organize musical information from their environments (Burton, 2002). Children create songs from those they know. They take these songs (like the lyrics or melodic motif) to restructure and integrate them into their own song. Thus, spontaneous songs are considered a key building block in song acquisition (Mang, 2005). Spontaneous songs transform musical occurrences from the environment and the songs from the children's culture. For instance, in the following example, a child combined two songs she knew to create her own song.

> At age 2 years 3 months, Clare sang the first phrase of Bingo but shifted to sing the first phrase of Old McDonald without a pause (Mang, 2005, p. 11).

"Pot-pourri" songs illustrate how children can merge melodic material from two songs they know. When a three-year-old girl previously sang most of the "Happy Birthday" song correctly and in tune, it is clear that she knew both songs. Many children create their spontaneous songs from fragments of songs they know (Mang, 2005).

Songs can be used in a variety of ways to promote other subject areas. The children's interest in certain songs can be adapted to a subject area and offer an opportunity to integrate songs to enhance several units in other subject areas.

*Musical Resources*

A variety of resources are available for classroom teachers including children's commercial music textbooks, books, and recordings such as those in Table 13.1 (Spodek & Saracho, 1994b). Teachers who are shy about teaching music in the classroom can always use a tape player, an MP3 player, or a CD player. Thousands of tapes and CDs can be obtained for music activities, enjoyment, and appreciation (Bryan, 2005). Teachers who are unable to read music can learn children's songs from CDs. Several music textbooks include recordings of the songs.

An assortment of children's songs can be used such as those that are specifically written for children, popular songs, and folk songs. The folk tradition is lively in children's songs, such as the nursery rhymes. Numerous folk songs are simple, have an abundance of repetitive musical phrases and words, and the children can learn them effortlessly. Children need to explore many types of music. Contemporary music is alluring in line, harmony, and meanings. Singing and listening activities need to incorporate jazz, folk, and rock.

Most traditions in the American culture contribute to the musical resources. For example, children can learn the music of the Mexican and Mexican American people, as well as the familiar artists and musicians. They can listen to music and learn how to dance *La Raspa*, a popular dance that is a combination of the "Hokey Pokey" and folk dancing. Records are available from music stores that carry Mexican American music. Teachers can

**TABLE 13.1.** Musical Resources

| Type of Resource | Publishing Information |
| --- | --- |
| Songbooks | Adams, P. (2007). *This old man*. Child's Play International |
| | Holmes, J. (2009). *There was an old lady*. San Francisco, CA: Chronicle Books |
| | Landeck, B. (1950). *Songs to grow on*. New York: Morrow |
| | Raffi. (1988). *The Raffi singable songbook*. New York: Crown Publishers, Inc. |
| | Raffi & Schuett, S.(2004). *This Little Light of Mine*. New York: Knopf Books for Young Readers |
| | Seeger, R. C. (2002). *American folk songs for children*. New York: Music Sales America |
| | Sharon, Lois, & Bram. (1989). *Mother Goose*. New York: Little, Brown & Co. |
| | Sickler, J. (2011). *Frère Jacques*. NY: Workman Publishing Company |
| | Winn, M. (1970). *What shall we do and allee galloo*! New York: Harper & Row |
| Recordings | Koch, F. (2007). Did You Feed My Cow? Lake Fluff, IL: Red Rover Records |
| | Palmer, H. (1982). Walter waltzing worm. Freeport, NY: Educational Activities |
| | Poelker, K. (1985). Amazing musical movements. Wheeling, IL: Look at Me Productions |
| | Raffi. (1996). Singable songs collection. Ontario, Canada: Troubadour |
| | Sharon, Lois, & Bram. (2008). Mainly Mother Goose. Canada: Elephant Records |

also introduce children to familiar Mexican American music artists—such as Jose Luis Orozco or Mariachi Azteca (Saracho & Martínez-Hancock, 2004). Music of different ethnic groups can be found in public libraries and should be provided for young children. The music of black Americans, Spanish-speaking people, Native Americans, and people from various European heritages can be part of the repertoire of resources. Recently, teaching multicultural or world music has been a forerunner in the music educators' minds. Music can be used to teach children about diverse cultures. However, teachers need to avoid assuming the role of expert. They can invite a guest musician to most authentically introduce unknown music. For example, a Japanese parent or community member may be invited to interpret the song, assist with its pronunciation, and offer the children with any contextual information that is important to the song's overall meaning (Peterson, 2006). As stated before, the songs should have a melodic phrase repetition, repeated word phrases, and the appropriate range for the children's particular stage of vocal development. Songs can be part of a unit of study, such as African songs for a black studies unit or songs for celebrated holidays. Children should find them appealing after numerous repetitions.

## Singing as a Movement Experience

Children combine singing with body movements (for example, "I'm a Little Teapot"). They sing a song and slowly add body movements. Sometimes children become captivated by their body movements and continue singing. Their body movements assume their interpretation of a song, whereas singing the melody and the words become a secondary role. In this instance, children become more fascinated with the word meanings of a song and sing it using body movement.

Jaques-Dalcroze tried to make music a means of expression. The source of the Dalcroze technique is the coordination of music and body movement. His goal was to improve rhythmic sense; therefore, his technique integrates a means of self expression. Based on the Dalcroze method, Carl Orff believed that music education for young children should develop their ability to create or to improvise. They need to be encouraged to create their own music based on their personal experiences in speaking and singing, moving, dancing, and playing. Orff believed that children can discover music by themselves. They need to be guided gradually from natural speech patterns to rhythmic activities; to melodies growing out of these rhythmic patterns; and to a simple harmony (Thresher, 1964).

Several early childhood educators have suggested teaching young children rhythm and movement in teaching music. Carl Orff's music is well-known for his creative treatment of rhythm, which he emphasizes in his educational music. His rhythmic element is natural, logical, and appropriate. Rhythm is the music component that is closely related to the human body. The children's development and refinement of rhythmic feeling is sensible (Frank, 1964). The rhythm of speech and movement motivates young children to explore music. Young children can develop rhythmic awareness; when they listen to natural speech, poetry, rhymes, and jingles, young children learn to determine rhythmic patterns. They can clap out the rhythms they hear and improvise movement patterns to follow them. Orff's approach to music education for young children had a basic premise that feeling is the main concern followed by intellectual understanding. Individual musical lyrics stimulate children to involve their imagination and enjoyment. Young children usually memorize several verses that have detailed song lyrics such as "I Know an Old Lady Who Swallowed a Fly" and "Supercalifragilisticexpialidocious."

The simple song "Old MacDonald Had a Farm" has a cheerful mood that encourages involvement. A tempo for the song can be placed in harmony. The lyrics propose a scene that young children can act out with ease. Different children can assume the role of various animals. Children can first accompany the rhythmic pattern of "Ee-i-ee-i-o" with body instruments (clap, stamp, knee-slap, snap). Children can express, discuss, and modify their ideas with their body movements, such as adding a finger snap at the second measure (after "o"). The original melody to "Ee-i-ee-i-o" may be used, but the children can create a different melody (Nichols, 1970).

## Playing Musical Instruments

Children learn that musical instruments are mainly to accompany singing and dancing or to illustrate poetry (Bacon, 1969). Instruments (such as the piano, autoharp, guitar) can be played to accompany the children's singing, although several music educators consider that instrumental accompaniment for singing with young children should be avoided. Several composers (Kodály, Dalcroze, Orff) contributed to music education for young children. For example, Kodály believed that human voices should accompany other human voices. Singing is basic and human, while the instruments are not alive in the same way as the voice or body. Usually when using instruments to accompany the children's singing, they want to play the instruments rather than sing (Bacon, 1969). The Kodály method proposes a consecutive technique where children sight sing, which helps them to understand musical notation.

Young children should be provided with opportunities to play a variety of musical instruments. They can engage in group playing, but young children should independently explore the use of musical instruments. A rigid pattern of music production needs to be avoided with young children. They need to experience activities with instruments that are of interest to them and that motivate them to test new ideas in sound. Even very young children need opportunities to explore and discover the importance of music through the use of instruments.

Children need to have the freedom to try out the instruments instead of requiring them to bang a specific rhythm. Drums, tambourines, rhythm sticks, maracas, and tone blocks are simple and appropriate instruments for young children. Simple tonal instruments need to be included with rhythm instruments except those where children place them in their mouth to play. Tone blocks in small sets, xylophones, marimbas, and tuned bells need to be made available for the children; they promote exploration of tonal and rhythmic relationships. Young children usually start to play simple tunes by themselves (Spodek & Saracho, 1994b). Orff believed that children should progress from hand rhythms (hand clapping, knee-slapping, stamping, finger-snapping) to instruments. Orff's music approach for young children provides an appealing collection of instruments such as several sizes of triangles, cymbals, and antique cymbals; various types of bells; coconut shells; tambourines; different sizes of hand drums (both one-headed and two-headed); wood blocks; rattles; castanets; the timpani and bass drum (Thresher, 1964).

Young children can make their own instruments. Simple instruments can be shakers made out of milk containers or plastic boxes containing beans or sand, where various items in the box create different tones to the shaker. Another appropriate instrument can be made out of sandpaper that is secured to wooden blocks that are rubbed against each other. Other instruments can be made out of numerous items that are lying around the house, no longer used and would be discarded (for instance, pot covers and automobile brake drums make percussion instruments). However, children need to experience commercially made instruments, because these instruments have a high quality of tone. Regardless of whether instruments are purchased or homemade, children need to treat them with respect.

Young children need to experience an assortment of instruments from several cultures and countries. Families can be encouraged to lend their instruments and demonstrate how to use them. These instruments can also be borrowed from music teachers or the music department of a local college. In addition to the instruments, photographs and maps that show each instrument's origin can be displayed in a bulletin board. The Diagram Group's (1997) publication *Musical Instruments of the World* is a source for ideas. Children will experiment with the instruments. They can compare and contrast the appearance and timbre (distinctive sound of a musical instrument) of the various instruments. Young children take pleasure in comparing the various ways to change the sounds of instruments (Kemple et al., 2004).

Musical instruments can be played along with the children's singing or movement to reproduce rhythmic or melodic patterns or to generate original compositions. They also offer a chance for children to experience free musical exploration. At times, just displaying instruments on top of a table can motivate young children to experiment with their sound. Occasionally children are able to extract patterns from the world around them (sounds such as someone running, the noise of the copying machine, noises in the streets). Children can replicate patterns of names, objects, or words in a story on a percussion instrument. When they listen to songs, they can abstract the meter or the accented beat and replicate it. Children can feel and create the shifts in tempo. Their individual explorations end up in playing in a group where children may play in harmony or in opposition to each other like in a dialogue.

When children play instruments, they should be told to concentrate on the range of sounds that each instrument can produce. For example, banging a drum with a hand has a different sound than if the drum is struck with a stick. The sound will differ when the drum is beaten in the middle than if it is struck at the edge. Children will learn to make a variety of sounds with the same instrument.

## Listening to Music

Children listen to the world around them and use its sounds to find out about their world. They also listen to the music components like pitch, intensity, rhythm, patterns, and themes. Listening to music helps children to:

- distinguish music and discover its mood, which provides them with the basis for singing or developing creative movement;
- become aware of different musical characteristics such as that music is loud, is soft; has fast tempo, is slow; has musical pitch that rises and falls; and
- understand and recognize the music components, design, and texture (Spodek & Saracho, 1994b).

Children can learn the different musical instruments and their sounds. Then they can learn the various families of instruments (e.g., brass, woodwind, strings, percussion) and the differences among the instruments in each family. Children can listen to recordings of musical compositions and concentrate on the different instruments as they look at pictures and charts of them. Live musicians can visit, play to the children, and answer their questions.

Young children usually listen to music actively where they respond to rhythm and melody through bodily movement, musical instruments, or voice. The children's active listening enhances their creative expression. The children's passive listening to music is similar to listening to a story. Class discussions improve their attentive and critical listening. Children can discuss their feelings when they hear the music and the types of activities that might evolve from the music they hear. They can also discuss the *uses* of music. For example, when children listen to music, they can relax, dance, make work easy, establish a mood, or listen to a story. For effective music listening, children need to listen to their favorite music and music with components that are most appealing to them. Creative movement experiences require children to respond and listen to music, which promotes their music listening.

Children can listen to music recordings, but they also need to listen to live musicians. Musicians can be invited to play to the class. Also talented teachers, parents, or older children can perform for the class. Several communities have local orchestras or groups that perform in schools. Young children can benefit from this experience. If the performance takes place with a large audience, young children should be taught "proper" audience behavior.

## Music Experiences for Children with Diverse Needs

In teaching music it is important to know the children's learning abilities. The musical achievement of children with disabilities is usually higher and has more depth than the teachers' expectations. Musical experiences assist them to develop social relationships. The basic music elements (singing songs, playing instruments, listening to music, rhythmic movement) can expand the possibilities for the children with disabilities. Music can attract children who are shy and withdrawn into a group; encourage children who are spastic to control their movements; and increase the vocabulary of English language learners (ELLs) through singing. ELLs use songs to learn vocabulary and speech sounds. When they sing repetitive refrains, they develop auditory discrimination, pronunciation skills, listening skills, and an awareness of language.

Children with an intellectual disability and orthopedic or physical disabilities are able to play in a rhythm band. A number of music pieces (such as "Shoemaker's Dance," "The Xylophone Dance," "Tambourine Waltz," "Drums of Parade") can effectively be modified for these children. When children with disabilities perform for others, they share a joyous and enriched experience.

The music goals for children with disabilities are the same as for typically developing children where they participate in all types of music activities, appreciate music, and develop musicianship. Children with disabilities can achieve these goals based on their capabilities and limitations. Edwards and Colleagues (2009) provide the following guidelines that apply to the musical experiences of children with disabilities:

1. Teach through creativity.
2. Teach through multisensory perception.
3. Teach at the appropriate developmental level and rate.
4. Repeat in a variety of ways.
5. Avoid drastic changes of gears.

6. Exclude distractions.
7. Provide instruction in small steps.
8. Offer success-assured activities.
9. Avoid overstimulation with too loud and/or rhythmic music.
10. Consider the children's level of social and language development.
11. Consider children's short attention span and/or other disabilities.
12. Repeat songs until children have learned them before attempting any variations.
13. Expect small successes; be ready for changes; be flexible.
14. Wait until the children have learned a song before accompanying it with instruments.
15. Share ideas with and seek them from others who work with and care for children with disabilities.

Since there is no competition, right, or wrong in music, children with disabilities feel comfortable. They enjoy singing songs about familiar persons or objects (names of family, pets), popular songs (such as "Happy Birthday," "Good Morning, I'm Pleased to See You"), and television jingles. They also like (a) singing nursery rhymes and action plays; (b) playing circle games; (c) listening to music that has humor or an element of surprise; and (d) singing songs with props (e.g., scarves, puppets), repetitive words or phrases, and directions.

## Children with Orthopedic or Physical Disabilities

Music experiences for children with orthopedic or physical disabilities need to be adapted to help them respond in any way they can (for instance, crawling, rolling over, clapping their hands). They can also listen to music, sing, hum, and play rhythm instruments. Rhythm activities allow them to sway to music, move their arms, and turn their bodies from side to side. During dance activities, they can watch, clap out rhythms, or have a peer move the wheelchair in time to music—back and forth, to the right and left, and in circles. Children with orthopedic or physical disabilities who are able to move their own wheelchairs can propel their wheelchair to the music.

Children with orthopedic or physical disabilities can watch gymnastic activities and use rhythmic activities at their physical therapy sessions. Rhythmic experiences can develop their muscles, coordination, and control. In a music experience, they can use instruments based on the degree of their coordination and ability to move. Children with gross motor skills can play drums or tambourines. Sand blocks, rhythm sticks, or sleigh bells can be used by tying them to the part of the body that children with orthopedic or physical disabilities can use.

## Children with Visual Impairments

Musical experiences for children with visual impairments also need to be adapted. These children are usually insecure and have poor coordination and poor balance in rhythmic movement. Rhythmic experiences can promote the mobility skills of children with visual impairments. In a music activity, they can use large movements, which become progressively refined. They can participate in rhythmic movements (e.g., rocks rolling, swinging, swaying, walking in the rain). Circle games (such as *Skip to My Lou, Looby Lou, London Bridge*) can develop their feelings of security.

The rhythmic ability of the children with visual impairments helps them understand and create rhythmic patterns that they can use with percussion instruments. During movement experiences, the class members can wear bells, tambourines, or other similar instruments with sounds to let the children with visual impairments know their classmates' positions and avoid crashing into them.

## Children Who Are Deaf and Hard-of-hearing

Children who are deaf and hard-of-hearing can listen and enjoy music when they use headphones or the music is amplified. They can also play and feel many of the musical instruments. Children who are deaf and hard-of-hearing can take pleasure in humming and clapping along with other children. They can detect the rhythmic sequence in several meters, clap or play instruments to replicate the patterns, and use movement to learn rhythms. The kinesthetic approach is an effective technique to teach rhythms.

Nursery rhymes help children who are deaf and hard-of-hearing acquire rhythm. They can also learn rhythm through tactile sensory perceptions, placing their fingers on a drum or another instrument playing the nursery rhymes. Much repetition is essential for them to feel the rhythm. In addition, nursery rhymes can also help the speech rhythm of children who are deaf and hard-of-hearing.

Children who have peculiar breathing patterns, poorly developed voices, and language problems have difficulty with singing. They can use movement or instruments to engage in rhythmic experiences. Children who are deaf and hard-of-hearing can develop their speech rhythm and bodily coordination when they participate in marching, hopping, skipping, and other strong rhythmic activities. Both movement and music experiences improve the ability, posture, and physical fitness of the children who are deaf and hard-of-hearing.

## Children with an Intellectual Disability

Music experiences that include rhythms create spontaneous interest, develop the listening skills, improve the attention span, and enhance the coordination of the children with an intellectual disability. After they reach the age of four, they are able to sing simple songs. They may have pitch problems, but they are usually able to listen for short periods of time to music that is of interest to them.

Children with an intellectual disability tend to be monotone singers, have short attention spans, lack auditory perception, and misunderstand their role in music, which can be improved when they engage in singing songs. They can learn simple songs when they repeatedly listen to them along with a variety of illustrative materials. They can learn songs (e.g., "I'm A Little Teapot," "Eency, Weency Spider") and different nursery rhymes when they are taught with colorful illustrations and movements, because these procedures strengthen the memory and concentration of the children with an intellectual disability. Action songs (e.g., "Row, Row, Row Your Boat") help them with moving their body, clapping, and brisk stepping to music. When they use large-muscle movements in action songs, children with an intellectual disability receive more reinforcement for their memory.

Musical experiences for children with an intellectual disability need to include playing instruments. Spodek and Saracho (1994a) recommend the following steps for playing musical instruments with them.

1. The children explore the musical instruments alone.
2. The teacher and a child play instruments together, labeling the sounds (e.g., "This is a drum—boom! This is a bell—jingle, jingle!").
3. The teacher asks the children to close their eyes and questions them ("What's this sound?" or "Is this a drum?").
4. The teacher taps a rhythm and asks the child to play that rhythm with her or him.
5. The teacher plays or sings a simple rhythm and then the child taps the rhythm.
6. The teacher plays increasingly difficult rhythms and asks the child to play them (p. 257).

Since the developmental rate for children with an intellectual disability is usually irregular or slow, their musical experiences need to be repeated in many different ways.

## Children Who Are Gifted

Children who are gifted need a music education that is challenging and appropriate to their intellectual levels. Their music experiences need to take into account the (a) characteristics of the children who are gifted, (b) practical and social situations, (c) organization of knowledge, and (d) current literature on these children's conditions of learning. One experience can be analyzing music. First children listen to a variety of recordings and discuss the musical elements that successfully communicated each work. They can discuss rhythm, music patterns, and instruments that contributed to the success of each piece of music. Then they can discuss a different musical genre (such as commercials, advertisements). Children can create and add music to an advertisement that is of interest to them. For example, a commercial about young children (such as the popular advertisement for Kelloggs) can stimulate the children's imagination. Then they might want to create a commercial (e.g., Burger King, cartoons) or advertisement (e.g., a classroom event, circus, children's museum) with music. The children create a melody (maybe 30 seconds long) for their advertisement. They can hum, whistle, or use instruments to test it. Throughout the process, children need to be encouraged to create music that is expressive and has rhythm to the beats and phrases of their advertisement.

## Children Who Have Linguistic and Cultural Differences

The children's identity is closely related to their families and culture. Music experiences for children who have linguistic and cultural differences need to integrate their language and culture. Audio tapings, music videos, and CD-ROMs that are based on these children's languages and cultures can be used. Teachers can integrate various cultural music activities into their classrooms, using music, songs, and dances. For example, the following are music experiences from two languages and cultures.

*Conjunto music* originated in South Texas and incorporates a distinct blend of different cultures. Children can be provided with a wide song selection of conjunto music. They can listen to recordings and view videos to introduce conjunto music to the children in the classroom. They can learn about and listen to the early recordings of music artists (such as Narciso Martínez, known as the father of conjunto music, and recent artists). They can listen to the songs and identify the stylistic characteristics of the instruments (for example, the accordion, bass, bajo sexto, drums). They can learn the songs and dance to the music, and role play being a band of conjunto musicians. The lyrics of the songs from conjunto music have been translated and can be found on several sites, such as the Smithsonian National Archive (see Smithsonian Global Sound at www.smithsonianglobalsound.org) (Soto, 2008).

*Korean folk music* can be introduced in the classroom. Children can learn and sing Korean folk songs. Children can easily learn "Pal Guen Dala" (Moon), which is a piece found on the album *Let's Sing Korean Folk Songs Together*. Children can listen to the different instruments (such as the taegum, a bamboo flute from Korea). Bowman (2008) recommends the following resources that are available in the United States.

- Michael Breen, *The Koreans: Who They Are, What They Want, Where Their Future Lies* (New York: St. Martin's, 2004).
- Mary C. Kimm Joh, *Folk Songs of Korea* (Dubuque, IA: Wm. C. Brown, 1950).
- Betty Warner and Thomas Choonbai Park, eds., *Folksongs of China, Japan, Korea* (New York: John Day Co., 1964).
- Byong-won Lee. 2003 Korean Traditional Music Workshop, "Social Aspect of Korean Music, II." Video retrieved from http://www.clickkorea.org/koreanstudies/learn10. asp?menubar=5.

It is important that teachers provide children who have linguistic and cultural differences with the opportunity to share the music that includes their language and culture. Several recordings, books, websites, and activities can be integrated into the classroom study of music to help children with linguistic and cultural differences better understand the language and culture of the other children in the classroom.

## Music Appreciation

Young children need to experience a balance of good listening activities to develop their musical appreciation. They need to be introduced to and encouraged to explore various kinds of music through informal exposure. The children's exposure to high quality musical literature improves their receptive and appreciative attitude toward different types of music (Edwards et al., 2009), including classical music.

### Classical Music

Classical music comes in many forms, but the most familiar are the symphony, opera, choral works, chamber music, Gregorian chant, the madrigal, and the Mass (Green, No date b). Specifically classical music relates to the music of the late 18th and early 19th centuries, but generally it is music that has stood the test of time and has exceeded the artistic standard (Funke, 2006). Classical music can be naturally integrated in the early childhood music program in many ways ranging from playing Bach's Preludes during quiet activities to marching around the room to the "March of the Toys" from Herbert's Babes in Toyland (Edwards et al., 2009).

Children's music experiences with classical music range from growing up in homes where classical music is frequently played and appreciated to growing up on a musical diet of rock-and-roll, rap, or "oldies." Young children have the capacity to listen to and enjoy sophisticated music. They need to be provided with opportunities to develop their musical experiences and the appreciation of classical music. The children's early participation with classical music promotes their enjoyment of music as a form of art and aesthetic awareness

(Cecil & Lauritzen, 1994). When young children are exposed to classical music, they add to their repertoire of musical experiences and musical expressions. Very young children respond sensitively to the music of great composers (such as Palestrina, Beethoven, Strauss, Prokofiev). They need to be introduced to great classical composers and their music to help them develop an appreciation for all music (Edwards et al., 2009). A good way to introduce them is through children's books that are usually displayed in art or music museums and found in bookstores. Examples of books that teachers can use to introduce classical music to young children are in Box 13.1, while Table 13.2 suggests ways to introduce classical music to young children (Green, no date a).

---

**Box 13.1. Examples of Books that Teachers Can Use to Introduce Classical Music**

- Koscielniak, B. (2000). *The story of the incredible orchestra: An introduction to musical instruments and the symphony orchestra.* New York: Houghton Mifflin Co.
- Sunshine, L., & Shange, N. (1994). *I live in music.* New York, NY: Stewart, Tabori & Chang, Inc.
- Venezia, M. (1995). *Wolfgang Amadeus Mozart.* Danbury, Connecticut: Children's Press
- Venezia, M. (1996). *Ludwig van Beethoven.* Danbury, Connecticut: Children's Press
- Venezia, M. (1998). *Johann Sebastian Bach.* Danbury, Connecticut: Children's Press
- Venezia, M. (1999). *Frédéric Chopin.* Danbury, Connecticut: Children's Press

---

**TABLE 13.2.** Ways to Introduce Classical Music to Young Children

| Method | Description |
| --- | --- |
| Listening to a Story with Classical Music | Young children can listen to a story as they listen to a classical music piece that corresponds to the story's emotion and actions. The story needs to be in time with the music. The same classical music should be played for each story. For instance, each time the children listen to *The Little Engine That Could* (Piper, 1930), it can be accompanied with Haydn's Symphony No. 94 (the upbeat rhythms of the second movement provide a dance feeling) |
| Interpret Classical Music through Dancing | Children can focus on classical music when they dance to their interpretation. The music can be combined. They can listen and respond to contrasting pieces of music. The children need to know the name of the piece, composer, and any relevant information to make it easier for them to remember the music |
| Identify Classical Music through Listening Games | Children listen to three pieces of music during the week. They identify the name of the song and its composer every time they listen to it. These pieces of music are selected from those musical pieces that the children know |

*(Continued)*

**TABLE 13.2.** *(Continued)* Ways to Introduce Classical Music to Young Children

| Method | Description |
|---|---|
| Listen to Classical Music during Play | Children can select classical music pieces and their composers to listen to while they play. When children select a piece of music, they can learn something about the composer. The young children will establish their personal classical music preferences and a basic knowledge of the composers. It is important that young children learn and select from a broad range of music |
| Interpret Classical Music during Art | Young children can listen to and interpret classical music when they are involved in art. They can listen to contrasting classical music pieces while they engage in art activities. They can listen to the music and draw the way the music makes them feel. When they finish, they listen to the music again and describe their art work. Children need to know the name of the classical music and the composer |

Several composers have created music pieces that are popular with young children. Some of these music pieces (*Swan Lake*, *Peter and the Wolf*, *Sleeping Beauty*) are described in Box 13.2 (Funke, 2006).

---

**Box 13.2. Music Pieces that are Popular with Young Children**

- *The Nutcracker* is a ballet suite by the Russian composer Tchaikovsky, who also wrote *Swan Lake* and *Sleeping Beauty*. The story is about the adventures of a 12-year-old girl and her nutcracker doll that magically comes to life. Young listeners are fascinated by this piece, because it has sword fights, fairies, and exotic characters. The music has a steady and upbeat tempo that causes it to be exceptionally danceable.
- *Peter and the Wolf*. Prokofiev's narrative is about Peter and his animal friends, who captured the wolf that was terrorizing the woods that surround his Russian farmhouse. This musical piece provides an excellent introduction to the timbre qualities of various instruments in the traditional orchestra.
- *Le Carnaval des Animaux* (*The Carnival of the Animals*) is a zoological piece that evolves from the first movement, *Introduction et marche royale du Lion*, through descriptions of elephants and donkeys ("Those with Long Ears") to a finale repeating many of the previous patterns. It is a 14 movement musical suite by the French Romantic composer Camille Saint-Saëns. There is a complete recording of all 14 movements by pianists Neil and Nancy O'Doan and the Seattle Youth Symphony conducted by Vilem Sokol.
- *Young Person's Guide to the Orchestra*. Benjamin Britten composed music that guides young children on a tour of the orchestra. In this tour, young children explore the sounds of each major section and are introduced to the way that the various instrument families work together to produce a full ensemble texture.

## Aesthetic Music Experiences

Children's aesthetic experiences represent artistic qualities, which orients them toward discovery. These experiences create a feeling of wonder and the facility to imagine, invent, and become creative. Young children's creative worlds provide them with a source of artistic beginning that is found in composers, performers, psychologists, and educators (Dewey, 1934). Cobb (1977) states that "the imaginative experiences of childhood could be found in the essential kernels of the highest forms of human thought" (p. 1).

Children focus on materials and human resources that are available in the environment. When they respond to such resources, children and artists become aesthetic agents and sensitive to both experience and the environment (DeNora, 2000). Play promotes the children's imagination and creativity (Singer & Singer, 1998). In Custodero's (2005) interviews, composers describe how these elements interact and are functioning in the musical play of children. Researchers support the importance of the preschool children's musical play.

## Music Play

Music education researchers show (a) that children develop musical abilities during their musical play (Smithrim, 1997), (b) the importance of musical play in the young children's development, and (c) several methods that offer and promote the children's musical play (Taggart, 2000; Tarnowski, 1999). Building on Piaget's developmental theory, Swanwick (1988) proposed that music represents play. Children who engage in play exhibit spontaneous behaviors that provide important information about them.

Play is a critical human characteristic that is inherently related to all artistic experiences such as painting, pictures, playing music, making and performing plays, and reading for pleasure. Piaget (1951) describes the children's basic progression that shows how they develop and understand their world. Play in early childhood relates to the absolute pleasure of exploring and mastering the environment, which Piaget refers to as "a feeling of virtuosity or power." This urge to master has an impact on the children's music experiences. In music the mastery components are considered when children manipulate voices and instruments, develop a collection of abilities and when appropriate, the children use notations or enjoy the virtuosity of others. For example, infants may achieve a mastery component when they experience pleasure after learning to repeat a vocal sound or to continuously shake a rattle (Swanwick, 1988).

Theorists (such as Piaget, 1951; Vygotsky, 1967) and researchers (such as Littleton, 1991; Moorhead & Pond, 1942; Taggart, 2000) support the notion of the children's need for play in music. Piaget first described cognitive play and identified three types of young children's play consisting of *practice play*, *symbolic play* and *games with rules*, which parallel his stages of intellectual development: *sensorimotor thought*, *preoperational thought*, and *concrete operational thought*. *Practice play* involves the infants and toddlers' manipulative play. *Symbolic play* is observed in the children's dramatic play. After kindergarten, children switch from dramatic play to playing more informal games. Later Smilansky (1968) modified Piaget's (1951) four types of cognitive play to study the preschool children's dramatic play. She described *functional play* as the routine or stereotyped use of play materials or basically a motoric activity. *Constructive play* characterized the sequential and purposive play that developed into a completed product. *Dramatic play* related to the thematic role play where situations or objects were transformed (Spodek & Saracho, 1994b). Specifically these types of play are defined below:

- *functional play* is when children run, jump, or repetitively manipulate objects to learn about their world;
- *constructive play* is when children manipulate objects to build structures or forms (e.g., painting, constructing with Legos, playing with sand);
- *dramatic play* is when children participate in role playing or the transformation of objects (for example, a child may pretend to be an adult or animal; a paper towel core may represent a microphone); and
- *games with rules* are activities where children create and/or use rules to set up play procedures (Tarnowski, 1999).

Littleton (1991) used three of Smilansky's (1968) types of play (functional, constructive, dramatic) to identify the children's music play behaviors. Young children engage in *functional* musical play when they explore vocal, instrumental, and environmental sounds. *Constructive* musical play goes beyond functional musical play, as when children explore with sounds and become aware of the music structure through patterns of rhythm, melody, tempo, dynamics, or tone color. *Dramatic* musical play is when children sing songs or play instruments within a music or nonmusic play theme. For example, four-year-old Peter introduced a dramatic musical play incident when he put on a cowboy hat, picked up a rhythm stick to use as a baton, and shouted, "I'm the conductor!" Children hurried to the instrument box to select an instrument to be able to play in Peter's band (Tarnowski, 1999). Table 13.3 compares Piaget's (1951) modified stages of cognitive play with those in music play.

**TABLE 13.3.** Piaget's (1962) Modified Cognitive Types of Play

| Cognitive Play | Cognitive Music Play |
| --- | --- |
| *Functional play* is when children run, jump, or repetitively manipulate objects to learn about their world | *Functional* music play is when children explore vocal, instrumental, and environmental sounds |
| *Constructive play* is when children manipulate objects to build structures or forms (e.g., painting, constructing with Legos, playing with sand) | *Constructive* music play goes beyond functional music play, as when children explore with sounds and become aware of the music structure through patterns of rhythm, melody, tempo, dynamics, or tone color |
| *Dramatic play* is when children participate in role-playing or the transformation of objects (e.g., a child may pretend to be an adult or animal; a paper towel core may represent a microphone) | *Dramatic* music play is when children sing songs or play instruments within a music or nonmusic play theme |
| *Games with rules* are activities where children create and/or use rules to set up play procedures (Tarnowski, 1999) | *Games without rules* are activities where children combine play and music, such as in Jack be nimble, Jack be quick, and Jumping Jack jumps up and down (Bridges, 1994) |

Young children find pleasure in playing games that they can combine with music. Numerous children initially associate games to music through movement. Games without rules can be part of music play (Maxim, 1997). Since young children learn mainly through play, folk songs that accompany action plays and games are a perfect repertoire. Songs and games present children with pitch and rhythm experiences while action play supports rhythmic reaction and imaginative play. When children listen to the songs and play games, they integrate new songs into their existing repertoire, which becomes the source for many of their musical creations and sound explorations (Turner, 1999).

Young children participate in various forms of musical play (see Box 13.3), which should be used in their musical play experiences (Littleton, 1998).

---

### Box 13.3. Forms of Music Play

- Co-operative musical play where children engage in sociable, interactive musical exploration;
- functional musical play where children explore the sound-making potential of a variety of materials and try-out different techniques;
- constructive musical play, an extension of functional play, where children explore creative improvisation and composition;
- dramatic music play where children combine music making with dramatic or pretend play;
- kinesthetic music play where children focus on movement or dance to playfully respond to music; and
- games with rules where children are involved in group-oriented, structured musical games such as singing games or clapping games (Littleton, 1998, as cited in Morin, 2001, p. 25).

---

Researchers observed the young children's behavior in play environments. Children had the freedom to self initiate their play and control the nature and direction of their play. Moorhead and Pond (1942) documented the children's self-initiated music play in a nursery school setting that displayed a range of instruments in an exposed environment. Their longitudinal 11-year study described the children's musical play experiences where preschool children played in a well-equipped and supportive environment.

Young children have a remarkable ability to respond to music when they are provided with a nurturing environment (Temmerman, 2000). The preschool children's musical behaviors emerge in a play environment. They explore sound by themselves and with others. During their music play, young children use statements, requests, gestures, and actions to express their needs to adults and other children. They need to be provided with appropriate materials in the play environment as well as with extended and continuous time for musical play (Berger & Cooper, 2003). In musical play three- and four-year-old children engage in (a) sound exploration, (b) long periods of absorbed activity, (c) teaching music to peers, (d) spontaneous games, and (e) unexpected ways of using music instruments. The musical play environment promotes the children's creative music making (Smithrim, 1997).

The characteristics of music play foster children's group activities (Taggart, 2000). In musical play, young children have the opportunity to explore, improvise, and create with sound on their own, which may be difficult in group music activities. In this case, group activities should be those that give the children opportunities to engage in music play (Littleton, 1991). Within group activities children should be "allowed to listen, watch, and musically explore as they wish" (Taggart, 2000, p. 24).

During musical play, children react naturally to music, lyrics, rhythms, and positive social interactions. Four- and five-year-old children engage in self-initiated music play. In a social and material environment children engage in music making (Dilkes, 1998). In musical play, young children participate in activities where they explore, improvise, and create with sound. Children focus on materials and human resources that are available in the environment. When they respond to such resources, children and artists become aesthetic agents and sensitive to both experience and the environment (DeNora, 2000).

## Elements of Musical Play

When preschool children play, they usually spontaneously sing or hum. Some of them have the need to hum while they are playing (Maxim, 1997). Children enjoy singing and playing. There is a relationship between music and play experiences, which are essential to the children's development. Musical play helps children establish an imaginary world that motivates their creativity. When children hear the music, they move their body the way they feel the music. They make up new words for a song. Children have a natural inclination to explore through play. In their musical play, children engage in music experiences that promote their inventiveness, imaginativeness, thinking, and expression. Very young children are able to invent their own music. Creative children usually enjoy music play, which prompts them to generate ideas and thoughts (Maxim, 1997).

Young children are naturally eager to engage in musical activities. Their favorite musical activity is moving. For example, a four-year-old boy commented:

> I like it best when I can experiment. Then I can be a galloping horse and sometimes go fast and crazy. One day I got tired and so I just moved some of my body slow, not all of it and I pretended to be a dinosaur. I like to make up dances (Temmerman, 2000, p. 56).

Music is a recurring element in young children's play and is reflected in their spontaneous singing, sound exploration, and dance. Many (Gluschankof, 2002; Littleton, 1998; Morin, 2001; Smithrim, 1997) acknowledge the value of play in the development of children's musicality. Children develop music abilities through exploration. Children who engage in musical play are more intensely involved in music experiences for long periods of time and have more diligence than when they engage in teacher-led group music experiences (Littleton, 1998; Smithrim, 1997).

In music play, young children move, dance, dramatize, or play instruments. They also participate vocally when they sing, chant, or make vocal sound effects and socially observe, imitate, lead, talk, and take turns with others. Young children also understand and emotionally appreciate the aesthetic perspective of music. They creatively participate in inventing or adapting lyrics, movements, or instrumental sound patterns. All of these music experiences are forms of play that help children to develop music knowledge and abilities (Niland, 2009).

Musical play also involves vocalizations, rhythmic movement of the body or objects, or playing instruments. Vocalizations are explorations of inflection and tone color (e.g., when children use a siren-like glissando or make high-pitched sounds to imitate wet boots squeaking on the floor), or rhythmic speech (e.g., when children repeat a rhythmic phrase such as saying, "no, no, macaroni" while they play with blocks), or songs. Children's songs are chants, original songs (may be nonsense syllables, regular songs, songs from a culture), standard songs, or song fragments. Song inventions develop both the children's language and their music abilities (Tarnowski, 1999). Movement is usually the children's first response to music, but movement also takes place in combination with the children's age group of their own music. When children walk, run, rock, or twist, they like to sing or speak in rhythm. They also like to rhythmically manipulate objects. For example, in a childcare center, Tarnowski (1999) observed

> a young boy playing with a farm set. As he sang a fragment of "Old MacDonald," he rhythmically moved toy cows, horses, and so on. Movement, or gestural representation, is also a part of instrument exploration. Repeating and stabilizing patterns of movement are as much a part of instrument playing as creating and recognizing melodic and rhythmic patterns (p. 28).

Four- and five-year-old preschool children prefer active music activities that involve movement and play. They strongly prefer free, unstructured playing activities where they have opportunities to explore, investigate, and produce their own sounds on different percussion instruments. A small group of these preschool children enjoy creating their own compositions. For example, a child said, "I like making sounds and listening to the sound and singing to the sound and dancing to my music." Another child said, "it's fun playing my loud and gentle sounds on the drum with my friend because I want to be in a band." These responses are typical of preschool children, who enjoy playing activities where they have the freedom to explore, create, and perform their own sounds and/or "compositions" on percussion instruments, because they get a feeling of accomplishment, ownership, and personal satisfaction (Temmerman, 2000).

## Compositions and Improvisations

Children can compose and improvise music during play. The following sections provide suggestions to encourage children to assume the role of composers and improvise during their play.

### Compositions

Young children are nurtured as artists, but they are rarely nurtured as composers. Composers use sound instead of paint to communicate their thoughts. Children may use a toy drum (usually with a dull sound). The kitchen cupboards have the most fascinating sounds (pots clang, pot lids ring, wooden spoons click). Pots differ in sounds that they make, which children can discover. Young composers need to learn that (a) sounds communicate ideas, (b) mixing long and short sounds create a bouncy feeling, (c) mixing ringing and clicking sounds make contrasting parts, (d) a pattern of strong and weak sounds produce a swinging or marching reaction, or (e) they control the loudness or softness of each sound (Kenney, 2007).

Kenney (2007) refers to the Anthropologist John Blacking's (1973) study on musical behaviors in Africa. She states,

> Blacking spent several years in Africa studying musical behaviors, particularly of the Venda. The Venda consider everyone musical. From Blacking's work I have an image of a young Venda mother responding to her toddler's banging on a pot by sitting down on the floor with the toddler, picking up another pot and making rhythm patterns along

8 Educational Perspectives

with the child. In such a setting, not only is the child learning about rhythm but he knows his sound-making is valued. He also begins to learn what ensemble playing is all about as he plays a duet with his mother. He will continue to explore sounds (compose) and his sounds will become more sophisticated as his mother continues to respond in positive, musical ways. Perhaps this pattern of toddler/adult interaction is why all Venda grow up musical (p. 32).

It is important to encourage promising young composers with an environment that cultivates their natural sound exploration. The young children's creative sounds need to be supported and they need to be viewed as young composers. Guidelines to encourage young composers to explore sound are in Box 13.4 (Kenney, 2007).

---

**Box 13.4. Guidelines to Encourage Young Composers to Explore Sound**

1. *Provide time and sources for sound exploration.* The classroom can have several areas besides the sound center for sound exploration. Young children need to have appropriate sound sources (such as traditional rhythm instruments, pitched percussion, pots and pans, and other resonating materials made out of metal, plastic, and wood). Schedule a daily time for children to explore with sounds.
2. *Observe and record musical behaviors.* Observe and record the children's musical behaviors to understand their compositional play. Children will range in their compositional abilities, from just exploring the sounds to keeping a beat on an instrument to creating short melodic or rhythmic patterns that they repeat over and over.
3. *Label and comment on their sounds.* The children's exploration of the different sounds need to be labeled with comments such as, "You are making sounds on wood (or metal, etc.)," or "Listen to the clicking (or ringing or swishing, etc.) sounds you are making," or "You made such high sounds, can you make low sounds, too?" The children's continuous beat or creation of motives can be labeled with comments such as, "You seem to really like to keep the beat," or "Listen to the musical pattern you just played. Can you play it again?"
4. *Become a member.* When children are playing instruments, the teacher can become a member of the group by playing a similar or a contrasting instrument. Playing should be spontaneous and fun by playing the beat or creating a rhythm. Children can play their own beat or rhythm and may sing as the group plays along. Discussing the composition can develop the children's vocabulary. The discussion can include words such as beat, motive, composition, duet, ensemble, band, and melody.
5. *Questions and comments develop the children's music concepts.* Asking appropriate questions and providing comments can develop the children's music concepts. Questions and comments can include
   - "What would it sound like if we made long and short sounds? It sounds like skipping."
   - "What if we play a pattern of strong and weak sounds in three? We could dance while we play to a meter of three."
   - "What if we play a pattern of four? We could march to a meter of four."

- "What if John played the drums first, then Jane played the bells, then John played the drums again. We could make a composition with the beginning and ending the same, and middle different."
- "What if John played his part softly and Jane began softly but ended louder?" (p. 33)

6. *Promote musical concepts in non music areas*. Children can experiment with many music sounds to accompany story reading or storytelling. For example, they can use (a) sounds on the wood block for walking, (b) a rain stick for falling leaves, and (c) a big drum with the fall of a cymbal or gong crash for chopping down a giant bean stalk.[1] Almost all fairy tales and picture storybooks can be embellished with music sounds.

7. *Record the compositions*. The children's compositions, unlike creative art, cannot be hung on the wall. However, they can be recorded. Children find pleasure in listening to their recorded compositions.

### Improvisations

A relationship exists between play and music composition and improvisation (Addison, 1991; Swanwick, 1988). Improvisation is when children act, sing, talk, respond, and create spontaneously to a stimulus in their environment and personal feelings. Their responses can be the creation of new thoughts, patterns, practices, structures, symbols, and/or behaviors. Improvisation can be viewed as an "on the spot" spontaneous activity. Improvisation abilities apply to a variety of forms of communication and expression in all artistic, scientific, physical, cognitive, academic, and non-academic disciplines (Shamrock, 1997).

Musical play develops the children's improvisatory and compositional behaviors in a different way than the ones that teachers direct for music experiences. The children's play should be integrated in their music experience to develop their improvisation and composition abilities (Custodero, 2005). Bruner's (1960) discovery approach to conceptual learning suggests that the different structural music components should be integrated into the children's musical experience. Then they can progressively learn each important component when they express and manipulate each one. Bradley (1974) tested Bruner's approach in relation to the total concept of music. Children participated in a one-year program of "total music experience." They were provided with opportunities to create their own music through improvisation, writing, playing, and listening to their own written music compositions. These children greatly improved their visual recognition, perception, and aural acuity because they engaged in active and creative experiences (Bradley, 1974).

## Developing a Play-based Music Program

A child-centered musical play curriculum supports young children's natural learning and development where music is completely integrated into the wider curriculum and the

---

1 Rain stick is a percussion instrument made from a dried cactus branch. It has a hole that is stuffed with small pebbles, and closed at both ends. When it is slanted, it produces a falling rain sound. Tribesmen from Chile used it in their ceremonies to ask for rain.

children's lives. They can participate in music in a variety of ways. They can participate in physical musical play when they move, dance, dramatize, or play instruments. Young children can participate in vocal musical play when they sing, chant, or make vocal sound effects. Children can participate socially when they observe, imitate, lead, engage in dialogue, and take turns with others. Young children can participate in cognitive music play when they interpret lyrics and emotionally show and interpret feelings and respond to aesthetic aspects of music. They can participate in creative music play when they invent or adapt lyrics, movements, or instrumental sound patterns. All of these forms of musical play can guide children into developing musical understandings and abilities (Niland, 2009).

A play-based music program needs to (a) include songs based on the children's interests and (b) permit a variety of playful responses. Children need to be provided with opportunities to select, adapt, and extend the songs; to explore sound, compose, improvise movement; and dramatize music experiences (Andress, 1998). Children need materials (such as audio and video recordings) that they can listen to and view to revisit their musical explorations (Niland, 2009). Addison (1991) studied children in a play-oriented music curriculum to identify properties mutual in both play and music, which consist of the following.

- Both are valued as a human activity.
- Both are essentially useful.
- Both play and engage in music for its own sake.
- Both are voluntary.
- Both provide pleasure.
- Both attract children to individually sing or play an instrument.

In a play-based, child-centered music curriculum for young children, the program's music elements will be the same with a different music approach that does not involve play. Children will continue to sing, move, and explore sound. They will also be provided with rich resources to help them experience a range of musical components and genres. Children will continue to develop awareness and abilities in singing and playing instruments. However, the music approach will differ. Children will collaborate with a repertoire of music experiences (Niland, 2009).

A play-based, child-centered music curriculum for young children can be designed based on the selection of materials and interactions with children. This play curriculum can consist of songs that relate to the children's interests and draws out a range of playful reactions. Young children need to select, adapt, and extend songs. They need opportunities to engage in musical play through exploration of sound, composition, improvised movement, and dramatic play. A play-based, child-centered music curriculum can use technology (such as audio and video recordings) to provide young children with opportunities to repeat their musical explorations (Niland, 2009).

In a music play program, children need a variety of rich resources to be able to experience the different musical components and genres. The children develop awareness and abilities in singing and playing instruments. A repertoire of music experiences needs to be planned in collaboration with the children based on their interactions with them and their responses during music play. Individual children will experience the music play program in their own unique way, but it should nurture their natural musicality to be able to become and continue to be music makers throughout their lives. Guidelines for a musical play program are in Box 13.5 (Niland, 2009).

**Box 13.5. Guidelines for a Musical Play Program**

- Children need to be allowed to share ideas and interests in selecting songs, instruments, recordings, and other music-making resources. They need to be allowed to share their interests, comments, and social interactions to make music an important part of the children's lives.
- Song selection needs to be based on the children's interests. They can be encouraged to develop new lyrics to a preferred traditional melody or to compose a new melody.
- Materials with illustrated song cards or books need to be provided. Children can select songs they would like on these cards and they can sketch them or photograph scenes that match their favorite songs. The children's versions or additions of lyrics can be written on the song cards.
- Learning stories (Carr, 2001) about songs and musical explorations can be developed through digital video, audio recording, and/or written on text to encourage children to revisit, reflect on, and extend their learning. Learning stories can be integrated into the song cards or books.

The play-based child-centered curriculum needs to be based on the children's ideas and interests, which should guide the selection of songs, instruments, recordings, and other music-making resources. In addition, the children's interests, comments, and social interactions need to be considered in developing such curriculum. For example, if children in a childcare center have a strong interest in whales, the teacher can initiate a number or activities under this theme. They can read, study, draw, paint, and create a two-dimensional model of a blue whale with hundreds of clear plastic milk bottles filled with blue water. The teacher can also compose a whale song that uses a call-and-response format and emphasizes the size of whales. The teacher can work with small groups to generate new verses about how whales eat, move, make sounds, and give birth. Some of the older children in the childcare center can use rhyme, meter, and rhythm to create the lyrics (Niland, 2009).

The music curriculum for young children needs to integrate the children's lives (Campbell, 2002), music, and play. Young children need to be provided with a musically enriched environment to encourage their musical abilities. It is important that young children explore their world in musical ways. In music, like in art education, the development of creativity is of critical importance. Young children need to be motivated to explore materials, tools, and media for a long period of time (Kolbe, 2007). They need to be provided with time to explore to help them develop their understanding of how to use the tools and materials (Kolbe, 2007). They also need to develop their thinking abilities through music making (Niland, 2009).

Young children need to be provided with opportunities to explore, play, compose, and improvise with musical instruments. A play-based environment that offers young children a range of "free choice" alternatives for them to engage in self-guided activity (Young, 2008) can be provided using music learning centers.

## Music Learning Centers

Young children need to be provided with opportunities to have the freedom to select, manipulate, explore, and experiment with objects that facilitate their learning. Many of the child-selected activities are provided in learning centers. During learning center time, children are free to choose from a range of developmentally appropriate activities. Children select the centers, materials, and activities to engage in music learning (Turner, 1999). In designing the music centers, it is important to consider:

- the purposes and possibilities of music in early childhood programs;
- the musical concepts and attitudes that young children can develop;
- the purposes and nature of music play;
- the ideas that introduce children to the joys of music.

Learning centers provide children with access to several areas in the classroom that are specifically designed to invite children to engage in music exploration.

Music centers need to be straightforward and display the highest quality of resources. Basic components for musical play centers are in Table 13.4 (Toth & Miranda, 1997).

**TABLE 13.4. Basic Components for Musical Play Centers**

| Component | Description |
| --- | --- |
| Something to do | An instrument to play or experiment with; cards or game pieces to manipulate; or something to write or draw |
| Something to listen to or move to | Pre-recorded listening examples |
| Something to learn about | Resources that introduce composers or instruments of the orchestra. Even simple matching games breed familiarity with musical subject |
| Something to share or take home | Tools for drawing, a CD recorder for recording onto a blank cassette, or materials from which to make a simple instrument |

## Materials for a Music Center

The music center can provide materials (see Box 13.6) for children to use in order to explore their world (Toth & Miranda, 1997).

### Box 13.6. Materials for the Music Centers

- *Musical and nonmusical instruments* that produce sound. Musical instruments need to be displayed in the music center. Children enjoy exploring nonmusical instruments such as rubber bands and cardboard tubes of different lengths.
- *High quality instruments* that (a) have different timbres, (b) are played in a variety of ways, and (c) represent various shapes and sizes. Children can make home-made instruments to stimulate their creativity.
- *Sturdy CD player designed for young children and blank CDs* can be used for individual recordings. Brief listening examples of both musical and environmental sounds can be included in these recordings.
- *Expressive movement props* (such as ribbons, scarves) can be displayed to encourage children to interpret music.
- *Books and recordings* that are appropriate for musical play that help children to learn about music.

> ■ *Resources* to introduce the instrument families, music and instruments from various cultures, and making homemade instruments.

This center can display music games and activities that allow young children to explore sounds. When young children explore sounds (1) they are able to discover the way the instruments' physical properties help to determine the sound it produces and (2) young children can mix and match several timbres. Homemade instruments and sound-producing devices can be provided. For example, five-gallon pickle buckets make excellent drums that are practically indestructible (Turner, 1999).

Children can also make and shake maracas. Paper plates, empty soda cans (with no sharp edges), plastic cups, pie tins, or paper towel rolls can be used. Materials (such as rice, sand, pennies, small jingle bells, marbles, beans) can be placed between two paper plates or pie tins stapled together. Alternatively, the materials can be poured into empty soda cans and tape fixed over the hole. Children can listen to everybody's maracas, compare the sounds, and identify the materials in their peers' maracas. A CD player and CDs with familiar songs can be displayed. Children might be encouraged to form a marching band and play the maracas to accompany a familiar recorded song (Kemple et al. 2004).

Music centers can be used to complement the units/themes that are being taught in the classroom. For example, the seashell center can encourage young children to listen to shells, to experiment with different sounds made with water, and to listen to Debussy's *La Mer*.[2] These centers will become more exciting for children and offer them opportunities for music learning when musical components, exploration of different cultures, seasons and holidays, transportation, zoo, farm, jungle, and other elements are added (Toth & Miranda, 1997).

Musical centers provide a perfect approach to cultivate children's spontaneous musical play. Music has a universal attraction that motivates young children to manipulate and experiment with musical paraphernalia that promotes their learning. An appropriately equipped music center communicates to young children that music is an essential and valuable component of life (Toth & Miranda, 1997).

## Dramatic Play Center

Young children can engage in dramatic play where they act out conducting and home life. The home life center can have rocking chairs and teddy bears. Young children can chant familiar finger plays (such as "This Little Piggy") and pretend the teddy bears are their babies. They can rock their teddy bear babies to sleep as they sing lullabies. Chanting familiar finger plays or conducting and singing lullabies assist young children to assume adult roles (Turner, 1999).

### Recording Studio

The dramatic play center can be a recording studio. Before setting up this center, children need to listen to stories about places where records, tapes, and CDs are recorded. A field

---

2 *La Mer*, which is French for *The Sea*, is an orchestral composition by the French impressionist composer Claude Debussy.

trip to a recording studio would be helpful. The center can be furnished with instruments, CD players, tape recorders, microphones, and other recording props. Occasionally the instruments can be changed to familiarize children with other musical genres (for example, jazz, country, classical). Markers and paper or software can motivate young children to make CD or audiotape labels. In this center children can explore the various instruments and record their sounds. They can listen to their recorded sounds and determine whether and how they can change their recordings. They can decide which instruments can be played alone, which to play together, and how to time the vocals. Children can later listen to their recordings with their classmates and family (Kemple et al., 2004).

### Musical Theater

The dramatic play area can become a musical theater by providing appropriate props (stage, costumes, instruments, seating for the audience, tickets, a real or pretend microphone). Prior to setting up this center, the concept of a musical show needs to be introduced. Children may have seen clips of a videotaped concert (such as Cathy and Marcy's Song Shop or Raffi on Broadway, or segments of a videotaped stage production). In this center, children act different roles (ticket seller, audience member, actor, musician, announcer). A guitar is a good instrument to include. Since a guitar pick is difficult to grasp and some children may need to develop their fine motor coordination, these children can substitute a pick with a rubber doorstopper, which will make a louder sound than a young child's finger strumming (Kemple et al., 2004).

## Non Music Centers

There are two types of music centers: music centers and non music centers. Music centers are those that only focus on music and have a specific music theme (singing, symbol, instrument, listening, drama). Non music centers (such as literacy, block, woodworking) that integrate music can also be considered music centers.

Music items that encourage music exploration can be added to non music centers. For example, a bell was placed on a cupboard in a kitchen center.

> . . . while "fixing dinner," five-year-old Jason picked up the bell and began singing "Jingle Bells" while ringing it. As he finished the chorus, he continued singing about the food he was preparing, creating his own little song.

Non music centers (see Table 13.5) can encourage music experiences with the addition of musical tools (e.g., a mallet, a CD player, resonator bells) (Kenney, 2004).

## Literacy Center

The literacy center can be set up in a quiet space in the room where young children can participate in quiet music activities. It can provide music books (see Box 13.7) to children in a large personal library that has picture books of familiar folk songs. Before placing these books in the literacy center, they need to be introduced and read to the whole class. Then children will be familiar with every book in this center (Turner, 1999). A variety of books can provide the children with a well-rounded knowledge of music genres.

**TABLE 13.5.** Non Music Centers

| Type of Center | Description |
| --- | --- |
| Book Center | Include picture song books and recordings of folk songs |
| Block Center | Leave mallets next to blocks |
| Playhouse Center | Add a CD player and recordings next to the dolls |
| Dress Up Center | Leave a CD player with classical music next to the dress up clothes |
| Doll House | Include tone bell steps to the house |
| Clay House | Children can create rhythmic chants as they roll or pat the clay |
| Woodworking Center | Include music with a strong beat such as the "Anvil Chorus" |
| Tree Branch Orchestra Center | Hang up instruments on branches of a tree or a hanging bar to test and explore instruments |

**Box 13.7.  Children's Books for Different Music Genres**

- *Sergei Prokofiev's Peter and the Wolf* by Prokofiev and Malone includes a fully orchestrated and narrated CD. Prokofiev's musical fairy tale is about a little boy (played by all the strings of the orchestra) who, with the help of a bird (played by the flute), outwitted the big, bad wolf (played by the French horns). The book and CD package allows children to see the story in the book and listen at the same time.
- *The 39 Apartments of Ludwig van Beethoven* by Jonah Winter tells the story of Beethoven and the five legless pianos on which he composed great works of music for the world.
- *The Girls' Guide to Rocking: How to Start a Band, Book Gigs, and Get Rolling to Rock Stardom* by Jessica Hopper tells how to start bands, write songs, get up on stage, and kick out the jams.
- *Sing Me a Story: The Metropolitan Opera's Book of Opera Stories for Children* by Jane Rosenberg retells the greatest operas at the children's developmental level. It gives children a clear understanding of plot, scene, and character.
- *Go In and Out the Window: An Illustrated Songbook for Young People* by Dan Fox is a songbook for young children.
- *Satchmo's Blues* by Alan Schroeder is about a boy who, on the hot summer nights in New Orleans, peeked under the big swinging doors of Economy Hall and listened to the jazz band. The world of New Orleans jazz is presented in this book as well as the young boy's experiences.
- *The Musical Life of Gustav Mole* by Kathryn Meyrick is about a baby mole who was born into a musical family. He and his animal friends begin a lifetime of learning pleasure.

A classroom with music centers will have noises such as the thump of a bucket drum, the crash of a tubular bell, children screaming out of enjoyment, instruments playing, children singing, children's conversations, and artistic differences. These are the sounds of young musicians who are discovering the beauty and joy of creating music both for themselves and with their friends.

## Summary

Musical experiences in the early years have a major impact on the children's later development and music interest (Temmerman, 2000; Young, 2003). Children's first five years are critical in their music development. The attributes of children's play have an impact on their learning and development, which encourages music educators to teach children music in a way that supports their natural learning and development by integrating music into their lives (Niland, 2009). The context and the circumstances are important in the types of music experiences, especially with young children. The importance of music in children's lives suggests that they should be provided with a musically enriched environment to draw out the musicality with which they were born. With young children music needs to help them to explore the world in musical ways. In music play, children communicate their ideas through different forms of expression including dancing, dramatizing, singing, exploring sound, drawing, and making things. In musical play, the children's music making is valued in its wider context.

When children engage in music play, they are motivated to continue their sensory, social, and imaginative ways of interacting with their world. First they explore the action of an object or person. Then they use this information to decide whether to interpret, re-create, or add to the original experience to be able to understand it. The children's responses to the musical prompt initiate newness through their sense of possibilities, using the available resources such as the mirror, the recording, the instruments, and the people in their environment to make it possible for them to imagine possible new interpretations (Custodero, 2005).

Play is essential to young children's involvement in their musical experiences and learning. When children play with music, they become involved in their world of make-believe. For example, Niland (2009) shared the incident below.

> "Let's go driving. Buckle up, start the car, and off we go. Where shall we drive today?" These are my words during a weekly early childhood music session as I give a laminated "steering wheel" to each child in preparation for the next song. Missie, age 3 1/2, grabs her steering wheel enthusiastically and begins to sing "driving, driving, a car, shopping, shopping, a car." She is only approximating the lyrics, but her sol-mi (falling minor third) is as perfectly in tune as any Kodály music educator could hope for. Missie's mum and I are amazed, and we both compliment her on her beautiful singing (p. 17).

This experience is important to Missie. The teacher had noticed in the classroom that children had a strong interest in cars. Each time the teacher handed out the steering wheels, the children would "drive" off around the room usually making engine and car horn sounds. The teacher planned the children's music experience based on their interest in transportation. Children tried "driving" in various directions, following, driving alongside, or moving ahead and pretending to have a passenger (Niland, 2009).

Music in early childhood education should allow preschool children to experience, enjoy, and relax with music. It should also develop their music abilities, skills, and knowledge. Music experiences provide young children with another way of expressing themselves. They also motivate young children to like sound, play instruments, and move with rhythm. The children's music interests and abilities are closely related to their initial music experiences (Denac, 2008). Five-year-old children's level of expressing interest in music is based on their ability to actively engage in music activities, which increases their interest in individual music activities (Temmerman (2000). Younger children are more interested in music activities than older ones (Bowles, 1998). Therefore, it is essential that young children be provided with a variety of musical experiences in an environment where they learn through active exploration in meaningful music activities. It is inappropriate to consistently have all children participate in the same music experience at the same time. Music learning should go beyond group activities, which are one element of the music curriculum. Young children need to engage in child-centered music learning where they are provided with an appropriate amount of time to create and interact with music in their own way.

Music centers can be used to extend the children's learning beyond group activities. Music centers are essential for the children's musical, social, emotional, and cognitive development. Music centers are not a frill, but they provide a way for children to learn; they are an essential element in the children's learning. Young children will develop abilities in the music centers that will last them a lifetime of active musical participation. In general, young children need to be provided with opportunities to direct their own learning in the music centers that have child-selected activities. Music centers are perfect in helping meet the children's individual developmental needs. An early childhood music program needs to allow young children to engage in (1) self-selected activities, (2) individual and small-group interactions, and (3) developmentally and educationally appropriate musical activities (Turner, 1999).

Music is a communicative and expressive art, loaded with opportunities for children to explore, improvise, and create. It is the ideal situation to acknowledge and promote young children's natural play (Tarnowski, 1999). In music play, the children's natural curiosity and desire to understand their world guides their learning experiences. Young children know their needs, which they communicate during their interactions with others. In music play children control their learning experiences at their own pace (Turner, 1999).

# Chapter 14
# Art-play Learning Experiences

Every child is an artist. The problem is how to remain an artist when he grows up.

Pablo Picasso

For more than four decades, art education in the United States has gone through several paradigm shifts ranging from creative self-expression movement, the discipline oriented movement, and lately the visual culture movement, which (possibly) is still in process (Tavin, 2010), and may have affected children's art education. Presently both art and early childhood educators are suggesting that art be integrated into children's play.

Schools usually neglect play, but it is extremely helpful in the children's art experiences. "The open and relaxed state of mind needed for making art derives from a sense of freedom to do whatever one likes to do. For adults, play is restricted to leisure time. For children, it is an integral part of working" (Szekely, 1983, p. 24). Artists continuously play with all objects in their environment such as paint or clay. Children play everywhere, at any time, and with everything in their surroundings. "Play is a way of research for both artist and child, allowing them to approach everything as if new and to work out any unknown or interesting idea" (Szekely, 1983, p. 24). In play children learn through experience, which is considered the most effective way for young children to learn. The purpose of this chapter is to describe artistic play, developmental stages in art, art media, play art environment, and children's understanding of classic works of art.

## Artistic Play

Art reflects children at play. A play experience is intrinsically motivated (doing for the sake of doing), freely chosen, pleasurable, spontaneous, flexible, and actively engaged both physically and psychologically, which are the characteristics of artistic play. Children's art has a fresh, spontaneous, and flexible quality. Art also supports children's play as they learn to cooperate, to share, to delay gratification of their impulses, and to imagine themselves assuming other people's roles. Art, like in play, promotes children's social, emotional, physical, and intellectual development. Art activities support their personal characteristics including persistence, self-confidence, independence of judgment, flexibility, openness to new experiences, tolerance of ambiguity, and even a good sense of humor.

Creative children become playfully curious about their world. Play should be emphasized to encourage children to test innovative ideas and become creative. During play, young children are not required to adhere to rules, regulations, and preconceived art functions. They are free to follow their own imaginations, to plan and challenge their work, to explore art methods, and to create impressive original art works. Teachers can motivate young children to behave like artists and create art works from within themselves instead of the teacher. Teachers can encourage the children's spontaneity, creative expression, and independence as they explore art techniques (Szekely, 1991).

## Playing Roles of Artists

Role playing in the arts helps children learn with meaning and helps them to learn the roles of people as they assume their roles. Young children pretend to be an artist and begin calling themselves "artists." Professional artists who talk to young children use this label by saying, "Now as artists, you . . .," or "As artists, we know . . ." The label will differ based on the artist (such as dancer, actor, painter, film maker) they are learning about. When the children assume an identity, they better learn the information of the artists in that profession and accept the rules of "the artistic community," which is the artistic term the community arts organizations use. When children assume the role of the artist, they become members of that artistic community and learn the elements and sets of abilities that artists need in their profession.

In the arts, the children's position toward a related situation is observed in the extent of their participation, cooperation, or observation. Members of the artistic community also suggest that children engage in "think time," "head space," or "breathing room." Young members of community arts organizations stress this position. They learn about the artists and their role and decide with their group how they are going to play their role. Assuming the type of role that Heath (2004) proposes requires the young artists to prepare through planning, practicing, and rehearsing for their artistic performance. Young children consider that within the arts learning is "play." They may say, "It's fun, just fun; sure, there's lots of hard work, but we're all in it together . . ." (Heath, 2004, p. 340).

Artists face problems that need to be solved. Children can anticipate situations that may affect their role. Kindergarten children can have a mini performance. In a few sessions they can plan and develop a story into a performance, and create and adapt a story using their own words and ideas. They can offer a mini performance and use their classmates and families for an audience. Since children become performers and bring the story events to life, they become "stars" (Morado & Koenig, 1999). Each mini performance works better with six to eight children.

Artistic play differs from other kinds of educational play in the classroom. Specific physical settings, materials, and teachers' actions relate to aesthetic expression and inquiry (Pitri, 2001). Artistic play needs to be flexible and spontaneous. "The spontaneity with which children turn art into play does not mean that specific planning for art need not take place" (Van Hoorn et al., 2011, p. 109). An artistic play environment allows young children the freedom of choice, a wide range of materials, and access to many tools. Children use their own experiences to create their art work rather than following the teachers' directions; they discover and plan on their own. In artistic play young children have the opportunity to absorb, examine, modify, restate, or even reject ideas (Pitri, 2001). The premises for art and play are found in Box 14.1 (Szekely, 1991).

---

**Box 14.1. Premises for Art and Play**

- All children are artists, born with the natural ability to observe, create art ideas, and complete their own works of art. For young children, play and art are integrated and foster the children's creativity.
- A playful environment influences the children's own ideas, sensations, and feelings to create art.
- Children's art experiences need to focus on the qualities of real materials within their environment instead of techniques to generate reflections of real objects.
- The best art depends on movements that stem from both mind and body. Children should be allowed to freely move in the art classroom to explore new movements, media, and subjects for expression.
- Art teaching needs to focus on the artistic spirit in every child. The art teacher provides situations that inspire the children to create their own ideas for making art.

---

Everybody needs to enjoy and appreciate art. Opportunities for art are everywhere including in the children's home, in their daily lives, and in their contacts with everyday objects. Art is a universal language that exists in all the cultures. Its organization and content communicate meaning without using words. It also relates culture to the time and situation where it occurs. Art provides children with a unique sense of cultural identity (Szekely, 1991).

Art related play for young children needs to offer open-ended activities which allow them to communicate their ideas based on their own experiences. Open-ended art experiences do not have a right or wrong way of functioning; therefore, there are no correct end results. The children's art experiences reflect the group's diversity where children are free to express their own narratives. Children engage in art experiences that have meaning and allow them to interact with their peers by observing and talking about each other's art (Thompson, 2005).

## Developmental Stages in Art

Children's art is fresh with a spontaneous quality that is easy to appreciate but difficult to explain. The children's developmental stages in art help teachers understand a child's artistic development. These stages help teachers establish a series of benchmarks that they can use to guide the children's learning. Teachers can use information about a child's developmental stage to provide art experiences that can lead them to a higher stage of using art media to express their ideas. Understanding the stages can help a teacher set developmentally appropriate expectations for children. These stages can be used to interpret the children's art products and plan a useful art program. Learning can be promoted by assessing the children's work and using this assessment to plan their art program.

Children's art products can guide the teacher in planning the children's art program and help them to progress from their present stage to a more mature one. For example, preschool children may have difficulty creating representational paintings and drawings, while kindergarten children may have difficulty drawing all objects shown in proper size and understanding their relationship to one another.

Levels of artistic development have been identified as being similar to those of intellectual development (see Table 14.1). Victor Lowenfeld (1957) describes a scheme of stages in the artistic development of children. In his scheme, the levels of development for young children consist of the *scribbling* stage (ages two to four), *preschematic* stage (ages four to seven), and *schematic* stage (ages seven to nine).

Between the ages of two and four, children in the scribbling stage have a kinesthetic experience through drawing. They move through longitudinal, then circular motions, becoming more coordinated as they mature. Children first experiment with materials, then find likenesses and differences within their drawings to objects in the real world, thus coming up with "names" to give to the drawing.

Between the ages of four and seven, children in the preschematic stage discover the relationships between drawing, thinking, and reality. Although a continuous change occurs in the symbols created in drawings, children start out with an idea of the objects they want to represent. They begin to draw in the picture representational forms that differ from reality. They are also developing form concepts.

**TABLE 14.1.** Lowenfeld Children's Developmental Stages in Art

| Stages | Ages | Characteristics |
|---|---|---|
| Scribbling | Two to four | a. *Disordered:* drawings show uncontrolled bold or light markings. Children have limited control over motor activities. |
| | | b. *Longitudinal:* drawings show controlled repetitions of motions. Children have a visual understanding and enjoy kinesthetic movements. |
| | | c. *Circular:* drawings show an exploration of controlled motions. Children seem to have the ability to draw more complicated forms. |
| | | d. *Naming:* drawings indicate a kinesthetic thinking ranging from movement to imaginative thinking. Children narrate stories about their scribble |
| Pre-schematic | Four to seven | Children draw human figures by sketching a circle with two dangling lines for legs. They usually make small marks inside the circle for facial features and draw a rectangle for trunks of bodies |
| Schematic | Seven to nine | Drawings indicate the children's thoughts rather than their actual observations. For example, they may draw a person riding a horse where both legs are showing, even if only one can actually be seen. They become aware of the concept of space. There is a spatial relationship in their drawings. Drawings of shapes and objects can be identified, although there is an exaggeration in their figures (e.g., humans are taller than a house) |

When children move to the schematic stage, between seven and nine, they begin to create realistic representations of people and things. They portray realism, color, space, and movement in pictures. The children then move on to more mature stages of artistic development.

Lowenfeld (1957) foresaw young children's developing abilities to create visual images of personal meaning in relation to artistic languages and knowledge. They are also able to critique the forms of the culture in which they live—both popular and traditional. Lowenfeld's stages provide guidelines that suggest a continuous artistic development in children starting in infancy and continuing into adolescence. His stages suggest that the baby in the carriage who is able to hold a crayon is ready to begin early drawing.

The children's early symbols document their "body action" (Matthews, 1984, p. 38). These are spontaneously made at the same time across cultures by both sighted and blind children. The children's drawings may be made on paper, sand, or even smeared on wet surfaces (Veale, 1988). According to Matthews (1984), "play . . . is a crucial component in the development of drawing," which continues because "Drawing, as it emerges, is assimilated into the area of play" (p. 38). The sequence in the emergence of spontaneous scribbling becomes drawing, because the children's playful exploration of the medium leads them to perceive its symbolic transformation. After the children have developed their perception, they become aware of the visual characteristics of the content (Golomb, 1974). Then "children begin to notice images" (Smith, 1982, p. 43) in their drawings. At this point, children will continuously repeat the new image and ultimately continue to explore the boundaries of their abilities.

Research on art related play reports that children begin drawing during infancy when they develop their sensory and perceptual systems and continue developing their artistic abilities throughout their life, which helps teachers understand the children's creative process. In considering the "parameters of stretching play in the context from its possible influence on the development of the creative process" (Veale, 1998, p. 111), it becomes apparent that play is the most natural medium in fostering the children's development in art.

The children's art develops as a result of their play. Three principles for an art program and its resources for young children are found in Table 14.2 (Arts Education Partnership, 1998).

**TABLE 14.2.** Principles for an Art Program

| Art Principle | Description |
| --- | --- |
| Child | Children should be encouraged to learn in, through, and about the arts by actively engaging in the processes of creating, participating in/performing, and responding to quality arts experiences, adapted to their developmental levels and reflecting their own culture |
| Arts Experience | Arts activities and experiences, while maintaining the integrity of the artistic disciplines, should be meaningful to children, follow a scope and sequence, and connect to early childhood curriculum and appropriate practices. They also may contribute to literacy development |
| Learning Environment and Adult Interactions | The development of early childhood arts programs (including resources and materials) should be shared among arts education specialists, practicing artists, early childhood educators, parents, and care givers; and the process should connect with community resources (p.2) |

In addition, the Arts Education Partnership (1998) identified the children's developmental benchmarks and stages (see Table 14.3) to use as a guide in using appropriate art activities.

The developmental benchmarks and stages described here can assist early childhood education programs to select arts-based early childhood programs and resources. The guiding principles are used as a basis in identifying examples of activities, programs, research, and resources. It is important that early childhood and arts education practitioners

**TABLE 14.3.**  Children's Developmental Benchmarks and Stages

| Age of Child | Art Experiences |
| --- | --- |
| Birth to three months | Stimulate eye movement and auditory development through contrasting images (such as black and white or colored objects) and voices (speaking or singing)<br><br>Increase awareness of space, movement, and sound by hanging mobiles, playing soothing music, and making animated faces. Babies discover that they can change what they see, hear, and touch |
| Three to eight months | Continue previous experiences<br>Encourage recognition of aspects of the environment through touching objects, listening to the names of the objects, and observing its uses<br>Use appropriate soft and colorful materials for babies to touch (such as blankets or toys) |
| Eight to 18 months | Continue previous experiences<br>Explore shapes and colors of everyday objects (such as clothing, cereal boxes, etc.)<br>Hang pictures at eye level. Name, describe, and point to items in the pictures<br>Provide opportunities to explore safe and appropriate media in visual arts (e.g., finger painting with water, drawing with crayons) |
| 18 to 24 months | Continue previous experiences<br>Have children make aesthetic choices (such as what color to paint the sky)<br>Provide activities with items as simple as a paper plate, nontoxic paint, and play dough<br>Supervise children as they experiment with materials<br>Take children to visit museums and appropriate child-friendly exhibits |
| 24 to 36 months | Continue previous experiences<br>Make arts-based activities a daily routine<br>Identify shapes, textures and colors in food and clothing<br>Use drawing and painting to promote several concepts such as light and dark<br>Develop hand–eye coordination with activities such as string beads or drawing on paper<br>Help children to use brushes and paint<br>Help children mold objects with clay<br>Take children to visit museums and appropriate child-friendly exhibits |
| Three to four years | Continue previous experiences<br>Have children cut with scissors<br>Make collages using paper, glue, scissors, and magazine cut outs<br>Allow children to choose by providing a variety of art materials such as clay |
| Five to eight years | Display the children's art work<br>Create scrapbooks or portfolios of the children's photographs and art work |

share current knowledge about the children's needs, the nature of their development, and the role of the arts in their lives. The statements provide guidance in selecting the most developmentally appropriate experiences for infants and young children. It starts from a baby's first lullaby, to a three-year-old's exploration with finger paint, and to a seven-year-old's dramatization of a preferred story. Art experiences must be developmentally appropriate. Art is critical for children of all ages and can be used naturally in the children's play to foster their learning and development.

## Art Media

Play allows children to engage in art experiences that are pressure free. The element of playfulness that marks the artist's creative qualities helps children generate new ideas and prolong the freedom to plan and carry out works of art. Children's imagination thrives on play that helps them create thoughtful and exciting art works of their own. When play is used in children's art, they draw ideas from their own experiences using a personal perspective.

Play is essential before and during the art making process. Children need to plan their art work where they manipulate materials and ideas and where they experiment with movements and images to decide the direction that their work will take. In developing plans, children need to learn to select the materials and space for their project to recognize possible solutions to an artistic challenge. They also need to select the kind of medium that they will use for their project. As children keep track of their play generated ideas and select from them, they begin to see the possibilities in the creation of their art project. Play allows children to generate various visions and ideas to discover beautiful color, space, lines, and interesting objects that they can use in their art. Play becomes a means of observing and rehearsing so that a better informed use of these elements can be made (Szekely, 1983).

Play offers children the opportunity to learn and develop, refine, and test their ideas. According to Jones and Reynolds (1992),

> Young children learn the most important things not by being told but by constructing knowledge for themselves in interactions with the physical world and with other children—and the way they do this is by playing (p. 1).

When children play in art, they experiment with a variety of media and materials. The following examples illustrate how children engage in play through art.

> A three year old sponge painting on sheets of newspaper, experimenting with different colors; young children adding a drop of food coloring to a bowl of water; children blowing through a straw into a puddle of paint or splattering paint with a toothbrush (Thompson, 2005, p. 4).

> Aaron is busily playing with a large lump of clay. He pounds it repeatedly against the table, then pulls off a large piece, breaks it into several small pieces and rolls them into balls. He soon grows tired of rolling, and so he flattens the balls into pancakes, which he distributes to each of the other three children seated at his table. Later he collects his pancakes and stretches them into hot dogs. Then he rolls them into balls again. Next he takes some of the balls, breaks them in half and makes smaller balls of the

broken pieces. Finally, when he begins to tire of the clay, he rolls the balls together in the following manner: First, he combines two small ones into a larger one; then he repeatedly adds another ball to the growing mass until he has a fairly large lump, which he proceeds to join to the original lump of clay that the teacher had given him (Hughes, 2010, p. 178).

Play with a variety of art media helps children understand the concept of what art is and what art can be made from. The manipulation of the different media helps children understand that the range of appropriate materials for art making is expanded. Golomb (1974) made the parallels between play and art in her statement, "Thus, in their origins symbolic play and the visual arts seem to share a number of characteristics. Representation begins with the child's playful exploration of the medium and its symbolic transformation, and comes increasingly under the domination of the visual attributes of the object, recreating its structural and dynamic characteristics" (p. 186).

Children need to be provided with a broad variety of art-making materials including reusable resources. Many art and play materials can be those that are disposed and donated by local businesses. Reusable materials include fabric, yarn, foam, plastic modeling, gold and silver Mylar, paper products, wood, wire, and a world of other reusable materials. Many businesses dispose of unwanted products, overruns, rejects, obsolete parts, and discontinued items. They pay an expensive fee to dispose of them or toss them in landfills and incinerators. Teachers can obtain reusable resources that can be used for art and creative play from a local Reusable Resource Center (see www.reusableresources.org).

The art media include a wide variety of materials that promote young children's creative processes in their art. Basic art materials such as paints, clay, and drawing and collage material are essentially shapeless and provide unlimited possibilities for modification, mastery, surprise, and self-reflection. Small drawing paper is needed with colored pens and pencils, whereas large drawing paper is needed with blunt instruments such as crayons and brushes. Young children need to have familiar and new experiences with materials that help them develop competency and continue to conceive brand-new possibilities in these media. Although the materials represent a spin-off of increased mastery and the more mature stage of artistic development, teachers need to introduce them in new ways throughout the years. Art media for young children consists of two- and three-dimensional art work.

## Two-dimensional Art Work

Most of the young children's art experiences consist of materials on a flat surface. Paints, crayons, and collage materials are used with only a single plane. Collage has an overlaying of various materials and textures that give the art some depth, but the children's art focuses directly on line, shape, and color.

### *Painting*

Painting is an engaging activity and essential in the early childhood education curriculum. In early childhood settings, painting plays a crucial role in extending art activities, although it has its own purpose and values. Young children like mixing paints and making brush strokes. This pleasurable experience establishes a basis for future aesthetic appreciation.

These vigorous painting characteristics enrich young children's learning through art (Lim, 2004; Schirrmacher & Fox, 2011). It is important to maintain painting activities in the art center to promote their aesthetic development.

Painting is usually a free exploratory activity. Teachers set out paint and paper for the children to freely express themselves. Painting can be extended by providing children with the opportunity to experiment with different textures such as sawdust, sand, flour, salt, or liquid soap. Plastic or Styrofoam meat trays and pie plates can be used as containers for these items. When children are provided with a piece of paper, a color of paint, and a brush, they can experiment with several materials to create a picture. For example, teachers can add materials (e.g., glitter) to the paint before painting or sprinkle the material on the paper after printing. Children can also paint with different tools such as rollers, a whisk broom, straws, marbles, or strings. For example, for string pictures, children can dip the string in paint and drag it or drop it on the paper. They can blow paint through a straw to create a pattern on the paper. The teacher's role in painting is (a) to encourage young children to explore the media, (b) to monitor their progress, and (c) to guide their artistic development by introducing new methods that match their developmental needs.

### Finger Painting

Finger painting is usually hard for children to control, but it helps to free their tension more than any other medium. Finger painting is better when applied to glazed shelf paper or glossy nonabsorbent paper that is sold in school supply houses. Children can paint on the plastic surface of a table. When they have completed such a painting, the children can make a print by carefully putting a paper over the painting, pressing it down tightly all over, and carefully picking it up.

### Tempera Painting

Tempera painting is an independent activity. Since the children's work is separated, they do not need to interact, even when two children paint together at an easel. However, children enjoy painting next to each other or in groups. A double easel, the floor, or mural painting encourages painting as a group activity. Tempera paints can be used in either powdered or liquid form. Primary colors (red, blue, yellow) as well as black and white should be available for young children. Later intermediate colors can be added. Powdered paints need to be mixed thick enough to make the colors look bright and the paint opaque. Paint brushes that are large and stiff need to be provided to facilitate the children's movement. Children also need to experiment with different sizes of brushes. They can paint on unprinted newsprint, newspaper, or wrapping paper with small designs. The standard size of the newsprint is 18-by-24-inches; but different sizes, shapes, or even textures of paper can lead children to find new ways of painting.

Children can experiment mixing the colors on a cookie sheet palette to find new shades or colors. They experiment with form and color, moving their own arms to spark the shapes on the paper. The children's experiments usually have rhythm, balance, and interest. They seem to possess an instinctive aesthetic feeling and their abstract paintings at times are similar to those of real artists. Children enjoy the tempera painting activity shown in Box 14.2.

**Box 14.2. Magazine and Tempera Pictures**

The teacher needs to carefully wash Styrofoam meat trays with soap and water to remove any residue from the meat. After the meat trays have dried completely, children can paint them with tempera paint (a second coat may be necessary). Painted trays need to dry for at least a day. The next day, children can cut out pictures from magazines and glue them onto the painted tray. The teacher attaches yarn to the top of the tray for hanging (Spodek & Saracho, 1994b, p. 463).

Young children need to be provided with the opportunity to explore and experiment. However, they need to learn how to use the materials correctly, as follows::

1. Wipe the brush to avoid having an excess of paint on their brush.
2. Clean brushes before dipping them in other colors.
3. Mix colors in fixed quantities for best results.
4. Dip the right brush into the matching container of paint, although accidental dips can provide a color mixture that can lead to an exciting discovery.

Most early childhood classrooms make an easel accessible for the children for most of the day. The top of a table or a small portion of floor space is just as good. The level surface limits the amount of dripping that falls during the painting. The art area should be arranged to make the cleanup as simple as possible. Children need to spread papers under the painting and have access to sponges and paper towels. Paints must be kept in containers that can be covered so that the art work can continue with a relative degree of administrative simplicity. The easel can be set up with five basic colors including red, yellow, blue, black, and white. There should be more white and yellow because these colors get dirty quickly.

*Electronic Painting*

Since the classroom environment is full of electronic and digital interactive devices, young children are experiencing the formation of very different developmental pathways. Their environment and playground have entries to electronic and virtual worlds in the form of television, digital still and video cameras, play stations, cell phone cameras, and computers. The appearance of electronic information technology and electronic digital interactive devices provide children with additional tools and playthings. Young children are able to transfer their mark-making media patterns across media areas. For example, young children can shift the representations and expressions that they make with pencil and paper technologies to electronic and digital media.

Through drawing young children sense that the marks and shapes they make on paper relate to events and objects that are part of the real world or may be part of the imaginary world (Stetsenko, 1995). Children are able to paint electronically. Matthews and Seow (2007) show how children can use a drawing and painting device utilizing mouse-driven computer painting programs. They studied the children's use of electronic and digital media (such as a camcorder and mouse-driven computer paint box). They had previously had the children use physical media such as ready-made objects, junk materials, and especially physical pigment and physical writing and drawing materials (pencils, pens, paper). Then they describe how young children (aged two to six) can use microcomputer paint box programs where they use a mouse-driven microcomputer and simultaneously coordinate at least three different motor-devices: (1) press the button on the mouse, (2) move the mouse, and (3) watch the screen. When children draw on a piece of paper, they directly and immediately make a mark, a trace, or a shape. In pencil and paper media, the marks in a drawing correspond (of course) spatially and visually to the marking actions made. In contrast, when children draw on the screen, their actions and visual trace are not direct or immediate. The drawing surface is separate, but it is next to the visual-display surface. Although the experience of drawing and painting with the mouse-driven computer paint box differs from drawing or painting with physical colors, young children are able to transfer several developmental principles across media areas. Children were able to virtually draw on the screen of a personal computer. They were told that this was a special drawing and painting device and they could draw on this screen with this pen that was located at the top left of the screen. Children could use it to draw like they would draw with a pencil on a piece of paper. When the children tried it, they drew anything they wished for an hour on the computer. Their paintings and drawings were printed and saved in the computer. Matthews and Seow (2007) described the following episode:

> one four-year old child, Glen, expressed disbelief that such a pen (which resembles a ball-point pen) was capable of drawing on what was, surely, a glass screen! This is an interesting example of a child's expectations of a new medium based upon prior experiences in the world. Glen was one of our subjects who had no experience of computers, but he did know that ball-point pens do not draw on glass! (p. 255).

It only took a stroke or a squiggle for the children to start on their own, to become self guided, and to be self-initiated in their drawing and painting. The children moved through successive generations of drawing actions, starting with those which reflect the natural actions of the skeletal and muscular frame to evermore differentiated structures which involve simple structural principles or drawing rules. Children moved through these structures in the same sequence as they did with their drawings on paper.

### Murals

Murals can be painted on large sheets of paper of different colors. At the beginning, murals can be collections of the young children's individual paintings. In creating a large mural, children paint on an assigned space on a large sheet of paper. With experience, children can learn to plan toward a theme for their mural where they use a variety of materials that can be from their environment or a supply house. For example, children can make a mural for an ocean unit. They can (1) finger paint an ocean on a wall size butcher paper, (2) add glitter to the paint to make salty water, and (3) cut ocean animals (e.g., dolphins, seahorses, sea stars, jellyfish, sharks) from magazines such as the *National Geographic* and glue them onto the mural (ProTeacher, 2006).

### Wax Crayons

Wax crayons are found in most early childhood classrooms; because they need little teacher preparation, rarely make any mess, and are easy to find. Large hexagonal or half-round crayons create bold, manageable strokes, and will not roll off the table. Children can have their own sets of crayons or share crayons in a class pool. Children can use crayons to color on large sheets of manila paper and other types of paper.

As the children gain experience using crayons, they can learn to combine them with other media. For example, painting the surface of a crayon drawing with a single coat of paint makes it stand out in an intriguing support.

### Colored Markers

Like crayons, these can be used for drawing. Teachers should only use washable markers, because permanent markers can easily tarnish clothing. They also need to teach young children the proper care of markers, such as covering them to keep them from drying out.

### Chalk

Chalk, whether colored or whitecap, can be used to draw on the board or on paper. To draw on paper, children wet the paper with water or buttermilk to make the colors show up more brilliantly. When they are finished, they can spray a fixative on the chalk drawings to protect them from rubbing off the paper.

### Cutting, Tearing, and Pasting Paper

This technique can form interesting designs. Children can fold papers that are fairly sturdy to make three-dimensional shapes. They can also make attractive designs at the two-dimensional level. Very young children tear pieces of colored paper that they can paste onto a background. When they are able to use scissors, they can cut the shapes.

### Collages

In making a collage, young children can use those materials that have a variety of textures, colors, and shapes. Materials from the environment and from a supply house can be used. These materials can be organized in a way that children can have access to them without any difficulty.

Different types of special paper and cardboard; pieces of fabric of various sizes, shapes, colors, and textures; bits of rope and yarn; feathers; buttons; colored sawdust; metal foil; and almost all materials can be shaped, cut, pasted, and used in an art experience. Children should use a variety of materials at any one time and be encouraged to consider new materials. They also need to consider ways of attaching the materials such as using rubber cement, white glue, staples, and cellophane tape.

### Printing Designs

Printing designs can be done in many ways. Children can dip an interesting textured or shaped object into a shallow dish of tempera paint and press it tightly onto a sheet of paper. Children can use a variety of colors and patterns to create an interesting medium. Printing designs can be made with many materials such as sponges, grainy ends of wooden boards, and vegetables such as carrots or potatoes. Teachers can carve a design into these materials to boost the printing. Children can also make a mural of hand prints on brown paper. They can put a blob of paint on their palettes and experiment with the texture of the paint for a while. When they have finished, they can make a hand print on the brown paper.

## Three-dimensional Constructions

Three-dimensional art media for young children consist of the creation of mobiles and stabiles, sewing, clay modeling, cardboard box constructions, and woodworking.

### Mobiles and Stabiles

Mobiles move, but stabiles remain stationary. A variety of materials are used to create mobiles and stabiles in interesting fashions. Materials can include dowels, tongue depressors, wire coat hangers, pipe cleaners, metal foil, yarn, balls, sponges, rubber bands, and many others. Clay and pieces of Styrofoam are used to make bases for stabiles. Since mobiles hang, they do not need a base. A coat hanger can be used where the materials are tied to it.

### Looms

"Loopers" can help young children weave on simple looms. They can start by using cotton loops and simple metal looms. Simple looms can be made out of squares of corrugated cardboard. Placing half-inch-deep slots in two opposite ends help children to thread the loom. They can then weave the yarn back and forth until they make a square. Simple looms are also made by driving nails into the edges of wooden boxes or frames.

### Sewing

Children can use tapestry needles to sew designs onto pieces of burlap. Later they can create interesting pictures by combining them with pieces of felt or a similar fabric. As young children explore materials in the classroom, teachers can praise their accomplishments and provide them with feedback through gentle guidance to help them to achieve further accomplishments. Sewing is also a way children use to express themselves, which becomes personally important.

### Clay Modeling

Working with clay strengthens the young children's development of small motor muscle control and encourages self-expression. Potter's clay is soft and flexible; it can be used many times. Clay that has the right consistency can be stored in a plastic bag for an indefinite length of time. If it dries, you just add water to it. If it is too wet, you can leave it out to dry. Clay needs to be soft enough to work with and thick enough to avoid having it stick to the fingers. Teachers can give young children a grapefruit-sized piece of clay for them to manipulate. They can knead it, pound it, roll it into balls or snakes, flatten it, break it up, and push it all together again. Playing with the clay is usually more important than constructing something. Children use their fingers and muscles differently when working with clay. Children manipulate clay in a sequence of stages which are similar to the stages in artistic development. These stages are in Table 14.4 (Neubert, 1991).

**TABLE 14.4.** Sequences in Stages when Children Manipulate Clay

| Stage | Description |
|-------|-------------|
| Stage 1 | When children first work with clay they beat and pound it without any purpose. This stage is similar to the one where children scribble in art |
| Stage 2 | Children form coils and balls. This stage is parallel to the one where children experience controlled scribbling |
| Stage 3 | Children pick up chunks of clay, making noises with this movement, and name their object such as an airplane or say, "This is a car." In this stage, the children's kinesthetic thinking has developed their imaginative thinking |
| Stage 4 | Clay accessories can be used |
| Stage 5 | Children make pinch pots, where they pull the clay into shapes and tear off the pieces |
| Stage 6 | Children create figures when they can add pieces of clay for heads, arms, and legs to a rolled body to create people and animals |
| Stage 7 | Children use the coil or slab method to build pots |

It is important for teachers to introduce the children to hands-on experiences with clay. Steps to introduce children to clay are in Box 14.3 (Koster, 1999).

> **Box 14.3. Steps to Introduce Children to Clay**
>
> 1. Cut the clay into pieces using a wire or old guitar string and offer young children balls of clay the size of a soft ball. When children are ready, they can work with bigger pieces.
> 2. Use a water-play table for children to work with clay.
> 3. Give children plastic lids filled with a small amount of water for them to rinse their hands when they get dry and dusty. They can dampen their hands with a small amount of water.
> 4. Teach children to return the clay to the storage container when they finish to keep it moist. To keep the clay moist, it can be stored in a tightly closed plastic bag inside a small covered plastic garbage can. Children also need to rinse their hands in a bucket of water after working with the clay before using the sink to avoid blocking the sink drain.
> 5. Tell children to keep their clay covered hands away from their faces and mouths.

Children enjoy working with clay. They enjoy poking, pushing, and modeling three-dimensional work. Clay meets the basic need to touch the earth and play in its life-giving soil. Children know this naturally when they make mud pies in the backyard. Clay and children have a unique relationship (Koster, 1999).

Plasticine is an oil-based clay that is sometimes substituted for potter's clay. Plasticine is not as sensitive to modeling and the children's work cannot be preserved. However, it can be used many times over again, because it does not dry out. Modeling dough can also be used. Although it is made out of simple household ingredients (salt, flour, water), it can be purchased commercially.

*Clay Accessories*

Two- and three-year-old children can gradually learn to use clay accessories such as wooden clay tools and small objects like shells, pods, and beads. Plastic and most metal tools should not be used. Plastic snaps, breaks, and any invisibly implanted in the clay can cut the children's hands; but metal cookie cutters encourage children to draw patterns.

When children are finished working with clay, they can save it in a crock. If they want to preserve their work, they can let it dry slowly and then paint it. If they have access to a kiln, children will enjoy watching the heat change the clay. Teachers need to be sure that work to be fired in the kiln is sturdy and that it does not contain air bubbles that will explode. Clay that has been used for a while may not need to be wedged. The pieces should be thin and the appendages should be securely attached. The children's work might be glazed.

Clay is smooth and cool, which gives a relaxing feeling. It fosters the children's imagination, creativity, and exploration. Clay accessories can also motivate young children to create sculptures out of clay. Teachers need to provide children with a few pottery tools, clay, space, and enough time to create. Children enjoy clay sculpture experiences (Kohl, 2005).

*Cardboard Box Constructions*

Simple cardboard constructions (such as houses, cash registers, rocket ships, model automobiles) can be made out of easy to get materials. Cardboard boxes and cartons can be cut up, pasted together, decorated with paper, painted, and colored. Byrum (1992) suggests that teachers collect egg cartons, corrugated cardboard, used wrapping paper, cardboard serving trays, and large chunks of Styrofoam to create a variety of sculptures. The children's skills that were developed in two-dimensional work can be expanded to use in creating endless constructions. Children can create a variety of sculptures (Kohl, 1988).

## Displaying the Children's Art Work

Children's art can be mounted, matted, or framed and then displayed. The children's art can be displayed on a bulletin board covered with burlap or some other attractive material. The children need to feel that their work is valued when they see their work displayed. Teachers can use a box of multicolor file folders to mount and display the children's art (Greenberg, 2000). Children's art can also be mounted and framed using colored mat board, oak tag, cardboard, heavy manila paper, and clear acrylic plastic. Materials that teachers can use to mount and frame the children's art can be gathered from local factories, craft centers, recycling centers, and glass manufacturers who like to donate frames, Plexiglas, paper, glue, scissors, tape, wire, string, tacks, and staples (Bakerlis, 2007). The children's work can also be placed in a picture frame and displayed like they do at the art galleries.

## Art Show

An art show can be planned to feature the children's art. Parents, teachers, children from other classrooms, and other staff personnel can be invited to the art show. Included in the children's art can be a variety of works in different media. An art show can include paintings, drawings, collages made out of clay, wood, and recycled materials. Teachers can have an art show in their classroom, the school library, the cafeteria, the school's hall, or any other available place in the school. The children's art needs to be mounted and framed with border edges. In addition, the pieces of art work must be labeled indicating the children's and teachers' names. The children's art can be displayed just like artists' work is displayed in a museum. Three dimensional art (such as sculptures) should be displayed in cases in the hallways. Signs need to be provided to inform the visitors about the art work. During the art show, children can pretend to be gallery tour guides who show and discuss the art that is on display. Two weeks before the show, brochures or announcements can be distributed to invite guests to the Children's Art Show.

At some point, children need to talk about their work to the class and compare their techniques with some of the artists they have studied. They can even pretend to be an artist agent who sets up the art work for display to be sold. They may also want to hold an auction for the children's drawings. Such experience can provide the children with more information about the world of art.

## Art Experiences for Children with Diverse Needs

Art experiences are valuable for *all* children including children with disabilities. Some children with disabilities may have difficulty in verbally expressing their feelings; however, they are able to use art materials to express themselves. Children with disabilities need to have opportunities to express themselves using a variety of media. Art helps children with disabilities become aware of their environment, develop relationships with their classmates, and express themselves in a positive or negative way. Children with disabilities use art to convey anger without fear of retribution. Children who are self-destructive find meaning in their art work. Children with delayed speech development are able to progressively see the sights of complex nonlinguistic symbolic forms. Art experiences are also valuable for the children with orthopedic or physical disabilities, visual impairments, and neurological impairments, because they have distorted sensory perceptions that generate peculiar responses of fragmentation and disorganization of cognitive processes.

Content, methods, materials, timing, and sequence in the art experiences of children with disabilities need to be adapted and presented in a climate of acceptance, openness, and empathy. Challenging art experiences assist children with disabilities to test their ideas, put an end to intense feelings, and gain some independence. Many children with disabilities are easily confused and upset. They need help in becoming self-motivated; expecting success; enhancing their receptive and expressive abilities; and expanding their attention span. In addition, children with disabilities need to improve their self-confidence, self-image, and self expectations in being successful. They need successful art experiences that make them feel comfortable with the materials and permit them to communicate their thoughts and feelings.

Children with limited receptive abilities need simple instructions with demonstrations. Children who lack self-direction need an enthusiastic demonstration to help them become interested and involved in art activities. Visual aids (films, slide presentations, pictures) capture their attention and motivate them. Rodríguez (1985) has suggested some of the discussed modifications for children with disabilities.

## Children with Orthopedic or Physical Disabilities

Children with orthopedic or physical disabilities usually have learning difficulties due to their orthopedic or central nervous system. However, their physical disabilities do not limit them from working independently. Their physical disabilities require them to use aids that help them move around their classroom, which promote their autonomy. Even children with orthopedic or physical disabilities who are only able to move their arms, hands, and fingers can engage in and enjoy art experiences. They need to have materials adapted to their specific needs (for instance, attaching materials to the wheelchairs, taping boards to a table for them to create collages).

Simple devices can be made or purchased for children with orthopedic or physical disabilities. Everyday objects can be used as adaptive devices. Since they cannot hold a brush because of limited manual dexterity, they can use a foam hair curler. They can slide the curler right over the brush handle or pencil. Foam, found in fabric stores, makes the tool thicker. Dowels that are drilled out can fit over a drawing tool or brush. Velcro strips are glued to drawing tools to attach to a Velcro band that children with orthopedic or physical disabilities can wear on their hand. If they have a weak grasp, children with orthopedic or physical disabilities can use this tool to keep the brush from slipping out of their hands.

For brushless painting, children with orthopedic or physical disabilities can use roll-on deodorant applicators or squeeze bottles, because these tools support good upper-body movement. Children who have limited fine motor skills may have trouble holding pencils, crayons, or paint brushes. The pencil, crayon, or brush can be wrapped around with a ball of clay or a foam rubber sponge to make the tools thick enough for them to be held. Children with orthopedic or physical disabilities who have jerky or uncoordinated movements will probably knock the paper from the easel or table, spill the paint, or knock other supplies to the floor. A different work area can be set up that has sturdy holders to tightly insert paint jars. Their papers can be attached (with tape or a clasp) to art easels or to the area on which they are working. Some children are not able to manipulate small objects and need large objects for their art work. Those who are not able to use paint can use crayons or work on a collage. They can also use felt-tip pens, soft-lead pencils, and ball-point pens to draw; because these objects require little pressure and are discarded when they are empty.

## Children with Visual Impairments

Children with visual impairments are usually excluded from most art experiences. Their participation is limited to appreciating art tactually and enjoying a variety of textures and forms. However, they need to be provided with opportunities to actively engage in the creative process and find their position in the art world. They need to be provided with developmentally appropriate experiences based on the degree of their disability, their perceptual experiences, and their age. Children with visual impairments need art experiences that are motivating but not overwhelming.

Children with visual impairments, whose sight losses range from mild to severe, use their senses (touch, smell, hear) for information. They learn through multisensory instruction, combining auditory, tactile, and kinesthetic experiences. They can try an extensive assortment of textures and refine their tactile sense. They can describe the medium they are using as they discriminate between the different materials and identify their distinguishing qualities. In addition, teachers can provide verbal directions as children with visual impairments feel the textures of the materials. For instance, when tying a knot, teachers can provide verbal directions and simultaneously direct children with visual impairments to use their fingers and hands through a series of actions. They need to have access to an assortment of materials (such as boxes, balls, cups, assorted kinds of paper, wood, textiles, sand, yarn, pipe cleaners, wires, rubber, plastic). Children with visual impairments begin to use only a small number of materials and progressively increase their repertoires.

Children with visual impairments enjoy modeling with clay, creating prints, gluing collages, and fingerprinting. Play dough can be dyed with a drop of food coloring combined with flavor extracts to give it color, flavor, and taste. For example, when orange coloring is mixed with orange extract, the play dough smells like orange, yellow coloring with lemon extract, or green with mint. Matching food extracts to the colors in poster paints will help the children with visual impairments to understand the relationship between colors and natural flavors. They need to be aware of the boundaries of the paper they are using. Teachers can take their hands and move them along the edges of the paper. Children with visual impairments need to have paper taped to their desk surface or table during their art work. If they are using paste, the container needs to be placed side up.

## Children Who Are Deaf and Hard-of-hearing

A hearing loss affects the communication, speech and language of the children who are deaf and hard-of-hearing. It is critical that they understand what they need to do in the art activity. They need to be provided with simple written directions or a small set of pictures that are displayed in a place where everybody can see them. An interpreter can sign for them to help understand the teachers' oral directions.

Children who are deaf and hard-of-hearing have refined observation skills, which can assist them in doing extremely well with their art projects. Art experiences can help them cope with their emotional detachment that has been affected by a lack of environmental awareness and interaction. Children who are deaf and hard-of-hearing can represent their feelings through their art experiences including three-dimensional art (such as modeling, carving). They can use their senses in their art experiences to acquire knowledge about themselves and their world and to substitute for information they are unable to hear. Children who are deaf and hard-of-hearing can use art experiences to identify and interact with the world of space and motion.

## Children with an Intellectual Disability

Art experiences are educationally valuable and personally satisfying for children with an intellectual disability. They exhibit slow but normal patterns of development in art expression. Children with an intellectual disability need systematic teaching and specific instructional materials to express themselves and learn some art concepts. When they draw with a heavy crayon, they develop kinesthetic skills and show their progress. They can create simple puppets to identify roles and develop conversations among the puppets. Children with an intellectual disability can easily make jewelry. They roll a salt-flour play dough mixture into beads, puncture them with toothpicks, and put them out to dry. After the beads are dried, they paint, varnish, and string them to wear as a necklace.

Children with an intellectual disability are interested in bright, shiny materials. Like the children with visual impairments, children with an intellectual disability benefit from textural and tactile art experiences (such as fabric or clay). Children with an intellectual disability need to become sensitive to form and space, improve their intellectual flexibility, increase their emotional sensitivity, enhance conceptual repertoire, and develop more social self-assurance. These needs require that children with an intellectual disability be provided with (1) planned activities, beginning with shape; (2) alternative activities that they can choose; (3) guidance to discover new forms; (4) an integration of art activities that they know (such as cutting, pasting, assembling); (5) a demonstration of art projects that have clear step-by-step progression; (6) materials of a size larger than the hand; and (7) numerous three-dimensional art activities.

## Children with Emotional Disabilities

Children with emotional disabilities display aggressive or withdrawn behaviors, which disrupt their learning. They have low self-esteem, which suggests that art experiences need to focus on their sense of self, such as a self-portrait. They can also create a collage. Objects (e.g., birthday cards, ticket stubs, photographs, letters, postcards) that are important to the children with emotional disabilities are placed in a brown bag. They use these objects to make a collage. They can create designs that include their names in them. Children with emotional disabilities can develop a positive self-concept and self-confidence through creative expression in their art experiences. They also develop positive feelings when they successfully complete their art work. Such positive feelings include empathy, respect, pride, and confidence.

Children with emotional disabilities can use their art experiences to communicate their feelings and moods (happy or sad, calm or tense, frightened, worried or confident). They can illustrate them using color and form. Their art experiences should be similar to their play activities, which have been used as a form of therapy for children with emotional disabilities. They use their art experiences to convey their ideas and feelings. They can also draw images that express their ideas. Their graphic symbols indicate the unconscious and usually repressed elements of their personality, concern, mood, and private fantasies. It is important to keep in mind that the goal of the art experiences for children with emotional disabilities, just like for *all* children, is to provide pleasure and satisfaction.

## Children with Learning Disabilities

Children with learning disabilities are intelligent, but they have difficulty processing information, which affects their academic learning. They seem to be like typically developing children, but they do not learn like them. They have a hidden disability. Children with learning disabilities are immature and lack the ability to organize themselves, to start something, to continue it, and to stop it. Therefore, they are unable to effectively use the freedom that is usually associated with expressive arts. During art experiences, children with learning disabilities need to have the teacher be their focusing mechanism and set up boundaries for them to learn effectively and to create fully. They can follow complex art procedures that are broken down into simple segments for them to learn step by step. Children with learning disabilities need to have limits with space, time, choices, quantity of materials to use, amount of work to be completed, directions, and discussion. Such limitations should not affect their ability to be creative and express themselves. It offers them parameters and borders in which to organize their creative expression. Children with learning disabilities need the adult's support, but they also need to be provided with assistance to become independent.

When children with learning disabilities make a mistake on an art project, they become upset. They need to work on art projects that can be reshaped or changed. For example, children with learning disabilities can draw on the board or finger paint. If they are unhappy with their art work, they can easily erase it and start a new drawing. They can use clay to mold and remold their art work until they are satisfied. Children with learning disabilities who are more advanced can weave, because their work can be easily modified.

Children with learning disabilities who have difficulty finishing a project can work on art activities that are of interest to them. They may wish to work on a simple art project like painting a picture of something they have recently seen or creating a print with a leaf, twig, or rock from the school yard.

## Children Who Are Gifted

Children who are gifted have an above average ability. Art materials need to be advanced and motivating to help them engage in complex art projects (such as a collage). They can collect items for a collage on a theme that is of interest to them. For instance, for a theme on winter children who are gifted can create a collage using pine cones, mistletoe, and a glove. For a theme on carpenters, they can create a carpenter collage and collect objects like nails, sandpaper, ruler, and screws. Collages generate class discussions, which are meaningful to the children who are gifted.

Creativity is usually related to giftedness. The originality and divergent thinking of children who are gifted must be valued in the arts. Teachers need to respect these children's creative thinking, encourage their creative expressions, and avoid forcing them to conform and create typical art work.

## English Language Learners

Since English language learners (ELLs) have difficulty expressing themselves in language, they can use art experiences as a means of communication. They may hear or see words but not understand them. Art experiences reinforce the ELLs' language concepts and develop their visual symbolism. For example, ELLs can draw a kite after they have seen one. They can name and describe the kite's characteristics (shape, color, texture, weight). When ELLs are drawing the kite, they can also describe it. ELLs can see pictures or slides of an assortment of kites and discuss their similarities and differences. Teachers can show a kite to the children. Next ELLs fly the kite or watch others fly it. They can observe and describe how the kite flies, how important the wind is (cause and effect), how the wind sounds when it blows the kite, how the kite moves, and how important the string is. ELLs can draw or paint to recall this experience. This art experience helps ELLs to expand their vocabulary and express themselves verbally and artistically.

Art experiences encourage ELLs to discuss their artistic projects. Positive questions and encouragement about the projects can assist ELLs to be comfortable when sharing their projects.

## Play Art Environment

A playful artistic environment encourages children to explore the art process. The children's art becomes a personal search and discovery where they become surprised with their discoveries. They can view everything in their environment as a potential source for display, selection, or manipulation. For example, a floor or a chair stands for a base; a wall represents a background, the room represents a space; and people symbolize objects within that space. The children's playful discoveries help them to look at their environment with fresh eyes and assume their role of artists as they work with the space and the objects in that environment (Szekely, 1991).

Teachers should motivate and provide young children with art experiences. They will learn best through their own discoveries. They are usually enthusiastic about searching for new locations, which can continuously help them to discover new environments. Young children are usually using their senses to investigate and collect information when they are on an outdoor walk or in a supermarket aisle. They touch, smell, and may taste when they see something new. Art lessons need to be investigative journeys in play settings. The children's explorations and discoveries will be regenerated in their art and later respect their art as adults (Szekely, 1991).

## Art Learning Center

An art learning center can be set up to provide young children with the opportunity to experiment and explore with a variety of materials. The area should be large enough to display and store a variety of materials and for children to work in their art projects, store them to finish later, and to display their work.

Children can be provided with the opportunity to select from a number of art activities, which are multisensory. Art experiences that require the use of several senses can help children understand fuller, richer, and visual imagery, which can be representations or abstract. Children enjoy drawing and displaying self-portraits. They may prefer to draw a portrait of a friend, pet, doll, animal, or anyone else (Szyba, 1999). It is important that children engage in spontaneous self-directed art experiences.

Basic open-ended materials at different levels of competence need to be provided. Children need to have daily access to art activities that are familiar to them such as painting and drawing. Collage, modeling with dough and clay, and sculpture with wood blocks and wire need to be provided when children are familiar with them. Appropriate new art experiences need to be introduced. A display table can have art experiences and materials available for children to self select and self manage, and to promote social interaction.

More than enough materials need to be provided in a learning center to allow young children to select and experiment with the different art media. Young children need to be encouraged to add materials (e.g., stones, twigs, leaves, flowers) that relate to their experiences and areas of study. Materials need to be changed when children lose interest in them.

Box 14.4 provides sample materials that can be included in art learning centers and Box 14.5 suggests ways to display the art materials.

---

**Box 14.4. Sample Materials for an Art Learning Center**

| | |
|---|---|
| Water | Water crayons |
| Spray bottles | Magic markers |
| Oil crayons | Pencils |
| Small sticks for etching | Pens in different colors |
| Watercolors | Glue |
| Termpera in different colors | Scissors |

Fingerpaint in different colors

Chalk in different colors

Brushes in several sizes

Sponges in several sizes

Water-based markers

Crayons (several boxes)

Small sticks or twigs

String

Small items to press into clay to create texture

Rolling pin

Scraps of wood

Packing materials

Cardboard tubes

Egg cartons

White paper in a variety of textures

Discarded newspaper

Sandpaper

Variety of different papers (foil, parcel etc.)

Fabric scraps

Feathers

Yarn

Clay (play dough, plasticine, salt dough)

Toothpicks

Straws

Buttons

Popsicle sticks

Cardboard shapes for base of structure

## Box 14.5. Ways to Display the Art Materials

Scissors

- Egg cartons can be used to display scissors or pencils. Tape the edges together so the carton remains closed when being carried. Empty spaces show how many scissors are missing.
- An empty coffee can also makes a good scissors holder. Glue the plastic lid to the open top, because there will be jagged edges inside when the holes have been punched. Then turn the can upside down and use a can puncher to make holes around the edge. Decorate the coffee can with contact paper.
- Another scissors holder can be made using elastic nailed to a wall or back of a cubby.

Paper holders can be made out of

- ice cream containers placed on the table; or
- newspaper cylinders placed on the table.
- Turn the ice cream containers or cylinders so that the opening faces the classroom. You can have several containers stacked up to put collage materials in them. Several containers stapled together make a case for a variety of small art activity items.

Crayons

- Frozen juice cans are good crayon holders. Colored paper covers tell the children where each crayon goes.

## Labeling the Materials

One of the goals for children is to become as independent in the classroom as possible and to take responsibility for themselves and their work. Labeled shelves and cubbies help children know where to find materials and where to put them back. It also makes clean up easier for everyone and helps keep the classroom neat. The labels have to be understandable to children. Pictures of what goes on the shelf help those children who are not able to read.

Since magic markers make permanent marks, vinyl adhesive paper (like contact paper) should be used; because it can be removed. Labeling with adhesive paper is not permanent and can be changed for a later arrangement. Dry mounting and laminating pictures makes them sturdier. Clear contact paper can also be used over a picture to keep pictures from getting torn or dirty. Sample pieces glued to the outside of an ice cream cylinder could label a container for collage materials. Collage materials can also be placed together in a box with a label to be easier to find.

## Storage Containers

Empty fruit baskets can be used for storage. They are labelled with their contents and placed in a cabinet. Teachers can ask for empty fruit baskets from the grocery store or produce distributor. Shirt boxes can also be used as storage containers with labels at the end of the box and placed in a storage cabinet. Shoe boxes and wine bottle boxes, which can be obtained at a liquor store, can be used as storage containers and labeled. A sheet of plywood is covered with colorful material such as burlap. Sheets of plastic or acetate are shaped to it to make pockets to create storage for all types of items.

## Children and Classic Works of Art

Art helps to develop children's imagination. It provides form to experience and to play, and also helps them to understand the real world. Young children's early experiences in relation to the arts are important. It opens the children's creative capabilities when they learn to recognize and appreciate the strength, beauty, and truth of their own ideas and feelings. In art, visual images of works of art help children learn free expression of ideas and feelings. In understanding the classic works of art, young children learn to analyze and discuss the work of artists. Children need to learn art content from a broad range of the visual arts in relation to "(1) conceptions of the nature of art, (2) bases for valuing and judging art, (3) contexts in which art has been created, and (4) processes and techniques for creating art" (Clark et al., 1987, p. 135). The role of the teachers is to help children learn to analyze, understand, and appreciate art. Basically children need to develop an understanding of the visual arts through a variety of art experiences to learn criticism and appreciation of art.

## Art Criticism

At an early age, young children can become art critics. Art museums provide experiences that allow very young children to enjoy, appreciate, and react to works of art. This valuable experience stimulates young children's curiosity and emotional interest. Museum personnel often have discussions with children about specific works of art and elicit their verbal responses. Preschool children can respond to questions that help them systematize their liberated art conversations. They are able to articulate their impressions of art work. Children learn to interpret lines, shapes, and clusters of marks to comprehend visual images in works of art even if they do not like the work. Spodek and Saracho (1994b) used several sources (e.g., Cole & Schaefer, 1990; Feldman, 1970) to identify four stages of art criticism with ways to promote young children's art criticism ability (See Table 14.5).

Art criticism prepares the way for the children's logical and creative thinking, which assists them in organizing their thoughts. Children acquire the pleasure of judging the artists' art work. They enjoy sharing their thoughts and emotional interest with others as well as discussing the works of art. Presently art museums encourage very young children to respond to and discuss works of art. They prepare discussions for young viewers about specific works of art and encourage them to respond and discuss these works.

## Art Appreciation

Appreciation of art is both possible and valuable for young children. Teachers need to help young children grow from art makers to art appreciators. Art appreciation can enhance their understanding of the world and enrich their lives in the process. It is a skill and an enjoyment that can last a lifetime. When children create their own art work, meaning enters their lives. However, they can also find meaning in art created by others, which is the core of art appreciation. Art experiences go beyond painting, drawing, and other art activities. They should include the idea of "thinking in art"; that is, children need to engage in the process of thinking about, feeling, and responding to art, while teachers need to provide children with opportunities to share their thoughts, insights, and feelings to be able to better understand the artist, the work, and themselves. Young children can gain an aesthetic experience that helps them to develop the foundation for a lifetime of enjoyment of art. This type of learning occurs when they are provided with the opportunities to create and appreciate beauty.

**TABLE 14.5.** Stages of Young Children's Art Criticism and Encouragement

| Stage | Description | Children's Activity |
|---|---|---|
| Description | Quantity of literal qualities that are visible to the child in a work of art | Pretend you're talking to me on the telephone. Can you name the things in this picture so that I'll be able to recognize it? |
| Analysis | Relationships the child finds between elements (such as line, shape, space, color, texture, balance) in a work of art | How do the colors get along? Are they quiet or noisy? Fighting or friendly? |
| Interpretation | The way the child understands the content (subject matter) of the artwork when they reply to questions that direct their thoughts to ideas, feelings, or moods | What happened just before or just after this scene? |
| Judgment | The child arrives at a conclusion based on information from the previous artwork | Which do you like the most? The story the art tells, the shapes and colors and designs in it, or the way it makes you feel when you look at it? |

*Experiences in Appreciation*

Teachers need to offer children direct opportunities for art appreciation. Teachers can help young children learn how to think about art. Although art appreciation is an academic and abstract concept, it is easy for young children to learn it. At their age, their senses and perceptions are very opened and attuned to their surroundings (Epstein, 2001; Scribbles, 2005). Children can learn to appreciate art, if art appreciation is presented in a concrete manner. Creative experiences, like those in Box 14.6, develop the children's knowledge base about art (Epstein, 2001; Scribbles, 2005).

---

**Box 14.6. Creative Experiences to Develop the Children's Knowledge Base about Art**

- Children need to feel safe and secure in expressing observations and opinions about art. When they share their feelings about a work of art, they are disclosing something that is highly personal. Children should feel comfortable enough to expose themselves in this way.
- Children need to gather reproductions and illustrations of fine quality art. Museum gift shops, bookstores, and libraries have reproductions of paintings, prints and drawings of master artists. Magazines and brochures feature reprints of their art work and newspapers have in the book review section illustrations from recently published art books.
- Children need to know about the art in their community. They can visit nearby museums, art galleries, and studios of artists. Children can also use the materials and tools that artists use.

---

Teachers can introduce artists through children's books such as those found in Box 14.7 (Collins, 2004).

---

**Box 14.7. Children's Books about Artists**

- Anholt, L. (1998). *Picasso and the girl with a ponytail: A story about Pablo Picasso*. New York: Barrons Educational Series, Inc.
- Bruna, D. (1998). *Miffy at the museum*. New York: Kodansha America, Inc.
- Burleigh, R. (2005). *Toulouse-Lautrec: The Moulin Rouge and the City of Light*. New York: Harry N. Abrams, Inc., Publishers.
- Frith, M. (2003). *Frida Kahlo: The Artist Who Painted Herself*. Grosset & Dunlap.
- Holub, J. (2001). *Vincent Van Gogh: Sunflowers and Swirly Stars*.
- Le Tord, B. (1999). *A Bird or Two: A Story about Henri Matisse*. Grand Rapids, MI: Eerdmans Books for Young Readers.
- Meyer, S. (1990). *First impressions: Mary Cassatt*. New York: Harry N. Abrams, Inc., Publishers.
- Minnerly, D. B., & Walker, G. (2004). *Molly meets Mona and friends: A magical day in the museum*. Glenview, IL: Crystal Productions.
- O' Connor, J. (2002). *Henri Matisse: drawing with scissors*. Illustrated by Jessie Hartland. (Smart about Art series.) New York: Grosset & Dunlap.

---

- Wolf, Aline D. (1984). *Mommy, it's a Renoir!* Parent Child Press, P. O. Box 767. Altoona, PA: 16603.
- Wolf, Aline D. (1985). *Child-sized masterpieces*. Parent Child Press, P. O. Box 767. Altoona, PA: 16603.

For example, the teacher can read to the children *Monet* (Venezia, 1989). When discussing the book, focus on page 21, where the book discusses his painting *Impression, Sunrise* (Monet, 1872). After discussing this painting with the children, Sabbeth (2002) suggests an activity that can be used with it, which she calls "Impressions, Me." Monet's painting (see http://www.artchive.com/artchive/M/monet/sunrise.jpg.html) shows that it is made of many short, choppy, and unblended strokes of color. Looking at the painting from a distance shows that these dabs and dashes merge together. According to Claude Monet,

> When you paint, try to forget what objects you have before you, a tree, a house, a field, or whatever. Instead think, "Here is a little square of blue, here an oblong of pink, here a streak of yellow," and paint it just as it looks (cited in Sabbeth, 2002, p. 24).

Children can make their own impressionist picture using Monet's ideas. Directions for making these pictures are in Box 14.8.

---

**Box 14.8. Directions for Making Impressionist Pictures**

1. Cut out a picture of a landscape or seascape from a magazine.
2. Although the picture seems to be in one solid color, it is actually painted with a combination of colors. For example, fluffy white clouds could also have shades of lavender, gray, and yellow. The blue water of a lake may have several colors (e.g., blue, green, purple); while a sunset might have pink in the color of the water.
3. Dip a cotton swab into a color of paint and make bold, short strokes with the swab on the top of the picture to add color to it. Continue painting short, separate splashes of different colors to the picture. Be sure to use a clean swab for each different color and make each stroke crisp without merging the colors together.
4. When finished, title your picture starting with: Impression, _____.

---

The work in the visual arts needs to (a) draw on the children's own experiences with their life and art materials and (b) explore how they approach and make sense of the artists' work. Children associate meaning based on their understanding of the artists' work. According to Korn-Bursztyn (2002), the children's early experiences need to be used to teach the visual arts. For example, drawing on the children's interest and their everyday experiences, the children and teacher may select Vincent Van Gogh's painting, *The Starry Night* (http://www.moma.org/collection/browse_results.php?object_id'79802). The night is an attractive theme for children who are fascinated with the sky and often afraid to go to sleep. The nighttime sky with rotating clouds can attract the interest of three- and four-year-olds. Children's literature books (see Box 14.9) related to the night sky and the children's concern about nighttime can be used and made available at the library corner for children to read over and over again.

Box 14.9. Books to Use with Van Gogh's Painting *The Starry Night*

- Asche, F. (1982). *Happy birthday moon*. Englewood Cliffs, NJ: Prentice Hall.
- Bradbury, R. (1983/1993). *Switch on the night*. New York: Knopf.
- Brown, M. W. (1947/1975). *Goodnight moon*. New York: Harper Trophy.
- Carle, E. (1998). *Little cloud*. New York: Philomel.
- Carle, E. (1992). *Draw me a star*. New York: Philomel.
- Carle, E. (1986). *Papa, please get the moon for me*. New York: Simon & Schuster Books for Young Readers.
- Cazet, D. (1992). *"I'm not sleepy"*. New York: Orchard Books.
- Dragonwagon, C. (1986). *Half a moon and one whole star*. New York: Macmillan.
- Grifalconi, A. (1987). *Darkness and the butterfly*. Boston, MA: Little, Brown.
- Gibbons, G. (1992). *Stargazers*. New York: Holiday House.
- Greenfield, E. (1991). *Night on neighborhood street*. New York: Books for Young Readers.
- Lucht, I. (1993). *In this night*. New York: Hyperion Books for Children.
- Ringgold, F. (1991). *Tar beach*. New York: Crown Publishers.
- Sendak, M. (1970). *In the night kitchen*. New York: Harper & Row.
- Troughton, J. (1986). *How night came*. New York: Bedrick/Blackie.

Children can also discuss these stories. A local artist can be invited to the classroom and participate in the children's discussion. Korn-Bursztyn (2002) shares a conversation between the children and an artist about Van Gogh's *The Starry Night*. Without hesitation, the children began telling the story and identified themselves with this work. The artist and the children engaged in the following conversation.

Teaching Artist: I hear that you were looking at things in the sky. I'm an artist and I love weather and the sky. There are a lot of cool paintings about the sky—I brought my favorite today, by an artist named Vincent Van Gogh (pointing to *The Starry Night* on a slide): What kinds of stories can you tell me about the painting? (pp. 41–42).

Teaching Artist: We're going to read the painting. There's a story in that painting. What do you see?

Sharon: (pointing at the moon) It's hiding!

Teaching Artist: Who do you think is hiding?

Sharon: The moons! It says you got to go to bed.

Jon: I like a dark room. I'm not scared of the dark.

Alicia: That's why the stars go all the way up (p. 41).

After reading books about nighttime, children can engage in art activities with different art materials than the ones they have been using. Teachers can make a washable palette, which is a thin board that artists use to lay and mix colors, for the children to carry around. The palette needs to be large enough for children to work on but light enough for them to carry. A palette can be made from a piece of tri-wall (three ply heavy cardboard—18 inches on a side is a convenient size). Then both sides are covered with washable vinyl self-sticking paper (like contact paper). A solid color is better because it is less distracting. The children can paint with a palette of blues ranging from pale to midnight blue, which highlights the shades of the night sky that appear in the night sky of Van Gogh's *The Starry Night*. The children can observe the deep colors, flowing lines, and swirling shapes that are found in the books that they read and discussed. Therefore, the children's paintings will reflect Van Gogh's *The Starry Night*.

Young children are artists who can learn the symbolic tools of literacy in the visual arts and the aesthetic symbols of their culture. They can use their intuitive knowledge to understand the qualities of their art work. Teachers can also introduce children to the art of famous artists. They learn about the artists, their techniques, and biographical information. Using this book, Thompson (2005) describes how an early childhood teacher introduced this artist's techniques (see Box 14.10).

---

### Box 14.10. Introducing and Discussing Van Gogh's Background Information

The teacher sat in a rocking chair with the children seated on the floor in front of her. On a small easel rested a print of Van Gogh's painting, *The Starry Night*. The teacher held a photograph of Van Gogh.

**Teacher** *(pointing to photograph)*: This artist was a great painter. His name was Vincent Van Gogh. He lived about 100 years ago.

**Chloe:** I wonder how old he is.

**Teacher:** Van Gogh was born in a country called Holland. *(The teacher and children look at the globe.)* This is where we are in the United States, and this is Holland. Holland is clear across the Atlantic Ocean.

**Salvador:** Like where the Leprechauns live!

**Teacher:** That's right, across the Atlantic Ocean, like Ireland. Van Gogh only lived 37 years. That's not very long, is it?

**Chloe:** Well, it kind of is.

**Teacher:** It seems kind of long to you but not to me, because I'm 38.

**Children:** Wow!

**Teacher:** Van Gogh loved to paint. He painted 800 paintings.

**Jesse:** That's almost a thousand paints!

**Avery:** I counted to 518 once.

**Teacher:** Then you know that 800 paintings is a lot (Thompson, 2005, p. 45).

---

The teacher linked the information about Van Gogh to the children's knowledge. She blended geography into the discussion. Locating Holland on the globe may be an abstract concept for young children; however, one child made the connection between the location for Ireland and the location for Holland. The teacher drew a comparison between her life of 38 years and Van Gogh's life span of 37 years to help the children understand the brevity of his life. The children used the context of their experiences with numbers and counting to understand that Van Gogh's 800 paintings consisted of a large number of paintings.

The teacher then discussed Van Gogh's painting techniques (see Box14.11).

---

**Box 14.11.  Discussing Van Gogh's Painting Techniques**

**Teacher** *(indicating "The Starry Night")*: This is a picture of one of Van Gogh's paintings. When we look at this painting, the first thing I want you to observe is what time of the day it is.

**Jaden:** Dark.

**Teacher:** It is dark. What's another word for dark time?

**Jaden:** Nighttime.

**Teacher:** It looks like nighttime. What tells you the painting that it's nighttime? Can you find some clues?

**Sam:** Blue color. It's kind of a dark color.

**Teacher:** What other colors did Van Gogh use to make it look kind of dark?

**Diego:** Yellow next to the dark color.

**Teacher:** You are right! Painting yellow next to blue really makes the dark colors show up. Now let's look at the way Van Gogh painted. *(Indicating paint strokes)* If you took a paintbrush and started to paint this picture, how would you describe your paint strokes?

**Faith:** Little blue strokes.

**Teacher:** Little blue strokes, yes. What else can you say about the paint strokes?

**Diego:** Straight and circled.

**Teacher:** Yes! Some strokes are straight and some go in circles. Are they short or long strokes?

**Kayni:** Short.

**Teacher:** You are very observant. That's right, Van Gogh used a lot of short strokes. Do you think he used thick paint or thin paint?

**Kayni:** Thick, because of the light blue where it kind of looks like people.

**Teacher:** Yes, thick paint. Can all of you see those strokes in the paint? Now, let's observe another thing about the colors Van Gogh chose. Let's look at the blue, for instance. Is blue a warm color or a cool color? Think of things in nature that are blue. Are they usually warm or cool?

**Brandon:** Cool! Because of the ocean.

**Teacher:** That's right. Most of the time we think of water as being cool. Did he use some colors that you would think of as warm colors?

**Kayni:** The moon.

**Teacher:** The moon is yellow. Do you have any ideas about what Van Gogh might have called this painting?

**Children:** "Spooky" . . . "The Burning House Picture" . . . "Hilltops" . . . "Twinkle Lights."

**Teacher:** "Twinkle Lights." What's up there in the sky that would make him call it "Twinkle Lights?" You are right on target, because this picture is called "The Starry Night" (Thompson, 2005, pp. 47–48).

---

Some might feel that the discussion is too long and detailed for this age group. However, the teacher kept the young children's attention as she led them to new ideas, related new knowledge to familiar knowledge, and built on their experiences. The children's responses are frequent estimates which other children responded to and built on. After this discussion, the teacher involved the children in a demonstration about Van Gogh's painting techniques (see Box 14.12).

---

### Box 14.12.  Demonstrating Van Gogh's Painting Techniques

**Teacher:** *(holding up a paper plate with finger paint on it)*: We talked about Van Gogh using thick paint. Is this thick paint?

**Trianna:** Yes, because you can hold it and it doesn't run.

**Teacher:** Can we do this with watercolors? What would happen to the paints then?

**Trianna:** They would drip down.

**Teacher:** That's right. This is special, thick paint. It is finger paint, but today we are going to paint with paint brushes instead of our fingers. *(Holds up two paintbrushes, one with thick bristles and one with thin.)* Do you think Van Gogh used a brush like this or a brush like this to paint thick, heavy strokes?

**Trianna** *(pointing to the thick-bristle paintbrush)*: The red one.

**Teacher:** He could have used both brushes, but when he wanted to get really thick strokes, he probably used this other brush, the thick one.

**Skye:** Do we have to paint that Van Gogh picture?

**Teacher:** Not unless you want to. You can paint a picture like it, with stars or planets if you want. It's up to you. I'm more interested in seeing you paint with thick paint and short strokes, like Van Gogh did. *(She tapes a large sheet of paper to the wall.)* We're going to try this out. Sarah, do you want to demonstrate? *(Sarah walks up and takes the thick paintbrush.)* Show us the way you think Van Gogh painted his strokes. *(Sarah paints a couple of short strokes.)* Yes, they are short strokes! He made some strokes here just using little, tiny, short strokes. *(Pointing to a group of paint strokes in "The Starry Night")*. What do you think these strokes represent?

**Children:** Wind . . . Clouds.

**Teacher:** I hear some good ideas. And down in here? What did he paint in here?

**Skye:** A house.

**Teacher:** Yes, little house made little, short strokes. Now let's try painting some pictures the way Van Gogh painted, with thick paints and short strokes (Thompson, 2005, pp. 48–49).

---

The children can learn about other artists. When they are provided with suitable experiences, children will remember each artist's techniques. For example, some time later, when the teacher placed thick paint onto paper plates for the children, a boy blurted, "Thick paint, just like Van Gogh uses!" (Thompson, 2005, p. 49). Teachers need to provide children with materials that they can use to experience the artists' style of art. These elements need to be taught in a framework that is developmentally appropriate for the children.

Children are realistic observers. After children have learned the techniques of several artists, they should be able to distinguish the paintings of each artist. When they determine what they see from an aesthetic perspective, they can appreciate the art work it inspires. Steps, like those in Table 14.6, help children appreciate works of art (Wolf, 1990).

**TABLE 14.6.** Steps to Help Children Appreciate Works of Art

| Steps to Encourage Appreciation | Description |
| --- | --- |
| Compare identical paintings | Young children can compare three identical pairs of simple subjects (e.g., a hare by Dürer, a chair by Van Gogh, and an abstract resembling a Tinkertoy by Miro). When children can do this task, teachers can add more pairs, one pair at a time (e.g., *A Girl with a Watering Can* by Renoir, then *Pot of Geraniums* by Matisse). The task becomes more difficult as children do each task successfully |
| Identify companion paintings by an artist | After young children can compare identical paintings, they can identify similar paintings by the same artist. For this task, children need to be able to identify two paintings by an artist that are similar in subject and style. For example, children can match two Degas with ballet dancers, two Audubons with birds, and two Mondrians with geometric designs. Then the difficulty in this task is gradually increased |
| Classify paintings by an artist | Children classify four paintings by three different artists. They start with extremely contrasting subjects such as four still lifes by Cezanne, four abstracts by Kandinsky, and four paintings of people by Goya. When children can do this task, teachers write the artist's last name under one of the four paintings. Children can capture a visual impression to relate to the style they are appreciating |
| Learn about artists and their times | The children's experiences can help them to read (a) the important artists' names and (b) the titles of their most famous paintings. Additional experiences can help them to identify paintings using the characteristics of some of the well-known art schools. Finally, they can group postcard size reproductions, which can be found at any art gallery or bookstore, sequentially on a time line, using a visual representation of the development of art through the centuries |

Preschool children perceive art appreciation as a favorable attitude toward different forms and styles of art. Children may prefer different forms; however, they need to be opened to art that is new to them and they need to know the value of different modes of expression. Teachers need to (a) help children understand that art is a personal form of expression, (b) introduce them to a wide range of art, and (c) engage them with art in ways that they are able to relate to it (Giorgis & Glazer, 2008). After children are able to recognize the different artists, they can engage in role playing situations.

## Role Play and Art Education

Role-playing experiences need to be very realistic, reflecting real-world situations. Role play is a form of dramatic play, where the children participate and observe to learn and to understand their interactions with others, the events, and the cause of these events. Role play prompts young children to improvise spontaneously, to solve problems, to assume roles in a situation, to observe the results of their response to their roles, and to make decisions.

Role-playing experiences promote the children's learning in a variety of situations. They also provide young children with an opportunity to develop social and critical thinking skills as well as develop positive attitudes. Role play is a versatile and cooperative learning experience that reduces the young children's nervous strain and encourages them to take risks.

Role play in art education was found in the Picture Study in the 1870s and 1880s. Young children role played that they were a model who posed for a painting (Hurll, 1914). Although this role lacked the dialogue of a role play drama, this experience provided them with an active and memorable learning experience. Role-playing experiences help young children learn art history (Szekely, 1997). Children can assume the role of art experts and pretend to be gallery owners, curators, or historians. They can communicate ideas that go "beyond narrow views and personal interpretations." Similar experiences help young children acquire verbal skills in art criticism (Jones, 1995). Children can pretend to be an artist's agent. They can study an artist's work, write a letter to describe the importance of the artist's work, and mail it to a museum or art gallery. This type of role play helps children to completely understand artists and their work.

## Summary

Many children in the United States have little or no opportunity to engage in high quality art learning experiences. Art has an important role in the early childhood play curriculum. Children use art as a form of their cognitive expression to communicate their ideas, feelings, and emotions. Art publicly communicates the children's private thoughts and concepts. It helps children to nonverbally express their ideas. Children express their thoughts and feelings in many ways. While language is the predominant mode of expression for most people, art is also important, especially during childhood.

Children use art to express their understanding and interpretations of their world before they are able to use words to communicate their thoughts and feelings. Their art becomes a symbolic communication, which may be better than language (Bae, 2004). They use art to communicate before they learn to write. They learn to interpret imagery and material culture before they are able to read texts (Barroquiero, 2010). Art provides young children with the opportunity to express themselves creatively in many ways. It also helps them to communicate and make sense of the world in a different way than language does. This form of expression should be accessible to all children, including those with disabilities, because art promotes the children's understanding of the world and motivates them to express their thoughts in a personal and unique way. Personal ways of knowing related to art are highly satisfying to young children, especially those children who are unsuccessful in using traditional forms of expression.

Very young children respond more to visual and tactile experiences than to representational art qualities. As they develop, they continue to use similar art media in more sophisticated ways, making prints, constructing, modeling, painting, stitching, and weaving (Spodek & Saracho, 1994b). Children can use those materials that have a variety of textures, colors, and shapes. Materials from the environment and from a supply house can be used. These materials can be organized in such a way that children can have access to them without any difficulty. Young children need to use the art media creatively by understanding what each medium can do. The role of the teacher is to function actively in helping children become better skilled and have greater knowledge in each of these areas. Developing a control of themselves combined with freedom provides young children with a basis for learning in art.

Art helps children learn and think. It contributes to the children's development including their self-esteem and creativity. In art children use their senses in open-ended play and develop cognitive, social–emotional and multi-sensory skills. According to Reyner (2010), "Art engages children's senses through open-ended play experiences and develops cognitive and socio-emotional competencies. Art provides opportunities for problem solving and divergent thinking." In art children engage in social interactions, collaboration, and discussion of ideas. The children's participation in art is essential to their lives.

# Chapter 15
# Block-play Learning Experiences

What are you able to build with your blocks?
Castles and palaces, temples and docks.
Rain may keep raining, and others go roam,
But I can be happy and building at home.

Robert Louis Stevenson (1885, p. 63)

Many educators assume that the early childhood education curriculum is made up of traditional subjects (like mathematics, science, social studies). They have considered block building a pastime activity that can be used in the children's play for learning. Perhaps it is best to think about block building as an activity that helps meet many of the present goals for the traditional subject areas. In that respect, it can be accepted as being part of the early childhood education curriculum. For example, in mathematics strands, the elements of number and operations and geometry are developed in *Principles and Standards for School Mathematics* (National Council of Teachers of Mathematics (NCTM), 2000). A joint position statement between the National Association for the Education of Young Children (NAEYC) and NCTM (2010) recommends the following mathematics objectives and activities for children ages three to six:

> In play and daily activities, children often explore mathematical ideas and processes; for example, they sort and classify, compare quantities, and notice shapes and patterns (p. 4).

Young children's learning is integrated into traditional subjects. Kamii and Colleagues (2004) offer the following example.

. . . when a 3- or 4-year-old begins to paint, the child is not learning about art. If children take a brushful of paint to the easel and drip some of it along the way, 3- and 4-year-olds learn about the effects of gravity and the nature of paint as a liquid. As they make the brush touch the paper and paint runs down, they learn more about the effects of gravity and how paint can move in space all by itself. If they go on to paint on the paper, they learn about the correspondence between the movement of their hand and the shape left on the paper. If they then apply another color without waiting for the first color to dry, they learn about mixing colors and go on to learn about the effects of evaporation. Science, mathematics, and art are completely undifferentiated in this example. Instead of learning science, mathematics, or art, the children are making all kinds of mental relationships that are the foundations of subjects that will become differentiated later (p. 44–45).

This example can be applied to the children's block building. Kamii and Colleagues (2004) examined the developmental interrelationships among various aspects of logico-mathematical knowledge. Children (ages one to four) were given 20 blocks and individually asked to build "something tall." They found that as children became older their new spatial relationships improved their classificatory, seriational, numerical, and temporal relationships. The researchers concluded that preschool children need to be motivated to think and make many mental relationships rather than simply to be taught specific subject matter. Such a conclusion provides support for block building. When children build with blocks, they sort, notice shapes and patterns, and develop a network of logical mathematical relationships. Blocks are materials that can be used to teach in the different subject areas. The purpose of this chapter is to describe the value of blocks in the curriculum, how block building contributes to adulthood, how blocks are used as a building toy, the different block categories, the unit or blocks by Caroline Pratt, the block building stages, the block accessories, the block center, and children as builders.

Early childhood education programs use a variety of equipment and materials to support learning through play. Among these materials are blocks and their accessories for building. Blocks are undecorated pieces of wood whose primary purpose is to build. Unit blocks are firm, clean, squarely cut, and solid pieces of hardwood. Their size is based on a common unit of measure and their shapes are repetitive. They are designed to fit together into sturdy structures (Cartwright, 1974). Blocks are safe, unthreatening, sturdy, flexible, and developmentally appropriate for children of all age levels. Blocks also develop the children's social, literacy, physical science, language, art, mathematical, motor, and problem-solving abilities. For example, in block play, young children may engage in the following activities:

- Jena accurately compares sizes, shapes, and numbers.
- Zena describes how she matched the shelf template with block shapes.
- Benny and Zach argue and solve the problem of which tower is taller—without a teacher's input.
- Shakela and Manny draw a picture of a bridge and then build it.
- Paula and Seth chart the weights of different sizes and numbers of blocks.
- Bill and LaTonya push toy trucks up an inclined plane and watch the trucks roll down again.
- Liz and Luis clap (and ask for a picture to be taken) when they finally achieve symmetry in their barn construction (Texas Child Care, 2009, p. 24).

Many times, early childhood teachers overlook the possibility of the children's learning and engaging in cooperative play that occurs when building with blocks. Teachers may find the usually noisy and exciting block play distracting. Nevertheless, block building is one of the activities that is most recommended for preschool, kindergarten, and first grade children. Unfortunately, many early childhood programs have meager supplies of blocks, which severely limits what can be done with them.

## The Value of Blocks

Blocks can be an important component of the early childhood program in relation to the total curriculum and their use has stood the test of time. Blocks are considered the "most important" material found in the preschool or kindergarten classroom (Stark, 1960). When children build, they encounter many puzzling questions that must be solved without any dictated answers. Block building challenges children to become resourceful and creative without restriction (Cartwright, 1974). Children have a driving force to engage in block building. They build and test their ideas about their physical and social world as children stack units, knock them down, enclose spaces, bridge gaps, and duplicate and refine their ideas without the adults' intervention.

Children develop their fine motor skills when they engage in block play, using small and large muscles and developing hand–eye coordination. Within block play, children learn to cooperate and respect their classmates' work, which develops their social skills. Block play is a noncompetitive activity that provides children with a feeling of accomplishment. In addition, block play promotes the children's thinking skills as they plan, organize, test, estimate, and create structures. Children extend their language vocabulary when they engage in conversations with each other as they compare, describe, and label structures. Blocks can promote the young children's geographic understanding as well as their science and mathematics learning (Mitchell, 1934). They develop math concepts when they measure, count, create patterns, add, subtract, compare, and discuss blocks. When children build towers and bridges, they acquire concepts of gravity and balance (Adams & Nesmith, 1996). Young children also develop art concepts in block play when they decorate their structures with painted signs, trees, backdrops, and add other details. Figure 15.1 shows the potential contributions of block play to the different subject areas.

As play materials, blocks are flexible and can be used in a variety of ways. For example, two-year-olds may only experience simple manipulations whereas older children build complex symbolic structures. When children play with blocks, they become aware of the materials' basic characteristics, the buildings that they can construct, the extent of their imagination, and rules when playing with others. Blocks have a dramatic quality. Children can build bold three-dimensional structures that they can see, touch, reach through, and sometimes bump into. When children use blocks to construct structures, change them, destroy them, and reconstruct them repeatedly, they gain skills and knowledge, while enjoying the activity.

Children as young as three years of age will build over long periods of time, trying to construct structures that will please them. Their determination and commitment in finishing a structure that satisfies them provides them with a valuable learning experience (Cartwright, 1974). This kind of learning provides them with a basic preparation for adulthood and their adult responsibilities.

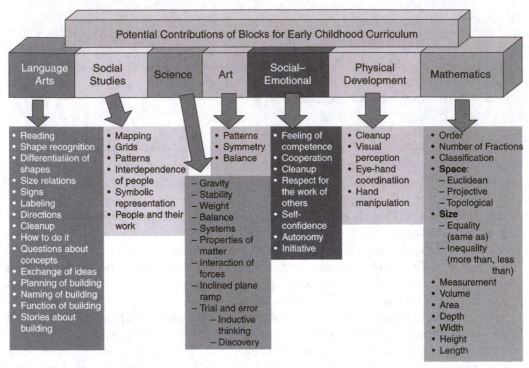

Adapted from Charlotte and Milton Brody. In E.S. Hirsch (Ed.), (1996), *The Block Book.* Washington, DC: National Association for the Education of Young Children. Reprinted with permission from the National Association for the Education of Young Children.

**FIGURE 15.1.** Potential Contributions of Block Play to the Early Childhood Curriculum Adapted from Charlotte and Milton Brody. In E. S. Hirsch (Ed.). (1996). *The Block Book.* Washington, DC: National Association for the Education of Young Children. Reprinted with permission from the National Association for the Education of Young Children.

## Block Building Contributes to Adulthood

Young children use blocks to create and structure their world. The children's configuration of practicality through block play can carry over into adult life. Block play helps young children learn the nature of basic materials, the purpose of things, the use of imagination, and rules that govern social interaction. Adults treat objects and spatial relations in similar ways to block building. For example, construction workers construct a building, storekeepers pack shelves with items to sell, and everyone organizes their closets (Moffitt, 1996). The builders and their inventions determine the size, design, and the materials for their construction (Provenzo & Brett, 1983).

Block building at an early age may influence the children's adult life. For example, as a young child, Albert Einstein became fascinated with building blocks and picture puzzles. His interest in toys may have helped him become a mature thinker while play may have assumed an important role in his work; Einstein explained that he developed the Theory of Relativity by asking himself questions of time and space that only children would ask (Erikson, 1977).

The architecture of block building in kindergarten also influenced two 20th century architects who were considered the greatest: Le Corbusier and Frank Lloyd Wright (Brosterman, 1997). Le Corbusier never attended architectural school; he used his experience more than his academic background in his profession. Since he attended a kindergarten that used Froebelian methods, his kindergarten training influenced his work.[1] Froebel's creative approach to geometry was reflected in all of Le Corbusier's buildings. He had a reliance on proportional systems and an almost religious adherence to the power of geometry, which connected the two practically and psychically. He integrated the concerns for symmetry and order in his work. He advised those who sought to learn architecture (a) to visit natural history museums and compare different types of seashells, (b) to walk through forests to draw leaves and trees, or (c) to observe spreading waves at beaches and the formations of the clouds (Brosterman, 1997).

Blocks also had an impact on the American architect Frank Lloyd Wright. In his autobiography, Wright (1951) describes how at the 1876 Philadelphia Centennial Exhibition his mother discovered an exhibit on Frederick Froebel's kindergarten toys or "Gifts." He states:

> After a sightseeing day, mother made a discovery . . . the Kindergarten! She had seen the "gifts" in the Exposition Building. The strips of colored paper, glazed and "matte," remarkable soft brilliant colors. Now came the geometric by play of those charming checkered combinations! The structural figures to be made with the peas and globes. The smooth shapely maple with which to build, the sense of which never afterwards leaves the fingers: *form* becoming *feeling* (Wright, 1951, p. 13).

> I soon became susceptible to constructive pattern *evolving in everything I saw*. I learned to "see" this way and when I did, I did not care to draw casual incidentals of Nature. I wanted to design (Wright, 1957, p. 2).

If one focuses on the structure and façades of his early buildings, one can become aware of their relationship to the block building activities that were an important part of his childhood (Provenzo & Brett, 1983).

## Blocks: A Building Toy

Most early childhood classrooms have toys that are miniature representations of the children's world. According to Barthes (1972)

> All the toys one commonly sees are essentially a microcosm of the adult world; they are reduced copies of human objects, as if in the eyes of the public the child was, all told, nothing but a smaller man, a homunculus to whom must be supplied objects of this own size (p. 53.)

Barthes believes that toys give children a structured way of seeing the world. Toys help children anticipate the activities of adult life. Early childhood classrooms have several toys that represent adult life such as the kitchen equipment (pots, pans, dishes), household furniture, dolls, cleaning equipment, plastic food, and other similar objects that motivate children to act out their representations of home life (Spodek & Saracho, 1994b). Other toys that help children represent the adult world into their experiences are the doctor's kit, the baby doll, the toy train, and automobiles; also cell phones, remote controls, and computer keyboards. Young children are fascinated by the buttons and lights and reach and grab

---

1  Many credit the first use of blocks as a medium for teaching young children in an educational environment to Froebel, German educator and "father of the kindergarten."

these objects. They observe their parents, family members, and other adults handling them and they want to, too. A set of wooden blocks is a toy that is more basic, versatile, and entertaining. Children can use them to build anything that they can imagine (Walker, 1995).

Blocks are relatively nonspecific and flexible, they are best opened to long-term use and can be combined with more specific playthings (such as block accessories) to motivate make-believe play (Spodek & Saracho, 1994b). Blocks have an inventive nature. Children use blocks to create and structure their personal world. Although blocks are not representative of the children's ready-made world, Barthes (1972) believes that:

> The merest set of blocks, provided it is not too refined, implies a very different learning of the world: then the child does not in any way create meaningful objects, it matters little to him whether they have an adult name, the actions he performs are not those of a user, but those of demiurge. He creates forms which walk, which roll, he creates life, not property: objects now act by themselves. They are no longer an inert and complicated material in the palm of his hand (p. 54).

A building block is a construction toy that is used to educate and entertain both children and adults. While children are building, blocks pose to the children many complicated questions, although the blocks do not prescribe the answers. The children are continuously motivated to be inventive and creative, because blocks are appealing to them. Rudolph and Cohen (1964) describe the children's enthusiasm when they look forward to block building.

> Joey, not yet five, hurriedly peels the sweater off his arms and stuffs the garment, inside out, into his cubby without looking at it. With a deft skip and a slide he lands in front of the richly stocked block shelves, clanks down several piles of blocks, and slaps possessively the smooth surfaces of the top ones. Joey's gestures and facial movements all bear an expression of appetite for those blocks (p. 41).

Joey's physical gestures, the satisfying physical exertion, the delight with the rhythm, and the sound of block building indicates how the children look forward to block building (Rudolph & Cohen, 1984).

## Block Categories

Teachers who are interested in using blocks with children have a wide variety of choices. Besides the unit or Caroline Pratt blocks, alphabet blocks and interlocking systems are among the many types of blocks that are currently available. The selections should be based on the children's interest, age, and developmental level. The different types of blocks are described in Box 15.1 (Provenzo & Brett, 1983).

---

**Box 15.1. Types of Blocks**

- *Picture and alphabet blocks*, which have been used since the end of the 17th century, are cubes with letters that are painted or printed on each of their sides. The best ones are those that have letters or pictures that children can see and touch the shape of. These types of blocks usually have letters, pictures, numbers, and mathematical symbols.

- *Discrimination blocks* include several types of blocks that are used for discrimination purposes. For example, *parquetry blocks* are brightly colored straight-edged geometric blocks that are shaped in triangles, diamonds, and squares. These blocks can be used on the table to build but are better used to create patterns and designs.
- *Pegboard sets* can also be set up with elastic bands to encourage the children to create a variety of shapes. Children can develop their visual perception when they match pattern cards with parquetry blocks. Since *parquetry blocks* are wooden pieces of varying shapes and colors and *pegboard* sets have pegs of different colors, teachers can use them to teach form and color discrimination and retention. Children acquire several skills that contribute to formal reading and mathematics instruction (Spodek & Saracho, 1994b).
- *Large hollow blocks* are made from kiln-dried hardwood with a protective finish so that they can be used both indoors and outdoors. Children can use these blocks to build large structures where they can stand, walk on, and enter them. These blocks can also be used to create settings (e.g., stores, puppet stages, etc.). Hollow blocks are typically established on a unit of one square foot. Its large sides are made of plywood or solid wood to use with open sides. Hollow blocks include half units and double units as well as triangle ramps and boards. Their size and sturdiness allows children to build large structures that represent buildings, vehicles, or furniture, which allow children to play in them.
- *Super blocks* are large plastic blocks that are hollow and are divided into several small compartments. Children find that these blocks have many interesting areas and holes where they can place objects.
- *Large cardboard blocks* are light and can be used to build structures on the floor. Since they are light and made out of cardboard, they are not durable and cannot be used outside. Their light weight causes the structures to be weak, and both the cardboard blocks and the children's structures only last for a short period of time (Spodek & Saracho, 1994b).
- *Bristle blocks* are interlocking plastic blocks that have bristles that stick out from their sides. Children use the bristles to stick the blocks together in arrangements that are not possible with the traditional blocks.
- *Legos* are interlocking plastic building blocks that were created in Denmark in the 1930s. The product is a line of construction toys that includes colorful interlocking plastic bricks with an additional assortment of gears, mini figures and several other pieces. Legos are of different sizes that can be used in a variety of ways. Bricks, tubes, beams, axles, gears, mini figures, and all other pieces in the Lego system are fitted together in a variety of ways. Children use these pieces to create elaborate constructions and patterns as well as use them in many activities. Teachers can also use Legos to introduce children to mathematical concepts such as place value, size, or making comparisons.
- *Construction sets*, which are small sets of constructive materials (e.g., *Lego, Tinker Toys, Lincoln Logs*, or similar materials), encourage children to make imaginative creations or to construct small buildings. The children's small size structures can be used to engage in miniature dramatic play with them.
- *Wooden unit blocks* are open ended materials that give children the opportunity to represent their world when they build their structures. These blocks were created by Caroline Pratt and will be discussed in the following sections.

## Unit or Caroline Pratt Blocks

In 1913 Caroline Pratt, an educator who received woodwork training in Sweden, developed the system of blocks for her experimental classroom located in New York City. In her book, *I Learn from Children*, Pratt (1948) stated:

> A child playing on his nursery floor, constructing an entire railroad system out of blocks and odd boxes he had salvaged from the wastepaper basket, taught me that the play impulse in children is a work impulse (p. 17).

Pratt wanted the children to use the blocks to construct their own world. She believed that her blocks were:

> so flexible, so adaptable, that children could use it without guidance or control. I wanted to see them build a world; I wanted to see them create on their own level the life about them, in which they were too little to be participants, in which they were always spectators (p. 18).

> A simple geometrical shape could become any number of things to a child. It could be a truck or a boat or a train. He could build buildings with it from barns to skyscrapers. I could see the children of my as yet unborn school constructing a complete community with blocks (p. 35).

To date, her blocks are frequently used (Cohen & Uhry, 2007, 2011) in most early childhood programs. The blocks in early childhood programs that were designed by Caroline Pratt (1948, 1970, 1990) decades ago are the large set of standard unit blocks, made of hardwood, and are distributed by educational equipment companies. The two types of blocks are the small unit blocks and the large hollow blocks. The set of smaller unit blocks lets the children miniaturize their world, while the set of larger hollow blocks helps them to build large structures that are appropriate for dramatic play. Unit blocks consist of solid, brick-like pieces of wood that are usually made of hard wood. The size of the basic unit is five and one-half inches by two and three-quarter inches, by one and three-eighth inches. The size of the double and quadruple units is two and four times the length of the single unit block, and half units of one-half its length. The block set also includes scaled proportions of ramps, triangles, pillars, and boards. Since the proportions are the same, children can build sturdy elaborate structures that will stay up on their own. Figure 15.2 illustrates the different types of blocks.

## Block Building Stages

Young children spend many hours stacking, balancing, building, grouping, sorting, spacing, ordering, and planning with blocks as they progress through developmental stages (Hirsch, 1996). Young children use unit block structures to build on the floor. At the beginning they may only pile blocks up or build simple enclosures. As children's block play progresses, they build more elaborate structures that may take them several days to finish. Johnson (1933) first identified these stages, which have been used and modified by others. She observed children while they were playing with unit blocks and found that children build several basic structures. When they are left alone, young children often begin by just carrying blocks around. They then move on to simple constructions, and

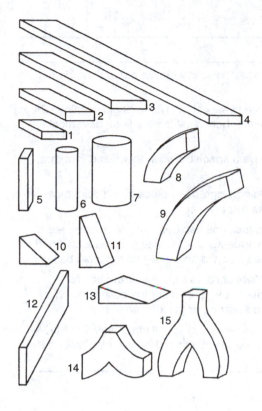

1. Half unit
2. Unit
3. Double unit
4. Quadruple unit
5. Pillar
6. Small cylinder
7. Large cylinder
8. Circular curve
9. Elliptical curve
10. Small triangle
11. Large triangle
12. Floor board
13. Ramp
14. Right-angle switch
15. Y switch

Blocks may come in other sizes and shapes as well.

**FIGURE 15.2.   Types of unit blocks.** From Bank Street College of Education. Publications; no. 70. Publisher: New York: Bank Street College of Education, 1962. Edition Reprinted with permission from the Bank Street College Archives, Bank Street College of Education, New York City.

then to building more elaborate structures that convey a dramatic content. Table 15.1 describes the different block-building stages (Johnson, 1933).

Children with disabilities may need some type of intervention to progress through these stages. For example, children with orthopedic or physical disabilities who are unable to carry blocks to their building area may need help in getting blocks with which to build. Children with orthopedic or physical disabilities who have difficulty holding a sitting

**TABLE 15.1. Block Building Stages**

| Building Stage | Description |
| --- | --- |
| Carrying Blocks | Before children are 2 years of age, they carry blocks around and do not use them for construction |
| Begin Building | At approximately age two or three years old, children begin building. They usually build rows, which are either horizontal (on the floor) or vertical (stacking) |
| Bridging | Children set up two blocks, leave a space between them, and roof that space with a third block |
| Enclosures | This is the children's early building stage. They place four blocks together in such a way that they enclose a space |
| Patterns | Between the ages of three and four, children begin to get so competent with blocks that another stage appears; that is, they build balanced and symmetrical patterns. At this stage, children usually do not label buildings |
| Representation | Between the ages of four and five, children label the structures for dramatic play. Such labels relate to the function of the building such as the garage, the bedroom, the play room, or the kitchen |
| Reproduction | Beginning at age five, children usually build actual structures that they know. They are strongly motivated to engage in dramatic play around the structures |

position need help with sitting close to the floor for block building. Teachers can cut one side of a large cardboard box, plastic trash can, or laundry basket. The other side is left complete and is used to offer the children with orthopedic or physical disabilities minimal support. A strap can be buckled under their arms to help them sit up. Casters are fastened under the can, box, or basket to help children with orthopedic or physical disabilities move by pushing off with their hands. Children with an intellectual disability may need adult modeling of representational play with the props. Children with visual impairments may need help in finding and tactfully exploring blocks. In addition, teachers can urge typically developing children to offer encouragement and support to the children with disabilities who need it. At all times, teachers must consider various interactions that respect the need for the children with disabilities to become independent and receive appropriate respect and support.

Teachers can become sensitive to the stages at which their children are building and use an understanding of these stages to guide children's block building. For example, when the children's structures become representational, they can add block accessories to represent places and to dramatize events that might occur in those places. Block accessories consist of props, miniature people, animals, vehicles, signs, and the like, and can be included as as children use the blocks.

## Block Accessories

Every early childhood classroom should have a good set of wooden unit blocks as a play material to facilitate constructive play. In addition, many kinds of block accessories can be used to supplement the children's block experiences.

Block accessories should be realistic (such as trucks, dolls, boats) to extend the children's block building structures. Young children can manipulate miniature objects or characters that become part of their world. Building with unit blocks can lead to miniature dramatizations, which can be encouraged by providing (a) appropriate accessories, (b) sufficient time to encourage children to go beyond manipulative building, and (c) resources to expand dramatic themes.

When children use blocks to build police stations, zoos, castles, or houses, they engage in dramatic and fantasy play. Props (such as human figures, animals, and cars) invite children to play in the building area. For example, a fire truck can encourage children to build a fire house, whereas farm animals can encourage dramatic play related to farming (Provenzo & Brett, 1983). Objects like sea shells, colored stones, pieces of cardboard, and paper stimulate the children's imagination, and they use the materials to represent a variety of things. Children may use a sea shell to represent a boat crossing an ocean and use a piece of colored paper for a bird flying through the air. Box 15.2 shows several accessories that can be provided in the block area (Spodek & Saracho, 1994b).

---

### Box 15.2. Block Accessories

- Toys are useful accessories. Small cars, rubber or wooden people and animals, pulleys, airplanes, and trucks can all be used.
- Colored cubes can be added to blocks, as can parquetry blocks or large dominoes. Assortments of odd shaped small blocks or sewing thread spools can be put into boxes for use in decorating buildings.
- Pebbles, small stones, and little sticks can serve as cargo for trains, boats, and trucks.
- Lumber scraps, especially flat pieces for constructing roofs and wide bridges, will enhance block constructions.
- Small, familiar signs such as "one way," "school crossing," or "bus stop" can be added to children's construction. Tongue depressors or popsicle sticks stuck in clay or play dough can be used to anchor these signs.
- Thin pieces of rubber tubing tacked to a cylinder block can become a simple gas pump.
- Excelsior (fine wood shavings that are used for stuffing or packing) makes good hay for farm animals.
- Trees can be drawn on paper, cut out, stapled to a tongue depressor or popsicle stick, and stuck into a piece of clay or play dough to stand.
- Pulleys, with ropes and containers, make wonderful elevators.
- Dry cell batteries with bell wire and flashlight bulbs are popular accessories.
- Magazine pictures of bridges, roads, constructions, or city scenes can be mounted on cardboard and displayed on the walls of the block area.
- Stories, photos, diagrams, poems, lists and informative texts can influence the children's construction.
- Children's books can be provided for the class to develop ideas for block construction. Since books that show interesting building structures can influence the children's construction work and play, they need to be accessible in the area

where children are building. For example, if a theme is "city scenes," the books might include:

1. Goodspeed, J. (1956). *Let's Go Watch a Building Going Up*. New York: G. P. Putnam's Sons.
2. Milich, Zoran (2005). *City*. Tonawanda, New York: Kids Can Press, Ltd.
3. Morris, Ann. (1995). Photographs by Ken Heyman. *Houses and Homes*. New York: Harper Trophy (HarperCollins).

Children who have special needs can use block accessories. Different figural characteristics of a toy can help the children with visual impairments to identify the various parts of the toy that represent the different parts of an animal such as the animal's face. Children with linguistic and cultural differences enjoy using block accessories during block building. Block accessories for these children can include collections of miniature people, representing people from a variety of ethnicities, of differing abilities, and of varying family constellations. Signs that are written in different languages can be used in their block structures, such as names of streets or shops in their block city.

Children can become master builders when they have access to many different materials including paper, scissors, crayons, and tape (Carter, 1985). These materials can be displayed in the block area. In addition, reading to the entire class, small groups, or individual children can also motivate children to build structures that are in the story they heard.

## Guidelines for Storing Blocks and Block Accessories

Blocks and their accessories need to have appropriate storage space that can help children store them properly and encourage block play. Box 15.3 suggests guidelines for storing blocks and their accessories (Adams & Nesmith, 1996).

---

**Box 15.3. Guidelines for Storing Blocks and their Accessories**

- The unit blocks need to be placed on open shelving where each shape is clearly identified using coded areas and spaces. The blocks need their own space and no other toys should be stored on these shelves. There should be sufficient shelves to store all available blocks in an area where children are able to easily grasp, remove, and shape them into neat stacks.
- The unit blocks need adequate storage space. Block structures that are built away from the main flow of traffic can be left on display overnight or for several days.
- Large portable blocks can be stored almost anywhere, placed in a crate with wheels, and moved to an open area that has room for motor play.
- Large blocks and unit blocks can be stored in large packing crates either inside or outside. Since they are durable and weatherproof, they can be stored outside under a covered area in large packing crates.

- Block accessories need to be proportionate in size to the blocks. They need to be stored in the block area.
- Children can take out different sizes, shapes, and numbers of blocks to build their structure. However, they need to know that they can take from the shelves only the number of blocks that they need to build their structures. After they start building, they can return and get more blocks. Taking the appropriate amount of blocks from the shelves makes clean up time easier.
- Children need to have sufficient time to store their blocks during the clean up period. They need to be informed when it is almost time to move to the next activity so that they get to a stopping point in their building. Children need a 10-minute signal (Cartwright, 1988).

## Rules for Builders

Children build their structures and discuss them. They also need to discuss with the class their expectations and routines for using, moving, and putting away blocks. Both the teacher and children discuss and decide on rules that will help them build safely and enjoy their block play. Such expectations can be recorded on a chart with words or pictures for children to follow. Rules, such as those in Box 15.4, are posted in the block building area (Chalufour & Worth, 2004).

### Box 15.4. Safe Rules for Builders

1. Blocks are used for building.
2. Take blocks off the shelves as you need them.
3. Blocks that fall onto the floor must be picked up and placed back on the table.
4. Take structures apart from the top down.
5. Do not crash the blocks.
6. Do not throw the blocks.
7. Do not walk on blocks.
8. Do not build higher than you are tall.

Teachers also need to arrange the block area so that blocks are easy to take out and put back. The following is a scenario in helping young children to store the blocks after they have finished playing with them.

### Example of Modeling

*Ms. Owen has noted that Richard has difficulty putting the blocks away at cleanup time. At times, he grabs blocks from another child who is also helping to clean up the block area. Ms. Owen kneels down next to Richard and begins picking up blocks alongside of him, placing them in the appropriate place on the shelf. As she does this she says to Richard, "see, there is work for each of us to do at cleanup time. But maybe it would be good to do it together. I will hand each block to you and you can put them on the shelf. That way we can work together and get cleaned up faster." They continue to cleanup together* (Spodek & Saracho, 1994b, pp. 175–176).

In addition, teachers should:

- Provide enough blocks to help children build representative structures. They need to have sufficient blocks, different blocks, and block accessories.
- Keep a storage area for toys that can be used as accessories (such as transportation toys, small toy animals, people).
- Initiate building with blocks at the beginning of the year.

Blocks are expensive and they take up a lot of space in the classroom. However, a great deal of learning can take place through the use of blocks, provided that (a) there is an adequate supply of them, (b) there is enough space for building, and (c) children are allowed to build elaborate block structures over several days.

## The Block Center

Most early childhood classrooms have a block center to support constructive and dramatic play. In constructive play children use materials to build or create something whereas in dramatic play children assume roles and act them out. For instance, Justin created a highway, using his mastery of spatial and motor skills. When he used a double unit block as a car to drive on the highway, he was engaging in drama. Justin used the blocks to cross back and forth between a concrete and an abstract representation or between physical and cognitive concept.

Thus, block play can contain both physical and dramatic elements. Related materials can promote both real and symbolic situations (Bender, 1978). Most children love playing with blocks; they find them to be appealing, familiar (Adams & Nesmith, 1996), dramatic materials, and easy to work with. They can actually build something with these three-dimensional materials as they are able to see, touch, reach through, and at times even crash them. Young children enjoy mastering their work as they build, use, change, destroy, and build again with blocks. Children as young as three years old work for long periods of time building and rebuilding a structure. Their persistence and involvement with blocks help make this material a valuable learning experience (Cartwright, 1974). Carter (1985) describes a conversation in the block center where children are talking to each other about their building projects.

"I need a block that arches like a moon," Jamal mutters to himself.

"This robot will be like R2D2 except that he can see through walls," said Chemeka. "Where are the clear blocks for his eyes?"

"This fort doesn't look right—on my pattern it shows a garage for the tanks, and the tanks won't fit in there," complains Tony (p. 8).

Their conversation suggests that they have clearly planned and designed a strategy for each of their structures. The children's designs can extend, expand, and promote their creative skills.

Building with unit blocks can also miniaturize their dramatizations when appropriate block accessories and ideas are provided to serve as sources for dramatic themes. Children also need to have sufficient time to go beyond manipulative building. Teachers can use a variety of resources to help children progress to the next stage in block play, such as reading books, showing videos, having discussions, inviting resource persons to class, and taking children on field trips. These resources also help children to distinguish between fantasy and reality during block play.

Children can walk through the school's neighborhood (Pratt & Stanton, 1926). When they return to the classroom, they can build block structures to represent their observations of the neighborhood. In the block center they can have the opportunities to build houses, stores, schools, and transportation systems. Children need to be provided with props to extend their play: a traffic light to control the movement of cars, toy farm animals and people to help them create a farm, or toy airplanes to motivate them to construct an airport. Teachers can introduce children to a dramatic role that they can assume while they build. A resource person (for example an architect, builder, engineer, mason, amateur carpenter, amateur builder) can visit the classroom and talk with the children about their work, then the children can act their role in the block area. When children are continually given access to blocks and time to experiment, they use blocks to symbolize objects from the real world and frequently intertwine block play with dramatic play. For example, children may plan their constructions before removing the first blocks from the shelf, and assign roles to each collaborative builder (Texas Child Care, 2009).

Many early childhood classrooms have (a) a set of blocks that includes a variety of sizes and shapes of blocks and (b) materials that will motivate children to build and role play their ideas. Children have their own ideas, interests, and beliefs about building based on their experience and developmental level. The classroom and the outdoors need to have an environment that communicates the excitement, challenge, and wonder of building with a variety of materials that are diverse, high quality, and can provide children with rich opportunities in their block building.

Block play can optimally facilitate the development of young children with disabilities. The environment needs to be modified for these children to fully participate in block building and interact with the other classroom children. With appropriate adaptations, children with disabilities can engage in block building. For example, children in wheelchairs can be at the floor level when they use a scooter (belly board or crawler) in different ways. The scooter board is a rectangular board of three-quarters of an inch thick plywood with heavy duty casters attached to each corner. For protection, the board is padded with a layer of foam or some other kind of cushion and covered with vinyl. Children with orthopedic or physical disabilities can lie on their stomachs on top of scooter boards while raising their heads, propelling themselves using their hands or elbows, reaching around themselves, and building with blocks, block accessories, or manipulative toys. Children with visual impairments can feel the various shapes of blocks and build with them. They can develop a sense of balance when they build structures that do not collapse.

A variety of blocks need to be available including natural color unit blocks of different sizes and shapes. Young children will enjoy building with blocks that have shapes typical of certain cultures. For example, there are sets that have domes for Russian buildings and other types of architecture. Box 15.5 suggests blocks and materials for the block center (Chalufour & Worth, 2004).

**Box 15.5. Blocks and Materials for the Block Center**

- Materials should differ in size, shape, weight, texture, and degrees of flexibility.
- Art materials should help interpret structures in many forms.
- Visual materials (e.g., books, videos, posters, photos) about building different structures need to be displayed in the block area.
- Posters of structures and large photographs of different buildings also can be displayed in the construction area. These should include different kinds of constructions (e.g., houses, towers, walls, fences, playground equipment, billboards) that people have created and natural ones (e.g., trees, cliffs, skeletons) that are found in the children's world. Such structures motivate children to build on their own.

The block center in the early childhood classroom promotes the children's dramatic play, especially when it includes block accessories such as dress-up clothes, steering wheels, toy cars and trucks, and innumerable other devices that support play activities. During block play, young children engage in other types of play such as dramatic or symbolic play. When children build based on themes, they also engage in dramatic and fantasy play. For example, they build police stations, zoos, castles, and houses. Block accessories (human figures, animals, cars) in the building area can motivate them to create a theme.

Block play provides children with opportunities to extend their thinking and building. The blocks center has the capacity to foster the children's creative thinking. It can provide children with many of the "building blocks" they need to develop their thinking skills. Children clearly understand that blocks are for building. They carefully space their creations. Teachers can guide the children with questions such as, "How high do the walls need to be to hold the elephants?" and "How can we make the castle tower very tall?" (Chalufour & Worth, 2004, p. 6). Often children will become intrigued with the building process and participate in exploratory play when they attempt to balance one block on another, determine which blocks will make the tallest tower, or build a foundation that is stable enough to hold up a wall (Chalufour & Worth, 2004). Adams and Nesmith (1996) describe how several young children engaged in block and dramatic play.

> Four boys and two girls sat comfortably on the floor in the block center sharing blocks and exchanging a few words occasionally, but mostly working intently on a "floor table." Six quadruple unit blocks formed the outer edge of a rectangular table, but there weren't enough to fill in the center evenly. "It doesn't look right," said Octavian as he started to remove an inside block. "Wait. Put this one in the corner," suggested LeMuel, passing a double unit block as he spoke. It must have been an acceptable solution because the remaining spaces were quickly filled with the double units. "Let's cover it up so we can eat," said Orlisa as she draped a cloth scrap over the "floor table." She then went to the housekeeping center and brought back teacups and paper plates (p. 87).

When children engage in block play, popular culture affects the children's ability to distinguish between their real world versus their imaginary world symbolism. According to Marsh and Millard (2000), "Children are constantly engaged in decoding the reality in the world around them, interpreting it according to their own sociocultural practices and experiences and then encoding it using whatever range of materials are available" (p. 49). For example, four- and five-year-old children remember facts and can tell the differences between a toy character from one medium (a stuffed animal) to another (a computer game). Children who construct block structures can interpret the virtual rules from a computer game to their play with blocks (Okita, 2004).

## Children as Builders

Children's urge to build is inherent. Block play is a basic experience in the education of young children. Playing with blocks provides them with many learning opportunities (Hewitt, 2001), including the acquisition of skills in symbolism, imagination, and pretending. Building with blocks can help young children achieve many complex and academic skills.

## Advanced Block Building Structures

Block building stimulates symbolic play when children act out the role of construction workers, architects, engineers, or masons. Teachers can display books, invite guest visitors, and provide props that have information that helps children understand these roles. In addition, the block area should include architectural drawing tools (drafting pencils, compasses, drawing /drafting triangles, architects' scales, erasers, books, DVDs) that children can use to build and to act out their roles (Chalfour & Worth, 2004). A working table nearby can encourage children to make three-dimensional models of their structures. Children can draw a sketch or take a photograph of the original structure before the modeling process. Individual or small groups of children can plan their construction and create a model. Children may need collage materials (wood, painters' tape, Q-tips, tracing paper, rags, paper towels, heavy paper) to create their model. When finished, children can share their models with the class and visitors.

Children need to learn that builders are careful planners, which helps them build better structures. Before they begin to build, they need to sketch, draw, and describe what they want to build, including the materials that are needed to build their structures (Chalufour & Worth, 2004). Lester Walker (1995), an award winning architect, recommends and illustrates several block building projects that he used with his young sons. First he provides a sketch of the "real" building, which is then followed by a suggestion of how it might be translated into a block construction. He includes designs for everyday buildings like car washes and drive-in restaurants. These also offer the opportunity for the young architects to compare their projects to the real things and to experience the mystery of scale that is such a big part of the architecture game. Children can build a variety of block projects, which can be displayed like they do in a museum. For example, Table 15.2 lists 18 block-building projects from around the world (Walker, 1995).

The following descriptions and sample prompts can be used with children during their block building activities (Walker, 1995).

### American Town Structures

This grouping of structures from the American countryside includes three commercial buildings that gained their popularity in the 1950s and are favorites among children. These projects are grouped from the least to the most challenging.

**TABLE 15.2. Block Building Projects from Around the World**

| Type of Structure | Examples |
| --- | --- |
| American Town Structures | Boat dock<br>Farm<br>House<br>Shopping center<br>Car wash<br>Drive-in restaurant |
| Great Civic Structures | Airport<br>Bridge<br>Train station<br>Skyscraper |
| Cities | Toy Store City<br>The Emerald City (Wizard of Oz)<br>City of the Future |
| Great Historical Structures | Greek temple<br>Synagogue<br>Cathedral<br>Mosque<br>Castle |

*Sample Prompts:*

Boat dock:       Imagine walking along the boat dock on a foggy night as fishermen unload their catches under bright spotlights, with the beam of the lighthouse streaking through the mist.

Shopping center:  Think about owning a store in the shopping center, the kind of store, the name of your store, and the items you would sell.

## Great Civic Structures

These are among the four best known and largest types of buildings in the world that are for public use. The bridge, train station, and airport developed as people began to travel by car, train, and airplane. The skyscraper, another American icon, is an exciting project, because a sudden blow of wind might cause the skyscraper to crash, leading to excitement during the construction.

*Sample Prompts:*

Airport:       Think about flying out of an airport on a clear sunny day and the excitement of looking out the window to watch the way the world below gets smaller and smaller as you go higher and higher.

Skyscraper:    Think about how you would feel to build the tallest building in the world and at the grand opening ceremony, ride to the top floor in a supersonic elevator.

## Great Historical Structures

These structures are the best known buildings throughout history. Greek temples were built as early as 500 B.C. Their elaborate details decorate their basic post and beam design, which continues to have an effect on Western architecture. Since synagogues have many unique forms, children can build their own style using their imagination. Cathedrals that were built in European cities and mosques that were built in the Middle East around the 13th century are among the most attractive and awe-inspiring religious structures ever built. The castle, which was built all over Europe and Asia during medieval times, has the most appeal to children.

*Sample Prompts:*

Synagogue:   Make a mental picture of a beautiful building that will be used for prayer. Think about how you will feel when the building is completed.

Cathedral:   Create a mental picture where you are standing inside a cathedral that was constructed with slender stone columns and beams that hold the huge walls of stained glass and the space inside is so high that clouds are at the top of the ceiling.

## Cities of the Future

Most cities everywhere have grown. There were routes and trials along rivers and around hills where people live. As industry developed, buildings for cities were constructed around these pathways. Traffic (such as trains, cars) grew around where people lived and worked. This grouping of structures forms different types of cities.

- *The Toy Store City* is a grid city with a crisscross pattern of north–south and east–west streets as its traffic pattern. Each block in the grid has a market, hardware store, clothing store, restaurant, apartments, and other necessary shops. Ideally each block is a concise little town within itself.
- *The Emerald City of Oz* is the capital city of The Land of Oz that was visited by Dorothy, her dog Toto, the Tin Man, the Lion, and the Scarecrow from the book and movie *The Wizard of Oz*. This city may include beautiful forests and farmlands that are surrounded by a large desert and populated with over half a million fairies.
- *City of the Future* may have a high speed monorail transit system running down its center for transportation to a narrow metropolitan area. This city will include parks, playgrounds, children's museums, zoo, countryside farm, and schools within walking distance from their home.

*Prompts:*

Toy Store City:   The Toy Store City can be devised with any toy store that the children have in mind. Any type of toy can be sold in this city. All they need to do is build the city around its streets. Imagine a city that has a different toy store on every block and you are the proud owner of several gift certificates. You can buy anything you want.

The Emerald City
of Oz:                  Create a mental image that you are walking on a road paved with
                        yellow bricks, across a wide field to a glowing, shiny green city
                        with your best friends, Dorothy, her dog Toto, the Tin Man, the
                        Lion, and the Scarecrow. When you go through the gates to
                        the city, you have the choice of meeting the wizard or going
                        sightseeing in this fantastic place.

City of the Future:     Think about riding a high speed monorail that is traveling at 80
                        miles an hour which will take you 10 minutes to visit a friend in a
                        different neighborhood in your city. When you get there, you can
                        decide if you want to walk to the downtown area, to the zoo, or to
                        the countryside to visit a farm.

Another prompt idea is the use of popular movies that preschoolers see. Teachers can use the movies and television shows that young children are seeing that are part of their culture and of which they have prior knowledge. Teachers can listen to the children's discussions and use them to provide the prompts in block play.

Block accessories can be used to motivate children to build authentic structures. Several block accessories (see Box 15.6) can be used to motivate young children with these projects (Walker, 1995).

---

**Box 15.6.  Block Accessories for Building Projects from around the World**

- Toy people of any scale can be used for almost any block building project.
- Cars, especially the metal ones that are about two and a half inches long, give a good scale to city, highway, and parking projects.
- Traffic signs are needed for any highway related construction and to direct vehicles.
- Toy animals stimulate block building projects such as zoos and farms.
- Modular windows and doors that can fit within the unit block dimensions and have the same scale as the dollhouses.
- Interconnecting train tracks with trains, a wooden toy that is compatible in size with the unit block system.
- Boats, trains, and airplanes are good transportation block accessories.
- Doll furniture can make a room look real. The doll furniture needs to be comparable in size to the unit blocks.
- Turnings that are store-bought wooden bed legs, railings, cabinet door handles, and newel post finials can make a block construction an exotic architectural masterpiece.
- Dowels that are store-bought can be cut into many narrow cylinders that can be used as supplements to a block set.

---

Children need to be introduced to the procedures of block building. Teachers can follow the procedures in Box 15.7 when children are working on their block building project (Walker, 1995).

**Box 15.7. Procedures to Follow When Children Are Block Building**

1. Children need a brief introduction before they begin each project.
2. During construction, children will learn something basic about architecture and architectural vocabulary. For example, they will learn about *flying buttresses* when they build a cathedral and the *column* and *beam* when they build a Greek temple.
3. Each project is meant to simply get the children started.
4. After children have completed their block building project, they can add to it or subtract from it based on their own designs. For example, they can add more stores, even a theater complex, to the shopping center or add more highways to the bridge project.
5. The project can stay on display in the block building area overnight or for several days.
6. Children can change it and play with it as they wish. But they need to make each project their own.

Children can chant, sing a song, or say a poem while they are building.

## Record the Children's Structures

Encourage children to observe, share, and examine the structures that they constructed. Children can have a walkabout every few days to look at the buildings that are still on display. Chalufour and Worth (2004) provide the following suggestions for the walkabout.

- At the end of the building period, the class can walk about the room to look at the buildings that their classmates built.
- Children can explain to the class their structures, including what they have been building and playing.
- The teacher can take photographs or make large drawings of the children's structures. The photographs can be enlarged, discussed, and displayed at the block building area.

Children's learning increases when they engage in building structures, representing them, and thinking about their experiences. Such experiences give children the opportunity to test and refine their ideas about their world, balance, stability, and materials.

## Summary

Early childhood educators authenticate the value of classroom materials for young children's development, which is promoted through block building. As a matter of fact, blocks are viewed as the most accepted and useful equipment in early childhood education programs. The blocks' different shapes, sizes, and weights contribute to the children's learning experiences from infancy through early childhood. In addition, blocks promote all of the children's development areas (physical, social, emotional, cognitive) (Cartwright, 1988).

The children engage in different developmental levels of block building based on their experiences. Younger and less experienced children need more support and motivation with their block constructions. The children's block-building stages range from carrying blocks around and not building (usually children under age two) to building structures that are more symbolic and focus on dramatic play (usually children over age five) (Johnson, 1933). Teachers need to determine the children's block building stages to understand their block play and offer them developmentally appropriate support and guidance.

Children carry blocks outside and around the classrooms. The openness of the unit and large blocks extends the number of different ways that the blocks can be used for teaching and learning. There is an indefinite number of ways that blocks can be used in the classroom (Adams & Nesmith, 1996). The presence of blocks in the classroom is increasing as educators are becoming aware of their importance in the children's learning. When children build, they

- act out stories using blocks as chairs, tables, and other props
- measure and stack blocks to make patterns
- study blocks and discuss how they are made.

Blocks, as classroom materials, determine the children's play activities. Their realism and usefulness contribute to the quality of the children's play. The flexibility, variety, and unconditional, satisfying qualities of blocks make them among the most proficient toys accessible for children. Children enjoy and learn with blocks, which makes them the best tool for both play and education. It is important that teachers understand the importance of blocks so that they can increase their use (Provenzo & Brett, 1983) in the classroom.

# References

Adams, P. K., & Nesmith, J. (1996). Blockbusters: Ideas for the block center. *Early Childhood Education*, 24(2), 87–92.

Addison, R. (1991). Music and play. *British Journal of Research in Music Education*, 8, 207–217.

Ahn, J., & Filipenko, M. (2007). Narrative, imaginary play, art, and self: Intersecting worlds. *Early Childhood Education Journal*, 34(4), 279–289.

Allen, J., Fabregas, V., Hankins, K. H., Hull, G., Labbo, L., Lawson, H. S., Michalove, B., Piazza, S., Piha, C., Sprague, L., Townsend, S., & English, C. U. (2002). PhOLKS lore: Learning from photographs, families, and children. *Language Arts*, 79(4), 312–322.

Almy, M. (2000). What wisdom should we take with us as we enter the new century? An interview with Millie Almy. *Young Children*, 55(1), 6.

Alschuler, R., & Hattwick, L. (1947). *Painting and personality*. Chicago, IL: University of Chicago Press.

American Association for the Advancement of Science. (1993). *Benchmarks for science literacy*. New York: Oxford University Press.

Anderson, D., Kisiel, J., & Storksdieck, M. (2006). Understanding teachers' perspectives on field trips: Discovering common ground in three countries. *Curator*, 49, 365–386.

Anderson, S., & Hoot, J. L. (1986). Kids, carpentry, and the preschool classroom. *Day Care and Early Childhood*, 13(3), 12–15.

Andress, B. (1998). *Music for young children*. Fort Worth, TX: Harcourt Brace.

Antell, S. E., & Keating, D. P. (1983). Perception of numerical invariance in neonates. *Child Development*, 54, 695–701.

Antonacci, P., & O'Callaghan, C. (2004). *Portraits of literacy development: Instruction and assessment in a well-balanced literacy program, K-3*. Upper Saddle River, NJ: Pearson.

Ariès, P. (1962). *Centuries of childhood: A social history of family life*. New York: Vintage Books, a division of Random House.

Aristotle. (1958). *The poetics*. New York: Pocket Books, Inc.

Aronoff, F. W. (1979). *Music and young children*. New York: Turning Wheel Press.

Arts Education Partnership. (1998). *Young children and the arts: Making creative connections*. A Report of the Task Force on Children's Learning and the Arts: Birth to Age Eight. Washington, DC: Arts Education Partnership.

Association for Library Service to Children (2007). *2007 notable children's books*. Retrieved on May 18, 2009, from http://www.ala.org/ala/alsc/awardsscholarships/childrensnotable/notablecbooklist/currentnotable.htm

Association of Children's Museums (2007). *Annual Report 2006B2007*. Retrieved on July 30, 2009, from http://www.childrensmuseums.org/docs/ACMAR08%20FINAL.pdf

Auden, W. H. (1965, April 3). As it seemed to us. *New Yorker*, 159–192.

Ault, Jr., C. R. (1987). The museum as science teacher. *Science and Children*, 25(3), 8–11.

Axline, V. (2002). *Play therapy*. New York: Elsevier Science Limited.

Bacon, D. (1969). Kodály and Orff report from Europe. *Music Educators Journal*, 55(8), 53–56.

Bae, J. (2004). Learning to teach visual arts in an early childhood classroom: The teacher's role as a guide. *Early Childhood Education Journal*, 31(4), 247–254.

Bagley, D. M., & Klass, P. H. (1997). Comparison of the quality of preschoolers' play in housekeeping and thematic sociodramatic play centers. *Journal of Research in Childhood Education*, 12(1), 71–77.

Bakerlis, J. (2007). Children's art show: An educational family experience. *Young Children*, 62(1), 88–91.

Bankauskas, D. (2000). Teaching chess to young children. *Young Children*, 55, 33–34.

Baquedano-López, P. (2003). Language, literacy and community. In N. Hall, J. Larson, & J. Marsh (Eds.), *Handbook of early childhood literacy* (pp. 66–74). Thousand Oaks, CA: Sage.

Barclay, K. D., & Walwer, L. (1992). Linking lyrics and literacy through song picture books. *Young Children*, 47(4), 76–85.

Barroquiero, D. (2010). The value of art in early childhood. Retrieved on December 23, 2010, from http://www.suite101.com/content/the-value-of-art-in-early-childhood-a292813

Barthes, R. (1972). *Mythologies*. New York: Hill and Wang.

Barton, B. (1981). *Building a house*. New York: Harper Collins.

Bateson, G. (1955). A theory of play and fantasy. *Psychological Abstracts Research Report*, 2, 39–51.

Becker, J., & Miltner, D. (2002). Developments in young children's mathematical reasoning. In O. N. Saracho & B. Spodek (Eds.), *Contemporary perspectives on early childhood curriculum* (pp. 131–154). Greenwich, CT: Information Age.

Bender, J. (1971). Have you ever thought of a prop box? *Young Children*, 26(3), 164–170.

Bender, J. (1978). Large hollow blocks: Relationship of quantity to block building behaviors. *Young Children*, 33(6), 17–23.

Benjamin, A. H. (1992) *What's up the coconut tree?* (Illustrated by Val Biro). New York: Oxford University Press.

Bergen, D. (1988). Introduction. In D. Bergen (Ed.), *Play as a medium for learning and development* (pp. 1–4). Portsmouth, NH: Heinemann.

Bergen, D. (2000). Linking technology and teaching practice. *Childhood Education* 76(4), 252–253.

Bergen, D. (2009). Play as the learning medium for future scientists, mathematicians, and engineers. *American Journal of Play*, 1, 413–428.

Berger, A. A., & Cooper, S. (2003). Musical play: A case study of preschool children and parents. *Journal of Research in Music Education*, 51(2), 151–166.

Berger, K. S. (2008). *The developing person through childhood and adolescence*. New York: Bedford, Freeman & Worth Publishing Group, LLC.

Berlyne, D. E. (1969). Laughter, humor, and play. In G. Lindsey & E. Aronson (Eds.), *Handbook of social psychology*, Vol 3 (pp. 795–852). Reading, MA: Addison Wesley.

Bernhard, J. K., & Pacini-Ketchabaw, V. (2010). The politics of language and educational practices: Promoting truly diverse child care settings. In O. N. Saracho & B. Spodek (Eds.), *Contemporary perspectives in language and cultural diversity in early childhood education* (pp. 21–41). Charlotte, North Carolina: Information Age Publishing.

Biber, B. (1984). *Early education and psychological development*. New Haven, CT: Yale University Press.

Bjorkvold, J. R. (1992). *The muse within: Creativity and communication, song and play from childhood through maturity*. New York: HarperCollins.

Blacking, J. (1973). *How musical is man?* Seattle, WA: University of Washington Press.

Blizzard, G. S. (1993). *Come play with me*. Charlottesville, Virginia: Thomasson-Grant, Inc.

Bobbit, F. (1918). *The curriculum*. Boston, MA: Houghton-Mifflin.

Bontempo, B., & Iannone, R. (1988). Creative drama: A special kind of learning. *Teaching K-8*, *18*(6), 57–59.

Booth, D. (2005). *Story drama: Creating stories through role playing, improvising, and reading aloud*. Portland, ME: Stenhouse Publishers.

Borstelmann, L. J. (1983). Children before psychology. In P. H. Mussen (Ed.), *Handbook of child psychology* (pp. 3–40). New York: Wiley.

Bowles, C. L. (1998). Music activity preferences of elementary students. *Journal of Research in Music Education*, *46*(2), 193–207.

Bowman, B. G. (2008). Korean folk music in your curriculum. *Music Educators Journal*, *95*(1), 48–53.

Bradley, I. L. (1974). Development of aural and visual perception through creative processes. *Journal of Research in Music Education*, *22*(3), 234–240.

Brewer, J. A. (2007). *Introduction to early childhood education: Preschool through primary grades*. Boston, MA: Allyn & Bacon.

Brody, C. (1996). Social studies through block building. In E. S. Hirsch (Ed), *The block book* (pp. 61–74). Washington, DC: National Association for the Education of Young Children.

Bromer, S. (1999). Review of *Where go the boats?: Play-poems of Robert Louis Stevenson*. *School Library Journal*, *45*(4), 125.

Bronfenbrenner, U. (1979). *The ecology of human development*. Cambridge, MA: Harvard University Press.

Brosterman, B. (1997). *Inventing kindergarten*. New York: Harry N. Abrams, Inc.

Brown, M. (1993). *Arthur's family vacation*. Boston, MA: Little, Brown and Company.

Brown, M. W. (2005). *Good night moon*. New York: HarperCollins.

Brown, W. H., Pfeiffer, K. A., McIver, K. L., Dowda, M., Addy, C. L., & Pate, R. R. (2009). Social and environmental factors associated with preschoolers' nonsedentary physical activity. *Child Development*, *80*(1), 45–58.

Bruner, J. (1960). *The process of education*. Cambridge, MA: Harvard University Press.

Bruner, J. (1972). Nature and uses of immaturity. *American Psychologist*, *27*(8), pp. 687–708.

Bruner, J. (1975). The ontogenesis of speech acts. *Journal of Child Language*, *2*, 1–19.

Bruner, J. (1976). *Play: Its role in development and evolution*. New York: Basic Books.

Bruner, J. (1990). *Acts of meaning*. Cambridge, MA: Harvard University Press.

Bruner, J. (1996). *The culture of education*. Cambridge, MA: Harvard University Press.

Bruner, J. S. (1983). Play, thought, and language. *Peabody Journal of Education*, *60*, 60–69.

Bryan, L. (2005). Play it again, teach: A contingency plan. *Education*, *126*(1), 143–147.

Byrum, L. S. (1992). Three-dimensional art and sculpture. *Day Care and Early Education*, *29*(1), 9–10.

Campbell, E. N., & Foster, J. E. (1993). Play centers that encourage literacy development. *Day Care and Early Education*, *21*(2), 22–26.

Campbell, P. S. (1998). *Songs in their heads: Music and its meaning in children's lives*. New York: Oxford University Press.

Campbell, P. S. (2000). What music really means to children. *Music Educators Journal*, *86*(5), 29–36.

Campbell, P. S. (2002). The musical cultures of children. In L. Bresler & C. Thompson (Eds.), *The arts in children's lives: Context culture and curriculum* (pp. 57–70). Dordrecht, Netherlands: Kluwer Academic.

Campbell, P. S., & Scott-Kassner, C. (2006). *Music in childhood: From preschool through the elementary grades*. Belmont, CA: Thomson Schirmer Press.

Carle, E. (1986). *Papa, please get the moon for me*. New York: Simon & Schuster.

Carle, E. (2008). *The very hungry caterpillar*. New York: Philomel.

Carney, S. (2004). *Folktales: What are they?* Retrieved on June 16, 2009, from http://falcon.jmu.edu/~ramseyil/tradcarney.htm

Carpenter, T. P. (1986). Conceptual knowledge as a foundation for procedural knowledge. Implications from research on the initial learning of arithmetic. In J. Heibert (Ed.), *Conceptual procedural knowledge: The case of mathematics* (pp. 113–132). Hillsdale, NJ: Erlbaum.

Carr, M. (2001). *Assessment in early childhood settings: Learning stories*. London: Paul Chapman.

Carson, R. (1956). *The sense of wonder*. New York: Harper & Row.

Carter, B. W. (1985). Master builders: Move over Frank Lloyd Wright. *Arithmetic Teacher, 33*, 9–11.

Carter, R. T., & Qureshi, A. (1995). A typology of philosophical assumptions in multicultural counseling and training. In J. G. Ponterotto, J. M. Casas, L. A. Suzuki & C. M. Alexander (Eds.), *Handbook of multicultural counseling and development* (pp. 239–260). Thousand Oaks, CA: Sage Publications, Inc.

Cartwright, S. (1974). Blocks and learning. *Young Children, 29*(3), 141–146.

Cartwright, S. (1988). Play can be the building blocks of learning. *Young Children, 43*(5), 44–47.

Caswell, H. L., & Campbell, D. S. (1935). *Curriculum development*. New York: American Book Co.

Cauley, L. B. (1981). *Goldilocks and the three bears*. New York: Putnam Berkley.

Caulfield, C. (2002). Babytalk: Developmental precursors to speech. *Early Childhood Education Journal, 30*(1), 59–62.

Cavitch, M. (2006). Emma Lazarus and the Golem of Liberty. *American Literary History, 18*(1), 1–28.

Cecil, N., & Lauritzen, P. (1994). *Literacy and the arts for the integrated classroom: Alternative ways of knowing*. White Plains, New York: Longman.

Ceglowski, D. (1997). Understanding and building upon children's perceptions of play activities in early childhood programs. *Early Childhood Education Journal, 25*(2), 107–112.

Chafe, W. L. (1986). Beyond Bartlett: Narratives and remembering. *Poetics, 15*, 139–151.

Chalufour, I., & Worth, K. (2004). *Building structures with young children*. St. Paul, MN: Redleaf Press.

Charlesworth, R. (1988). Integrating math with science and social studies: A unit example. *Day Care and Early Education, 15*(4), 28–31.

Chenfeld, M. B. (2004). Guest editorial: On behalf of children. The geography of play. *Early Childhood Education Journal, 32*(3), 141–142.

Chinn, C. A., & Malhotra, B. A. (2002). Children's responses to anomalous scientific data: How is conceptual change impeded? *Journal of Educational Psychology, 19*, 327–343.

Christie, J. F. (1980). The cognitive significance of children's play: A review of selected research. *Journal of Education, 162*(4), 23–33.

Christie, J. F. (1982). Sociodramatic play training. *Young Children, 37*(4), 25–32.

Christie, J. F. (1990). Dramatic play: A context for meaningful engagements. *The Reading Teacher, 43*(8), 542–545.

Clark, G., Day, M., & Greer, D. (1987). Discipline-based art education: Becoming students of art. *The Journal of Aesthetic Education, 21*(2), 129–193.

Clark, H. H. (1994). Discourse in production. In M. A. Gernsbacher (Ed.), *Handbook of psycholinguistics* (pp. 985–1021). San Diego, CA: Academic.

Clay, M. M. (1972). *Reading: The patterning of complex behavior*. Auckland: NZ: Heinemann.

Clay, M. M. (1975). *What did I write?* Auckland, NZ: Heinemann.

Clay, M. (1991). *Becoming literate: The construction of inner control*. Portsmouth, NH: Heinemann.

Clements, D. H. (2004). Major themes and recommendations. In D. H. Clements, J. Sarama, & A-M. DiBiase (Eds.), *Engaging young children in mathematics: Standards for early childhood mathematics education* (pp. 7–72). Mahwah, NJ: Erlbaum.

Cobb, E. (1977). *The ecology of imagination in childhood*. New York: Columbia University Press.

Cohen, L., & Uhry, J. (2007). Young children's discourse strategies during block play: A Bakhtinian approach. *Journal of Research in Childhood Education, 21*(3), 302–315.

Cohen, L., & Uhry, J. (2011). Naming block structures: A multimodal approach. *Early Childhood Education Journal, 39*(1), 79–87.

Cole, E., & Schaefer, C. (1990). Can young children be art critics? *Young Children, 45*(2), 33–38.

Collins, S. (2004). Books for young children about the creative arts. *Young Children, 59*(4), 18–20.

Conezio, K., & French, L. (2002). Science in the preschool classroom: Capitalizing on children's fascination with the everyday world to foster language and literacy development. *Young Children 57*(5), 12–18.

Consortium for Interdisciplinary Teaching and Learning & Endorsed by the National Council for the Social Studies (1994). *Interdisciplinary learning, Pre-K-Grade 4.* Retrieved on August 24, 2008, from http://www.socialstudies.org/positions/interdisciplinary/

Coody, B. (1996). *Using literature with young children.* New York: McGraw-Hill Humanities/Social Sciences/Languages.

Cook, M. (2000). Writing and role play: A case for inclusion. *Reading. 34*(2), 74–78.

Cook, S. (1996). *Math in the real world of architecture.* Nashville, TN: Incentive Publications.

Coon, D., & Mitterer, J. O. (2008). *Introduction to psychology: Gateways to mind and behavior.* Belmont, CA: Wadsworth/Thompson Learning.

Copley, J. V. (2000). *The young child and mathematics.* Washington, DC: National Association for the Education of Young Children.

Copple, C., & Bredekamp, S. (2009). *Developmentally appropriate practice in early childhood programs: Serving children from birth through age 8.* Washington, DC: National Association for the Education of Young Children.

Courtney, R. (1977). *Play: Drama and thought.* New York: Viking.

Courtney, R. (1982). *Replay: Studies of human drama in education.* Toronto: Canada: The Ontario Institute for Studies in Education.

Creasey, G., & Jarvis, P. (2003). Play in children: An attachment perspective. In O. N. Saracho & B. Spodek, (Eds.), *Contemporary perspectives on play in early childhood* (pp. 133–151). Greenwich, CT: Information Age.

Creasey, G. L., Jarvis, P. A., & Berk, L. E. (1998). Play and Social Competence. In O. N. Saracho & B. Spodek (Eds.), *Multiple Perspectives on Play in Early Childhood Education* (pp. 116–143). New York: State University of New York Press.

Cuffaro, H. (1996). Dramatic play: The experience of block building. In E. S. Hirsch (Ed.), *The block book* (pp. 75–102). Washington, DC: National Association for the Education of Young Children.

Cuffaro, H. (1999). A view of materials as the texts of the early childhood curriculum. In B. Spodek & O. N. Saracho (Eds.), *Yearbook of Early Childhood Education: Issues in Early Childhood Curriculum.* Troy, New York: Educator's International Press.

Curry, N. E. (1974). Dramatic play as a curricular tool. In D. Sponseller (Ed.), *Play as a learning medium* (pp. 59–73). Washington, DC: National Association for the Education of Young Children.

Curtis, A., & O'Hagan, M. (2008). *Care and education in early childhood.* New York: Routledge.

Custodero, L. A. (2002). The musical lives of young children: Inviting, seeking, and initiating. *Zero to Three, 25*(1), 4–9.

Custodero, L. A. (2005). "Being With": The resonant legacy of childhood's creative aesthetic. *The Journal of Aesthetic Education, 39*(2), 36–57.

Custodero, L. A. (2006). Singing practices in 10 families with young children. *Journal of Research in Music Education, 54*(1), 37–56.

D'Addesio, J. A., Grob, B., Furman, L., Hayes, K., & David, J. (2005). Social studies: Learning about the world around us. *Young Children, 60*(5), 50–57.

Danilov, V. J. (1986). Discovery rooms and kidspace: Museum exhibits for children. *Science and Children, 24*(4), 6–11.

Darvill, D. (1982). Ecological influences on children's play: Issues and approaches. In D. J. Pepler & K. H. Rubin (Eds.), *The play of children: Current theory and research* (pp. 144–153). Basel, Switzerland: Karger.

Davis, G. (1976). *Childhood and history in America.* New York: Psychohistory Press.

Denac, O. (2008). A case study of preschool children's musical interests at home and at school. *Early Childhood Education Journal, 35*(5), 439–444.

DeNora, T. (2000). *Music in everyday life.* Cambridge: Cambridge University Press.

Dewey, J. (1900). Froebel's educational principles, *Elementary School Record, 1,* 143–145.

Dewey, J. (1902). *The child and the curriculum.* Chicago, IL: University of Chicago Press.

Dewey, J. (1916). *Democracy and education.* New York: Free Press.

Dewey, J. (1934). *Art as experience.* New York: Berkley Publishing Group.

Dewey, J. (1943). *The school and society.* Chicago, IL: University of Chicago Press.

DeZutter, S. L. (2007). Play as group improvisation: A social semiotic, multimodal perspective on play and literacy. In O. N. Saracho & B. Spodek (Eds.), *Contemporary perspectives on social learning.* Charlotte, NC: Information Age.

Diagram Group. (1997). *Musical instruments of the world: An illustrated encyclopedia.* New York: Sterling.

Diamond, K. E., Hong, S., & Tu, H. (2008). Context influences preschool children's decisions to include a peer with a physical disability in pay. *Exceptionality, 16*(3), 141–155.

Dickens, C. (1861). *Great expectations.* London: Chapman & Hall.

Dickinson, P. (2003). Choosing books you can count on. In *Teaching and Learning about Math,* from the National Association for the Education of Young Children's *Beyond the Journal.* Retrieved on October 26, 2009, from http://www.naeyc.org/files/yc/file/200301/ChildrensBooks.pdf

Dilkes, H. (1998) The Octopus Project – "I was making bing and bong": Children's conceptions of their own musical improvisations. *Australian Journal of Early Childhood Education, 23*(2), 13–18.

Dissanayake, E. (2000). *Art and intimacy.* Seattle, WA: University of Washington Press.

Division for Early Childhood. (2007). Promoting positive outcomes for children with disabilities: Recommendations for curriculum, assessment, and program evaluation. Missoula, MT: DEC. Division for Early Childhood of the Council for Exceptional Children.

Dobbert, M. L. (1985). Play is not monkey business: A holistic bioculture perspective on the role of play in learning. *Educational Horizons, 63*(4)158–163.

Doyle, A., Doehring, P., Tessier, O., de Lorimier, S., & Shapiro, S. (1992). Transitions in children's play: A sequential analysis of states preceding and following social pretense. *Developmental Psychology, 28,* 137–144.

Dudley-Marling, C., & Searle, D. (1988). Enriching language learning environments for students with learning disabilities. *Journal of Learning Disabilities, 21* (3), 140–142.

Dyson, A. H. (1989). *Multiple worlds of child writers: Friends learning to write.* New York: Teachers College Press.

Dyson, A. H. (1997). *Writing superheroes: Contemporary childhood, popular culture, and classroom literacy.* New York: Teachers College Press.

Dyson, A. H. (2005). Crafting the humble prose of living: Rethinking oral/written relations in the echoes of spoken word. *English Education, 37,* 149–164.

Eberbach, C., & Crowley, K. (2009). From everyday to scientific observation: How children learn to observe the biologist's world. *Review of Educational Research, 79*(1), 39–68.

Edwards, C. P. (2000). Children's play in a cross-cultural perspective: A new look at the six cultures study. *Cross-Cultural Research, 34*(4), 318–338.

Edwards, C. P., & Willis, L. M. (2000). Integrating visual and verbal literacies in the early childhood classroom. *Early Childhood Education Journal, 27*(4), 259–265.

Edwards, L. C., Bayless, K. M., & Ramsey, M. E. (2009). *Music and movement: A way of life for the young child.* Columbus, OH: Merrill.

Einstein, A. (1949). Autobiographical notes. In P. A. Schilpp (Ed.), *Albert Einstein: Philosopher scientist.* (pp. 1–95). Evanston, IL: The Library of Living Philosophers.

Einstein, A. (1954). *Ideas and opinions.* New York: Crown Publishers.

Eisenwine, M. J., & Hunt, D. A. (2000). Using a computer in literacy groups with emergent readers. *The Reading Teacher, 53*(6), 456–458.

Elkind, D. (1987). *Miseducation: Preschoolers at risk.* New York: Knopf.

Elkind, D. (1999). Educating young children in math, science, and technology. In *American Association for the Advancement of Science, Dialogue on Early Childhood Science, Mathematics, and Technology Education*. Washington, DC: American Association for the Advancement of Science.

Ellis, M. J. (1973). *Why people play?* Englewood Cliffs, NJ: Prentice-Hall.

Ensley, S. (1987). The significance for music education of Johan Huizinga's study of the play element in culture. *Canadian Journal of Research in Music Education*, 29, 31–46.

Epstein, A. S. (2001). Thinking about art: Encouraging art appreciation in early childhood settings. *Young Children*, 56(3), 38–43.

Erikson, E. (writing as Erik Homberger). (1937). Configurations in play – Clinical notes. *The Psychoanalytic Quarterly*, 6(1), 139–214.

Erikson, E. H. (1940). Studies in the interpretation of play. *Genetic Psychology Monographs*, 22, 557–671.

Erikson, E. H. (1950). *Childhood and society*. New York: Norton.

Erikson, E. H. (1977). *Toys and reasons: Stages in the ritualization of experience*. New York: Norton.

Evans, J. (2000). Young writers and the nursery rhyme genre. *Reading*, 34(1), 17–23.

Fagen, R. (1981). *Animal behavior*. New York: Oxford University Press.

Falconer, I. (2003) *Olivia and the missing toy*. New York: Atheneum/Anne Schwartz Books.

Fein, G. G. (1981). Pretend play: An integrative review. *Child Development*, 52, 1095–1118.

Fein, G. G., & Schwartz, P. M. (1982). Developmental theories in early education. In B. Spodek (Ed.), *Handbook of research in early childhood education* (pp. 82–104). New York: Free Press.

Feldman, E. (1970). *Becoming human through art: Aesthetic experience in the school*. Englewood Cliffs, NJ: Prentice-Hall.

Fenson, L. (1984). Developmental trends for action and speech in pretend play. In I. Bretherton (Ed.), *Symbolic play: The development of social understanding*. New York: Academic Press.

Ferreiro, E. & Teberosky, A. (1983) *Literacy before schooling*. Portsmouth, NH: Heinemann.

Fertig, G. (2007). Teaching history and social studies to young children. In O. N. Saracho & B. Spodek (Eds.), *Contemporary perspectives on social learning in early childhood education*. Charlotte, NC: Information Age.

Fox, J. E. & Schirrmacher, R. (2011) *Art and creative development for young children*. Florence, KY: Cengage.

Frank, P. L. (1964). Orff and Bresgen as music educators. *Music Educators Journal*, 50(4), 58–60, 62, 64.

French, L. (2004). Science as the center of a coherent, integrated early childhood curriculum. *Early Childhood Research Quarterly*, 19, 138–149.

French, V. (1977). History of the child's influence: Ancient Mediterranean Civilizations. In R. Q. Bell & L. V. Harper (Eds.), *Child effects on adults* (pp. 1–28). Hillsdale, NJ: Lawrence Erlbaum.

Freud, A. (1937). *The ego and the mechanism of defenses*. London: Hogarth.

Freud, S. (1938). *The basic writing of Sigmund Freud*. New York: Modern Library.

Friedman, S. (2005). Social studies in action. *Young Children*, 60(5), 44–47.

Froman, R. (1974). Dead tree. *Seeing things: A book of poems*. New York: Crowell.

Fromboluti, C. S., & Seefeldt, C. (1999). *Early childhood: Where learning begins: Geography with activities for children, ages 2 to 5 years of age*. Washington, DC: National Institute of Early Childhood Development and Education.

Frost, J. L., & Dongju, S. (1998). Physical environments and children's play. In O. N. Saracho & B. Spodek (Eds.), *Multiple perspectives on play in early childhood education* (pp. 255–294). New York: State University of New York Press.

Fuller, G. (1974). *Woodworking with children*. New York: Bank Street College of Education.

Funke, S. C. (2006). Classical music for children: Swan Lake, Peter and the Wolf, Sleeping Beauty, The Nutcracker, and more! Retrieved on November 23, 2009, from http://classicalmusic. suite101.com/article.cfm/childrensmusic

Gág, W. (1928). *Millions of cats*. New York: Coward-McCann, Inc.

Galda, L., Cullinan, B. E., & Sipe, L. (2009). *Literature and the child*. Belmont, CA: Wadsworth.

Galdone, P. (1962). *The hare and the tortoise*. New York: McGraw-Hill.

Galdone, P. (1985). *The three bears*. New York: Clarion Books.

Galdone, P. (1985). *The three bears*. New York: Clarion Books.

Ganschow, R., & Ganschow, L. (2006). Playfulness in the biological sciences. In D. P. Fromberg & D. Bergen (Eds.), *Play from birth to twelve and beyond: Contexts, perspectives and meanings* (pp. 455–460). New York: Routledge.

García, E., & Jensen, B. (2010). Language development and early education of young Hispanic children in the United States. In O. N. Saracho & B. Spodek (Eds.), *Contemporary perspectives in language and cultural diversity in early childhood education* (pp. 43–64). Charlotte, NC: Information Age Publishing.

Garvey, C. (1990). *Play*. Cambridge, MA: Harvard University Press.

Garvey, C., & Hogan, T. (1973). Social speech and social interaction: Egocentrism revisited. *Child Development, 44*(3), 562–568.

Garvey, C., & Kramer, T. L. (1989). The language of social pretend play. *Developmental Review, 9*, 364–382.

Gee, J. P. (2000). The New Literacy Studies: from 'socially situated' to the work of the social. In Barton, D., Hamilton, M., & Ivanic, R. (Eds.), *Situated literacies: Reading and writing in context* (pp. 180–196). New York: Routledge.

Geisert, A. (1991) *Oink*. New York: Houghton Mifflin.

Geist, E. (2001). Children are born mathematicians: Promoting the construction of early mathematical concepts in children under five. *Young Children, 56*(4), 12–19.

Gelman, R., & Brenneman, K. (2004) Science learning pathways for young children. *Early Childhood Research Quarterly, 19*, 150–158.

Gibbons, G. (1986). *How a house is built*. New York: Holiday House.

Ginsburg, H. P. (1980). Children's surprising knowledge of arithmetic. *Arithmetic Teacher, 28*(1), 42–44.

Ginsburg, H. P., Lee, J. S., & Boyd, J. S. (2008). Mathematics education for young children: What it is and how to promote it. *Social Policy Report Giving Child and Youth Development Knowledge Away, 22*(1), 3–24.

Giorgis, C., & Glazer, J. I. (2008). *Literature for young children: Supporting emergent literacy*. Upper Saddle River, NJ: Prentice Hall.

Giorgis, C., Johnson, N. J., Bonomo, A., Colbert, C., Conner, A., Kauffman, G., & Kulesza, D. (1999). Children's books: Visual literacy. *Reading Teacher, 53*(2), 146–153.

Gluschankof, C. (2002). The local musical style of kindergarten children: A description and analysis of its natural variables. *Music Education Research, 4*(1), 37–50.

Gluschankof, C. (2004). *Music and play: Diverse aspects of 4–6 year olds' self-initiated musical play*. Paper presented at the Second International Conference on Questions of Quality, Dublin Castle, Ireland.

Golomb, C. (1974). *Young children's sculpture and drawing*. Cambridge, MA: Harvard University Press.

Göncü, A., Tuermer, U., Jain, J., & Johnson, D. (1999). Children's play as cultural activity. In A. Goncü (Ed.), *Children's engagement in the world: Sociocultural perspectives* (pp. 148–170). New York: Cambridge University Press.

Goodman, J. R. (1990). *A naturalistic study of the relationship between literacy development and dramatic play in 5-year-old children*. Unpublished doctoral dissertation, Vanderbilt University, Nashville, TN.

Gopnik, A. (2010). How babies think. *Scientific American, 303*(1), 76–81.

Gould, S. (1997). *Full house: The spread of excellence from Plato to Darwin*. New York: Three Rivers Press.

Graham, P. (2008). Susan Isaacs and the Malting House School. *Journal of Child Psychotherapy, 34*(1), 5–22.

Green, A. (No date a). Classical music for children: Five ways to introduce classical music to young children. Retrieved on November 25, 2009, from http://classicalmusic.about.com/od/classicalmusictips/a/childrenclassic.htm

Green, A. (No date b). Intro to classical music: A beginner's guide to classical music. Retrieved on November 25, 2009, from http://classicalmusic.about.com/od/classicalmusic101/a/intro072104.htm

Greenberg, P. (2000). Display children's art attractively. *Young Children, 55*(2), 89.

Greene, W. P. (1998/2001). *Museums and learning: A guide for family visits.* Washington, DC: U.S. Department of Education and Smithsonian Office of Education.

Griffin, S. (2004). Teaching number sense. *Educational Leadership, 61*(5), 39–42.

Griffin, S., & Case, R. (1997). Rethinking the primary school math curriculum: An approach based on cognitive science. *Issues in Education, 3*(1), 1–49.

Groos, K. (1898). *The play of animals.* New York: Appleton.

Groos, K. (1901). *The play of man.* New York: Appleton.

Guha, S. (2002). Integrating mathematics for young children through play. *Young Children, 57*(3), 90–92.

Hadjigeorgiou, Y. (2001). The role of wonder and 'romance' in early childhood science education. *International Journal of Early Years Education, 9*, 63–69.

Hall, G. S. (1906). *Youth: Its education, regimen, and hygiene.* New York: Appleton.

Hall, J. S. (2000). Psychology and schooling: The impact of Susan Isaacs and Jean Piaget on 1960s science education reform. *History of Education, 29*(2), 153–170.

Hall, N. (1987). *The emergence of literacy.* Portsmouth, NH: Heinemann.

Hall, N. (1998). Real literacy in a school setting: Five-year-olds take on the world. *Reading Teacher, 52*(1).

Hall, N., & Robinson, A. (2003). *Exploring writing and play in the early years.* London: David Fulton Publishers.

Halliday M. (1969). Relevant models of language. *Educational Review, 21*(3): 26–37

Handel, G. (2005). Socialization and the social self. In G. Handel (Ed.), *Childhood socialization* (pp. 11–19). New Brunswick, NJ: Aldine Transaction.

Harlen, W. (2006). *Teaching, learning and assessing science 5–12.* London: Sage.

Hartley, R. E., Frank, L. K. & Goldenson, R. M. (1952). *Understanding children's play.* New York: Columbia University Press.

Hartley, R., & Goldenson, R. (1963). *The complete book of children's play.* New York: Crowell.

Hawkins, D. (1965). Messing about in science. *Science and Children, 2*(5), 5–9.

Hawkins, D. (1983). Nature closely observed. *Daedalus, 112*(2), 65–89.

Heath, S. (1983). *Ways with words: Language, life and work in communities and classrooms.* New York: Cambridge University Press.

Heath, S. B. (2004). Language and strategic thinking through the parts. *Reading Research Quarterly, 39*(3), 338–342.

Henniger, M. L. (1987). Learning mathematics and science through play. *Childhood Education, 63*(3), 167–71.

Henshon, S. E. (2010). Talent development across the lifespan: An interview with Margie Kitano. *Gifted Child Today, 33*(2), 32–35.

Herman, C. (1987). Through the magnifying glass. *Science and Children, 25*(3), 36–38.

Hewitt, K. (2001). Blocks as a tool for learning: Historical and contemporary perspectives. *Young Children, 56*(1), 6–13.

Hiebert, J. (1986). *Conceptual and procedural knowledge: The case of mathematics.* Hillsdale, NJ: Erlbaum.

Hill, P.S. (1913). Second Report in Committee of Nineteen, *The kindergarten.* Boston, MA: International Kindergarten Union.

Hirsch, E.S. (Ed.). (1996). *The block book.* Washington, DC: National Association for the Education of Young Children.

Hirsh-Pasek, K., Golinkoff, R. M., Berk, L. E., & Singer, D. (2009). *A mandate for playful learning in preschool: Compiling the scientific evidence.* New York: Oxford University Press.

Hoberman, M. A. (2000). Nadine Bernard Westcott (Illustrator). *Eensy weensy spider.* Boston, MA: Little, Brown & Company.

Hoberman, M. A. (2004). Nadine Bernard Westcott (Illustrator). *I know a lady who swallowed a fly.* Boston, MA: Little, Brown & Company.

Hohmann, M., Weikart, D. P., & Epstein, A. S. (2008). *Educating young children: Active learning practices for preschool and child care programs* (3rd Ed.). Ypsilanti, MI: High/Scope Educational Research Foundation.

Holdaway, D. (1979). *The foundations of literacy*. Portsmouth, NH: Heinemann.

Hommerding, M. (2007). Science prop boxes. *Science and Children, 45*(3), 42–45.

Hopkins, L.B. (1998). *Pass the poetry, please!* New York: Harper Collins Publishers.

Howarth, M. (1989). Rediscovering the power of fairy tales: They help children understand their lives. *Young Children, 45*(1), 58–65.

Howes, C., & Lee, L. (2007). If you're not like me can we play? Peer groups in preschool. In O. N. Saracho & B. Spodek (Eds.), *Contemporary perspectives on social learning in early childhood education* (pp. 269–278). Charlotte, NC: Information Age.

Hsiung, P. (2005). *A tender voyage: Children and childhood in late imperial China*. Stanford, CA: Stanford University Press.

Huck, C., Kiefer, B., Hepler, S., & Hickman, J. (2004). *Children's lilterature in the elementary school*. New York: McGraw-Hill.

Hughes, F. P. (2010). *Children, play and development*. Thousand Oaks, CA: Sage.

Huizinga, J. (1950). *Homo ludens: A study of the play element in culture*. Boston, MA: Beacon Press.

Hurll, E. M. (1914). *How to show pictures to children*. Boston, MA: Houghton Mifflin Company.

Hurwitz, S. C. (2002–2003). To be successful – let them play! *Childhood Education, 79*(2), 101–102.

Hymes, D. (1972). *Reinventing anthropology*. New York: Random House.

Illick, J. E. (1974). Child-rearing in seventeenth-century England and America. In L. DeMause (Ed.), *The history of childhood* (pp. 303–350). New York: Psychohistory Press.

International Children's Digital Library (n.d.). The International Children's Digital Library. Retrieved on November 7, 2010, from http://en.childrenslibrary.org/books/activities/index.shtml

International Reading Association (1986). *Literacy development and pre-first grade*. Newark, DE: Author.

Isaacs, S. (1930). *Social development in young children*. New York: Routledge.

Isenberg, J. P., & Quisenberry, N. (2002). Play: Essential for all children. *Childhood Education, 79*(1), 33–39.

Jacob, E. (1984). Learning literacy through play: Puerto Rican kindergarten children. In H. Goelman, A. Oberg & F. Smith (Eds.), *Awakening to literacy* (pp. 73–86). Exeter, NH: Heinemann.

Jacobs, G. (n.d.). *Preschool rhymes for community helpers*. Brooklyn: Rainbow Resource Room. Retrieved from http://www.preschoolrainbow.org/helper-rhymes.htm

Jenness, M. (1987). Schoolyard hikes. *Science and Children, 24*(6), 23–25.

Johnson, H. (1933). *The art of block building*. New York: John Day Co.

Johnson, J. E., Christie, J. F., & Wardle, F. (2005). *Play, development and early education*. Boston: Allyn & Bacon.

Jones, E., & Reynolds, G. (1992). *The play's the thing . . . Teachers' roles in children's play*. New York: Teachers College Press.

Jones, I., Lake, V. E., & Lin, M. (2008). Early childhood science process skills: Social and developmental considerations. In O. N. Saracho & B. Spodek (Eds.), *Contemporary perspectives in science and technology* (pp. 17–39). Charlotte, NC: Information Age.

Kaderavek, J., & Sulzby, E. (1998). Parent–child joint book reading. An observation protocol for young children. *American Journal of Speech-language Pathology, 7*, 33–47.

Kalmar, K. (2008). Let's give children something to talk about: Oral language and preschool literacy. *Young Children, 63*(1), 88–92.

Kamii, C., Miyakawa, Y., & Kato, Y. (2004). The development of logico-mathematical knowledge in a block-building activity at ages 1–4. *Journal of Research in Childhood Education, 19*(1), 44–57.

Kantor, R., Miller, S. M., & Fernie, D. E. (1992). Diverse paths to literacy in a preschool classroom: A sociocultural perspective. *Reading Research Quarterly, 27*(3), 185–201.

Karplus, R., & Thier, H. D. (1967). *A new look at elementary school science*. Skokie, IL: Rand McNally.

Kavanaugh, R. D. (2006). Pretend play. In B. Spodek & O. Saracho (Eds.), *Handbook of research on the education of young children* (pp. 269–278). Mahwah, NJ: Erlbaum.

Kavanaugh, R. D., & Engel, S. (1998). The development of pretense and narrative in early childhood. In O. N. Saracho & B. Spodek (Eds.), *Multiple Perspectives on Play in Early Childhood Education* (pp. 80–99). New York: State University of New York Press.

Kean, E. (2006). Chemists and play. In D. P. Fromberg & D. Bergen (Eds.), *Play from birth to twelve and beyond: Contexts, perspectives and meanings* (pp. 468–472). New York: Routledge.

Kemple, K. M., Batey, J. J., & Hartle, L. C. (2004). Music play: Creating centers for musical play and exploration. *Young Children, 59*(4), 30–37.

Kenney, S. (1989). Music centers: Freedom to explore. *Music Educators Journal, 76*(2), 32–36.

Kenney, S. (2004). The importance of music centers in the early childhood class. *General Music Today, 18*(1), 28–36.

Kenney, S, (2007). Every child a composer. *General Music Today, 20*(2), 31–33.

Kiefer, B. Z. (2004). Children's literature and children's literacy: Preparing early literacy teachers to understand the aesthetic values of children's literature. In O. N. Saracho & B. Spodek, *Contemporary Perspectives on Language Policy and Literacy Instruction in Early Childhood Education* (pp. 161–180). Greenwich, CT: Information Age.

Kilpatrick, W. H. (1918). *The project method.* New York: Bureau of Publications, Teachers College, Columbia University.

Kimmel, E. (1993). *The gingerbread man.* (Illustrated by M. Lloyd). New York: Holiday House Inc.

Kirkland, L. D., & Patterson, J. (2005). Developing oral language in primary classrooms. *Early Childhood Education Journal, 32*(6), 391–395.

Kleibard, H. (2004). *The struggle for the American curriculum,1893–1958.* New York: Routledge.

Kohl, M. A. (1988). Creative art experiences: Sculpture. *Day Care and Early Education, 15*(3), 44–46.

Kohl, M. A. (2005). *Group clay sculpture from big messy art.* Bellingham, WA: Bright Ring Publishing.

Kohlberg, L. (2008). The development of children's orientations toward a moral order: Sequence in the development of moral thought. *Human Development, 51*(1), 8–20.

Kolbe, U. (2007). *Rapunzel's supermarket: All about young children and their art.* Byron Bay, Australia: Peppinot.

Koralek, D. (2009). Mathematics in the early years. *Young Children, 64*(3), 10–1.

Korat, O., Bahar, E., & Snapir, M. (2002/2003). Sociodramatic play as opportunity for literacy development. *The Reading Teacher, 56*(4), 386–393.

Korn-Bursztyn, C. (2002). Scenes from a studio: Working with the arts in an early childhood class-room. *Early Childhood Education Journal, 30*(1), 39–46.

Koste, V. G. (1995). *Dramatic play in childhood: Rehearsal for life.* Portsmouth, NH: Heinemann.

Kostelnik, K. M., Lynch, J. A., Grimm, J. W., Corbett, E. S. (1989). Sample size requirements for estimation of through fall chemistry beneath a mixed hardwood forest. *Journal of Environmental Quality, 18,* 274–280.

Koster, J. B. (1999). Clay for little fingers. *Young Children, 54*(2), 18–22.

Kounin, J., & Sherman, J. (1979). School environments as behavior settings. *Theory into Practice, 28,* 145–150.

Krasnor, L. R. & Pepler, D. J. (1980). The study of children's play: Some future directions. In K. H. Rubin (Ed.), *New directions for child development: Children's play* (pp. 85–95). San Francisco: Jossey-Bass.

Krown, S. (1975). *Threes and fours go to school.* Englewood Cliffs, NJ: Prentice-Hall.

Labbo, L. D. (1996). Beyond storytime: A sociopsychological perspective on young children's opportunities for literacy development during story extension time. *Journal of Literacy Research, 28*(3), 405–428.

Labbo, L. D. (1998). Social studies play in kindergarten. *Social Studies and the Young Learner, 10*(4), 18–21.

Labbo, L. D. (2000). 12 things young children can do with a talking book in a classroom computer center. *The Reading Teachers, 53*(7), 542–546.

Ladd, G. W. (2007). Social learning in the peer context. In O. N. Saracho & B. Spodek (Eds.), *Contemporary perspectives on socialization and social development in early childhood education* (pp. 133–164). Charlotte, NC: Information Age.

Lamont, A. (2006). Toddler's musical worlds: Musical engagement in 3.5-year-olds. In M. Baroni, A. R. Addessi, R. Caterina, & M. Costa (Eds.), *Proceedings of the 9th International Conference on Music Perception & Cognition*, Bologna/Italy (pp. 946–950). Society for Music Perception & Cognition.

Lazarus, M. (1883). *Die Reize des Spiels.* (Berlin. Fred. Dummlers Verlagsbuchhandlung).

Lee, E., Hong, Y., Cho, K., & Eum, J. (2001). A study of children's traditional play in Korea. *The Journal for the Study of Early Childhood Education*, 21(1), 117–140.

Leslie, A. M. (1987). Pretense and representation: The origins of '"theory of mind"'. *Psychological Review*, 94(4), 412–426.

Levy, A. K., Schaefer, L., & Phelps, P. C. (1986). Increasing preschool effectiveness: Enhancing the language abilities of 3- and 4-year-old children through planned sociodramatic play. *Early Childhood Research Quarterly*, 1, 133–140.

Lewin, K. (1935). *A dynamic theory of personality.* New York: McGraw-Hill.

Lewin-Benham, A. (2006). One teacher, 20 preschoolers, and a goldfish: Environmental awareness, emergent curriculum, and documentation. *Young Children*, 61(2), 28–34.

Lieber, J., Horn, E., Palmer, S., & Fleming, K. (2008). Access to the general education curriculum for preschoolers with disabilities: Children's School Success. *Exceptionality*, 16(1), 18–32.

Lillard, A. (1998). Playing with a theory of mind. In O. N. Saracho and B. Spodek (Eds.), *Multiple perspectives on play in early childhood education* (pp. 11–33). New York: SUNY Press.

Lilley, I. M. (1967). *Friedrich Froebel: A selection from his writings.* New York: Cambridge University Press.

Lim, B. Y. (2004). The magic of the brush and the power of color: Integrating theory into practice of painting in early childhood settings. *Early Childhood Education Journal*, 32(2), 113–119.

Littleton, D. (1991). *Influence of play settings on preschool children's music and play behaviors.* Ph.D. Dissertation, University of Texas at Austin.

Littleton, D. (1998). Music learning and child's play. *General Music Today*, 12(1), 8–15.

Logan, W. (1978). Relationships between language and literacy. In R. Beach & P. D. Pearson (Eds.), *Perspectives on literacy.* Minneapolis, MN: University of Minnesota.

López, E. E., & Mulnix, M. (2004). Educating the next generation: Culture-centered teaching for school-aged children. In O. N. Saracho & B. Spodek (Eds.), *Contemporary perspectives on language policy and literacy instruction in early childhood education* (pp.259–280). Greenwich, CT: Information Age.

Lowenfeld, M. (1931). A new approach to the problem of psychoneurosis in childhood. *British Journal of Medical Psychology*, 11, 194–227.

Lowenfeld, M. (1979). *Understanding children's sandplay: Lowenfeld's world technique.* Great Britain: Antony Rowe Ltd.

Lowenfeld, V. (1957). *Creative and mental growth.* New York: Macmillan.

Luria, A. R. (1932). *The nature of human conflicts.* New York: Liveright.

Lynch-Brown, C. & Tomlinson, C. (2004). *Essentials of children's literature.* Boston, MA: Allyn and Bacon.

MacCleod, F. (2004). Literacy identity and agency: Linking classrooms to communities. *Early Child Development and Care*, 174(3), 243–252.

Malcom, S. (1999). Making sense of the world. In American Association for the Advancement of Science, *Dialogue on early childhood science, mathematics, and technology education.* Washington, DC: American Association for the Advancement of Science.

Mang, E. (2005). The referent of children's early songs. *Music Education Research*, 7(1), 3–20.

Marsh, J., & Millard, E. (2000). *Literacy and popular culture. Using children's culture in the classroom.* Thousand Oaks, CA: Sage.

Marsh, K. (2005). World of play: The effects of context and culture on the musical play of young children. *Proceedings of the Seminar of the Commission for the Early Childhood Music Education.* Barcelona, Spain.

Martin, B. (1986). Eric Carle (Illustrator). *Brown bear, brown bear. what do you see?* New York: Holt, Rinehart & Winston.

Martin, C. L., Fabes, R. A., Hanish, L. D., & Hollenstein, T. (2005). Social dynamics in the preschool. *Developmental Review*, 25(3–4), 299–327.

Mason, J. (1980). When do children begin to read: An exploration of four year old children's letter and word reading competencies. *Reading Research Quarterly*, 15, 203–227.

Matthews, J. C. (1984). Children's drawing: Are children really scribbling? *Early Child Development and Care*, 18, 1–39.

Matthews, J., & Seow, P. (2007). Electronic paint: Understanding children's representation through their interactions with digital paint. *International Journal of Art & Design Education*, 26(3), 251–263.

Matthews, W. S., & Matthews, R. J. (1982). Eliminating operational definitions: A paradigm case approach to the study of fantasy play. In D. J. Pepler & K. H. Rubin (Eds.), *The play of children: Current theory and research* (pp. 21–29). Basel, Switzerland: Karger.

Maxim, G. M. (1997). The very young: Guiding children from infancy through the early years. Englewood Cliffs, NJ: Prentice-Hall.

Mayfield, M. I. (2005). Children's museums: Purposes, practices and play? *Early Child Development and Care*, 175(2), 179–192.

Maynard, T., & Thomas, T. (2009). *An introduction to early childhood studies*. Thousand Oaks, CA: Sage.

McAloney, K., & Stagnitti, K. (2009). Pretend play and social play: The concurrent validity of the Child-Initiated Pretend Play Assessment. *International Journal of Play Therapy*, 18(2), 99–113.

McCaslin, N. (2006). *Creative drama in the classroom and beyond*. Boston, MA: Allyn & Bacon.

McDonald, D. (1979). *Music in our lives: The early years*. Washington, D.C: National Association for the Education of Young Children.

McGee, L. M., & Richgels, D. J. (2004). *Literacy's beginnings: Supporting young readers and writers*. Boston, MA: Allyn & Bacon.

McGinnis, J. R. (2002). Enriching the outdoor environment. *Young Children*, 57(3), 28–30.

McKinney, J. D., & Golden, L. (1973). Social studies dramatic play with elementary school children, *The Journal of Educational Research*, 67(4), 172–176.

McNaughton, C. (2000). *Oops!: A Preston pig story*. New York: Voyager Books.

McRobbie, C. & Tobin, K. (1997). A social constructivist perspective on learning environments. *International Journal of Science Education*, 19(2), 193–208.

Meigs, C., Eaton, A. T., Nesbitt, E., Viguies, R. H. (1969). *A critical history of children's literature*. New York: Macmillan.

Meinbach, A. M. (1991). *Sources and resources: Ideas and activities for teaching children's literature*. New York: HarperCollins.

Mellou, E. (1994). Play theories: A contemporary view. *Early Child Development and Care*, 102, 91–100.

Meltzoff, A., & Moore, M. K. (1989). Imitation in newborn infants: Exploring the range of gestures imitated and the underlying mechanisms. *Developmental Psychology*, 25, 954–964.

Mendoza, J., & Katz, L. G. (2008). Introduction to the special section on dramatic play. *Early Childhood Research & Practice*, 10(2). Retrieved on June 5, 2009, from http://ecrp.uiuc.edu/v10n2/introduction.html

Micklethwait, L. (1996). *A child's book of play in art*. New York: DK Publishing, Inc.

Miller, E., & Almon, J. (2009). *Crisis in the kindergarten: Why children need to play in school*. College Park: Alliance for Childhood. Retrieved on December 28, 2010, from http://www.allianceforchildhood.org/sites/allianceforchildhood.org/files/file/kindergarten_report.pdf

Mindes, G. (2005). Social studies in today's early childhood curricula. *Young Children*, 60(5), 12–18.

Mitchell, E. D., & Mason, B. (1948). *The theory of play*. New York: A. S. Barnes and Co.

Mitchell, L. S. (1934). *Young geographers*. New York: Bank Street College of Education.

Moffitt, M. W. (1996). Children learn about science through block building. In E. S. Hirsch *The block book* (pp. 27–34). Washington, DC: National Association for the Education of Young Children.

Montessori, M. (1912). *The Montessori method*. New York: Schocken.

Mooney, B. J. (2008). *Cooking with kids*. Retrieved on July 18, 2009, from www.ChildrensRecipes.com.

Moorhead, G., & Pond, D. (1942). *Pillsbury Foundation Studies: Music of young children*. Santa Barbara, CA: Pillsbury Foundation for the Advancement of Music Education.

Morado, C., & Koenig, R. (1999). Miniperformances, many stars! Playing with stories. *Reading Teacher*, 53(2), 116–123.

Moran, K. J. K. (2006). Nurturing emergent readers through readers theater. *Early Childhood Education Journal*, 33(5), 317–323.

Morin, F. (2001). Cultivating music play: The need for changed practice. *General Music Today*, 14(2), 24–29.

Morris, A. (1990). *On the go*. New York: A Mulberry Paperback Book.

Morrow, L. M. (2009). *Literacy development in the early years: Helping children read and write*. Boston, MA: Allyn & Bacon.

Murphy, K. L., DePasquale, R., & McNamara, E. (2003). Meaningful connections: Using technology in primary classrooms. *Young Children*, 58(6), 12–18.

Murphy, L. (1956). *Methods for the study of personality in young children*. New York: Basic Books.

Murphy, L. (1962). *The widening world of childhood*. New York: Basic Books.

Myhre, S. M. (1993). Enhancing your dramatic play area through the use of prop boxes. *Young Children*, 48(5), 6–11.

Nāone, C. K., & Au, K. (2010). Culture as framework versus ingredient in early childhood education: A Native Hawaiian perspective. In O. N. Saracho & B. Spodek (Eds.), *Contemporary perspectives in language and cultural diversity in early childhood education* (pp. 147–165). Charlotte, North Carolina: Information Age Publishing.

National Association for the Education of Young Children. (1996). Position statement: Technology and young children – ages three through eight. *Young Children*, 51(6), 11–16.

National Association for the Education of Young Children. (1999). Museums: Hands-on and more! Retrieved on June 17, 2009, from http://74.125.95.132/search?q'cache:3Yx9RHu2hAUJ:www.naeyc.org/ece/1999/01.pdf+Museums:+Hands-on+and+More!&cd'7&hl'en&ct'clnk&gl'us&client'firefox

National Association for the Education of Young Children (NAEYC) & National Association of Early Childhood Specialists in State Departments of Education (NAECS/SDE) (2003). Early childhood curriculum, assessment and program evaluation: Building an effective, accountable system in programs for children birth through age 8. Joint Position Statement. Washington, DC: NAEYC.

National Association for the Education of Young Children (2005). Exploring social studies through children's books. *Young Children*, 60(5), 60.

National Association for the Education of Young Children (2006). Museums: Hands-on and more! Retrieved on July 27, 2009, from http://www.naeyc.org/ece/1999/01.asp

National Association for the Education of Young Children. (2008). Creative teaching with prop boxes. *Teaching Young Children*, 2(4), 5.

National Association for the Education of Young Children and National Council of Teachers of Mathematics. (2010). *Position statement. Early childhood mathematics: Promoting good beginnings*. Retrieved on December 29, 2010, from http://www.naeyc.org/files/naeyc/file/positions/psmath.pdf

National Council for the Social Studies (1984). *Social studies for young children*. Prepared by the National Council for the Social Studies Elementary/Early Childhood Education Committee. Retrieved on August 23, 2009, from http://www.socialstudies.org/positions/children/

National Council for the Social Studies (1988). *Social studies for early childhood and elementary school children preparing for the 21st century*. A Report from the National Council for the Social Studies Task Force on Early Childhood/Elementary Social Studies. Retrieved on May 26, 2009, from http://www.socialstudies.org/positions/elementary

National Council for the Social Studies (2008a). *Expectations of excellence curriculum standards for social studies*. Update-Draft. Prepared by the NCSS Curriculum Review Task Force. Retrieved on May 26, 2009, from http://www.socialstudies.org/system/files/StandardsDraft10_08.pdf

National Council for the Social Studies (2008b). *Revision of NCSS Elementary Education Position Statement* (Draft, 11/10/08). Retrieved on May 26, 2009, from http://communities.socialstudies.org/system/files/Revision+of+NCSS+Elementary+Education+Position+Statement.doc

National Council for the Social Studies (2009). *Powerful and purposeful teaching and learning in elementary school social studies*. A position statement prepared by the Task Force on Early Childhood/Elementary Studies and members of the NCSS Board of Directors, approved by the

NCSS Board of Directors in June 2009. Retrieved on July 25, 2009, from http://www.social studies.org/positions/powerfulandpurposeful

National Council of Teachers of English (2006). *What we know about writing, Grades K-2*. Retrieved on December 13, 2010, from http://www.ncte.org/writing/aboutearlygrades

National Council of Teachers of Mathematics (1989). *Curriculum and Evaluation Standards for School Mathematics*. Reston, VA: National Council of Teachers of Mathematics.

National Council of Teachers of Mathematics (2000). *Principles and standards for school mathematics*. Reston, VA: National Council of Teachers of Mathematics.

National Council of Teachers of Mathematics (2000–2004). Overview: *Prekindergarten through Grade 2*. Retrieved on November 22, 2009, from http://standards.nctm.org/document/chapter4/index.htm

National Reading Panel (2000). *Teaching children to read: An evidence-based assessment of the scientific research literature on reading and its implications for reading instructions*. Bethesda, MD: The National Reading Panel.

National Research Council (1996). *National Science Education Standards*. Washington, DC: National Academy Press.

National Research Council (1998). *Preventing reading difficulties in young children*. Washington, DC: National Academy of Sciences.

Neubert, K. (1991). The care and feeding of clay. In L. Y. Overby, A. Richardson, & L. S. Hasko *Early childhood creative arts* (pp. 121–127). Reston, VA: American Alliance for Health, Physical Education, Recreation and Dance.

Neuman, S. B., & Roskos, K. (1989). Preschoolers' conceptions of literacy as reflected in their spontaneous play. In S. McCormick & J. Zutell (Eds.), *Cognitive and social perspectives for literacy research and instruction* (pp.87–94). Chicago, IL: National Reading Conference.

Neuman, S. B., & Roskos, K. (1990a). Play, print, and purpose: Enriching play environments for literacy development. *The Reading Teacher*, 44(3), 214–221.

Neuman, S. B., & Roskos, K. (1990b). The influence of literacy-enriched play settings on preschoolers' engagement with written language. In J. Zutell & S. McCormick (Eds.), *Literacy theory and research: Analyses from multiple paradigms* (pp. 179–187). Chicago, IL: National Reading Conference.

Neuman, S. B., & Roskos, K. (1991). Peers as literacy informants: A description of young children's literacy conversations in play. *Early Childhood Research Quarterly*, 6(2), 233–248.

Neuman, S., & Roskos, K. (1993). *Language and literacy learning in the early years: An integrated approach*. New York: Harcourt Brace Jovanovich.

Neuman, S. B., & Roskos, K. (1997). Literacy knowledge in practice: Contexts of participation for young writers and readers. *Reading Research Quarterly*, 32(1), 10–32.

Nichols, E. L. (1970). Orff can work in every classroom. *Music Educators Journal*, 57(1), 43–44.

Nicolopoulou, A. (2009). Rethinking character representation and its development in children's narratives. In J. Guo, E. Lieven, N. Budwig, S. Ervin-Tripp, K. Nakamura & S. Ozcaliskan (Eds.), *Crosslinguistic approaches to the psychology of language: Research in the tradition of Dan Isaac Slobin* (pp. 241–262). New York: Routledge.

Nicolopoulou, A. (2010). The alarming disappearance of play from early childhood education. *Human Development*, 53(1), 1–4.

Niland, A. (2009). The power of musical play: The value of play-based, child-centered curriculum in early childhood music education. *General Music Today*, 23(1), 17–21.

Norris, D. J., Eckert, L., & Gardiner, I. (2004). *The utilization of interest centers in preschool classrooms*. Paper presented at the National Association for the Education of Young Children Annual Conference, Chicago, IL.

Nourot, P. M. (1998). Sociodramatic play: Pretending together. In D. P. Fromberg & D. Bergen (Eds.), *Play from birth to twelve and beyond: Contexts, perspectives, and meanings* (pp. 378–390). New York: Garland Publishing, Inc.

Numeroff, L. (1998). *If you give a pig a pancake*. New York: HarperCollins.

Odom, S. L., Zercher, C., Li, S., Marquart, J. M., Sandall, S., & Brown, W. (2006). Social acceptance and rejection of preschool children with disabilities: A mixed-method analysis. *Journal of Educational Psychology*, 98(4), 807–823.

Okita, S. Y. (2004). Effects of age on associating virtual and embodied toys. *Cyber Psychology & Behavior*, 7(4), 464–471.

Opie, I., & Opie, P. (1959). *The lore and language of schoolchildren*. Oxford: Oxford University Press.

Opie, I., & Opie, P. (1969). *Children's games in street and playground*. New York: Oxford University Press.

Osborne, M. D., & Brady, D. J. (2001). Constructing a space for developing a rich understanding of science through play. *Journal of Curriculum Studies* 33 (5) 511–24.

Osborne, M. D. & Brady, D. J. (2002). Imagining the new: Constructing a space for creativity in science. In E. Mirochnik, D. Sherman (Eds.), *Passion & pedagogy: Relation, creation, and transformation in teaching* (pp. 317–332). New York: Peter Lang.

Pace, J. P. (December 19, 2007). Commentary: Why we need to save (and strengthen) social studies. *Education Week*, 27(16), 26–27.

Pan, W. H. L. (1994). Children's play in Taiwan. In J. Roopnarine, J. Johnson, & F. Hooper (Eds.), *Children's play in diverse cultures* (pp. 31–50). New York: SUNY Press.

Parten, M. B. (1932). Social participation among preschool children. *Journal of Abnormal Psychology*, 27, 243–269.

Patrick, G. T. W. (1916). *The psychology of relaxation*. Boston, MA: Houghton-Mifflin.

Peller, L. E. (1952). Models of children's play. *Mental Hygiene*, 36, 66–83.

Peter, M. (2003). Drama, narrative and early learning. *British Journal of Special Education*, 30(1), 21–27.

Peterson, E. M. (2006). Creativity in music listening. *Arts Education Policy Review*, 107(3), 15–21.

Peterson, N. (1987). *Early intervention for handicapped and at-risk children: An introduction to early childhood special education*. Denver, CO: Love.

Petrakos, H., & Howe, N. (1996). The influence of the physical design of the dramatic play center on children's play. *Early Childhood Research Quarterly*, 11(4), 63–77.

Piaget, J. (1947). *The psychology of intelligence*. Totowa, NJ: Littlefield.

Piaget, J. (1951). *Play, dreams, and imitation in childhood*. New York: Norton.

Piaget, J. (1976). Symbolic play. In J. S. Bruner, A. Jolly, K. Sylva (Eds.), *Play: Its role in development and evolution* (pp. 555–569). Bergenfield, NJ: Penguin Books.

Pigdon, K., & Woolley, M. (1993). *The big picture: Integrating children's learning*. Portsmouth, NH: Heinemann.

Pinchbeck, I., & Hewitt, M. (1969). *Children in English society Vol I: From Tudor times to the 18th century*. New York: Routledge.

Pinnell, G., & Jaggar, A. (2003). Oral language: Speaking and listening in elementary classrooms. In J. Flood, D. Lapp, J. Squire, & J. Jensen (Eds.), *Handbook of research on teaching the English language arts* (pp. 881–913). Mahwah, NJ: Erlbaum.

Piper, W. (1930). *The little engine that could*. New York: Grosset & Dunlap.

Pitri, E. (2001). The role of artistic play in problem solving. *Art Education*, 54(3), 46–51.

Plato, F. M. (1941). *The republic of Plato* translated by F. Cornford. Oxford: Oxford University Press.

Poest, C., Williams, J., Witt, D., & Atwood M. (1990). Challenge me to move: Large muscle development in young children. *Young Children*, 45(5), 4–10.

Pollard-Durodola, S. D., Gonzalez, J. E., Simmons, D. C., Kwok, O., Taylor, A. B., Davis, M. J., Kim, M., & Simmons, L. (2011). The effects of an intensive shared book-reading intervention for preschool children at risk for vocabulary delay. *Exceptional Children*, 77(2), 161–183.

Potts, R. (1996). *Humanity's descent: The consequences of ecological instability*. New York: Avon.

Poydar, N. (1996). *Cool Ali*. New York: Margaret K. McElderry.

Pratt, C. (1948). *I learn from children*. New York: Simon & Schuster.

Pratt, C., & Stanton, J. (1926). *Before books*. New York: Adelphi Co.

ProTeacher (2006). Ocean theme. In *ProTeacher Community*. Retrieved on July 14, 2009, from http://www.proteacher.net/discussions/showthread.php?t'9683

Provenzo, E. F., & Brett, A. (1983). *The complete block book*. Syracuse, New York: Syracuse University Press.

Raut, S. (1985). Identifying the inaccurate singer in your classroom. *General Music Journal, 3*(2), 28–30.

Raymo, C. (1973). Science as play. *Science Education, 57*(3), 279–289.

Raymo, C. (April 15, 2007). Science as play. *Science Musings.* Retrieved on July 24, 2009, from http://www.sciencemusings.com/2007/04/science-as-play.html

Rea, R. E., & Reys, R. E. (1971). Competencies of entering kindergartners in geometry, number, money, and measurements. *School Science and Mathematics, 71,* 389–402.

Regnier, V. (1987). The children's museum: Exhibit and location issues. *Children's Environmental Quarterly, 4*(1), 55–59.

Reifinger, J. L. (2009). An analysis of tonal patterns used for sight-singing instruction in second-grade general music class. *Journal of Research in Music Education, 57*(3), 203–216.

Reyner, A. (2010). Art and creativity in early childhood education. Retrieved on December 23, 2010, from http://artandcreativity.blogspot.com/

Riley, J. L. (1996). The ability to label the letters of the alphabet at school entry: A discussion on its value. *Journal of Research in Reading, 19*(2), 87–10.

Riley, J., & Savage, J. (1994). Bulbs, buzzers and batteries: Play and science. In J. Moyles (Ed.), *The excellence of play* (pp. 136–144). Buckingham: OUP.

Ringgenberg, S. (2003). Singing as a teaching tool: Creating story songs. *Young Children, 58*(5), 76–79.

Roberts, W. P. (2001). Symbolic play and the evolution of culture: A comparative life history perspective. *Theory in context and out, 3,* 97–108.

Robinson, L. (no date). Computers for young children: Gold or "fool's gold?" retrieved on March 26, 2010, from www.wiu.edu/thecenter/articles/gold.html

Rodríguez, S. (1985). Art for special needs . . . it's exceptional. *Arts and Activities, 98*(4), 44–46.

Rogers, C. S., & Sawyers, J. K. (1988). *Play in the lives of children.* Washington, DC: National Association for the Education of Young Children.

Rogoff, B. (1990). Apprenticeship in thinking: Cognitive development in a social context. New York: Oxford University Press.

Rogoff, B., Mistry, J., Goncü, A., & Mosier, C. (1993). Guided participation in cultural activity by toddlers and caregivers. *Monographs of the Society for Research in Child Development, 58* (8).

Roopnarine, J. L., Lasker, J., Sacks, M., & Stores, M. (1998). The cultural contents of children's play. In O. N. Saracho and B. Spodek (Eds.), *Multiple perspectives on play in early childhood education.* (pp. 194–219). New York: SUNY Press.

Roopnarine, J. L., Suppal, P., Shin, M., & Donovan, B. (2007). Sociocultural contexts of dramatic play: Implications for early education. In K. Roskos & J. Christie (Eds.), *Play and literacy in early childhood: Research from multiple perspectives* (pp. 205–230). Mahwah, NJ: Lawrence.

Rosen, M. (1995). Robert Louis Stevenson and children's play: The contexts of A child's garden of verses. *Children's Literature in Education, 26*(1), 53–72.

Rosen, D., & Hoffman, J. (2009). Integrating concrete and virtual manipulatives in early childhood mathematics. *Young Children, 64*(3), 26–29, 31–33.

Roskos, K. (1988a). Designing and using play centers that promote literacy: Two examples. *Day Care and Early Education, 15*(4), 26–27.

Roskos, K. (1988b). Literacy at work in play. *The Reading Teacher, 41* (6), 562–566.

Roskos, K. (1991). An inventory of literate behavior in the pretend play episodes of eight preschoolers. *Reading Research and Instruction, 30*(3), 39–52.

Roskos, K., & Neuman, S. B. (1998). Play as an opportunity for literacy. In O. N. Saracho & B. Spodek (Eds.), *Multiple perspectives on play in early childhood education* (pp. 100–115). New York: State University of New York Press.

Roskos, K., & Vukelich, C. (1991). Promoting literacy in play. *Day Care and Early Education, 19*(1), 30–34.

Ross, M.E. (2000). Science their way. *Young Children, 55* (2), 6–13.

Rossie, J.P. (1998). *Toys in changing North African and Saharan societies.* Paper presented at the Culture of Toys Conference, Emory University, Atlanta, GA.

Rousseau, J. J. (1762). *Émile.* (Translated by Barbara Foxley.) London: Dent.

Rowe, D. W. (1988). *The impact of author/audience interaction on preschoolers' literacy learning*. Paper presented at the Annual Meeting of the American Educational Research Association, New Orleans, LA.

Rowe, D. W. (1998). The literate potentials of book-related dramatic play. *Reading Research Quarterly, 33*(1), 10–35.

Rubin, K. H. (1976). Relation between social participation and role-taking skill in preschool children. *Psychological Reports, 39*, 823–826.

Rubin, K. H. (1982). Early play theories revisited: Contributions to contemporary research and theory. In D. J. Pepler & K. H. Rubin (Eds.), *The play of children: Current theory and research*, Vol 6 (pp. 4–14). Basel, Switzerland: Karger.

Rubin, K. H., & Copla, R. J. (1998). Social and non-social play in childhood: An individual differences perspective. In O. N. Saracho & B. Spodek (Eds.), *Multiple perspectives on play in early childhood education* (pp. 144–170). New York: State University of New York Press.

Rudolph, M., & Cohen, D. H. (1964). The many purposes of block building and woodwork. *Young Children, 20*, 40–44.

Rudolph, M., & Cohen, D. H. (1984). *Kindergarten and early schooling*. Englewood Cliffs, NJ: Prentice Hall.

Ruiz, N. T. (1995). A young deaf child leaves to write: Implications for literacy development. *The Reading Teacher, 49*(3), 206–217.

Rupiper, M., & Zeece, P. D. (2005). Fee, fi, fo, fum: Folktales are for everyone! *Early Childhood Education Journal, 32*(6), 377–382.

Russell, Y. (2007). Folktales categories. *Writing for Kids & Teens*. Retrieved on November 9, 2009, from http://www.growyourwritingbusiness.com/?p=66

Ryan, S., & Hyland, N. (2010). Preparing early childhood teachers to enact social justice pedagogies. In O. N. Saracho & B. Spodek (Eds.), *Contemporary perspectives in language and cultural diversity in early childhood education* (pp. 235–249). Charlotte, NC: Information Age Publishing.

Rylant, C. (1988) *All I see*. New York: Orchard Books.

Sabbeth, C. (2002). *Monet and the impressionists for kids*. Chicago, IL: Chicago Review Press.

Saltz, E., & Johnson, J. (1974). Training for thematic-fantasy in culturally disadvantaged children: Preliminary results. *Journal of Educational Psychology, 66*(4), 623–630.

Sapora, A. V., & Mitchell, E. D. (1961). *The theory of play and recreation*. New York: Ronald Press.

Saracho, O. N. (1983). Cognitive style and Mexican American children's perceptions of reading. In T. Escobedo (Ed.), *Early childhood education: A bilingual perspective* (pp. 201–221). New York: Teachers College Press.

Saracho, O. N. (1984). Construction and validation of the play rating scale. *Early Child Development and Care, 17*, 199–230.

Saracho, O. N. (1986). Play and young children's learning. In B. Spodek (Ed.), *Today's kindergarten: Exploring the knowledge base, expanding the curriculum* (pp. 91–109). New York: Teachers College Press.

Saracho, O. N. (1987). Evaluating reading attitudes. *Day Care and Early Education, 14*, 23–25.

Saracho, O. N. (1990). Developmental sequences in three-year-old children's writing. *Early Child Development and Care, 56*, 1–10.

Saracho, O. N. (1993). Literacy development: The whole language approach. In B. Spodek & O. N. Saracho (Eds.), *Yearbook of early childhood education: Early childhood language and literacy*, Vol. IV. New York: Teachers College Press.

Saracho, O. N. (1997). *Teachers and students' cognitive styles in early childhood education*. Westport, CT: Greenwood.

Saracho, O. N. (1998a). Socialization factors in the cognitive style and play of young children. *International Journal of Educational Research, 29*(3), 263–276.

Saracho, O. N. (1998b). What is stylish about play? In O. N. Saracho & B. Spodek (Eds.), *Multiple perspectives on play in early childhood education* (pp. 240–254). New York: State University of New York Press.

Saracho, O. N. (1999a). A factor analysis of preschool children's play strategies and cognitive style. *Educational Psychology, 19*(2), 165–180.

Saracho, O. N. (1999b). The role of play in the early childhood curriculum. In B. Spodek & O. N. Saracho (Eds.), *Early childhood education: Issues in early childhood curriculum* (pp. 86–105). Troy, New York: Educator's International Press, Inc.

Saracho, O. N. (2001). Exploring young children literacy development through play. *Early Child Development and Care, 167,* 103–114.

Saracho, O. N. (2002a). Developmental play theories and children's social pretend play. In O. N. Saracho & B. Spodek (Eds), *Contemporary perspectives on early childhood curriculum* (pp. 41–62). Greenwich, CT: Information Age.

Saracho, O. N. (2002b). Teachers' roles in promoting literacy in the context of play. *Early Child Development and Care, 172*(1), 23–34.

Saracho, O. N. (2002c). Young children's literacy development. In O. N. Saracho & B. Spodek (Eds.), *Contemporary Perspectives on Early Childhood Curriculum* (pp. 111–130). Greenwich, CT: Information Age.

Saracho, O. N. (2002d). Young children's creativity and pretend play. *Early Child Development and Care, 172*(5), 431–438.

Saracho, O. N. (2003) Young children's play and cognitive style. In O. N. Saracho & B. Spodek (Eds.), *Contemporary perspectives on play in early childhood* (pp. 75–96). Greenwich, CT: Information Age.

Saracho, O. N. (2004). Supporting literacy-related play: Roles for teachers of young children. *Early Childhood Education Journal, 31*(3), 203–208.

Saracho, O. N. (2008). Developmental theories of children's play. *International Journal of Early Childhood Education, 14*(1), 119–132.

Saracho, O. N. (2010a). A culturally responsive literacy program for Hispanic fathers and their children. *Journal of Hispanic Higher Education, 9*(4), 281–293.

Saracho, O. N. (2010b). Children's play in the visual arts and literature. *Early Child Development and Care, 180*(7), 947–956.

Saracho, O. N. (2010c). The interface of the American family and culture. In O. N. Saracho & B. Spodek (Eds.), *Contemporary perspectives in language and cultural diversity in early childhood education* (pp. 117–146). Charlotte, NC: Information Age Publishing.

Saracho, O. N., & Shirakawa, Y. (2004). A comparison of the literacy development context of United States and Japanese families. *Early Childhood Education Journal, 31*(4), 261–266.

Saracho, O. N., & Spodek, B. (1993). Language and literacy in early childhood education. In B. Spodek & O. N. Saracho (Eds.), *Yearbook of early childhood education: Early childhood language and literacy,* Vol. 4 (pp. v–xiii). New York: Teachers College Press.

Saracho, O. N., & Spodek, B. (1995). Children's play and early childhood education: Insights from history and theory. *Journal of Education, 177*(3), 129–148.

Saracho, O. N., & Spodek, B. (1996). Literacy activities in a play environment. *International Journal of Early Childhood Education, 1,* 7–19.

Saracho, O. N., & Spodek, B. (1998a). A historical overview of theories of play. In O.N. Saracho & B. Spodek (Eds.), *Multiple perspectives on play in early childhood education* (pp. 1–10). New York: State University of New York Press.

Saracho, O. N., & Spodek, B. (1998b). A play foundation for family literacy. *International Journal of Educational Research, 29,* 41–50.

Saracho, O. N., & Spodek, B. (2002). Introduction: The backbone of the early childhood curriculum. In O. N. Saracho & B. Spodek (Eds.), *Contemporary perspectives on early childhood curriculum* (pp. vii–xii). Greenwich, CT: Information Age.

Saracho, O. N., & Spodek, B. (2003a). Recent trends and innovations in the early childhood education curriculum. *Early Child Development and Care, 173*(2–3), 175–183.

Saracho, O. N., & Spodek, B. (2003b). Understanding play and its theories. In O. N. Saracho, & B. Spodek (Eds.), *Contemporary Perspectives on Play in Early Childhood* (pp. 1–19). Greenwich, CT: Information Age.

Saracho, O. N., & Spodek, B. (2006). Young children's literacy-related play. *Early Child Development and Care, 176*(7), 707–721.

Saracho, O. N., & Spodek, B. (2007a). Developmental perspectives on social development. In O. N. Saracho & B. Spodek (Eds.), *Contemporary perspectives on socialization and social development in early childhood education* (pp. 301–315). Greenwich, CT: Information Age.

Saracho, O. N., & Spodek, B. (2007b). Social learning in the early childhood years. In O. N. Saracho & B. Spodek (Eds.), *Contemporary perspectives on social learning in early childhood education* (pp. ix–xx). Greenwich, CT: Information Age.

Saracho, O. N., & Spodek, B. (2007c). Social learning as the basis for early childhood education. In O. N. Saracho & B. Spodek (Eds.), *Contemporary perspectives on social learning in early childhood education* (pp. 303–310). Greenwich, CT: Information Age.

Saracho, O. N., & Spodek, B. (2008a). Introduction: Trends in research in early childhood mathematics. In O. N. Saracho & B. Spodek (Eds.), *Contemporary Perspectives in Mathematics* (pp. vii–xx). Charlotte, NC: Information Age.

Saracho, O. N., & Spodek, B. (2008b). Research perspectives in early childhood mathematics. In O. N. Saracho & B. Spodek (Eds.), *Contemporary Perspectives in Mathematics* (pp. 309–320). Charlotte, NC: Information Age.

Saul, J. D. (1993). Ready, set, let's go! Using field trips in your curriculum. *Early Childhood Education Journal, 21*(1), 27–29.

Schartzman, H. B. (1978). *Transformations: The anthropology of play.* New York: Plenum.

Schickedanz, J. & McGee, L. (2010). The NELP report on shared story reading interventions (Chapter 4): Extending the story. *Educational Researcher, 39*(4), 323–329.

Schiller, J., & Tillett, B. (2004). Using digital images with young children: Challenges of integration. *Early Child Development and Care, 174*(4), 401–414.

Schlosberg, H. (1947). The concept of play. *Psychological Review, 54,* 229–231.

Scholastic (2004). Dreamy rhymes. *Early Childhood Today, 19*(1), 52.

Scribbles. (2005). Appreciation in young children. *Scribbles Kids Art Site.* http://www.scribbleskidsart.com

Seefeldt, C., Castle, S. D., & Falconer, R. (2009). *Social studies for the preschool/primary child.* Columbus, OH: Merrill.

Seidel, S., Tishman, S., Winner, E., Hetland, L., & Palmer, P. (2009). *The qualities of quality: Understanding excellence in arts education.* Cambridge, MA: Harvard University Press.

Seo, K.-H. (2003). What children's play tells us about teaching mathematics. *Young Children, 58*(1), 28–33.

Severide, R. C. & Pizzini, E. L. (1984). The role of play in science. *Science and Children, 21*(8), 58–61.

Shaftel, F. R., & Shaftel, G. (1967a). Role-playing for social values: Decision-making in the social studies. Englewood Cliffs, NJ: Prentice-Hall.

Shaftel, F. R., & Shaftel, G. (1967b). *Words and action.* Photo pictures for *Role Playing with young children.* New York: Holt, Rinehart & Winston.

Shaftel, F. R., & Shaftel, G. (1982). *Role playing the curriculum.* Englewood Cliffs, N.J.: Prentice-Hall, Inc.

Shamrock, M. (1997). Orff-Schulwerk: An integrated method. *Music Educators Journal, 83* (6), 41–44.

Shedlock, M. L. (2004). *The art of the story-teller.* Oxford, MS: Project Gutenberg Literary Archive Foundation.

Sher, B. T. (2003). Adapting science curricula for high-ability learners. In J. V. Baska & C. A. Little (Eds.), *Content-based curricula for high-ability learners* (pp. 191–218). Waco, TX: Prufrock Press.

Short-Meyerson, K. J., & Abbeduto, L. J. (1997). Preschoolers' communication during scripted interactions. *Journal of Child Language, 24,* 469–493.

Siks, G. B. (1983). *Drama with children.* New York: Harper & Row.

Singer, D. G., & Singer, J. L. (1998). Fantasy and imagination. In D. P. Fromberg & D. Bergen (Eds.), *Play from birth to twelve and beyond: Contexts, perspectives, and meanings* (pp. 313–318). New York: Garland Publishing, Inc.

Singer, J. L. (1973). Theories of play and the origins of imagination. In J.L. Singer (Ed.), *The child world of make-believe* (pp. 1–26). New York: Academic Press, Inc.

Sipe, L. R. (2008). *Storytime: Young children's literary understanding in the classroom.* New York: Teachers College Press.

Slobodkina, E. (1989). *Caps for sale.* New York: HarperCollins.

Smilansky, S. (1968). The effects of sociodramatic play on disadvantaged preschool children. New York: Wiley.

Smith, B. O., Stanley, W. O., & Shores, H. J. (1957). *Fundamentals of curriculum development.* New York: Harcourt Brace Jovanovich.

Smith, N. R. (1982). The visual arts in early childhood education: Development and the creation of meaning. In B. Spodek (Ed.), *Handbook of early childhood education* (pp. 295–317). New York: The Free Press.

Smith, P. K., & Vollstedt, R. (1985). On defining play: An empirical study of the relationship between play and various play criteria. *Child Development, 56,* 1042–1050.

Smith, R. B. (1970). *Music in the child's education.* New York: Ronald Press.

Smithrim, K. L. (1997). Free musical play in early childhood. *Canadian Music Educator, 38*(4), 17–22.

Smolucha, L., & Smolucha, F. (1998). The social origins of mind: Post-Piagetian perspectives on pretend play in children. In O. N. Saracho & B. Spodek (Eds.), *Multiple perspectives on play in early childhood education* (pp. 34–58). New York: State University of New York Press.

Soderman, A. K., & Farrell, P. (2008). *Creating literacy-rich preschools and kindergarten.* Boston, MA: Allyn & Bacon.

Sokal, R. R. (1974). Classification: Purposes, principles, progress, prospects. *Science, 185,* 1115–1123.

Sommerville, J. (1982). *The rise and fall of childhood.* Thousand Oaks, CA: Sage.

Soto, A. C. (2008). Conjunto in the classroom. *Music Educators Journal, 95*(1), 54–59.

Soundy, C. S., & Gallagher, P. W. (1992). Creating prop boxes to stimulate dramatic play and literacy development. *Day Care and Early Education, 20*(2), 4–8.

Spodek, B. (1999). Early childhood curriculum and cultural definitions of knowledge. In B. Spodek & O. N. Saracho (Eds.), *Early childhood education: Issues in early childhood curriculum* (pp. 1–20). Troy, New York: Educator's International Press, Inc.

Spodek, B., & Saracho, O. N. (1987). The challenge of educational play. In D. Bergen (Ed.), *Play as a medium for learning and development* (pp. 11–28). Olney, MD: Association for Childhood Education International.

Spodek, B., & Saracho, O. N. (1994a). *Dealing with individual differences in the early childhood classroom.* New York: Longman.

Spodek, B., & Saracho, O. N. (1994b). *Right from the start: Teaching children ages three to eight.* Boston, MA: Allyn & Bacon.

Spodek, B., & Saracho, O. N. (2003a). Early childhood educational play. In O. N. Saracho, & B. Spodek (Eds.), *Contemporary Perspectives on Play in Early Childhood* (pp. 171–179). Greenwich, CT: Information Age.

Spodek, B., & Saracho, O. N. (2003b). "On the shoulders of giants": Exploring the traditions of early childhood education. *Early Childhood Education Journal, 31*(1), 3–10.

Spodek, B., Saracho, O. N., & Davis, M. D. (1991). *Foundations of early childhood education: Teaching three-, four-, and five-year-old children.* Englewood Cliffs, NJ: Prentice-Hall.

Stamp, L. N. (1992). Music time? All the time? *Day and Early Education, 19*(4), 4–6.

Stark, E. B. (1960). *Blockbuilding.* Washington, DC: American Association of Elementary-Kindergarten Nursery Education & National Education Association.

Starkey, P., Spelke, E. S., & Gelman, R. (1990). Numerical abstraction by human infants. *Cognition, 36,* 97–127.

Steig, W. (1969). *Sylvester and the magic pebble.* New York: Simon and Schuster.

Steig, W. (1997). *Zeke Pippin.* New York: HarperCollins.

Stetsenko, A. (1995) The psychological function of children's drawing: A Vygotskian perspective. In C. Lange-Kuttner & G. V. Thomas (Eds.), *Drawing and looking: Theoretical approaches to pictorial representation in children* (pp. 147–158). New York: Harvester Wheatsheaf.

Stevenson, R. L. (1885). (Illustrator: Tasha Tudor). Block city. In *A child's garden of verses*. New York: Simon & Schuster Children's Publishing.

Stevenson, R. L. (1930). *Child's play: Virginibus Puerisque and other papers, memories and portraits*. Bangalore: Standard Book Company.

Stevenson, R. L. (1987). From a railway. *In A child's garden of verses* (Illustrated by Brian Wildsmith). New York: Oxford University Press.

Stevenson, R. L. (1998). *Where go the boats?: Play-poems of Robert Louis Stevenson*. San Diego, CA: Browndeer/Harcourt Brace.

Stone, J. I. (1987). Early childhood math: Make it manipulative. *Young Children, 42*(6), 16–23.

Stone, S. J. (1995–1996). Teaching strategies: Integrating play into the curriculum. *Childhood Education, 72*(2), 104–107.

Suh, J. M., Moyer, P. S., & Sterling, D. R. (2003). Junior architects: Designing your dream clubhouse using measurement and geometry. *Teaching Children Mathematics, 10*(3), 170–179.

Sulzby, E. (1991). Assessment of emergent literacy: Storybook reading. *The Reading Teacher, 44*(7), 498–500.

Sulzby, W., & Teale, W. H. (1991). Emergent literacy. In P. D. Pearson, R. Barr, M. L. Kamil, and P. Mosenthal (Eds.), *Handbook of reading research* (pp.727–757). New York: Longman.

Sulzby, W., & Teale, W. H. (2003). The development of the young child and the emergence of literacy. In J. Flood, D. Lapp, J. R. Squire, & J. Jensen (Ed.), *Handbook of research on teaching the English language arts* (pp. 300–313). Mahwah, NJ: Erlbaum.

Sunal, C. S. (1990). *Early childhood social studies*. Englewood Cliffs, NJ: Prentice Hall.

Sunal, C. S. (1993). Social studies in early childhood education. In B. Spodek (Ed.), *Handbook of research on the education of young children*. New York: Macmillan.

Sunal, C. S., & Haas, M. E. (2007). *Social studies for the elementary and middle grades: A constructivist approach*. Boston, MA: Allyn & Bacon.

Sutterby, J. A., & Frost, J. (2006). Creating play environments for early childhood: Indoors and out. In B. Spodek & O. N. Saracho (Eds.), *Handbook of research on the education of young children* (pp. 305–322). Mahwah, NJ: Erlbaum.

Sutton-Smith, B. (1967). The role of play in cognitive development. *Young Children, 22,* 361–370.

Sutton-Smith, B. (1995). Conclusion: The persuasive rhetorics of play. In A. Pellegrini (Ed.), *The future of play: A multidisciplinary inquiry into the contributions of Brian Sutton Smith* (pp. 275–305). New York: State University of New York Press.

Sutton-Smith, B. (2001). *The ambiguity of play*. Cambridge, MA: Harvard University Press.

Sutton-Smith, B., & Kelly-Byrne, D. (1984). The idealization of play. In P. K. Smith (Ed.), *Play in animals and humans* (pp. 305–321). Oxford: Basil Blackwell.

Sutton-Smith, B., & Magee, M. A. (1989). Reversible childhood. *Play & Culture, 2,* 52–63.

Sutton-Smith, B. & Roberts, J. M. (1981). Play, games and sports. In H. Triandis & A. Heron (Eds.), *Handbook of cross-cultural psychology: Developmental psychology*, Vol. 4, pp. 425–71. Boston, MA: Allyn & Bacon.

Swanwick, K. (1988). *Music, mind and education*. New York: Routledge.

Sylva, K., Bruner, J. S., & Genova, P. (1974). The role of play in the problem solving of children. In J. S. Bruner, A. Jolly, & K. Sylva (Eds.), *Play: Its role in development and evolution* (pp. 97–109). Bergenfield, NJ: Penguin.

Szekely, G. (1983). Preliminary play in the art class. *Art Education, 36*(6), 18–24.

Szekely, G. (1991). *From play to art*. Portsmouth, NH: Heinemann.

Szyba, C. M.. (1999). Why do some teachers resist offering appropriate, open-ended art activities for young children? *Young Children, 54*(1), 16–20.

Taggart, C. C. (2000). Developing musicianship through musical play. In *Spotlight on early childhood music education* (pp. 23–26). Reston, VA: The National Association for Music Education.

Takhvar, M. (1988). Play and theories of play: A review of the literature. *Early Child Development and Care, 39,* 221–244.

Tarnowski, S. M. (1999). Musical play and young children. *Music Educators Journal, 86*(1), 26–29.

Tavin, K. M. (2010). Six acts of miscognition: Implications for art education. *Studies in Art Education, 52*(1), 55–68.

Taylor, S. I., Morris, V. G., & Cordeau-Young, C. (1997). Field trips in early childhood settings: Expanding the walls of the classroom. *Early Childhood Education Journal, 25*(2), 141–146.

Temmerman, N. (2000). An investigation of the music activity preferences of pre-school children. *British Journal of Music Education, 17*(1), 51–60.

Terr, L. (1999). *Beyond love and work: Why adults need to play.* New York: Scribner.

Texas Child Care. (2009). Block play: Classroom essentials. *Texas Child Care,* 24–33.

Thompson, C. M. (2005). *Children as illustrators.* Washington, DC: National Association for the Education of Young Children.

Thresher, J. M. (1964). The contributions of Carl Orff to elementary music education. *Music Educators Journal, 50*(3), 43–48.

Tolstoy, L. (1852). *Childhood, boyhood, youth.* New York: Penguin Classics.

Toth, B., & Miranda, L. (1997). Musical play centers. *Early Childhood Connections, 3,* 37–39.

Trentacosta, C. J., & Izard, C. E. (2007). Feeling, thinking, and playing: Social and emotional learning in early childhood. In O. N. Saracho & B. Spodek (Eds.), *Contemporary perspectives on socialization and social development in early childhood education* (pp. 59–77). Charlotte, NC: Information Age.

Trevarthen, C., & Aitken, K. J. (2001). Infant intersubjectivity: Research, theory, and clinical applications. *The Journal of Child Psychology and Psychiatry and Allied Disciplines, 42,* 3–48.

Tucker, M. J. (1974). The child as beginning and end: Fifteenth and sixteenth century English childhood. In L. DeMausse (Ed.), *The history of childhood* (pp. 229–258). New York: Psychohistory Press.

Tureil, E. (1973). Stage transition in moral development. In R. M. W. Travers (Ed.), *Second handbook of research in teaching* (pp. 732–758). Chicago, IL: Rand McNally.

Turnbull, W., & Carpendale, J. I. M. (2001). Talk and the development of social understanding. *Early Education and Development, 12*(3), 455–478.

Turner, B. (2004). *H.G. Wells' Floor Games: A father's account of play and its legacy of healing.* Cloverdale, CA: Temenos Press.

Turner, B. A. (2009). *The history and development of sandplay therapy.* Middletown, PA: Sandplay Therapists of America.

Turner, M. E. (1999). Child-centered learning and music programs. *Music Educators Journal, 86*(1), 30–33 & 51.

Twain, M. (1876). *The adventures of Tom Sawyer.* London: Chatto & Windus.

Twain, M. (1884). *Adventures of Huckleberry Finn.* New York: Charles L. Webster.

Twain, M. (2000). *The prince and the pauper.* New York: Charles L. Webster.

Tyler, R. W. (1957). The curriculum then and now. In *Proceedings of the 1956 Conference on Testing Problems.* Princeton, NJ: Educational Testing Service.

Udry, J. M. (1987). *A tree is nice.* (illustrator Marc Simont). New York: HarperCollins.

Uttal, D. H. (2003). On the relation between play and symbolic thought: The case of mathematics manipulatives. In O. N. Saracho & B. Spodek (2003). *Contemporary Perspectives on Play in Early Childhood* (pp. 97–114). Greenwich, CT: Information Age.

Vacca, R. T., Vacca, J. L., & Mraz, M. E. (2011). *Content area reading: Literacy and learning across the curriculum.* Boston, MA: Allyn & Bacon.

Van Hoorn, J., Nourot, P. M., Scales, B. P., & Alward, K. R. (2011). *Play at the center of the curriculum.* Columbus, OH: Merrill.

Vandermass-Peler, M. (2002). Cultural variations in parental support of children's play. In W. J. Lonner, D. L. Dinnel, S. A. Hayes, & D. N. Sattler (Eds.), *Online Readings in Psychology and Culture.* Bellingham, WA: Western Washington University.

Veale, A. (1988). Art development and play. *Early Child Development and Care, 37,* 109–117.

Vinovskis, M. A. (2008). *The birth of Head Start: Preschool education policies in the Kennedy and Johnson administrations.* Chicago, IL: University of Chicago Press.

Vukelich, C. (1990). Where is the paper? Literacy during dramatic play. *Childhood Education, 66*(4), 205–209.

Vygotsky, L. S. (1934). *Thought and language.* Cambridge, MA: MIT.

Vygotsky, L. S. (1935). Predistoria peismennoy rechi [The prehistory of written language]. In *The mental development of children during education* (pp. 73–95). Moscow/Leningrad: Uchpedgiz.

Vygotsky, L. S. (1967). Play and its role in the mental development of the child. *Soviet Psychology, 12,* 62–76.

Vygotsky, L. S. (1978). *Mind in society.* Cambridge, MA: Harvard University Press.

Vygotsky, L. S. (1983). School instruction and mental development. In R. Grieve & C. Pratt (Eds.), *Early childhood development and education* (pp. 263–269). New York: Guilford.

Vygotsky, L. S. (1987). Thinking and speech. In R. Rieber, A. S. Carton (Eds.), & N. Minick (Trans.), *The collected works of L. S. Vygotsky: Vol. 1: Problems of general psychology* (pp. 37–285). New York: Plenum.

Wadsworth, O. A. (2003). (Illustrator AnnaVojtech). *Over in the meadow.* New York: North-South Books.

Walker, L. (1995). *Block building for children.* New York: Penguin.

Wardle, F. (2003). *Introduction to early childhood education: A multi-dimensional approach to child-centered care and learning.* Boston: Allyn & Bacon.

Wassermann, S. (1988). Play-debrief-replay: An instructional model for science. *Childhood Education, 64*(4), 232–235.

Wassermann, S. (1992). Serious play in the classroom: How messing around can win you the Nobel Prize. *Childhood Education, 68,* 133–139.

Watson, J. B. (1925). *Behaviorism.* New York: Norton.

Wattenberg, J. (2000). *Henny Penny.* New York: Scholastic.

Way, B. (1967). *Development through drama.* New York: Humanity Books.

Webster (2008). *Merriam-Webster's dictionary.* Springfield, MA: Webster.

Wehman, P., & Abramson, M. (1976). Three theoretical approaches to play. *The American Journal of Occupational Therapy, 30*(9), 551–559.

Wells, G. (1986). *The meaning makers.* Portsmouth, NH: Heinemann.

Wells, H. G. (1911). *Floor Games.* Alexandria, VA: Skirmisher Publishing.

Whitehurst, G. J., & Lonigan, C. J. (1998). Child development and emergent literacy. *Child Development, 69*(3), 848–872.

Whiting, B. B. & Whiting, J. M. W. (1975). *Children of six cultures.* Cambridge, MA: Harvard University Press.

Williams, K. L. (1998). *Painted dreams.* New York: HarperCollins.

Williams, M., & Hask, H. (2003). Literacy through play: How families with able children support their literacy development. *Early Child Development and Care, 173*(5), 527–533.

Wimmer, H. & Perner, J. (1983). Beliefs about beliefs: Representation and constraining function of wrong beliefs in young children's understanding of deception. *Cognition, 13,* 103–128.

Witte Museum (No date). *Creative dramatics.* San Antonio, Texas. Retrieved on May 30, 2009, from www.wittemuseum.org/pdfs/SocialStudiesDramaticsEducatorGuide.pdf

Wolf, A. D. (1990). Art postcards – Another aspect of your aesthetics program? *Young Children, 45*(2), 39–43.

Wolf, D. & Grollman, S. H. (1982). Ways of playing: Individual differences in imaginative style. In D. J. Pepler & K. H. Rubin (Eds.), *The play of children: Current theory and research, Contributions to human development* (pp. 46–64). Basel, Switzerland: Karger.

Wolf, J. (1992). Let's sing it again: Creating music with young children. *Young Children, 47*(2), 56–61.

Wolff, A. L., & Wimer, N. (2009). Shopping for mathematics in Consumer Town. *Young Children, 64*(3), 34–38.

Wolfson, B. J. (1967). Values and the primary school teacher *Social Education, 31,* 37–38.

Woodard, C.Y. (1984). Guidelines for facilitating sociodramatic play. *Childhood Education, 60*(3), 172–177.

Woods, C. S. (2000). A picture is worth a thousand words: Using photographs in the classroom. *Young Children, 55*(5), 82–84.

Woodson, B., & Johnston, J. M. (1989). Listening: The key to early childhood music. *Day Care and Early Education, 16*(3), 11–17.

Wright, F. L. (1951). *An autobiography*. New York: Modern Library.

Yim, H. Y. B., & Ebbeck, M. (2009). Children's preferences for group musical activities in child care centres: A cross-cultural study. *Early Childhood Education Journal*, 37(2), 103–111.

Yopp, H. K. (1992). Developing phonemic awareness in young children. *Reading Teacher*, 45(9), 696–703.

York, S. (1998). *Big as life*. St. Paul, MN: Redleaf Press.

Young, S. (2002). Young children's spontaneous vocalizations in free-play: Observations of two- to three-year-olds in a day care setting. *Bulletin of the Council for Research in Music Education*, 152, 43–53.

Young, S. (2003). Time-space structuring in spontaneous play on educational percussion instruments among three- and four-year-olds. *British Journal of Music Education*, 20(1), 45–59.

Young, S. (2008). Collaboration between 3- and 4-year-olds in self-initiated play on instruments. *International Journal of Educational Research*, 47(1), 3–10.

Zeece, P. D. (2008). Linking life and literature in early childhood settings. *Early Childhood Education Journal*, 35(6), 565–569.

Zimmerman, C. (2005). *The development of scientific reasoning skills: What psychologists contribute to an understanding of elementary science learning*. Washington, DC: National Research Council's Board of Science Education.

Zur, S. S., & Johnson-Green, E. (2008). Time to transition: The connection between musical free play and school readiness. *Childhood Education*, 84(5), 295–300.

# Index

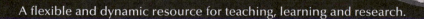